D0146334

Movements in the Arts
Series Editor: Stanley Trachtenberg

The Postmodern Moment
Edited, with an introduction, by Stanley Trachtenberg

Postmodern Fiction

A Bio-Bibliographical Guide

EDITED BY
LARRY McCAFFERY

MOVEMENTS IN THE ARTS, NUMBER 2

Greenwood Press

NEW YORK • WESTPORT, CONNECTICUT • LONDON

Library of Congress Cataloging-in-Publication Data
Main entry under title:

Postmodern fiction.

  Movements in the arts, ISSN 8756–890X ; no. 2)
  Includes index.
  1. Fiction—20th century—Bio-bibliography.
  2. Fiction—20th century—History and criticism.
  3. Postmodernism. I. McCaffery, Larry, 1946–
  II. Series.
  PN3503.P594 1986   809.3'04   85–17723
  ISBN 0–313–24170–8 (lib. bdg. : alk. paper)

Library of Congress Catalog Card Number: 85–17723
ISBN: 0–313–24170–8
ISSN: 8756–890X

First published in 1986

Greenwood Press, Inc.
88 Post Road West
Westport, Connecticut 06881

Printed in the United States of America

The paper used in this book complies with the
Permanent Paper Standard issued by the National
Information Standards Organization (Z39.48–1984).

10 9 8 7 6 5 4 3 2 1

Copyright Acknowledgment

We gratefully acknowledge permission to reprint the following copyrighted material: excerpt
of a song from *Ratner's Star*, by Don DeLillo, by permission of Alfred A. Knopf, Inc.

For Larry McCaffery, Sr.—the Wild Mustang

Contents

Preface

The organization of *Postmodern Fiction: A Bio-Bibliographical Guide* is designed to facilitate easy access by scholars and general readers to information about specific postmodern authors and critics, as well as to broader, theoretical issues that have shaped postmodern fiction. With this in mind, the volume has been divided into two sections. Part I contains 15 overview articles dealing with a variety of issues, themes, and stylistic tendencies; individually and collectively, these articles define the chief features of postmodern fiction, isolate specific aesthetic tendencies within the movement, and discuss the major themes and topics central to postmodernism. Part I concludes with two articles dealing specifically with postmodern criticism and its interaction with recent fiction and other relevant areas of learning, such as linguistics, philosophy, and science. Part II contains individual author entries, arranged in alphabetical order, which provide a summary of the writer's life and literary career, a critical assessment of the major works, and a selected bibliography; these bibliographies are usually divided into Primary Sources, which list the author's works chronologically, and Secondary Sources, which provide information about the major critical essays and books that examine the works of the individual authors.

In addition to the two major sections, this volume also contains a selected bibliography of critical books and essays that focus on postmodernism in general or that provide useful background information about the sources of postmodern experimentalism. In the Introduction to this volume, I have outlined my own views on what constitutes postmodernism, discussed the aesthetic, philosophical, social, and political issues that precipitated the outbreak of experimentalism typical of postmodern fiction during the 1960s, and analyzed the important tendencies of the movement. To assist readers in their research, the volume has provided a general subject index, as well as asterisked cross-references whenever an overview essay or individual author entry mentions a writer who is included in a separate author entry.

In the course of preparing this volume over several years, I have been constantly aware that the elements that constitute this area of study—i.e., postmodern fiction—are in a constant state of flux, with new (and neglected) authors emerging, new critical approaches and themes suggesting themselves, and (inevitably) new books appearing by the authors and critics examined herein. Without the ongoing help supplied by numerous students, professors, secretaries, and friends, it would have been impossible for this volume to have been completed. Michael Davidson, Lori Chamberlain, Tom LeClair, Harold Jaffe, Sinda Gregory, Ron Silliman, and Jerome Klinkowitz all offered specific suggestions about topics and individual author entries. Neil Barron provided assistance in compiling bibliographical information for the science fiction entries, Mary Wagner assisted me in updating the bibliographies for all the individual author entries, Paula Bryant proofread the manuscript in various stages, and Lissa Findley helped out in compiling the index. San Diego State University supplied me with several units of release time which allowed me to complete this work. Special thanks of a more personal nature go to Maurice and Yvonne Couturier, Elise Miller, Kim Cox, Jan Jarrell, Robert Coover, Kathy Sagan, Edie Jarolim, Dana Jackson, John and Stephanie Mood, Lisa Jackson, Doug Capps, Lisa Levesque and Jeff Uniacke. Finally, Sinda Gregory (wife, colleague, rock-and-roller) and Mark Urton (son, good buddy) were unfailingly generous in giving me the time and encouragement I required, space on the kitchen table, a beer and a Springsteen song when I needed a lift. That love and friendships were somehow involved here goes without saying.

Larry McCaffery

Introduction

This bio-bibliographical guide is designed to serve a number of purposes both for scholars specializing in the field of contemporary fiction and for the general reader. Chiefly, of course, this guide should provide easy access to significant biographical and bibliographical information, as well as critical assessments, about many of the important figures in the field of postmodern literature. It also supplies a series of overview articles dealing with various aesthetic tendencies and other issues central to the field. What this volume does not do, however, is attempt to create a single sharply delineated definition of postmodernism that will, once-and-for-all, explain the meaning of this mysterious term. This volume does not develop such a definition simply because postmodernism is, in fact, not a unified movement but a term that serves most usefully as a general signifier rather than as a sign with a stable meaning. I am beginning the introduction to the volume, then, with a warning common to many postmodern texts: beware of labels, lest you be tempted into a fruitless search for something that in reality exists in language only. "Postmodernism" is exactly such a label, a term that was invented by critics (among several other, competing terms are parafiction, surfiction, metafiction, and postcontemporary fiction) when no others seemed to work and that points in a general direction toward a highly complex set of ideas or tendencies. I have attempted to organize this volume without forcing its contents to cohere to any narrowly conceived definition of postmodern in the hopes of avoiding the pitfalls, evident in many critical discussions of the topic, of reductionism, of facile category-making, of isolating individually developed conventions and then assigning them more universal significance than they deserve.

Getting a sense of what *does* constitute postmodernism is perhaps best approached in the same way readers should approach one of Faulkner's multi-narrated novels: one reads one section, one tendency, one subjective opinion to get a feel for the territory, and then one moves on into another expanse, examines *that* area for its distinctive features, and so on. Eventually, after looking at several of these views (some of which complement each other and others which openly contradict one another), one begins to assemble a rough picture of what all the perspectives collectively seem to be suggesting. This volume has been devised with this analogy very much in mind. Although I have selected topics and authors that seem especially useful in developing a sense of the variety and scope of postmodernism, I gave the critics who wrote these articles almost complete freedom to develop the specific direction of their discussions. They were supplied only one basic guideline: the primary focus of the volume was to be on fiction that had rejected traditional notions of representation, mimesis, or realism, or that was attempting to redefine what realism is. This freedom, I felt, would encourage a variety of viewpoints which, in their *différances* (to appropriate Jacques Derrida's* most famous term), would suggest some of the key features of postmodern fiction.

To say that postmodernism is not a unified movement, however, is not at all to suggest that there aren't cogent ways of analyzing its tendencies, its background, the sources of its vitality. What seems crucial from the outset is the realization that there is no sharp demarcation line between what constitutes modernism and postmodernism except such arbitrary designations that critics may find useful. For the purposes of this volume, for example, it would be very convenient to list November 22, 1963 (the day John Kennedy died) as the day postmodernism was officially ushered in— at least in the United States—since that was the day that symbolically signaled the end of a certain kind of optimism and naivete in our collective consciousness, the end of certain verities and assurances that had helped shape our notion of what fiction should be. This is a great oversimplification, of course, for many of the disturbances and uncertainties that affected the aesthetic sensibilities of the authors of this period had much deeper roots in philosophy (in the Kantian revolution, in the discoveries of Wittgenstein, Gödel, the existentialists, and so on), in science (as with developments in quantum physics, the theory of relativity, the Uncertainty Principle), in the aesthetic revolutions undergone by most of the other major art forms in this century, and in a deeper awareness in most fields of learning about the role which subjectivity plays in the nature of our systems of thought. Given such a context, it is not surprising that realistic fiction—a form whose origins are intimately related to the assurances and optimism of empiricism and Western rationalism—would seem less attractive to writers anxious to express a sense of a world that suddenly seemed much less stable and predictable than the plots of most novels had led us to believe.

The resulting attack on or reinterpretation of mimesis thus becomes one tendency which, in various guises, can be found in almost all works that today seem recognizably postmodern in orientation. In looking at some of

the central postmodern texts, for example—books like Thomas Pynchon's*
V., Vladimir Nabokov's *Pale Fire*, John Barth's* *Giles Goat-Boy*, Robert
Coover's* *Pricksongs and Descants*, Donald Barthelme's* *Snow White*,
Italo Calvino's* *Cosmicomics*, Gabriel García Márquez's* *One Hundred
Years of Solitude*, Kurt Vonnegut's* *Slaughterhouse-Five*, John Fowles'*
The French Lieutenant's Woman, Jorge Luis Borges' *Ficciones*—we find a
shared heightening of artifice, a delight in verbal play and formal manipulation of fictive elements, the widespread use of fantasy and surrealism,
a tendency to present obviously fictive characters working out their destinies in landscapes of pure language, dream, or other fiction. As will be
discussed more fully in a moment, this sort of flaunting of artifice was
receding in importance by the late 1970s as the next generation of fictional
experimenters was busy grafting the innovations of the 1960s to more
traditional concerns or redefining what could be done with realistic structures. The result is that by the mid–1980s, postmodern experimentalism is
moving in many different directions. A book like Barth's *Letters* or Pynchon's *Gravity's Rainbow* is operating on some very different aesthetic
principles than, say, Raymond Carver's* *Will You Please Be Quiet, Please*,
and yet all three seem distinctly postmodern in spirit. Barth's and Pynchon's
mammoth, encyclopedic narratives, with their enormous cast of major
characters moving through a dizzying series of landscapes and times, their
massive transformations of history, science, myth, and popular culture,
clearly aim at devising grand, multi-layered structures that can deal with
contemporary experience through a wide range of allusions, symbols, and
language forms. Meanwhile, Carver's minimalist fiction approaches the
problem of capturing a sense of contemporary life from a different direction: its pared-down prose, stripped of all ornamentation, its focus on the
small, unarticulated mysteries of daily life, its lack of traditional resolution
or progression—these, too, are features of nontraditional vision, one that
seeks a means of capturing the emptiness, the bewilderment and misguided
illuminations, of Carver's ordinary characters.

There are dozens of other tendencies in postmodern fiction, several of
which I have tried to group together into categories that could be discussed
in individual articles. But because the focus of this volume is on nontraditional fiction, I have omitted from the categories and individual author
entries all writers whose basic impulses seemed to be conventional realism.
Thus, many significant and very wonderful writers who are important to
contemporary fiction—writers like Saul Bellow and Larry McMurtry and
John Updike and Larry Woiwode and Peter DeVries—are not included in
this volume. This omission, it should be emphasized, is not due to an
evaluative judgment on my part (some of the best writing remains realistic
and traditional in orientation, and will likely to continue to be so) but
results from my desire to create a relatively clear focus for the volume. In
making individual selections for author entries, I narrowed my choices to

those writers whose careers were established during the postmodern era (roughly 1960 until the present). This selection process necessarily forced me to eliminate from consideration various significant precursors of postmodern experimentalism, some of whom—such as Samuel Beckett, Nabokov, Borges, and John Hawkes—continued to write fiction that had a major impact on our contemporary literary sensibility. These omissions were made reluctantly, but to do otherwise would have created the unsolvable dilemma of where and how else to draw the line of demarcation. To include Borges but not Kafka, for example, would seem highly questionable—and, for that matter, what about Céline and Faulkner and Joyce (or even Melville, Sterne, or Cervantes himself)? Fortunately, the complex swirl of interactions between these precursors and the more recent authors is discussed at some length in the overview articles; and, of course, for most of these precursors there is already ample biographical and bibliographical information readily available for scholars and interested readers.

THE EVOLUTION OF POSTMODERNISM:
SOME PRECURSORS AND BACKGROUND

As I've already suggested, there is no sharp demarcation line separating modernism and postmodernism, and the alleged differences between the two become especially difficult to pinpoint if one is examining the development of fiction in a global context and not just focusing on what has been occurring in the United States. (The impulses behind the experimentalism of, say, Latin American or Eastern European fiction are clearly different from those that motivated U.S. authors in the 1960s.) In the United States what occurred in the postmodern outburst of the 1960s seemed very radical in part because fiction in the United States during the previous 30 years had seemed, for the most part, conservative aesthetically. This is not to say that experimenting wasn't taking place in the United States at all during this period—some of the great innovators of the previous generation continued to explore new forms (Faulkner, Stein, Fitzgerald), and a few newcomers with an experimental bent appeared (Djuna Barnes, Kenneth Patchen, Nathaniel West, John Hawkes, Jack Kerouac); but for the most part, U.S. authors during this period were content to deal with the key issues of their day—the Depression, World War II, existential angst—in relatively straightforward forms. The reasons behind this formal conservatism are certainly complex, but part of its hold on writers has to do with the way the times affected many writers, especially the sense that with such big issues to be examined authors couldn't afford the luxury of innovative strategies. At any rate, for whatever reasons in the United States from the period of 1930 until 1960 we do not find the emergence of a major innovator—someone equivalent to Beckett or Borges or Alain Robbe-Grillet or Louis Ferdinand Céline—except in the person of perhaps postmodern fiction's most important precursor, Vladimir Nabokov, who labored in obscurity in this country for 25 years until the scandal of *Lolita* made him suddenly very visible indeed (though for all the wrong reasons). As a result, by the late 1950s the United States was just as ripe for an aesthetic revolution as it was for the cultural revolution that was soon to follow. The two are, of course, intimately related.

Much of the groundwork for the so-called postmodern aesthetic revolution had already been established earlier in this century in such areas as the theoretical work being done in philosophy and science; the innovations made in painting (the rejection of mimesis and fixed point perspective, the emphasis on collage, self-exploration, abstract expressionism, and so on); in theater in the works of Pirandello, Brecht, Beckett, Genet, even Thornton Wilder; the increasing prominence of photography, the cinema, and eventually television, which coopted certain alternatives for writers while opening up other areas of emphasis. And if one looks carefully enough, there were many modernist literary figures who had called for a complete overhaul of the notion of representation in fiction. It is a commonplace to note that *Tristram Shandy* is a thoroughly postmodern work in every respect but the period in which it is written, and there are dozens of other examples of authors who explored many of the same avenues of experimentalism that postmodern writers were to take: for instance, the surreal, mechanically produced constructions of Raymond Roussel; the work of Alfred Jarry, with its black humor, its obscenity, its confounding of fact, fiction, and autobiography, its general sense of play and formal outrageousness; André Gide's *The Counterfeiters*, with its self-reflexiveness and self-commentary; Franz Kafka's matter-of-fact surrealistic presentation of the self and its relationship to society (significantly, Kafka's impact on American writing was not strong until the 1950s); William Faulkner, with his multiple narrators and competing truths, and whose own voice is so insistently foregrounded throughout his fiction as to obliterate any real sense that he is transcribing anything but his own consciousness; and, looming over the entire literary landscape, is the figure of James Joyce, the Dead Father of postmodern fiction, who must be dealt with, slain, the pieces of his genius ritually eaten and digested.

The wider social and political forces that galvanized postmodern writers and provided a sense of urgency and focus to their development were similar, in some ways, to those that provided such a great impetus to artistic innovation during the 1920s. In both cases, an international tragedy—World War I for artists in the 1920s, and Vietnam (along with a host of more diffused insanities, like the proliferation of nuclear weapons and the ongoing destruction of the environment) for postmodern American writers—created the sense that fundamental reconsiderations had to be made about the systems that govern our lives. Such systems included the political, social, and other ideological forms that had helped lead us to the position we were in, and also the artistic forms through which we could express a sense of ourselves and our relationship to the world around us. Thus, World War I was a global disaster of such unprecedented proportions, and had been produced by the very features of society that were supposed to ennoble and "civilize" us (reason, technology), that artists were forced to rethink the basic rationalistic, humanistic principles that had formed the basis of Western art since the Renaissance. One predictable response to the view that reality had become a fragmented, chaotic "Wasteland" was to turn to art as a kind of last retreat, a last source of reason, stability, and harmony. (One thinks of the magnificently ordered private systems of Joyce, Yeats, Pound, Proust, and Hemingway.) Another tactic was to develop art that turned its back on the barbarism and entropy of reality and explored instead the more abstract, rarified realm of art itself; here was a place where poets could examine language without regard to referents, where painters could explore the implications of lines, shapes, textures, and colors freed from outer correspondences. A third possibility was the development of artistic strategies that affirmed rather than denied or ignored the disorder and irrationalism around it, that joined forces with the primitive, illogical drives that Freud claimed lay within us all—the strategy of the dadaists and surrealists in painting and poetry, and of a few fiction writers as well (Anaïs Nin, Céline, Robert Desnos, Michel Leiris). Interestingly enough, all three tendencies would be evident in postmodern fiction 40 years later: the huge, intricately structured work (Pynchon, William Gaddis*, Barth, Don DeLillo*, Coover, Joseph McElroy*, Alexander Theroux*); the work that concerns only itself, its own mechanisms, the pure relationship of symbol and word (in William H. Gass*, Richard Kostelanetz*, Robert Pinget, Coover, Steve Katz*, Barthelme); and the fractured, delirious text whose process mirrored the entropy and fragmentation outside (William S. Burroughs, Barthelme, Raymond Federman*, Kathy Acker*). The difference between the two periods, then, is finally one of degree—the degree to which contemporary writers have turned to these strategies, the degree to which they have moved away from realistic norms (even in elaborately ordered works), especially in the degree to which artifice, playfulness, and self-consciousness—features not so common to the innovative fictions of the 1920s—have been consistently incorporated into the fabric of postmodern fiction.

It probably seems initially peculiar that postmodernism emerged in the 1960s rather than in the years that immediately followed World War II. It may be that the war, with its Hitlers and Mussolinis, its Hiroshimas and Normandy Beaches and Dresdens, its other unthinkable horrors (the concentration camps, collective suicides, and so on), was too dreadful or overwhelming to be directly confronted. In any case, the great innovators of the 1940s and 1950s tended to be, at least at first glance, nonsocially conscious writers. Beckett, Borges, and Nabokov—the three authors from this

period who were to have the most direct impact on postmodern writing—
all appeared to turn their backs on the world outside in favor of a movement
inward, toward the world of language, dream, and memory, to examine
the nature of subjective experience, of the way words beguile, mislead,
and shape our perception, of the way imagination builds its own realm out
of symbols. I emphasize the word "appear" in these three cases because
all three of these authors were, in fact, very much political writers in a
very basic sense, for each was profoundly aware of the importance that
language plays in shaping the world around us, the way power-structures
use this world-building capacity of words, the way that reality and commonsense are disguised versions of ideologies that are foisted on individuals
by institutions that profit from the popular acceptance of these illusions.
From this perspective, the postmodern emphasis on subjectivity, language,
and fiction-making is hardly as irrelevant, self-indulgent, and narcissistic
as many unsympathetic critics have charged. Indeed, many of the most
important postmodern works, for all their experimentalism, metafictional
impulses, self-reflexiveness, playfulness, and game-playing, have much more
to say about history, social issues, and politics than is generally realized.

Another writer very aware of the need to examine the role of language
within larger contexts was George Orwell, whose *1984* remains the most
famous fictional treatment of political language manipulation. *1984*, which
grew out of science fiction's dystopian tradition and which was specifically
influenced by Yevgeny Zamiatin's remarkable experimental novel, *We* (a
"postmodern" novel published in 1920), points to another important tendency in postmodern fiction: the increasing attention being paid by serious,
highly sophisticated authors to paraliterary forms such as science fiction
and detective fiction—forms that proved attractive to the postmodern spirit
partly because mimesis was never their guiding concern to begin with. Such
genres were thus free to generate forms and conventions that were entirely
different from those of traditional fiction, and that proved to be surprisingly
rich and suggestive. Developments in these paraliterary forms need to be
examined more thoroughly by scholars—there are fertile areas of investigation into, for example, the use of pornographical conventions by Acker,
Coover, Samuel Delany*, and Clarence Major (not to mention Nabokov);
or the appropriation of detective novel forms by many postmodern writers
(Nabokov, Stanislaw Lem*, Michel Butor, Robbe-Grillet, William Hjorts-
berg, McElroy). But the most significant evolution of a paraliterary form
has been that of science fiction. Long respected in Europe and never as
clearly separated from literature there as it has been in the United States
(cf. the European tradition of H.G. Wells, Zamiatin, Karel Čapek, Olaf
Stapledon, Orwell, Aldous Huxley, Arthur C. Clark, J.G. Ballard), SF
emerged in the United States from its self-imposed "ghetto status" into a
major field of creative activity during the 1960s. Although many literary
critics remain suspicious of and condescending toward SF, it is obvious

today that a number of the most significant postmodern innovators have been SF writers. This is certainly the case with Philip K. Dick*, a writer misunderstood both inside and outside his field. Because his publishers forced him onto a treadmill of rapid-fire production, Dick's novels are always plagued by a certain amount of sloppiness, lack of verbal grace, and two-dimensional character portrayals. Nevertheless, Dick had a brilliant fictional imagination capable of inventing plots of considerable intricacy and metaphorical suggestiveness. In his best works—*The Man in the High Castle, Martian Time-Slip, Ubik, Do Androids Dream of Electric Sheep?*—he devised highly original central plot structures that deal with many of the same issues common to postmodernism: metaphysical ambiguity, the oppressive nature of political systems, entropy, the mechanization of modern life.

Similarly, other major SF figures—including Ursula LeGuin,* Delany, Gene Wolfe,* John Varley,* Lem, Roger Zelazny*—have been creating complex, ingenious fictional forms that tell us a great deal about the fantastic world around us but that do so with structures whose conventions and language differ fundamentally from that of "mundane fiction" (as Delany refers to it). Indeed, one indication of the richness and diversity of this field can be seen in the number of "mainstream" authors who have turned to SF—Doris Lessing, Anthony Burgess, Italo Calvino, Marge Piercy, Thomas Berger,* Nabokov, Raymond Federman, and dozens of others.

There were, of course, other developments occurring before 1960 that would influence the direction of postmodernism. One of the most important of these has been the rapid emergence of the cinema and television as major artistic forms. It is probably no accident that postmodern experimentalists were the first generation of writers who grew up immersed in television, or that many of these writers were as saturated with the cinema as their forefathers had been with literature. The specific influences of television and the movies on postmodern fiction are diffuse, generalized, difficult to pinpoint, but obviously an awareness of the process through which a movie is presented—its rapid cutting, its use of montage and juxtaposition, its reliance on close-ups, tracking shots, and other technical devices—is likely to create some deeply rooted effects on writers when they sit down at their collective typewriters. (The process is also symbiotic: Eisenstein's theory of montage had a profound effect on an entire generation of writers, but so did Flaubert's use of montage in the famous "country-fair" scene in *Madame Bovary* affect filmmakers.) And as important as movies and television were in suggesting to writers what could be put in to their works was the example they supplied for what could be left out profitably. Not only did writers quickly realize that television and the cinema could deal with certain narrative forms more effectively than fiction (photography had similarly made certain forms of painting instantly obsolete), but a number of cinematic shorthand devices proved useful in fiction as well. Audiences trained in the conventions of the nineteenth-century novel may have required certain connections, certain details and transitions, but cinematic directors quickly discovered that many of these could be eliminated once the audience became acquainted with a different set of conventions. (Consider a typical cinematic juxtaposition of a man walking up a street and a shot of him sitting in the interior of a house—there's no need to supply the sights he saw on his walk, a view of the house approaching, the pause while knocking on the door or inserting the key, and so on.) Similarly, the pacing of television—and of television commercials, whose significance is also substantial in this regard—is directly apparent in many postmodern works (one thinks of *Slaughterhouse-Five*, *Ragtime*, of Coover's and Barthelme's short fiction, of Manuel Puig* and Jonathan Baumbach). The more specific influences of individual directors cannot be discounted: Jean-Luc Godard probably had as much impact on the imaginations of writers during the 1960s as any literary figure; and in various ways, movies like *8*, *Blow Up*, *Belle de Jour*, *Repulsion*, *2001*, *Dr. Strangelove*, and a host of other innovative films, have deeply imprinted themselves in the body of postmodern fiction.

THE POSTMODERN AWAKENING: 1960–1975

The early 1960s saw the publication of a number of fictional works that indicated that American fiction was heading in some very different directions than it had been during the preceding 25 years. Signaling this change in aesthetic sensibility was the appearance within a relatively short period of time (1960–1965) of a number of major works that decisively broke with the traditions of conventional realism. These key works included John Barth's *The Sot-Weed Factor* (1960) and *Giles Goat-Boy* (1966), Joseph Heller's *Catch–22* (1961), Vladimir Nabokov's *Pale Fire* (1962), Thomas Pynchon's *V.* (1963), Donald Barthelme's *Come Back, Dr. Caligari* (1964), and Robert Coover's *The Origin of the Brunists* (1965). These works were all produced by young, obviously ambitious writers (Nabokov is an exception, in terms of age). This fiction owed its unusual effects to a wide variety of sources, such as the absurdist theater (which had been flourishing in New York's Off-Broadway scene during the late 1950s), jazz and rock and roll, pop art, and other developments in the avant-garde art scene, the growing appreciation of Kafka and other experimenters (many of whom were first being translated during this period: Céline, Robbe-Grillet, and the other French New Novelists, Jean Genet, Borges, Günter Grass*), the energy and hot-wired delirium of the Beats. The result was a peculiar blend of dark humor, literary parody, surrealism, byzantine plots full of improbable coincidences and outrageous action, all presented in a dazzling variety of excessive styles that constantly called attention to themselves. Postmodern fiction had arrived.

What was to characterize the direction of postmodern fiction during the rest of the decade—the push to test new forms of expression, to examine conventions and solutions critically and seek new answers, to rethink so-called natural methods of organizing perception, expose their ideological origins, and pose new systems of organization—was hardly born in an ivory-towered, academic vacuum. The art of the 1960s, including the postmodern fiction, reflected the basic ways in which the ideologies on which the U.S. order had traditionally relied, together with the cultural values by which it rules, were in deep turmoil. Fiction reflected the sense, shared by many of our most thoughtful and articulate citizens, that we had been led (and misled) into the age of nuclear nightmare, into Vietnam, into ecological apocalypse, into political oppression, and into an insane and immoral sense of values that devalued human beings by glorifying abstractions and the inanimate—all this in the name of certain labels and covert ideologies that badly needed overhauling. A natural extension of this feeling was the desire to tear down the ruling ideologies (political, sexual, moral, social, aesthetic, all of which proved to be remarkably integrated) and reveal them for what they were: arbitrary structures imposed as a result of various complex, historical, and economic forces, instated into societies as natural and commonsensical, all of which served, in one way or another, to reinforce the status quo and insure the continued world view (and hence the continued power) of those who established these ideologies. Thus, the aggressive, radicalized poetics of postmodernism was an extension of a larger sense of dissatisfaction and frustration. "Don't trust anyone over 30" was an expression commonly heard among young people in the 1960s who were fed up with the content and structure of their lives. A similar distrust of one's "elders" was equally apparent in postmodern fiction writers.

By the late 1960s and early 1970s, a new generation of writers had firmly established itself. During this period experimental fictions appeared by authors who were eventually characterized by critics as being postmodern in outlook: William Gass' *In the Heart of the Heart of the Country*, Jerzy Kosinski's* *Steps*, Robert Coover's *Universal Baseball Association* and *Pricksongs and Descants*, John Fowles' *The French Lieutenant's Woman*, Peter Handke's* *The Goalie's Anxiety at the Penalty Kick*, García Márquez's *One Hundred Years of Solitude*, Steve Katz's *The Exagggerations of Peter Prince*, Donald Barthelme's *City Life*, *Snow White*, and *Unspeakable Practices, Unnatural Acts*, Pynchon's *The Crying of Lot 49*, Richard Brautigan's *Trout Fishing in America*, Tom Robbins'* *Another Roadside Attraction*, Raymond Federman's *Double or Nothing*, Rudolf Wurlitzer's *Nog*, Nabokov's *Ada*, and Joseph McElroy's *A Smuggler's Bible*. The point is not that these authors approached the issue of fictional innovation in a fundamentally unified fashion. Rather, quite the opposite was true: writers were busy exploring a host of innovative strategies, many of them very different in intent and effect. (One can hardly imagine, for example, two works so opposed in aesthetic orientation as, say, Federman's *Double or Nothing* and Gass' "In the Heart of the Heart of the Country.") What these experimentations did share, however, was a general sense that fiction needed to acknowledge its own artificial, constructed nature, to focus the reader's attention on how the work was being articulated rather than merely on what was happening. Distrustful of all claims to truth and hypersensitive to the view that reality and objectivity were not givens but social or linguistic constructs, postmodern writers tended to lay bare the artifice of their works, to comment on the processes involved, to refuse to create the realist illusion that the work mimics operations outside itself. In the ideology of realism or representation, it was implied that words were linked to thoughts or objects in essentially direct, incontrovertible ways. On the other hand, postmodern authors—operating in an aesthetic environment that has grown out of Saussaurian linguistics, Wittgenstein's notion of meaning-as-usage, structuralism, and deconstructive views of language—tend to manipulate words as changeable entities determined by the rules of the particular sign-system (the fiction at hand). Hardly a translucent window on to an object (the world, reality) or a mind, the language in many postmodern texts becomes "thickened," played with and shown off, and frequently becomes just another element to be manipulated by a self-conscious author.

Other conventions of the realist narrative were challenged. The notion of the unified subject living in a world of stable essences (one of the cornerstones of traditional fiction) was one such notion that was frequently mocked by postmodern authors, either by so obsessively emphasizing the schizophrenic, subjective nature of experience as to obliterate the distinction between subject and reality (as in Philip Dick or Jonathan Baumbach or Federman) or by creating characters with no definable personality or who changed from scene to scene (as with Ronald Sukenick's* figures who change "like a cloud," or Ron Silliman's* prose experiments in which narrator and setting disappear into the process of language selection). The commonsensical distinction between fact and fiction, author and text, also became increasingly difficult to make. "Real" authors began making increasingly common excursions into their fictional worlds (as Vonnegut did in *Breakfast of Champions* and Fowles did in *The French Lieutenant's Woman*, or as Sukenick and Federman and Katz did in nearly all their works); fragments of real events, real reportage, and news often became incorporated into works, collage-fashion, making it impossible to untangle what was being made up from what had really happened. (Here one thinks of Barthelme, Burroughs, Vonnegut, Harold Jaffe,* Coover, and William Kennedy.*) This tendency to break down the seam between the real and the invented, or to deny the relevance of this distinction altogether, was also evident in the writing of the New Journalists, like Tom Wolfe,* Truman Capote, Norman Mailer, and Hunter Thompson. These authors, along

with other writers who blurred the fact/fiction dichotomy (Robert Pirsig*
in *Zen and the Art of Motorcycle Maintenance*, Maxine Hong Kingston*
in *The Woman Warrior* and *China Men*, Peter Handke in *A Sorrow Beyond
Dreams*, V. S. Naipaul in *In a Free State*, and so on), not only employed
various conventions borrowed from fiction to heighten a sense of drama
and plot development, but they also thrust their own subjective responses
into the forefront of their works rather than making claims that their texts
were objective. Likewise, the distinction between poetry and prose was
also often dissolved, not just by fiction writers who emphasized poetic
qualities in their prose (Gass, Barry Hannah,* Stanley Elkin,* Nabokov,
Hawkes), but also by poets who began to explore longer forms of prose.
(See Ron Silliman's discussion of this important phenomenon in this volume.) Even the familiar "look" of books—the conventions of typography,
pagination, and other visual elements that actually govern the process of
reading itself—was freely tampered with, in works of such visual ingenuity
as Federman's *Double or Nothing*, Katz's *The Exaggerations of Peter
Prince*, Gass' *Willie Masters' Lonesome Wife*, Julio Cortázar's* *Ultimo
Rundo*, Barthelme's *City Life*, or Butor's *Mobile*. In short, virtually all of
the elements that make the reading experience what it is were being reexamined by postmodern experimenters during the 1960s. Not surprisingly,
many of the experiments proved to be dead ends or were rapidly exhausted
and then discarded. This seems to be the case with the New Novel experiments and with a lot of the typographical experimentation, for example.
But even these innovations were useful in that they suggested avenues that
writers need no longer explore.

POSTMODERN CRITICISM

As should be evident from the focus of the two critical articles dealing
with postmodern criticism and from the critics I selected to be included in
the individual author entry section, I have tried to emphasize critical thought
that shares features of postmodern thought rather than focusing on criticism
that deals with postmodern fiction. Indeed, it seems evident to me that
many of the same principles and tendencies that were shaping the direction
of postmodern fiction are central to the development of the most important
critical schools of the past 25 years: structuralism, deconstruction, and
Marxist-oriented criticism. (For a good overview of this interaction, see
Charles Caramello's *Silverless Mirrors: Book, Self & Postmodern American
Fiction* [Tallahassee, Fla.: University Presses of Florida, 1983].) For example, the Marxist and structuralist emphasis on the constructedness of
human meaning is similar to postmodern fiction's sense that reality is not
given and that our way of perceiving it is hardly natural or self-evident.
Terry Eagleton's fine summary of the chief tenets of structuralism in his
survey of critical thought, *Literary Theory* (Minneapolis: University of

Minnesota Press, 1983) helps clarify the interrelationship between structuralism and postmodern aesthetics very clearly. Structuralism, he notes, emphasizes that:

Meaning was neither a private experience nor a divinely ordained occurrence: it was the product of certain shared systems of signification. The confident bourgeoise belief that the isolated individual subject was the fount and origin of all meaning took a sharp knock: language pre-dated the individual, and was much less his or her product than he or she was the product of it. Meaning was not "natural," a question of just looking and seeing, or something eternally settled; the way you interpreted your world was a function of the languages you had at your disposal, and there was evidently nothing immutable about these. Meaning was not something which all men and women everywhere intuitively shared, and then articulated in their various tongues and scripts; what meaning you were able to articulate depended on what script or speech you shared in the first place. There were the seeds here of a social and historical theory of meaning, whose implications were to run deep within contemporary thought. It was impossible any longer to see reality simply as something "out there," a fixed order of things which language merely reflected (pp. 107–108).

For structuralism, then, reality and our experience of reality need not necessarily be continuous—a view that is intimately connected with postmodern fiction's refusal to rely on fixed notions of reality, its emphasis on reproducing the human being's imaginative (subjective, fictional) responses to what is "out there" rather than trying to convince the readers that they are experiencing a transcription of reality unfiltered by a mediating process. Roland Barthes' early ventures into structuralist criticism produced a notion that also bears some striking relevance for what would develop in fiction during the 1960s. For example, Barthes' analysis of the healthy sign is directly applicable to what postmodern authors suggest about healthy fiction: in both cases the artifact is healthiest which draws attention to itself and to its own arbitrariness—one that makes no effort to pass itself off as natural or inevitable but that, in the very act of conveying a meaning, communicates something of its own relative, artificial status as well. Thus, very much like postmodern fiction writers, Barthes rightly perceives that one of the functions of ideologies and power-structures of all sorts is always to convert culture into nature—to make it appear that conventions, signs, and social realities are natural, innocent, commonsensical. The obvious literary analogy to this natural attitude can be found in realist fiction, which implies that it possesses the means (a natural language) to represent something else with little or no interference with what it mediates. Such a realist sign is for Barthes—and for the postmodern authors of the 1960s—essentially unhealthy, for it proceeds by denying its own status as a sign in order to create the illusion that we are perceiving reality without its intervention.

Deconstruction and poststructuralism, as developed by Derrida, Paul de Man,* Barthes, and others, was essentially an attempt to topple the logic by which a particular system of thought (and behind that, a whole system of political structures and social institutions) maintains its force. By demonstrating that all meaning and knowledge could be exposed as resting on a naively representational theory of language, poststructuralism provided still another justification for postmodernism's emphasis on the free play of language, of the text-as-generating-meaning. The later Barthes (as in *The Pleasure of the Text*, 1973) suggested that only in writing (or in reading-as-writing) could the individual be freed momentarily from the tyranny of structural meaning, from ideology, from theory. As Eagleton notes, one product of this emphasis on the unnaturalness of signs was admittedly the tendency by some poststructuralists (and some fiction writers) to flee from history, to take refuge in the erotic play of writing/reading, and conveniently to evade reality and all political questions completely:

If meaning, the signified, was a passing product of words or signifiers, always shifting and unstable, part-present and part-absent, how could there be any determinate truth or meaning at all? If reality was constructed by our discourse rather than reflected by it, how could we ever know reality itself, rather than merely knowing our own discourse? Was all talk just talk about talk? Did it make sense to claim that one interpretation of reality, history or the literary text was "better" than another? (p. 143)

Such questions cut to the heart of the debate that was to rage during the mid- to late 1970s about the moral responsibility of fiction—a debate most famously summarized in the series of public discussions between the late John Gardner*, whose study *On Moral Fiction* sparked considerable public interest in this issue, and William Gass, whose eloquent defense of fiction's irrelevancy to conditions outside the page (in *Fiction and the Figures of Life*) became a seminal aspect of postmodern aesthetics. (The Gass-Gardner "Debate" in *Anything Can Happen*, eds. Tom LeClair and Larry McCaffery [Urbana: University of Illinois Press], pp. 20–31. This issue recurs in many of the 18 interviews collected in this volume.) The outline of this debate centered on Gardner's claim, echoed by a number of other critics (perhaps most effectively in Gerald Graff's *Literature Against Itself* [Chicago: University of Chicago Press, 1979]), that postmodern experimentalism, with its willful artifice and subjectivity, its metafictional impulses and emphasis on the play of language, is fundamentally trivial, vain, self-absorbed, and narcissistic. Gass, on the other hand, took essentially the familiar art-for-art's-sake position but developed his views with considerable rigor, supporting them with theories of language and aesthetics formulated by Wittgenstein and Max Black (both of whom Gass had studied under at Cornell), Paul Valéry, and Gertrude Stein. Words, said Gass, are the writer's chief concern, for the writer's final obligation is to build something (a world of language, with its own rules and systems of transformations), not to describe something. One senses in Gass a longing for a safe and human refuge in this world of language, a place controlled and purified, an escape from an ugly, petty reality in which history becomes a destructive monument to human greed, in which discourse has been degraded into instruments of commerce, politics, and bureaucracy. Paradoxically, then, although Gass's emphasis on fiction as an interaction of signifiers had a liberating effect on the formal concerns of postmodern authors, there was also a potentially troubling elitism about his position, with its emphasis on formal complexity and beauty, and its lack of self-irony and play. This tendency is also obvious (and troubling) when one examines the important Yale School of Critics (Geoffrey Hartman,* J. Hillis Miller,* de Man, and, with some reservations, Harold Bloom*). These latter critics have argued, often brilliantly, that literary language—indeed, all forms of discourse—constantly undermines its own meaning. But in their tendency to view all elements of reality, including social reality, as merely further texts to be deconstructed as being undecidable, there emerges the sense that one has found a means to demolish all opinions without having to adopt any of one's own. Perhaps the key factor that needs to be emphasized in this regard is that, as Derrida and Barthes, among others, have demonstrated, there is no fundamental opposition between a fiction that emphasizes its unnaturalness, its arbitrariness, that reveals (and revels in) its *différances*, and one that deals with history, politics, and social issues in a significant fashion. Indeed, by opening up a radical awareness of the sign systems by which men and women live, and by offering exemplars of freely created fictions that oppose publicly accepted ones, postmodern fiction contains the potential to rejoin the history which some claim it has abandoned. Thus, although most critics have been largely blind to the political thrust of postmodern experimentalism, it will surely soon be recognized that the fiction of Barthelme, Coover, Sukenick, Federman, Gaddis, Barth, Pynchon, DeLillo, Silliman, and other innovators of postmodernism is very much centered on political questions: questions about how ideologies are formed, the process whereby conventions are developed, the need for individuals to exercise their own imaginative and linguistic powers lest these powers be coopted by others.

POST-POSTMODERNISM: THE EVOLUTION OF CONTEMPORARY CONSCIOUSNESS

If a single work may be said to have provided a model for the direction of postmodern fiction of the 1970s and 1980s, it is probably García Márquez's *One Hundred Years of Solitude*, a work that admirably and brilliantly combines experimental impulses with a powerful sense of political and social reality. Indeed, Márquez's masterpiece perfectly embodies a tendency found in much of the best recent fiction—that is, it uses experimental strategies to discover new methods of reconnecting with the world outside the page, outside of language. In many ways, *One Hundred Years of Solitude* is clearly a nonrealistic novel, with its magical, surreal landscape, its dense reflexive surface, its metafictional emphasis on the nature of language and how reality is storified from one generation to the next, its labyrinthine literary references, and other features. Yet for all its experimentalism, *One Hundred Years of Solitude* also is a highly readable, coherent story, peopled with dozens of memorable characters; and it also urgently speaks to us about political, historical, and psychological realities that are central to our experience. It thus becomes an emblem of what postmodernism can be, being self-conscious about its literary heritage and about the limits of mimesis, developing its own organic form of experimentalism, yet managing to reconnect its readers with the world around them. When one examines some of the major works that have appeared since 1975—Barth's *Letters*, for example, or Gaddis' *JR*, or Salman Rushdie's* *Midnight's Children*, or William Kennedy's *Ironweed*—one can see a similar synthesis at work.

This synthesis between experimentalism and more traditional literary concerns is explainable on many levels. Partly it has to do with the predictable, dialectical process that seems to govern most revolutions (aesthetical and otherwise), with the radicalism of one era being soon questioned, reexamined, and then counterattacked by more conservative attitudes. If the public spirit of rebellion, distrust, and unrest was reflected in the disruptive fictional forms of the 1960s, so, too, has the reactionary, conservative political and social atmosphere of the late 1970s and early 1980s inevitably been manifested in the literature of this period. This is not to say that experimentalism has dried up completely, but certainly it is obvious that authors today are less interested in innovation per se than they were ten or fifteen years ago—especially innovation in the direction of reflexive, nonreferential works. And, of course, the source of this shift in sensibility lies beyond the political climate alone. For one thing, the experimental fervor that seemed to sustain postmodernism for several years has been subjected to repeated counterattacks by authors and critics (one thinks of Gardner, Carver, Gore Vidal, and Graff). More significantly, we find authors simply exploring new grounds, different methods of innovation, redefining notions like realism and artifice in much the same way that, for example, photorealists did in painting. This is a familiar scenario: so-called artistic revolutions have a natural life span, and they are inevitably succeeded by a new artistic situation, with its own demands and needs, its own practitioners who do not share the enthusiasms of the previous group and who are anxious to define themselves as individuals in their own way. Thus, when we examine a number of the highly regarded writers who have emerged since 1975—authors like Ron Hansen, Ian McEwan,* Frederick

Barthelme, William Kennedy, Toni Morrison,* Jayne Anne Phillips,* Stephen Dixon,* Raymond Carver, or Ann Beattie*—we discover a very different aesthetic sensibility in their work than that which characterized earlier postmodern writers, a sensibility that seems interested in what I would term experimental realism. (Note that Professor Jerome Klinkowitz* presents a different notion of this term in his article in this volume.) By experimental realism I mean fiction that is fundamentally realistic in its impulses but that develops innovative strategies in structure (the nonendings of Beattie, Carver, Barthelme, the absence of character and plot in Silliman), language (the poetic prose of Phillips or Maxine Hong Kingston or Marilynne Robinson, the collage-assemblage of Silliman), the use of unusual materials (as with the use of "found" materials in Beattie, the manipulations of legend and history in Hansen, Kennedy, Leslie Silko, and Kingston), and so on. Of course, some of the sense of the decline of experimentalism results from our greater familiarity with the innovative strategies that once seemed so peculiar and difficult. Because later fiction which uses these experimental strategies seems more familiar and hence less threatening, its subsequent appearance is less likely to be remarked on—it is, in fact, no longer considered to be experimental at all. To take an obvious example, it might not occur to most readers or critics to discuss John Irving's* *The World According to Garp* as an experimental novel, although it obviously employs many of the same metafictional techniques— the book-within-a-book, the interweaving of fiction and reality, playful self-references to its author's previous works—that other, more radical texts were using back in the 1960s. This isn't to say that Irving's book isn't experimental or metafiction—it clearly is; it just may seem beside the point to label it as such.

Much the same point can be made about many of the best works of fiction that have appeared in the United States from 1975 to 1984. Books like Tim O'Brien's* *Going After Cacciato*, Alexander Theroux's *Darconville's Cat*, John Barth's *Sabbatical*, Ann Beattie's *Falling in Place*, Kurt Vonnegut's *Jailbird*, Toni Morrison's *Song of Solomon*, William Kennedy's Albany trilogy, and John Calvin Batchelor's* *The Further Adventures of Halley's Comet* (to give just a sampling) incorporated postmodern experimental strategies into their structures so smoothly that they have often been seen as being quite traditional in orientation. Naturally, more radical experimental works continue to be written, but with a few notable exceptions—most of the books published by the Fiction Collective, the remarkable prose experiments of Ron Silliman, Lyn Hejinian,* Barrett Watten,* and Charles Bernstein,* Joseph McElroy's *Plus*, Gilbert Sorrentino's* *Mulligan Stew*, Kathy Acker's* "punk novels," Walter Abish's* works—most of the important, vital fiction of the last decade were neither exclusively experimental in an obvious, flamboyant manner, nor representational in a traditional, realist sense. Again, this situation recapitulates what we see in the other arts, in which the advances and new directions adopted by artists of one period (say, the break with representation and fixed perspective in painting) are gradually assimilated by artists of succeeding generations until a new period of stagnation arises which subsequently produces a new revolution. Thus, like the operations that are endlessly forming and transforming the nature of reality itself (and the nature of our lives within this flux), the transformations of art will surely continue, heedless of the desires of critics for clear patterns, unassailable definitions, and useful labels.

PART I
OVERVIEW ARTICLES

POSTMODERN FICTION

LORI CHAMBERLAIN

Magicking the Real:
Paradoxes of Postmodern Writing

"There is a specter haunting fiction—the specter of realism." This para-phrase of Marx's opening to *The Communist Manifesto* characterizes a pervasive attitude toward realism in contemporary writing. It captures both the vociferous derogation of the term "realism," especially as that term is used in opposition to experimental writing, and its ghostly persistence. Authors and critics alike, championing the cause of postmodern experi-mentation, have repeatedly raised the specter of "the traditional realistic novel" as that which threatens to choke—perhaps even kill—the novel as a genre; the realistic novel is seen to rely on naive, even dangerous, pre-suppositions. From the point of view of experimental fiction, the following is a fairly typical description of the traditional novel:

Realistic fiction presupposed chronological time as the medium of a plotted nar-rative, an irreducible individual psyche as the subject of its characterization, and, above all, the ultimate concrete reality of things as the object and rationale of its description.[1]

This characterization of realism belies not simply an aesthetic quibble but an epistemological one; realist aesthetics are seen to be unquestioningly empiricist and rationalist, while experimental fiction calls into question any such post-Cartesian certainties. In response, postmodern experimental fic-tion has attempted to redefine the possibilities of plot, character, and narration, challenging both traditional fiction and the discourse about it.

This ominous picture of realism has, of course, been overdrawn; few of the great realist writers exhibit the kind of confidence, hubris even, that has been attributed to them. The same periods that have nurtured realism, Larry McCaffery has pointed out in his *The Metafictional Muse*, have also spawned its double. Thus, the nineteenth century, for example, saw both the height of realist narrative and

the demolition of the faith in rational, empirical investigation, the frank acknowl-
edgement of the subjective nature of our mental operations and their relationship
to the world, and the injection of the concept of relativity into the very fabric of
the universe itself.[2]

Yet, in the genealogy of literary history, it was probably necessary to distort
the nature and authority of realism in order to open up a *new* space for a
genre many thought was already exhausted. Such a misreading was directed
not only against some of the obvious precursors to postmodern writing,
but more importantly also against a more popular and contemporary form
of realism that enjoyed the favor both of the large publishing houses and
of the major reviews—perhaps even of the public. As an alternative to
what they perceived to be the traditional and contemporary orthodoxy of
realism, writers such as Ronald Sukenick,* Raymond Federman,* William
H. Gass,* and Steve Katz* offered experimental works of self-reflexive
writing, reveling not in the reality principle but in the pleasure principle.
Such works argued for the value of fiction-making per se, rather than
measuring the value of a work of fiction against the ethics of mimesis.

But this is also to divide the world of contemporary fiction too neatly
into two, presumably exclusive camps. Somewhere between these two poles
lies a body of writing difficult to classify, writing made possible, in some
senses, by the very debate. Lacking most of the external signs of experimentation and most of the self-conscious, self-reflexiveness of experimental
fiction, this writing at first glance seems to share those realist assumptions
of the traditional novel. The opening paragraph of William Kennedy's*
Ironweed, for example, does not overtly threaten our expectations concerning character or narration:

Riding up the winding road of Saint Agnes Cemetery in the back of the rattling
old truck, Francis Phelan became aware that the dead, even more than the living,
settled down in neighborhoods. The truck was suddenly surrounded by fields of
monuments and cenotaphs of kindred design and striking size, all guarding the
privileged dead. But the truck moved on and the limits of mere privilege became
visible, for here now came the acres of truly prestigious death: illustrious men and
women, captains of life without their diamonds, furs, carriages, and limousines,
but buried in pomp and glory, vaulted in great tombs built like heavenly safe
deposit boxes, or parts of the Acropolis. And ah yes, here too, inevitably, came
the flowing masses, row upon row of them under simple headstones and simpler
crosses. Here was the neighborhood of the Phelans.[3]

This is an unobtrusive, third-person narrator using the simple past tense
to begin the story. It is true, Kennedy's description of the cemetery relies
on a metaphoric language that seems to animate the inanimate, yet metaphor per se is certainly a conventional strategy of realist representation.

The second paragraph, however, clearly defies any realist depiction of the dead:

Francis's mother twitched nervously in her grave as the truck carried him nearer to her; and Francis's father lit his pipe, smiled at his wife's discomfort, and looked out from his own bit of sod to catch a glimpse of how much his son had changed since the train accident (pp. 1–2).

While this is not a realist description, it does not, as much experimental fiction might, call attention to the problem of its representation. Instead, it treats these ghosts in the cemetery as matters of fact, and we are supposed to take them as "real" characters. The metaphoric language ("the dead . . . settled down in neighborhoods") is to be taken literally.

The oxymoron "magic realism" defines this aesthetic limbo for *Ironweed* and the considerable body of writing for which realism is a very real specter. Although there is no clear consensus among critics about the precise boundaries of magic realism, it refers broadly to that fiction propelled by the tension between realistic elements and fabulous, magical, or fantastic elements. The work of such writers as William Kennedy, Tim O'Brien,* Stanley Elkin,* Toni Morrison,* Max Apple,* Thomas Pynchon,* Robert Coover,* Harry Mathews,* Donald Barthelme,* and many others integrates both an attention to the real and to the power of the imagination to construct that reality.

Although there is an impressive body of magic realist writing in America and a tradition for such writing, only recently have critics put the term together with that writing. The term itself developed not in literary circles but in painterly ones; it was borrowed by Latin American writers, in fact, from Franz Roh's book *Nachexpressionismus, magischer Realismus: Probleme der neuesten europäischer Malerei* (Leipzig: Klinkhard and Biermann, 1925), which was translated into Spanish soon after its publication. This may explain why the term has been used more frequently in Latin America than in North America, despite the fact that it could as well describe phenomena in both. And in fact, the term has been used in North American art circles as well; the New York Museum of Modern Art held a 1943 exhibition entitled *American Realists and Magic Realists*. Roh, in attempting to distinguish magic realism from other movements, outlined some of its defining features. Magic realism, he said, is representational, tending, indeed, toward a sharp focus on objects to make them appear more than real. But the sharp focus does not necessarily serve the aims of representation; instead, it invests the object with a kind of magic aura, calling attention to the illusion of reality as in the paintings of Henri Rousseau and Giorgio de Chirico.[4]

In literary circles, the term has previously been used primarily to describe certain tendencies in Latin American narrative; its currency in those circles is indebted specifically to discussions of Alejo Carpentier's work. In the often quoted introduction to his *El reino de este mundo*, a novel based historically in Haiti during the period of the French Revolution, Carpentier observes that the entire history of America is but a chronicle of "lo real-maravilloso," the marvelous-real.[5] For Carpentier, the marvelous-real is something to be found in the quotidian; it is surprising—terrible and awesome, perhaps—but not fantastic. The marvelous-real might more properly denote our way of seeing or conceptualizing the real, re-presenting it as if it were seen for the first time. For an example of this sense of the marvelous, we might look at the opening section of Gabriel García Márquez's* *One Hundred Years of Solitude*. José Arcadio Buendía takes his two sons to see the gypsies, who have brought, among their many treasures, a pirate chest:

Inside there was only an enormous, transparent block with infinite internal needles in which the light of the sunset was broken up into colored stars. . . .

"It's the largest diamond in the world."

"No," the gypsy countered. "It's ice."[6]

Struck by the mystery of the ice, José Arcadio Buendía proclaims, "This is the great invention of our time."

As both García Márquez and Carpentier point out, the New World was full of such marvelous realities. For those who came to conquer, the Americas presented an unimaginable landscape, fabulous cities, exotic peoples, and potential dangers. Colonization lent an air of the carnivalesque to the political landscape, and the many brutal, repressive dictatorships that followed matched the cruelty of the environment. The New World seemed to oscillate between the poles articulated by Domingo Sarmiento, a nineteenth-century Argentine writer—between civilization and barbarity. It was a world that demanded a new language to refer to this marvelous reality. Thus, García Márquez, for example, insists that even the more fantastical elements of his *One Hundred Years of Solitude*, such as the ascension of Remedios the Beauty, are real. The fact of Remedios' ascension is based, he says in an interview with Plinio Apuleyo Mendoza, on "a woman whose grand-daughter had run away from home in the early hours of the morning, and who tried to hide the fact by putting the word around that she had gone up to heaven."[7] This is a reality produced by the imagination and shaped by a specific cultural and historical situation. García Márquez reinvents ice for us and invents a world in which the ascension of Remedios the Beauty is as real as that ice.

That magic realism has developed both a literary and a critical currency in Latin America is at least partly due to the social circumstances of colonialism. That it is developing a currency in North American literary terminology may reflect both the increasingly fantastical quality of life in late capitalism—where people walk on the moon, go to drive-in churches, and have pet rocks—and the emergence of writing by those who have previously been largely excluded from conventional publishing outlets— women and writers of color, for example.

It is difficult to sort out the genealogy of magic realist writing in America in the contemporary period. There is no doubt that Latin American narrative has exercised a powerful influence on American writing. Translations brought the work of Jorge Luis Borges here in the early 1960s; García Márquez's *One Hundred Years of Solitude*, translated in 1971, has been widely read and enormously influential. Other Latin American magic realist authors whose works have been translated include Carpentier, José Donoso, Mario Vargas Llosa,* Miguel Angel Asturias, and Julio Cortázar,* among others. However, while it would be easy to chronicle the influence of, say, Borges on such writers as Barthelme, John Barth,* and Coover, it would be wrong to imply thereby that magic realism originated in Latin America and was imported to the United States in translation. The revival of magic realism in roughly the last 20 years is part of the larger context of postmodernism which exceeds the boundaries of national literatures. In practical terms, for example, it is difficult now to speak of writers in terms merely of a national literary tradition; although these traditions are important, writers from both South and North America share a common cross-cultural literary heritage. Kafka, for instance, is frequently cited by writers of both Americas as an important forebear, and his "The Metamorphosis" certainly lies in the tradition of magical realist writing. Surrealist writers and painters also were important, both to the nascence of magic realism and to its later revival in Western literary circles. In addition, magic realist writers in Latin America fed from the translations of certain key figures from the Anglo-American tradition—such writers as Poe, Hawthorne, Faulkner, and Hemingway. A more accurate way of characterizing the nature of influence, then, would be to note the cross-fertilization that results from translation north and south as well as such European movements as surrealism that were common to both South and North American writers.

For writers in the United States, there is an indigenous tradition for magic realism beginning at least with the gothic tales of Poe and the romances of Hawthorne—that is, with certain strands of American romanticism. Romanticism is itself torn by contradictions similar to those of magic realism: its imaginative view of the world, informed primarily by an idealist metaphysics, often sought in the irrational powers of the individual a sort of mystical unity of the world of nature and the world of the spirit, yet such an idealist project stood always in potential conflict with the empiricist and rationalist epistemology that was informing the rise of experimental

science at the same time. Nathaniel Hawthorne's *The Scarlet Letter* provides an archetype of this sort of conflict. Framed by the pseudo-realist
prologue "The Custom House," *The Scarlet Letter* projects the real world
of Puritan New England—the problems of theological authority and secular
guilt—onto a psychological landscape. Hawthorne describes his technique
in a famous passage from "The Custom House":

Moonlight, in a familiar room, falling so white upon the carpet, and showing all
its figure so distinctly,—making every object so minutely visible, yet so unlike a
morning or noontide visibility,—is a medium the most suitable for a romance-writer
to get acquainted with his illusive guests. There is the little domestic scenery of
the well-known apartment; the chairs, with each its separate individuality; the
centre-table, sustaining a work-basket, a volume or two, and an extinguished lamp;
the sofa; the book-case; the picture on the wall; —all these details, so completely
seen, are so spiritualized by the unusual light, that they seem to lose their actual
substance, and become things of intellect. Nothing is too small or too trifling to
undergo this change, and acquire dignity thereby. A child's shoe; the doll, seated
in her little wicker carriage; the hobby-horse; —whatever, in a word, has been
used or played with, during the day, is now invested with a quality of strangeness
and remoteness, though still almost as vividly present as by daylight.[8]

It is this moonlight that allows the narrator of the custom house section
to press the scarlet letter to his chest and feel it burning him as it later
does Hester Prynne. For it is in this space that "the Actual and the Imaginary may meet, and each imbue itself with the nature of the other" (31).
In this imaginative vision, such real objects as a sofa or a book-case are
"invested with a quality of strangeness and remoteness," while the supernatural is made to seem part of everyday life. This tension is articulated
with different emphases in the works of Edgar Allan Poe, Herman Melville,
and Henry James, authors who bear a natural affinity to the principles of
magic realism and who have been influential in both Europe and the
Americas.

More recent forebears for magic realism in America may be found in
the modernist period in such authors as Faulkner and Hemingway. Faulkner, of course, has frequently been cited as an important influence on the
work of García Márquez, Carlos Fuentes,* and other Latin American
magic realists. Faulkner's depiction of Yoknapatawpha, peopled with
strange, obsessive characters whose lives repeat themselves in later generations, is a kind of double for the world García Márquez creates around
Macondo. In both cases, it is a world where metaphor becomes literal,
where what we are accustomed to take as realistic detail is rendered in a
highly figurative language. Faulkner's description of Miss Coldfield in the
opening pages of *Absalom, Absalom!* provides an example of this confusion
of realms:

Her voice would not cease, it would just vanish. There would be the dim coffin-smelling gloom sweet and over-sweet and the twice-bloomed wistaria against the outer wall by the savage September sun impacted distilled and hyperdistilled, into which came now and then the loud cloudy flutter of the sparrows like a flat limber stick whipped by an ideal boy, and the rank smell of female old flesh long embattled in virginity while the wan haggard face watched him above the faint triangle of lace at wrists and throat from the too tall chair in which she resembled a crucified child; and the voice not ceasing but vanishing into and then out of the long intervals like a stream, a trickle running from patch to patch of dried sand, and the ghost mused with shadowy docility as if it were the voice which he haunted where a more fortunate one would have had a house.[9]

Faulkner's main task here seems to be to show the transformation of a voice into silence without our noticing that transformation; he accomplishes this through a number of other transformations that confuse the realms of the animate and inanimate, the living and the dead: the flutter of sparrows becomes a flat limber stick; a woman becomes a crucified child; the voice becomes the trickle of a stream disappearing through the sand. The past is thus made to inhabit the present like a ghost haunting the language of this description. Compare this with the following passage from García Márquez's *One Hundred Years of Solitude*, a description of the death of José Arcadio:

A trickle of blood came out under the door, crossed the living room, went out into the street, continued on in a straight line across the uneven terraces, went down steps and climbed over curbs, passed along the Street of the Turks, turned a corner to the right and another to the left, made a right angle at the Buendía house, went in under the closed door, crossed through the parlor, hugging the walls so as not to stain the rugs, went on to the other living room, made a wide curve to avoid the dining-room table, went along the porch with the begonias, and passed without being seen under Amaranta's chair as she gave an arithmetic lesson to Aureliano José, and went through the pantry and came out in the kitchen, where Ursula was getting ready to crack thirty-six eggs to make bread.

"Holy Mother of God!" Ursula shouted (pp. 129–130).

The difference, we see in these two passages, is that Faulkner relies on the simile to both separate and confuse the realms of fact and fiction, whereas García Márquez has made what might have been a simile ("the news arrived *like* a trickle of blood...") into something we are to take as fact, the truth now stranger than fiction. In literalizing the metaphor, however, García Márquez does not simply become a new symbolist or allegorist. His narratives lack the shining metaphysics of the symbolist period, and they are far too complex to be read in allegorical terms.
    Although Faulkner shares at least some elective affinities with the Latin American tradition of magic realist writing, he is also one of the obvious

precursors to Stanley Elkin, one of the major contemporary American magic realists. Elkin, who wrote a dissertation on Faulkner, shares Faulkner's baroque language, a language that seems to grow in grotesque tendrils, transforming what might begin as an ordinary landscape into something rich and strange. Relying frequently on the simile, Elkin extends it and obscures it in an accumulation of phrases and clauses. His characters, like the language itself, tend to be obsessive, their obsessions circling around the twins of sex and mortality, grounded in the real and exaggerated by the pressures of fantasy and everyday life.

Elkin's novella *The Making of Ashenden* is in some ways paradigmatic of magical realist writing. Although it draws clearly on the American romance tradition—on such values as innocence, purity, heroism—it projects these onto a grotesque landscape that is at once wildly savage and completely artificial or invented. Hawthorne's forest scenes are not so far from such scenes as the following, where Brewster Ashenden is taking a moonlit walk on his friend's game reserve:

He was in a sort of clearing. Though he knew he had not retraced his steps nor circled round behind himself, it seemed familiar. He stood on uneven ground and could see a line of low frigid mountains in the distance. High above him and to his right the great tea of the moon, like the drain of day, sucked light. At his feet there appeared the remains of—what? a feast? a picnic? He bent down to investigate and found a few clay shards from an old jug, a bit of yellow wood like the facing on some stringed instrument and swatch of faded, faintly biblical cloth, broadly striped as the robe of a prophet. As he fingered this debris he smelled what was unmistakably bowel. "Have I stepped in something?" He stood and raised his shoe, but his glance slid off it to the ground where he saw two undisturbed lumps, round as hamburger, of congealing lion waste. It came to him at once. "I *knew* it was familiar! 'The Sleeping Gypsy.' This is where it was painted!"[10]

Ashenden has stepped into a painting, but the painting has taken on life:

He looked suspiciously at the mangled mandolin facing and smashed jug and at the tough cloth which he now perceived had been forcibly torn. My God, he thought, the lion must have eaten the poor fellow. The picture had been painted almost seventy-five years earlier but he understood from his reading that lions often returned to the scenes of their most splendid kills, somehow passing on to succeeding generations this odd, historical instinct of theirs (p. 38).

Ashenden's search for purity brings him ironically full circle to the bestial, in a scene where he makes love with a bear. Elkin's magic realism exposes the twin sides of passion, its beauty and its vulgarity.

Elkin and writers like him may seem more magical than realist; he is an exuberant writer whose language tends to be highly poetic and who seems at least partially indebted to the tradition of romance, gothicism, and the baroque, where the imagination has traditionally been the term valued over reality. One of the paradoxes of magic realism, however, is that it is also sometimes referred to as the new objectivity; its heirs in art are such movements as photorealism and hyperrealism, where sharply focused attention to detail renders the familiar strange. We see this heightened attention to the real in such writers as Raymond Carver,* Marilynne Robinson, Robert Coover, and others. One of the precursors to such new objectivity in the American literary tradition is Ernest Hemingway. Where Faulkner projects the psychological dimensions of his characters into the language of description, Hemingway attempts to repress that dimension, focusing instead on the minute details of an objective world. The force of that repression, however, magnifies or distorts that object, making it seem more than real. Take, for example, Hemingway's "Big Two-Hearted River"; as Nick heads out for the river on his fishing trip, he stops at the bridge in Seney and watches the trout in the water:

He watched them holding themselves with their noses into the current, many trout in deep, fast moving water, slightly distorted as he watched far down through the glassy convex surface of the pool, its surface pushing and swelling smooth against the log-driven piles of the bridge. At the bottom of the pool were the big trout. Nick did not see them at first. Then he saw them at the bottom of the pool, big trout looking to hold themselves on the gravel bottom in a varying mist of gravel and sand, raised in spurts by the current.[11]

What makes this passage odd is that juxtaposed to these minute observations is a studiously vague evaluation: "They were very satisfactory." The fish and water have the magical clarity of, say, a landscape in a hyperrealist painting, where all things near and far have the same quality of focus, and, for being more focused than our eyes can see, seem almost mystical.

It is this quality of focus that characterizes Raymond Carver's work, for example. His stories magnify the repressed violence of so-called ordinary life in a style deceptively direct and simple. The stories provide the illusion, then, of realism, yet always with a twist. "Viewfinder," for example, a story from *What We Talk About When We Talk About Love*, begins thus: "A man without hands came to the door to sell me a photograph of my house. Except for the chrome hooks, he was an ordinary-looking man of fifty or so."[12] Even though the chrome hooks are not ordinary, we are to take them as a matter of fact. As the story progresses, the narrator becomes increasingly obsessed with the man and his chrome hooks and behaves in an increasingly bizarre fashion; he ends by standing on the roof lobbing rocks and demanding that the man with the hooks take more pictures. Narrated in a simple, matter-of-fact manner, the events seem unlikely but not impossible—and this is the point. Carver's man with the hooks is as strange as García Márquez's child (in *One Hundred Years of Solitude*) with the tail of the pig; both authors attempt to capture what is strange and marvelous about ordinary life.

It is no accident, then, that Hemingway, one of the culminating figures of American realism, is so frequently cited as one of the important figures for the Latin American and American magic realists. A writer such as Tim O'Brien, who sees himself in the realist tradition, values the efficiency and drama of Hemingway's prose.[13] O'Brien's *Going After Cacciato* alternates between the unimaginable reality of the Vietnam War and a fantasy of escape; the fantasy gives the main character, Paul Berlin, a way to come to terms with his experience. It also allows him to explore the morality of the individual's involvement in the war, countering it with the possibility of desertion. Thus, the death of a soldier who has been ordered into a tunnel and is shot there is juxtaposed against the fantasy of falling into a tunnel and meeting "the living enemy," a man who turns out to have been condemned to the tunnel for resisting fighting the war. On the one hand, this is a sort of wish-fulfillment ("if you go down a tunnel, you will not be killed"), but it also attempts to understand the human other side of the tunnel as well.

The fantasy sections of the book are as realistic as the other sections, peopled with the same characters who behave according to the same sets of fears and desires. O'Brien insists that the fantasies *are* real, that "it wasn't dreaming—it wasn't even pretending, not in the strict sense. It was an idea. It was a working out of the possibilities. It wasn't dreaming and it wasn't pretending. It wasn't crazy."[14] O'Brien's premise—that events of the imagination are equivalent to other kinds of events—could be seen as *the* central tenet of magic realism. Thus, for O'Brien, *Cacciato* is as much a book about the imagination as it is about the war—the imagination as a power and reality in its own right. It is precisely for this reason that O'Brien claims that this novel is the most realistic novel he has written.[15]

What O'Brien's work also points to is that war itself seems magical real. Writers as different aesthetically as Kurt Vonnegut* and Michael Herr show us a picture of war that is perhaps too true to be believable. Herr is a particularly interesting example because, as a journalist, he could be thought to owe more allegiance to representing reality than a novelist, who we are prepared to allow these fantasies. Yet Herr's *Dispatches* is as magical as O'Brien's book.

Going out at night the medics gave you pills, Dexedrine breath like dead snakes kept too long in a jar. I never saw the need for them myself, a little contact or anything that even sounded like contact would give me more speed that I could bear. Whenever I heard something outside of our clenched little circle I'd practically flip, hoping to God that I wasn't the only one who'd noticed it. A couple of rounds fired off in the dark a kilometer away and the Elephant would be there kneeling on my chest, sending me down into my boots for a breath.[16]

Herr is attempting to capture, through figurative language, not just the war but the experience of war, an experience that surely lies somewhere between two points of vision, the real and the magical. Indeed, Herr, like O'Brien, asserts the validity of both:

When I think of it [Khe Sanh] quickly, just seeing the name somewhere or being asked what it was like, I see a flat, dun stretch of ground running out in an even plane until the rim of the middle distance takes on the shapes and colors of jungled hills. I had the strangest, most thrilling kind of illusion there, looking at those hills and thinking about the death and mystery that was in them. I would see the thing I knew I actually saw: the base from the ground where I stood, figures moving across it, choppers rising from the pad by the strip, and the hills above. But at the same time I would see the other, too; the ground, the troops and even myself, all from the vantage of the hills. It was a double vision that came to me more than once there. . . . It doesn't matter that memory distorts; every image, every sound comes back out of smoke and the smell of things burning (p. 107–8).

It remains to point out how important magic realism is as an aesthetic for women's fiction, particularly Afro-American women's fiction. Writers such as Toni Morrison or Alice Walker* make use of a specifically African heritage and its dislocations in America in order to represent the reality of that experience. The imagination plays a powerful role both in escaping the cruel realities of racial discrimination, for example, and in creating the possibility of overturning those conditions. Take, for example, Toni Morrison's *Song of Solomon*. When the protagonist Milkman is taken to jail for having stolen a bag of bones (in the mistaken belief that it was a bag of gold) from his aunt Pilate, she comes to the jail to bail him out:

Alone, without Macon, he let the events of the night come back to him—he remembered little things, details, and yet he wasn't sure these details had really happened. Perhaps he made them up. Pilate *had* been shorter. As she stood there in the receiving room of the jail, she didn't even come up to the sergeant's shoulder—and the sergeant's head barely reached Milkman's own chin. But Pilate was as tall as he was. When she whined to the policeman, verifying Milkman's and Guitar's lie that they had ripped off the sack as a joke on an old lady, she had to look up at him.[17]

In the presence of the white police authorities, Pilate, ordinarily a tall, strong, proud woman, shrinks in size and becomes a helpless old lady; she becomes, in short, exactly what the social situation of racial discrimination demands. This literalization functions at larger levels of the text as well. In fact, the novel takes as its thematic center the lyrics to a traditional slave song:

Sugarman done fly away

Sugarman done gone

Sugarman cut across the sky

Sugarman gone home.

The song records a folk legend, the belief that slaves sometimes escaped by simply flying back to Africa. In investigating the social circumstances that produced such a belief, the novel works with both the literal and metaphoric possibilities of flight, where "flying" can be seen as escape or as freedom. In many ways, this work seems closer to that of the Latin American authors, for they share an eye for the marvelous reality of folklore and superstition.

Although American writers have consistently been working within the aesthetics of magic realism in the contemporary period, their writing has not always been so labeled. Much of it has gone under the term "fabulism," following Robert Scholes' book *The Fabulators* and his later book *Fabulation and Metafiction*. Scholes defines the term as follows: " . . . modern fabulation, like the ancient fabling of Aesop, tends away from the representation of reality but returns toward actual human life by way of ethically controlled fantasy."[18] Fabulism, an alternative to the realist novel, is closely linked to romance, satire, and fable; Lawrence Durrell, Kurt Vonnegut, John Hawkes, and John Barth are the paradigmatic authors Scholes discusses in his first book.

If there is a difference between fabulism and magic realism as I have been describing it, it would be a matter of emphasis and usage. With its competing connotations—the fable and the fabulous—American critics have used fabulism to refer to work that is more consistently allegorical than magical realist. Donald Barthelme's *The Dead Father*, for example, concerns the problem of transporting an oversized dead father to his grave, allegorizing the problem of family history and the individual (particularly in the Oedipal family structure). Jonathan Baumbach's *Babble* is likewise structured around an allegory of the loss of innocence, projected onto its child hero. Pynchon's *The Crying of Lot 49*, many of Robert Coover's stories, the work of I. B. Singer and Kurt Vonnegut, all depend on the projection of a cultural fantasy onto an allegorical scene. It is important to say, however, that these works cannot be reduced to simple allegory, as all of them work assiduously against that defining term.

A third term has recently been proposed by Alan Wilde in his essay " 'Strange Displacements of the Ordinary': Apple, Elkin, Barthelme, and the Problem of the Excluded Middle." Wilde, arguing for a less dogmatic approach to both the concepts of mimesis and of representation that the experimental fiction writers have objected to, outlines a course lying between realism and experimentalism. His term is "midfiction," which he defines as follows:

Midfiction describes a narrative form that negotiates the oppositional extremes of realism and reflexivity (both their presuppositions and their technical procedures). Further, it seeks to reveal the extraordinariness of the ordinary, frequently and paradoxically by trafficking in limit situations—thereby subjecting to interrogation the very foundations of the writer's (and the reader's) beliefs. And, finally, it invites us not *through* but *in* the relationships and actions of its characters—and by way of some strategic *ecart* or swerve in its fabric—to perceive, obliquely and ironically, the moral perplexities of inhabiting a world that itself, as "text," ontologically ironic, contingent, and problematic.[19]

Wilde rejects Scholes' term "fabulism" as being too general and, he says, "too aesthetically resolved in its quasi-modernist emphasis on complexity compelled into unity" (197, note 9). Yet, while acknowledging the similarity between midfiction and Carpentier's "lo real maravilloso," he apparently fails to recognize the similarities between midfiction and magic realism. Wilde's readings of Apple, Elkin, and Barthelme are insightful and persuasive; but in an age where terminology proliferates, it was probably not necessary for him to coin a new one.

It would be wrong to draw too firmly the distinction between fabulist and magic realist writing. Both terms refer to mixed genres and styles, to authors caught in between, to writing that works both within and against the aesthetics of realism. It is not surprising that the postmodern era would generate an aesthetics pulled in such apparently contradictory directions, for postmodernism is itself a kind of oxymoron, defying our ordinary sense of temporality. As both a historical and a critical term, the postmodern has struggled with the changing world of production and reproduction, presentation and representation. It is a world where the boundaries of the known have exploded—but so have the boundaries of the unimaginable. I have borrowed my title from the postmodern poet Jack Spicer, whose sense of magic and the real makes him a magic realist of the first order. The real is for him a kind of jigsaw puzzle, and, he says, "It does not fit together." The writer's task is not to make the pieces fit—the way, we might say, the realist novel did—but to build around those pieces:

Not as a gesture of contempt for the scattered nature of reality. Not because the pieces would not fit in time. But because this would be the only way to cause an alliance between the dead and the living. To magic the whole thing toward what they called God.[20]

In searching for the alliance between the real and the imaginary, the dead and the living, reality and pleasure, magic realist writers are investigating both realms. Magic realism serves an essential binding function in the larger context of postmodern writing, a binding that links the dailiness of realism and the risks of experimentalism.

NOTES

1. Ronald Sukenick, "The Death of the Novel," in *The Death of the Novel and Other Stories* (New York: Dial Press, 1969), p.41.

2. Larry McCaffery, *The Metafictional Muse: The Works of Robert Coover, Donald Barthelme and William H. Gass* (Pittsburgh: University of Pittsburgh Press, 1982), pp. 10–11.

3. William Kennedy, *Ironweed* (New York: Penguin Books, 1984), p. 1.

4. For a history of magic realism in art, see Seymour Menton, *Magic Realism Rediscovered* (Philadelphia: Art Alliance Press, 1983).

5. In later essays elaborating the aesthetic implications of this assertion, Carpentier attempts to distinguish the marvelous real from magic realism, but in fact the two terms tend to be used interchangeably.

6. Gabriel García Márquez, *One Hundred Years of Solitude*, trans. Gregory Rabassa (New York: Avon Books, 1971), pp. 25–26.

7. Plinio Apuleyo Mendoza, *The Fragrance of Guava*, trans. Ann Wright (London: Verso Edition, 1983), p. 37.

8. Nathaniel Hawthorne, *The Scarlet Letter* (New York: W. W. Norton & Co., 1978), pp. 30–31.

9. William Faulkner, *Absalom, Absalom!* (New York: Random House, 1972), p. 8.

10. Stanley Elkin, *The Making of Ashenden* (London: Covent Garden Press, 1972), p. 38.

11. Ernest Hemingway, *In Our Time* (New York: Charles Scribner's Sons, 1925; 1970), p. 134.

12. Raymond Carver, *What We Talk About When We Talk About Love* (New York: Vintage Books, 1982), p. 11.

13. Interview with O'Brien in *Anything Can Happen: Interviews with Contemporary American Novelists*, Tom LeClair and Larry McCaffery (Urbana: University of Illinois Press, 1983), p. 270.

14. Tim O'Brien, *Going After Cacciato* (New York: Delacorte Press/Seymour Lawrence, 1975), p. 29.

15. Interview with McCaffery/LeClair, pp. 272–73.

16. Michael Herr, *Dispatches* (New York: Avon Books, 1978), pp. 4–5.

17. Toni Morrison, *Song of Solomon* (New York: New American Library, 1977), p. 208.

18. Robert Scholes, *The Fabulators* (New York: Oxford University Press, 1967), p. 11.

19. Alan Wilde, " 'Strange Displacements of the Ordinary,': Apple, Elkin, Barthelme, and the Problem of the Excluded Middle," *boundary 2* 10, no. 2 (Winter 1982): 192.

20. Jack Spicer, *The Collected Books of Jack Spicer* (Santa Barbara: Black Sparrow Press, 1975), p. 176.

SELECTED BIBLIOGRAPHY

Primary Sources

Apple, Max. *The Oranging of America*. New York: Grossman Publishers, 1976.

Asturias, Miguel. *El Señor Presidente*. New York: Atheneum, 1964.

————. *Mulata*. New York: Delacorte Press, 1967.

————. *Strong Wind*. New York: Delacorte Press, 1968.

————. *The Green Pope*. London: Jonathan Cape, 1971.

————. *The Eye of the Interred*. New York: Delacorte Press, 1973.

Barth, John. *Giles Goat-Boy*. Garden City, N.Y.: Doubleday, 1966.

————. *Letters*. New York: G. P. Putnam, 1982.

Barthelme, Donald. *The Dead Father*. New York: Farrar, Straus & Giroux, 1968.

Barthelme, Frederick. *Moon Deluxe*. New York: Farrar, Straus & Giroux, 1984.

Baumbach, Jonathan. *Babble*. New York: Fiction Collective, 1978.

Boyle, T. C. *Water Music*. Boston: Little, Brown, 1971.

————. *Greasy Lake & Other Stories*. New York: Viking Press, 1985.

Brautigan, Richard. *Trout Fishing in America*. New York: Delta, 1967.

Bumpus, Jerry. *Things in Place*. New York: Fiction Collective, 1975.

————. *Special Offer*. Poweroy, Ohio: Carpenter Press, 1975.

Calvino, Italo. *t zero*. New York: Harcourt Brace, 1969.

————. *Cosmicomics*. New York: Collier, 1970.

————. *The Baron in the Trees*. New York: Harcourt Brace, 1977.

————. *The Nonexistent Knight and the Cloven Viscount*. New York: Harcourt Brace, 1977.

Carpentier, Alejo. *Explosion in the Cathedral*. Trans. John Sturrock. London: V. Gallency, 1963.

Carver, Raymond. *Will You Please Be Quiet, Please*. New York: McGraw-Hill, 1976.

————. *What We Talk About When We Talk About Love*. New York: Vintage, 1981.

Coover, Robert. *The Origin of the Brunists*. New York: G. P. Putnam, 1966.

————. *Pricksongs and Descants*. New York: E. P. Dutton, 1969.

————. *The Public Burning*. New York: Viking Press, 1980.

Cortázar, Julio. *Blow Up and Other Stories*. Trans. Paul Blackburn. New York: Collier, 1963.

Donoso, José. *The Obscene Bird of Night*. Trans. Hardie St. Martin and Leonard Mades. New York: Alfred A. Knopf, 1973.

Eastlake, William. *Castle Keep*. New York: Simon & Schuster, 1965.

————. *Dancers in the Scalp House*. New York: Viking Press, 1977.

Elkin, Stanley. *A Bad Man*. New York: Random House, 1967.

————. *The Dick Gibson Show*. New York: Random House, 1971.

————. *Searches and Seizures*. New York: Random House, 1973.

————. *The Franchiser*. New York: Farrar, Straus & Giroux, 1976.

————. *The Living End*. New York: E. P. Dutton, 1979.

————. *George Mills*. New York: E. P. Dutton, 1982.

Faulkner, William. *Absalom, Absalom!* New York: Random House, 1972.

García Márquez, Gabriel. *One Hundred Years of Solitude*. Trans. Gregory Rabassa. New York: Harper & Row, 1970.

————. *Leafstorm and Other Stories*. Trans. Gregory Rabassa. New York: Harper & Row, 1972.

————. *The Autumn of the Patriarch*. Trans. Gregory Rabassa. New York: Harper & Row, 1976.

————. *Innocent Erendira and Other Stories*. Trans. Gregory Rabassa. New York: Harper Colophon Books, 1979.

Gardner, John. *Grendel*. New York: Alfred A. Knopf, 1971.

Hawkes, John. *The Cannibal*. New York: New Directions, 1962.

————. *Second Skin*. New York: New Directions, 1964.

————. *The Blood Oranges*. New York: New Directions, 1971.

————. *Death, Sleep and the Traveler*. New York: New Directions, 1974.

Hawthorne, Nathaniel. *The Scarlet Letter*. Boston: Ticknor, Reed & Fields, 1850.

Hemingway, Ernest. *In Our Time*. New York: Charles Scribner's Sons, 1925; 1970.

Herr, Michael. *Dispatches*. New York: Alfred A. Knopf, 1977.

Kafka, Franz. *The Metamorphosis and Other Stories*. New York: Vanguard Press, 1946.

————. *The Castle*. New York: Alfred A. Knopf, 1954.

————. *The Trial*. New York: Alfred A. Knopf, 1956.

————. *America*. New York: Alfred A. Knopf, 1959.

Katz, Steve. *Moving Parts*. New York: Fiction Collective, 1975.

Kennedy, William. *The Ink Truck*. New York: Dial Press, 1969.

————. *Ironweed*. New York: Viking Press, 1983.

Morrison, Toni. *Song of Solomon*. New York: Alfred A. Knopf, 1977.

O'Brien, Tim. *Going After Cacciato*. New York: Delacorte Press, 1978.

Pynchon, Thomas. *V*. Philadelphia: Lippincott, 1963.

————. *The Crying of Lot 49*. Philadelphia: Lippincott, 1966.

————. *Gravity's Rainbow*. New York: Viking Press, 1973.

Reed, Ishamel. *Yellow Back Radio Broke-Down*. Garden City, N.Y.: Doubleday, 1971.

Robbins, Tom. *Another Roadside Attraction*. New York: Ballantine, 1971.

————. *Even Cowgirls Get the Blues*. New York: Bantam, 1976.

————. *Still Life with Woodpecker*. New York: Bantam, 1980.

————. *Jitterbug Perfume*. New York: Bantam, 1984.

Rushdie, Salmon. *Midnight's Children*. New York: Alfred A. Knopf, 1980.

Vonnegut, Kurt. *Slaughterhouse-Five*. New York: Delacorte Press, 1969.

————. *Breakfast of Champions*. New York: Delacorte Press, 1973.

————. *Jailbird*. New York: Delacorte Press, 1979.

Walker, Alice. *The Color Purple*. New York: Harcourt Brace Jovanovich, 1982.

Secondary Sources

Brooke-Rose, Christine. *A Rhetoric of the Unreal: Studies in Narrative Structure, Especially of the Fantastic*. Cambridge: Cambridge University Press, 1981.

Manlove, C. N. *The Impulse of Fantasy Literature*. Kent, Ohio: Kent State University Press, 1957.

Menton, Seymour. *Magic Realism Rediscovered, 1918–1981*. Philadelphia: Art Alliance Press, 1983.

Scholes, Robert. *Fabulation and Metafiction*. Urbana: University of Illinois Press, 1979.

Wilde, Alan. " 'Strange Displacements of the Ordinary': Apple, Elkin, Barthelme, and the Problem of the Excluded Middle." *boundary 2* 10, no. 2 (Winter 1982): 180–95.

WELCH D. EVERMAN

The Paper World: Science Fiction in the Postmodern Era

> (L)iterature is not representative in the same sense that certain sentences of everyday speech may be representative, for literature does not refer . . . to anything outside itself.
>
> Tzvetan Todorov[1]

There is something strange about the very idea of a science fiction. In our times, science has come to mean the knowledge of and the search for the real. Science is truth. Fiction, on the other hand, is fiction. And as Todorov reminds us in his study of the fantastic in literature, literary language does not point beyond itself and into the real world. Unlike the language of science, the language of fiction is not intended to tell the truth. "Science fiction," then, would seem to be a contradiction in terms.

In fact, however, the literary genre that, for better or worse, has come to be known as science fiction calls into question the languages of both science and fiction, and this is particularly true of those SF works that might be termed postmodern in their orientation toward literature and the world. For the postmodern mind, language is not equal to objective reality or representative of reality but a hole in the real, a self-contained negativity, an absence, or rather a tool by which the absent appears to become present. As Todorov points out, literary language does not refer to anything outside itself but is rather a coherent verbal structure that is purposely not the real; it creates a separate realm of fictive characters and situations which are absent from the real world that exists beyond language. And, as we will see, postmodernist works of science fiction also suggest that the languages of the real—the languages of the physical sciences, psychology, sociology, history, and so on—might also create only fictive realms, the formal structures we use to bring order to reality but which are absent from the world that does not need these verbal models to be what it is.

Science fiction draws on the languages of science and fiction to create a very special literary genre. In the passage quoted above, Todorov speaks of all literature as nonrepresentational, but his book *The Fantastic* (1975) deals specifically with those literary works that are overtly nonrepresentational—texts of the impossible, of the absent. Works of SF are such texts, as are tales of fantasy and the supernatural—texts that do not point beyond themselves to a corresponding reality because that reality does not exist. Unlike works in the realist tradition that present characters, settings, and situations that seemingly could find counterparts in the world beyond language, these texts of the imagination create worlds that exist only as words in books—as paper worlds.

Science fiction, then, is a literature of absence, because the language of science fiction makes that which is absent present to the reader. In general, the absence that works of SF offer is the future, the not-yet, though some works of the sword and sorcery subgenre make present a mythical past beyond memory (the no-longer), and others propose the not-at-all of alternate history—our own world as it might have been if certain historical events had happened differently. All science fiction—from Jules Verne and H. G. Wells to the present day—is rooted in and dependent on the language that makes the impossible possible, at least on the surface of the page.

In the 1960s, a number of younger writers began to write self-referential science fiction texts that called attention to their own verbal structure and betrayed their own fictivity by making use of the innovative techniques that were being developed in other literary quarters. Termed the New Wave by critics, these authors work within the traditional boundaries of science fiction while simultaneously pushing against those boundaries, creating texts that are not intended to be realistic or even believable. Rather, these works are coherent and separate realities, language structures that reflect on themselves, on the nature of science fiction in particular and of literature in general, and on the relationship between the language of fiction and the language of fact. With the works of Samuel R. Delany,* Thomas M. Disch, Roger Zelazny,* Michael Moorcock, and others, the science fiction genre—a realm of adolescent pulp for decades—became an arena for serious literature.

The New Wave movement inspired controversy in the SF ranks, and, though the controversy and the radical innovation of the 1960s have all but passed away, the New Wave era has had a major influence on many writers who came after. In the past 20 years, science fiction has attracted any number of modern masters—Italo Calvino,* Doris Lessing, Kobo Abe, Joseph McElroy,* Raymond Federman.* SF has also created its own masters—Stanislaw Lem* and Kurt Vonnegut, Jr.,* among others—who have been successful with hardcore science fiction fans, the general reading public, and even the critics who once considered SF novels to be little more than childish Westerns set in outer space instead of Dodge City.

In a very real sense, postmodern SF writers are parodists, playing with and within the genre they have chosen to champion, self-consciously questioning the rules that their forerunners simply accepted without thinking. Writers like Delany, Disch, and others create works *of* science fiction that are also *about* science fiction, that lay bare the very structure of the SF text, like a perfectly crafted sonnet that explains the rules by which a sonnet is written. These works are both individual and universal, unique examples of SF texts, and, insofar as they also expose and examine the literariness of this literary genre, all possible SF texts as well. The successful postmodern work of science fiction adds to the genre and exhausts it at the same time.

The premier parodist of postmodern science fiction is the Italian writer Italo Calvino, and in his books *Cosmicomics* (1970) and *t zero* (1969), he creates tales that call the languages of both science and fiction into question by exposing the means by which SF texts come into being. As Calvino makes clear, the science fiction text adopts a scientific hypothesis (intergalactic or time travel is possible, extraterrestrial beings exist, and so on) and proceeds as if that hypothesis were true. The given hypothesis is, of course, a text in its own right, and the SF story becomes a rather elaborate and idiosyncratic translation of the original.

To establish the link between the language of science (the hypothesis) and the language of fiction (the story), Calvino begins each of his tales with the scientific premise that gave rise to the piece. For example, he introduces "All at One Point" with the following: "Through the calculations begun by Edwin P. Hubble on the galaxies' velocity of recession, we can establish the moment when all the universe's matter was concentrated in a single point, before it began to expand in space."[2] In the story that follows, Calvino's ageless narrator Qfwfq tells of the days when he and everyone else lived in the single point that, millennia ago, was the universe. ("Naturally we were all there . . . where else could we have been?"[3]) The tale is absurd and hilarious, of course, and avowedly fictive, possible only as a verbal construct, because it would be impossible for the reader even to form a visual image of a situation in which there is no space and time.

But if Calvino's "translation" of the scientific hypothesis is self-consciously fictive, what of the hypothesis itself? By implication, the scientific premise, like the text of "All at One Point," is yet another story about the universe, a fiction, a verbal construct that orders reality in a serviceable way but that need not be true and is always open to question and possible revision. Like the language of fiction, the language of science is the source of stories, of fictions, of literature.

Although American readers are still discovering Poland's Stanislaw Lem, he is probably the best-selling science fiction writer in the world. Some of Lem's work is traditional, but the best of it is wildly innovative and deeply self-reflexive, consciously combining the basic structural elements of SF—science and folktale/myth—to generate unique parodies of the genre.

Ijon Tichy is Lem's favorite futuristic hero, the featured character in a number of stories and, like Calvino's Qfwfq, an obsessive storyteller. In Lem's fictive future, Tichy and his adventures have become objects of scholarly study by the Scientific Council of the Tichological Institute and the Associated Institute of Tichology, Tichography and Tichonomics Descriptive, Comparative, and Prognostic. Tichologist Professor A. S. Tarantoga provides occasional commentaries on Tichy's space logs, reflecting on these strange texts that already reflect on themselves.

Like Calvino, Lem uses his SF tales to illustrate and to translate the language of science into the language of fiction, thus questioning the authenticity of scientific truth. In "The Seventh Voyage" of *The Star Diaries* (1970), Tichy notes that "the bending of the direction of the flow of time in the presence of gravitational fields of great intensity . . . might even on occasion lead to the complete reversal of time and the 'duplication of the present.' "[4] Then, by passing through a number of black holes, Tichy comes into contact with his past and future selves until his entire space ship is full of Tichys, arguing and vainly trying to form governing committees to maintain order within the conflicting ranks of Tichy's selves.

Also like Calvino, Lem is fascinated by the fictivity of fictions, the storiness of stories. In *The Futurological Congress* (1976), Tichy finds himself in the futuristic projection of our own drug culture where hallucinogenic drugs are so all-pervasive that there is no longer a difference between hallucinations (fictions) and reality. Tichy's adventures in this world are doubly fictive—hallucinations and hallucinations-within-hallucinations, all concocted by the imaginative skill of Stanislaw Lem. These stories about stories, again rooted in the "truths" of science, place Tichy's tales at a far greater distance from the real than the shadows in Plato's cave, and Lem suggests that it is within such realms of storiness that we live out our individual and collective lives, using words to create reality as we go along.

In many ways, the archetypical Lem story is the "Tale of the Three Storytelling Machines of King Genius" in *The Cyberiad* (1976), subtitled *Fables for the Cybernetic Age* in which robots have replaced humans. In this particular tale, the inventor-robot Trul creates three storytelling devices for King Genius which in turn create stories "to (1) exercise, (2) entertain and (3) edify the mind."[5] The stories the machines tell also contain stories within stories, each reflecting on the others while Trul and his client listen attentively. At last Trul suggests: "Suppose that which is taking place here and now is not reality, but only a tale, a tale of some higher order that contains within it the tale of the machine."[6]

And, of course, this is the case. Lem's story is the machine that creates the machines that create stories just as the science fiction genre is the machine that creates Lem's story, just as the languages of science and fiction form the machine that creates the genre. And so on. For Lem, and for the rest of us, there seems to be no escape from storiness. Telling/

writing and hearing/reading tales seem to give us ourselves and guarantee that we exist. When Tichy doubts his own existence, he need only read the words he has written. "(A) ship's log can't very well read itself. So I do exist, yes, because I read it."[7]

Samuel R. Delany's brand of SF is a language-conscious art. In fact, his novel *Bable–17* (1966) is a space opera that parodies itself and turns itself inside out by reflecting on its own language within the context of a new language, "Bable–17," a language that controls and denies its speakers/receivers because it has no word for "I." In *The Einstein Intersection*, (1967), Delany presents his own variation of the boy-adventure novel (a favorite SF theme), though the boy is a member of an extraterrestrial society that has taken over a depopulated Earth in the distant future. There is a mythic quality here, as in all of Delany's fictions, and the use of myth focuses the reader's attention on the storiness of a story that is both familiar and defamiliarized by the futuristic context. In addition, Delany betrays the fictivity of the fiction by including sections of his own journal written at the same time as the novel. The journal comments on and modifies the fiction, and the juxtaposition of the two texts collapses the distinction between factual and fictive language, between work and commentary. *The Einstein Intersection* becomes it own self-reflexive critique. In a very real sense, the work reads itself.

On the other hand, *Nova* (1969), another mythic space opera, writes itself from within. Like so many Delany novels, *Nova* has a resident writer who seems to have written himself into existence by writing the novel in which he appears as a character. Young Katin understands that the work he writes/lives is based on the quest for the Holy Grail, projected into the distant not-yet. But he also knows that many other writers of Grail stories have died before they completed their works. And so, in the closing paragraph of *Nova*, he resolves: "The only way to protect myself from the jinx, I guess, would be abandon it before I finish the last."[8]

Dhalgren (1975), Delany's ambitious 900-page tour de force, both writes and reads itself, again within the boy-adventure form. The boy, Kid or Kidd, a Kaspar Hauser character without a past, is author and reader of the text that describes an urban world in the not-too-distant future, a world of violence, decay, and death. *Dhalgren* makes this absent future present and yet betrays the original absence by reflecting on itself in texts within texts and commentaries within commentaries. For Delany, the language that makes the not-yet realm of science fiction possible also becomes the primary topic of fiction, the form and the content, the what and the how. As such, his works question the very nature of language itself and the possibility of using language to say something we might be willing to call true.

Like Delany, Gene Wolfe* also parodies the SF genre from within by emphasizing the linguistic form of the work, the textuality of the text, the storiness of the story. *The Fifth Head of Cerberus* (1972) is a collection of three novellas that form a single complex and mysterious piece. The title work is a rather straightforward story about life on a French space colony where cloning allows individuals to repeat themselves to infinity, thus confusing and destroying traditional notions of personality and individuality. The background of the tale is fascinating. The planet of St. Croix is a highly civilized metropolis, but its sister planet of St. Anne is still quite primitive. Once the home of the native abo who have become extinct since the beginning of colonization, St. Anne is now inhabited by rugged human pioneers. Little is known about the abo culture, but some colonists believe they were shape-shifters who did not die out at all but assumed human form in order to survive during the time of colonization. Since then, the abo have forgotten their original forms and culture and have continued to live among the colonists as humans.

Wolfe's first novella introduces a minor character, John V. Marsch, an anthropologist from earth who is visiting St. Croix/St. Anne to try to gather information about the abo and to see whether any still survive. There is at least the suggestion that Marsch himself could be an abo in human form, and Wolfe's second novella, " 'A Story,' by John V. Marsch," is a document by Marsch himself, a text on abo life and culture on St. Anne that could be either a fictive account based on his anthropological studies or a factual treatise based on his own racial memories as an abo. In the third novella, "V.R.T.," Marsch is in prison on St. Croix, and an investigator there studies transcripts of interviews with him and the journals Marsch kept of his field work on St. Anne in the attempt to discover who he really is. The notes document his travels with Victor Trenchard—the V.R.T. of the title—a young guide who claims he is a descendant of the original abo. According to Marsch's journal, Victor dies mysteriously in the field, and the anthropologist makes his way back to civilization alone. The notes suggest, however, that Marsch might have been the one who died and that Victor the abo has assumed his form and name, though it is also possible that Marsch's search for the abo has consumed his personality so thoroughly that he now believes he is one of them. Wolfe does not resolve these questions. There is no absolute truth in the worlds of St. Croix and St. Anne, any more than there is absolute truth in our own world; there are only documents, texts, always open to interpretation.

Thomas M. Disch is a master of subtle parody, and his works assume that the reader has at least a basic knowledge of the traditional elements of science fiction—elements that Disch proceeds to distort and pervert. *Echo Rounds His Bones* (1967) is a fascinating SF text and in some ways a more or less traditional "end-of-the-world" story in which humankind is saved at the last instant by the hero of the work. But Disch plays with this ordinary format by calling attention to the way his novel follows the rules of the genre, from the opening segment to the last chapter entitled "The

Happy Ending." The author addresses the reader again and again in digressions that comment on the complexities of writing futuristic fiction, the inevitability of the love story in all popular literature, and the unavoidability of contrivances that challenge the reader's suspension of disbelief but that also advance the plot. In *The Genocides* (1967), Disch goes one step further. The novel is a straightforward "alien invasion" tale in the tradition of *War of the Worlds* and countless books and films. But in the closing chapter where the rules demand that humankind be saved from apparently inevitable extinction, Disch simply and matter-of-factly lets the human race expire.

Because science fiction is a literature of the impossible, of absence, it has always maintained an air of the fabulous, and, as we have seen, postmodern writers in the genre have emphasized the literariness of their paper worlds by self-consciously drawing on established myths and fables as the structural bases for their works. By retelling tales that have already been told time and again, these writers betray the fictivity of the fundamental stories that form the basis of our culture. As Delany questions the story of the Grail Quest in *Nova,* Disch's *Camp Concentration* (1980) addresses the Faust myth, the "Faustian urge to secure knowledge at any price,"[9] that has come to typify our own age. In *This Immortal* (1966), Roger Zelazny retells the story of Ahasuerus, the Wandering Jew who is cursed with eternal life. But Zelazny, among others, has also drawn on more modern tales, re-creating contemporary literary works in futuristic contexts that repeat and distort our own central myths. Zelazny's novella *The Doors of His Face, the Lamps of His Mouth* (1974) is Melville's *Moby Dick* set on Venus where an obsessed hunter tracks the most monstrous ocean creature imaginable, an extraterrestrial beast that has already cost him far too much.

Philip José Farmer is the most literary-minded writer in the SF ranks, for he has created many volumes of literature-about-literature, including the "true" stories of Edgar Rice Burroughs' Tarzan and Jules Verne's Phineas Fogg. His novel, *The Wind Whales of Ishmael* (1971), is an extension of *Moby Dick* is which Melville's young hero, rescued by the ship "Rachel," is again wrecked by a strange storm that casts him millions of years into a future where men hunt flying whales in lighter-than-air craft.

Farmer's finest piece of literary play is "Riders of the Purple Wage" (1969). Although the title refers to a Western classic by Zane Gray, the text is a playful parody of *Finnegans Wake,* James Joyce's modern masterwork that, in turn, parodies all of Western literature, including itself. Like Joyce, Farmer revels in the well-turned pun ("They taught me at school that puns are cheap and vulgar"). His hero, Grandpa Winnegan, stages an elaborate scam to cheat tax collectors out of their share of $20 billion—a complicated plot known popularly as Winnegan's Fake. Farmer's tale charts the progress of Winnegan's hilarious efforts to cause disruption in his utopian (and crashingly dull) society of the future.

Although Farmer enjoys toying with the texts of his predecessors, he is not opposed to poking fun at his contemporaries as well. Kurt Vonnegut, Jr., created a hack science fiction writer named Kilgore Trout in his novel *God Bless You, Mr. Rosewater* (1965) and Trout's fictive fictions returned in Vonnegut's later works, *Slaughterhouse-Five* (1969) and *Breakfast of Champions* (1973). Trout's works and ideas for works are stories within Vonnegut's stories that provide commentary on the novels in which they appear and suggest that "science fiction can help reinvent reality, which is itself just an arbitrary convention."[10] Trout's fictive existence implies that Vonnegut himself could also be the product of a literary work, the vast and complicated work that creates all of us and all that we call reality. In a sense, Trout's bizarre works are ideal texts that Vonnegut can draw from but need never write.

Farmer has complicated this situation by writing the novel *Venus on the Half-Shell* (1975) under the pen-name Kilgore Trout in a brilliant parody of Vonnegut's style. Trout's hero is Simon Wagstaff the Space Wanderer who travels the universe asking the question posed implicitly or explicitly by so many Vonnegut protagonists: "Why are we created only to suffer and die?"[11] Curiously, like Eliot Rosewater in Vonnegut's novel, Simon also has a favorite science fiction writer, Jonathan Swift Somers III, and *Venus on the Half-Shell* contains synopses of a number of Somers' strange tales. Somers is a fictive creator of fictions, created by another fictive creator who in turn was created by an author who could be nothing more than the product of another's words. The fictions-within-fictions of Vonnegut/Trout/Farmer/Somers seem to be only fictions-within-the-fiction of our own everyday world.

The writer of futuristic fiction must create a vocabulary for his realm of the not-yet. He generates his paper world as we generate ours—by naming it. In *Stand on Zanzibar* (1969), John Brunner* coins words like "shiggy" (a live-in female friend), "drecky" (derogatory adjective), "mucker" (a madman), and "Shalmeneser" (a super computer), and the reader comes to know Brunner's overpopulated Earth of the future by learning this alien vocabulary as he goes along, as he reads. But in addition, following the elaborate structural ideas of John Dos Passos' *U.S.A.*, Brunner includes fictional newspaper and TV broadcasts, advertising, and quotes from futuristic books in his narrative, all of which serve to delineate this fictive world in the language Brunner has created to describe and define it. For the reader, the effect is of living in two worlds at once, Brunner's and his own, each with its own distinctive vocabulary, each seemingly quite real because each takes shape in words.

With the knowledge that words create worlds, Anthony Burgess wrote *A Clockwork Orange* (1965) entirely in the futuristic street slang of his young narrator. In the process of reading, this strange language becomes the reader's own, as does the terrifying and familiar world that Alex and his friends speak into being, a world of violence, immorality, and alienation. (" 'There was never any trust,' I said, bitterly, wiping off the krovvy with my rooker, 'I was always on my oddy knocky.' ")[12]

The narrator of Russell Hoban's* *Riddley Walker* (1980) also creates his own fictive world in his own fictive language. In Riddley Walker's England of the future, centuries after a nuclear holocaust, people live in primitive tribal groups, follow a religion based on puppet shows, and speak and write a semiliterate English, but this world is not so very different from our own. As Riddley says: "Our woal life is a idear we dint think of nor we dont know what it is. What a way to live."[13]

By stressing the development of language, by creating vocabularies that in turn create fictions distinct from our own reality and the language we use to describe it, Brunner, Burgess, and Hoban show that their paper worlds exist only as words, that they are spoken into being. But the implication here is that our own world also depends on the words we have created to speak of it. A new vocabulary would mean a new reality.

Most works of science fiction are set in a more or less distant future, a not-yet, but many works of the sword and sorcery subgenre—tales of the mythical no-longer—show a similar concern with language, stories, and the speaking of the world. These tales of the distant past are rooted in myth and folklore and often represent a search for the origin of our culture, for the fundamental stories that have shaped our civilization. In his most recent fictions, Samuel R. Delany proposes a search for the origin of writing itself and the stories that writing has made possible.

Delany has said that sword and sorcery fables "are all rewrites of the same story,"[14] a recombining of traditional elements: magicians, witches, brave warriors, travelers on elaborate quests. Certainly this is true of the stories in Delany's own *Tales of Neveryon* (1979) and *Neveryòna* (1983)— stories that rewrite each other and any number of earlier sword and sorcery tales in the attempt to write again what may well be the origin of writing itself. The *Tales* are stories of Gorgik the Liberator, an ex-slave who has sworn to eradicate slavery from the empire, his companion Small Sarg, Raven the female warrior, and other familiar characters from the ranks of sword and sorcery fiction. But Delany has also added a curious appendix to his volume of stories, an essay by archaeologist S. L. Kermit on the Culhar' Text, "a narrative fragment of approximately nine hundred words (that) has been known and noted in many languages for centuries."[15] Drawing on a new translation of the text by linguist/mathematician K. Leslie Steiner, Kermit presents a brief history of the fragment, its links with other texts like Gilgamesh and the Dead Sea Scrolls, and the modern scholarship surrounding the codex, then concludes that "apparently, over a good deal of Europe and Asia Minor, during ancient times, the Culhar' Text was thought to be the origin of writing, or the archtrace."[16]

The text is not a coherent tale; it is only bits and pieces of a narrative that refuse to fit together. But for Kermit, the Culhar' Text is fascinating.

... it is impossible not to find one's imagination plunging into the images thrown up by this archeological oddity, this writing on and around and within writing, and not come up with myriad narrative possibilities that might meet, or even cross, in this ancient fragment. If some writer were to actually put down these stories, just what sort of reflection might they constitute, either of the modern world or our own past history?

Could one perhaps consider such an imaginative expansion simply another translation, another reading of the text, another layer of the palimpsest?[17]

Delany includes the Kermit essay as an appendix to his *Tales of Neveryon* because these are tales *are* the rewriting of the Culhar' Text, "another translation, another reading," another writing of the first writing. The *Tales* are an attempt to repeat the origin of writing, to discover again the absence that is the source of absence, the source of all stories, including the *Tales* themselves.

The Neveryon stories are, as Delany explains, "in dialogue" with the Culhar' Text. The "hero (feminine) carrying a double blade" who is mentioned in the fragment is Delany's character Raven. "The love of the small barbarian slave for the tall man from Culhare" is the basis for the story of Small Sarg and Gorgik. The *Tales of Neveryon* seek out the stories contained in the fragments and write them again.

The novel *Neveryòna* also has its source in the Culhar' Text, in the tale the heroine Pryn first hears from "an old woman on the island, putting colored 'memory marks' on unrolled reeds." This tale is the *Tales of Neveryon*, and in following the story, Pryn meets the original characters— Gorgik, Sarg, Raven, and the others. In fact, *Neveryòna* is a rewriting of the *Tales*, as the Tales rewrite the Culhar' fragments. In *Neveryòna,* Delany writes a writing which rewrites a writing which in turn rewrites a writing. *Neveryòna* is the story of a story of a story.

And the chain of stories does not end here. To the layman, the Culhar' scholarship in the appendix to the *Tales* seems flawless. But something is wrong here. Kermit's essay is dated January 1981. The publication date for *Tales of Neveryon* is September 1979. The Kermit essay is a not-yet, an absence. The origin of the writing, the source of the Neveryon fictions, is itself a fiction. Delany is a science fiction writer, and the sciences he fictionalizes are archaeology and linguistics, the sciences that seek out the origins of culture. But for him, there is no origin, no really real, only stories and stories of stories.

Some of the most fascinating works of science fiction are those that question another science of culture: history. These stories play with the texts of history in much the same way that futuristic SF tales play with the texts of science.

Philip K. Dick's* works of futuristic fiction are well known, but his 1962 novel *The Man in the High Castle* is firmly within the realistic tradition— the characters are precisely drawn, the settings are presented in fine detail, the time frame is familiar, and the plot is intricate and logically developed. But Dick's is an alternate reality. *The Man in the High Castle* is set in the United States of the 1960s, but in this version of reality, the Axis powers have won the Second World War. Germany occupies the Eastern states, Japan controls the West Coast, and the Rockies are a buffer between these two nations whose alliance has become painfully tenuous.

As SF novels create the absent future, Dick creates an absent present based on an absent past. *The Man in the High Castle* is a curious work that is made even more curious by a fiction within the fiction. Dick's fictive universe also has its novelists, and one of them, Hawthorne Abendsen, has written a novel, *The Grasshopper Lies Heavy*, that has been banned by both occupying forces. The revolutionary idea behind Abendsen's novel is a fictive history in which the Allies win World War II. But like the historical text of *The Man in the High Castle*, the historical text of *The Grasshopper Lies Heavy* is not the history of our world. According to Abendsen's text, there was no Pearl Harbor attack, and the United States never became involved in the European theater—Britain and Russia defeated the Nazis on their own.

The interplay of historical texts in Dick's work suggests that our reality, like the realities of *The Man in the High Castle* and *The Grasshopper Lies Heavy*, is based on yet another historical text that explains or seems to explain the structure of the world we know but that may well be a fiction. Like the historical texts that underlie Dick's novel and his novel-within-the-novel, the historical text that underlies our world is only words. Facts seem to escape the history that tries to contain them.

Norman Spinrad's novel *The Iron Dream* (1972) raises the same points through an ingenious distortion of history. In fact, Spinrad's work is only a brief introduction and an afterword by "Homer Whipple," framing a novel entitled *Lord of the Swastika* by Adolf Hitler. It is the novel Hitler might have written if he had come to America after the First World War and eventually become a hack science fiction writer. His work is an appalling exercise in racism, violence, and cruelty—and shockingly similar to many authentic pulp SF works. But *Lord of the Swastika* is less important than the historical text that underlies the "writing" of it. According to Spinrad's alternate history, there was no World War II, no Holocaust, no Hiroshima—the crucial events of our time never happened. In many ways, Spinrad's time is more believable than our own. As Homer Whipple says of the fictive world conqueror in Hitler's work: "Of course, such a man could gain power only in the extravagant fancies of the pathological science-fiction novel."[18] To those in Spinrad's world, the unthinkable need not be thought. Their history need not try to speak the unspeakable, as our history must. But, of course, any history of our time that believes it has encompassed the unspeakable in words is a fiction. The unspeakable events of our reality must remain unspoken.

The paper worlds of postmodern science fiction may be nothing more than words, but the works of Calvino, Lem, Delany, Dick, and others exist to question the truths of our own world, our science, our history, our language. In our time, science fiction has come of age.

NOTES

1. Tzvetan Todovov, *The Fantastic: A Structural Approach to a Literary Genre*, trans. Richard Howard (Ithaca, N.Y.: Cornell University Press, 1975).
2. Italo Calvino, *Cosmicomics*, trans. William Weaver (New York: Collier Books, 1970), p. 5.
3. Ibid.
4. Stanislaw Lem, *The Star Diaries*, trans. Michael Kandel (New York: Avon Books, 1970), p. 5.
5. Stanislaw Lem, *The Cyberiad: Fables for the Cybernetic Age,* trans. Michael Kandel (New York: Avon Books, 1976), p. 145.
6. Ibid., p. 160.
7. Lem, *Star Diaries,* p. 318.
8. Samuel R. Delany, *Nova* (New York: Bantam Books, 1969), p. 215.
9. Thomas M. Disch, *Camp Concentration* (New York: Bantam Books, 1980), p. 115.
10. Jerome Klinkowitz, *Kurt Vonnegut* (London and New York: Methuen & Co., Ltd., 1982), p. 60.
11. Philip José Farmer (as Kilgore Trout), *Venus on the Half-Shell* (New York: Dell Publishing Co., 1975), p. 34.
12. Anthony Burgess, *A Clockwork Orange* (New York: Ballantine Books, 1965), p. 148.
13. Russell Hoban, *Riddley Walker* (New York: Washington Square Press, 1980), p. 7.
14. Samuel R. Delany, *The Jewel-Hinged Jaw: Essays on the Language of Science Fiction* (Elizabethtown, New York: Dragon Press, 1977), p. 203.
15. Samuel R. Delany, *Tales of Neveryon* (New York: Bantam Books, 1979), p. 248.
16. Ibid., p. 253.
17. Ibid., pp. 262–63.
18. Norman Spinrad, *The Iron Dream* (New York: Avon Books, 1972), p. 255.

SELECTED BIBLIOGRAPHY

Primary Sources

Ballard, J. G. *The Drowned World*. New York: Berkley Books, 1962.
———. *The Crystal World*. New York: Berkley Books, 1966.
———. *Love and Napalm: Export U.S.A.* New York: Grove Press, 1969.
———. *Chronopolis*. New York: Berkley Books, 1972.
———. *The Disaster Area*. London: Panther Books, 1973.
———. *The Drought*. London: Penguin Books, 1974.

————. *The Wind from Nowhere*. London: Penguin Books, 1974.

————. *The Terminal Beach*. London: Penguin Books, 1974.

————. *Vermilion Sands*. London: Panther Books, 1975.

Benford, Gregory. *In the Ocean of Night*. New York: Dell Publishing Co., 1978.

————, and Gordon Eklund. *Find the Changeling*. New York: Dell Publishing Co., 1980.

————. *Timescape*. New York: Pocket Books, 1980.

Brunner, John. *Stand on Zanzibar*. New York: Ballantine Books, 1969.

————. *The Sheep Look Up*. New York: Harper & Row, 1972.

Burgess, Anthony. *A Clockwork Orange*. New York: Ballantine Books, 1965.

Calvino, Italo. *t zero*. Trans. William Weaver. New York: Harcourt, Brace & World, 1969.

————. *Cosmicomics*. Trans. William Weaver. New York: Collier Books, 1970.

Capek, Karl. *War with the Newts*. Trans. M&R Weatherall. New York: Berkley Books, 1976.

Delany, Samuel R. *The Fall of the Towers*. New York: Ace Books, 1966.

————. *Babel–17*. New York: Ace Books, 1966.

————. *The Einstein Intersection*. New York: Ace Books, 1967.

————. *Nova*. New York: Bantam Books, 1969.

————. *The Jewels of Aptor*. London: Sphere Books, 1971.

————. *Driftglass*. New York: New American Library, 1971.

————. *Dhalgren*. New York: Bantam Books, 1975.

————. *Triton*. New York: Bantam Books, 1976.

————, and Howard V. Chaykin. *Empire*. New York: Berkley/Putnam, 1978.

————. *Heavenly Breakfast*. New York: Bantam Books, 1979.

————. *Tales of Neveryon*. New York: Bantam Books, 1979.

————. *Neveryòna*. New York: Bantam Books, 1983.

Dick, Philip K. *The Man in the High Castle*. New York: Berkley Books, 1962.

————. *Flow My Tears, the Policeman Said*. New York: Daw Books, 1974.

————, and Roger Zelazny. *Deus Irae*. New York: Dell Publishing Co., 1974.

————. *The Golden Man*. New York: Berkley Books, 1980.

Disch, Thomas M. *Triplicity: Echo Rounds His Bones, The Genocides, The Puppies of Terra*. New York: Nelson Doubleday Co., 1967.

————. *334*. New York: Avon Books, 1974.

————. *Getting into Death and Other Stories*. New York: Pocket Books, 1977.

————. *Camp Concentration*. New York: Bantam Books, 1980.

————. *Fundamental Disch*. New York: Bantam Books, 1980.

————. *The Man Who Had No Idea*. New York: Bantam Books, 1982.

————. *Ringtime*. West Branch, Iowa: Toothpaste Press, 1983.

Eklund, Gordon. *The Grayspace Beast*. New York: Pocket Books, 1977.

Farmer, Philip José. "Riders of the Purple Wage." In *Dangerous Visions #1*. Harlan Ellison, ed. New York: Berkley Books, 1969.

————. *The Wind Whales of Ishmael*. New York: Ace Books, 1971.

———— (as Kilgore Trout). *Venus on the Half-Shell*. New York: Dell Publishing Co., 1975.

Hoban, Russell. *Riddley Walker*. New York: Washington Square Press, 1980.

Lafferty, R. A. *Arrive at Easterwine: The Autobiography of a Ktistect Machine*. New York: Ballantine Books, 1973.

———. *Apocalypses*. Los Angeles: Pinnacle Books, 1976.

Lem, Stanislaw. *Solaris*. Trans. Joanna Kilmartin and Steve Cox. New York: Berkley Books, 1971.

———. *The Futurological Congress*. Trans. Michael Kandel. New York: Avon Books, 1976.

———. *Memoirs Found in a Bathtub*. Trans. Michael Kandel and Christine Rose. New York: Avon Books, 1976.

———. *The Investigation*. Trans. Adele Milch. New York: Avon Books, 1976.

———. *The Cyberiad: Fables for the Cybernetic Age*. Trans. Michael Kandel. New York: Avon Books, 1976.

———. *The Star Diaries*. Trans. Michael Kandel. New York: Avon Books, 1977.

———. *Return from the Stars*. Trans. Barbara Marszal and Frank Simpson. New York: Harcourt Brace Jovanovich, 1980.

Lessing, Doris. *Canopus in Argos: Archives—Re: Colonised Planets Shikasta, Personal, Psychological, Historical Documents Relating to Visit by Johor (George Sherban) Emissary (Grade 9) 87th of the Period of the Last Days*. New York: Vintage Books, 1981.

———. *Canopus in Argos: Archives—The Marriages Between Zones Three, Four, and Five (as Narrated by the Chroniclers of Zone Three)*. New York: Vintage Books, 1981.

———. *Canopus in Argos: Archives—The Sirian Experiments: The Report by Ambien II, of the Five*. New York: Vintage Books, 1982.

McElroy, Joseph. *Plus*. New York: Alfred A. Knopf, 1977.

Miller, Walter M. *A Canticle for Leibowitz*. New York: Bantam Books, 1976.

Moorcock, Michael. *Behond the Man*. New York: Avon Books, 1970.

———. *The Cornelius Chronicles*. New York: Avon Books, 1977.

Russ, Joanna. *The Female Man*. New York: Bantam Books, 1975.

Spinrad, Norman. *The Iron Dream*. New York: Avon Books, 1972.

———. *Bug Jack Barron*. New York: Pocket Books, 1972.

———. *No Direction Home*. New York: Pocket Books. 1975.

Vonnegut, Kurt. *God Bless You, Mr. Rosewater*. New York: Holt, Rinehart & Winston 1965.

———. *Slaughterhouse-Five*. New York: Delacorte Press, 1969.

———. *Breakfast of Champions*. New York: Delacorte Press, 1973.

Wolfe, Gene. *The Fifth Head of Cerberus*. New York: Ace Books, 1972.

———. *The Shadow of the Torturer*. New York: Pocket Books, 1981.

———. *The Claw of the Conciliator*. New York: Pocket Books, 1982.

———. *The Citadel of the Autarch*. New York: Pocket Books, 1983.

———. *The Sword of the Lictor*. New York: Pocket Books, 1983.

Zelazny, Roger. *This Immortal*. New York: Ace Books, 1966.

———. *Jack of Shadows*. New York: Signet Books, 1972.

———. *The Doors of His Face, the Lamps of His Mouth and Other Stories*. New York: Avon Books, 1974.

———. *Roadmarks*. New York: Ballantine Books, 1979.

———. *Changeling*. New York: Ace Books, 1980.

———. *The Last Defender of Camelot*. New York: Pocket Books, 1980.

———. *The Changing Land*. New York: Ballantine Books, 1981.

Secondary Sources

Aldis, Brian. *Billion Year Spree*. New York: Schocken Books, 1974.

Apter. T. E. *Fantasy Literature*. London: Macmillan, 1982.

Baron, Neil. *Anatomy of Wonder*. New York: R. R. Bowker Co., 1976.

Bleiler, Everett F. *The Guide to Supernatural Literature*. Kent, Ohio: Kent State University Press, 1983.

Brooke-Rose, Christine. *A Rhetoric of the Unreal*. Cambridge: Cambridge University Press, 1981.

Burns, Alan, and Charles Sugnet, eds. *The Imagination on Trial: British and American Writers Discuss Their Working Methods*. London: Allison & Busby, 1981; New York: Schocken Books, 1982.

Clareson, Thomas D., ed. *SF: The Other Side of Realism; Essays on Modern Fantasy and Science Fiction*. Bowling Green, Ohio: Bowling Green University Press, 1972.

Delany, Samuel R. *The American Shore: Meditations on a Tale of Science Fiction by Thomas M. Disch—Angoul Me*. Pleasantville, N.Y.: Dragon Press, 1978.

————. *The Jewel-Hinged Jaw: Notes on the Language of Science Fiction*. Elizabethtown, N. Y.: Dragon Press, 1977.

Greenland, Colin. *The Entropy Exhibition: Michael Moorcock and The British 'New Wave' in Science Fiction*. London and Boston: Routledge & Kegan Paul, 1983.

Hillegas, Mark Robert. *The Future as Nightmare: H.G. Wells and Anti-Utopias*. New York: Oxford University Press, 1967.

Holdstock, Robert, ed. *Encyclopedia of Science Fiction*. London: Octopus Books, 1978.

Jackson, Rosemary. *Fantasy: The Literature of Subversion*. New York: Methuen, 1981.

LeGuin, Ursula K. *The Language of the Night: Essays on Fantasy and Science Fiction*. New York: Berkley/Putnam, 1982.

Magill, Frank N., ed. *Survey of Modern Fantasy Literature*. 5 vols. Englewood Cliffs, N.J.: Salem Press, 1983.

Moscowitz, Samuel. *Seekers of Tommorow: Masters of Modern Science Fiction*. New York: Ballantine, 1966.

Myers, Robert E., ed. *The Intersection of Science Fiction and Philosophy*. Westport, CT.: Greenwood Press, 1983.

Nadeau, Robert. *Readings from the New Book on Nature: Physics and Metaphysica in the Modern Novel*. Amherst: University of Massachusetts Press, 1981.

Nicholls, Peter, ed. *The Science in Science Fiction*. London: Roxby, 1982; New York: Alfred A. Knopf, 1983.

Parrinder, Patrick. *Science Fiction: Its Criticism and Teaching*. New York: Methuen, 1980.

Riley, Dick, ed. *Critical Encounters: Writers and Themes in Science Fiction*. New York: Frederick Ungar, 1978.

Rosinsky, Natalie M. *Feminist Future: Contemporary Women's Speculative Fiction*. Ann Arbor, MI: UMI Research Press, 1984.

Rose, Mark. *Alien Encounters: Anatomy of Science Fiction*. Cambridge, Mass: Harvard University Press, 1981.

Sadler, Frank. *The Unified Ring: Narrative Art & the Science Fiction Novel.* Ann
     Arbor, MI: UMI Research Press, 1984.
Schlobin, Roger C., ed. *The Aesthetics of Fantasy Literature and Art.* Notre Dame,
     IN.: University of Notre Dame Press, 1982.
Scholes, Robert. *Structural Fabulation: An Essay on Fiction of the Future.* Notre
     Dame, IN: University of Notre Dame Press, 1975.
————,and Eric S. Rabkin: *Science Fiction: History, Science, Vision.* New York:
     Oxford University Press, 1977.
Slusser, George E., Eric S. Rabkin, and Robert Scholes, eds. *Bridges to Fantasy.*
     Carbondale: Southern Illinois University Press, 1982.
————. *Coordinates: Placing Science Fiction and Fantasy.* Carbondale: Southern
     Illinois University Press, 1983.
Smith, Nicholas D., ed. *Philosophers Look at Science Fiction.* Chicago: Nelson
     Hall, 1982.
Suvin, Darko. *Metamorphoses of Science Fiction: On the Poetics and History of a
     Literary Genre.* New Haven, CT: Yale University Press, 1979.
Todorov, Tzvetan. *The Fantastic: A Structural Approach to a Literary Genre.* Trans.
     Richard Howard. Ithaca, N.Y.: Cornell University Press, 1975.

GEOFFREY GREEN

The Extremities of Realism

Yet half I seemed to recognize some trick

Of mischief happened to me, God knows when—

In a bad dream perhaps. Here ended, then,

Progress this way. When in the very nick

Of giving up, one time more, came a clink

As when a trap shuts—you're inside the den!

Burningly it came on me all at once,

This was the place! those two hills on the right,

Crouched like two bulls locked horn in horn in fight;

While to the left, a tall scalped mountain . . . Dunce,

Dotard, a-dozing at the very nonce,

After a life spent training for the sight!

With these words, the narrator of Robert Browning's " 'Childe Roland to the Dark Tower Came' " (1855) expresses his abrupt realization that the strange, grotesque landscape through which he has been journeying in search of his goal is, in fact, his goal—the place he has been seeking all along. The location remains the same; what has changed is his perception of where he is. But this perceptual modification alters everything.

The features of reality are the same, yet the world, somehow, is different. Such an awareness necessitates a questioning of the senses: have I perceived correctly? Am I sane? But when the answer is yes, the conclusion suggests that beneath the familiar surface of reality lurks a fundamental strangeness—an otherness of perceptual dislocation that occurs within us as we react to life. Hence, what we thought to be sanity may perhaps now be madness. And the ability to perceive "correctly" may be seen as an illusion. Furthermore, our perception as readers of the text about this misperception may itself be called into question: reality or fiction?

An example of this perceptual alteration occurs in an enlightening conversation between John Hawkes and Robert Scholes about Hawkes' novel *The Blood Oranges*:

Scholes: I wonder in a way, and I suppose in a very ordinary way, whether one in the world of the living could achieve the gorgeous grace of Cyril with respect to sexuality, or whether one should attempt, let's say, to achieve the ideal set forth in the novel. In other words, this seems to me an ideal which is so ideal in fact, and Illyria a place which is so gorgeous in its way, that it almost prevents one from thinking of emulating it at all.

Hawkes: Gorgeous? As a matter of fact, the world of Illyria as described in *The Blood Oranges* actually consists of an arid landscape with a few broken-down stone huts, some villagers, a few boats, a lot of sun, a lot of desolation, some lemons, and four people. And here you are, Bob, sitting in a blue, short-sleeved shirt, a pair of striped, short, ragged trousers, an enormous grey-black beard, some hair sticking out of the side of your head, a smile that is enormous, eyes that are gleaming, a Protean man angled and at perfect ease in a corner of this room. You look like Cyril, you talk like Cyril, you live on the sea, you love, you're alive. So what are you talking about? *You* exemplify the possibility of living fully, honestly, truly, benignly, joyously. This is all my character does.[1]

In this exchange, both speakers are right: the fictional world of Illyria as created by Hawkes' Cyril (by way of Shakespeare's *Twelfth Night*) is indeed gorgeous as Scholes suggests, yet its appearance, as Hawkes reminds us, is drab, ordinary. To what does it owe its beauty? To the language of its depiction.

Here are the opening lines of Hawkes' *The Blood Oranges* spoken by the lyrical voice of Cyril, the first-person narrator:

Love weaves its own tapestry, spins its own golden thread, with its own sweet breath breathes into being its mysteries—bucolic, lusty, gentle as the eyes of daisies or thick with pain. And out of its own music creates the flesh of our lives. If the birds sing, the nudes are not far off. Even the dialog of the frogs is rapturous.

As for me, since late boyhood and early manhood, and throughout the more than eighteen years of my nearly perfect marriage, I always allowed myself to assume whatever shape was destined to be my own in the silken weave of Love's pink panorama.[2]

Is a squalid reality described by lyrical and ornate language yet squalid? Or does it become lyrical? The very nature of reality is thus seen to depend on the way in which its discrete elements are depicted. I hope it may be seen that Hawkes and Scholes reflect the two sides of the perceptual spectrum: the reality is the same! and yet it is different! And, of course, both are aware of this. The possibilities of this realization are sketched by Hawkes when he proceeds to include Scholes as an extension of the world within his novel. His voice becomes more like Cyril's—more detailed, poetic; the effect is to break down our own perceptual boundaries between what we are certain is real and what is imaginary.

To speak of the extremities of realism is to accept the notion that reality may at times be unreal—nonrealistic, fantastic, beyond our standard expectations for the norms of reality—and yet be anchored in the actual world. The sense of displacement that occurs when the world is thought to be the world and, simultaneously, is not the world is at the center of postmodern fiction. Particular objects may appear to be under our control but on closer examination their imaginary nature looms dangerously beyond our grasp, as in this passage from *The Blood Oranges* about the excavation of a medieval chastity belt:

> ... all four of us stared down at the pliant and yet indestructible thin loop of iron that was large enough to encircle a human waist and was dissected by a second and shorter loop or half circle of iron wrought into a deliberate and dimly functional design.

> ... we were scrutinizing the single tissue-thin contraption that had already revealed its purpose to Fiona and now, I suspected, was slowly suggesting itself to Catherine as something to wear.

> "It looks like a belt," I heard her saying.
> "But what are all those little teeth ... "

> ... the delicate and time-pocked iron girdle was lying on the gray stone and, I saw in this hard light, was the brown and orange color of dried blood and the blue-green color of corrosion.[3]

What is being described here? Is it the belt itself, now a decrepit relic? Or is it the brutal sexual possessiveness embodied by the *idea* of the belt? Or is it the possibility (contained within the partner-swapping scenario of the plot) for the contemporary use of such a contraption? To answer yes to all of these queries is to ask whether the details mean what they say. If so, how do our associations derive from the details?

When what we perceive takes on qualities that belie our perceptions, we are faced with the notion that reality is ultimately groundless, without orientation. Thomas Berger's* work explores this state of dissociation. "A work of fiction," he declares in the epigraph to *Killing Time* (1967), "is a construction of language and otherwise a lie." Berger's novel *Neighbors*

(1980) is structured around the ambiguities of perception that occur within what we identify as typical or ordinary reality. Here is a description of the protagonist, Earl Keese:

Were Keese to accept the literal witness of his eyes, his life would have been of quite another character, perhaps catastrophic, for outlandish illusions were, if not habitual with him, then at least none too rare for that sort of thing. Perhaps a half-dozen times a year he thought he saw such phenomena as George Washington urinating against the wheel of a parked car (actually an old lady bent over a cane), a nun run amok in the middle of an intersection (policeman directing traffic), a rat of record proportions (an abandoned football), or a brazen pervert blowing him a kiss from the rear window of a bus (side of sleeping workingman's face, propped on hand).[4]

The matter-of-fact narrative voice that so clearly discerns the truth behind Keese's earlier misperceptions conceals the profound crisis of misunderstanding that subsequently ensues in the novel. The reader is lured into a perceptual complacency that mirrors Keese's own failure to recognize that the senses are not reliable because the world eludes our ability to understand. Overnight, Keese is changed from an upstanding man of propriety to a wild man who "respond[s] to the particular situation."[5] His supposed enemies, Harry and Ramona, are now seen to be "probably the finest people I've ever met. It just takes a while to perceive their unique quality, but once you do, you're not the same."[6]

   Similarly, in Grace Paley's fiction, actual events evoking a recognizable reality are described in a manner that alters our reactions to these events. In the title story from her collection *Enormous Changes at the Last Minute* (1974), we assume that Alexandra's sickly father will further deteriorate at the news that she has had a baby out of wedlock. On the contrary, we are told:

Alexandra's father's life was not ruined, nor did he have to die. Shortly before the baby's birth, he fell hard on the bathroom tiles, cracked his skull, dipped the wires of his brain into his heart's blood. Short circuit! He lost twenty, thirty years in the flood, the faces of nephews, in-laws, the names of two Presidents, and a war. His eyes were rounder, he was often awestruck, but he was smart as ever, and able to begin again with fewer scruples to notice and appreciate.[7]

The effect is of having the carpet pulled from beneath our assumptions. Although the father's health does worsen, this "does not ruin" his life. His "short circuit" does not interfere with his intelligence; rather, it allows him "to notice and appreciate" reality "with fewer scruples"—which is the point of the fiction.

   When supposedly dire consequences instantaneously become benefits, our previous conception of the purpose and use of things is likewise modified. Edward Whittemore's novels are set in a recognizable and superficially accurate historical milieu, but beneath the surface, nothing is as it seems. Here is an account of Baron Kikuchi's heroism during the 1905 war between Japan and Russia from *Quin's Shanghai Circus* (1974):

On a barren plain near Mukden his regiment was surrounded by Cossack cavalry. The fierce horsemen swept repeatedly through the Japanese lines, cutting down the soldiers with their pikes. Kikuchi alone was able to hold his unit intact, a triumph attributed to his decision to use the dead horses of the Cossacks as a barrier against their attacks. Like most of the Japanese officers, his Buddhist background had bred in him an abhorrence of meat, but that didn't stop him from saving his men in the only way open to him.

At the end of three days and three nights Japanese reinforcements broke through the Cossack encirclement to find the lost regiment largely massacred. Only Kikuchi's company had survived, safe behind the walls of rotting meat, eight feet high, that he had erected. The young Captain was awarded Japan's highest combat decoration and singled out as an officer likely to become the youngest general in Japanese history. . . .

It turned out that his decision to defy Buddhist custom on the plains of Manchuria had an immediately harmful effect on him. A fly feeding on the rotting carcass of a horse during the siege had infected his right eye. He was not back in Japan many days before the sight in the eye began to fail.

Kikuchi went to a specialist who was also a family friend. The doctor told him that the infection could be treated and the eye saved but that nearly total blindness was inevitable. He would be left with a gray film over the eye, an ability to distinguish light and darkness but not shapes.[8]

The Baron's cleverness is rooted in his being able to see beyond the apparent form of things to their inherent function. But in so doing, he violates Buddhist custom in order to save his company of men. The eye infection is presented as a consequence of that violation, rather than as the price he paid to remain alive. His eye infection leaves him with "an ability to distinguish light and darkness but not shapes." Was the Baron's heroism actually an infection or a disease? In a sense, he already had the ailment before the battle: the light and darkness he could see insisted that his men must be saved. What he could not distinguish was the shape of the horses as merely horses, and this saved his life. But from the perception of Buddhist morality, he had succumbed to an affliction that destroyed his soul while saving his life.

When the people and things of the world are presented as ambiguous entities, our familiar associations no longer seem to follow in a logical manner. Thus, the very duties of a position may be precisely what estranges an individual from his calling. Such is the case with the Pope in Celia

Gittelson's *Saving Grace* (1981). In this description, the Pope's general dissatisfaction focuses on his bathroom:

As simple as the Papal bedroom was—bed, bureau, plain chair, wooden crucifix—the decor of the Papal bathroom (over which *il Papa* exercised less control) were ornate. Its opulence distressed him. The four walls were of the finest marble, and on the one facing the door, over the toilet, hung a gold crucifix from the seventeenth century. It was not that he liked this room too little, he thought, but that he liked it too much. There were mornings when he spent nearly a quarter of an hour dawdling in the bathtub, preparing to face the day.

Long enough and deep enough for two grown persons, the tub—riding on immense brass claws—appeared ready to pounce. White towels drooped like luxuriant jungle flowers from metal bars beside the sink, behind the door.[9]

What in the world is a pope's bathroom supposed to look like? The inappropriateness of the subject matter only intensifies the effect of the realistic details: that before he was Pope, the Pope, too, was a person who could not conceive of what the Papal bathroom should look like. The creation of a specific milieu here serves to reinforce the sensation of alienation—and this will be achieved in the novel by the Pope's abandoning the Vatican and hiding in disguise in order to attain a higher sense of his calling.

Or else an accumulation of specific details may act to assault our assumption that the reader is detached, uninvolved, outside the world of the fiction. In this passage from Marilynne Robinson's *Housekeeping* (1981), the orientation of the description is basically realistic. But the breathless and elongated phrasing serves to reinforce the grandfather's claustrophobia for the reader:

Through all these generations of elders we lived in one house, my grandmother's house, built for her by her husband, Edmund Foster, an employee of the railroad, who escaped this world years before I entered it. It was he who put us down in this unlikely place. He had grown up in the Middle West, in a house dug out of the ground, with windows just at earth level and just at eye level, so that from without, the house was a mere mound, no more a human stronghold than a grave, and from within, the perfect horizontality of the world in that place foreshortened the view so severely that the horizon seemed to circumscribe the sod house and nothing more. So my grandfather began to read what he could find of travel literature.[10]

Ultimately, the label "extreme" for realism depends on a norm or standard of reality. We suppose that reality functions in this way; thus, the fictional depiction of reality ought to reflect our conception of the world. However, when people and things in fiction are represented in accordance with our expectations about the world, but the consequent fictional world created seems profoundly different from those expectations—then our sense of reality is disoriented by the mirror we had thought would reflect it. Jerome Charyn's fiction is born in precisely that disruptive atmosphere. Here is a description of the descendant of a convert family from the Inquisition, now living in the Bronx; it is taken from his *Blue Eyes* (1974):

Having already been reduced to penniless scratchers, they attended church (which they called El Synagoga), and mumbled secret prayers at home, cooking vast amounts of pork outside their doors to mislead their Christian neighbors and protect themselves from future Inquisitions. Thus Mordeckay inherited his role as a cooker and eater of pork. . . .

He performed a few specific services for his cousins from North America in the Bronx, for which he was adequately paid. He sought no other employments, spending his hours praying over his pots of boiling pork. Mordeckay had prayers for the da Silvas, living and dead, for his Bronx cousins and *chuetas* everywhere, for El Dia del Pardon (the Day of Atonement), for the pigs that were slaughtered so that the da Silvas could survive, for the darkness that protected the *chuetas*, for the Portuguese language that had succored them, for the Spanish they spoke in America, and for his own apostasy, his forced departure from the laws of Moses. He worshipped Cristóbal Colón (Christopher Columbus), whom he considered a *chueta* out of Portugal, and Queen Esther, who married a Persian king to save the Jews, becoming the first Marrano in history. The *chuetas* had holy obligations to Santa Esther; on her feast day they were forbidden to spit, urinate, or consume pork. Mordeckay would only eat spinach for Esther's day. And no matter how hard his kidneys throbbed, he wouldn't pass water until sundown.[11]

Certainly, Mordeckay's world is ordered and structured, but from a world perspective that seems strange and fantastic in comparison with our own. At no point does this world become magical or otherworldly, yet the effect is that our reality is transformed. For how else may it coexist with such an alternative world?

Although the world may at times seem spectral and illusory despite its reality, it is comprised of human beings engaged in living. But how human are they? What happens when the reality of the world confronts our own humanity? Jerzy Kosinski's* fictions address this issue. The following passage from *Steps* (1968) pits the human urge to live against the very humanity by which we live:

The commander of our group ordered the prisoners to turn and face the wall. I was certain that they were about to be shot. Not wanting to participate in the execution, I gestured to the man next to me, offering to exchange my rifle for his long knife. The man agreed. I was just about to hide behind one of the trucks when I was roughly pushed forward by men also armed with knives. Each of us was ordered to stand directly behind one of the prisoners.

I glanced around me: the armed men, tense and ready, stood at my sides and behind me. Only then did I realize that the prisoners were about to be beheaded. My refusal to obey orders would mean my being executed with those who stood in front of me. I could no longer see their faces, but their shirts were only a few inches from the blade of my knife.

It was inconceivable, I thought, that I would have to slash the neck of another man simply because events had placed me behind his back. What I was about to do was inescapable, yet so unreal that it became senseless: I had to believe I was not myself any more and that whatever happened would be imaginary. I saw myself as someone else who felt nothing, who stood calm and composed, determined enough to stiffen his arms, to grasp and raise the weapon, to cut down the obstacle in his path. I knew I was strong enough to do it. I could recall the precision with which I had felled young trees: I could hear their moaning and creaking, and see their trembling, and I knew I could jump aside as they cracked and fell, their leaves brushing my feet.[12]

When faced with a choice between his own life and another man's life, the narrator is forced to extreme measures: were he to say "better him than me" his humanity would be lost. Instead, he convinces himself of the unreality of his reality: "What I was about to do was inescapable, yet so unreal that it became senseless." He has to wish himself out of his reality: "I had to believe I was not myself any more and that whatever happened would be imaginary." Thus the narrator, upon completion of the act, would recall the experience of chopping down a young tree—but a man would be dead. The unwilling executioner would have momentarily transcended his reality in order to carry out its odious task. But we, as readers of the fiction, are stirred by this fictional being escaping into the imaginary not least of all because we are doing the same thing by reading the fictional text. Or are we?

What could be more extreme than to question the boundaries between fiction and reality, between the self of the character who reads and the self of the character being read about? But Norman Mailer's works probe the meaning of reality when conceived from the vantage point of our mortality. His *The Executioner's Song* (1979), termed a "true life novel," recreates through fiction events that already had occurred in reality. Here is the scene of mass murderer Gary Gilmore's post-execution autopsy:

Now, the fellow who was at the head of Jerry's table made an incision from behind Gary's left ear all the way up across the top of his head and then down below to the other ear, after which he grabbed the scalp on both sides of the cut, and pulled it right open, just pulled the whole face down below his chin until it was inside out like the back of a rubber mask. Then he took a saw and cut around the skull. Picked up something like a putty knife, and pried the bone open, popped the top of the head off. Then, he stuck his hand inside the cavity and pulled the brain out, weighed it. Pound and a half, it looked like to Jerry Scott. Then they removed the pituitary, put it aside, and sliced the brain like meat loaf. "Why are you doing that?" asked Jerry Scott. "Well," said one of the doctors, "we're looking for tumors." They started explaining to him about the different areas of the brain, and how they were looking to see if there were any problems in Gary Gilmore's motor system. Everything, however, looked to be just fine.

Then they took pictures of his tatoos. "Mom" had been written on his left shoulder, and "Nicole" on his left forearm. They took his fingerprints, and then they took all the organs they did not need for dissection and put them back into the body and head cavities, and drew his face up, pulled it right back taut over the bones and muscles, like putting on the mask again, fit the sawed-off bone-cap back on the skull, and sewed the scalp, and body cavity. When they were all finished, it looked like Gary Gilmore again.[13]

All along we have followed Gilmore from his parole to his violent murders to his incarceration and execution. But is the matter then concluded? By continuing to refer to the corpse as "Gary" while describing its dissection, we are thrown into a disarray of turbulent associations: why are human beings doing this? The senselessness of all crime and punishment is thus highlighted. Beyond this, however, the dismantling of the cadaver encourages us to question what it is that makes us alive? that makes us murder? When the autopsy is finished, "it looked like Gary Gilmore again." But was it Gary Gilmore? Was the true Gary Gilmore the man who murdered or the man who loved? Is Norman Mailer's "true life novel" about Gilmore fact or fiction? Are we as responsible as the fictional (?) society depicted within the pages of the text? If life is as simple as the taking apart and putting together of corpses, why is reality so elusive and challenging?

These are some of the issues investigated by those postmodern works that situate themselves at the extremities of realism. I have only been able to discuss a few of the exemplary writers operating today in order to provide a sketch of the contours of the field. But there are many other talented authors: Rudolph Wurlitzer, Thomas McGuane,* Barry Hannah,* Joan Didion,* Richard Price, Harry Crews,* William Burroughs, Joy Williams, Cynthia Ozick, Russell Hoban,* John Gregory Dunne.

> There they stood, ranged along the hill-sides, met
>
> To view the last of me, a living frame
>
> For one more picture! in a sheet of flame
>
> I saw them and I knew them all. And yet
>
> Dauntless the slug-horn to my lips I set,
>
> And blew.
>
> ("Childe Roland to the Dark Tower Came")

At the end of Browning's poem, the narrator, having realized that the world is altered irrevocably in a moment's perceptual reassessment, raises his trumpet and plays the very song whose lyrics comprise the lines of the poem we have just completed reading.

If postmodern reality seems unreal, then there is nothing to do but to confront the extreme nature of that reality through fiction—as a means of attaining enunciation and insight. Thus, we come to know our reality through the fictional evocation of that reality. And vice versa. Read on! Live on!

NOTES

1. "John Hawkes and Robert Scholes: A Conversation," *Novel* 5, no. 3 (Spring 1972): 203.
2. John Hawkes, *The Blood Oranges* (New York: New Directions, 1971), p. 1.
3. Ibid., pp. 206–207.
4. Thomas Berger, *Neighbors* (New York: Delacorte Press, 1980), pp. 1–2.
5. Ibid., p. 270.
6. Ibid., p. 271.
7. Grace Paley, *Enormous Changes at the Last Minute* (1974; rpt. New York: Laurel, 1975), p. 139.
8. Edward Whittemore, *Quin's Shanghai Circus* (New York: Holt, Rinehart & Winston, 1974), pp. 114–15.
9. Celia Gittelson, *Saving Grace* (New York: Alfred A. Knopf, 1981), p. 5.
10. Marilynne Robinson, *Housekeeping* (1981; rpt. New York: Bantam, 1982), pp. 3–4.
11. Jerome Charyn, *Blue Eyes* (New York: Simon & Schuster, 1974), p. 106.
12. Jerzy Kosinski, *Steps* (1968; rpt. New York: Bantam, 1969), pp. 145–46.
13. Norman Mailer, *The Executioner's Song* (1979; rpt. New York: Warner, 1980), p. 983.

SELECTED BIBLIOGRAPHY

Primary Sources

Berger, Thomas. *Killing Time*. New York: Dial Press, 1967.
———. *Neighbors*. New York: Delacorte Press, 1980.
Burroughs, William. *Naked Lunch*. New York: New Directions, 1974.
Busch, Frederick. *Manual Labor*. New York: New Directions, 1974.
———. *Domestic Particulars: A Family Chronicle*. New York: New Directions, 1976.
———. *The Mutual Friend*. New York: Harper & Row, 1978.
Carver, Raymond. *Will You Please Be Quiet, Please?* New York: McGraw-Hill, 1976.
———. *What We Talk About When We Talk About Love*. New York: Vintage, 1981.
———. *Cathedral*. New York: Alfred A. Knopf, 1983.

Crews, Harry. *The Gospel Singer*. New York: William Morrow, 1968.

―――. *Karate Is a Thing of the Spirit*. New York: William Morrow, 1971.

―――. *Car*. New York: Morrow, 1972.

―――. *A Feast of Snakes*. New York: Atheneum, 1976.

Didion, Joan. *Play It As It Lays*. New York: Farrar, Straus & Giroux, 1970.

Elkin, Stanley. *Boswell*. New York: Random House, 1964.

―――. *The Dick Gibson Show*. New York: Random House, 1967.

―――. *Searches and Seizures*. New York: Random House, 1973.

―――. *The Franchiser*. New York: Farrar, Straus & Giroux, 1976.

Gittelson, Celia. *Saving Grace*. New York: Alfred A. Knopf, 1981.

Hannah, Barry. *Geronimo Rex*. New York: Viking Press, 1972.

―――. *Airships*. New York: Alfred A. Knopf, 1978.

―――. *Ray*. New York: Alfred A. Knopf, 1980.

Hawkes, John. *The Lime Twig*. New York: New Directions, 1961.

―――. *The Cannibal*. New York: New Directions, 1962.

―――. *Second Skin*. New York: New Directions, 1964.

―――. *The Blood Oranges*. New York: New Directions, 1971.

Hoban, Russell. *Riddley Walker*. New York: Summit Books, 1980.

―――. *Pilgermann*. New York: Summit Books, 1983.

Irving, John. *The 158-Pound Marriage*. New York: Random House, 1974.

―――. *The World According to Garp*. New York: E. P. Dutton, 1978.

Kosinski, Jerzy. *The Painted Bird*. Boston: Houghton Mifflin, 1965.

―――. *Steps*. New York: Random house, 1968.

McGuane, Thomas. *Ninety-Two in the Shade*. New York: Farrar, Straus & Giroux, 1973.

―――. *Panama*. New York: Farrar, Straus & Giroux, 1977.

―――. *Nobody's Angel*. New York: Farrar, Straus & Giroux, 1982.

Mailer, Norman. *The Executioner's Song*. 1979; rpt. New York: Warner, 1980.

Paley, Grace. *The Little Disturbances of Man*. New York: Viking Press, 1968.

―――. *Enormous Changes at the Last Minute*. New York: Farrar, Straus & Giroux, 1974.

Robinson, Marilynne. *Housekeeping*. New York: Farrar, Straus & Giroux, 1981.

Stone, Robert. *A Hall of Mirrors*. Boston: Houghton Mifflin, 1967.

―――. *Dog Soldiers*. Boston: Houghton Mifflin, 1974.

Whittemore, Edward. *Quin's Shanghai Circus*. New York: Holt, Rinehart & Winston, 1974.

―――. *Sinai Tapestry*. Holt, Rinehart & Winston, 1977.

Williams, Joy. *State of Grace*. Garden City, NY: Doubleday, 1973.

Wurlitzer, Rudolph. *Nog*. New York: Random House, 1969.

―――. *Flats*. New York: E. P. Dutton, 1970.

―――. *Quake*. New York: E. P. Dutton, 1972.

JOHN HELLMAN

Postmodern Journalism

Plausible, if debatable, forerunners of the nonfiction novel and the New Journalism can be traced from James Agee's *Let Us Now Praise Famous Men* (1941) all the way back to Daniel Defoe's *A Journal of the Plague Year* (1722). Nevertheless, the serious presentation of journalistic subject matter in the form of fiction first consistently appears in the *New Yorker* magazine in the years following World War II. John Hersey (writing on the nuclear holocaust at Hiroshima), Lillian Ross (on Hemingway and on the making of a Hollywood motion picture), and Truman Capote (on an opera company's tour of Russia and on Marlon Brando) demonstrated that journalistic observation and research could be rendered more powerfully, even more fully, with the reconstruction of setting, dialogue, and narrative pattern associated with fiction than with the flat unfolding of the "five w's" found in modern journalism. With the publication of Capote's exhaustively researched and beautifully crafted *In Cold Blood: A True Account of a Multiple Murder and Its Consequences* (1965), accompanied by his well-publicized claims to having invented a new literary form, the concept of a nonfiction novel combining the highest fidelity to journalistic fact with the highest effects of literary art became a matter of fierce debate.

The *New Yorker* writers were experimenters only in giving the unique authority of a journalist's relation to the world to the traditional forms of the fiction writer. Although that combination in itself startlingly revealed the power of fictional shape and texture to breathe the wholeness of represented life into reported observation, these writers confined themselves to realistic methods sharing the same assumptions of a solid external reality that could be mirrored as did the conventions of modern journalism. The author remained invisible, the style styleless, the point of view objective. Not surprisingly, this realistic nonfiction has been favored over the years mainly by journalists presenting an inside story, such as Gay Talese in *The Kingdom and the Power* (1969), or recounting a sensational story, such as

Thomas Thompson in *Blood and Money* (1976). Like the muckraking exposé and the lurid pot-boiler, realistic nonfiction seeks no disruptions of the reader's notions of reality but rather the aim of nineteenth-century realism of revealing the "true" reality lurking behind the illusory public image.

In the 1960s, other writers responded to the alterations in American reality being brought about by the mass media with a much more experimental combination of journalistic subject and fictional form. These experimenters—Norman Mailer, Tom Wolfe,* Hunter Thompson, Joan Didion,* and Michael Herr—published stories about the celebrities, subcultures, and events that were now intruding into the living rooms of mainstream American life. Although their styles and techniques varied as strikingly as their sensibilities, these writers all approached public fact through a frank, obtrusive, liberated assertion of their private consciousness. These New Journalists, as they came to be called, recognized that the mass media were confronting personal consciousness with the most remote and strange facts, while at the same time further disorienting that perceiving consciousness by fictionalizing this vastly enlarged reality in fragmented, superficial, and stereotypical formulas. Mailer, Wolfe, Thompson, Didion, and Herr followed the corporate shapers of the news in presenting the phenomena of a rapidly changing American culture through fictional forms; they countered the media by casting aside the pretenses and restraints of objectivity for a self-referential focus on personal consciousness, as well as by casting off formulas of simple conflict and balanced analysis for the fresh perspectives of experimental form.

This meant entering at the same time more deeply into the world of public fact and more deeply into the world of private consciousness. At their best, the New Journalists would attempt to get inside their subjects, either through lengthy first-hand observation and even participation or through exhaustive research of first-hand sources. Frankly presenting their resulting perceptions as perceptions, they would then proceed to bring the full resources of their interpretive powers as sense-making beings. The results looked remarkably like the nonrealistic fables with which writers working in the invented realm of the novel and short story in the 1960s were abandoning depiction of an increasingly elusive, seemingly irreal, postmodern reality. Allegory, black humor, picaresque or fragmented narrative, metafiction—the characteristic modes of John Barth,* Donald Barthelme,* Thomas Pynchon,* Robert Coover,* Kurt Vonnegut,* and Jerzy Kosinski* were to be found dispersed as well among the works of the New Journalists.

Although the fables of the experimental fiction writers took the world of private imagination as their ostensible subject and the New Journalists took the world of public fact, both were leaping over the limited techniques and purposes of realism. Avoiding its naive assumptions about reality, they both attempted to overcome its inadequacies in the face of the fragmenting, changing world of the postmodern. The experimenters in both fiction and journalism were insisting on the tentative nature of all perception while exploiting the power of that perception when liberated from rigid convention and preformulated response. By respectively promising no defined relation to actuality whatever, or promising the quite definite relation of journalistic observation, neither postmodern fictionists nor postmodern journalists had any need to limit themselves to misleading considerations of the plausible, the commonsensical, the typical. Instead, they could both use the full resources of their own consciousness in seeking out a deeper pattern and meaning.

Recognizing the inevitably transforming nature of human consciousness—so that the choice confronting a journalist was not the commonly supposed one of fact versus fiction and objectivity versus subjectivity, but rather one of formula versus form and disguised perspective versus open perspective—the New Journalists presented their observations and research through modes of fiction representing modes of consciousness. Thus, a journalistic subject could be presented factually through a whole range of styles, from Didion's precise melancholia to Wolfe's pyrotechnic playfulness, from Mailer's existential drama to Thompson's comic bestiality. The subject could be patterned as an epic, if also funny, narrative, as in Wolfe's presentation of the test pilots and early astronauts as symbolic warriors in *The Right Stuff* (1979). Or it could be patterned as an obsessive search back through one's memories, as in Herr's fragmented depiction of the Vietnam War in *Dispatches* (1977) and in Didion's similar "flash-cut" technique for reporting the coming apart of California culture in *The White Album* (1979). All of these writers created works in which their consciousness, instead of passively accepting the fictions both reported and created by the media, self-consciously confronted fact, self-reflexively shaping it into tentative but personally achieved meanings of their own. If the effects were not realistic, they nevertheless possessed a greater verisimilitude in presenting a reality pervaded by fictions.

Mailer and Thompson have been the two boldest and most innovative of these journalistic fictionists. Mailer's *The Executioner's Song* (1979) and Thompson's *The Curse of Lono* (1983) afford an opportunity to observe how two strikingly different works share the essential assumptions of postmodern journalism. In addition, because each work represents a significant development in the context of its author's previously well-established approach to the form, *The Executioner's Song* and *The Curse of Lono* also provide revealing examples of the unique demands and opportunities the genre presents to its artists.

DEEPER INTO FACT: MAILER'S *THE EXECUTIONER'S SONG*

In his several journalistic works prior to *The Executioner's Song*, Mailer developed a metafictional journalism in which he overtly imposed his ideas

and fantasies on the events he reported, and in which he openly manipulated narrative form to suit his purposes. Presenting *The Armies of the
Night* (1968) as an accurate report of his knowledge as participant at the
march on the Pentagon, Mailer uses the simple strength of the reporter's
"I was there and this is what I saw" author-reader contract. But he also
contemptuously casts off the objective restraints of conventional journalism
to present the events and characters of this media event as they exist in
the elaborate world of his own observing, experiencing consciousness. As
mock-epic hero and mock-epic stylist, Mailer dominates the event, presenting it through separate and highly self-conscious personae—Mailer as
witnessing participant, Mailer as reflecting novelist, Mailer as omniscient
historian—and from each of these perspectives playfully adopting and violating conventions. With somewhat decreasing impact, Mailer continued
this practice in such works as *Miami and the Siege of Chicago* (1968), *Of
a Fire on the Moon* (1970), *St. George and the Godfather* (1972), and *The
Fight* (1975).

Thus, Mailer surprised the literary world when he produced a 1,050-
page book that abandoned this stance. In *The Executioner's Song*, which
narrates the events leading up to and surrounding murderer Gary Gilmore's
execution, he instead imitates the conventions of journalism and realistic
fiction. Keeping himself invisible behind a resolutely objective stance and
reportorial prose, Mailer seems in *The Executioner's Song* to be going
considerably further than the great realists whom he emulated at the start
of his novelistic career—Theodore Dreiser, James Farrell, John Dos Passos—in seeking to give up the fancies and intuitions of his own consciousness for a capturing of society simply as it is. Yet the effect of this
determinedly factual report is anything but that of the raw life sought by
realism and naturalism. It is instead that of a highly crafted artifice lacking
a final authority, of a world the reader experiences more on the psycho-
symbolic and tentative plane of fabulation than on the seemingly solid
surfaces of realism. *The Executioner's Song* is a document with a firm
journalistic connection to the world, but it is a social novel in which the
object of depiction is not the manners and mores of realism but rather the
private visions of a nation's consciousness.

In *The Executioner's Song* Mailer still follows the strategy and aims of
his previous journalism—to seek in the interaction of exterior fact and
interior consciousness the mysteries of contemporary American society
lurking beneath the confusing surfaces. In this book, however, Mailer
eliminates his previous roles as protagonist and self-conscious narrator to
focus on the interior consciousness of a mass of people in various classes
of America. The eerie effect of the book results most basically from Mailer's
collapsing of opposed prose forms shaping the divided realm of the collective consciousness of American society. Adhering to the material of a
huge body of interviews, Mailer narrates the events of *The Executioner's*

Song completely through the successive and alternating points of view of approximately 100 characters. The interviews were clearly conducted with the aim of probing the subject, not simply for their observations of the relevant events but also for their private thoughts and emotions and even for their past lives. The book includes these elements, and as a result it is in effect a compendium of confessions, of voices (Mailer divides his narrative into two parts called "Western Voices" and "Eastern Voices") recounting their personal troubles, triumphs, anxieties, joys, and guilts.

This material is precisely the world of private longing and anxiety found in the pulp "true" confession magazines of crime and romance. In the manner of *True Confessions* or *True Love* magazines, virtually every fact in *The Executioner's Song* is presented as the interior experience of people the reader comes to know well. This connection, which Mailer implies by calling the book a "true life novel" on the jacket and in the afterword, is reinforced on the original jacket flap when the reader is promised the voyeuristic thrill and final ennobling value characteristic of a pulp magazine blurb: "the true tale of violence and fear, jealousy and loss, of a love defiant even in death."

Mailer narrates the characters' confessional material, however, in the precise, neutral manner of the newspapers which in reporting events determinedly leave such material out. By presenting the intensely human material of his characters' confessions in the manner of the flat unfolding of the "five w's" of conventional journalism, Mailer makes painfully obvious the loss involved in the newspapers' removal of events from inner human experience while he brings to that larger context the serious attention represented by the conventions of journalism.

Above all, this objective, neutral, precise recording of people's subjective confessions as he reconstructs the events leading up to Gilmore's execution is a carefully crafted novelistic strategy for achieving the portrait of American society eluding realistic approaches. Enjoying the strong credibility and sense of actuality afforded by the journalistic author-reader contract, with the added effect of objective fairness created by the journalistic conventions, Mailer is able to keep to a minimum the details of setting as well as of dress, gestures, expressions—in other words, manners—by which a realist labors to establish authenticity and to convey the reality of a stable social class. Enjoying the innate fascination his material holds in its factual look into human territory largely unknown to the reader of the news and even of contemporary serious novels, Mailer is likewise able to avoid the realist's need to sustain interest by building toward a climax or by telescoping bits of narrative.

Instead, he is able to leap directly into his characters' consciousness, reporting their longings, actions, conflicts, ways of thinking, their ways of ordering; to move up and down the social strata of America without getting lost in the surface phenomena of its multiple and transmitting codes; and

to unfold his material at a steady pace, allowing him to explore along the
way all the characters and incidents contributing to his picture of society.
His resulting portrait is of Americans explaining themselves—the fables
by which they live, kill, commit suicide, grow, accommodate, and serve.
In these stories lies the secret lore of American society, the private myths
by which its citizens make sense of their lives. In the afterword Mailer,
after detailing the extraordinary amount of interviewing involved in getting
the "revelations" out of which the book is built, does not hesitate to add
that "this does not mean it has come a great deal closer to the truth than
the recollections of the witnesses." Because the truth he is after is those
recollections, the seeming qualification only directs the reader back to the
actual subject of the book.

Mailer has constructed *The Executioner's Song* so that it is a constant
contradiction: flatly episodic, yet symmetrically ordered into two books of
seven chapters dividing the story precisely at the middle; exhaustively
detailed with small facts of incidents and thoughts, yet curiously insubstantial because of a very spare depiction of physical setting; reading like
a flat news account, yet crystallizing each event into such concrete language
and framed isolation that the effect pushes toward that of poetry; following
the course of tensions and conflicts, yet never shaping into a strong, controlling pattern. The ultimate effect is that of a fable lacking a moral or
meaning known to its author; he is, after all, finally only a chronicler.

The paradox of *The Executioner's Song* lies in its being a chronicle of
fables. Unlike the exterior stories of the newspaper it imitates, it provides
a mass of interior stories that take the reader into the human lives of the
characters in the event. Stripped as they are by Mailer of surface details,
these stories read like allegories conveying abstract meaning in action. In
a sense they are, for as the memories of the characters they are orderings
and selections of the characters' consciousness, revelations not simply of
what happened but of the meaning "what happened" has taken on in their
orderings of reality. Mailer with each character traces their thoughts, their
past biographies, and their actions relevant to the Gilmore narrative according to the configuration the characters themselves perceive in them.
In effect, then, Mailer presents their private myths, the stories by which
they explain the facts of their experience. This accounts for the presence
of patterns in the book that never seem to connect into an encompassing
one conferred or approved by the author.

In the sections centering on Gilmore's California attorney Dennis Boaz,
for instance, the narrative is shaped by the character's lifelong sense of
being divided between seeking goal-oriented advancement and "the underground thing about the right to play, and the pursuit of happiness"; in
the sections devoted to small-newspaper reporter Tamera Smith, her sense
of division between being "so active and true-believing a Mormon on the
one hand" and "having such crazy impulses on the other" shapes a narrative

conflict between passionately social and personal longings; in the Lawrence Schiller sections, his secular version of the quest for grace through good works, consisting of an effort to submit his highly developed skills as a purveyor of sensationalism to the service of a serious history of Gilmore, makes his story one of middle-class redemption. Mailer's resolute lack of irony or favor leaves these visions without any conclusive interpretation.

Of course, Mailer's own personal mythos, which has long included a perception of schizophrenia in American society, has clearly contributed to his focusing on such patterns. Nevertheless, Mailer has refrained from imposing on them the easy dualities that with *Of a Fire on the Moon* seemed to become prepackaged formulas of his own. Instead, the collective authorship is allowed to force a more open vision of American society: what Mailer calls his discovery in the book that perhaps American society is not evil after all, but rather a "sad comedy" of people all striving to do the "right thing." Mailer's vision, focusing on but also subduing itself to the patterns evident to him in his characters' confessions, produces a richly complex portrait of a society ever more fragmented by multiple divisions at the base of its culture.

The logic of Mailer's document is thus largely the same logic of dream, myth, and the unconscious that shapes a fabulist novel such as Barth's* *Giles Goat-Boy*. Writing a book of objective fact, which is also a highly stylized artifice, and which is finally a tracing by the author of what seem to him the significant orderings of one character's consciousness after another, Mailer has given us a document comprised of factual fables without the final closure of an author's controlling allegory, without a center. The result is a social novel that could not be further from the determinist world of the naturalist novels Mailer started out emulating in *The Naked and the Dead*, and that takes him and the reader out of the trap which his absorption in his own consciousness was becoming in his previous journalism.

DEEPER INTO CONSCIOUSNESS: THOMPSON'S *THE CURSE OF LONO*

Thompson's *The Curse of Lono* offers a striking contrast to *The Executioner's Song*. After first winning fame with the feat of reporting on a notorious motorcycle gang in *Hell's Angels: A Strange and Terrible Saga* (1966), Thompson developed in *Fear and Loathing in Las Vegas: A Savage Journey to the Heart of the American Dream* (1971) and *Fear and Loathing: On the Campaign Trail '72* (1973) a disruptingly original technique. Like Mailer in his journalism prior to *The Executioner's Song*, Thompson presented himself as both the protagonist and the narrator of his works.

His persona, however, was a self-caricature, a flattened and exaggerated version of his self-perceived inclination toward innocent idealism and savage bestiality, a comic-book character he put to use in presenting the news as a parodic allegory of an America caught in a struggle between its dark and light impulses. As narrator, this persona—usually disordered by drugs— was an obviously unreliable witness who thus freed his creator to bring an expressionistic vision to the world of journalistic observation. As protagonist, he was a picaro who could respond with entertaining antics to the evil of the story in which he found himself enmeshed. Through his persona, Thompson offered the reader a vicarious opportunity to cast off a passive relation to the news and to assert one's outraged consciousness with humor and aggression.

In his writings following *Campaign Trail*, collected in *The Great Shark Hunt: Strange Tales from a Strange Time* (1979) along with his early, more conventional reportage, Thompson seemed—like the Mailer of *Of a Fire on the Moon* and *The Fight*—increasingly trapped within the confines of his persona. His articles from this period seem repetitive and stale, imitations of his earlier work lacking the original passion and invention. His persona had become a cult figure, a self-parody in the first place now parodied by others in film and comic strip, and by himself in interviews and on the college lecture circuit. Toward the end of the 1970s he dropped virtually out of sight amid rumors that he had turned to writing a novel and was suffering from writer's block.

In *The Curse of Lono* Thompson resurfaces to take the persona to an event (the Honolulu Marathon) and setting (Hawaii) on the periphery of American news. Thompson's subject is always ultimately the spiritual condition of the nation, a soul he finds mirrored equally in the public setting in which he finds himself and in the private landscape of his own psyche. *The Curse of Lono* succeeds because here, as in the earlier *Fear and Loathing* works, he finds both without and within something new to report. In *The Curse of Lono* Thompson reprints excerpts from Mark Twain's *Letters from Hawaii* and describes himself at one point as struggling in the "land of Po." *The Curse of Lono* is simultaneously a Twain-like journey through nature and society and a Poe-like descent into one's own dark unconscious. As such, it is a wild fictional contrivance making a journalistic report on the state of the American errand in the 1980s as perceived by an acutely sensitive, yet aggressive, consciousness. Repulsive yet humorous, it is a literary work providing the instruction of a warning and the delight of an aggressive vision.

Thompson centers his narrative on two sporting events: running, which he characterizes as the "Last Refuge of the Liberal Mind, or at least the Last Thing that Works"; and marlin fishing, which he sees as a Darwinian contest for status epitomizing the macho spirit dominating Reagan's America of the 1980s. But his larger topic is the setting of Hawaii, which fascinates him as the furthest western edge of America, a frontier in which Texaco stations and McDonald's hamburger stands are placed over ground haunted by pagan gods, and where the misnamed Pacific Ocean manifests the falseness of the American vision of nature as benign and controllable. Thompson unifies these unlikely subjects into a tall tale exemplifying his vision of the state of the nation in the aftermath of its failed quests of the 1960s and 1970s for social justice and personal fulfillment. With the American dream of an ever-expanding frontier and ever-progressing society given over to the masochistic marathon and status-seeking hunt, Thompson presents the tragic Hawaiian legend of Lono (a god self-condemned to lengthy fighting and wandering by his irrational killing of his wife) as a myth more appropriate to contemporary America than the Christian one of a redeemer nation.

Thompson constructs his tale as a journey from the rational to the irrational, the civilized to the savage, and sets it off against excerpts from Richard Hough's *The Last Voyage of Captain James Cook* (1965) which he reprints in accompanying blocks. This parallel narrative of the eighteenth-century British explorer's discovery of Hawaii, reception by the natives as their returning god Lono, and eventual murder by them suggests the danger of Western hubris in trying to control and remain aloof from a world of savage and irrational nature. In contrast to Cook, Thompson himself survives by willingly taking on the persona of Lono. In the course of the tale he becomes increasingly savage, hurling verbal abuse and huge quantities of firecrackers at the society and nature threatening him. Little happens in the story, and far less can be trusted as actually happening. Nevertheless, through wildly comic little vignettes (including a literal shaggy dog story about a flea-infested poodle improbably at the center of a drug-smuggling scheme, and a literal fish story climaxing in the conquest of a giant marlin with a Hawaiian war club), a savagely evocative prose, the artfully contrived collage of parallel narratives, and letters that are obviously false documents, Thompson constructs an artful adventure of the mind.

The Curse of Lono is a playful representation of how a consciousness, through art, can contemplate and probe an experience otherwise both bland and terrible. The alternatives are the retreat to civilization he parodies in the character of his illustrator-companion Ralph Steadman (who flees back to England) or the atavistic entry into the spirit of the time and place he portrays in a grimly humorless projection of himself called Gene Skinner. Thompson ends *The Curse of Lono* with an epigraph describing a legendary Hawaiian prophetess who found her visions alone in a hut, a clear analogue to Thompson's practice here of journalism as introspection as prophecy— in other words, as literature.

WORLD AND CONSCIOUSNESS

Postmodern journalism presents a direct confrontation of fact with form, of world with consciousness, of journalism with fiction. Mailer's *The Ex-*

ecutioner's Song imitates both the content and form of a document, but that subtle imitation shapes a highly crafted and sly artifice. Thompson's *The Curse of Lono* is an extended exercise in the tall tale, yet it never gives up its claim to being written by an actual consciousness speaking from and about an actual place and time. Between these extremes, Wolfe goes behind the fictions of the media to find the facts of the psychedelic movement and the early space program, then asserts the interpretations of his consciousness to present tales of mythic shape and resonance in *The Electric Kool-Aid Acid Test* (1968) and *The Right Stuff*; dealing with California and Vietnam, respectively, Didion and Herr each combine personal essay with deeply subjective report to collapse the private and public worlds, separated for the rest of us by the television screen, into a psychodrama at once national and personal.

Such works are a form of fiction in which both the authority and trickery of journalism are self-consciously recognized and appropriated to the uses of the personal, rather than corporate and technological, consciousness. Once dismissed as a passing style of the 1960s, this postmodern journalism is far more likely to be around as long as it continues to be obvious that public reality is a fiction of the mass media, one demanding to be countered by fuller facts and more imaginative fictions.

As in fiction, the danger for even the most original and energetic of experimental journalists is that their vision will harden into their own private set of conventions, stereotypes, and cliches. Thus, the work of experimental journalists, in addition to a struggle with the external world, offers a dramatization of struggle with one's own consciousness. In *The Executioner's Song* and *The Curse of Lono*, we see instances of two authors successfully choosing quite different strategies for overcoming a formulaic rigidity that was slipping over their perceptive—and thus both reportorial and fictive—powers. Like the postmodern fictionist, the postmodern journalist assumes the inevitability of fictions in the making of reality, and pursues reality through a search for fictions emerging from an inventive, fresh interaction of world and consciousness.

SELECTED BIBLIOGRAPHY

Primary Sources

Capote, Truman. *In Cold Blood: A True Account of a Multiple Murder and Its Consequences*. New York: Random House, 1966.
Castaneda, Carlos. *The Teachings of Don Juan*. Berkeley: University of California Press, 1968.
———. *A Separate Reality*. New York: Simon & Schuster, 1971.
———. *Journey to Ixtlan*. New York: Simon & Schuster, 1972.
———. *Tales of Power*. New York: Simon & Schuster, 1974.

Didion, Joan. *Slouching Towards Bethlehem*. New York: Farrar, Straus & Giroux, 1968.

————. *The White Album*. New York: Simon & Schuster, 1979.

————. *Salvador*. New York: Simon & Schuster, 1983.

Herr, Michael. *Dispatches*. New York: Alfred A. Knopf, 1977.

Kingston, Maxine Hong. *The Woman Warrior: Memoirs of a Girlhood Among Ghosts*. New York: Alfred A. Knopf, 1976.

————. *China Men*. New York: Alfred A. Knopf, 1980.

Mailer, Norman. *The Armies of the Night: History As a Novel/The Novel as History*. New York: New American Library, 1968.

————. *Miami and the Siege of Chicago*. New York: New American Library, 1968.

————. *Of a Fire on the Moon*. Boston: Little, Brown, 1970.

————. *St. George and the Godfather*. New York: New American Library, 1972.

————. *The Fight*. Boston: Little, Brown, 1975.

————. *The Executioner's Song*. Boston: Little, Brown, 1979.

Thompson, Hunter S. *Hell's Angels: A Strange and Terrible Saga*. New York: Ballantine, 1966.

————. *Fear and Loathing in Las Vegas: A Savage Journey to the Heart of the American Dream*. New York: Popular Library, 1971.

————. *Fear and Loathing: On the Campaign Trail '72*. San Francisco: Straight Arrow Books, 1973.

————. *The Great Shark Hunt: Strange Tales from a Strange Time*. New York: Summit Books, 1979.

————. *The Curse of Lono*. New York: Bantam Books, 1983.

Wolfe, Tom. *The Kandy-Kolored Tangerine-Flake Streamline Baby*. New York: Farrar, Straus & Giroux, 1965.

————. *The Electric Kool-Aid Acid Test*. New York: Farrar, Straus & Giroux, 1968.

————. *The Pump House Gang*. New York: Farrar, Straus & Giroux, 1968.

————. *The Painted Word*. New York: Farrar, Straus & Giroux, 1975.

————. *Mauve Gloves and Madmen, Clutter and Vine and Other Stories, Sketches, and Essays*. New York: Farrar, Straus & Giroux, 1976.

————. *The Right Stuff*. New York: Farrar, Straus & Giroux, 1979.

Secondary Sources

Hellman, John. *Fables of Fact: The New Journalism as New Fiction*. Urbana: University of Illinois Press, 1981.

Johnson, Michael. *The New Journalism: The Underground Press, the Artists of Nonfiction, and the Change in the Established Media*. Lawrence: University of Kansas Press, 1971.

Zavarzadeh, Mas'ud. *The Mythopoeic Reality: The Postwar American Nonfiction Novel*. Urbana: University of Illinois Press, 1976.

JEROME KLINKOWITZ

Experimental Realism

The first point to make about experimental realism, whether in fiction or, under its more common name in painting, superrealism, is that it is not a return to simple realism. Indeed, it is not a return to anything, certainly not to the tradition of verisimilitude, but is rather a logical progression from innovative fiction in literature and abstract expressionism in art. Art follows culture, and culture has in no sense regressed to the high realism of the nineteenth century. Literature and painting have always dealt with not reality itself (whose definition is utterly relative), but rather with what a given culture sees as reality—in the nineteenth century surely an approximation of the thing in itself, but in our own times an entirely more problematic matter. A typical fiction by Walter Abish*or canvas by Richard Estes incorporates within its vision both the new technology in our lives and the equally new modes of perception within which we see. No artist of 150 years ago was faced with the plethora of highly polished reflective surfaces such as confront Abish and Estes on every urban street corner; no Victorian or Belle Epoque writers might suspect that so much of contemporary reality lay on the surface, or that the artistic glance might include more information than real-life perception might ever contain.

Abstract expressionist painting, notably that by Jackson Pollock, Hans Hofmann, Franz Kline, and Willem de Kooning, offered the paradigm for self-reflexive fiction, the penultimate step toward total self-apparency in fiction. "At a certain moment," Harold Rosenberg has noted, "the canvas began to appear to one American painter after another as an arena in which to act—rather than a space in which to reproduce, re-design, analyze or 'express' an object, actual or imagined. What was to go on the canvas was not a picture but an event."[1] As Rosenberg explained in a later essay on Hofmann, "The innovation of Action Painting was to dispense with the representation of the state in favor of enacting it in the physical movement of painting. The action on the canvas became its own representations."[2]

Abstract expressionist paintings thus capitalized on line because "a line is the direct manifestation of an act" (p. 159), just as the self-consciously flat surface of these works celebrated, rather than regretted, what earlier artists had considered anti-realistic limitations of the medium. So, too, would fiction appreciate, rather than obliterate, the materiality of its construction: authorial presence would become not something to efface but rather the substance of the work itself, and meaning would become less a property of subject matter than of the process of composition. Action painting suggests action writing, and action writing is just what the self-reflexive novelists, notably Ronald Sukenick* and his close associates, were attempting in the 1960s.

Superrealism, as a movement, comes nearly a decade and a half after abstract expressionism; yet as painting anticipates the other arts, so too does this history reflect the historical distance between the heyday of self-reflexiveness (the mid-1960s) and the introduction of experimental realism in fiction (circa 1980). And just as there is a logical movement from fictional reflexiveness to experimental realism, so, too, does the analogue in art follow as a logical development. One by one, the major principles of action painting—qualities that describe the central work of Pollock, de Kooning, and the rest—can be applied to superrealism, in a way that highlights the new form's essential features. As one might expect, the metaphor transfers directly to the style of avant-garde fiction being developed in the 1980s, with equally revolutionary results.

ALL OVER

A typical abstract expressionist canvas is painted in an "all-over" manner—the drip paintings of Jackson Pollock, with their border-to-border swirl of splashed color and tangled lines, are the image to conjure for this most important principle of action painting. Nothing could be farther from the familiar rubrics of realism, for the interest of a Pollock painting literally fills the canvas, every inch of it, as opposed to the ordered perspective so essential to realism. Hofmann used this same quality to display his "push and pull" of color forces on the canvas; Kline used it for his arm's length gesture of black paint thrust across the white canvas, while de Kooning saw it as the arena for his many-layered dance of color and staining.

Superrealism embraces the "all over" aesthetic as the central principle of its art. The urban landscapes of Richard Estes seem like expeditions in search of street corners, diners, rows of phone booths, facades, show windows, shop rows, or any reflective surfaces conducive to the indiscriminate spread of perception over a broad, flat surface. Estes' *Drugs* defies selection as it depicts a vision of a corner pharmacy most notable for its highly reflective surface, each highly polished square of marble, glass, or chrome filling the canvas with a superabundance of information. An upstairs window is painted with the same precision as the central display windows, and understandably so, for each pane of glass is doing its job to the fullest of mirroring whatever falls within its plane of reflective reference—here indeed are mindless signs whose signifying process yields nothing to the hierarchy of its referent. No human presence enters the frame; none is needed, for either range or focus, because the drugstore is a totally inanimate object which nevertheless is central to human concern. As a sign itself, it is fully opaque, for there is no emotional narrative here: the drugstore simply *is*, an artifact added to the world like the finest of self-apparent fictions.

Can fiction itself be written in an all-over manner? To do so it would have to seize the otherwise negative limitations of its form and embrace them as positive aids, just as Estes uses the flat extent of his canvas as the key compositional element. Stephen Dixon's* story "Said" does just this, taking the redundant problematics of identifying each line of dialogue and making that very convention not a transparent signifier but rather a self-apparently opaque sign, a true thing in itself:

He said, she said.
She left the room, he followed her.
He said, she said.
She locked herself in the bathroom, he slammed the door with his fists.
He said.
She said nothing.
He said.
He slammed the door with his fists, kicked the door bottom.
She said, he said, she said.
He batted the door with his shoulder, went into the kitchen, got a screwdriver, returned and started unscrewing the bathroom doornob.
She said.
He said nothing, unscrewed the doornob, pulled the doornob out of the door, but the door stayed locked. He threw the doornob against the door, picked it up and threw it down the hall, banged the door with the screwdriver handle, wedged the screwdriver blade between the door and the jamb and tried forcing the door open. The blade broke, the door stayed locked.
He said, she said, he said.
He got about 15 feet down the hall and charged at the door.
She said.
He stopped.
She said nothing. Then she said, he said, she said, he said.
He got about 10 feet down the hall this time and charged at the door. . . . [3]

By dropping out the content which can be imagined to precede each pair of "saids," Dixon foregoes artistic centering in favor of an all-over effect—which is, after all, just as appropriate to the substanceless nature of most marital fights as the widespread flatness of Estes' canvas is to the urban facades he seeks out. Few people can accurately remember what a corner in Walgreen's looks like in perspective, and no one can remember what a lover's spat was about; each has an all-over quality to its experience, to which this style of writing and painting is nicely suited. Not reality itself but *how we perceive it* is what determines this choice of effect.

ANTI-HIERARCHAL

In surveying one of Jackson Pollock's drip paintings, Franz Kline's broad slashing gestures, or Hans Hofmann's dynamics of color in push and pull, no single element takes precedence over the others. Standing back, one is taken with the grand sweep of each canvas. In Pollock's case the lines and splashes fill the canvas, with just as much action happening in the corners as in the center. The tension in Hofmann's work results from his energies playing against themselves from frame to frame, the most literal example of Harold Rosenberg's arena of action—no single area of the canvas is privileged above another, but rather all are equal in creating the dynamic effect. Even close inspection, as of a painting by de Kooning, yields the same anti-hierarchal effect, for here the close examiner sees that there are many layers of paint imposed on each other so thoroughly that no single plane dominates. Instead, the effect is that of gazing into a deep pool where the water's clarity has collapsed all perspective among the many-shaped and colored rocks, weeds, and shadows. *What you see is what there is*, the abstract expressionists tell us, and discarding any sense of hierarchal importance is a key element in their aesthetic practice.

This same principle of the anti-hierarchal has become the most striking feature of superrealism, and expresses a peculiarly postmodern sense of how reality is perceived. Throughout the modern period artistic interpretation was the favored mode, the more intellectually radical the better, from the Cubist vision (decidedly a mental affair) through the various *isms* of the Teens and Twenties, climaxing in the very literary readings of psychology in the Surreal. Postmodernism's visual tool, however, is the camera, which with the improved techniques of our own time (sharp focus, broader field, deeper color) has been able to restore the visual to its former primacy. Indeed, the camera's picture is so visual that it excludes the intellectual. Allowing for no privileging of focus or conceptual center of interest, the camera presents an unstructured overload of information, with every detail just as sharp and clear as the rest, and with lines from every square inch of surface sharpened with identical clarity. Superrealistic canvases seize this camera-like vision and exploit it even further, expanding the scale to gigantic size (beyond the point where a printed photo or projected size would become fuzzy in detail) and compositing in even more subject matter. (Estes often combines three or four photographs of a site, maximizing depictable content.) A lack of hierarchy such as the camera's mechanical focus allows also yields brilliant, mentally impossible effects, such as the ability to focus on several planes at once. In human practice, looking through a highly reflective window can yield alternate visions, either of the image through the glass or of the reflected image behind— but never both at the same time. The camera, however, does not have to choose at which depth to perceive, for its range of focus can be adjusted to capture both and then display them on the single plane of its print.

"Through the avoidance of a hierarchy that is related to values outside the actual work, language has a chance of becoming what Roland Barthes* refers to as a field of action"—so Walter Abish describes this same principle's usefulness for self-apparent fiction.[4] Anti-hierarchal means divest the perceived sign of its anthropomorphic qualities, and also of the intellectualism which through the mind's inhibiting factors censors out supposedly extraneous information and highlights what it considers central. Alain Robbe-Grillet and the other makers of the *nouveau roman* followed a somewhat similar practice, but with the precisely opposite goal: to capture the thing itself, the pure object now clearly seen through a purified signifier, rather than the absolute opacity of sign to which Abish and Estes aspire. But in either case projective anthropomorphism must be banished, which for fiction means using all of the familiar conventions not as indices of attitudes but rather as verbal collages of self-apparent signs, as in these three introductory paragraphs from Kenneth Gangemi, Howard McCord, and Leonard Michaels, respectively:

Olt knew he would never see a meteor striking an iceberg, a bat falling into snow, or a clown on a nun. He knew he would never go to a party and talk to thunderstorm experts, roller-coaster experts, vampire experts, sailplane experts. He knew that he would never design bear grottos, furnish a time capsule, live in an orange grove, wade in a vat of mercury, work in the Dead Letter Office, find narwhale tusks on a beach, see a tampax string at the ballet, smell a burning spice warehouse, overhear two call girls talking shop, or attend a meeting of the Junior League.[5]

"The Geography of Ohio"

Ohio lies fifteen thousand feet below see level in a great rift valley bisecting the western portion of the northeastern corridor. The border with Indiana is considered by some impassable, and by all as rivalled only by lunar structures of yet undetermined origin. A stone dropped from Pennsylvania does not land in Ohio, but in Indiana, the prevailing upward westerlies prohibiting all but a few major airlines from landing anything in Ohio.[6]

"In the Fifties"

In the fifties I learned to drive a car. I was frequently in love. I had more friends than now.

When Khrushchev denounced Stalin my roommate shit blood, turned yellow, and lost most of his hair.

I attended the lectures of the excellent E. B. Burgum until Senator McCarthy ended his tenure. I imagined N.Y.U. would burn. Miserable students, drifting in the halls, looked at one another.

In less than a month, working day and night, I wrote a bad novel.

I went to school: N.Y.U., Michigan, Berkeley—much of the time.

I had witty, giddy conversation, four or five nights a week, in a homosexual bar in Ann Arbor.

I read literary reviews in the way people suck candy.

Personal relationships were more important to me than anything else.

I had a fight with a powerful fat man who fell on my face and was immovable.

I had personal relationships with football players, jazz musicians, ass-bandits, nymphomaniacs, non-specialized degenerates, and numerous Jewish premedical students.

I had personal relationships with thirty-five Rhesus monkeys in an experiment on monkey addiction to morphine. They knew me as one who shot reeking crap out of cages with a hose.[7]

Traditional realists would accumulate such details as a way of indicating sensibility (the character's, the writer's), and the best way to judge such style would be on the level of absolute transparency. "I know a writer who wished his prose to be transparent so that only a movement and growth of his story would be in evidence," Gilbert Sorrentino* writes in *Splendide-Hotel* (1973),[8] but for the experimental realists these descriptive items do just the opposite work. There is no window here, just a self-contained circuit of odd details that do best when read as referring to themselves. The movement is full interior, from the roommate's shitting blood to the monkey excrement the narrator must flush away, from the personal relationships with old friends to the business with the addicted primates. Gangemi's details in like manner resist narrative effacement; instead, both reader and character are treated to an experiential sense of life itself, undiluted by craft or program. As Philip Stevick has indicated in *Alternative Pleasures*, using the two latter examples, these paragraphs imply no audience and explain nothing.[9] They are not background for anything else. Their only meaning is in the assemblage of verbal collage, which the reader must appreciate for the integrity of its compositional elements. Above all there is no explaining, no meaning, no *world-making*, as Stevick says; these descriptions simply mean themselves. And as themselves, they are delightfully funny and inventive, so different from the leaden, self-conscious thing-making of the *nouveau roman*. The joy of self-apparent signs is the lack of hierarchy and informed meaning, which allows the reader to experience them with a full sense of their being.

MATERIALITY: HARD AND FLAT

For the abstract expressionists, a sign, of course, meant only itself. But as the signs of this style became the action of the paint of the canvas, the materials of this process took on added importance. Even before color and line came the physical property of paint itself. De Kooning laid it on thick and heavy, with one color swirling into another. Flat areas of Hofmann's canvases were virtually three-dimensional, the knife-applied paint so thick that mountains and valleys formed a recognizable terrain; to heighten this effect in his own work, Pollock would mix glass and sand into his already thickened industrial-base paint. Although there might be sensations of depth thanks to variations of light and dark color, there would never be an illusion of perspective: in action painting everything was up front, happening on the surface with a self-apparent use of materials. "A sensual interest in materials comes first," says Robert Motherwell to Frank O'Hara, who adds his own analysis:

a painting is a sheer extension, not a window or a door; collage is as much about paper as about form; the impetus for the painting or a drawing starts technically from the subconscious through automatism (or as he may say "doodling") and proceeds toward the subject which is the finished work.[10]

Paint, then, becomes its own subject, and so do surface and scale. What were in earlier times limitations for art—the textural qualities of paint, the hard flatness of canvas surface—quickly became the dominant features of abstract expressionism, for materiality of process was now the painting's point.

Superrealistic paintings are hard and flat as well. Although there is, as opposed to action painting, a recognizable subject on the canvas, it has been sought out precisely because its own highly polished reflective surfaces, urban iconography of stark image and harsh color, and absence of any depictable human presence all yield themselves to an absolutely material representation. The superrealist's tools enhance this flatness: quick-drying paints, often applied with an airbrush, on a canvas gelled to the point of impenetrability. The amount of concrete, steel and chrome, and glass and neon in the average superrealistic painting is as remarkable as the quantities of splashed paint and swirled line in a work of action painting, and the effect is in principle the same: a flatness that defies image in favor of the materials that make it up.

The experimental realists know that the materials of their fictions are signs as well—opaque signifiers which by virtue of superrealistic treatment can become self-apparent materials, just as the painter's line and color. Stephen Dixon, whose story of "saids" demonstrates the all-over quality of experimental realism, also shows a mastery of other conventions in and for themselves, to the point that he can construct entire stories on the materiality of signs, which for other writers would only be transfer points toward larger meaning. "Mac in Love" sacrifices even the movement of "Said" so that a line of dialogue can slowly expand to become the whole story, both technically and thematically. Dixon's lovers are forever parting, so much so that their tendency to break up is what cements their relationship, since they will always come back to this point. The breakups, of course, must be signaled by conventions of dialogue or behavior, and so it is this act of signification that creates a truly textual sense to their affair. In this story from Dixon's first collection, the narrator prolongs their parting by sustaining a single sentence. Real time stands still while he builds a syntactic temporality and movement-in-stasis within the sentence: " 'Jane,' I yelled. 'Will you thank Ruth for telling Mrs. Roy for telling you to tell Ruth to tell you to tell Mrs. Roy to tell Ruth to tell you your watering can's on the window ledge.' "[11] Similarly, in a typical Dixon story plots will go on forever, weaving themselves in a self-apparency of material to the extent that the reader can only take delight in the process itself, for any attempt to see through the signifiers to some ulterior meaning is quickly frustrated. "14 Stories," itself the title work for a collection that assembles only thirteen short fictions, uses materiality of plot in the same way painters use the limitations of paint and canvas. "Eugene Randall held the gun in front of his mouth and fired," this piece begins, just where more conventionally plotted stories might end. "The bullet smashed his upper front teeth, left his head through the back of his jaw, pierced an ear lobe and broke a window that overlooked much of the midtown area."[12] Already we know more about the shell's trajectory than about the reasons for poor Eugene's demise, but Dixon is being true to his own materials—plot lines, of Eugene in action and of the bullet in flight, are all there is. These are the real materials, more real in fact than the cozily humanistic touches that more conventional writers might demand of their signs. Eugene is dead, but the bullet goes on until it stops but in turn inaugurates another line of action, frightening a boy who comes rushing down from the roof to cross paths with another character: "I never should have left my flat for cigarettes—never should have been smoking in fact. Cancer I'll get, and also a jail sentence. In fact, I never should have taken my first puff, Willy, because it will lead to bad things. Little did they know. Do you smoke, Warren?" (p. 8) Meanwhile, the suicide note has blown out of the broken window and drifted to the street where it is found by another person whose life takes off in a plot line from this event. The maids clean up the mess, the police come to investigate. "14 Stories" summarizes the techniques of experimental realism noted so far, from the all-over distribution of its plot to the anti-hierarchal consideration of each human interest as equal. But above all it is a materially flat story, thanks to the emphasis on conventions as conventions rather than as indices to greater meaning.

SURFACE

In abstract expressionism, everything happens on the surface, for it is the arena of the artist's act. Franz Kline's arm-length gesture cannot go through the canvas, only across it, on the same plane where Hans Hofmann's blocks of color push and pull. Even figuration is flat and fully frontal, a surface dance of action found in Willem de Kooning's *Woman* series. An exploitation of the limits of surface is the crowning touch to all-over, anti-hierarchy, materiality, color field, and scale.

Superrealism, though dealing with figurative material, collapses perspective down to a single plane; Richard Estes' title *Facade* says it all. But as in Sol Le Witt's sculpture, the implication is cultural: we are after all living, perceiving within an urban landscape made of rectilinear planes with absolutely nothing behind. (Le Witt's cubes are vacant, just as Estes' windows rarely show a human presence.) Yet the effect is very human, for this is the world we've made; superrealists simply emphasize the way we see it.

Surface is the central principle of superrealism which the experimental realists in fiction have taken for their own. Although other effects, such as materiality and field, can be applied analogically, the linguistic surface of behavior is at once central to both fictive theory (from Ludwig Wittgenstein and Ferdinand de Saussure to Jacques Derrida* and Julia Kristeva) and practice. "This is a familiar world," Walter Abish begins his novella, "This Is Not a Film. This Is a Precise Act of Disbelief"(1975):

It is a world crowded with familiar faces and events. Thanks to language the brain can digest, piece by piece, what has occurred and what may yet occur. It is never at a loss for the word that signifies what is happening this instant. In Mrs. It's brain the interior of her large house with a view of the garden and the lake are surfaces of the familiar. She is slim, and moves quite gracefully from one familiar interior to the next. Her movements are impelled by familiar needs.[13]

The novella's plot follows from this same theory, that human needs are shaped by the surface of what is available—in this case, by language. Abish creates the situation of a French filmmaker, modeled on Jean-Luc Godard, who has come to America so he might examine the plans and construction of an inter-city shopping mall (an actual project later built in Cedar Falls, Iowa, by developer Garth Huffman). Abish, trained and once employed as a city planner, sees that the three levels of activity—mall building, filmmaking, and language—are all predicated on the availability of surface (urban topography and economic life, the celluloid strip, the generative syntax), and his novella works its way out in just the same manner as his more obviously and mechanically disciplined novel, *Alphabetical Africa* (1974). What he has said of that novel applies to "This Is Not a Film" as well: "I was fascinated to discover the extent to which a system could impose upon the contents of a work meaning which was fashioned by the form, and then to see the degree to which the form, because of the conspicuous obstacles, undermined that very meaning."[14]

Abish's most complete work of experimental realism is his novel *How German Is It* (1980), winner of the first Faulkner/PEN Award for Fiction in 1981. Here there are no obvious devices such as the alphabet or linguistic proscription. Instead, like a superrealist painter, Abish has sought out circumstances from real life which confirm our culture's unique patterns of sight, feeling, and thought. As a result, the quality of life in *How German Is It* is just as apparently artificial as what one might encounter on Richard Estes' street corners. As his introduction to the "new" postwar Germany, Abish's account is painstakingly empirical:

What are the first words a visitor from France can expect to hear upon his arrival at a German airport?
  Bonjour?
  Or, Guten Tag?
  Or, Passport bitte?[15]

And what is the first thing such a visitor might notice? Here is what the new German surface, remade since the war, asks one to note:

Undoubtedly the cleanliness. The painstaking cleanliness. As well as the all-pervasive sense of order. A reassuring dependability. A punctuality. An almost obsessive punctuality. Then, of course, there is the new, striking architecture. Innovative? Hardly. Imaginative? Not really. But free of that former somber and authoritative massivity. A return to the experimentation of the Bauhaus? Regrettably no. Still, something must be said in favor of the wide expanse of glass on the buildings, the fifteen, twenty-story buildings, the glass reflecting not only the sky but also acting as a mirror for the older historical sites, those clutters of carefully reconstructed buildings that are an attempt to replicate entire neighborhoods obliterated in the last war (pp. 2–3).

This paragraph is almost self-consciously syntactical, with careful qualifications of each original detail much like Richard Estes sharpening the focus on a superrealistic painting. Following these initial qualifications come a series of adjectival questions answered by adverbs in a self-apparently parallel manner. Then for the paragraph's statement: that the key element is glass, one highly polished surface reflecting another (for as reconstructions, the historical sites can have no depth, only surface). Depth and meaning have been obliterated by something whose presence has now been entirely removed. Unlike the East, which has left the ruins as a memorial to and indictment of the wartime past, West Germany has tried to efface the war entirely, and what remains is a self-apparency of signs that mean only themselves.

Abish's cast of characters live and build on this surface. Of the two Hargenau brothers, one works with steel and glass (as architect of the new municipal buildings), and the other with words (as a novelist). The latter also has terrorist connections, a reference to those who would tear down what the former brother constructs over the war's ruins. To show the received quality of this life we are given a smart young couple, straight from the cover of *Stern*—Egon and Gisela, all glitter and surface, whose real life is a sickening morass of ego and autism. All is described in an austere, defamiliarized manner, almost as in a student's copybook. All hierarchal values are removed from Abish's perceptions, not so that we see the thing in itself (a *nouveau roman* attitude he satirizes through the philosopher Brumhold) but rather to emphasize the opaque nature of the sign. Once we humanize, Abish implies, we become subject to the same flawed rules of communication from which his characters suffer.

Besides the qualities of "all over," "surface," and the like, there are more particular analogues to superrealism which indicate the special quality of experimental realism in fiction. Each genre wishes to emphasize sign over subject, and one way to accomplish this is to choose as image something wholly inappropriate to conventional art, so that the view-reader is discouraged from passing through the sign to a romanticized or idealized image of the actual thing. Here the superrealists are most characteristic, from Richard Estes' resistant facades to John Salt's junked cars resting in the weeds. Neither subject would be usable in any previous tradition of realism, and here the harsh windowfronts and rusted out autos remind one that there's more to the picture than *nature mort*. In effect, the blinds are drawn on the signifier, arresting the viewer's vision at the canvas with the opacity of sign itself. Kenneth Gangemi's "Lydia" works much the same, as a simple listing of a 16-year-old nymphet's venereal qualities—not for the implication of some Nabokovesque lyric but simply in and of themselves as outrageously unclean thoughts, yet so simply and directly that the reader is stuck on them as objects rather than passing through them to the forbidden territory of teenage sex. Moreover, these signs are removed from context: we have no idea what's around the corner from Estes' drugstore or what Lydia may do later in the day. There is no meaning, no story; rather, we are given a syntax of signs, as in the mix of pickup trucks in a Ralph Going's parking lot. Above all, the painter or writer has no involvement with the scene, for all selection and framing have been taken care of by the photograph. With that out of the way, both creator and viewer are free to deal with the purely artistic problems of execution and reception—and these on the level of sign.

Flatness of sign is also important, for when dealing with an icon there's no need for anything else to be said. As if a picture can be worth a thousand words, Ken Gangemi writes his *Interceptor Pilot* (1980)[16] as a purely visual treatment: copy of *Le Monde* tossed on the journalist's car seat, two columns of smoke rising from the crash scene in the jungle. Here we have pure narrative, ignoring everything except what can be seen, which is another way of avoiding contamination of sign by reality. Peter Handke* writes with a similarly visual sense, finding a narrative in which a character is so alienated from life that all he can do is rehearse the semiotic process, as in this scene from *The Goalie's Anxiety at the Penalty Kick* (1972):

Bloch was irritated. With the segments themselves he saw the details with grating distinctness: as if the parts he saw stood for the whole. Again the details seem to him like nameplates. "Neon signs," he thought. So he saw the waitress's ear with one earring as a sign of the entire person; and a purse on a nearby table, slightly open so that he could recognize a polka-dotted scarf in it, stood for the woman holding the coffee cup who sat behind it and, with her other hand, pausing only now and then at a picture, rapidly leafed through a magazine. A tower of ice-cream dishes dovetailed into each other on the bar seemed a simile for the cafe owner, and the puddle on the floor by the coat rack represented the umbrella hanging above it. Instead of the heads of the customers, Bloch saw the dirty spots on the wall at the level of their heads.[17]

Handke's meditation on his mother's suicide, *A Sorrow Beyond Dreams* (1975), uses a similar scene to show not only how a character can become caught up within the semiotics of her world but be defined by it as well:

the GOOD OLD ironing board, the COZY hearth, the often-mended cooking pots, the DANGEROUS poker, the STURDY wheelbarrow, the ENTERPRISING weed cutter, the SHINING BRIGHT knives, which over the years had been ground to a vanishing narrowness by BURLY scissors grinders, the FIENDISH thimble, the STUPID darning egg, the CLUMSY OLD flatiron, which provided variety by having to be put back on the stove every so often, and finally the PRIZE PIECE, the floor and hand-operated Singer sewing machine.[18]

Yet it must be emphasized that a superrealistic painting is not a copy of a photograph or an equivalent for what the camera can do. Nor is an experimental fiction in any respect like the news. Although there is a superficial resemblance for both, on the technical level there are great differences, noticeable as well in final effect.

In fiction, the closest incorporation of news and history may be found in the works of Guy Davenport,* but here there is a careful shift from the camera-view of events so that the work of fiction (as the Estes, the work of painting) may take place. "My Tatlin is not Tatlin, nor my Poe Poe," Davenport insists. "But my stories are stories about them,"[19] just as the superrealists paint pictures of pictures. "History is a dream that strays into innocent sleep," Davenport says within his "necessary fictions," and "the mind is what it knows." Therefore, he creates imaginative exercises involving characters who are within the knowable past but who do not match up with our memory of it. Leonardo inventing a bicycle on which lancers would ride into battle full tilt; Gertrude Stein reading the Sunday comics to Picasso; Greek philosophers inventing, in all seriousness, a mechanical pigeon; Richard Nixon bombing the DMZ to impress Chairman Mao, his host; Kafka taking in the airshow at Brescia and brushing shoulders with Wittgenstein—these startling juxtapositions indicate the way our imaginations create the world, for the encounters Davenport presents seem so necessarily real.

Several of these stories, pertinently enough, use the chance of photography to make Davenport's point: Lenin snapped at a Zurich cafe while in the background James and Nora Joyce haggle with a taxi driver, a paleolithic fossil at the Museum of Natural History captured in an early experimental daguerreotype where a bystander, Edgar Allan Poe, is incorporated for scale. Why photography? Because "for the first time in the history of art the accidental becomes the controlling iconography of a representation of the world"[20] and hence a perfect analogue for the human imagination at work in the creation of our world.

We know reality only through our fictions, which is the task experimental realism takes on itself anew. In its process, the full range of techniques from self-apparent fiction are incorporated in the rediscovery of life itself, the noblest role for literary art and the surest way for fiction to be something added to the world and therefore something important in itself.

NOTES

1. Harold Rosenberg, *The Tradition of the New* (New York: Horizon, 1959), p. 25.

2. Harold Rosenberg, *The Anxious Object* (New York: Horizon, 1966), p. 158.

3. Steve Dixon, "Said," *boundary 2* 8 (Spring 1980): 99–100.

4. Jerome Klinkowitz, "Interview with Walter Abish," *Fiction International* 4, No. 5 (Fall 1975): 95.

5. Kenneth Gangemi, *Olt* (New York: Orion Press, 1969), pp. 49–50.

6. Howard McCord, "The Geography of Ohio," *Fiction International* 2, No. 3 (Fall 1974): 121.

7. Leonard Michaels, "In the Fifties," *I Would Have Saved Them If I Could* (New York: Farrar, Straus & Giroux, 1975), pp. 59–60.

8. Gilbert Sorrentino, *Splendide-Hotel* (New York: New Directions, 1973), p. 13.

9. Philip Stevich, *Alternate Pleasures* (Urbana: University of Illinois Press, 1981), p. 103.

10. Frank O'Hara, *Art Chronicles* (New York: Venture/Braziller, 1975), pp. 71–72.

11. Stephen Dixon, "Mac in Love," *No Relief* (Ann Arbor, Mich.: Street Fiction, 1976), p. 17.

12. Stephen Dixon, "14 Stories," *14 Stories* (Baltimore: Johns Hopkins University Press, 1980), p. 1.

13. Walter Abish, "This Is Not a Film. This Is a Precise Act of Disbelief," *Minds Meet* (New York: New Directions, 1975), p. 31.

14. Klinkowitz, "Interview," p. 96.

15. Walter Abish, *How German Is It* (New York: New Directions, 1980), p. 1.

16. Kenneth Gangemi, *The Interceptor Pilot* (London: Marion Boyars, 1980); originally published in a translation by Samantha Martin and Livia Standersi as *Pilote de chasse* (Paris: Flammarion, 1974).

17. Peter Handke, *The Goalie's Anxiety at the Penalty Kick*, trans. Ralph Mannheim (New York: Farrar, Straus & Giroux, 1972), p. 88; originally published as *Die Angst des Tormanns beim Elfmeter* (Frankfurt: Suhrkamp, 1970).

18. Peter Handke, *A Sorrow Beyond Dreams*, trans. Ralph Mannheim (New York: Farrar, Straus & Giroux, 1975), pp. 41–42; originally published as *Wunschloses Ungluck* (Salsburgh: Residenz Verlag, 1972).

19. Guy Davenport, "Ernst Mach Max Ernst," *The Geography of the Imagination* (San Francisco: North Point Press, 1981), p. 383.

20. Guy Davenport, "The Invention of Photography in Toledo," *Da Vinci's Bicycle* (Baltimore: Johns Hopkins University Press, 1979), p. 123.

SELECTED BIBLIOGRAPHY

Primary Sources

Abish, Walter. *Alphabetical Africa*. New York: New Directions, 1974.

———. *Minds Meet*. New York: New Directions, 1975.

———. *In the Future Perfect*. New York: New Directions, 1977.

———. *How German Is It*. New York: New Directions, 1980.

Davenport, Guy. *Tatlin!* New York: Scribner's, 1974.

———. *Da Vinci's Bicycle*. Baltimore: Johns Hopkins University Press, 1979.

———. *Eclogues*. San Francisco: North Point Press, 1981.

———. *The Geography of the Imagination*. San Francisco: North Point Press, 1981.

Dixon, Stephen. *No Relief*. Ann Arbor, Mich.: Street Fiction Press, 1976.

———. *Quite Contrary*. New York: Harper & Row, 1979.

———. *14 Stories*. Baltimore: Johns Hopkins University Press, 1980.

———. *Movies*. Berkeley, Calif.: North Point Press, 1983.

———. *Fall and Rise*. Berkeley, Calif.: North Point Press, 1984.

———. *Time to Go*. Baltimore: Johns Hopkins University Press, 1984.

Gangemi, Ken. *Olt*. New York: Orion Press, 1969.

———. *The Interceptor Pilot*. London: Marion Boyars, 1980.

Handke, Peter. *The Goalie's Anxiety at the Penalty Kick*. Trans. Michael Roloff. New York: Farrar, Straus & Giroux, 1972.

———. *A Sorrow Beyond Dreams*. Trans. Ralph Manheim. New York: Farrar, Straus & Giroux, 1975.

———. *A Moment of True Feeling*. Trans. Ralph Manheim. New York: Farrar, Straus & Giroux, 1977.

———. *Short Letter, Long Farewell*. Trans. Ralph Manheim. New York: Farrar, Straus & Giroux, 1977.

———. *The Left-Handed Woman*. Trans. Ralph Manheim. New York: Farrar, Straus & Giroux, 1978.

Michaels, Leonard. *I Would Have Saved Them If I Could*. New York: Farrar, Straus & Giroux, 1975.

O'Hara, Frank. *Art Chronicles*. New York: Venture/George Braziller, 1975.

Sorrentino, Gilbert. *Splendide-Hotel*. New York: New Directions, 1973.

JEROME KLINKOWITZ

Writing Under Fire: Postmodern Fiction and the Vietnam War

American novels and stories about Vietnam reveal a common, desperate search for meaning—a search for any shred of authenticity in this experience—that may be traced back decades before "our" Vietnam War and that extends forward to the decade that has now passed since the American withdrawal from Vietnam. Although many important novels about Vietnam have recently appeared—Tim O'Brien's* *Going After Cacciato* (1978), Robert Butler's *The Alleys of Eden* (1981), John Cassidy's *A Station in the Delta* (1979), Charles Durden's *No Bugles, No Drums* (1976), Winston Groom's *Better Times Than These* (1978), among others—this article focuses on the fiction published during our actual involvement there. But the central thesis of this article remains true for more recent works: Vietnam affected our literary imagination in ways that no other war has, and the result has been a body of fiction that relies on various innovative formal devices, similar to the experimental features that characterize other postmodern fiction, to capture a sense of that war's assault on language and on our sense of reality.

The first Western novelist to write about Vietnam was André Malraux, who as early as 1930 saw that the Indochina experience could be a metaphor for man's anguished alienation from an absurd society within a meaningless universe. Malraux's *The Royal Way* (1930) was the beginning of a line of books that followed the Western involvement in Vietnam from colonial exploitation to ideologically based warfare.[1] By 1966 Norman Mailer could state, "If World War II was like *Catch-22*, this war will be like *Naked Lunch*."[2] Malraux's anguished alienation had become a full-blown nightmare, suggesting that this shard of the Asian continent was indeed bound up with the subconscious of Europe and America, and that to deal with it in art would take on the dimensions of a dark encounter with the more unpleasant aspects of our lives.

The processes of art inevitably tell us more about ourselves than the matter at hand. But the Indochina experience is especially self-revealing, and with Malraux's *The Royal Way* the measure of self begins. In the jungles of what we now call Thailand, Cambodia, and Vietnam, Malraux explores the roots of what two subsequent generations of novelists must face: "that fabulous aura of scandal, fantasy, and fiction which always hovers about the white man who has played a part in the affairs of independent Asiatic states" (p. 7). The jungle itself is a strange and exotic contrast to the civilizations of the West, a place where Malraux's protagonist finds that he was "growing aware of the essential oneness of the forest and had given up trying to distinguish living beings from their setting, life that moves from life that oozes" (p. 101). Even in 1930 Vietnam is a place where "some unknown power assimilated the trees with fungoid growths upon them, and quickened the restless movements of all the rudimentary creatures darting to and fro upon a soil like marsh-scum amid the steaming vegetation of a planet in the making" (p. 101). In such a place one asks, "Here what act of man had any meaning, what human will but spent its staying power?" (p. 101).

The overt action in *The Royal Way* is colonial adventure. The soldier of fortune, Perken, would plunder the land of its treasures and organize a military force to become its political ruler as well. But as in every subsequent Vietnam fiction there is a deeper current turning back upon the characters. As Perken explains his motives to his skeptical assistant Claude:

"And then—only try to grasp all that this country really is. Why, I'm only just beginning to understand their erotic rites, the process of assimilation by which a man comes to identify himself, even in his sensations, with the woman he possesses—till he imagines *he is she*, yet without ceasing to be himself! There's nothing in the world to match it—sensual pleasure strained to the point where it becomes intolerable, the breaking-point of pain! No, for me these women aren't merely bodies; they're . . . instruments. And I want . . . " Claude guessed his unseen gesture, the gesture of a hand crushing out life. " . . . as I once wanted to conquer men."

What he's really after, Claude mused, is self-annihilation. I wonder is he more aware of it than he admits. Anyhow he'll achieve it easily enough (pp. 93–94).

Perken's immediate quest fails. He cannot take his plunder out of Vietnam, and his private army is decisively beaten. But his greatest defeat is just as Claude supposed:

Frenzied with self-centered passion, her body was withdrawing itself from him irrevocably. Never, never would he apprehend, never share, this woman's sensations; never could the frenzy which thrilled her body be for him anything but a proof of the unbridgeable gulf between them. Without love there can be no passion. Carried away by forces he could not control, unable even to make her realize his presence by tearing himself away from her, he too closed his eyes, thrown back upon himself as on a noxious drug, drunk with a wild desire violently to crush out of existence this stranger's face that urged him on to death (pp. 249–50).

It would be 35 years before American fiction came to grips so closely with these dark matters of the self. Westerners in this novel took their first steps into an experience destined to constrain and diminish their imperial selves, but the challenge was irresistible.

Two dozen novels about the war were published during America's active involvement in it. In 1965, Robin Moore first introduced the war to a literary audience with *The Green Berets*, which concluded: "What the outcome in Vietnam will be is anybody's guess, but whatever happens, Special Forces men will continue to fight Communism and make friends for America in the underdeveloped nations that are the targets of Communist expansion."[3] The war did not turn out that way, and neither did our country's appreciation of it. Coming to a final understanding, and expressing it in art, has become an ongoing effort as arduous as any trial described in the existential novels of Kafka, Sartre, or Malraux. From a European perspective it would have been nothing new. But in Vietnam, America lost its innocence and by that process grew immeasurably in its art.

Some historians date the beginning of American involvement in Vietnam from 1954, with Vice-President Richard M. Nixon's advocacy of intervention at Dien Bien Phu against Eisenhower's wish to remain neutral. Graham Greene's Vietnam novel of 1955, *The Quiet American*, witnesses the awesomely quiet birth of American interest in this country recently deserted by the French. The narrator is a British journalist, seasoned by events in his personal life as well as by his nation's experience, before whom the quiet American Agency for International Development (AID) official, Pyle, is the epitome of collective innocence: "He was absorbed already in the dilemmas of democracy and the responsibilities of the West; he was determined—I learned that very soon—to do good, not to any individual person, but to a country, a continent, a world. Well, he was in his element now, with the whole universe to improve."[4] This innocence, of course, is Pyle's downfall. As the journalist tells him, "I wish sometimes you had a few bad motives; you might understand a little more about human beings. And that applies to your country too, Pyle" (p. 173). Innocence, we learn, "is like a dumb leper who has lost his bell, wandering the world, meaning no harm" (p. 40). The young, well-intentioned man with a crew cut and a black dog at his heels is as out of date as an Errol Flynn movie where the hero "rescued a girl and killed his enemy and led a charmed life. It was what they call a film for boys, but the sight of Oedipus emerging with his bleeding eyeballs from the palace at Thebes would surely give a better training for life today" (p. 240). Vietnam was already gaining a reputation as "an experience," and Americans were from the first cast as hapless (if dangerous) innocents.

Greene's novel portrays the personal and national havoc created by Pyle's "involvement," the consequences of which are a vivid preview of what was to happen from 1962 to Christmas week of 1972. During these same years *The Quiet American* went through 17 printings in the United States; but few Americans came forward to write a Vietnam novel with such a measured and controlled view. The first attempt was Robin Moore's *The Green Berets*. Its tone was set by the dust-jacket advertisement, boasting that Moore "was paid the 'supreme compliment' of being sent along as the second Special Forces 'sergeant' on all-Vietnamese or Montagnard patrols. On one such patrol Moore so distinguished himself that the Montagnard commander offered him the rare privilege of cutting off the ear of a dead VC!"

In the years since 1965 Robin Moore has remained an apologist for the war in Vietnam. David Halberstam is not. A journalist in Vietnam the same time as Moore, Halberstam incurred Administration disapproval for his Saigon dispatches, which Graham Greene characterized as not taking at all "the conventional line about the American presence in Vietnam." In 1967 Halberstam wrote *One Very Hot Day*, a novel that follows an American advisor through a day's patrol—the same role Moore took for his own book, but with very different results. Halberstam's Captain Beaupré is the first American literary character to face Malraux's jungle, the first to sense that "the heat was the enemy of all white men, but it was more an enemy of his, he had less resistance and resilience."[5] It is 1963; he is only a military advisor; and there is a strict limit to his tour of duty, so the magnitude of Malraux's primeval landscape need be nothing more than "his imagination turning Vietnam into 365 days of this." But the artificial limits on time and on his military role are distressing. "He wished the troops would go faster, would move it out, and he wished he were a real officer, someone who could give commands and then see them obeyed, who could send a patrol here and another there, could make the troops go fast, go slow, be brave, be strong; wished to be hated, to be feared, even to be loved, but to be an officer and in charge" (p. 155). His experience is perplexing, because Vietnam is a different kind of war for him. A veteran of World War II and Korea, the sergeant can instruct his young lieutenant (a scene that is to reappear in several Vietnam fictions) in just how strange things are compared to the war against Hitler:

We didn't know how simple it was, and how good we had it. Sure we walked but in a straight line. Boom, Normandy beaches, and then you set off for Paris and Berlin. Just like that. No retracing, no goddam circles, just straight ahead. All you needed was a compass and good sense. But here you walk in a goddam circle, and then you go home, and then you go out the next day and wade through a circle, and then you go home and the next day you go out and reverse the circle you did the day before, erasing it. Every day the circles get bigger and emptier. Walk them one day, erase them the next. In France you always knew where you were, how far you had walked, and how far you had to go. But this goddam place, Christ, if I knew how far I had walked, it would break my heart. From Normandy to Berlin and back, probably (p. 79).

Halberstam's novel also begins the search for structure common to most subsequent Vietnam novels: how to organize this war that defies all previous military and political patterns. The novelist starts with basics, a single day's patrol, but on it his veteran sergeant loses all sense of purpose and achievement. Even in the simplest of conventional terms, the experience of Vietnam makes little sense.

Whether experienced by journalists on Guggenheims or by literate infantrymen on patrol, Vietnam proved to be a war unlike any other. Tom Mayer, a representative of the first group, writes about such difficulties in his collection of stories, *The Weary Falcon* (1971), which includes the situation of "the US Marines landing at Chu Lai where the troops came storming out of the amtracks and up the beach like John Wayne in 'The Sands of Iwo Jima' only to find twenty photographers on the top of the first dune taking pictures of it all."[6] In similar terms William Pelfrey's *The Big V* (1972) fails as a realist combat novel, because the war, measured first against its familiar image on television, never has the chance to escape the tired pop-art cliches assigned to every act. "I fired one round on semiautomatic. His body jerked erect, almost like a gangster blown back by a sawed-off shotgun, only screaming, hoarse, with his mouth gaping; more like an Indian, his arms flying up and dropping the rifle."[7] Pelfrey's narrator can find no vocabulary for the war beyond that of its television images because his vision extends no further than the video-adventures of his youth. That Vietnam was fought on such a level is less frightening than the thought that it was so comprehended, by soldiers and citizens alike.

Outstripping the politics and military theories of earlier wars and older generations, the truth of Vietnam became a test of the artist's imagination. Hence, three of the best books about the war were written by authors who were never there as participants, and who remove the action of their books to points of broader perspective. In *The Prisoners of Quai Dong* (1967) Victor Kolpacoff suggests the sense of Vietnam by writing about a military jail, where the order of life has all the tedium, uncertainty, and senselessness of the war going on outside—particularly when the narrator is asked to participate in the interrogation/torture of a Viet Cong suspect.[8] William Eastlake's *The Bamboo Bed* (1969)[9] finds an even more appropriate perspective on this surreal war—above the jungle combat, above even the monsoon engulfing that action, in a rescue helicopter used for inflight trysts by a modern Captain Tarzan and Nurse Jane. The ship is more noted for the people it has not rescued, including an infantry company directed by its captain into a ritualistic re-creation of Custer's Last Stand, with the Viet Cong as obliging Indians. Asa Baber sets his *The Land of a Million Elephants* (1970) in a place of make-believe not unlike Vietnam in its geography, and quite like Vietnam in its role in our international fantasies. Baber's strategists submit that America has been deadened by civil unrest and political assassination: "I submit that if you had a National Blood Pressure Monitor at the moment people heard the news you would have found virtually no response. No orgasm."[10]

Baber's depiction of the lack of imaginative possibilities in Vietnam may be closest to the truth of what the war really meant. But within the limits of actual events, it remained the role of fictionists to find a structure. Ronald J. Glasser's *365 Days* (1971) admitted the problem: "There is no novel in Nam, there is not enough for a plot, nor is there really any character development. If you survive 365 days without getting killed or wounded you simply go home and take up again where you left off."[11] Yet within this artificially imposed structure of a duty tour Glasser sketches many aspects of the war: the suicidal role of helicopter pilots, the medics' psychotic altruism, and the case of a veteran commander who against the military silliness of Vietnam applies World War II tactics with great success until he is fragged by his most decidedly Vietnam-era troops. Airmen's routines—bombing Vietnam on office-hour schedules, from comfortable bases in Thailand while intimately involved in affairs back home in Washington, D.C., or Schenectady, New York—are used by George Davis as the structure for *Coming Home* (1971). In counterpoint, Davis places the problems of a black officer, unique even in the Vietnam-era Air Force, for whom "this war is like Harvard. Nothing in it seems real. Everything is abstract. Everything is an argument or a question."[12]

In terms of structure, the most successful novel to portray the military situation in Vietnam is Josiah Bunting's *The Lionheads* (1972). A major and former commander in Vietnam teaching history at West Point, Bunting finds the essence of the Vietnam insanity simply by viewing it through the traditional form of Army chain-of-command. His novel begins at the top, where a major general knows that

commanding a Division in the combat theatre can be the capstone of an excellent career of service, leading to one further assignment . . . or, if he truly distinguishes himself, the assignment will lead to another promotion—the big step to three stars (only 15 percent of two-star generals are promoted to the three star rank). . . . He wants to be Chief of Staff—of the Army.[13]

With the visit of a branch secretary imminent, the general mounts a campaign, the implications of which are carried down-staff with the orders. At brigade, he charges one of his colonels in the manner of a sales director:

"Your body-count is a standing joke. Tell you what, Robertson, you have one week to produce" (p. 66). Among the three brigades, there is a scramble for the division's helicopter assets; inevitably, one brigade is shorted and sustains a frightening number of deaths, but overall the casualties are "moderate" enough for the general to claim a significant victory. As the battle has progressed from planning to execution, Bunting has followed the action down to company, platoon, and squad, until he reaches what the Army calls the "real sharp individual"—the soldier in the field, in this case PFC Compella, the single person in the book devoid of all but purely human ambitions. In the first chapter, at division, he has been temporarily assigned as an aide, displaying maps for the coming battle. "PFC Compella notes that the officers take no notice of him, but follow only the movements of the tip of his pointer as it plots the new locations on the briefing map" (p. 6). His presence is as unreal as the deaths orchestrated by these same commanders. At the novel's conclusion, when he himself is the fine point of the war's action, the officers again take no note, for he is killed on a day for rejoicing, when casualties are light. His experience in Vietnam is absolute but unmeasurable.

But the Vietnam experience was bewildering even to the military. To Army veterans, the war made little sense. Confused sergeants, whose 20 years of service span the end of World War II, Korea, and the beginnings of Vietnam, are familiar characters in fiction emerging from the war—and in few cases do they find a solution, or even an understanding of what is going on. The larger dimensions of America's involvement remain the province of the professional novelist. Two young novelists wrote their first books about the war, James Park Sloan with *War Games* (1971) and William Crawford Woods with *The Killing Zone* (1970). Both have since broadened their writing careers, but these first novels are two of the best to come out of the Vietnam War.

For *War Games* Sloan faces the familiar problem of finding a structuring device. This is why his protagonist has joined the Army—he has two theories to test, one of which he hopes to use for a novel:

Theory One

The timid hero goes to Vietnam like a sissy dipping his toe in the pool. Suddenly he realizes that he can be a cold-water swimmer. This happens because Vietnam provides him with a character-molding experience. It is both purposeful and earth-shaking. There is a flash of insight. He realizes that he is now fully mature. He has become a soldier and a man.

This is only a hypothesis. Then there is Theory Two.

Theory Two

A tough-minded young man, who unsuspectingly has above-average sensitivity goes to Vietnam. For the first time in his life he encounters genuine brutality and tragedy—perhaps his first tragic love affair. The experience shocks him into his

own humanity. There is a flash of insight. He comes home in total revulsion at war
and probably writes a book.[14]

This story of his book becomes the story of his attempts to write the
definitive novel of Vietnam, and its structure becomes natural and unique
to the young college dropout ripping off the Army in Vietnam. Discovering
that if the service does dental work on any tooth it is responsible for the
care of that tooth, and the two adjacent, for the rest of the soldier's life,
Sloan's protagonist begins a program of systematically complaining about
every third tooth. The organization of his dental chart becomes the structure of his novel.

The chart is the most real thing in the book. Like other writers before
him, Sloan finds that there are many unreal things in this new war: airliners
that race the sun across the Pacific, serving breakfast every hour; APO
mail that sends the same letter back and forth across the world 27 times;
a peacetime army staffed by uniformed civil servants who must suddenly
fight for their careers; and dozens of other incongruities that suggest that
Vietnam and its war are a world apart from anything America has previously known. Officially, the Army contrives its own unreality to match. It
is a nonlinear war, with no objectives to seize or end-date in sight:

Each departure is festive in its own way. . . . Since the rotations after one-year tours
are staggered, victory is a continuous process. It is thus more sustained than the
sword tendering, paper signing, and ticker-tape marching of previous wars. On the
other hand, it is followed by an equally continuous reappraisal (p. 40).

The service treats it as a game, a matter of duration and a simple modal
exercise:

We lead by a steady three-to-one. Which is good, but not good enough. Any worse
and there would be alarm. Any better and the statistics would be checked. . . . I
never bother with the facts. When a town comes up on my roster, I put the monthly
battle there. That's the way it is with this war (p. 87).

Sloan's protagonist learns that if he is to have a real war, he must make
it up himself. "I shall remember to cite Hamlet: devise the play, then act
in it!" (p. 9). As he makes progress through his war, which has become
his novel, he wonders, "Have I begun inventing things? A man who goes
to war should return with tales to tell. . . . Is my life merging with my
imagination?" (p. 125). He fears that he is "tramping, step by step, in the
direction of the implausible" (p. 133). On patrol with a group of ARVN
rangers, his dream catches up with him: sickened by his allies' torture of
villagers and disgusting acts with animals, he sets his rifle on automatic fire
and destroys them all. For this he expects court-martial and execution, but

at least he has performed a significant act in this otherwise insignificant war.

The writer and his "separate war" are saved by his new boss, Colonel Rachow, who has authored the Army manual *Creative Leadership and Collective Tunnel Vision*, and who in other times "would have been magnificent . . . as a paper lawyer in the twelfth century. Or perhaps as the head of a noble family encroaching on its vassals." Rachow sympathizes with the protagonist's behavior because he can articulate many of the young soldier's feelings about the unreal war against Vietnam:

War, said Rachow, has ceased to be tied down by facts. It has become metaphysical; one might say a platonic form. He asked me to picture an amphibious landing across Lake Michigan. Then imagine, he said, such things as landings by Martians; invaders from liquid planets formed of molten lava, surprised and threatened by our exploration. This is the future of military planning. War is no longer waged merely to achieve ends; it is waged as proof of its own possibility (p. 144).

Moreover, technologically "war had come to a state of entropy! It was more and more complex, but in the process its energy was spent. If he had known sooner, he might have quit the army and written a book—on the war which had made his profession obsolete" (p. 154). And so Sloan's protagonist ends his tour with the creation of his small novel about a small war, *War Games*.

In *The Killing Zone* William Crawford Woods employs even more artifice to come to terms with this most artificial of wars. A confused sergeant stands at the center of the action, which Woods places not in Vietnam but rather in a New Jersey training camp where the strategies of Vietnam are first rehearsed. Sergeant Melton has rejected a career that would have led him to Josiah Bunting's managerial officer caste of Vietnam. Instead, he finds himself first sergeant of a company with no executive officer, its C.O. having been stricken with a heart attack on the golf course; and so he is in a position of command when a new lieutenant arrives to test a demonstration plan of computerized warfare—a plan being implemented in the Vietnam War for which the inductees are training. The war and its methods, of course, are like no other. The lieutenant helping to plan it is equally new:

Twenty-four years old. BS and MS in electrical engineering from the University of California. Master's thesis on some military application of information retrieval. ROTC commission deferred until after graduate school. Part-time programmer for Armed Resources Corporation—one of those ambiguous concerns that hide in the rolling countryside of Maryland and Virginia within fifteen minutes by chopper of the Pentagon.[15]

Lieutenant Track's experiment is to find out how closely and how well a computer can perform with a small line unit in a rapidly changing combat

situation. The unit chosen is led by Sergeant Cox, who is of Track's age
but in spirit is more akin to Melton's Army. Despite the strange nature of
the war and the even more incongruous circumstances in which one trains
for it ("the training area . . . was a parking lot; they were learning to kill
like cavemen in a place where the pizza truck would stop that night,"
[p. 25]), he resists computerized warfare in favor of the personal virtues
of soldiery.

Track's computer plans an action, issues plastic-headed wargame ammunition, and follows the training exercise with all the deliberation of a
division commander, receiving information from the field and determining
the best strategies to continue. But an error is made: the operator has not
routinely cleared the computer's storage, and as a result two boxes of live
ammunition have been used. There is no way the computer can discover
or correct its action. That remains the prerogative of the common foot
soldier, in this case Sergeant Cox, who has but one way to save his men
from total slaughter:

He had been hit four times by the gunner who was still firing when he reached
him. Mr. Track's computer had provided an unbeatable realism which had gone
into his belly, and one bit of realism had ruined his left arm, taken it out altogether.
So it was with the rifle in one hand that he came over the barrel, calmly, indiffer-
ently, almost sweetly, and with practiced smoothness and precision slid the bayonet
into the boy's chest. . . . The sergeant and the private fell together behind the finally
silent gun (p. 164).

Because he has attacked the technology itself, Sergeant Cox can affirm
both himself and the real matter of death, each of which the military
technicians of the Vietnam War try to efface. *The Killing Zone* probably
stands as the best novel to define, amid the surreal confusion of a war
planned by computers and practiced in parking lots, what field remains for
honor. The villains are those who disavow such honor, whether they be
technocrat lieutenants who fight weekday wars with weekends in New
York, or a military establishment that has lost sight of the purpose of
soldiering. Again, the sergeants, both young and old, suffer. But in Woods'
novel their acts have meaning and their minds comprehend the meaning
of what's going on. The lieutenant can drive away in his red Corvette,
radio blaring; the first sergeant remains, to write letters of bereavement
but also to understand:

Melton paused, because the melody from Track's radio was surfacing in his mind,
and he wanted to name it. It mingled with the others, then came clearer. Rock
and roll, or what they now called just rock, the new music—he hated most of it—
but he had heard before, and liked, this quiet tune—there it was: "Ruby Tuesday,"
by the Rolling Stones. A really beautiful song (p. 179).

The fact that amateur and professional writers of all ages and abilities wrote on every aspect of the war in a wide range of styles and modes demonstrates that writing, that telling stories, is an essential reflex to the human dilemma. More specifically, these works of fiction argue that literature is a person's private weapon against lies and hypocrisy, that a precise and concrete use of language is a moral act. The Vietnam conflict made less of an immediate impression on domestic America than any other war in history; there was no mobilization of the homefront, and America was, simultaneously, going through one of the most culturally fertile periods in recent times. In his book *Standard Operating Procedure: Notes of a Draft-Age American* (1971), James S. Kunen ponders what he will be able to tell his future grandchildren:

They won't understand why the war did not become the center of our lives, why stopping it did not pre-empt all other concerns, why opposition did not progress far beyond *dissent*. They won't understand how it was possible that, while the war was going on, a new football league grew and merged with the old, hemlines rose and fell amid great controversy, and the nation rediscovered romance.[16]

The task of making such explanations ultimately falls on literary artists. The peculiar nature of Vietnam, both at home and abroad, has made that task all the more difficult. But long after the politics, economics, military theories, and sociologies of the war have been outdated, the fictions of those artists will remain as evidence of how the war affected our imagination. And for all its struggles, their writing is perhaps our most reliable record of just what Vietnam was.

NOTES

1. André Malraux, *La Voie royale* (Paris, 1930), trans. Stuart Gilbert as *The Royal Way* (New York: Harrison Smith and Robert Haas, 1935), photographically reproduced as a Vintage paperback in 1955 by Random House, New York; subsequent references are to the Gilbert translation.

2. Norman Mailer, *Cannibals and Christians* (New York: Dial Press, 1966), p. 85.

3. Robin Moore, *The Green Berets* (New York: Crown Publishers, 1965), p. 286.

4. Graham Greene, *The Quiet American* (London, 1955; American edition published in 1956 by Viking Press, New York, and photographically reproduced as a Compass Book in 1957, from which this and subsequent quotes are taken), p. 13.

5. David Halberstam, *One Very Hot Day* (Boston: Houghton Mifflin, 1967), pp. 18–19. Subsequent references in text.

6. Tom Mayer, *The Weary Falcon* (Boston: Houghton Mifflin, 1971), p. 95.

7. William Pelfrey, *The Big V* (New York: Liveright, 1972), p. 36.

8. Victor Kolpacoff, *The Prisoners of Quai Dong* (New York: New American Library, 1967).

9. William Eastlake, *The Bamboo Bed* (New York: Simon & Schuster, 1969).

10. Asa Baber, *The Land of a Million Elephants* (New York: William Morrow, 1970), p. 95.

11. Ronald J. Glasser, M.D., *365 Days* (New York: George Braziller, 1971), p. xii.

12. George Davis, *Coming Home* (New York: Random House, 1971), p. 77.

13. Josiah Bunting, *The Lionheads* (New York: George Braziller, 1972), p. 15. Subsequent references cited in text.

14. James Park Sloan, *War Games* (Boston: Houghton Mifflin, 1971), p. 4. Subsequent references cited in text.

15. William Crawford Woods, *The Killing Zone* (New York: Harper's Magazine/Harper & Row, 1970), p. 5. Subsequent references cited in text.

16. James S. Kunen, *Standard Operating Procedure: Notes of a Draft-Age American* (New York: Avon, 1971), p. 365.

SELECTED BIBLIOGRAPHY

Primary Sources

Allen, George W. *Ri*. Englewood Cliffs, N.J.: Prentice-Hall, 1978.

Archibald, Joseph. *Special Forces Trooper*. New York: McKay, 1967.

Baber, Asa. *The Land of a Million Elephants*. New York: William Morrow Co., 1970.

Balaban, John. *After Our War*. Pittsburgh: University of Pittsburgh Press, 1974.

Ballard, J. G. *Crash*. New York: Farrar, Straus & Giroux, 1973.

Bernard, Edward. *Going Home*. Philadelphia: Dorrance, 1973.

Berrigan, Daniel. *Night Flight to Hanoi War Diary*. New York: Macmillan, 1968.

————. *The Trial of the Catonsville Nine*. Boston: Beacon Press, 1970.

Berry, D. C. *Saigon Cemetery*. Athens: University of Georgia Press, 1972.

Briley, John. *The Traitors*. New York: G. P. Putnam's Sons, 1969.

Briscoe, Edward G. *Diary of a Short-timer in Vietnam*. New York: Vantage, 1970.

Bryan, C. D. B. *Friendly Fire*. New York: G. P. Putnam's Sons, 1976.

Bunting, Josiah. *The Lionheads*. New York: George Braziller, 1972.

Burdick, Eugene and William J. Lederer. *The Ugly American*. New York: W. W. Norton, 1958.

Caputo, Phillip. *A Rumor of War*. New York: Holt, Rinehart and Winston, 1977.

Casey, Michael. *Obscenities*. New Haven: Yale University Press, 1972.

Cassidy, John. *A Station in the Delta*. New York: Charles Scribner's Sons, 1979.

Clark, Alan. *The Lion Heart: A Tale of the War in Vietnam*. New York: Morrow, 1969.

Coe, Charles. *Young Man in Vietnam*. New York: Four Winds Press, 1969.

Coleman, Charles. *Sergeant Back Again*. New York: Harper & Row, 1980.

Connell, Robert. *Firewinds: Poems on the Vietnam War*. New York: Macmillan, 1976.

Connolly, Edward. *Deer Run*. New York: Charles Scribner's Sons, 1971.

Corder, E. M. *The Deer Hunter*. New York: Jove, 1978.

Davis, George. *Coming Home*. New York: Random House, 1971.

Downs, Frederick. *The Killing Zone—My Life in the Vietnam War*. New York: W. W. Norton, 1978.

Duncan, Donald. *The New Legions*. New York: Random House, 1967.

Durden, Charles. *No Bugles, No Drums*. New York: Viking Press, 1978.

Eastlake, William. *The Bamboo Bed*. New York: Simon & Schuster, 1969.

Ehrhart, Bill. *A Generation of Peace*. Flushing, N.Y.: New Voices Publishing, 1975.

Emerson, Gloria. *Winners and Losers: Battles, Retreats, Gains, Losses and Ruins from a Long War*. New York: Random House, 1972.

Ford, Daniel. *Incident at Muc Wa*. Garden City, N.Y.: Doubleday, 1967.

Giovannitti, Len. *The Man Who Won the Medal of Honor*. New York: Random House, 1973.

Glasser, Ronald J. *365 Days*. New York: George Braziller, 1971.

Groom, Winston. *Better Times Than These*. New York: Summit Books, 1978.

Halberstam, David. *One Very Hot Day*. Boston: Houghton Mifflin, 1967.

Halderman, Joe W. *War Year*. New York: Holt, Rinehart & Winston, 1972.

Harrison, Jim. *A Good Day to Die*. New York: Simon & Schuster, 1973.

Hasford, Gustav. *The Short-timers*. New York: Harper & Row, 1979.

Heinemann, Larry. *Close Quarters*. New York: Popular Library, 1974.

Herr, Michael. *Dispatches*. New York: G. P. Putnam's Sons, 1973.

Huggett, William Turner. *Body Count*. New York: G. P. Putnam's Sons, 1973.

Hughes, Larry. *You Can See a Lot Standing Under a Flare in the Republic of Vietnam: My Years at the War*. New York: William Morrow, 1969.

Just, Ward S. *To What End*. Boston: Houghton Mifflin, 1968.

———. *Stringer*. Boston: Little, Brown, 1974.

Karlin, Wayne, Basil T. Paquet, and Larry Rottman, eds. *Free Fire Zone*. New York: McGraw Hill, 1974.

Kirkwood, James. *Some Kind of Hero*. New York: Crowell, 1975.

Kolpacoff, Victor. *The Prisoners of Quai Dong*. New York: New American Library, 1967.

Kovic, Ron. *Born on the Fourth of July*. New York: McGraw-Hill, 1976.

LeGuin, Ursula K. *The Word for World is Forest*. New York: Harper and Row, 1976.

Lifton, Robert J. *Home from the War: Vietnam Veterans, Neither Victims Nor Executioners*. New York: Simon & Schuster, 1973.

McGinnis, Joe. *Heroes*. New York: Viking Press, 1976.

Mailer, Norman. *Why Are We In Vietnam*. New York: G. P. Putnam's Sons, 1968.

Mayer, Tom. *The Weary Falcon*. Boston: Houghton Mifflin, 1971.

Moore, Gene D. *The Killing at Ngo Tho*. New York: W. W. Norton, 1967.

Moore, Robin. *The Green Berets*. New York: Crown, 1967.

Morrison, C. T. *The Flame in the Icebox*. Jericho, N.Y.: Exposition, 1968.

O'Brien, Tim. *If I Die in the Combat Zone, Box Me Up and Send Me Home*. New York: Delacorte, 1973.

———. *Going After Cacciato*. New York: Selacorte, Seymour Lawrence, 1978.

Pelfrey, William. *The Big V*. New York: Liveright, 1972.

Rabe, David. *The Basic Training of Pavlo Hummel, Sticks and Bones*. New York: Viking Press, 1973.

Rivers, Gayle and James Hudson. *The Five Fingers*. Garden City, N.Y.: Double-
    day, 1978.
Roth, Robert. *Sand in the Wind*. Boston: Little, Brown, 1973.
Rottman, Larry, Jan Barry, and Basil T. Paquet. *Winning Hearts and Minds*. New
    York: McGraw-Hill, 1971.
Russ, Martin. *Happy Hunting Ground*. New York: Atheneum, 1968.
Santolini, Al. *Everything We Had*. New York: Random House, 1981.
Sloan, James Park. *War Games*. Boston: Houghton Mifflin, 1971.
Sontag, Susan. *Trip to Hanoi*. New York: Farrar, Straus & Giroux, 1968.
Stone, Robert. *Dog Soldiers*. Boston: Houghton Mifflin, 1974.
Taylor, Clyde, ed. *Vietnam and Black America: An Anthology of Protest and
    Resistance*. Garden City, N.Y.: Anchor Books, 1973.
Tiede, Tom. *Coward*. New York: Trident Press, 1968.
Tregaskis, Richard. *Vietnam Diary*. New York: Holt, Rinehart & Winston, 1963.
Vance, Samuel. *The Courageous and the Proud*. New York: W. W. Norton, 1970.
Webb, James H. *Field of Fire*. Englewood Cliffs, N.J.: Prentice Hall, 1978.
Willwerth, James. *Eye in the Last Storm: A Reporter's Journal of One Year in
    Southeast Asia*. New York: Gorssman, 1972.
Wolfe, Michael. *Man on a String*. New York: Harper & Row, 1973.
Woods, William Crawford. *The Killing Zone*. New York: Harper's Magazine Press,
    1970.

Secondary Sources

Beidler, Philip D. *American Literature and the Experience of Vietnam*. Athens:
    University of Georgia Press, 1982.
Colonnese, Tom and Jerry Hogan. "Vietnam War Literature, 1958–1979: A First
    Checklist." *Bulletin of Bibliography* 38, No. 1 (1981): 26–29, 50–51.
Hellman, John. *Fables of Fact: The New Journalism as New Fiction*. Urbana:
    University of Illinois Press, 1981.
Klinkowitz, Jerome. *The American 1960s: Imaginative Acts in a Decade of Change*.
    Ames: Iowa State University Press, 1980.
McInerney, Peter. "Straight and Secret History in Vietnam War Literature." *Con-
    temporary Literature* 22 (Spring 1981): 187–204.
Saltzman, Arthur M. "The Betrayal of the Imagination: Paul Brodeur's *The Stunt
    Man* and Tim O'Brien's *Going After Cacciato*." *Critique* 22 (1980): 32–38.
Taylor, Gordon O. "American Personal Narrative of the War in Vietnam." *Amer-
    ican Literature* 54 (May 1980): 294–308.
Tetlow, Joseph A. "The Vietnam War Novel." *America*, July 1980, 32–36.
Wilson, James C. *Vietnam in Prose and Film*. Jefferson, N.C.: McFarland & Com-
    pany, Inc., 1982.

SARAH E. LAUZEN

Notes on Metafiction: Every Essay Has a Title

> Once an angry young man dragged his father along the ground through his own orchard. "Stop!" cried the groaning old man at last, "Stop! I did not drag my father beyond this tree."
>
> Gertrude Stein, *The Making of Americans*

Certain things will always be with us. Stories and fathers. Scotty dogs. Romanians. (Yes, aurochs and angels.) The desire for certainty and the need for paradox. The inevitability of judging ourselves against the tradition. The chiaroscuro—the fluctuating borders and teasing lines—of the world and art. (This mirror. That nature.) Tradition and continuity. And yet *not* going further than the father before. Postmodernism burdened with "the overwhelming fatherhood of modernism"—A. Wilde.[1] The father and its bedwetting child. Questioning ourselves and our materials, our reasons and results. Narrative is a primary human function. Tell us a story daddy. But now we seem to be less sure, more angry. We feel abandoned. (By the tale? The tellers?)

But who can we blame for the predicament we're in? That old man on our back. Our muffled head-in-pillow protests are no use, for the modernists are all gone, or don't seem to matter much anymore. Who to blame for their clean swipe of our twentieth century slate? We are, we seem to be, what was left over and behind. There are hostilities. We feel cheated. We are only going through the motions: dad on back, march out to orchard, dump. Knowing full well nothing will come of it. The march has lost its cadence, the journey its purpose, the ritual its resolution. The reasons don't matter any more. How can we go to the orchard if we have no tangible father to leave there?

She felt the terror of terminology.

> Why weren't there any decent words?
>
>   William Gass, *Willie Masters' Lonesome Wife*

Okay, be brief. Yes, metafiction is a formal term: "That is, a reader, or lepidopterist, or critic, handed the text and deprived of further data, can still say, 'Oh sure, here's some metafiction. You can see it clearly in the first chapter and the bright eye-spots on the wings.'"[2] Somewhere early on it should read: Metafiction is characterized by the prominence of metafictional devices. A metafictional device or element is one that foregrounds some aspect of the writing, reading, or structure of a work that the applicable canons of standard (realistic) practice would expect to be backgrounded; or is such a foregrounded element itself. Metafiction uses techniques to *systematically* heighten its own status as fiction. Metafiction is therefore more a formal term than an historical one, and is not solely a postmodern (or modern) possession.

A cluster of terms hovers around metafiction: experimental and innovative, avant-garde, ludic, areal or irreal, disruptive, anti-, neo-, para-, sur-, superfiction, post-realistic, post-contemporary, the introverted novel, the self-begetting novel, and the new fiction.[3] Brief paragraph describing jargon, whose and where, depending on space. Especially note the intersection of innovation and metafiction.[4] Then back to fictional propriety. Avoiding the mistake of deriving critical rules from forms of fiction different from those being currently considered. Metafictional novels are quest novels: they contain within themselves the means for their own examination and elucidation as well as a critique of the current status of the literary species.

WHAT IS THE TITLE OF THIS SECTION?

> "The Trees. 'I think that I shall never see slash A poem as lovely as a tree.'"
>
>   —Donald Barthelme, "The Leap"

> "Oh God comma I abhor self-consciousness."
>
>   —John Barth, "Title"

Metafiction is marked by many invalid misconceptions and an equal number of healthy paradoxes. "Self-conscious" fiction carries a taint: trivial, self-absorbed, decadent. "Self-reflexive" might be synonymous with "metafiction" or it might lack a referent, but in any case, it's not the same as self-conscious fiction which is a narrower classification of metafiction. A text can probably be self-reflexive without being self-conscious. Self-conscious fiction is the most noticed, most prototypical, and most overt kind of metafiction, but it is only a segment. Self-conscious fiction—to which most critics refer when they speak of "metafiction"—played out its current cycle in the late 1960s and reached its zenith in works like John Barth's* *Lost in the Funhouse*. Other paradigmatic examples of self-conscious fiction: Flann O'Brien's *At Swim-Two-Birds* (1939) and Gilbert Sorrentino's* *Mulligan Stew* (1979). Writing about writing—in promoting overt textual self-interrogation as the norm—readies us to receive self-reflexive fiction of a more covert, and ultimately more interesting, sort.

HOW METAFICTIONAL IS IT?

Degree and Intent. What makes a novel metafictional is both abundant and systematic use of metafictional devices. A sprinkling of one or two strange and metafictional moments may serve to give the reader a jolt, without giving the whole work a metafictional cast. In the lighthearted but generally conventional mystery *The Moving Toyshop* by Edmund Crispin, the protagonist, Fen, having some extra time on his hands, reflects on a few titles for his author: "Murder Stalks the University . . . The Blood on the Mortarboard. Fen Strikes Back." Prototypical self-consciousness and frame-breaking, but for only a moment and not enough to make us usher this work into the metafictional canon.

If that's a retreat from full metafictional degree, a retreat from full metafictional intent occurs when metafictional devices serve not so much to lead the reader to reflect on the unnaturalness of conventional naturalistic devices, as much as to create an eerie effect or simply to back up the realist/symbolic story intent. Some critics, for instance, consider John Irving's* *The World According to Garp* (1978) and D. M. Thomas's* *The White Hotel* (1984) metafictional. Yet every device used in these novels directs its energy toward the story or message (pathos) of a fairly traditional, non-self-conscious sort. The message in all fully metafictional novels is at least partly "art is artifice"; we are made conscious in some way that any message comes to us via processing of language by both author and reader. In a metafictional work, the device that points to itself (and us) has some significant weight in the novel as a whole.

Let's examine the methods themselves, the local metafictionalities that (with sufficient degree and genuine intent) contribute to a work's global metafictionality. And we want to examine them not in the abstract, but as they have actually been instantiated. So the discussion centers on examples—the chart is meant to be a classification of techniques, not books, providing a backbone for a fairly orderly traversal of an interesting range of possibilities in metafiction. *All* charts operate in an ideal world. Here, we cite tendencies and indications rather than exclusive categories, and in the true metafictional spirit, we summon our readers to pick up their pens and supply their own examples.

Our typology is an extension of one proposed by Linda Hutcheon in

Hutcheon's Typology of Textual Narcissism

	covert	overt
diegetic		
linguistic		

Narcissistic Narrative (1984). Her examination of the formal types of self-reflexivity employs two cross-cutting binary features to yield a four-way classification. On one dimension, she distinguishes between texts that are *diegetically* self-aware (conscious of their own narrative processes) and those that are *linguistically* self-reflective. (She uses "diegetic" in place of the more common "narrative" to indicate her rejection of the split between the process of storytelling and its product, the story told.) Along the other axis, she separates *overt* (or thematized) narcissism from *covert* narcissism (also called structuralized, internalized, and actualized).[5]

We subdivide her categories a bit further. Our "overt" corresponds to hers, and our "exaggeration"/"reduction"/"eccentric" are versions of her "covert." Down the left, we include "language" and "medium" approximating her "linguistic," with the remainder of our categories subdividing her "diegetic": narration and point-of-view; content, itself further broken down into plot and action, characterization, setting and theme; and structure. These are intended to capture, in a rough-and-ready way, the familiar facets of the classic well-made realist story. The double lines on our chart reconstruct Hutcheon's four-way division.[6]

The ways in which metafiction foregrounds conventional technique are by overdoing it, by suppressing it, by standing it on its head or otherwise distorting it, and, of course, by explicitly subjecting it to direct scrutiny and discussion. All the lines tend to bend and overlap, but let's push on since we want only a *catalogue raisonné*, not a well-greased theoretical machine.[7]

NARRATION AND POINT OF VIEW

The realist presumption is that there *is* a narrator or implied author that is more or less stable and more or less behind the curtain for our benefit.

Typology of Metafictional Devices

	Overabundance or exaggeration	Absence or reduction	Eccentric execution	Overt self-consciousness
NARRATION & POINT OF VIEW				
CONTENT:				
Plot/action				
Characterization				
Setting				
Theme				
STRUCTURE				
LANGUAGE				
MEDIUM				

Point of view is essentially non-self-conscious, first person, omniscient third person, limited third person—all consistent internally, or if unreliable, this is easily known. Narrator-Pal is one of the built-in conventions of fiction that urges us, paradoxically, to trust in the illusion before us.

An obvious overabundance of narration is the presence of multiple narrators (without self-conscious indications) such as those in Faulkner's *As I Lay Dying*. Discursive narrators, authorial intrusion, and the traits and symptoms of direct address to the reader can operate within a range, from well within the frame of the fiction through overt disruption of the fictive world. The struggle of the "divided I" to achieve a single voice is the story of Raymond Federman's* fourth book of fiction, *Voice in the Closet* (1979). The restraining presence, the overriding voice of the *un*named Manager of Gilbert Sorrentino's* *Aberration of Starlight* (1980) prods and pokes the characters, asks leading questions, footnotes their conversations, and in general defers our interest from their cliched, struggling story to the book.

The absent narrator of Alain Robbe-Grillet's *Jealousy* (1965) is the example par excellence of reduction in narration: we observe all details from a particular vantage point—walk down corridors, see place settings, sip drinks, spy on a probable infidelity—but never does this point-of-view narrator get directly referred to or acknowledged. And speaking of absence, there are the disembodied voices of Samuel Beckett's narratives, prosing out of their existence in empty rooms (urns). A mysterious, traveling point of view—like an unattended movie camera on a dolly—is our guide through the fog in "The Beak Doctor" by Eric Basso (*Chicago Review*, 29:1); a speculating "he or she or it" (and sometimes "you"), dematerialized, unaccountable, perhaps dreaming.[8]

Another manifestation of reduced narration is the matter of *no* explicit narration as in the pure dialogue in stories by the Barthelme Boys, Frederick and Donald ("Storytellers," *CR* 32:1 and *Great Days*, respectively). Perhaps Nathalie Sarraute's "sub-conversation" dialogue in *The Golden Fruits* (1965) belongs here, as well as the multi-character narration in the overheard conversations of William Gaddis'* *J R* (1975). Also add under too little narration the profusion in a text of absurd lists, questionnaires (such as the one that appears in the middle of Donald Barthelme's *Snow White*). "Zero point of view" is a name we've hitched to the device that operates in texts like A. B. Paulson's "The Minnesota Multiphasic Personality: a diagnostic test in two parts," with reading passages and true/false sections (*TriQuarterly* 29, Winter 1974) and Stewart Justman's "The Books Are Tallied After the Fair" (*CR* 30:2), or, for that matter, Marcia Adamson's "Nutritional Information Per Serving" (CR 33:2). All masquerade as documents—albeit absurd ones—with no more than an indication to the reader as to what to make of them.

"Suspect narration" falls on the line between absence or reduction of narration and eccentric execution. This technique is related to the realistic "unreliable narrator," but the latter is much more rational, communicable, and trustworthy in its unreliability. Suspect narration casts doubt on the veracity of the narrative by using words like "probably," "perhaps," and "maybe," including, paradoxically, words of assurance (that do not assure) like "undoubtedly," "of course," "certainly." This technique operates in many of the French New Novels, but especially see Robbe-Grillet's *The Voyeur* (1963).

When the narrating—the telling-the-story—becomes a major part of the subject matter, we are in the realm of overt self-consciousness. In several stories of John Barth's *Lost in the Funhouse* (1968), the narrator(s) or implied author(s) are visibly engaged in the act of composition. Raymond Federman's *Double or Nothing* (1971) opens with the struggle of at least three speakers for control of the text. Also overt: explicit dramatization of the reader, as in the opening pages of Italo Calvino's* *If on a winter's night a traveler* (1979), among many others.

CONTENT

Plot & Action

The conventional assumptions are that there *is* some sort of plot/incident; that chronology is at least logically consistent (retraceable); that it is realistic, that is, plausible—cause and effect—and that in a necessarily vague, general, or "organic" sense, the incidents all hang together to satisfy our craving for pattern.

Overabundance of incident often turns into a reduction of real plot, blocking the reader's detection of the figure in the carpet. We have the wandering narrative thwarting unity, the difficulty of connecting things up, which is the hallmark of *Finnegans Wake*. Thomas Pynchon's* *V.* (1963) also deploys profusion of incident while withholding overall connection, at the same time thematizing the search for connection as an imporant part of its subject. There are books where we get practically all the elements of plot—connection, continuity, cause and effect, consquential amusement, cohesion—and yet we are left with the impression that it all lacks a point, that it's a shaggy dog story. See Harry Mathews'* three extended works, *The Conversions* (1962), *Tlooth* (1966), and *The Sinking of the Odradek Stadium* (1975).

A kind of absence or reduction of plot—its subordination to an externally imposed artificial organizing principle—is discussed below under the heading "Structure." Sometimes a metafictional device works to supplement a plot or storyline, such as the Question/Answer mode used in Robert Pinget's *The Inquisitory* (1967). And sometimes motivic relationships replace plot lines as in the story "Sheep" by Pamela Zoline.[9] Another kind of absence of overall shape is assemblage or collage. Kathy Acker,* in her novel *Great Expectations* (1983), calls this "Plagiarism": texts made up of sections or snippets taken from various sources (some perhaps original) and arranged together in a new combination. The new arrangement may be determined by chance, by formula, or by conscious, artful placement of each piece.[10] Gilbert Sorrentino's *Mulligan Stew* (1979) is an unholy goulash of texts-within-texts, lists, puns, poems, rejection letters, along with borrowed plots and characters (Martin Halpin once worked for James Joyce, Ned Beaumont for Dashiell Hammett, Daisy Buchanan for F. Scott Fitzgerald—but we're jumping ahead a row.) Clarence Major's *Emergency Exit* (1978) is an assemblage of discrete bits of fantasy, dream, images, anecdotes, surrealism, and story. This Open Door (or Revolving Door) Novel operates on the principle of formal diversity, accommodating all kinds of brief excursions out of the ordinary frames of consistency, coherence, genre. *Emergency Exit* is written in short, discontinuous takes, with units ranging from a single sentence to three- or four-page clusters; the interweaving is so thorough and the sequence so arbitrary that any single sentence appears without local context.

When reduction/absence of plot shifts the scope of connection down to individual sentences, we have texts that some call prose poetry. A specimen that merits the honorific term "fiction" is Ron Silliman's* *Ketjak* (1978). More extended local connectivity with hints of cohesive plot development may nonetheless fizzle out and withhold global unity, even with the presence of occasional book-length threads; such is the case with Frederick Ted Castle's *Anticipation* (1984).

The simplest kind of eccentric execution of plot is grotesquerie: nonplausible story, simply outrageous or blatantly unlikely incidents. (See "Dwarf School," under the heading "Characterization.") Steve Katz's* "Parcel of Wrists" section in *Moving Parts* (1975) comes to mind. The most dramatic kind of eccentric execution is the inclusion of inconsistencies: contradictory information, false scenes, complicated flash-forward and flashbacks that cannot be resolved into a unified plot although the reader is urged to try. This technique is a conscious part of Robbe-Grillet's armamentarium, displayed particularly well in *Jealousy* (1959) and *La Maison de rendez-vous* (1966).

But the most important kind of eccentric execution of plot is nonrealism, irrealism: disavowal in whole or in part of the pretense that all of this did happen or could have happened to somebody somewhere, refusal to encourage or collaborate in the reader's much-vaunted suspension of disbelief. Go ahead, says the irrealist, *disbelieve!* After all, you're right: *it's not true*. No one example will do. Ultimately, some version of irrealism is the goal of all the metafictional techniques in this catalogue.

Characterization

The Dwarf School of Metafictional Poetics is characterized by generalized weirdness of content, be it grotesque character, eccentric theme, or bizarre setting. The term seems to have sprung up sometime around the publication of Harold Jaffe's* "The Blood Donor" (CR 33:1). (Early Dwarf School, and a precursor to metafiction, is Carson McCullers' *Ballad of the Sad Cafe* [1944] and, by extension, *Reflections in a Golden Eye* [1941].) It is not just the presence of hunchbacks, whores with hearts of gold and red stiletto heels, wombats, Nazis, toilets (and, of course, dwarfs)—it's the fact that nothing in particular is done with them. They are not there to emphasize the extremities of experience against the drolling banalities of daily life. They're just flatly, simply there as part of the pomp and circumstance, the happily perverse imaginative celebration of fiction.

Concerning the identity of fictional characters: a question of verisimilitude. "Description of physical appearance and mannerism is one of several standard methods of characterization used by writers of fiction," says a speaker in John Barth's "Lost in the Funhouse." But when this stock literary convention is parodied, we have the stuff of metafiction.

Initials, blanks, or both were often substituted for proper names in nineteenth-century fiction to enhance the illusion of reality. It is as if the author felt it necessary to delete the names for reasons of tact or legal liability. Interestingly, as with other aspects of realism, it is an illusion that is being enhanced by purely artificial means.[11]

The use of grotesque, comical, or obtrusive proper names in Pynchon and Gaddis and the omission of any name or the use of only an initial in many French New Novels covertly mocks the humanity of the characters. Doppelgängers of parodic or symmetric intent such as those in Nabokov are another version of dehumanization of character. The deliberate flattening out of character reveals the personality to be a cardboard or cartoon-like representation. See the novels of Robbe-Grillet, especially *In the Labyrinth* (1965). In *Mulligan Stew*, characters become tired of perfecting vacant stares with watery blue eyes and curling their lips into thin mirthless smiles. And readers become dramatized—more characters to be mocked or cajoled, further illusions spawned by the author. "Draw your chair closer to the fire, trusting friend," writes a character in *Mulligan Stew*. Another responds: "You gentle listener, have your feet in the flames." Characters who are aware of their fictional status, addressing their author with complaints, suggestions, or revisions for the work-in-progress are a feature of overt self-consciousness. See especially Flann O'Brien's *At Swim-Two-Birds* (1939).

Setting

> "Those are not real moons that your Grace is knocking over, maiming and killing, but pasteboard figures."
>
> (*Don Quixote*)

Description that defeats the purpose of description through the over-abundance of minute detail that either contradicts itself or proves impossible to visualize or map out is a prime feature in Claude Simon's *Triptych* (1973), one of the many French New Novels to use this device.

Synthetic worlds. For an absence or reduction of setting find Samuel Beckett. In most of the late novels, for example, *Company* (1980) and *Worstward Ho* (1983), no real indication of place is given. In the earlier *The Lost Ones* (1972), the setting is a large cylindrical room: an isolated place perhaps outside our normal universe, but decidedly not the alternate universe of science fiction.

Some works, such as Nabokov's *Ada* (1969), create a world different from our own, perhaps parallel and perhaps not. John Mella's *Transformations* (1975) couples Elizabethan England with modern Chicago in a merging of two disparate (real) times.

Theme

When the extraordinary—the mad, brutal, vulgar—is coupled with "the droning banalities of our 'dailiness'," we may be in the presence of a kind of metafiction that challenges the ordinary, denying it solidity. See Philip Stevick's *Anti-Story: An Anthology of Experimental Fiction.*[12] His "Against the Middle Range of Experience" category includes George P. Elliott's "In a Hole" and Robert Coover's* "A Pedestrian Accident."

For fiction as a game (fiction as a tarot deck, as a secret library) disavowing symbolism, politics, real world applications, see most of Borges and Nabokov.

Considering its prominence in conventional fiction, theme plays a surprisingly small role in metafiction.

STRUCTURE

Here the disclaimer that we are exploring techniques rather than works reaches its greatest strain, for in this section we talk of principles of organization that are inherently pervasive. The relevant presupposition for standard realism is that structure is "organic," given by the content, and not arbitrarily imposed.

On the side of overabundance or exaggeration, we find in otherwise more or less realistic texts an externally imposed set of principles used to determine *some* elements of the text. Joyce's familiar chart for the episodes of *Ulysses* (see Stuart Gilbert's *Joyce's Ulysses: A Study.* New York: Vintage, 1955) certainly fits here, as does Gilbert Sorrentino's scheme for *Aberration of Starlight.* For the latter, we can discover a structure based on a 4 by 10 matrix, with each of the four major characters controlling a section of the book, and ten chapters in each section using varied narrative techniques (letters, dialogues, associational streams of consciousness, projected fantasies, question/answer) which correspond across the main sections.

Those can pass as organic until the pattern is noticed, but other kinds of overdetermination are more insistent. Here we find external or artificial organizing principles that operate to the exclusion or subordination of plot. The experience of reading Walter Abish's* *Alphabetical Africa* (1974) is thoroughly dominated by his alphabetical technique: every word in the first chapter begins with the letter A, the second chapter allows both A and B words, and so on through twenty-six chapters, after which the possibilities shrink back accordingly. Richard Horn's *Encyclopedia* (1969) is an interesting hybrid, for a major share of the reader's concern ultimately goes to the rather conventional story about rather realistic characters; but all the information about the underlying plot, as well as an amusing collection of miscellanea, is presented through the device of alphabetized encyclopedia entries, complete with cross-references. The reader is presented with a choice of reading straight through or following up the references; alternate reading order also plays a part in Julio Cortázar's* *Hopscotch* (1966), where the jump pattern is achieved by numbering all sections and concluding each one with the number of its successor.

Number sequences have been used in similar ways, although where the alphabet serves in part to control *what* we get, numbers often control *how many* of something we get in successive instances. Ronald Sukenick's* *Out* (1973) is printed in small blocks of text with ten lines to the block in the first chapter, nine in the next, and so on (incidentally providing the author with a simple way to end). The number of sentences per section (or extended paragraph) in Ron Silliman's *Ketjak* follows the successive powers of two, while his *Tjanting* (1981) uses the Fibonacci series. These two works also contain complex, but not unfathomable, rules for deciding which sentences get repeated (or repeated with variation) from one section to another. Probably the logical extreme of numerical control (a degenerate case) can be found in Richard Kostelanetz's* peculiar attempts to type out numbers in geometric patterns and claim that they capture the essence of plot.

Although their application may be complicated, the alphabet and number sequences are themselves simple structures, in some sense available in advance. But authors have been known to impose on their works various ornate, byzantine, or idiosyncratic patterns. In Osman Lin's *Avalovara* (1973), the sequence of chapters is determined by an opening graphic: the movement of a spiral superimposed on the ancient magic square SATOR AREPO TENET OPERA ROTAS. The 88-letter descriptive subtitle ("An old time epistolary novel by seven fictitious drolls & dreamers each of which imagines himself factual") to John Barth's mammoth epistolary novel *Letters* (1979) is printed so as to provide the block-letter shape of the main title, this pattern then being superimposed on calendar months turned sideways. This determines which correspondent writes on what date, and the not quite chronological order in which the letters are presented in the book. (A Book-of-the-Month Club featured alternate. No kidding.)

Related to the alphabetical and numerical is an organizing principle which we call serial structure by analogy to the overdetermining serialism that grew out of twelve-tone music. In literature, the organizing method is not as strict: a succession of similar scenes provides the ground against which any variation stands out, with the variations perhaps dictated by some scheme but perhaps not. Robert Coover's *Spanking the Maid* (1981) achieves a sense of progress within this technique, not through the illusion of passing time, but rather through variations of the emotional tone. The reader cannot consistently account for the repetition as entirely being a matter of successive days or as entirely being a matter of a character's fantasy-expectations or mental replayings of a one-time event. A similar dilemma provides the core technique for Coover's deservedly well-known story "The

Babysitter." A strict application of serial technique is found in David Lee's "Trailer" (*CR* 33:2); here the method creates an uncannily menacing atmosphere as the reader begins to suspect foul play in what has been left unsaid. Tom Beckett's "Volumes" (*CR* 33:2) achieves a remarkable expressiveness, creating within its serialism a heightened awareness of linguistic rhythms. A related technique, characteristic of one trend in the New Novel, is generative structure. A small number of initially selected elements—the generative cell—are transformed and recombined to produce or license everything in the text. For a detailed application of this principled expansion from one section to the next, see Jean Ricardou's *La Prise de Constantinople* together with his explanation of how the title, his name, and the publisher's name and emblem (i.e., all and only the items that appear on the cover of the book) generate the rest of the work.[13]

Besides these diverse external schematisms that often substitute for or supplement linear plot structure, various kinds of play with frames and levels also count among overabundance of structure.[14] The simplest case, which hardly need be considered metafictional, is the story within the story. (A recent example where the device is used prominently but not metafictionally is John Gardner's* *October Light* (1976), but this tradition stretches back through Joseph Conrad to *Hamlet* and, for that matter, the problem was Scheherazade's in *The 1001 Nights*.) Italo Calvino's *If on a winter's night a traveler* makes do with only two main levels and a bit of a third, but teases the reader with the possibilities enough that we can easily call it metafiction; the use of levels comes closer to overtness than simple overabundance. A more clearly nonstandard offshoot is the suggestion of infinite recursions and circularities (the latter can even be carried out). The interplay of mazes and mirrors of thought—the "vertiginous symmetries"—is the realm of Jorge Luis Borges' metaphysical fictions. His "The Circular Ruins" gives us three levels (with the relations of each one to the next that of reality to dream), with the suggestion that they extend infinitely in both directions.

So far, our examples of levels of framing have been stable and consistent: scenes that turn out to be part of a film some character is viewing remain exactly that, and whenever the narration emerges up or out of that particular frame, it reaches the same level each time. Or, if there are several exclusive but simultaneous frames (scenes of settings for action) as in Welch D. Everman's "Marathon" (*CR* 30:2), each remains self-contained. But this presumption can very readily be canceled, producing paradoxically mixed or inconsistent frames. The point may be to exploit the paradox directly as thematic material, as Julio Cortázar's "Continuity of Parks" turns the reader into the victim, or to have fun with it and make it overt, as in *At Swim-Two-Birds* and *Mulligan Stew*. In David Lee's "Reporter" (CR 31:2), a voice (that may be a surfacing figment of the protagonist's frenzied paranoia, but not likely) reports on the thoughts and activities of a criminal while he waits in a rented room; the story becomes disturbing only when the Reporter reaches through and violates the frame, resetting the criminal's alarm clock, unloading his gun. The levels may be inconsistent from the very first, so that there is neither paradox nor stability; see Claude Simon's *Triptych* (1973) and Alain Robbe-Grillet's *La Maison de rendez-vous*. The paradox may be not so much structural or topological (pattern of connection between levels), but a matter of contradiction between the kind of frame some level nominally has and the way it actually behaves in the text. For example, in the second section of Robbe-Grillet's *In the Labyrinth*, an etching—explicitly identified as such—is described in careful detail. Over the course of four pages, this etching slowly animates into a live scene with moving, speaking characters.

One last variation on frames and levels in interior duplication or *mise en abyme*, where some work or object described in the text seems to correspond in some way to the work in hand. In Robbe-Grillet's *Jealousy*, there are two slightly different instances of this inner duplication: the African novel passed back and forth by two of the characters which is about marital infidelities—the situation within *Jealousy* itself—and the native song, the description of whose structure seems to be trying to tell us something about the structure of the novel. *Magnetic Field(s)* (1983) by Ron Loewinsohn displays effects that are akin to both paradoxical levels and interior duplication; rather covertly, there are hidden correspondences between scenes and recurrences of language; objects pop up under varying ownership; and the people and things in a model railroad layout have a disturbing isomorphism with those in the fictively real world.

Absence or reduction of structure seems a reasonable category to hold the now familiar practice of writing in semi-disconnected short takes, which looked radical and startling when its current cycle was launched in 1968 by Jerzy Kosinski's* *Steps*. This book is more memorable than Kosinski's *The Painted Bird* (1965), which shares its bleak vision but embodies it in a conventional continuous narrative, precisely because the intensity of the experience of reading *Steps* is distilled and concentrated through this technical (metafictional) innovation of short takes.

This brand of fragmentation is still going strong. A good recent example is Renata Adler's *Speedboat* (1976). Fragmentation can happen on virtually any scale, of course, but let's resist treating it as a unified phenomenon. There seems to be a qualitative difference of effect, for example, when we reach micro-fragments—passages limited to a single sentence or just a few lines, perhaps only a word or two. The practice is endemic in the short story today and was used with devastating power by Samuel Beckett in *How It Is* (1964).

Strangely akin to this trend, though seemingly just the opposite, is William Gaddis' *J R*, 726 pages long without a single chapter break or other typographically acknowledged formal division. This in itself clearly qualifies as a reduction or absence of structure, but in addition there is something fragment-like about the way the individual live-action scenes are strung together with practically no background narration or summary. Instead of leaving vertical white space, Gaddis jump-cuts in the middle of connected prose; typically, the transition is buried in the middle of a dense paragraph and may elude the inattentive reader.

A nearly unclassifiable technique, which pops up as eccentric execution of structure, is the thoroughgoing faithful parodic imitation of some other (generally nonfiction) form. The modern fountainhead for this genre is in the mock essays of Borges, and it can claim a true world-class masterwork in Nabokov's *Pale Fire* (1962), a novel that half-pretends it's a scholarly commentary on a poem, with all the appropriate apparatus. Recent exponents include Herbert Lindenberger with *Saul's Fall: A Critical Fiction*, which rather thoroughly masquerades as a critical edition of a famous historical drama, complete with critical essays, important background materials, and an introduction; and Stanislaw Lem's* *A Perfect Vacuum* (1979)—"Perfect Reviews of Nonexistent Books." An author might include reviews of his novel *within* the novel itself, or parody reviews of his recent work. For an amusing example of the latter, see William Gaddis' *J R* for crazy capsule reviews of ridiculous books, all of whose titles are exact or imperfect anagrams of the title of Gaddis' earlier novel, *The Recognitions* (1955). This metafictional method disturbs the placid uni-level surface expected in conventional realism.

Sometimes the author seems to regard it as more prudent to describe a good idea than to try carrying it out in full. For example, Borges states: "The composition of vast books is a laborious and impoverishing extravagance. To go on for five hundred pages developing an idea whose perfect oral exposition is possible in a few minutes! A better course of procedure is to pretend that these books already exist, and then to offer a resume, a commentary."[15] For application, see the novels attributed to the eponymous character in Nabokov's *The Real Life of Sebastian Knight* (1941). A slippery and somewhat elegiac variation of this device occurs in Nabokov's *Look at the Harlequins* (1974). In place of a list of other books by the author, we read "Other Books by the Narrator." From their titles and later descriptions, we understand them to partly be confused, recombined, and inferior versions of Nabokov's own work, just as the narrator's biography is a bad imitation of the author's.

LANGUAGE AND STYLE

The key assumption of the conventional use of language in fiction is that it should serve as a neutral conduit for the content (taking content to be something besides language). It should be transparent; it should not call attention to itself and distract us from the real business of the novel (whatever that might be): noses to the grindstone, please.

Ornate or euphuistic language, as in Barth's syntactically complicated *The Sot-Weed Factor* (1960), can be counted as an overabundance or exaggeration of style—as can rhetorically vivid prose like Stanley Elkin's* in *The Franchiser* (1976), among other works, when it reaches the point of serving more for enjoyment of its surface than for communication. Another sort of exaggeration is the literalization of figurative language, and the peculiar situation where the language of a text leaks over its boundaries and begins to affect what happens in the text. Simple excess of faithfully recorded run-on (realistic) dialogue is what gave Stephen Dixon's* fiction the name superrealism.

An almost *sui generis* example that belongs here is Raymond Queneau's *Exercises in Style* (1947). The same pointless anecdote is retold 99 different ways. The notion of style used here is very broad, ranging from what everyone would accept as stylistic variation to mathematical permutations of letters. It is only almost *sui generis* because Harry Mathews' *Trial Impressions* (1977) undertakes something similar on an initial poetic text.

Presumably there's no way to achieve a complete and literal absence of language and still produce something that can be called writing. But some writers have come remarkably close. At least we can call it an absence of the usual function of language, ranging from nonsense (in the Edward Lear sense), double talk, and incantations, to extreme opacity. Nabokov (in *Ada*) and Harry Mathews have incorported passages of code in their novels. Peter Inman's *Platin* (1979) does without most levels of linguistic function, retaining only the phonetic and a bit of the lexicon (we recognize some words). It serves to point up how powerful even that little bit is: we understand that this is not just a sample of nonlanguage in general but very particularly non-English, recognizably distinct from the equivalent sort of non-French or non-German (not to mention non-Chinese, non-Djirbal, non-KiRundi, and so on). We also get wisps of meaning and proceed to weave them into our own elaborate fabrics. *Une Semaine de bonté* by Max Ernst is a work of graphic collage, largely without text except for its several title pages; yet its author presents it as a surrealistic novel. Perhaps this illustrates the extreme of fiction without language.

When the language in a work manages to convey meanings without severe opacity, yet noticeably deviates from the rules of ordinary prose, we count it as eccentric execution. The mountain visible from everywhere on the plains is *Finnegans Wake*. Subordinating the primacy of meaning to accidents of form in language, on a local, intermittent level—puns, anagrams, palindromes—is not truly unusual when you consider the accident of rhyme that has operated in poetry for centuries. Distorted words and a few portmanteaux show up in "Instuns uh apply dighdacdics" by Richard Flint (*CR* 33:2)—though the author maintains that he is just providing phonetic spellings of regional speech. For all its distortion of words, the *Wake* was remarkably respectful of normal English syntax. The notable innovator in this area was Gertrude Stein, in *Lucy Church Amiably* among other works. A recent example violating expectations both of syntax and discourse structure is James Sherry's *In Case* (1981). Beth Tashery Shannon's departures from standard language are less radical but manage to challenge assumptions in several components of language at once.[16] For *Men in Aida* (1983) David Melnick took the sound of Greek words in the first book of the *Iliad* and found sequences of English words that approximated the Greek text phonetically, while remaining roughly within correct English syntax.

A school of linguistic experimenters goes under the name Oulipo (a semi-acronym for *OUvroir de la LIttérature POtentielle*, or the workshop for potential literature—though one is tempted to hear it as a lament for Chinese poetry: Where is Li Po?).[17] Georges Perec was not the first to write a novel-length lipogram (and he cheats a bit with invented spellings), but his *La Disparition* (1969) (lipogram on *e*) and *Les Reventes* (1972) (lipogram on *a i o u*, leaving *e* as the only true vowel) are the most accomplished literary works within this special genre. *La Disparition* thematizes the notion of disappearance, missing people and objects, for the first time creating something like a reason for the lipogrammatic method. Harry Mathews, an American member of Oulipo, has been cited elsewhere in this catalogue for his linguistic and structural experimentation. Perhaps the most famous concoction from the Oulipo school is the N plus 7 rule: take an existing text, find each noun, substitute for that noun the seventh one following it in your dictionary.

MEDIUM

While this category includes language, we separated that out because of its prominence. In medium, we are dealing with all other aspects of how the text reaches the reader. Generally, this means the physical presentation of the text in a book.

The relevant convention is twofold. First of all there is a long list of standard practices, all aimed at making the medium a transparent path to the text: the book is a physical object; it is typeset or at least typed; it is printed in dark ink on more or less white paper in a legible font; it is bound in a fixed order (the *right* order); only a very limited range of things besides the text may appear on the page (page numbers, headings, printer's ornaments, and true illustrations: representations of characters or scenes from the text, treated as an adjunct and not strictly part of the work); and in principle the text could be reassembled into a single straight line, a unique string of words (the actual lines and pages being just an inevitable convenience). The second part of the convention is that none of this matters at all: so long as some reasonably standard choice is made for each aspect of the presentation, the particular choices are accidents and not even a small part of the essence of the work. A reprint publisher can change all these parameters, yet still be issuing *the same work*.

Although medium may not officially be part of a fiction, there can be ways of making it so through overabundance or overt techniques—still without violating any of the specific conventions. Any reference to page numbers, "the next chapter," and so on, is potentially metafictional.

A departure from the norm, on the other hand, automatically makes the relevant aspect of medium into a nonaccidental part of the work. A novel printed in black ink is not notably printed in black ink—but print it in purple ink and suddenly ink color becomes part of the work. Write one word after another in the usual linear manner and the novel isn't peculiarly linear—but break up the linearization with double columns, footnotes, marginalia, and so on, and the lack of linearization becomes an inherent part of the work. These simple violations of linearity are the most common kind of metafictional play on medium. See *Finnegans Wake* for marginalia; Manuel Puig's* *Kiss of the Spider Woman* (1979) for footnotes; and *Hopscotch* (discussed under "Structure" above) for alternate orders of linearization. H. C. Turk (from *Inertia*, CR 28:2) multiplies his split columns, eventually reaching six across the page.

Willie Masters' Lonesome Wife (1968) by William H. Gass* uses a variety of typefaces and miscellaneous typographic hijinks, as well as nontext markings on the page (e.g., a coffee-cup stain). Donald Barthelme went through a period, well represented in his collection *City Life* (1970), of including nonillustration graphics that had to be counted as part of the work. Each page of Raymond Federman's *Double or Nothing* is typed in its own special shape, sometimes apparently decorative or arbitrary and sometimes resonating from the text on that page. His *Voice in the Closet* (1979) is a true book-object. Each of two texts (an English "Voice in the Closet" and a French version) begins with its own front cover at opposite edges of the volume (never attaining closure with a back cover). In the center, "Echoes" by Maurice Roche is a single ribbon of continuous letters that spreads over 12 pages and leaves its negative mirror imprint on the reverse, suggesting, if superimposed, a solid block of black ink. The text of the English "Voice" consists of 20 perfectly square pages with 18 lines of 68 characters each; stressing the accidental aspect of language, this technique—which is not as noticeable as it might sound—elevates the number of letters in a word or line to the pivotal factor determining content. *Sleepers Awake* (1946) by Kenneth Patchen presents a very diverse surface, with a variety of type sizes, nonlinear layouts, and both alphabetic and geometric graphics. The interplay of text and image reaches an extreme in the extraordinary and beautiful *A Humument: A Treated Victorian Novel* (1982) by Tom Phillips. Taking the first book he could find for a threepence

(*A Human Document* by W. H. Mallock), Phillips proceeded to graphic out portions of the original text with an almost infinite variety of designs, crosshatchings, and paintings, creating in the process the character Bill Toge (from the pages originally containing "together" of "altogether") and his adventures.

Nonlinearization and eccentric binding combine in Raymond Queneau's *100,000,000,000,000 Poems* (1961). The pages are sliced into strips in such a way that ten alternative first lines lie atop one another, ten second lines, and so on. The reader is to select one choice from each group independently, and open the book so that only 14 selected lines will be showing together; they create a sonnet, correct in rhyme scheme and generally forming syntactically correct sentences.

Without stretching the point too far, we may see absence or reduction of medium in anything that renders the text unreadable or difficult to read, dating all the way back to the blank page of *Tristram Shandy*. A recent instance is a handwritten section in Frederick Ted Castle's *Anticipation*. There have also been experiments with the absence of binding: works issued as loose sheets in a box, with the implied or express directive that the reader should shuffle them. More radical reductions abandon the book itself. *Five Traditions of Art History, An Essay* and *Some Poetry Intermedia* by Dick Higgins are posters, and would surely be metafictional were they not some kind of nonfiction. Raymond Federman's *Rumor Transmissible Ad Infinitum in Either Direction* (1976) is an indubitable case of poster-fiction, which furthermore violates the unique-linearization principle. Paper can also be abandoned, as with texts incorporated into paintings, and fiction published only on-line for a computer-equipped audience. Even these still maintain an alphabetic representation of the text as words made up of letters (ultimately visual even if stored electronically). As a final step we have works represented only nonvisually, nonalphabetically. John Barth suggested that some of the stories in *Lost in the Funhouse* should be presented via sound or should be read as though they were; he even specified, for different stories, live or recorded voice, phonograph record or tape, mono or stereo. Yet these are failed ambitions since the only existence these stories have is in print. When carried out more seriously, this extreme of nonstandard medium has a difficult time remaining literature: it slides into looking like less radical cases of some other genre or art form—radio drama, performance art, conceptual art. Some conceptual art is classed with fine arts only because of the historical-biographical accident that its perpetrators were painters and sculptors; internally and formally, it shows many of the signs of literature, either drama or fiction, depending on whether the action itself or the documentation is taken as central. So let us reach out and reclaim it, with the long arm of metafiction.

NOTES

1. Alan Wilde, *Horizons of Assent: Modernism, Postmodern, and the Ironic Imagination* (Baltimore: Johns Hopkins University Press, 1981), p. 47.

2. M. Marks, conversation with the author.

3. Some of this critical neologism results from the manifestoes (more prescriptive than descriptive) of the era. See my "Men Wearing Macintoshes, the Macguffin in the Carpet, (Aunt Martha—still?—on the Stair)" in Part II of A Special Section on In/Renovative Fiction in *Chicago Review*, 33, no. 3 (Winter 1983):57–77.

4. Once techniques have become familiar departures, they are no longer innovative, but they still might be metafictional. Metafiction exploits conventions to call attention to them. Innovation does something unaccountably different. For more on the nature of innovation, see my Introduction "This Old Text/This New Text" to Part I of A Special Section on In/Renovative Fiction in *Chicago Review*, 33, no. 2 (1982):4–8.

5. Linda Hutcheon, *Narcissistic Narrative: The Metafictional Paradox* (New York: Methuen, 1984). Overt linguistic narcissism, for instance, manifests itself in at least three ways: parody of a certain style of writing; overtness as printed or written text (marginal commentary, and so on); and thematized word-play in the manner of puns, anagrams, and the like. On the overt diegetic level, the reader is made aware that he is actively creating a fictive universe as the text displays itself as narrative; this corresponds to self-consciousness as we've used the term. Hutcheon illustrates the covert diegetic level with four commonly used models: the detective story or murder mystery plot; fantasy, in which the reader is forced—not overtly asked—to create an autonomous fictive world separate from our own; game structure—codes and rules and the process of using them, as with Soller's chess board in *Drame* or Robert Coover's *The Universal Baseball Association*; and the erotic, in which the text tantalizes and seduces the reader and yet also escapes possession (LH 28–33). Hutcheon has some difficulty providing examples for her fourth category, the covertly linguistic, but finally offers puns (again) and anagrams (34).

6. Patricia Waugh lists "features typical of postmodernism," *Metafiction: The Theory and Practice of Self-Conscious Fiction* (New York: Metheun, 1984), pp. 21–22, some of which we have incorporated into our chart. We have also helped ourselves generously to "The Repertoire of Self-Consciousness," a list of devices in Brian Stonehill's 1978 Ph.D. dissertation "Art Displaying Art: Self-Consciousness in the Novels of Joyce, Nabokov, Gaddis, and Pynchon" (University of Chicago, pp. 31–34). Most of Stonehill's devices operate in the "overt self-consciousness cell."

7. A tip of the typological hat to M. Marks.

8. Henceforth the many references in the text to example fiction in the pages of the literary magazine *Chicago Review* will read *CR* vol: no.

9. A superb collection by a fine press, *Likely Stories: A Collection of Untraditional Fiction*, selected by Bruce R. McPherson (New Paltz, N.Y.: Treacle Press, 1981).

10. The phenomena of aleatory and total formulaic control, of course, go beyond

collage, for example, for *Mohawk*, Ron Silliman chose 26 words and determined their placement with a deck of cards. Randomness itself is an absence of structure. Yet, to the extent that there's some system for using random input, an external arbitrary system of chance, it is excess of structure.

While often considered opposites, aleatory and highly controlled formulaic systems defeat the sense of organic unity by substituting nonsubjectivity for the subjectivity of thematic/associational coherence. If the method of such a text is not disclosed, the reader may be unable to read the principle off the surface of the text, and the effect of either might be the same. (John Cage knows this.)

11. John Barth, *Lost in the Funhouse, Fiction for Print, Tape, Live Voice* (New York: Doubleday & Co., 1968).

12. Published by the Free Press/Macmillan Company, New York, 1971.

13. Jean Ricardou, "Birth of a Fiction," *Critical Inquiry* 4, no. 2 (Winter 1977):221–30. *La Prise de Constantinople/La Prose de Constantinople* (Paris: Les Editions de Minuit, 1965).

14. Frames and levels may be a matter of nesting various narrative perspectives on the same fictive world (e.g., *Wuthering Heights*) or of creating a new fictive world that operates on a different level of reality from the original. The latter kind more easily provides ontological play, but both are equally grounds for metafiction. Hence, the following discussion doesn't distinguish them too fastidiously. See Erving Goffman's *Frame Analysis* (New York: Harper & Row, 1974) for a thorough investigation of how this phenomenon operates in life as well as in art.

15. From the Prologue in *Ficciones* (New York: Grove Press, 1962), p. 15.

16. See "Bons" in *Chicago Review* 28, no. 2; "Nibbid-Bodies: A Nimmage" and "Black Wholes" in *CR* 30:2; and "Asilomarian Lecture" and "Satday Afternoon with a Cold. When I Lett it Out, and it Only Started Crawsing Back too thee House" in *CR* 33:2.

17. For essays and texts, see *Oulipo: La littérature potentielle (Créations Recréations Récréations)*, (Paris: Editions Gallimard, 1973). Also see Martin Gardner's illuminating discussion of Oulipo in "Mathematical Games: The Flip-Strip Sonnet, the Lipogram and Other Mad Modes of Wordplay," *Scientific American*, February 1977.

SELECTED BIBLIOGRAPHY

Primary Sources

Abish, Walter. *Alphabetical Africa*. New York: New Directions, 1974.

Acker, Kathy. *Great Expectations*. New York: Grove Press, 1983.

Adler, Renata. *Speedboat*. New York: Random House, 1985.

Barth, John. *Lost in the Funhouse*. Garden City, NY: Doubleday & Co., 1968.

———. *The Sotweed Factor*. New York: Bantam Books, Inc., 1969.

—. *Letters*. New York: G. P. Putnam's Sons, 1979.

Barthelme, Donald. *Snow White*. New York: Atheneum, 1967.

———. *City Life*. New York: Farrar, Straus & Giroux, 1970.

———. *The Dead Father*. New York: Farrar, Straus & Giroux, 1975.

———. *Sixty Stories*. New York: G. P. Putnam's Sons, 1981. Currently in print from E. P. Dutton Publishers, New York, 1982.

Beckett, Samuel. *How It Is*. Trans. from French by author. New York: Grove Press, 1964.

———. *Three Novels: Molloy, Malone Dies, The Unnamable*. Trans. from French by author and Patrick Bowles. New York: Grove Press, 1965.

———. *The Lost Ones*. Trans. from French by author. New York: Grove Press, 1972.

———. *Company*. New York: Grove Press, 1980.

———. *Ill Seen Ill Said*. Trans. from French by author. New York: Grove Press, 1981.

———. *Worstward Ho*. New York: Grove Press, 1983.

Beckett, Tom. *Dump*. San Fransisco, California: AfterHours Press, 1982.

———. *Soluble Senses Census*. Atwater, Ohio: Tonsure Press, 1984.

Berry, R. M. *Plane Geometry and Other Affairs of the Heart*. Normal, IL: Illinois State University; New York: Fiction Collective Series, 1985.

Cabrera-Infante, Guillermo. *Three Trapped Tigers*. Trans. from Cuban by Donald Gardner and Suzanne Jill Levine in collaboration with the author. New York: Harper & Row, 1971. Currently in print from Avon/Bard, New York, 1985.

Calvino, Italo. *If on a winter's night a traveler*. Trans. from Italian by William Weaver. New York: Harcourt, Brace Jovanovich, 1979.

Castle, Frederick Ted. *Anticipation*. New Paltz, NY: McPherson & Co., 1984.

Coover, Robert. *The Universal Baseball Association, Inc., J. Henry Waugh, Prop.* New York: Random House, 1968.

———. *Pricksongs and Descants*. New York: E. P. Dutton, 1969.

———. *Spanking the Maid*. New York: Grove Press, 1982.

Cortázar, Julio. *Hopscotch*. Trans. from Spanish by Gregory Rabassa. New York: Random House, 1966.

———. *Blow-Up and Other Stories* (originally titled *End of the Game and other stories*). Trans. from Spanish by Paul Blackburn. New York: Pantheon/Random, 1985.

Dixon, Stephen, *Quite Contrary. The Mary and Newt Story*. New York: Harper & Row, 1979.

———. *14 Stories*. Baltimore: Johns Hopkins University Press, 1980.

Elkin, Stanley. *The Franchiser*. New York: Farrar, Straus & Giroux, 1976. Currently available from David R. Godine, Boston, MA, 1980.

Ernst, Max. *Une Semaine de bonté*. Trans. by Stanley Appelbaum. New York: Dover Publications, 1976.

Federman, Raymond. *Double or Nothing: a real fictitious discourse*. Chicago, IL: Swallow Press, 1971.

———. *Rumour Transmissible Ad Infinitum in Either Direction* (poster). Supplement to *Sixth Assembling*, ed. by Richard Kostelanetz, Brooklyn, NY: Assembling Press, 1976.

———. *Take It or Leave It*. New York: Fiction Collective, 1976.

———. *The Voice in the Closet/La Voix Dans le Cabinet de Debarras* (plus *Echoes* by Maurice Roche). Madison, WI, Coda Press: 1979.

Gaddis, William. *The Recognitions*. New York: Harcourt, Brace and Co., 1955.

Currently available from Viking/Penguin, Contemporary American Fiction Series, New York, 1985, (corrected edition).

———. *J R*. New York: Knopf, 1975. Currently available from Viking/Penguin, Contemporary American Fiction Series, New York, 1985.

———. *Carpenter's Gothic*. New York: Elisabeth Sifton Books, Viking/Penguin, 1985.

Gass, William. *Willie Masters' Lonesome Wife*. Evanston, IL: A TriQuarterly Book, Northwestern University Press, 1968.

Gins, Madeline. *Word Rain or A Discursive Introduction to the Intimate Philosophical Investigations of G,R,E,T,A, G,A,R,B,O, It Says*. New York: Grossman Publishers, 1969.

Higgins, Dick. *Five Traditions of Art History, an Essay* (poster). Reprinted in *A Dialectic of Centuries: Notes towards a Theory of the New Arts*. New York: Printed Editions, 1978.

———. *Some Poetry Intermedia* (poster). Reprinted in *The Avant-Garde Tradition in Literature*, edited by Richard Kostelanetz. Buffalo, NY: Prometheus Books, 1982.

Horn, Richard. *Encyclopedia*. New York: Grove Press, 1969.

Inman, Peter. *Platin*. Los Angeles, CA: Sun & Moon Press, 1979.

Katz, Steve. *The Exagggerations of Peter Prince*. New York: Holt, Reinhart and Winston, 1968.

———. *Moving Parts*. New York: Fiction Collective, 1977.

Kelley, William Melvin. *Dunfords Travels Everywheres*. Garden City, NY: Doubleday & Company, Inc., 1970.

Kosinski, Jerzy. *Steps*. New York: Random House, 1968.

Lem, Stanislaw. *A Perfect Vacuum: Perfect Reviews of Nonexistent Books*. New York: Harcourt, Brace Jovanovich, 1979.

Leyner, Mark. *I Smell Esther Williams*. New York: Fiction Collective, 1983.

Lindenberger, Herbert. *Saul's Fall: A Critical Fiction*. Baltimore, MD: Johns Hopkins University Press, 1979.

Lins, Osman. *Avalovara*. Trans. from Portuguese by Gregory Rabassa. New York: Knopf, 1980. Originally published 1973.

Loewinsohn, Ron. *Magnetic Fields*. New York: Knopf, 1983.

Major, Clarence. *Reflex and Bone Structure*. New York: Fiction Collective, 1975.

———. *Emergency Exit*. New York: Fiction Collective, 1979.

Mathews, Harry. *The Conversions*. New York: Doubleday & Co., 1962.

———. *Tlooth*. New York: Doubleday & Co., 1966.

———. *The Sinking of the Odradek Stadium and Other Novels* (incl. *The Conversions* and *Tlooth*). New York: Harper & Row, Publishers, 1975. Currently available from Carcanet, New York, 1985.

———. *Selected Declarations of Dependence*. Calais, VT: Z Press, 1977.

———. *Trial Impressions*. Providence, R.I.: Burning Deck, 1977.

Mella, John. *Transformations*. Chicago, IL: Chicago Review Press, 1975.

Melnick, David. *Men in Aida*. Berkeley, CA: Tuumba Press, 1983.

Nabokov, Vladimir. *Invitation to a Beheading*. Trans. from Russian by Dmitri Nabokov and author. New York: G. P. Putnam's Sons/Capricorn Books, 1959.

————. *The Real Life of Sebastian Knight*. New York: New Directions, 1959. Originally published 1941.

————. *Pale Fire*. New York: G. P. Putnam's Sons, 1962.

————. *Ada*. New York: McGraw Hill, 1969.

————. *The Defense*. Trans. from Russian by Michael Scammell and author. New York: Capricorn Books, 1970.

————. *The Gift*. Trans. from Russian by Michael Scammell and author. New York: Capricorn Books, 1970.

————. *Look at the Harlequins!* New York: McGraw Hill, 1974.

O'Brien, Flann. *At Swim-Two-Birds*. New York: New American Library, 1976. Originally published 1939.

Patchen, Kenneth. *Sleepers Awake*. New York: Padell Book Company, 1946. Reprint: New Directions, NY, 1969.

Perec, Georges. *Les choses: a story of the sixties*. Trans. from French by Helen R. Lane. New York: Grove Press, 1967.

————. *La Disparition*. Paris, France: Editions Denoël, 1969.

————. *Les Revenentes*. Paris, France: Julliard, 1972.

Phillips, Tom. *A Humument: A Treated Victorian Novel*. New York: Thames and Hudson, 1982.

Pinget, Robert. *The Inquisitory*. Trans. by Donald Watson. New York: Grove Press, 1967.

Puig, Manuel. *Kiss of the Spider Woman*. Trans. from Spanish by Thomas Colchie. New York: Knopf, 1979.

Pynchon, Thomas. *V*. Philadelphia, PA: Lippincott, 1963.

Queneau, Raymond. *Exercises in Style*. Trans. from French by Barbara Wright. New York: New Directions, 1981.

————. *100,000,000,000,000 Poems*. Trans. by John Crombie. Kickshaws, 1983. Originally published 1961.

Ricardou, Jean. *La Prise de Constantinople*. Paris, France: Les Editions de Minuit, 1965.

Robbe-Grillet, Alain. *In the Labyrinth*. Trans. from French by Richard Howard. New York: Grove Press, 1960. (Also in *Two Novels*, Grove, NY, 1965).

————. *The Voyeur*. New York: Grove Press, 1963.

————. *Jealousy*. Trans. from French by Richard Howard. New York: Grove Press, 1959. (Also in *Two Novels*, Grove, NY, 1965).

————. *La Maison de rendez-rous*. Trans. from French by Richard Howard. New York: Grove Press, 1966. Originally published 1965.

Sarraute, Nathalie. *The Golden Fruits*. New York: George Braziller, 1964.

Sherry, James. *In Case*. Los Angeles, CA: Sun & Moon Press, 1981.

————. *Popular Fiction*. New York: Roof Books, 1985.

Silliman, Ron. *Ketjak*. San Fransisco, CA: This, 1978.

————. *Tjanting*. Berkeley, CA: The Figures, 1981.

Simon, Claude. *Triptych*. Trans. from the French by Helen R. Lane. New York: Viking Press, 1976.

Sorrentino, Gilbert. *Imaginative Qualities of Actual Things*. New York: Pantheon/Random, 1971.

————. *Mulligan Stew*. New York: Grove Press, 1979.

————. *Aberration of Starlight*. New York: Random House, 1980.

Stein, Gertrude. *Lucy Church Amiably*. New York: Something Else Press, 1969.
————. *Ida*. New York: Random House, 1941.
Sukenick, Ronald. *Out*. Chicago, IL: Swallow Press, 1973.
Sumner, Melody. *The Time Is Now*. Oakland, CA: Burning Books, 1983.

Secondary Sources

Alter, Robert. *Partial Magic: The Novel as a Self-Conscious Genre*. Berkeley, CA:
    University of California Press, 1975/1978.
Barth, John. "The Literature of Exhaustion" and "The Literature of Replenish-
    ment" reprinted in *The Friday Book*. New York: G. P. Putnam's Sons,
    1984.
Federman, Raymond. *Surfiction: Fiction Now and Tomorrow*. Chicago IL: Swallow
    Press Books, 1975. Second edition: Ohio University Press, Athens, 1981.
Gass, William. *Fiction and the Figures of Life*. New York: Knopf, 1971.
————. *Habitations of the Word*. New York: Simon and Schuster, 1985.
————. *The World within the Word*. New York: Knopf, 1978.
Hayman, David, and Elliott Anderson, eds. *In the Wake of the Wake*. Madison,
    WI: The University of Wisconsin Press, 1978. Originally *TriQuarterly 38*,
    Winter 1977.
Hutcheon, Linda. *Narcissistic Narrative: the metafictional paradox*. New York:
    Methuen, 1984.
Kellman, Steven G. *The Self-Begetting Novel*. New York: Columbia University
    Press, 1980.
McCaffery, Larry. *The Metafictional Muse: The Works of Coover, Gass and Bar-
    thelme*. Pittsburgh, PA: University of Pittsburgh Press, 1982.
Newman, Charles. *The Post-Modern Aura: The Act of Fiction in an Age of Inflation*.
    Evanston, IL: Northwestern University Press, 1985.
Scholes, Robert. *Fabulation and Metafiction*. Urbana, IL: University of Illinois
    Press, 1979.
Tanner, Tony. *City of Words: American Fiction, 1950–1970*. New York: Harper
    & Row, 1971.
Waugh, Patricia. *Metafiction: the Theory and Practice of Self-Conscious Fiction*.
    New York: Methuen, New Accents Series, 1984.

THOMAS LeCLAIR

Postmodern Mastery

Postmodernism exists. Pages of illustration are here dispensed with. After categorizing comes criticism: which are the best postmodern novels? Which writers achieve mastery? Not just mastery of innovative or postmodern methods, but also mastery of extraliterary experience such as commerce, technology, politics, and history; mastery of the reader; and mastery of new, truly contemporary modes of understanding the world, particularly the contributions of systems theory.

Mastery is a category usually excluded by both traditionalists and postmodernists. Alfred Kazin—speaking for John Gardner,* Gerald Graff, Mary McCarthy, John W. Aldridge, and other Philistines—says "our writers are weak in the legs, part of the drift instead of exercising some mastery."[1] Representing the defensive position of some experimentalists is Richard Kostelanetz* who claims "that the dynamics of artistic change invariably sabotage the masterpiece mentality."[2] The two sides have split over the fundamental issues of representation and performance, with both sides generally ignoring a set of novels published in the last decade that achieve mastery by combining illusion-breaking performance and what I'll call for now recording rather than representation. The books I have in mind are William Gaddis'* *J R* (1975), Joseph Heller's *Something Happened* (1974), Robert Coover's* *The Public Burning* (1977), Joseph McElroy's* *Lookout Cartridge* (1974), Thomas Pynchon's* *Gravity's Rainbow* (1973), John Barth's* *Letters* (1979), and Don DeLillo's* *Ratner's Star* (1976). Several have been widely praised, some have been half-read or half-heartedly read, and a couple—*Lookout Cartridge* and *Ratner's Star*—are largely unknown. Although they are different from each other in many ways, taken together they give us our most ambitious, most inventive, and best work.

In *The Pleasure of the Text* (1975), a description and manifestation of postmodern responses, Roland Barthes* says that only "the absolutely new" can create bliss. Although the seven novels mentioned above are not qualitatively and militantly and exclusively new, and although they might even be taken as the last dinosaurs of modernism, they do have the post-modern effects Barthes praises in "texts of bliss." Each "imposes a state of loss . . . discomforts (perhaps to the point of a certain boredom), un-settles the reader's historical, cultural, psychological assumptions, the con-sistency of his tastes, values, memories, brings to a crisis his relation with language."[3] To perform these negations, the texts are self-conscious and frequently self-reflexive; they sometimes seem to sacrifice or even cancel themselves as part of their deconstructive purposes. Yet they are also bulky with representation and insistent in their powers of formulation, asserting literary authority despite all of their postmodern uncertainties. Both de-constructive and reconstructive, they achieve these dual effects with quan-tity, with an art of excess.

They initially solicit the reader with traditional genre expectations and with conventional interests in character and plot. They are not experimental insults, but they do confute the expectations they encourage by eventually deforming the text with excess of one kind or another. This usually means exaggerating some fictional element, skewing proportion and propriety, creating styles that disturb the usual principles of selection, balance, and, especially, scale. *Something Happened* is probably the most solicitous and is taken the least seriously. It looks like another New York ad man's confession until Heller exceeds the demands of verisimilitude with his narrator's triviality and suspends interest in "what happened?" with frus-trating redundancy and repetition. Excessive familiarity makes newly strange a much-treated situation, as well as offering a systems-based critique of mechanistic thinking. The book is American Beckett, its narrator a sub-urban Watt whose futility is ultimately understood as a mistake in con-ceiving the world in purely cause and effect terms.

The novelists' purposes are not just literary parody, the intent of some other postmodern novels of excess such as Gilbert Sorrentino's* *Mulligan Stew* or Alexander Theroux's* *Darconville's Cat.* Parodic or distancing techniques are combined with an exhaustive knowledge of materials outside literature. Kazin claims that American realities, especially science, cripple our writers. In these novels the external world supplies new languages, new sources of metaphor and modes of attention. The writer's business is transformation of these materials, of the text as it proceeds, and of the reader, who is first solicited and then trapped or amazed or forced into an imitative form rather different from the form he entered. For example: *The Public Burning* begins as an entertainment offering what Coover says are the staples of American amusement—fact and sensationalism—but he transforms his three-ring circus into a sacrificial festival. The public burning for entertainment partakes of a public burning in Times Square. Readers whose appetites parallel the public's in the novel must recognize their own complicity.

Economic, social, political, and psychological subjects occupy the novelists of excess, but the reader is denied an integrated mid-range of experience where the interpretations offered by these disciplines would suffice. Underinformed, overloaded with information, or in the middle of paradoxes, the readers find their paradigms won't account for the data of the texts. They must find within or outside the book new ways of thinking about it and, just posssibly, the world. McElroy has said of *Gravity's Rainbow*, "it shows forth the processes of which human life is an instance."[4] It is true of Pynchon's novel, McElroy's own *Lookout Cartridge*, and the other novels of excess: a concern with processes and principles that underlie the usual explanatory disciplines. In these seven novels we have a new naturalism: a combination of microscopic attention and planetary system-making, both plenitude and abstract elegance—but without the mechanistic determinisms of nineteenth-century naturalism. It is now a naturalism of information rather than mechanism. The novels are all about communication exchanges, the relations between information and energy and forces, the methods of storing, retrieving, and using new kinds of information. Their excess presses us to read them as stores of information—as large sets of improbable signals—rather than as messages of a familiar kind. Of the seven, *Lookout Cartridge* is the most explicitly located in what McElroy calls "The great multiple field of impinging information."[5] Conceived as an imitation of an analogue computer, it compels the reader, who begins the book as a story of detection, to perform high-speed, simultaneous, and collaborative operations of mind. In a way, the computer is the model for all these novels: a collection of minute bits that, because of the size of its collection and its connections, can show us abstract patterns and relations we could not invent before.

Barth's *Letters* may be the best example of the new ecological naturalism. Its epistolary form is appropriate for information exchange, and the sequel form recycles the past into a grand new open system. Its excess of both minute facts and abstract codes has its rationale in a statement by William James which Barth quotes early in the novel: "To get enough of anything in nature, one has to take too much."[6] By including more than readers want or need, the novelist reminds them of how much is left out of the book, out of any communication exchange, and especially out of the traditional novel. The positive effect of this "too much" is an awareness of new relations and concepts to comprehend quantity and complexity. Barth's definition of plot—"the incremental perturbation of an unstable homeostatic system and its catastrophic restoration to a complexified equilibrium"[7]— along with the qualities of *Letters* mentioned earlier illustrate the degree to which Barth has been influenced by systems theory, a primary means by which all the novelists of excess understand and formulate the diffuse contemporary experience they present. Some years ago Pynchon was called "the first systems novelist." Talking with the other six, I found each had read in systems theory, or a closely allied discipline (such as anthropology or mathematics), an influence not always evident on the surface of their texts, perhaps because systems theory has an eye for all the invisible realities that channel us and make us channels, but an influence largely responsible for their originality and mastery.

Much of the early modern science that influenced modernist and postmodernist writers was a source of relativity and disorder, an extraliterary inspiration for deconstruction or what Ihab Hassan* calls in *The Right Promethean Fire* (1980) "unmaking."[8] Now systems theorists in various scientific disciplines are moving beyond the fragmentation produced by specialization and the infinite regresses of experimental sciences to propose new, reconstructive models. I can't summarize here the work of Ludwig von Bertalanffy, the initiator of general systems theory, or his more notable followers—Gregory Bateson, Kenneth Boulding, Ervin Laszlo, and Anthony Wilden—but their concern with large perspectives and new wholes makes systems thinking a literally postmodern approach to interior and exterior reality, as well as all of reality's interfaces. Some of the qualities of systems thinking that carry over into or directly influence the novels I've mentioned are as follows:

1. Acceptance of relativity, fragmentation, and the artifices of knowledge as givens;
2. Interest in new intellectual maps, the crossing of disciplines, and communication with nonspecialists;
3. A method more like that of mathematics than of the physical sciences: hypothetical, imaginative, abstract, comprehensive; and
4. A series of contrasts with mechanistic science (mechanism—systems): phenomena—relations; functions—formal properties; sequences—homologies; linearity—hierarchy, circularity; causes and effects—processes of communication and restraints; one-way relations—reciprocity; isolation—collaboration; laws—probabilities; and closed systems—ecosystems.

Describing precisely how systems thinking governs each of the novels of excess, giving them new interior processes and large outer frames, is beyond the scope of this article, though I can describe the kinds of representation and performance that characterize the surfaces of these systems-influenced novels and can illustrate how mastery of technique, external reality, system, and reader is achieved in two of the seven, *JR* and *Ratner's Star*. All the novelists of excess are dissatisfied with the book as book or, at least, with fiction that imitates the static pictorial. They want to achieve either the power of some living communication exchange with an element of reciprocity (such as the theater) or the power of formula, something more abstract, encompassing, and elegant than the book. Whatever the ultimate intention, the books are mostly "talk" or, more precisely, they are largely composed of public discourses, usually oral: the entertainment routines of *Gravity's Rainbow*, the political and media rhetoric of *The Public Burning*, the therapeutic "confessional" of *Something Happened*, the white noise of *JR*, the technologisms of *Lookout Cartridge*, the battles of scientific lingoes in *Ratner's Star*, and the private talk made public in Barth's *Letters*. Because representation has a pictorial connotation, I call the novelists' collecting a talk "recording." A traditional realistic novel—say *The Great Gatsby*—that mixes description and dialogue has a spatial perspective of background and foreground; a built-in illusion of referentiality because the dialogue is about the world described, thus making an internal model of the world itself; a commitment to proportion and balance between speech and act; and nostalgia for the pictorial whole seen at once. A novel that collects discourses—one that is made of language, as William H. Gass* insists—follows more closely the temporal nature of the speech act. Instead of perspective, we have collage; an interest in the sources and relations of languages before the referent; different kinds of proportions and scales, more true to the permutations of language itself; and a sense that succession and displacement—not the whole seen at once—are the rule of language. In order to more thoroughly combat the spatial assumptions of fictions that are reinforced by the artifact of the book (a collection of numbered spaces), the novels of excess should be recorded on tapes invisible to the auditor's eye. That way, he or she would not know how long they would last, a modification of scale impossible in print but at least suggested by the length of the excessive novels. No novel is long enough, no language large enough—these are the lessons of length.

If representation is "recording," the collection and transformation of public languages, performance is artful ventriloquism. The authors perform others' voices in these novels. The writers offer little metalanguage; conventional literary language is generally absent. The authors record, arrange, and play the role of editor, but not for the kind of first-person realism of traditional fiction. As performers, they are visible—or audible—because of the various kinds of excess they practice and because in the drama of voices they enact they do not ask that the characters who speak be accepted as persons—only as plausible mouthpieces, interesting or illustrative sources. Most of the characters in these books turn out to be linguistic habits, and so the conflicts of the novels come to be between languages or between languages and circumstances. Because the languages come from a variety of extraliterary sources, reality or, at least, its coding enters the books. The limitation of language has been a common theme in postmodern fiction; the novelist in trouble is now too hoary a metaphor for words. What the artists of excess do is take the theme out of the workshop to measure its consequences in the world of multiple languages and multiple insufficiencies.

Despite the performances of these authors, the books remain in some ways illusionistic. They are not, after all, tapes. But the representation of discourse seems closer to possibility than representation of reality, pictorially considered. The novelists also practice the anti-literary illusion that their books are out of artistic control, that what I call their excess is really excess instead of being functional extravagance. This illusion usually demands a sacrifice; the novelist may have to give up the artful sentence-making of a William Gass or Stanley Elkin.* Elkin's work offers a good contrast to the writers I mentioned here, for it, too, is excessive as he is proud to admit. But the excess is in the mid-range of literary language, in the continuous and elaborate transformation of shop-talk into metaphor. The seven novelists discussed here often sacrifice this local metaphor-making for the illusion of recording some often banal or ugly or specialized language and for the construction of large homologies. Their art is usually in arrangement rather than in sentence-to-sentence creation.

The risks of the kinds of performance discussed here—the "living" act, the breaking of illusions, the desire of public power—are summed up in Coover's little story "The Hat Act," an epigraph to excess, his own and others'. Set up on the page as stage directions for a play, the story describes a magician's acts and an audience's responses. The magician uses conventional props—hat, rabbits, beautiful assistant—and does some traditional tricks, always topping the previous trick or suffering criticism from the audience. When the magician becomes the subject as well as the performer of the acts, the recorded as well as the recorder, the entertainment becomes increasingly visceral, the acts featuring sex and pretending to accidental death and murder, the audience more and more wild in its applause. But when the magician seems to kill his lovely assistant, the audience rebels and pleads for his punishment. The magician is ushered off the stage by two men who had helped him perform the tricks. Although the audience in the story does not suspect that they have been tricked by the magician's illusionist skill into experiencing real revulsion and rage, the reader of the story sees that possibility as well as the possibilities that the magician may have exceeded the compact of what is permissible in a performance or may have exceeded his powers, actually killing his assistant and destroying himself. Urged by the audience to give an extreme performance, the artist does that and more, putting the audience through an emotional experience it does not want or does not know it wants, and risking his or her own banishment.

Readers of excessive novels may not be willing to participate in talk so distant from conventional art-speech or their own common tongue; if they do participate, they may not finally recognize the alternative system being built out of the excess. Like the audience in "The Hat Act," the reader may not see the formal control and manipulation in the performance, may not see the other meaning of "performance," a meaning not usually mentioned in the criticism of postmodernism: performance as full exploitation of the means at hand, excellence, quality, mastery. The novelists of excess balance their extrinsic performances—of others, for others—with intrinsic performance, what Barth calls "loyalty to the text,"[9] the attempt to exhaust all of its possibilities. Coover might call this execution. The other writers who have commented on their novels, including Gaddis, share this sense of loyalty to the necessity of the text, to following its demands for fulfill-ment, to making the system whole.[10] Performance in postmodernism usu-ally has the connotation of effete artifice, self-indulgence, showing off. In some shorter works of experimental fiction, it often seems so. In the novels of excess, however, performance (in its double meaning) is a means of radical communication, a risk-filled attempt to break through the haze of conventional wisdom and to ease uncertainties. Brecht's theories about the epic theater and the alienation effect correspond to the rhetoric of excess— the desire to defamiliarize the ordinary, the splitting of response to create a critical attitude, the mixture of modes, the solicitation of amazement and instruction, a concern with historical and scientific processes. These are the intents and means of the novelistic epic theaters described here.

Questions remain: is mass necessary for mastery? can mastery become masochism? These fictions are no longer than some conventional works of the same period—Larry Woiwode's *Beyond the Bedroom Wall*, John Gard-ner's* *Sunlight Dialogues*, Saul Bellow's *Humboldt's Gift*, for example. The mass of excess is a deformation of conventional proportions. This deformation—the proliferation of material within some chosen con-straints—gives at least the illusion of comprehensiveness and completion. Perhaps a narrow fullness, yet also a full commitment. Mass warrants. The massiveness of these novels also imitates the changes of scale in the practical and speculative experience of contemporary persons, their lives in the geometrical progressions that surround them, their investigations of the unimaginably remote, the magnitude of their computations and exactitude of their measurements. Multiplicity mutates; more becomes many. But large and encompassing new wholes are also being identified or invented by collaborations of the open system. In more practical terms, mass can help have effect: can make a splash in heavy commercial waters; can con-ribute to the possibility of assent in a media-land that miniaturizes thought; and can—once in a while, at great risk—transform readers, show them into a new system by which they can apprehend the world. For all the density and information of these books, I see with them, think about the world through the systems they construct. They displace other fictions less total than they. The knowledge of the world which the authors offer is often bitter or satiric, and to the extent that they rub the reader's ears in the culture's foolish talk they are masochistic, punishing as well as prom-ising, yet for all their negations the authors' assembling of grand constructs is itself an affirmation of art's morality. Committed to their constructs, the novelists are also committed to their audience. When those commitments are large-minded, the result is mastery.

Gaddis' *J R* and DeLillo's *Ratner's Star* provide two illustrative extremes of excess. Whereas *J R* is composed of an excess of the concrete, *Ratner's Star* is abstract. *J R* is familiar, fragmented, and redundant talk; *Ratner's Star* is unfamiliar in its materials, a nonrepetitive whole. *J R* is in the metonymic mode of combination and association: an excess of the local that requires the recognition of system. *Ratner's Star* is in the metaphoric mode of substitution and similarity that explicitly creates its own system. Both books are "sacrificial," *Ratner's Star* because its subject—higher mathematics—is a secret code for most readers, and *J R* because its subject—commerce in America—is an all-too-familiar code. Gaddis' vision of America is a land of excess, or quantitative values and uncontrolled bigness, a place where time, people, and language are atomized. Although Pynchon, Coover, and others share aspects of this vision, *J R*, more than any of their books, imitates what it hates, relentlessly insists that the author and the reader occupy in fiction what they inhabit in America. The excess of *J R* is its consistency; about the proliferating opportunities for the waste of American energies, the novel is itself prodigal and is composed almost entirely in the "recorded," unmediated language of waste, the gibbering jargons and double-talk in which America does its business.

In *J R* the deformation of the prose and the quantity of it turn the reader from interests in character and plot to the question: what kind of fictional system is this? To accommodate and reinforce all of the meanings of waste, Gaddis constructs *J R* as a set of nestling analogues in which a large master system is replicated by smaller systems within it. The master system is a runaway system, a term coined by Gregory Bateson and developed by Anthony Wilden in *System and Structure* (1972):

The present relationship of the industrial system and those who control it (state or private capitalism) to the biosocial environment (to me, to you, to nature, to its "resources") is known as a positive feedback or runaway relationship: the more you have, the more you get. Unlike the primary control system of nature, negative feedback, which seeks out deviation and neutralizes or transforms it, positive feedback increases the deviations. . . . In the short run, this is fine for those who invest their money at compound interest or who draw their profits from underdeveloped countries, but in nature, all runaway systems (such as a forest fire or a supernova) are inexorably controlled, in the long run, by negative feedback at a second level.[11]

This second level, Wilden goes on to say, is elaboration of a new ecological system or extinction. In mechanical or social systems that imitate the negative feedback of natural ecology, a governor is built in to trip off destructive runaway processes. In *J R*, the industrial conglomerate that reaches into every area of the world and the book is headed by Governor John

"Black Jack" Cates, whose name is appropriate in several ways. "Cates" is an archaic word meaning buy or seize; "Governor" suggests the interlocking of business and politics as well as the control of any system of growth. Cates is an ironic governor, for his obsessional drive for expanded production, organization, and control increases positive feedback—"the more you have, the more you get"—in the economic system. Temporary setbacks, changes, and threats occur, but they do not interrupt the growth of Cates' conglomerate or the increase in deviations between rich and poor, developed and undeveloped countries, the powerful few and the powerless many. In attempting to rid his system of waste, Cates reduces the chances for a natural homeostatic balancing of economic processes and accelerates toward an ultimate waste the runaway system he is supposed to be "governing."

The boy wonder of the novel, J R, forms an empire out of Cates' leftovers; it is both a small analogue of Cates' operations and a prophetic example of the eventual fate of the runaway. Wilden summarizes the consequences: "Through unlimited imposition of order and organization, it (industrial capitalism) drives the biosphere and sociosphere to disorder and disorganization. Capital thus becomes equivalent to rigidity, to bound energy, to waste."[12] To communicate these consequences fully—to both defamiliarize business and show its underlying processes—Gaddis makes his novel a runaway fictional system: a system characterized by growth through positive feedback; by fragmentation at local, personal levels; by order at high and abstract levels of organization; and by a lack of flexibility and variety. Minute trivialization and enormous power, consistent in their waste, are the proportions of the runaway and J R. Despite the assault of indeterminacy, Gaddis offers a set of ordering or reordering principles derived from systems theory. Excess is a means of local understanding and global recognition.

If J R is the extreme of performance—a long, long-playing recording of the real—*Ratner's Star* is the extreme of representation. Like J R, *Ratner's Star* is a performance of multiple voices. Most of the characters do not survive from one chapter to the next. The novel begins as a science fiction— a child prodigy is brought to a faraway setting to decode a signal from outer space—but this expectation is soon dispensed with as little Billy Twillig moves through the voices he meets. Science fiction becomes fictional science, for the novel takes as its subject and inspiration for its method the science most distant from the human mid-range. A song in the book expresses this extremity:

> But physical significance
>
> And theories vague and sure
>
> And modern relativity and empirical proclivity

All yield the abstract field

To mathematics pure.[13]

Like the materials of other large novels of the 1970s cited above, the ideas of *Ratner's Star* are diffuse, excessive in quantity and in the degree of their abstraction. But excessive to a purpose: resisting a ready-made order, they fit only the conceptual pattern that the author creates. In *Ratner's Star* this pattern is derived from the history of mathematics: characters in the novel pass through or dramatize the beginnings of mathematics in concrete experience, its 2,500 years of increasing abstraction, and the radical uncertainties of modern mathematics. To this verifiable history, DeLillo appends his own imagined epilogue in which contemporary practitioners of high abstraction circle backward to concrete forms of irrationality, thus tying what a character calls the "unsolvable knot of science and mysticism" and providing a model of Western thought as a boomerang of abstraction, a model simple in its outline but intricate with the analogues and corollaries DeLillo builds in. Difficult in its allusiveness, demanding in it abstract connections, *Ratner's Star* ultimately moves toward the elegant clarity of formula, what DeLillo calls in an interview "naked structure."[14]

Looked at from the present thicket of Gödelian undecidability, the history of mathematics assumes a mirror structure: moving away from its foundations in concrete experience toward increasing abstraction, then in the twentieth century moving backward to investigate those foundations. This, too, is the structure of *Ratner's Star*. Part I or "Adventures," subtitled "Field Experiment Number One," indirectly recounts key developments in mathematics from Mesopotamia to the late nineteenth-century set theory of George Boole and Georg Cantor. Part II or "Reflections," as its name and subtitles ("Logicon Project Minus One") suggest, is the mirror history—"Minus One" reflecting "Number One," "Logicon Project" referring to the characters' attempt to invent a characteristically modern metamathematics, rigorously logical and expressed in its own notation. The names of the mathematicians whose ideas give form to "Adventures," unmentioned in that part, are subtly, almost surreptitiously inserted into the text of "Reflections" in mirror order. The pattern of progress and regress is not just one of simple opposites. The mirror of *Ratner's Star* is curved, the end identical with the beginning. By having the novel circle back upon itself and by imposing on historical concepts his own pattern and extrapolation, DeLillo makes *Ratner's Star* an independent structure full of internal correspondences that must be understood as such before the reader can send it out to do work in the world.

Ratner's Star is a world of multiple representations but is not representational in the pictorial sense in which realistic novels are representational. The novel represents, by using their language, the concepts of dead mathematicians; it represents abstractions in abstractions, and it represents itself in its doubling. It is an abstract kind of recording. DeLillo knows and shows that in our "press to measure and delve . . . in annotated ivory tools, lengths of notched wood, in the waveguide manipulation of light and our nosings into the choreography of protons, we implicate ourselves in endless uncertainty" (p. 432). Yet, despite the boomerang fiction that he has constructed, mathematics—the system of systems—remains for DeLillo the symbol not of release but of "the will to live . . . the prolongation of order" (p. 432). Somewhere between the excess of the brutally concrete and the excess of the impossibly abstract, between *J R* and *Ratner's Star*, "At the contact line of nature and mathematical thought is where things make sense" (p. 431). There are in *Ratner's Star* the systems theorist's simultaneous recognitions: that the purest representations are inadequate; that the representations must continue to be performed and invented; and that comprehension of the world is inseparable from comprehensiveness. The novel attempts that comprehensiveness, mastery of its own form, mastery of its inspiration, and mastery of the readers who are conducted into a system they can use as a lens to see both elaborate, encompassing orders and the mystery that slips through them. They can see how humankind has not yet consumed itself. That seems to me to be the final point of postmodern mastery.

NOTES

1. Alfred Kazin, "American Writing Now," *The New Republic*, October 18, 1980, p. 29.

2. Richard Kostelanetz, "New Fiction in America" in *Surfiction*, ed. Raymond Federman (Chicago: Swallow Press, 1975), p. 86.

3. Roland Barthes, *The Pleasure of the Text*, trans. Richard Miller (New York: Hill & Wang, 1975), p. 14.

4. Joseph McElroy, "Neural Neighborhoods and Other Concrete Abstracts," *TriQuarterly* 34 (1975), 216.

5. McElroy, *Lookout Cartridge* (New York: Alfred A. Knopf, 1974), p. 465.

6. John Barth, *Letters* (New York: Putnam's, 1979), p. 82.

7. Ibid., p. 767.

8. Ihab Hassan, *The Right Promethean Fire* (Urbana: University of Illinois Press, 1980.

9. "A Dialogue: John Barth and John Hawkes" in *Anything Can Happen: Interviews with Contemporary American Novelists*, eds. Tom LeClair and Larry McCaffery (Urbana: University of Illinois Press, 1983), p. 15.

10. Thomas LeClair, "Missing Writers," *Horizon* 24 (October 1981): 52.

11. Anthony Wilden, *System and Structure* (London: Tavistock, 1972), pp. 208–209.

12. Ibid., p. 394.

13. Don DeLillo, *Ratner's Star* (New York: Alfred A. Knopf, 1976), p. 174; subsequent references in parentheses.

14. "Interview with Don DeLillo" in *Anything Can Happen*, p. 86.

SELECTED BIBLIOGRAPHY

Primary Sources

Barth, John. *Letters*. New York: G. P. Putnam's, 1979.
Coover, Robert. *The Public Burning*. New York: Viking Press, 1977.
DeLillo, Don. *Ratner's Star*. New York: Alfred A. Knopf, 1976.
Gaddis, William. *J R*. New York: Alfred A. Knopf, 1975.
Heller, Joseph. *Something Happened*. New York: Alfred A. Knopf, 1974.
McElroy, Joseph. *Lookout Cartridge*. New York: Alfred A. Knopf, 1974.
Pynchon, Thomas. *Gravity's Rainbow*. New York: Viking Press, 1973.

FRED MORAMARCO

Postmodern Poetry and Fiction: The Connective Links

The writing of poetry and the writing of fiction in contemporary America are activities as distinctive as baseball and ballet. Although this analogy may evoke certain clichés such as suggesting that fiction writers are macho types, while poets are genteel and sensitive souls, it is meant not at all in that sense. Rather, the analogy carries the idea that both ballplayers and ballet dancers require agility, grace, coordination, and other highly developed physical skills, but they display these skills in a totally different manner for almost totally different audiences. Likewise, poets and novelists share similar verbal talents but utilize those talents in strikingly different ways for almost wholly separate groups of readers. The worlds of poetry and fiction in the United States are in fact separately institutionalized with regard to publishers, university courses and academic specialties, and even many literary magazines devoted to one genre or the other, such as *Fiction International* or *The American Poetry Review*.[1]

The audiences for each of these genres are similarly segregated. The audience for poetry is very small and is generally associated with universities, libraries, and specialized bookstores where poetry readings are often scheduled at regular intervals. The sales of poetry collections in this country are miniscule. Commercial publishers keep a few books of poetry on their lists largely for the prestige associated with well-established contemporary poets and, more importantly, from an economic viewpoint, as a tax write-off. These days poets write largely for other poets, and contemporary American poetry may be quite accurately defined as that area of literary activity where the number of readers equals the number of writers. By contrast the audience for fiction is large and varied. Although new and experimental fiction writers also have difficulties publishing their work with commercial presses, the outlets for fiction, which include film and television, lead to a much wider exposure. Ask the average person on the street to name five living novelists and he or she will produce five names (even though those names are likely to be Robert Ludlum, Sidney Sheldon, Lawrence Sanders, James Michener, and Harold Robbins); ask a person to name five poets and he or she will probably be stumped after Rod McKuen. In addition, newly published fiction gets substantial attention in all the major reviewing outlets, whereas books of poetry are generally reviewed in clusters or not at all. Erica Jong, who writes both fiction and poetry, has observed that even the reviewers of the two genres seem to keep separate company. "I am always hoping," she writes in a recent collection of poetry, "that someone will recognize the poet and the novelist as two different aspects of the same soul—but alas, the genres are reviewed by two different groups of people, so no one ever seems to notice this in print."[2]

A few of our well-established novelists continue to write poetry—Jong, Joyce Carol Oates, John Updike, and Gilbert Sorrentino* (to name a highly unlikely quartet) come to mind. And some of our most highly regarded poets have tried their hand at fiction—Robert Creeley, James Dickey, John Ashbery, and the late Sylvia Plath. But for the most part, poetry and fiction in America are separate worlds, intersecting only slightly like Boolean circles of nearly separate sets. Perhaps this separation occurs because fiction is essentially a narrative art, whereas poetry is essentially a lyric art. Regardless of how arcane and experimental their methods may get, fiction writers are storytellers and aim to engage us by keeping us guessing about what happens next. Poets are more attuned to producing memorable, if not always musical, language, in brief and usually tightly controlled and contained verbal expressions. Although both poetry and fiction are literary and verbal, the act of writing a poem is so vastly different from the act of writing a novel or even a short story, that very few writers are able to develop the expansive sensibility necessary to do both.

These obvious distinctions and separations granted, it is equally true that the self-contained worlds of postmodern fiction and poetry have clear areas of thematic, formal, and stylistic convergence, because developments in the literary arts are almost always analagous. Poets, novelists, dramatists, and even essayists sharing the same cultural-historical moment are in a sense prisoners of the world view of that period, whether they are innovators who deconstruct and disassemble that world view, or traditionalists who defend and preserve it.

The poetry and fiction of postmodernism is no exception to this rule and may in fact illustrate it more clearly than any other literary period in our history. Living as we do in a period of an extraordinary revolution in communications and access to information, the artists of our time share more than ever a homogeneous cultural-historical tradition. For poets and novelists, as for all of us, it has been a period of acute psychological stress, of traumatic and unprecedented worldwide upheavals, of devastating and unrelenting social, political, economic, and even spiritual change. The postmodern period has been the age of the Cold War, assassinations, Vietnam, Watergate, the women's movement, the civil rights movement, the moon landing, and the Energy Crisis. Our litany of traumas also includes environmental destruction, Jim Jones, the Middle East, Black Power, Chicano Power, and the awesome, overbearing shadow of nuclear power. The response of the fiction writer and the poet to these consecutively unnerving events has been, in a collective sense, dualistic. That is, we have had writers in both genres whose primary attention has been directed toward the major social changes of their time—Norman Mailer, Allen Ginsberg, Adrienne Rich, and Joan Didion* are a representative sample of this group—and we have had writers who have directed their major creative energies toward revolutionizing the aesthetic conventions of their art: John Barth,* John Ashbery, Donald Barthelme,* the late Charles Olson. Many writers, like Thomas Pynchon,* Kurt Vonnegut,* Robert Coover,* and Ed Dorn have done both. This combination of social concern and aesthetic innovation characterizes the collective literary climate we call postmodernism. Its permeations and influences transcend genres, and an examination of some of the central tendencies in postmodern poetry and fiction reveals important areas of convergence.

A place to begin to examine these convergences is with the rebellious emergence of the Beat Generation in the mid–1950s. Though often regarded more as a social than a literary phenomenon, the Beats had an important impact on successive generations of writers, even though they produced little enduring literature of their own. In fact, an argument can be made to date the postmodern period from 1956, the year Allen Ginsberg published *Howl*, or from 1957, the year Jack Kerouac published *On the Road*. The work of Ginsberg in poetry and Kerouac in fiction provoked an enormous negative response from the literary establishment of their day because they shook the modernist foundations of both arts.[3] What Kerouac and Ginsberg proposed, in their separate but clearly related ways, was to reestablish the experiential self as a primary source of material for both genres. Thomas Wolfe, William Carlos Williams, and Theodore Roethke had attempted this reaffirmation earlier, but their work was, for the most part, outside the modernist aesthetic developed by T. S. Eliot, Ezra Pound, James Joyce, Wallace Stevens, and others. Countering the modernist emphasis on allusion, tradition, historicity, and ironic distancing, Kerouac and Ginsberg exploded on the literary scene with an abrupt reassertion of long-abandoned romantic tenets. Both writers included brief statements on poetics in Donald Allen's influential and widely read anthology, *The New American Poetry* (1960). These little manifestos emphasized spontaneity and speed in the compositional process in contrast to the deliberate and revisionary method of Pound and Eliot in poetry and Joyce and Hemingway in prose. Kerouac wrote "The rhythm of how you decide to 'rush' yr statement determines the rhythm of the poem, whether it is a poem in verse-separated lines, or an endless one-line poem called prose . . . (with its paragraphs)."[4] This poetry, and the form of much Beat writing, was a kind of free-flowing poetic prose characterized by cadence, repetition, and free association. Its closest analogue was the improvisational riffs of the modern jazz of the period, and Kerouac's clearest inspiration was probably the legendary jazz alto saxophonist, Charlie Parker. Ginsberg, in his statement, underscored the connection between poetry, prose, and music, as he described the method by which he composed *Howl*: "So the first line of *Howl*, 'I saw the best minds,' etc. the whole first section typed out madly in one afternoon, a huge sad comedy of wild phrasing, meaningless images for the beauty of abstract poetry of mind running along making awkward combinations like Charlie Chaplin's walk, long saxophone-like chorus lines I knew Kerouac would hear *sound* of—taking off from his own inspired prose line really a new poetry."[5] These sentiments, as well as the widely reported fact that Kerouac composed his novels on long rolls of newsprint (so as not to have to stop to change sheets of paper) over a period of nine or ten days, provoked Truman Capote's widely quoted remark, "That's not writin', that's typin'!"

Although the work of Kerouac and Ginsberg gained wide popular acceptance, writers of the late 1950s and early 1960s may have been more influenced by William Burroughs, whose work revealed a new sense of language liberated from its traditional moorings. Actually, it was Burroughs' sense of irreverence toward language and his impatience with the pretensions of literary artists generally that led him to experiment with the "cut-up" technique, creating passages of prose and poetry out of previously existing words and documents, rearranged in a collage format to produce a new literary artifact. Burroughs utilized this technique extensively in *Nova Express* (1965), *The Ticket That Exploded* (1967), and *The Soft Machine* (1966), as well as in many short pieces he published throughout the 1960s in the little magazines. Together with Brion Gysin, he developed a rather elaborate rationale for disassembling and reassembling previous literary works and documents.[6] This method, though widely regarded as ludicrous and a throwback to the Dadaist aesthetic of the early twentieth century, focused attention on the idea of the writer as a manipulator of words, on the literary artifact as an assemblage, and on the very physicality of the compositional process. Ihab Hassan has noticed an important connection between the pioneering work of Burroughs and the parodic and language-oriented direction of much postmodern fiction. Speaking generally of the work of John Barth, Thomas Pynchon, Donald Barthleme, Robert Coover, Rudolph Wurlitzer, and Ronald Sukenick*, he asks " . . . do not these authors share with Burroughs a complex desire to dissolve the world—or at least to recognize its dissolution—and to remake it as an absurd or decaying or parodic or private—and still imaginative construct?"[7]

A fourth theorist of the postmodern sensibility in America was Charles

Olson, an important figure at Black Mountain College, a haven for innovative artists and writers thoughout the 1950s. Olson's essay on projective verse appeared in *Poetry New York* in 1950 but reached a much wider
audience when it was reprinted in the Allen anthology a decade later. The
terms of Olson's literary manifesto were more academic and intellectual
than either Kerouac, Ginsberg, or Burroughs; it contained similar emphasis
on a heightened awareness of the compositional moment, and on the rapid
movement from one perception to another. Olson insisted that the literary
voice of the writer emanated from the writer's very breath and promoted
what he called "open form" and "composition by field." These were methods by which the work at hand was shaped by the writer in the very act
of composing it without preconception as to its ultimate formal structure.
He argued, citing the poet Robert Creeley, that FORM IS NEVER MORE
THAN AN EXTENSION OF CONTENT and citing the novelist and essayist
Edward Dahlberg, that ONE PERCEPTION MUST IMMEDIATELY AND DI-
RECTLY LEAD TO A FURTHER PERCEPTION.[8]

These theoretical underpinnings created a climate of intense self-
consciousness among the emerging writers of the late 1950s and early 1960s.
This self-consciousness became manifest in two almost entirely contradictory ways. One the one hand, there was a heightened focus on the writer's
ego and unconscious, a new personal psychological dimension that allowed
for the exploration of one's deepest and most private impulses in a public
forum. Following the publication of Robert Lowell's *Life Studies* in 1959,
critics became fond of using the term "confessional poetry" to describe
the intense inward direction of the verse of Lowell and his followers. The
term had connotations of sin and penance associated with the Catholic
confessional, as well as sensationalistic aspects associated with pulp magazines like *True Confessions*. A writer could now tell all in print and
unburden himself or herself of repressed guilt and compulsive neurotic or
even psychotic tendencies. This new openness extended to fiction as well
as poetry. The year 1959 was also the year that Norman Mailer published
Advertisements for Myself, an unprecedented and unclassifiable book in
which Mailer personally commented on his aspirations, his reaction to
criticism, and his fascination with violence, as he generally strutted his ego
across the literary landscape in a manner that made his personal life as
much a part of the fictional mode as the characters and personae in his
work. The term "confessional novel" emerged during this period as well
and could be applied to books like Sylvia Plath's *The Bell Jar* (1971) or
Philip Roth's *Portnoy's Complaint* (1969), which seemed barely disguised
fictional re-creations of personal traumas and which dealt with subjects
(suicide and masturbation in the case of Plath and Roth respectively) previously considered taboo.

On the other hand, a different sort of self-consciousness began to become
a prominent part of both the fiction and poetry of the period. This aspect

of a newly emerging aesthetic was a keen awareness of the writer as a
literary performer, capable of dazzling the reader with a vast assortment
of literary pyrotechnics. In a popular poem of the time, Lawrence Ferlinghetti spoke of the poet as an acrobat, impressing his audience with
"high theatrics."[9] More and more writers began to bring the reader into
the compositional process itself, allowing the reader to look, not only over
the writer's shoulder, but also into the actual workings of the creative mind
at work as it formulates one aesthetic decision after another. What Michael
Davidson has noted about the poetry of the period is equally true about
much of the fiction: namely, its tendency to present the writer "directly in
the acts of thinking and reflecting." Instead of preconceived forms that
structured writing in some traditionally sequential order, the new poetry
and fiction often seemed chaotic and random because its focus was not the
external world of reality, but rather, "the moment to moment attentions
of an inquisitive mind."[10] More and more poems and novels began to
include commentary about themselves and about the process of their coming into being. From Frank O'Hara's chronicles of individual moments in
his life which characteristically begin with a specific statement of the time
and place of composition ("It is 12:20 in New York a Friday") to A. R.
Ammons' *Tape for the Turn of the Year* (published in 1974, but written
during the winter of 1964–1965), poetry appeared to be revelling in self-
referentiality. In 1972, John Ashbery published the long and complex *Three
Poems* which seemed at once to summarize and extend this tendency.
Though called "poems," the three sections of the book—"The New Spirit,"
"The System," and "The Recital"—appear as blocks of prose. "The New
Spirit" immediately engages the question that confronts every writer in
every moment of the compositional process: what to put in the work, and
what to leave out. The poem progresses to develop as a kind of meta-
poetry—a prosaic music hovering beyond the limits of the poetic art.

In fiction, self-referentiality had become so widespread that it was widely
parodied by the very writers who practiced it. A famous example is Donald
Barthelme's *Snow White*, which includes a brief questionnaire for the reader
in the midst of it, asking for commentary on characters in the novel and
evaluations as to its success or failure: "Holding in mind all works of fiction
since the War, in all languages, how would you rate the present work, on
a scale of one to ten, so far?" And there is John Barth's beginning of "A
Life Story," which makes this self-depreciating observation: "What a dreary
way to begin a story he said to himself. . . . Another story about a writer
writing a story! Another regressus in infinitum! Who doesn't prefer art that
at least overtly imitates something other than its own processes?" But the
tour de force of self-referentiality may be Vladimir Nabokov's *Pale Fire*,
a book that turns traditional notions of fiction upside down, presenting us
a "novel" that includes a foreword, a 999-line poem in four cantos, 160

pages of commentary on the poem, and a scrupulously annotated scholarly 10-page index.

The self-consciousness of self-referential literature is the antithesis of the confessional mode because it eschews personal details in favor of a heightened awareness of the forms and processes of literary composition. By contrast to the mainstream poetry of Lowell, Plath, and others of the confessional school, or the mainstream fiction of Mailer, Roth, Bellow, and others, which clearly has its sources in actual events of major significance in the writers' lives (the war, growing up Jewish in America, a friendship with Delmore Schwartz, and so on), the "alternate" fiction and poetry of Ashbery, Olson, Barth, Barthelme, and Nabokov was remarkably impersonal. Language itself became the subject matter of much of this new work that seemed to be following the lead of the American abstract expressionist painters in taking the very materials and processes of composition as a major point of departure. Just as much abstract expressionist art was about painting and the act of painting, much of the new writing was about writing and the act of writing. At its most extreme, this widely imitated practice moves toward stripping language of any mimetic pretensions whatsoever.[11] The world described or evoked in a work of this sort is not the physical world of reality as we experience it in our daily rounds; rather, it is a world that never before existed, created by the generative properties of language itself.[12]

This sense of literature as a world apart is the position eloquently developed in the essays of William H. Gass,* which appeared throughout the 1960s and 1970s and were collected in *Fiction and the Figures of Life* (1970) and *The World Within the Word* (1978). In "Philosophy and the Form of Fiction," Gass asserted that "There are no descriptions in fiction, there are only constructions."[13] And those constructions, of course, are made purely of language. The aesthetic aim of the fiction writer, he proposed, was to create a verbal world that had an intrinsic vitality, not necessarily related to what that world revealed about reality. "It seems a country-headed thing to say," he begins an essay called "The Medium of Fiction," "that literature is language, that stories and the places and the people in them are merely made of words as chairs are made of smoothed sticks and sometimes of cloth or metal tubes."[14] Gass' observation does indeed seem obvious, but his careful examination of the implications of literature as a linguistic construct focused additional attention on the writer as a manipulator of language, a creator of verbal artifacts. In Gass' view, fiction has only a broadly metaphorical connection with actual life, and fiction writers shaped their verbal structures in a compositional field with care and the precision of poets.

The poetic fiction of John Hawkes, one of our most original and meticulous prose stylists, seems as illustrative of these views as Gass' own fiction is. In works like *The Lime Twig* (1961), *Second Skin* (1964), *The Blood Oranges* (1967), and other novels, Hawkes produces a palpably poetic prose, derived from his surrealist-symbolist aesthetic. As Eliot Berry has observed, Hawkes' "care with language, his manipulation of the novel form as if it were a poem, not only separates him from the prosaic writers of event and detail, but links him with a tradition . . . in American literature . . . one finds a number of the most original and powerful American writers at this same junction of fiction and poetry—Brockden Brown, Hawthorne, Melville and West, to cite just a few."[15] Hawkes' revival of the romance tradition, his precise and haunting evocation of the images of dream and nightmare, his fixation of the terror and poetry of violence and sexuality, make him a unique figure among the postmodern writers—our most poetic writer of prose, or our most novelistic poet.

Thus far I have been discussing primarily formal and aesthetic similarities between the poetry and fiction of the postmodern period, but there have obviously been thematic connections as well. When Allen Ginsberg wrote, "I saw the best minds of my generation destroyed by madness" as the famous opening lines of *Howl*, he hit upon the metaphor that was to preoccupy the talents of many of our most ambitious poets and novelists for several decades to come. Writing about madness, in all its variant social forms, began to dominate the literary landscape. There were various kinds of madness competing for writers' attention: the madness of the Cold War, the arms race, the racial tensions in America, the riots and assassinations of the 1960s, the emerging madness of Vietnam. And, of course, there was individual madness of nearly infinite variety as well—neurotic, psychotic, and suicidal impulses that writers in unprecedented numbers began to explore with new energy and depth. The unspoken query behind many of these explorations was, "How do we live in an insane world without going insane?" The British psychiatrist R. D. Laing probed this question in some depth and became something of a guru by suggesting that schizophrenia might be a normal and even healthy response to an insane world.[16] To be destroyed by madness came to be regarded by many of our writers as the only way to cope with the bizarre irrationality of contemporary life.

Four of the most important and influential novels of the 1960s played variations on this theme. Ken Kesey's *One Flew Over the Cuckoo's Nest* (1962), Joseph Heller's *Catch–22* (1961), Kurt Vonnegut's* *Slaughterhouse-Five* (1969), and Nabokov's *Pale Fire* (1962) all feature protagonists who are certifiably insane. Kesey's book, the most direct application of the metaphor of madness, is actually set in a mental institution and its hero is a convicted rapist. The Big Nurse, who represents stability and order in the novel, is the villain. Yossarian, Heller's protagonist, is regarded by everyone around him as crazy because he puts personal survival ahead of submission to authority. Billy Pilgrim, in Vonnegut's fiction, believes he can travel in time and to other planets. In each case, an individual's madness is an attractive alternative to the madness of the society. And Kinbote in *Pale Fire* has transfigured his dull, unappreciated life as a gay academician into his magnificent (if paranoid) existence as Charles-the-beloved, ex-ruler of Zembla.

This same preoccupation with madness virtually saturated the poetry of the early 1960s. Following the publication of Robert Lowell's *Life Studies* (1959), in which a mainstream American poet had written "My mind's not right/I myself am hell,/nobody's here," poets began to write about personal traumas in unprecedented numbers, producing a poetry of the exposed inner self, the raw nerve ends seeming to cling to the very words on the page. Lowell's work was followed by Anne Sexton's *To Bedlam and Part Way Back* (1960), which chronicled her experiences in a mental hospital; Sylvia Plath's *Ariel* (1965) revealed her persistent flirtations with suicide; and John Berryman's *The Dream Songs* (1969) exposed the tormented pysche of a very troubled man. All three of these poets took their own lives, and in retrospect their work seems appropriately to bear the collective title of one of Leroi Jones' early collections of poetry published in this same period: *Preface to a Twenty-Volume Suicide Note* (1961). Although these poets were briefly influential, the confessional wave subsided after their deaths, when it became clear that working in this mode involved considerable psychic risks.

Another area of thematic convergence between postmodern fiction and poetry was the emergence in both genres of powerful literary voices articulating the frustrations of long repressed groups in this country: blacks, gays, ethnic minorities, and women. The civil rights movement and the women's movement had divergent literary manifestations, often ignored by critics focusing exclusively on formal or stylistic matters. When Leroi Jones, a fairly well-established black poet associated with the Beat movement of the 1950s changed his name to Imamu Amari Baraka, the gesture was literarily symbolic as well as personal. Baraka became a prominent literary and political presence in America, touring the country, lecturing on campuses and elsewhere, laying the groundwork for an evolving black nationalist consciousness both in literature and in politics. Ralph Ellison's *Invisible Man*, originally published in 1952, was widely revived in the 1960s, integrated into university literature courses. And the astonishing success of Alex Haley's *Roots*, first as a novel and then as an immensely successful television mini-series, brought black literature and black history into the forefront of national awareness. Following the leads of Baraka, Ellison, Haley, and James Baldwin—black writers whose political values covered a broad spectrum—minority writers like June Jordan, Toni Morrison,* Nikki Giovanni, Gwendolyn Brooks, and many others began to reach wide audiences and achieve very wide attention. To a more limited degree, other ethnic literatures were being discovered and institutionalized in various university ethnic studies programs. Chicano and Native American literature particularly gained an important foothold in the academy, and the experience of the oppressed in America became widely accessible, at least literarily, to the majority culture.

No cultural changes in America in the 1960s and 1970s have had such a far-reaching effect as the changes that occurred in the lives of millions of American women. And few changes were more closely chronicled, both in fiction and in poetry. Poets and novelists like Adrienne Rich, Louis Glück, Carolyn Forché, Erica Jong, Joyce Carol Oates, Anne Tyler, Ursula LeGuin,* Marge Piercy, Gail Godwin, Joan Didion,* Alice Walker,* and many others, could no longer be relegated to subservient positions in the hierarchy of American literary values. Although not all these writers identified themselves as feminists, they wrote with an authority and force rarely seen before in literature by American women. Adrienne Rich perhaps best expressed the gender revolution that was occurring (and continues to occur) in American life and literature in her 1972 poem, "Diving into the Wreck," in which the wreck may be taken metaphorically as the deteriorating values of Western civilization. The diver's task is to assess the damage and find what remains salvageable.

This is the task that preoccupied the politically and socially conscious writers of the 1970s and 1980s, whether or not they belonged to a minority group: to use words to calculate the damage done by Western civilization at its exploitative and corrupt worst, and to cull from the wreckage of the 1960s some sense of the continuity of humankind. For all their formal innovations, the fiction writers and poets of the postmodern period have been, for the most part, serious critics of contemporary culture, and their books have been delineations of their particular critique of our social fabric. Whether it is Adrienne Rich offering us *A Dream of a Common Language* (1978) (in her collection of poems of that name); Thomas Pynchon relating the laws of physics to the dynamics of contemporary culture; Kurt Vonnegut pointing to the absurd contradictions inherent in a presumably Christian society with imperialistic tendencies; William Styron exploring the continuing legacy of racial hatred and the dawning of the Holocaust on an innocent American mental landscape; Allen Ginsberg proclaiming an end to the Vietnam War in "Wichita Vortex Sutra"; Joseph Heller dissecting the intricate and surreal workings of bureaucracies; John Ashbery finding the images that bespeak our collective consciousness; or John Updike exploring the fractured terrain of contemporary human relationships—the poetry and fiction of postmodernism is intimately connected to the events of its time and committed to broadly humanistic values. It is a mistake to see the generation that succeeded Pound and Eliot in poetry and Faulkner and Hemingway in fiction as merely concerned with literary rebellion and technical innovation. Their work defines, explores, and reflects back to us the continuing dilemmas and contradictions inherent in the cacophonous and otherwise indefinable American culture of the latter twentieth century.

NOTES

1. The list, of course could be greatly expanded to include *Poetry*, *Poetry Northwest*, *Concerning Poetry*, *American Poetry*, *Short Story*, *Modern Fiction Studies*, *Studies in the Novel*, and so on. There are, to be sure, many magazines that include discussion and examples of both genres.

2. Erica Jong, *Ordinary Miracles* (New York: New American Library, 1983), Preface.

3. See Norman Podhoretz, "The Know Nothing Bohemians," *Partisan Review* 25 (Spring 1958): 305–11, 313–16, 318, for the characteristic establishment response.

4. Donald Allen, *The New American Poetry, 1945-1960* (New York: Grove Press, 1960), p. 414.

5. Ibid., p. 415.

6. The collaborative work of Burroughs and Gysin has been collected and published as *The Third Mind* (New York: Viking Press, 1978).

7. Ihab Hassan, "The New Gnosticism: Speculations on an Aspect of the Postmodern Mind," *boundary 21*, no. 3 (Spring 1973), p. 565.

8. Allen, *The New American Poetry*, pp. 387–88. The caps are Olson's way of drumming something into his readers' heads.

9. Lawrence Ferlinghetti, *A Coney Island of the Mind* (New York: New Directions, 1958), p. 30.

10. Michael Davidson, "Ekphrasis and the Postmodern Painter-Poem," *Journal of Aesthetics and Art Criticism* 49, no. 1 (Fall 1983):71.

11. An extremely influential poetic work in this tradition is John Ashbery's *The Tennis Court Oath* (Middletown, Conn.: Wesleyan University Press, 1962). Drawing significantly on the work of the French surrealist Raymond Roussel, Ashbery unleashed language from its normal referential and syntactic constraints. See my extended discussion of this book in David Lehman, ed., *Beyond Amazement, New Essays on John Ashbery* (Ithaca, N.Y.: Cornell University Press, 1982), pp. 150–62.

12. The excesses of this approach are illustrated by the recent work of the language-centered writers—Ron Silliman,* Charles Bernstein,* Lyn Hejinian,* Bob Perelman, and others—who have developed a substantial theoretical basis for their work in periodicals like $L=A=N=G=U=A=G=E$ and *Poetics Journal*. Silliman, the leading theorist of the group, argues that the dominance of descriptive and narrative aspects of language in capitalistic societies turns art into a commodity that reproduces "the optical illusion of reality in capitalist thought." Almost all the language-centered writers are Marxist-oriented and seem intent on jettisoning traditional sequential and logical linguistic order in their work in favor of what Silliman calls "the new sentence," in which there is a deliberate discontinuity of narrative or descriptive movement from one sentence to the next in favor of a kind of cumulative pattern of repetition with variation and recombining of sentence elements interspersed throughout the text like an embroidered verbal tapestry. Although it is too early to tell whether this work will have any enduring value, it seems to be a consistent phase in the development of postmodern self-referentiality. The characteristic form of the language writers is the prose-poem, and in their work the merging of the poetic and fictional impulses seems almost total.

13. William Gass, *Fiction and the Figures of Life* (New York: Alfred A. Knopf, 1970), p. 17.

14. Ibid., p. 27.

15. Eliot Berry, *A Poetry of Force and Darkness, The Fiction of John Hawkes* (San Bernardino, Calif.: Borgo Press, 1979), p. 4.

16. See especially R. D. Laing, *The Divided Self* (Chicago: Quadrangle, 1960), passim.

SELECTED BIBLIOGRAPHY

Primary Sources

Allen, Donald, ed. *The New American Poetry, 1945–1960*. New York: Grove Press, 1960.

Ammons, A. R. *Tape for the Turn of the Year*. Ithaca, N.Y.: Cornell University Press, 1965.

Ashbery, John. *The Tennis Court Oath*. Middletown, Conn.: Wesleyan University Press, 1962.

———. *Three Poems*. New York: Viking Press, 1972.

Barthelme, Donald. *Snow White*. New York: Atheneum, 1967.

Berryman, John. *The Dream Songs*. New York: Farrar, Straus & Giroux, 1969.

Burroughs, William. *Nova Express*. New York: Grove Press, 1965.

———. *The Soft Machine*. New York: Grove Press, 1966.

———. *The Ticket That Exploded*. New York: Grove Press, 1967.

———, and Gysin, Brion. *The Third Mind*. New York: Viking Press, 1978.

Ellison, Ralph. *Invisible Man*. New York: Random House, 1952.

Ferlinghetti, Lawrence. *A Coney Island of the Mind*. New York: New Directions, 1958.

Gass, William. *Fiction and the Figures of Life*. New York: Alfred A. Knopf, 1970.

———. *The World Within the Word*. New York: Alfred A. Knopf, 1978.

Ginsberg, Allen. *Howl, and Other Poems*. San Francisco: City Lights, 1956.

Haley, Alex. *Roots*. Garden City, N.Y.: Doubleday, 1976.

Hawkes, John. *The Lime Twig*. Norfolk, Conn.: New Directions, 1961.

———. *Second Skin*. New York: New Directions, 1964.

———. *The Blood Oranges*. New York: New Directions, 1967.

Heller, Joseph. *Catch–22*. New York: Simon & Schuster, 1961.

Jones, Leroi (Imamu Amiri Baraka). *Preface to a Twenty-Volume Suicide Note*. New York: Totem & Corinth Books, 1961.

Kerouac, Jack. *On the Road. New York: Viking Press, 1957.*

Kesey, Ken. One Flew Over the Cuckoo's Nest. New York: Viking Press, 1962.

Laing, R. D. *The Divided Self*. Chicago: Quadrangle, 1960.

Lowell, Robert. *Life Studies*. New York: Farrar, Straus & Cudahy, 1959.

Mailer, Norman. *Advertisements for Myself*. New York: G. P. Putnam's, 1959.

Nabokov, Vladimir. *Pale Fire*. New York: G. P. Putnam's, 1962.

Plath, Sylvia. *Ariel*. New York: Harper and Row, 1965.

———. *The Bell Jar*. New York: Harper & Row, 1971.

Rich, Adrienne. *Diving into the Wreck*. New York: W. W. Norton, 1973.

————. *A Dream of a Common Language, Poems 1974–1977*. New York: W. W. Norton, 1978.
Roth, Philip. *Portnoy's Complaint*. New York: Random House, 1969.
Sexton, Anne. *To Bedlam and Part Way Back*. Boston: Houghton Mifflin, 1960.
Vonnegut, Kurt. *Slaughterhouse-Five*. New York: Delacorte Press, 1969.

MARTINA SCIOLINO

Mourning, Play, and the Forms of Fiction in Europe

There is an homology between the forms of the postmodern novels in Europe and the process of mourning. The chief formal tendencies of these works include circular systems, storylines that spiral, seemingly linear narratives that don't progress, fragmentation underlined by the multifaceted point of view, and shifts in space and time. Most postmodern novels resist closure (or conclude self-consciously, ironically). This irresolution indicates that these authors are working-through loss.

World War II erupted in a Europe beset by radical changes. During the 1920s and 1930s, the revolutionary ideas of Darwin, Marx, and Freud began to widely affect the world view of many European artists and intellectuals; with the advent of war, genocide, and atomic annihilation, writers had more reason than ever to question what had for so long been taken for granted as absolute. Advances in technology, including Einstein's relativity theory, added to this increasing decomposition of the world. Not surprisingly, the chief forms of contemporary fiction revolve around lost ideals: what was meaning, or truth, is now multifarious and temporal. The notion of identity as a unified entity is obsolete. Time is no longer perceived as a continuous, universal experience but appears relative and fragmented. As a result of advances in transportation as well as postwar revisions of boundaries between countries (and the exile of so many European writers), space has lost its traditional relationship to the novel. We can't consider all of these losses without conceding that our perceptions of reality and human nature have changed; this makes the issue of mimesis in fiction problematic. Postmodern authors don't represent the world but create fiction that is overtly subjective, narcissistic—charges commonly leveled at much postmodern literature.

The chief tendencies of postmodern European fiction are experimentation and self-consciousness. The latter seems analogous to the Freudian process of mourning. Fiction takes fiction-making as topic just as the mourning subject replaces his or her own ego temporarily for the lost love-object or idea. Hence the narcissistic impetus of contemporary texts. But the distinction between the mourning subject and the contemporary novel is an important one. The term "narcissism" must be applied to this fiction in a qualified, and almost contradictory, sense: it is other-directed. The self-conscious style of these novels prevents any created value-system within them from seeming noncreated, that is, self-evident or doctrinaire. In reminding readers that the fiction in their hands is indeed fiction, metafiction allows writers to show social responsibility by insisting that all meanings are provisional.

The notion of propaganda in literature was not an imperative one for American critics until the modern period, a gradual result of Marxist influence, American involvement in World War I, and the Depression. The Continent, however, had been more or less beset by shifts of power, for instance, from aristocratic to bourgeois control as the Industrial Revolution progressed. France, in particular, already had a tradition of viewing literature suspiciously for possible propagandistic content by the time the subject became *au courant* in the United States. Resistance to propaganda has evolved into the postmodern tendency to proceed self-consciously, insisting on its own fraudulent nature as a way of protecting the many against the one.

Experimentalism often serves this political purpose. Literary free play proceeds first of all through an acknowledgment that all of the rules of novel writing are arbitrary. There is no logocentric law that says a plot must begin by introducing X characters, developing them via rising action which puts them in predictable conflicts. By what authority? The novelistic conventions that grew in the last two centuries were largely governed by readership. This consensus was composed of the rapidly growing bourgeoisie; as the class gained power, one of their means of control was subsequently realized in the novel: in the early twentieth century, the novel presented a reality created by the desires of the governing class as *reality itself*. Avant-garde authors such as the French surrealists followed the method adopted in the other fine arts, one of using the art-object as a means of changing rather than perpetrating the viewer's perspective. Samuel Beckett, whose *oeuvre* is a cornerstone for postmodernism, seems to employ a similar method in all of his fiction. His fictional world is based on the premise that all art distorts the world. We are accustomed to exaggerations within the art-object, although conventionally these include an hyperbolization of harmoniousness, consistent psychology, or resolution, to name a few. Postmodernism suggests that these are all distortions, albeit pleasant ones. Beckett distorts in a negative manner; the cripple Malloy, the bedridden Malone: his Everyman is a diseased, disfigured vagrant who plods onward, whose speech is the victory of the will to proceed. Thus, his fiction does not stroke the reader, but rather forces the reader to consider realities outside of the bourgeois success story.

But there is humor in his fiction, comedy in the lame Malloy attempting to ride a bicycle. The sense of loss is nowhere as marked in tone as it is in Beckett's work. (It is so emphatic that critics speak of his work as a silence.) Yet, one does his work an essential disservice by failing to acknowledge the playfulness of Beckett's humor, black as it is. Similarly, the correspondence between mourning and fiction may excessively tint one's picture of the contemporary European scene. Although experimentalism in postmodern writing demonstrates the need to reconstruct values (aware all the while that these are constructs and not real), much of its experimentalism is also playful. Because there is no consensus on what reality is, what human nature is, therefore what a novel is, the writer is free to create. For instance, Italo Calvino* reacts most joyfully to the void of postmodernism. *T zero* (1969) and *Cosmicomics* (1970) immediately come to mind as some of contemporary fiction's most festive works. But again, Calvino has his political motives. One of his earlier short stories, "The Watcher," is about an Italian election day. He describes the happenings of a particular polling place, significantly housed in a public sanitarium. The protagonist, an ordinary man of modest circumstance, must collect votes from bedridden inmates. Some can't see, some can't hold a pen to sign their names on the ballot, others can't even understand the procedure. Thus, Calvino metaphorically relates the problems of the new republic in a land so recently impoverished by monarchy and fascism. In his later work, Calvino's political statements are much less overt, although they are an inseparable part of his narratives. In *If on a winter's night a traveler* (1979), the reader experiences the vertiginous shifting of fictional realities through a novel that dissolves into different ones. The search of the original novel becomes the plot, but at the heart of the mystery lies an essentially public issue: government censorship.

When those readers who have not yet acquired a taste for postmodern fiction call its playful means self-indulgent, they forget that literary free play emphasizes the imagination as the means of breaking through suppressive ideologies hidden in the discourse of the Few. In *Juan sin tierra* (1977), Juan Goytisolo unites the subject of his book, the enslavement of blacks on sugar plantations in old Spain, with one of the book's major themes, the Judeo-Christian ideology integrated within the Spanish language. Such an ideology is sustained by metaphors; these metaphors, in turn, sustain servitude. The correlation justifies Goytisolo's choice of the metafictional mode which exploits and undermines such analogies as the one that promises the slave's redemption through selfless duty to the master: the blackness of the slave will be perfected as crude sugar into the purified whiteness of the Christian soul. Goytisolo catalogues metaphors like this one throughout his novel, showing us that poetical means may also be political means, culminating with "the stunted existence of millions upon millions of human beings condemned for centuries to the ideological servitude consubstantial with your native tongue" (p.168).

Paradoxically, then, the loss of absolute meaning may provide an occasion both to mourn and to rejoice. Postmodern aesthetics is intimately connected with the view that reality is no longer a given that can be apprehended and defined by a single perspective. Within these works, we may observe the negation of omniscience—a negation that has concrete effects on the novel form. Readers became accustomed to the all-knowing, all-seeing narrator as the novel evolved in the last century. *Juan sin tierra* also treats this subject. Within the Spanish system of suppressive metaphors, God is the great plantation master in the sky. The comparison allows the earthly master to terrorize his slaves into obedience even when he isn't looking (for God always is). Omniscience within the novel is the subject of parody in Flann O'Brien's *At Swim-Two-Birds*. This book is formed as a text-within-a-text (a common postmodern technique). The story's protagonist is a writer, and most of the story is the text he's writing. Within this interior text is an author who creates a set of characters and demands that they all live under his roof so that he may keep watch over them, and insure that they relate to each other only in the ways he desires for the complications of the plot he has in mind. These characters react to his manipulation by drugging him so that the author/master spends most of the day asleep; now the characters may upset his plan. They're free to form relationships according to their own desires.

Sometimes the story-within-the-story sets up an implied analogy to the old correspondence of the microcosm to the macrocosm, a conjoining of humanistic notions and literary forms with roots in the ancients, with its full expression in the critical theory of the Renaissance. But, four centuries later, the correspondence is, of course, obsolete. Now, the relationship between microcosm and macrocosm isn't an artistic alliance as it was, for instance, in Spencer's *Defense of Poesie*, but an autism. We can view this happening particularly in Beckett whose title in the last work of his famous trilogy characterizes the idea of God as Unnameable. Language can't mediate between human and maker. This triad between God-author and author-character is also the subject of the second part of Beckett's *Stories and Texts for Nothing* (1976): the author's manipulation of the Malloy character (and his various manifestations: Malone, Watt, and so on) is analogous to the hopelessly problematic and unspeakable relationship between the author and his Author.

European literary forms are still enmeshed with the Judeo-Christian heritage. That's why the movement from monotheism to polytheism in Joyce's *Portrait* has serious ramifications within the form of the novel. Earlier writers could understand their role as omniscient author by making a comparison to God's omniscience, so that the humanistic idea of a single perspective's centrality remained intact. This notion is systematically destroyed in Michel Butor's *L'Emploi du temps*. Jaques Revel sets out on a journey through the city of Bleston. That journey, at the novel's start, will be recorded in a diary, the most personal of literary forms. However, Revel soon finds his diary, indeed, his personal view, a quite unsatisfactory way of rendering the labyrinthine, temporaneous meanings that Bleston yields. The personal view is not central. What's needed is a literary form that allows a collective view, a mode that permits heterogeneity within the world.

Jorge Luis Borges, whose influence on postmodern European fiction is immense, frequently traces the contours of the mystical experience. He typically focuses on certain philosophical phenomena that have produced theory-making since literature began (evident in the poetical myths of the ancients). In Borges' fictional realism, as in Homer, Job, and Boethius, humankind is not equal to its fate. Individual will struggles against Providence, creating fictions that are hopelessly ill-equipped to define this struggle. It's important that Borges doesn't personify the providential agency. Fate appears in his fictional world as it would seem to appear in our postmodern experience: without origin, with no source we can trace, much less re-create within the limits of grammar and diction. The Babylon lottery has always been. The Babylonians accept it as a will greater than their own. The issue of servitude reappears: "divine will" may be a trope that attempts a rendering passive of the masses and encourages the exploitation of a lesser caste. But again, predestiny isn't personified in Borges' texts; rather, he resists particular classifications and transcends cultural boundaries. Moreover, Borges treats universal questions as questions: his fiction doesn't answer but demonstrates the unanswerable. His *ficciones* are queries, myths; variations on universal mysteries.

Writer-as-Theseus, world-as-labyrinth is a motif that can be observed in the tapestry in *L'Emploi du temps*, and the minimalistic environs of Beckett: streets, pasture, forests, and sea become maze when one is crippled, at the mercy of the elemental hazards that intrude, accidentally, against the individual's will. The maze appears in one of Julio Cortázar's* short stories, as the Paris metro in "Manuscript Found in a Pocket." One may aptly describe the plot of Umberto Eco's *The Name of the Rose* (1983) as a labyrinthine journey through a monastary, through texts, through detection. The ironic use of the conventions of the detective novel is essential to the framework of Eco's tour de force—and to many other postmodern works—for it underscores the impossibility of detecting. (The novel ends on a note of uncertainty, which in turn reads back on the entire text.) Alain Robbe-Grillet's *Erasers* (1964) and Nabokov's *The Eye* (1930) also fall into this category, for they demonstrate, via their manipulations of the usual implications of the novel, the limits of human knowledge.

In Borges, the maze signifies a meticulous, thoroughly unknowable order. In "The Garden of Forking Paths," political intrigue is a subjective plot in the mind of Dr. Yu Tsun whose alliance with Germany in World War I leads him to create "an incredibly risky plan" to assassinate a British agent. But the tone of the narrative, and its imagery, are mystical. Borges traces the cosmic resonance of murder (here, not a deadly sin, but a sorry fate). Yu Tsun discovers his own fate at the same time that he discovers the lost texts of his grandfather. Posterity has left him a map of a labyrinth hidden in the pages of a story. The vertigo evoked in the reader (both Yu Tsun and myself) results from the crossing-over of fictional levels in the text. The mystery of this maze unites grandfather, grandson, and victim. Yu Tsun's motive for killing the agent is not political—he says he doesn't care at all for Germany. There is a hint of insanity within his taking of the assignment, since he is pursued by a rival, Madden. The murder has the flavor of a self-fulfilled prophecy, with its seeds sown long before Yu Tsun's birth. Borges achieves a similar vertigo in "The End" and "The South."

Postmodernism proceeds through a gradual deconstruction of humanism which includes the limits of the individual's sight and language. The book itself is the only viable ontology. Systems are arbitrary, but once adopted or created as the framework for a book, the system becomes a series of rules that must not be broken in the course of the narrative. This is the chief notion underlying the work of the Oulipo Group, a French-based group of experimental authors whose members includes Calvino, Harry Mathews,* Raymond Queneau, and George Perec. One representative work is Calvino's *Castle of Crossed Destinies* (1969), where a group of characters enter a castle and find themselves mute. In order to tell their stories to one another, they use the Tarot deck. The "teller" must employ the images on the faces of the cards, arbitrarily drawn. Similarly, Calvino must create various tales from the limited number of pictures within the Tarot. The results of this scheme have been compared, among critics of postmodern novels, to the improvisation of the jazz musician: creative freedom exists in juxtaposition to a rigorous system, the finite set of notes in the restricted pattern of melody. Perec's *Alphabets* (1976) is of this order. The author creates his text according to a system at once arbitrary and fixed (for which the book is named—a framing device that becomes a commentary on the limits of language itself). Roland Barthes* adopts this design in *A Lover's Discourse*, (1978), as does American writer Walter Abish* with *Alphabetical Africa* (1974). Marc Saporta's *Composition No. One* (1962) approaches these formal issues in a different fashion. The pages of this work are unbound and are held in a box. The reader shuffles them and creates a completely unique ordering, thus an original story. These works show us that order in the novel is at once necessary and arbitrary. Their success depends on an active reader, demanding that readers help create the text as they read. The theory is put into action because the writers resist the conventional novelistic form, forcing us to change our ways of perceiving.

One explanation for the emphasis on an essentially mathematical scheme in postmodernism is the current usurpation of industry by technology. Often, European writers exploit the control inherent in technology parlance in order to parody theory. Calvino's artificial constructions exhibit human passions and desire for symmetries and final truths while retaining a fundamental epistemologic skepticism. Again, Eco's *Rose* shares this mode because the author uses the machinery of the mystery novel as a formula. The setting of Eco's novel is a monastary, which emphasizes a turning away from the world. In addition, this retreat is renowned for its library, and as the speaker describes it, he speaks as a clerk—he expects his interlocutor to be as learned as he in the theological canon of the fifteenth century. Surprisingly, *The Name of the Rose* has enjoyed considerable commercial success in both Europe and America, which helps counter the view that postmodernism no long attempts to communicate with the average reader.

Overt didacticism is another ironic postmodern technique. Although a reader might find the excessively technical experiments within the canon as works for critics only (repeating Joyce's alleged purpose for *Ulysses*), writers like Stanislaw Lem,* Borges, and Nabokov delight in playing with intellectual chaos and mocking the usual theoretical forms (book reviews, the scientific or philosophical treatise) as a means of parodying the notion of high-brow literature. In *A Perfect Vacuum*, (1979), Lem satirizes scholarly, literary, and scientific forms. The book is a collection of critical essays on novels or technical works that don't exist. *A Perfect Vacuum* proposes to help the critic find humor in his own meaning-making, and as Borges in *Ficciones*, Lem creates a bewilderingly elaborate Chinese-box structure so common in postmodern fiction. He makes it apparent that the methodology of the intellect is comically unable to reduce the flux of the world which postmodernism views as basically a phenomenological experience. (D. M. Thomas'* *The White Hotel* should also be mentioned in this regard, for it parodies Freudian theory with similar results—experience overcomes the idea.)

The technical orientation of the Oulipo Group and others, including Beckett's minimal psychomachy, subtly emphasizes Europe's pervasive sense of loss, a kind of vacuum at the core of the postmodern mind that pulls the thinker further into his or her psyche. There's a chaos in this absence which can neither be reduced nor contained within a single intellectual matrix. Concurrently, a concern for method indicates a realization of insurmountable problematics, a deep need for order, a respect of phenomena. Metaphysical questions universal to all ages are reformulated in highly technical jargon, or a new form, but remain as enigmatic as ever.

Some of the impetus toward mocking theory surely includes a new view of the relation between man and his flesh. The notion that the body is evil has the power of centuries of conditioning, born, of course, within the Judeo-Christian trope: human beings as a hierarchy unto themselves, with baser instincts and greater inspiration. Transcending the bestial was an important aspect of literature's high purpose. Of course, through the centuries, the danger of this view was realized in the sexual repression that actuated Freud's theories. Partly in reaction to this repression, modernists such as Joyce, Proust, and Virginia Woolf boldly evoked the sensuality of experience in their books. This had an influence on literary style that is very important for writers today. *Portrait of the Artist as a Young Man* is a postmodern precedent in this sense. (One recalls that an essential conflict in the book is that between Stephen's sexual awakening and his strict Catholic upbringing. The fruition of this conflict results in the making of the writer.) Similarly, *À la recherche du temps perdu* is an archetype for the circuitous course of desire in contemporary fiction. Marcel wants to remember, but the richest moments of his past are mnemonic products of the senses, arbitrary collisions between the writer's consciousness and a cake dipped in tea, or a broken piece of pavement. These accidents bring a flood of memories and an essence irretrievable by all the tricks of the intellect. Proust's syntax is a winding path that follows the form of the essence it desires, but it never attains it, never becomes it.

The importance of sensuality to the postmodern literary experience can't be understated. For instance, Goytisolo's *Juan sin tierra*, already cited as a political-linguistic critique of slaveowning in Spain, includes a discussion of sexuality by an overt contrast of the natural freedom of the slaves (in matters of sexuality only) and the hypocritically repressed family that owns the plantation. Goytisolo's style is beautifully sensual. It seems, in his own words, born of the "symbiotic contact that draws forth from the primordial substance the life force." On the other hand, what is liberating in Beckett's work is an implied view of human nature as primitive, achieved through minimalism and frequent references to sex and excretion. Hence, Beckett frees the novel from pseudo-moralistic implications.

Freud, modern novelists, and other thinkers of the early twentieth century don't compose the whole of what created the pervasive presence of desire in the postmodern narrative. Clearly, for example, the pattern of exhaustion-creation-exhaustion, demonstrated in the structure of so many contemporary novels, corresponds to the capitalist mentality in various ways. The literature of exhaustion literally displays built-in-obsolesence. British author Ian McEwan's* work often carries a critique of capitalistic consumption. "Dead as They Come," from his collection *In Between the Sheets* (1978), is an excellent anatomy of desire, both commercial and sexual. Here a wealthy man falls in love with a clothes store manikin. He brings her home, buys her an extravagant wardrobe, and begins his life anew, inspired. He returns from work to his inanimate lover and a romantic dinner, followed by an intimate evening by the fireside. The tongue-in-cheek humor of the story is successful, especially when the man reads every possible emotion into the dummy's blank expression: love, pride, compassion, fear, and, finally, the traces of infidelity! The process of overinterpretation, the imaginative distortion of what's perceived, is a mechanism of desire. That McEwan begins the affair with a purely visual relationship between the rich man and the figure in a boutique window aptly designates desire to a primarily visual category, related to a capitalistic necessity: for where would the free market be if the consumer wasn't tempted to buy? An appeal to the sight is an efficacious method of temptation.

Now, what has all this to do with loss? Desire—whether it's consumer-oriented, sexual, or both—results from absence, or from the subject's belief that he or she lacks something. The Tel Quel movement and its novel of surfaces is related to the phenomenology of sight. This can be readily seen in *Jealousy* (1965), where Robbe-Grillet refuses to penetrate the psychological depths of the main character, rendering this obsession instead via the excessive detailing of objects in his environment (which includes, of course, his wife). With this method, the author achieves a more sophisticated demonstration of jealousy, writing how it proceeds without labeling what it is. The protagonist is convinced he'll lose his wife to another, and we receive the effect that this projected loss has on his perception.

Seeing postmodern fiction as the machinery of mourning parallels reading the same as an algebraic of desire. In both cases, a system develops out of lack. Both systems are at work in D. M. Thomas' recent novel, *Ararat* (1983), which deals with the Armenian genocide. *Ararat* opens with a character who is himself an author, an *improvisatore*. He begins the story of another author who, in turn, tells his stories. Such improvisation and the story-within-the-story frame are, as already noted, common postmodern techniques. Thomas' concern for improvisation is clear, for it is repeated throughout *Ararat*. Each author is an *improvisatore*. The novel is a subjective journey but is also firmly rooted in the reality of the horrible Armenian massacre. *Ararat* inscribes the process of mourning where the subject's consciousness revolves indefinitely around the memory of a lost object. Because the novel proceeds as a story-within-a-story, concluding with a visit to the Armenian mountain Ararat, it repeats the circular process of a mourner who works his way through grief to its cause. Thomas is also concerned here with the process of sexual desire. The story of his protagonist is told via a number of sexual affairs he has as he journeys to Armenia. Finally, Thomas' work may be classified as postmodern, for one must read it as a fabric of analogies rather than for plot or story. Thomas employs several characters alike in old age, bad health, and profession. All are proud of their crude sexuality, which Thomas contrasts with intellectual discourse within the novel's dialogue. This use of several protagonists portrays a single consciousness fragmented by its memories of a tragic past, anticipating its own individual death as it clings violently to the life force, spinning within the matrix of sexual desire.

Parallel concerns are evident in the works of Raymond Federman,* a French-born author who has been living in the United States since the 1940s. What has been said here of *Ararat* could well apply to his pseudo-biographical *The Twofold Vibration* (1982). In fact, most of his early work issues from similar content varied through meaningful changes in form. Fragmentation, cyclical progression, multiplied narrators—these are some of his variations. The content is usually an account of the speaker's past, the deportation of his family to concentration camps, a young boy's escape, a man's exile from France to America. For Federman, the story is not as important as the variations of its tellings. In his earlier work, *Double or Nothing* (1971) and *The Voice in the Closet* (1979), he fragments and decomposes his tale, even obfuscating it through typography. In *The Twofold Vibration*, the text is more readable, although it resists summation. Federman's work exemplifies the progress of postmodern fiction in Europe—an unresolved response to loss, a temporary inability to proceed until one has fully mourned existing concurrently with the need to progress—all this grounded in an explosive sexuality and an authentic appreciation for the world through the senses.

I spoke earlier of an algebraic of desire, a tendency that frequently takes the form of metonymy and metaphor. Metonymy implies a working-through time, a healing process that perhaps never ends but is part of the human condition itself. (Gabriel García Márquez's* wonderful epic *One Hundred Years of Solitude* brilliantly demonstrates this process.) Metaphor has been cited by Jean Ricardou as a "fabric of analogies" in the work of Philippe Sollers, although the notion may be extended to include all postmodern works in which seemingly unrelated objects occupy the same space. Both terms, metonymy and metaphor, find perhaps their fullest demonstration in the texts of Borges and Barthes, respectively.

Allusions to the Tower of Babel and 1001 Arabian Nights pervade Borges' work. The first defines language as governed by need, specifically the need to discover origin (Nimrod's tower was built to reach God), a journey both essential and futile. Thus, the text functions within the desire to speak the unnameable. The Arabian Nights suggests that the process of speaking may never be resolved into product (or, solution): in Arabic, "1001" means "infinite." Finally, there is an intriguing fact: the frame story of Arabian Nights pivots on disillusionment (the loss of an ideal). A sultan discovers the infidelity of his queen and harem. He kills them. He plans to remarry indefinitely. Soon, the only virgin left in his kingdom is Scheharezade. She begins telling him stories on the wedding night, foregoing the conclusion until the next day so that the sultan's curiosity about the outcome coerces him to let Scheharezade live. She's literally speaking to save her life. Bruno

Bettelheim sees this frame story—the process of storytelling—as thera-peutic, as, metaphorically, a way for the sultan to work-through his dis-illusionment. But again, the Arabic meaning of "1001" implies that this process is indefinite. Borges' frequent allusions to this ancient collection reveals his idea that storytelling doesn't work toward closure. Indeed, nearly every postmodernist writer resists it.

If one agrees that this fiction responds to absence, one may wonder if its response is generally more melancholic than mournful. The distinction is a fine one and must really be addressed in terms of particular works, which, of course, a general discussion of postmodern fiction doesn't allow. But both processes are characterized by repetition. Jacques Derrida's* much quoted phrase "repetition with a difference" seems to signify mourn-ing, which, according to Freud, differs from the repetition inherent in melancholia because it proceeds through progressive substitution. Meta-phor is a type of repetition; in the works of postmodern Europeans, met-aphor works with an infinite metonymy, as already noted, within an algebraic of desire that finds its fullest expression in the uncategorizable works of Roland Barthes.

The fragmentation prevalent in the postmodern novel causes the reader numerous problems. For instance, Peter Handke's* *The Goalie's Anxiety at the Penalty Kick* (1977) and *The Left-Handed Woman* (1978) both ob-scure the meaningful relation between cause and effect, forcing the reader into a new way of understanding, respectively, murder and divorce. One experiences a similar frustration in Cortázar's *Hopscotch* (1963) where seemingly unrelated objects occupy the same space. The "fabric of anal-ogies" which Jean Ricardou suggests underlies the work of Philippe Sollers can be viewed as the subject and the mode of Barthes' *A Lover's Discourse* (1978) where the arbitrary and rigid alphabetical organization of content stops us from a structural reading and encourages us to look for a literary mode which we traditionally reserve for poetry: metaphor. In *A Lover's Discourse*, writing is a performance space and the desired other is the audience. The act of writing is a sublimation. Speech is a way for the writer to inscribe his being (the verb) in the text. Style is a subconscious insist-ence—a nondeliberate selection of content from the "image-repertoire" (Barthes' term). This image-repertoire, in turn (and by turns), is governed by the "Demon Analogy." Barthes, of course, is fully aware of the con-notation of this original term. In the process of passionate desire, the subject is caught up in a machine that he or she cannot control. Barthes inscribes a limit *and* a freedom: because style is not a conscious develop-ment, one is free to improvise.

I would like to repeat my correlation of desire and capitalism only so I may move on, finally, to a notion that is central to all postmodern texts (whether they're American or European): alienation. As we see in Beck-ett's work, the self is split into many selves, and plenty of critics have treated the subject. Post-Holocaust writers do express splits within the self, for instance, survivor's guilt, in their fiction, but here our concern is with a more objective alienation, of the Marxist stamp, a paradigm that helps illuminate Thomas Bernhard's* *Gargoyles* (1967).

The excessive concern with language in postmodern fiction is really a traditional concern for German-speaking intellectuals inasmuch as the culture's very geography lends itself to fragmentation. Of course, the world wars caused further shifts of boundaries. German culture is not a product of geographical, socioeconomic, or political unity but a nation formed by language itself. For Thomas Bernhard, language seems a means of transcending alienation, be it personal or communal. Bernhard treats a juncture between Austria's past and present by creating a student-teacher relationship in *Gargoyles*. Three quarters of the novel presents an old, aristocratic consciousness in the lengthy monologue of Prince Sarrau who faces the obsolescence of monarchy. His twisted, suffering speech is filled with contradictions within pseudo-logical rhetoric, rendering a sad irony within the novel. His captive audience is a young man, significantly a student, who perhaps represents Austria's nebulous future. Because Bernhard doesn't describe the young man's reaction to the prince's speech, we don't really know the purpose of this interior narrative. (Again, we see the postmodern resistence to closure.)

The novel begins with this student's initiation to the Austrian countryside which he had left to attend a university. His father, a doctor in a poor province, receives his son from school and intends to further his education. There follows a series of visits to the homes of exploited laborers, all of which include illness, death, and frequent allusions to insanity. Their final stop is the castle of Prince Sarrau, where the theme of insanity reaches a climax. Bernhard here continually contrasts the old aristocratic order with the industrial order, supporting a belief that progress hasn't actually improved the condition of Austria's people. Perhaps we don't know how the student responds to the dark lesson, for Bernhard doesn't know how Austria will work-through industrialization. The obscure geographical feature of the gorge (which leads from the town to the castle where the prince's monologue ends the book) is a central image in the text. This gorge becomes synecdochic, representing Austria's unknowable future as well as alienation both public and private. The process re-created here is seen in the novel's form which moves from a topographical journey to the meanderings of a seeking consciousness. The final monologue evokes an infinite Hamletesque soliloquy precariously set on the edge of a precipice.

Postmodern men and women live in the middle of a circle, a zero where full recourse into the past or present is impossible. What characterizes such a moment is a hesitation not unlike Hamlet's. One can move neither forward nor backward: history can't be trusted, for like the ghost of Hamlet's father, it may be a fabrication and an evil one at that (i.e., propagandistic).

And, if the past is untrustworthy, the possibly apocalyptic future, unknowable in the first place, is doubly so. But what to do in the interim? Doodle in the margins? Unlike what we usually think of as virtuosity, such doodlings, such paraliterary gestures, aren't made for their grandiloquence alone. Like Barthes' wrestlers, postmodern authors show on the page *a series of signs that create their own meaning*. The analogy between Denmark's state and Hamlet's mind still holds for those writing in Europe. Postmodern fiction substitutes a new referent, new references where humanism has failed it: its evolving self, the ability for the self to evolve to meet the demands of a postwar era, the joy of the visceral. By exploiting arbitrary or overly complicated order as Lem in his pseudo-critical works, Márquez in *One Hundred Years of Solitude*, Robbe-Grillet in *Jealousy*, and Eco in *Rose*, writers emphasize the process of creation, juxtaposing the necessity to proceed despite an uncertain source and obscure fate. Such is the theme of Beckett's *Malone Dies:* one lives, one speaks. One speaks, one lives.

SELECTED BIBLIOGRAPHY

Primary Sources (*European fiction available in English translation.*)

Barthes, Roland. *The Pleasure of the Text*. Trans. Richard Miller. New York: Hill & Wang, 1975.
———. *A Lover's Discourse*. Trans. Richard Howard. New York: Hill & Wang, 1978.
Beckett, Samuel. *Malone Dies*. New York: Grove Press, 1956.
———. *The Unnameable*. New York: Grove Press, 1958.
———. *Molloy*. New York: Grove Press, 1965.
———. *Stories and Texts for Nothing*. New York: Grove Press, 1967.
Borges, J. L. *Ficciones*. New York: Grove Press, 1962.
Calvino, Italo. *t zero*. Trans. William Weaver. New York: Harcourt, Brace & World, 1969.
———. *Cosmicomics*. Trans. William Weaver. New York: Collier, 1970.
———. *If on a Winter's Night a Traveler*. Trans. William Weaver. New York: Harcourt Brace Jovanovich, 1979.
Eco, Umberto. *The Name of the Rose*. Trans. William Weaver. San Diego: Harcourt Brace Jovanovich, 1983.
Federman, Raymond. *Double or Nothing*. Chicago: Swallow Press, 1971.
———. *Take It or Leave It*. New York: Fiction Collective, 1976.
———. *The Voice in the Closet*. Madison, Wis.: Coda, 1979.
———. *The Twofold Vibration*. Bloomington: Indiana University Press, 1982.
Grass, Günter. *The Tin Drum*. Trans. Ralph Manheim. New York: Pantheon Books, 1963.
———. *Dog Years*. Trans. Ralph Manheim. New York: Harcourt, Brace & World, 1965.

————. *The Meeting at Telgte*. Trans. Ralph Manheim. New York: Harcourt Brace Jovanovich, 1981.

Goytisolo, Juan. *Juan sin tierra*. New York: Viking Press, 1977.

Handke, Peter. *The Goalie's Anxiety at the Penalty Kick*. Trans. Michael Roloff. New York: Farrar, Straus & Giroux, 1977.

————. *The Left-Handed Woman*. Trans. Ralph Manheim. New York: Farrar, Straus & Giroux, 1978.

Lem, Stanislaw. *A Perfect Vacuum*. Trans. Michael Mandel. New York: Harcourt Brace, 1979.

McEwan, Ian. *In Between the Sheets*. New York: Simon & Schuster, 1978.

O'Brien, Flann. *At Swim-Two-Birds*. London: Walker and Company, 1939.

Perec, George. *Alphabets*. Paris: Galiée, 1976.

Ricardou, Jean. "Writing Between the Lines." In *Surfiction*. (Ohio: Swallow Press Books, 1975).

Robbe-Grillet, Alain. *The Erasers*. New York: Grove Press, 1964.

————. *Jealousy*. New York: Grove Press, 1965.

RON SILLIMAN

New Prose, New Prose Poem

Genres bedevil literature, even as they increase writing's accessibility to a public reluctant to embark on any reading that is not immediately cozily familiar. The rise of the novel, which accompanied the "descent" of literacy onto the masses, was itself an index of just how thinly spread the capacity to tease meanings out of written signs would be. Even today, according to figures derived from the 1980 census, 21.7 percent of all adult Americans are functionally illiterate.[1] And the skill with which reading proceeds beyond the bare minimum is hardly uniform. From the other side, as readers, even writers are aware of the difficult negotiation that occurs at the start of a given text, and of how often this is the moment at which the project is abandoned. Genres, by focusing and fixing expectations, lower the performance anxiety of the reader, allowing works to be consumed.

This common enough psychological process is reinforced throughout the social structures that envelop writing. Publishers, even before the producers of Hollywood films or prime-time television, understood the market value of imitations. And that performance anxiety (sometimes, when blame is shifted onto the text, referred to as difficulty) could be a more powerful impediment to a sale than price. The evolution of sci-fi cover art signals an attempt on the part of designers and publishers alike to pre-assure prospective readers that one can indeed tell the book by its packaging.

In a more subtle fashion perhaps, the categorical divisions set forward by libraries and bookstores are no less complicit. If all possible texts were arranged simply by the alphabetical sequence of authors and titles (or, as in one private collection in New York, by color of cover), the responsibility placed on the potential reader would be immense. To choose the latest compendium of Garfield comics would then be perceptible as a rejection of Aristotle and Louis Zukofsky alike.

The administrative necessity of developing curricula would appear to put literature departments into this same business of converting the sum of all published texts into an orderly sequence of characteristic types. This is not to suggest that pattern recognition is unimportant (or wrong) in the consumption of writing. Shakespeare's plays do share more than just the fact of staging, and authors, even as they produce their works in isolation, invariably position texts (i.e., select distinctive features) with regard to their own individual understanding of this group behavior called literature.

Which is why genres bedevil it. Literature in this sense is always an abstraction. The process of learning to read itself is significantly one of coming to recognize such distinctions as might exist between, say, exposition and the fictive. By virtue of their own literacy, writers are never free to compose unaware of the options that might be available. These alternatives, which preexist any given act of writing (and which will differ from moment to moment, and place to place, within history), track the emerging text just as certainly as educational tracks predetermine which student will go to Stanford and which to San Quentin. Genres form a kind of prior restraint, segmenting the real into the discrete. In the same moment that the devices which yield identifiability relieve authors of certain decisions and responsibilities, they strip them also of the freedom inherent in responsibility itself.

This problematic is nowhere more evident than in the breach between fiction and verse, the terrain of what has traditionally been conceived of as the prose poem, an entity or genre whose name alone suggests a bastardized, hybrid existence. Increasingly within the past decade texts have appeared, often written by persons with established reputations as poets, which are in prose and may or may not be fiction. To say that they are in prose is only to indicate the existence of a right-hand margin, and that the sentence (or something like the sentence) and not the verse line is the predominant compositional unit. To say that they might be fiction is only to say that the bulk of these writings do not visibly partake of the conventions that have come to be associated with the prose poem in America. Several of these works, such as Lyn Hejinian's* *My Life* (1980), James Sherry's *In Case* (1981), or Clark Coolidge's *Mine: The One That Enters the Stories* (1982), are the length of novels. In fact, Coolidge has referred to *Mine* as such, and this is also how Hejinian's publisher lists *My Life* in the catalog.

The confusion that has attended this development in writing is considerable and ironically enough has served to erase still further any clear sense of margin between these two domains of literature. A writer who conceives of her work in terms of the novel, Kathy Acker,* finds an excerpt of her *Great Expectations* (1984) included in a sampling of language poetry in the French journal *Change*. The first work in a recent *Chicago Review* devoted to new fiction is a piece by Sherry. A writer who has made extensive use of the story form, Carla Harryman, is, by virtue of where she has published, almost always identified in print as a poet.

This obliteration of generic distinction is neither restricted to the border between poetry and fiction, nor is it entirely new. "Realism" by Steven Benson, which appeared in a collection of poetry by that name in *Ironwood*, was composed originally as a theoretical statement for use by Hejinian in a talk. The title piece of David Bromige's *My Poetry* (1980) is in the form of an essay, a mode that had it been written by Jorge Luis Borges, would have been taken as fiction. Yet Borges, Kafka, and Julio Cortázar* all have short works included in Michael Benedikt's *The Prose Poem: An International Anthology* (1980), although no evidence exists to support a thesis that these writings were intended as poems. Although Benedikt's book focuses heavily on what might be considered the conventional prose poem, excluding, for example, Gertrude Stein's *Tender Buttons* and William Carlos Williams' *Kora in Hell: Improvisations* (both classic texts that were written with a conscious, although not imitative, relation to the French prose poem in mind), he does include a section of Lautréamont's *Maldoror*, a 200-page work that owes far more to gothic novels such as *Melmoth the Wanderer* than it does the writing of Aloysius Bertrand or Charles Baudelaire.

To date, poet and critic Michael Davidson has offered the most articulate analysis of this situation. Between poetry and fiction in America there have come to exist not one, but two distinct genres: the conventionalized prose poem and this more recent work which he has called the new prose or (more descriptively, if less felicitously) non- or intergeneric prose.

The conventional prose poem of Robert Bly, James Wright or W. S. Merwin is scenic; it projects a *paysage moralise*, a landscape upon which is grafted a series of psychological speculations. However desultory the pattern of speculations, this prose depends upon some contingency between all elements of the landscape and the discourse which surrounds it. Disjunctions at the level of the sentence are expressive; they dramatize the fragmented emotional state of the author.[2]

Davidson is correct to identify the primary convention of these poets, whose work in the 1960s first brought sustained American attention to the prose poem fully a century after its arrival in France, as that mainstay of Victorian verse, the dramatic monologue. They were essentially a band of maverick academics who rebelled against the metrics-centered, sonnet-oriented devices that dominated that tendency via Robert Lowell and Richard Wilbur in the 1950s. Their solution was, through prose, to rehabilitate a genre that had fallen into disuse. The wider prosodic possibilities of a sentence no longer fixed to an a priori measure enabled their writing to assume voices ranging from the self-pityingly prosaic working stiff (Wright, Ignatow) to the mystical astonishments of an openly spiritual poetics (Bly, Merwin). Furthermore, by identifying their work with an historic European tradition, these writers were able to claim an internationalist prestige for their poetics that would have been difficult to duplicate had they declared themselves the sons of Robert Browning.

In spite of their staking out the term "prose poem," there is little reason to equate the work of Bly et al. with the European, and particularly the French, tradition first identified by Baudelaire. In his dedication of *Paris Spleen* (1947 [1869]) to Arsène Houssaye,

the miracle of a poetic prose, musical, without rhythm and without rhyme, supple enough and rugged enough to adapt itself to the lyrical impulses of the soul, the undulations of reverie, the jibes of conscience.[3]

is said to have occurred in response to Alyosious Bertrand's *Gaspard de la Nuit*—a novel. What distinguishes Bertrand's book is the absence of a frame story (Baudelaire, of his own work, writes, "I do not keep the reader's restive mind hanging in suspense on the threads of an interminable and superfluous plot"[4]): it is more precisely a collection of short pieces unified through the narrating presence of Gaspard, some secondary characters, and its setting in ancient Flanders. Parallel in time of composition to the mysteries of Poe, Bertrand's work anticipates both the short story and the poem in prose.

Inseparable from the history of fiction at its moment of origin, Baudelaire's *Spleen* also evidences a fundamentally anti-generic impulse:

From the very beginning I perceived that I was not only far from my mysterious and brilliant model, but was, indeed, doing something (if it can be called *something*) singularly different, an accident which any one else would glory in, no doubt, but which can only deeply humiliate a mind convinced that the greatest honor for a poet is to succeed in doing exactly what he set out to do.[5]

Ironic wit and false modesty aside, the point is well taken. Can the prose poem be called *something*, or does its existence depend exactly on this process of being written *away from* models and categories? Baudelaire's own verse, centered as heavily as it was on the use of closed forms, rhyme, meter, and other devices of symmetry, may have made his sense of the distance between the two possibilities seem especially large. (Indeed, that distance may have been what made it feasible to imagine a middle path at all.) Yet, the writing of later French prose poets, such as Arthur Rimbaud, Max Jacob, and Francis Ponge, authors as different in temperament as they were in time, also suggests that a transgeneric drive is at least as defining an element as the use of sentences and paragraphs.

Although both Rimbaud and Ponge had far greater range and control over their materials than Picasso's friend Jacob—Ponge's "Fauna and Flora" is sometimes cited as the apotheosis of the French prose poem—it was *The Dice Cup* that ultimately popularized the form in Europe, with Jacob's preface to the 1916 edition making a singular attempt to actually set down some governing principles. More telling than any position taken, however, is the crankiness of this essay. In the name of classicism, he dismisses *all* of his predecessors. He writes, "A page of prose isn't a prose poem, even when it frames two or three lucky finds. . . . The poem is a constructed object and not a jewelry store window. Rimbaud is a jewelry store window, he's not the jewel: the prose poem is a jewel."[6] Yet he offers a work entitled "Poem Lacking Unity" and "The Cock and the Pearl," a long collection of discrete paragraphs, not unlike a prose anticipation of Robert Creeley's *Pieces* (1969). The poem counters directly Jacob's main thesis, that the prose poem, like all art, "is only style," and that "one recognizes that a work has style if it gives the sensation of being self-enclosed" (p. 8).

If Jacob's prescription for the formal constitution of a prose poem serves only to reveal an anti-prescriptive nature, his works themselves play an even greater role in the historic evolution of what still might not be a genre: the model of the sentence, for the first time, is derived from the prose, and not the verse, side of the equation.[7] Thus, into the space first opened by Baudelaire a half century earlier, Jacob triggers a dynamic that will lead eventually to the *recit*, to the text that is itself first and that may or may not bear a significant relation to an identifiable convention, as with the work of Edmond Jabès.

The turn toward prose in French poetry, which marked the onset of modernism there, was not duplicated in England or the United States largely because it had been preempted by another compelling model of postclassical discourse—speech. In this sense, the English-language equivalent to Baudelaire's dedication to Houssaye would be Wordsworth's preface to the second edition of *Lyrical Ballads*. In fact, the term that Wordsworth chooses to identify the plainspeaking of the common person, his paradigm for direct communication, is prose. Six decades before the publication of *Paris Spleen*, he writes:

it has been shown that the language of Prose may yet be well adapted to Poetry; and it was previously asserted, that a large portion of the language of every good poem can in no respect differ from that of good Prose. We will go further. It may be safely affirmed, that there neither is, nor can be, any *essential* difference between the language of prose and metrical composition.[8]

Incorporating prose style into verse formats reverses the dynamics of the prose poem while retaining its basic components. This same strategy still dominates conventional Anglo-American poetry 183 years later. And the counter-poetics, sometimes referred to as the Pound-Williams-New American tradition, which evolved in opposition to this increasingly academic verse, can likewise be read as a dispute over emphasis within the same framework put forward by Wordsworth. Rather than insert prose, a sense of sentence structure derived from Latin grammar and the advent of writing, into predetermined stanzaic patterns, these more modernist poets sought to develop poetic forms that accurately represented the paratactic, as distinct from syntactic, orders of the speech chain.

It was from within this oppositional poetics that the new prose, or prose poem, appeared. By equating the free verse line with the quantity of speech that could occur between two pauses for breath, Charles Olson in 1950 made available an enormously refined system for scoring the habits of dialect and idiolect on the printed page. Both transcending and codifying that which had been merely intuitive in the poetry of William Carlos Williams, Olson's breakthrough in "Projective Verse" gave rise to a generation of brilliant speech transcriptionists, including Creeley, Denise Levertov, Robert Duncan, LeRoi Jones, Ed Dorn, Paul Blackburn, Lew Welch, Philip Whalen, Joanne Kyger, and Gary Snyder.

Already inscribed within this achievement of a genuinely speech-based poetics were the terms of its demise. On one level, the work of the first wave of projectivists amounted to a sketching out of a possible linguistic atlas of the United States. Would younger writers be content merely to fill in the missing regional variations? Furthermore, once an adequate depiction of an individual's speech was possible, the limits this placed on what could then be written became clear. One could record little daily events, the sort of diaristic occasional verse that is often found in the work of Blackburn, Whalen, or Welch. Or one could construct a persona and compose, from that perspective, a dramatic monologue. Such an option is taken seriously (at least at the outset) in Olson's *Maximus* (1960), parodied in Dorn's *Slinger* (1968) and carried out in the name of autobiography by Clayton Eshleman. Not only does either alternative lead circuitously back to the resurrection of a previously discarded genre, but also both depend on the poet adopting a psychology of the person as an essentially unified subject, one capable of knowing who speaks (and, equally, who is spoken) with the utterance of the word "I." It is worth noting that Olson, in *Maximus*, and Creeley, following a critique of language he derived from the poetry of Louis Zukofsky, systematically subvert and attack that notion of the subject, and that not one of the surviving projectivists listed above can now be said to be practicing a specifically speech-based poetics.

It was not until the first issue of *This* magazine in 1971 that a poet, Robert Grenier, would "for our time proclaim an abhorrence of 'speech' designed as was (Williams') castigation of 'the sonnet' to rid us, as creators of the world, from reiteration of the past dragged on in formal habit. I HATE SPEECH".[9] From that moment, the theoretical and historical distance to the publication of Clark Coolidge's "prosoid," "Karstarts," in the same magazine four issues later is practically nil. Coolidge's earlier works had typically made use of poetic devices such as line and stanza, into which lists of words studiously void of any syntax had been inserted. In "Karstarts" syntax enters in, but not as a stepping stone toward some narrative or expository whole:

The cave without a ceiling, blouses without shirts tied by Julie Harris. An internally organized ceiling closed to the public. Nobody, push-pull, takes the blouses for the breasts. Some pulled tight so pissed off. I know the idea that comes next: blouses for breasts (Wittgenstein). Julie Harris without shirts breasts tied tight with shirts without shapes no thought of the women who own them. Probably the landgrubbers who don't even live around here. Breasts without definition as bodies of thought. Alphabet blouses. The thought of ceilings and their word equivalents. Nobody home.

Some blouses means the breasts invested in them. Peer in vague windows a ceiling goes on in. Try next house. The caverns in the bodies of thought of the women who define them (Julie Harris). The shape of Julie Harris' breasts studying Wittgenstein. The thoughts of women a little ways in caves. See-thru photographs of marble ceilings. A page, pushpull, nobody finishes, tied in black. Around in back would have been where this is. The which idea.[10]

Although "Karstarts" may have been the first prose text to be perceptible to poetry readers as of another genre, it was neither without kin nor precedent. During this same period, Grenier was composing a box (not a book) of 500 five by eight inch cards, whose texts were sometimes only two or three words long and which never opted for the form of the paragraph, but which he entitled *Sentences*.[11] David Bromige published a collection called *Tight Corners & What's Around Them* (1974), in which the "tight corners" were sequences of short prose works which, while closer in style to Jacob than Coolidge, had "corners" drawn about their upper left-hand (first) letter.

Even before this, poets in the nonacademic tradition had been periodically experimenting with prose forms. In addition to Stein and Williams (whose *Spring & All*, even more than *Kora*, has proven to be a rich source of ideas for the writers of new prose), Robert Duncan, in his "Structure of Rime," and Jack Spicer, in "A Textbook of Poetry," demonstrated that a paragraph-centered poetry, informed but not limited by the French tradition, offered possibilities that went beyond a speech-based poetics. Similarly, Louis Zukofsky, one of the most influential (and, with Stein, least speech-centered) writers of this counter-tradition, described *Bottom: On Shakespeare* (1963)—his book-length meditation on the bard's writing in an attempt to find an end to ontology—as a prose poem. Finally, in 1972, both Creeley and John Ashbery, poets who had matured in the 1950s, published major intergeneric prose works. Although Ashbery's *Three Poems* (1972) is the closest thing to a French *recit* yet composed in English, Creeley's *A Day Book* (1972) reflects the influence of both Stein and Williams, as well as the fragmented, open poetics of his own *Pieces*. Creeley followed with two other prose sequences, *Presences* (1974) and *Mabel: A Story* (1976). Although the organizational unit of *A Day Book* had been, with one exception, that of the day, defined as what could be written single-spaced on one sheet of paper, *Presences* carries this quantitative aspect to a new level of formal construction. In typescript, each section equals six pages, divided into subunits of one, two, and three pages, variously ordered. Whereas Baudelaire had, on some occasions, counted the number of sentences per paragraph, so as to lend the interrelation between paragraphs the same sense of symmetry that an *a,b,b,a* rhyme scheme can impose on a quatrain, no other prose poet in the intervening 110 years had so clearly posed the possibility of quantity itself as an alternate organizing principle to narrative or exposition. With this step, all of the strategies that had evolved throughout the history of poetry with regard to the formal uses of number, from haiku to double canzone, become relevant to prose. Lyn Hejinian's *My Life*, written within two years of the publication of *Presences*, is composed of 37 paragraphs of 37 sentences each.

Although written using a similar quantitative strategy, *Mabel*, intended as "an imagination of women," approaches narrative and, in that process, carries with it a textual surface quite close to Stein's prose. It also brings Creeley back in the direction of *The Island* and *The Gold Diggers*, a novel and collection of short stories written in the 1950s. These works place Creeley, who began as a prose writer, within another particular tradition that rests between the margins of fiction and verse: prose intended as fiction, but whose primary audience is to be located within the poetry community. "Poetic fiction" in a sense almost as social as it is literary, this alternative storytelling prose can be traced back through the later novels and short stories of Williams to the writing of Joyce and Stein. But it was not until the 1950s, with its flowering of New American poetries (every one of them indebted heavily to Williams), a phenomenon that both expanded and differentiated the poetry reading public in the United States, that a sufficient *social* base was established for a prose stressing values normally associated with verse, such as an evident concern for prosody. This prose acquired something akin to a genre status of its own, a condition by no means shunned in a collection such as *New American Story* (1967), edited by Creeley and Donald Allen.

Given the period, it is not surprising that several of the practitioners of this new fiction, like Creeley, Ed Dorn, Larry Eigner, LeRoi Jones (Amiri Baraka), or Robert Kelly, were known primarily as projectivist poets, whereas others, such as Fielding Dawson, Douglas Woolf, Michael Rumaker, or Hubert Selby, Jr., showed a parallel concern with the accurate presentation of speech rhythms on the page. Just as the Black Mountain school was only one tendency within New American poetry, the new writers of poetic fiction likewise reflected the broader gamut of possibilities, from Beats Jack Kerouac and William Burroughs, to the French-influenced side of the New York School in the work of Harry Mathews* (a French resident and member of the Oulipo Group centered around the games-playing Raymond Queneau and Georges Perec), to the laidback side of the San Francisco Renaissance with Richard Brautigan.*

Precisely because of their relationships to preexisting poetry communities, audiences, and values, these writers differ from the meta- or surfictionists. Gilbert Sorrentino,* Toby Olson, and Bobbie Louise Hawkins, like Brautigan, had established reputations as poets before concentrating on fictive prose. In contrast, the verse of Steve Katz* has remained aloof from any of the larger tendencies in recent poetry, an alienation explicit in the concluding section of his novel *Saw* where members of the St. Marks scene at a party are conveyed as cliquish through the simple device of referring to them by their (identifiable) initials.

As always, categorical distinctions such as this have no firm borders, and someone like Fanny Howe could fit either. More noteworthy is the degree to which poetic fiction, as it has grown dramatically in the past two decades, making room for all manner of maverick authors (Lydia Davis, Walter Abish,* Paul Metcalf, Tom Ahern, Dale Herd, Michael Amnasan), has begun finally to generate its own internal tendencies, most notably the writing, much of it overtly political, by gay men such as Melvyn Freilicher, Jeff Weinstein, Bruce Boone, and Bob Gluck. Weinstein and Freilicher share with Clay Fear, Constance DeJong, Marsha Campbell, and Laurie Anderson the tangible influence of Kathy Acker, a major novelist whose work has emerged entirely framed within the context of fiction-for-poets-and-other-artists. Had Jack Kerouac allowed the pioneering forms of *Visions of Cody* to evolve, rather than progressively taming them toward an a priori model of the novel, Acker's writing decades later might not look so extreme.

Acker's persistent formula (plagiarism + pornography = autobiography) is both a method of composition and the bleakest imaginable vision of meaning in the world. In exposing the constructedness of any reality posed as a narrative, texts such as *Great Expectations* function within the genre of the novel subversively, calling attention to the stitching of tropes in what ostensibly is without seams. As such, Acker's writing shares its oppositional strategy with Coolidge's early de-syntaxed stanzas, Grenier's unpunctuated one- and two-word "sentences," and Bromige's graphically marked margins in "Tight Corners." Making perceptible that which exists "below the line," sub/version represents one pole or limit of possibility in recent inter- (or anti-) generic literature.

In *In Case*, James Sherry offers the detective novel absent narrative or character. A tour de force of prosody and wit, the text demonstrates just how far beyond the lumbering machinations of plot the distinctive features of the thriller extend, particularly with regard to verb tense and sentence length.

Erica Hunt, in a untitled three-piece sequence published in a 1981 issue of *Vanishing Cab 4*, performs equally deconstructive operations on the devices of a more personal mode, the letter. All are unsigned. The first is addressed "Dear Dear," and the next two "Dear." Within each there is a surface of coherent narrative or exposition, yet there is no apparent connection between letters. The degree to which the artifice of character is built on such elements as context and continuity of name becomes evident. Are there one, two, or three expositors present? The presence of the "Dear Dear" contrasts with the other salutations to prevent an unproblematic reading of a "ping-pong" volley of correspondence. The same difficulty occurs as to the number of persons addressed. Hunt's critique extends further than the context-dependent devices of exposition and their structural (if not historical) origins in dramatic monologue, to the textual nature of intimacy itself. The most narrative of the three pieces is, by this fact, the most removed: what demands telling is that which has not been shared.

In these works Hunt and Sherry proceed by elimination, an almost Brechtian disruption of the illusionist or natural claims of their genres. Hannah Weiner utilizes supplementation to demonstrate and transcend the ego-centered limits of the diary. In *Clairvoyant Journal* (1978) and elsewhere, Weiner inserts statements that she claims to have seen appear on foreheads, walls, in the air, or on the page. These statements, presented in italics, capitals, or large boldface type (and even between lines or over other words in the text), dominate the work rendering the narrative—that of a middle-aged woman's life of intense material poverty within the arts community of New York's Lower East Side—a counterpoint. Leaving virtually no sentence complete, these insertions are as important for their prosodic implications as for their metacommentary (much of which a Freudian might read as emanations of a displaced superego) on the exposition. Unfortunately, Weiner's claim to clairvoyance has been used by some as one more reason not to take a woman writer seriously. Nonetheless, the result of her process is a series of remarkably complex and subtle works that often share a view of the individual found in the writing of other recent practitioners of what Davidson calls the new prose.

This view is a deep distrust in the unity, identity, or inherent naturalness of the self, of the subject that writes or professes to narrate. It is not simply that one cannot compose anything, let alone a dramatic monologue, without the presence of a writer, but that inscribed within all of the genres of Western literature is the presumption of a fundamentally stable and unified perspective. Self-centered in the most literal sense, these traditional categories communicate a vision of human existence and action entirely consistent with the evolution of Euro-American societies driven by impulses that, at the level of the state, are expressed as imperialism and the denial or repression of contradiction and difference.

The degree to which the distrust on the part of recent authors of this view of humanity exists can be gauged by contrasting Weiner's ensemble of voices with Lyn Hejinian's *My Life*. Equally autobiographical in its focus, Hejinian's use of an externally visible plan, one paragraph for each year of her life, presents the self as a construct. Her rigor and passion for order makes *My Life* a much more optimistic text than *Clairvoyant Journal*; yet underlying each is a rejection of the simplistic psychology which is the ideological foundation for the whole of Western civilization.

Hejinian's constructivist approach also represents the far pole of possibility from Weiner's subversive technique. Although it *is* autobiography, *My Life* neither starts from, nor works toward, issues that might be contained within that genre.

Another writer often associated with the constructivist approach to text generation is Barrett Watten.* In his prose at least, this has less to do with any use of a numeric pattern principle than with the extraordinary degree to which his works operate outside any constraints of genre. This is particularly visible in his two books from Tuumba Press, *Plasma/Paralleles/ "X"* (1979) and *Complete Thought* (1982). In the title poem of the latter collection, each section is composed of two double-spaced sentences, such as

> The world is complete.
>
> Books demand limits.[12]

Through their brevity, the question of margins (and through this the distinction between verse line and prose sentence) is successfully evaded. Are these two lines or two paragraphs? One stanza or two? What is the relationship between the sentences, or between this section and the next? In Watten's prose such issues are never idle or academic. The meaning of any given statement depends precisely on the amount of autonomy which the reader grants to its words and syntax versus the dependency it has on a larger linguistic and literary context. Recognizing that the essence of form is passion, Watten's texts maximize the tension between these opposing sources of signification, an intensity heightened by a refusal to proceed through the logic of existing prose genres.

It is a mistake to confuse this constructivist approach with superficially similar moments in earlier literary history, just as it is to read the subversive tendency as only an ironic critique. Even here, categories of this sort are a reductivist shorthand, the reality being that almost every writer mentioned combines elements of both impulses. A clear instance of this is Bob Perelman, some of whose pieces in *7 Works* (1978) could be described as constructivist subversions, submitting generic source materials to editing and rewriting processes. Similarly, Bernadette Mayer's *Memory* (1975) is a prose journal whose subversive element lies in its composition through formal procedure.

Carla Harryman makes use of the devices of fiction, including character and narrative, without producing works that, in any usual sense, would ever be called stories. Yet, although her writing is filled with play, in addition to its exact shadings of style and sometimes awesome emotional range, a book such as *Property* (1982) is not a subversion of the novel. Unlike *In Case*, the text does not foreground the genre, using its techniques instead in a more methodological manner that is closer to Hejinian's use of number.

In contrast, Charles Bernstein* employs strategies associated with the formal method to subvert everything, including the formal method. Like *Complete Thought, The Occurrence of Tune* (1981) is neither prose, poem, nor prose poem. Yet where Watten establishes his text and its rapid-fire shifts through a consistent tone and overall surface texture, Bernstein's writing is full of stops and starts, languid passages surrounded by manic bursts. The most unrelentingly ironic of the writers here, Bernstein has also gone further in bringing in the prosaic, the deliberately banal, into the verse line.

Kit Robinson's "A Sentimental Journey," published in *Hills 8*, might be read as subversive if one recognizes the pun between journey and journal, and that the text alluded to in the title (in addition to being quoted and its format of small paragraphs taken as a model) is the collection of memoirs by the Russian Formalist critic Viktor Shklovsky. Although no text can be said to be without themes or development, Robinson's "Journey" stands alongside the best of Watten and Bernstein as a fully realized instance of plotless literature, a term coined by Shklovsky to describe the pre-Revolutionary Russian prose stylist Vasily Rozanov.

Other writers occupying this middle ground include Steve Benson, Peter Seaton, and Lynne Dreyer. Benson's largely unpublished *Blue Books* begins with a formal premise: fill 50 college blue books, defining a paragraph as a single sitting. The result, however, is neither a parody of a final exam nor a journal, as it is a series of meditations that also function as writing. Seaton's texts, such as *The Son Master* (1982) initially appear more foreboding—walls of words composed with an exquisite sense of prosody, in which themes sparkle and flicker like gems embedded in rock. Here the writing pursues its own course, informed by but apart from either constructive or subversive strategies. Dreyer's *Step Work* (1983) is equally a self-determining text, aspects of fiction, diary, and essay coming into play on an almost sentence-by-sentence basis.

Beyond these poets of prose are a large number of others who likewise produce texts that call into question the margin of either genre. Among these are Bruce Andrews, Jean Day, DeLys Mullis, Larry Price, Alan Davies, Rae Armantrout, Tom Mandel, Michael Gottlieb, Alan Bernheimer, Michael Palmer, and Michael Davidson. In another, related direction, writers who, to varying degrees, conceive of their audiences as specifically feminist are increasingly turning poetry to prose. Judy Grahn's work (which is perhaps the founding document of contemporary lesbian-feminist letters) uses only techniques associated with fiction, but was originally published as the title piece in a volume she carefully named *The Psychoanalysis of Edward the Dyke and Other Poems* (1981). Beverly Dahlen's *A Reading* (1985), the first writing by a woman on the scale of Pound's *Cantos*, Williams' *Paterson*, or Olson's *Maximus*, is in prose. Others who have demonstrated the usefulness of prose in opening up a literary terrain left invisible by the male-defined traditions of verse include Kathleen Fraser, Gloria Frym, and Barbara Einzig.

Genres are not innate. Stephane Mallarmé once went so far as to argue that there is no prose, that all organization of language beyond the simple filing system of the alphabet was versification. Genres represent historically determined ensembles of features around which the many possible tendencies within writing may gather for a time. And as they gather, so are they permitted to disperse should the social conditions change. The collapse of a speech-based poetics after a reign of nearly two centuries and the withdrawal of corporate capital from the field of serious fiction have profoundly destabilized either side of this equation. On a broad scale what is taking place is nothing less than a social struggle over the organization of the literary arts. A struggle over categories, over status, over meaning. Whatever the future of these categories might be, we can trust that it will not be a simple reflection of the past.

NOTES

1. *U.S. News and World Report*, May 17, 1982, p. 22.
2. Michael Davidson, "After Sentence, Sentence," *American Book Review* (September-October 1982): 3.
3. Charles Baudelaire, *Paris Spleen*, trans. Louise Varese (New York: New Directions, 1947), pp. ix-x.
4. Ibid., p. ix.
5. Ibid., p. x.
6. Max Jacob, *The Dice Cup*, Preface translated by Zack Rogow (College Park, MD.: Sun & Moon Press, 1979), p. 7.
7. Contrast the prose of *The Dice Cup* with Mallarmé's "The Pipe," for example. This is not to say that rhythms consciously derived from nonliterary prose were not working their way into French poetry prior to Jacob. In contrast with Mallarme's prose poems, his "A Throw of the Dice"—most widely known for its departure from the stanzaic form and its literally graphic utilization of the entire page—uses just such prose rhythms.

8. William Wordsworth, *Selected Poems and Prefaces by William Wordsworth*, ed. Jack Stillinger (New York: Houghton Mifflin, 1965), p. 451.

9. Robert Grenier, *This* 1 (1971): n.p.

10. Clark Coolidge, *This* 5 (1974): n.p.

11. It may not be a coincidence that the modern prose poem movement in Japan was initiated by writers who had previously been identified as members of the "small poem movement."

12. Barrett Watten, *Complete Thought* (Berkeley, Calif.: Tuumba Press, 1982), p. 1.

SELECTED BIBLIOGRAPHY

Primary Sources

(This listing does not include volumes by these authors in which prose is not substantially represented. Most items still in print can be found through either Small Press Distribution, 1794 Shattuck Avenue, Berkeley, California, or Seque Distribution, 300 Bowery, New York City, New York. A selection of prose from several of these authors, plus those who have yet to publish a volume—notably Erica Hunt—is included in the poetry anthology *In the American Tree*, edited by Ron Silliman, National Poetry Foundation, Orono, Maine.)

Acker, Kathy. *The Childlike Life of the Black Tarantula*. New York: TVRT Press, 1978.

———. *The Adult Life of Toulouse Lautrec*. New York: TVRT Press, 1978.

———. *Kathy Goes to Haiti*. Toronto: Rumour Publications, 1978.

———. *I Dreamt I was a Nymphomaniac: Imagining*. New York: Traveler's Digest Editions, 1980.

———. *Hello, I'm Erica Jong*. New York: Contact II, 1982.

———. *Implosion*. New York: Wedget Press, 1983.

———. *Blood and Guts in High School, Plus Two*. London: Picador, 1984 (also includes *Great Expectations* and *My Death, My Life, by Pier Paolo Pasolini*).

Andrews, Bruce. *Wobbling*. New York: Roof, 1981.

———. *R + B*. New York: Segue, 1981.

Armantrout, Rae. *The Invention of Hunger*. Berkeley, Calif.: Tuumba Press, 1979.

Beckett, Tom. *Dump*. San Francisco: After Hours Press, 1982.

———. *Soluble Senses Census*. Alwater, Ohio: Tonsure, 1984.

Benedetti, David. *Nictating Membrane*. Berkeley, Calif.: The Figures, 1976.

———. *Social Climax Text*. Self-published, 1981.

———. *Ideas Imagine Passion*. Self-published, 1983.

Benson, Steve. *As Is*. Berkeley, Calif.: The Figures, 1978.

———. *Blindspots*. Cambridge, Mass.: Whale Cloth, 1981.

———. *Blue Book 42*. San Francisco: Tottel's, 1981.

Bernheimer, Alan. *Cafe Isotope*. Berkeley, Calif.: The Figures, 1980.

———. *State Lounge*. Berkeley, Calif.: Tuumba Press, 1981.

———. *The Hamlet of the Bees*. Trans. Valery Larbaud. Cambridge, Mass.: Whale Cloth, 1981.

Bernstein, Charles. *Controlling Interests*. New York: Roof, 1980.

————. *The Occurrence of Tune*. New York: Segue, 1981.

————. *Islets/Irritations*. New York: Jordan Davies, 1983.

Boone, Bruce. *My Walk with Bob*. San Francisco: Black Star, 1979.

————. *Century of Clouds*. San Francisco: Hoddypell, 1980.

————. *La Fontaine* (with Robert Gluck). San Francisco: Black Star, 1981.

————. *The Truth About Ted*. Oakland, Calif.: e.g., 1983.

Bromige, David. *Birds of the West*. Toronto: Coach House Press, 1973.

————. *Three Stories*. Los Angeles: Sparrow, 1973.

————. *Out of My Hands*. Los Angeles: Sparrow, 1974.

————. *Tight Corners & What's Around Them: Prose & Poems*. Los Angeles: Black Sparrow, 1974.

————. *My Poetry*. Berkeley, Calif.: The Figures, 1980.

————. *P-E-A-C-E*. Berkeley, Calif.: Tuumba Press, 1981.

————. *Red Hats: Fit the First*. Unpublished manuscript.

Burns, Gerald. *Towards a Phenomenology of Written Art*. New Paltz: Treacle, 1979.

————. *Prose*. Quincy, Ill.: Salt Lick, 1980.

Campbell, Marsha. *Dear Daddos*. Oakland, Calif.: e.g., 1983.

Chester, Laura. *Proud and Ashamed*. Santa Barbara: Christopher's Books, 1978.

————. *My Pleasure*. Berkeley, Calif.: The Figures, 1980.

Child, Abigail. *From Solids*. New York: Segue, 1983.

————. *De-Multiplying Phenomenon*. Oakland, Calif.: Qu, 1984.

Coolidge, Clark. *Quartz Hearts*. San Francisco: This Press, 1978.

————. *Smithsonian Depositions & Subject to a Film*. New York: Vehicle Editions, 1980.

————. *American Ones*. Bolinas, Calif.: Tombouctou, 1981.

————. *A Geology*. Needham, Mass.: Potes & Poets, 1981.

————. *Mine: The One That Enters the Stories*. Berkeley, Calif.: The Figures, 1982.

Creeley, Robert. *The Gold Diggers and Other Stories*. New York: Scribner's, 1965.

————. *Mabel: A Story, and Other Prose*. London: Marion Boyars, 1976.

Dahlen, Beverly. *A Reading*. San Francisco: Momo's Press, 1985.

Darragh, Tina. *My Hands to My Self*. Washington, D.C.: Dry Imager, 1975.

————. *Pi in the Skye*. New York: Ferguson/Franzino, 1980.

————. *On the Corner to Off the Corner*. College Park, Md.: Sun & Moon, 1981.

Davidson, Michael. *The Mutabilities*. Berkeley, Calif.: Sand Dollar, 1976.

————. *The Prose of Fact*. Berkeley, Calif.: The Figures, 1981.

————. *The Landing of Rochambeau*. Providence, R.I.: Burning Deck Press, 1985.

Davies, Alan. *Mnemonotechnics*. Hartford, Conn.: Potes & Poets, 1982.

————. *Active 24 Hours*. New York: Roof, 1982.

Davis, Lydia. *The Thirteenth Woman*. New York: Living Hand, 1976.

————. *Story and Other Stories*. Great Barrington, Mass.: The Figures, 1983.

Day, Jean. *Linear C*. Berkeley, Calif.: Tuumba Press, 1983.

————. *A Bronzino*. Oakland, Calif.: Jimmy's House of Knowledge, 1984.

Dewdney, Christopher. *A Paleozoic Geology of London Ontario*. Toronto: Coach House, 1973.

————. *Fovea Centralis*. Toronto: Coach House, 1975.

————. *Spring Trances in the Control Emerald Night*. Berkeley, Calif.: The Figures, 1978.

———. *Alter Sublime*. Toronto: Coach House, 1980.

DiPalma, Ray. *Between the Shapes*. East Lansing, Mich.: Zeitgeist, 1970.

———. *Soli*. Ithaca, N.Y.: Ithaca House, 1974.

———. *Accidental Interludes*. Cranston, R.I.: Turkey Press, 1975.

———. *January Zero*. West Branch, Iowa: Coffee House, 1984.

Dreyer, Lynne. *Stampede*. Washington, D.C.: Eel Press, 1976.

———. *Step Work*. Berkeley, Calif.: Tuumba Press, 1983.

Drucker, Johanna. *The Surprise Party, or: on not going, not ongoing*. No location: Chased Press, 1977.

———. *'S crap 'S ample*. No location: Druckwerk, 1980.

———. *Italy*. Berkeley, Calif.: The Figures, 1980.

———. *Tongues: A Parent Language*. No location: Druckwerk, 1982.

———. *Just As*. No location: Druckwerk, 1983.

Eigner, Larry. *Country/Harbor/Quiet/Act/Around*. San Francisco: This Press, 1978.

Einzig, Barbara. *Disappearing Work, A Recounting*. Berkeley, Calif.: The Figures, 1979.

Faville, Curtis. *Wittgenstein's Door*. Berkeley, Calif.: The Figures, 1979.

Fear, Clay. *Susan Hayward Has Brain Surgery, or As the Music Fades*. San Francisco: Self-published, 1974.

———. *I Don't Expect You'll Do the Same*. San Francisco: Self-published, 1974.

Fischer, Norman. *Like a Walk Through the Park*. Berkeley, Calif.: Open Books, 1980.

Fixel, Lawrence. *The Book of Glimmers*. Berkeley, Calif./London: Cloud Marauder/Menard, 1979.

Fraser, Kathleen. *Each Next: Narratives*. Berkeley, Calif.: The Figures, 1980.

———. *Something (even human voices) in the foreground, a lake*. Berkeley, Calif.: Kelsey St. Press, 1984.

Friedman, Ed. *Black Star Pilgrimage*. New York: Frontward Books, 1976.

Frym, Gloria. *Back to Forth*. Berkeley, Calif.: The Figures, 1982.

Gluck, Robert. *Family Poems*. San Francisco: Black Star, 1979.

———. *La Fontaine* (with Bruce Boone). San Francisco: Black Star, 1981.

———. *Elements of a Coffee Service*. San Francisco: Four Seasons Foundation, 1982.

Gottlieb, Michael. *Ninety-Six Tears*. New York: Roof, 1981.

Greenwald, Ted. *Smile*. Berkeley, Calif.: The Figures, 1981.

Grenier, Robert. *Sentences*. Cambridge, Mass.: Whale Cloth, 1978.

Harryman, Carla. *Percentage*. Berkeley, Calif.: Tuumba Press, 1979.

———. *Under the Bridge*. Oakland, Calif.: This Press, 1980.

———. *Property*. Berkeley, Calif.: Tuumba Press, 1982.

———. *The Middle*. San Francisco: Gaz, 1983.

Harwood, Lee. *The Sinking Colony*. London: Fulcrum, 1970.

———. *All the Wrong Notes*. Durham, U.K.: Pig Press, 1981.

Hejinian, Lyn. *A Thought Is the Bridge of What Thinking*. Willits, Calif.: Tuumba Press, 1976.

———. *Gesualdo*. Berkeley, Calif.: Tuumba Press, 1978.

———. *My Life*. Providence, R.I.: 1980.

Howe, Fanny. *For Erato: The Meaning of Life*. Berkeley, Calif.: Tuumba Press, 1984.

Korzeniowsky, Carol. *Breastwork*. New York: Self-published, 1977.

Kuenstler, Frank. *Lens*. New York: Film Culture, 1964.

Lally, Michael. *Oomaloom*. Washington, D.C.: Dry Imager, 1975.

———. *In the Mood*. Washington, D.C.: Titanic, 1975.

———. *Catch My Breath*. Quincy, Ill.: Salt Lick, 1978.

McCaffery, Steve. *Panopticon*. Toronto: Blewointment Press, 1984.

Mandel, Tom. *Erat*. Providence, R.I.: Burning Deck Press, 1981.

Mayer, Bernadette. *Moving*. New York: Angel Hair, 1971.

———. *Studying Hunger*. New York/Bolinas: Adventures in Poetry/Big Sky, 1975.

———. *Memory*. Plainfield, Vt.: Atlantic Books, 1975.

———. *Midwinter Day*. Berkeley, Calif.: Turtle Island Foundation, 1982.

———. *Utopia*. New York: United Artists, 1984.

Meyer, Sandra. *To Turn Over in the Mind*. San Francisco: Tramen, 1982.

Mullis, DeLys. *As If*. Oakland, Calif.: e.g., 1984.

Palmer, Michael. *Blake's Newton*. Los Angeles: Black Sparrow, 1972.

———. *The Circular Gates*. Los Angeles: Black Sparrow, 1974.

———. *Without Music*. Santa Barbara: Black Sparrow, 1977.

———. *Notes for Echo Lake*. Berkeley: North Point, 1981.

———. *First Figure*. Berkeley, Calif.: North Point, 1984.

Perelman, Bob. *Braille*. Ithaca, N.Y.: Ithaca House, 1975.

———. *7 Works*. Berkeley, N.Y.: The Figures, 1978.

———. *a.k.a.* Great Barrington, Mass.: The Figures, 1984.

Price, Larry. *Proof*. Berkeley, Calif.: Tuumba Press, 1982.

Reese, Marshall. *Writing*. Baltimore: Pod, 1980.

Robinson, Kit. *Chinatown of Cheyenne*. Iowa City: Whale Cloth, 1974.

———. *Down and Back*. Berkeley, Calif.: The Figures, 1978.

Scalapino, Leslie. *Considering How Exaggerated Music Is*. Berkeley, Calif.: North Point, 1982.

Seaton, Peter. *Agreement*. New York: Asylum's, 1978.

———. *The Correspondence Principle*. New York: A Hundred Posters, 1978.

———. *The Son Master*. New York: Roof, 1982.

———. *Crisis Intervention*. Berkeley, Calif.: Tuumba Press, 1983.

Sheidlower, David. *The Consolation of Prose*. Oakland, Calif.: Jimmy's House of Knowledge, 1984.

Shein, Keith. *Pictures Words Threes and Other Numbers*. San Francisco: Trike, 1977.

———. *An Intimate Distant*. San Francisco: Trike, 1982.

Sherry, James. *In Case*. College Park, Md.: Sun & Moon, 1981.

Shurin, Aaron. *The Graces*. San Francisco: Four Seasons Foundation, 1983.

———. "Codex." Unpublished manuscript.

Silliman, Ron. *Ketjak*. San Francisco: This Press, 1978.

———. *Sitting Up, Standing, Taking Steps*. Berkeley, Calif.: Tuumba Press, 1978.

———. *Tjanting*. Berkeley, Calif.: The Figures, 1981.

———. *Bart*. Hartford, Conn.: Potes & Poets, 1982.

———. *ABC*. Berkeley, Calif.: Tuumba Press, 1983.

———. *Paradise*. Providence, R.I.: Burning Deck Press, 1985.

Thorpe, John. *Exogeny*. San Francisco: Trike, 1981.

Warshawski, Morrie. *Out of Nowhere*. No location: Press 22, 1980.

Watten, Barrett. *Opera—Works*. Bolinas: Big Sky, 1975.

———. *Decay*. San Francisco: This Press, 1977.

———. *Plasma/Paraelleles/"X"*. Berkeley, Calif.: Tuumba Press, 1979.

———. *1 = 10*. San Francisco: This Press, 1980.

———. *Complete Thought*. Berkeley, Calif.: Tuumba Press, 1982.

Weiner, Hannah. *Clairvoyant Journal*. Lenox, Mass.: Angel Hair, 1978.

———. *Spoke*. College Park, Md.: Sun & Moon, 1984.

Yau, John. *Sometimes*. New York: Sheep Meadow Press, 1979.

———. *The Sleepless Night of Eugene Delacroix*. Brooklyn: Release Press, 1980.

———. *Corpse and Mirror*. New York: Holt, Rinehart, & Winston, 1983.

Young, Geoffrey. *Subject to Fits*. Berkeley, Calif.: The Figures, 1980.

BONNIE ZIMMERMAN

Feminist Fiction and the Postmodern Challenge

Feminism, from its modern emergence during the French Revolution to its contemporary manifestations, has always allied itself with the progressive and revolutionary forces that have overthrown conventions, hierarchies, and orthodoxies. But feminism has even knocked away the underpinnings of the revolutionary theories that made the twentieth century an age of transformation, uncertainty, and experimentation. Marx challenged political philosophies; Darwin, biblical creation; Freud, theories of the self: feminism provides a meta-discourse about these very challenges. If the history of thought in the Western world has been that of progressive blows to Man's centrality in the universe, feminism today questions the very identification of Man with men. Feminism is perhaps the ultimate overthrow of authority.

Necessarily, then, feminism is also a challenge to the authority of authorship. At least since Mary Wollstonecraft's day, women have been subverting male control of cultural expression by writing themselves into the picture. And because many of the techniques and tactics of mimetic fiction were developed to express the rhythms and realities of male life (the *bildungsroman*, the picaresque, the symbolic inscription of the "Eternal Feminine"), women writers have turned to experimental movements in order to freely inscribe their own words. In the eighteenth century, when English women in large numbers began to write, the novel itself was a new and experimental genre. Women were central to early twentieth-century modernism: Virginia Woolf, Dorothy Richardson, Gertrude Stein, and Djuna Barnes among the fictionists; Amy Lowell, H.D., and Mina Loy among the poets. For Woolf and Stein in particular, language arose from lived experience and thus from sex or gender. Later in the century, Nathalie Sarraute and Anaïs Nin (the latter very popular with feminist readers) helped write the theory of the New Novel. Finally, Doris Lessing—one of the gurus of contemporary feminism—brought realism to and then beyond its extreme limits. *The Golden Notebook*, a phenomenonally influential feminist text, is also a metafiction that questions the possibility of writing a realistic novel, or any novel at all, in our violent, chaotic, and fragmented modern era.

The women's liberation movement that began in the 1960s continued this fighting and writing tradition of feminism by rebelling against androcentric definitions of all social, political, and cultural forms that make up reality. We might expect that a feminist literary program would demand the rejection of realism as inherently male-defined. And indeed, critics have either described or prescribed feminist writing as experimental, nonlinear, associational, and allied with postmodernism.[1] Nevertheless, there are relatively few examples of truly postmodernist feminist novels. In consideration of why this is so, we should recall that literary expression and production in the 1960s was highly male-dominated. The women's movement arose at this particular time for very good reasons. The political and cultural expansion brought about by nineteenth-century feminism atrophied as men reasserted cultural hegemony after the Depression and wars. By the time postmodernism disrupted twentieth-century realism, it was generally accepted that men were writing the Great American Novels and women were typing them. Furthermore, when women read these new fictions, they often found the same old stereotypes, sexual violence, or avoidance of the female that they found in representational fiction. Postmodernism seemed no more a women's movement than any other movement of the time. Finally, feminists shared the commonplace perception of this fiction as the literature of alienation and exhaustion. Feminist writers did not feel alienated or exhausted, however; they felt angry and energized. Self-reflexive fiction about the structure of fiction was perceived to be an apolitical luxury not yet affordable by an "undercapitalized" cultural group.

Inspired by a grassroots political movement, many critics and writers argued instead that women's fiction should be a true realism presenting honest, authentic, factual stories of women's lives, and thus inspire social and political change.[2] After all, white men had defined themselves as existing at the center of what is considered real, including literary reality. Women—like people of color, Jews, and homosexuals—existed outside or at the margins of reality. In the Bloomian battle between representational fathers and experimental sons, the daughter cried out, "What do you mean, realism is dead? Whose reality? Not mine—I haven't had a chance yet to define it!" For women's relation to literary tradition has been that of an "anxiety of authorship," and the task of feminist fiction has been to create an authoritative voice, not to undermine an already existing one.[3] Women's liberation novels, such as *The Women's Room* (Marilyn French), *Small Changes* (Marge Piercy), and *Memoirs of an Ex-Prom Queen* (Alix Kates Shulman), are, therefore, unrelentingly realistic. It is also noteworthy that prominent female authors not directly connected with, or even hostile to, the feminist movement (such as Gail Godwin, Anne Tyler, Diane Johnson, Rosellen Brown, Joyce Carol Oates, and Cynthia Ozick) seem committed to an audience, to meaning, to everyday life. Is this a uniquely female quality, linked to biology, or at least to the way in which society constructs biology? Rosellen Brown articulates the commonly held position that, because women are predisposed to "respond and nurture," it is possible that "women will be more engaged by the social than by the reflexive function of writing."[4] With the strong caveat that this is a socialized, not inherent, quality, I would agree with Brown, at least about women writing in the 1970s and 1980s.

Nevertheless, I do find a demonstrably reflexive, experimental tendency in some feminist fiction.[5] Anti-mimetic fictions inscribe the absurdities of domesticity, the fragmentation of female life, the circularity of female time, the construction of female selfhood, the vision of women's community, and the possibilities of female sexuality. There is a difference, however, between male and female experimentalism. Feminist fiction seldom is as self-conscious and artificial as are male metafictions, and experimentation usually serves the ultimate end of realism. The conflict between representationalism and experimentalism is resolved in this manner: it is women's real lives that defy the laws of the text; as women write their selves, so do they destroy the laws.

A central theme of both mimetic and anti-mimetic feminist fiction is the construction and deconstruction of the female self. Consider the examples of books that seem, on the surface, conventional *bildungsroman*, indeed, confessions so personal that fact and fiction cannot be distinguished. Both *Fear of Flying* (1973), by Eric Jong, and *Flying* (1974), by Kate Millett, were accepted by readers and critics alike as factual stories of their authors' lives, the first cast in the mode of novel and the second of autobiography. Feminists as well as literary critics criticized both books for being self-indulgent and overly personal confessions. And yet both books present constructions of a self who is *not* the author as self-consciously and self-reflexively as do those of Henry Miller or Norman Mailer. In *Fear of Flying*, Erica Jong inscribes herself as Isadora Wing who, in its sequel, *How to Save Your Own Life* (1977), writes a novel called "Candida Confesses." This tri-level narrator—Erica/Isadora/Candida— creates an ironic distance that undermines the reality of any one voice. To further emphasize that these novels are about the constructions of self by life/literature/psychoanalysis, Erica/Isadora constantly steps outside the narrative to abolish its authority: "I had written myself into his hackneyed plot" (*Fear of Flying*, p. 173). "Surely you don't suppose that I'm telling the literal truth here either?" (p. 183). "I started believing I was a fictional character invented by me" (p. 258). "I knew I did not want to be trapped in my own book" (p. 288). As in other metafictions, Isadora searches for some fiction or fantasy to make sense of a senseless reality, whether it be psychoanalysis, the famous zipless fuck, or—the most traditional of metarealities—writing itself: "That was how we parted. Loss piled on loss. My life spilling out into the street, and nothing but a slim volume of verse between me and the void" (p. 272). Despite Jong's attempt to create a "deceptive realism," critics and readers alike read only a bawdy tale about the author's sexual escapades. So Jong gave them a bawdy tale they could not confuse with life, by turning, like John Barth,* to eighteenth-century self-conscious narrative in *Fanny*, a feminist rewriting of Richardson and Fielding.

Whereas Jong followed the path of (deceptive) self-exposure to conscious literariness, Kate Millett moved in the opposite direction. After achieving celebrity for her literature dissertation, *Sexual Politics* (1970), Millett turned to even more daring confessions than those of Jong. Jong at least wrote within the fiction of fiction; Millett adopted the more dangerous genre of autobiography. But, like Jong, she overdetermines her confession. The "Kate" who is writing *Flying* (and *Sita*) during the book's real time is a conscious artifact, like the text itself. Indeed, *Flying* is a book about the consequences of writing a book and becoming the person that the move-ment and media say you are. Painfully, "Kate" explores the self she finds herself to be and tries on a self she would like to become: "And now I will be who I am becoming. Alone in the bus I am pleased with myself. I will put on my blue glasses, the glamorous ones, the ones where people can recognize me. . . . I will go ahead then and be Kate Millett" (p. 300). Although there is certainly a correspondence between the "Kate" of *Flying* and the Kate Millett who wrote the book, even in the most deceptively realistic novel or memoir a meta-discourse exists: what kind of self can be written in words?

Millett illustrated what Simone de Beauvoir argued in *The Second Sex*, that women are split (often by literature and the media) between conscious self and reified other. In feminist fiction, this may be expressed through a split in the main character between an "I" (woman as subject) and a name (woman as object): for example, I/Mira (*The Women's Room*), I/Norma Jean (*Norma Jean the Termite Queen*, 1975, by Sheila Ballantyne), or I/ Elisheva (*The Law of Return*, 1983, by Alice Bloch). Furthermore, central to feminism is the definition of a communal, not just individual, self: the connection of one woman to her mother or foremothers, her sisters, her historical or literary role models. Thus, we find multiple narrators and multiple points of view common in feminist novels, such as Bertha Harris' *Lover* (1976), Sheila Ortiz Taylor's *Faultline* (1982), and Toni Cade Bam-bara's *The Salt Eaters* (1980). The author creates commonality from the fragments of many women's (and sometimes men's) lives. Unlike the com-munal realism of such Victorian authors as George Eliot, continuity is not provided by an omniscient narrator, but by the reader's weaving of a literary tapestry from the materials given her by the author. The titles of E. M. Broner's novels, *Her Mothers* (1975) and *A Weave of Women* (1978), suggest this intent and technique, as does the weaving profession of the family of women in Ntozake Shange's *Sassafrass, Cypress & Indigo* (1982). Finally, a few novels actually transform their protagonist from female to male in order to explore the ambiguities of selfhood and gender roles. In June Arnold's *Applesauce* (1977), four separate characters—Gus and his three wives—are revealed to be aspects of one single woman. And in Lois Gould's disturbing novel about violence and sex roles, the female protagonist resolves her anger at and fear of male violence by herself undergoing *A Sea Change* (1976) into the very man who has terrorized her.

It may have become evident that contemporary women writers, feminist and nonfeminist alike, have eagerly seized upon the images and metaphors of domestic life. *Flying* captures the unstructured, overflowing quality of everyday life, sometimes to a fault. Domestic life further informs the content and structure of many interesting experimental fictions. Indeed, in Marilynne Robinson's neo-realist *Housekeeping* (1981), housework is the central activity and metaphor for controlling life, a control that the narrator and her aunt choose to abandon. In Pamela Zoline's brilliant short story, "The Heat Death of the Universe," Sarah Boyle's loss of control over domestic details and her ultimate dissolution are metaphorically related to the decay of civilization and the physical law of entropy (the heat death of the universe). In Gail Godwin's story, "Interstices," a slowly melting freezer-full of food tempts the housewife-protagonist to plot her unsuspecting family's death from botulism. In "Good Housekeeping," by Rosellen Brown, a housewife photographs the evidence of her life—the baby's bottom, its open crying mouth, the toilet bowl, the laundry—in an ultimately insane attempt to structure meaning. In these fictions, domestic tasks are presented as the only source of meaning evident in the random, shapeless movement of women's lives, and yet, at the same time, the locus of a futility that turns women into "mad" housewives.

In another way the domestic rhythms of women's lives—interruption (the baby, the telephone, the deliveries), fragmentation, and isolation—are used to structure the text itself. Many feminist fictions are fragmented into sections—as short as a paragraph or as long as a chapter—headed by some metafictional device which are then quilted or woven by the writer into a narrative structure. One prototype for this structure is *The Golden Notebook*, which uses journals, fragments of story plots, newspaper clippings, and dreams in an intentionally unsuccessful effort to get at reality. The 54 numbered sections of "The Heat Death of the Universe" present Sarah Boyle's disintegration almost as a progression of scientific propositions. In Monique Wittig's* *Les Guérillères* (1971) and *Le Corps Lesbien* (1975), short discrete paragraphs are randomly interrupted by lists of female names or anatomical parts set in larger type, or by an occasional page empty save for a large "O"—her symbol for both female sexuality and the absence of women in patriarchal discourse. *Her Mothers* often separates its narrative sections with ballad- or joke-like dialogues between an archetypal mother and daughter; these comment ironically on the narrative by mouthing conservative values or radically undercutting the heroine's liberal idealism. Shange interrupts the storyline of *Sassafrass, Cypress & Indigo* with folk tales and remedies, recipes, letters, keys to playing the numbers, poems, journal entries, and the conjured presence of Billie Holiday and Mamie Smith. In *Lover*, each chapter is headed by a story of a female saint who died defending her chastity. Midway through the novel the stories become increasingly outlandish until they are obviously absurdist reflections on both saints and the novel.

In feminist fictions, mimetic and anti-mimetic, every fictional element undergoes "a sea change": character, metaphor, narration, and genre as well. As with many contemporary writers, feminists find the line between fiction and nonfiction, novel and autobiography, thin and permeable. Some texts—*Flying*, *The Woman Warrior* (1976, Maxine Hong Kingston*), and *Zami: A New Spelling of My Name* (1982, Audre Lorde)—ostensibly memoirs, write about the self with novelistic abandon, using deliberately fictive or mythic shadings. Moreover, several of the finest works of feminist imagination are neither novels, poetry, nor nonfiction prose, combining instead elements of all three. Susan Griffin's *Woman and Nature* (1978) is a poetic essay that reads like a *nouveau roman*; Mary Daly's word-play in *Gyn/Ecology* (1978) anticipates the deconstruction of language theorized by proponents of *écriture féminine*; and Michelle Cliff's *Claiming an Identity They Taught Me to Despise* (1980) combines poetic prose, literary criticism, etymology, and philosophy in an autobiographical exploration of the self. Joanna Russ, in a 1972 article, further suggested that women writers would turn to popular fiction genres in order to find plots and myths more amenable to female life than those of conventional realism.[6] To an extent this was already true; the gothic had always been a favorite form for women, used, in the twentieth century, by many serious writers (such as Carson McCullers, Flannery O'Connor, and Shirley Jackson) to create chilling views of social and private life. Gothic forms of subtexts were used later by Margaret Atwood in *Lady Oracle*, Gail Godwin in *Violet Clay*, and Joyce Carol Oates in *A Bloodsmoor Romance*. Furthermore, mysteries appealed to Diane Johnson (*Lying Low* and *The Shadow Knows*) and M. F. Beal (*Angel Dance*), and the picaresque to Erica Jong (*Fanny*), Lisa Alther (*Kinflicks*), and Rita Mae Brown (*Rubyfruit Jungle*).

But the genre most popular with feminist writers, as with many postmodern male writers, is speculative fiction. Lessing turned to SF in her *Canopus in Argos* series, as did Marge Piercy in her only excursions outside realism (*Dance the Eagle to Sleep*), inspired by the youth culture of the 1960s, and *Woman on the Edge of Time*, immensely popular because of its marvelous feminist utopia). Suzy McKee Charnas' *Walk to the End of the World* and *Motherlines*, Chelsea Quinn Yarbro's *False Dawn*, Vonda

McIntyre's *Dream-Snake*, Sally Gearhart's *The Wanderground*, and Pamela Sargent's collections of short stories (beginning with *Women of Wonder*) all have explicit feminist messages. Ursula LeGuin,* among the most celebrated of SF writers, has never been as explicitly feminist, but she does explore sex roles in her works. The writer most committed to SF, feminism, and serious experimental fiction, however, is Joanna Russ herself. Russ' most successful novel, *The Female Man* (1975), is also her most feminist and most metafictional. Like the novels I have discussed, it probes the fragmentation of personality as experienced by a woman standing at the crossroads of past, present, and future(s). The protagonist, an Everywoman, is the product of past definitions of the feminine; she is also a "female man" trying to be human in the present time; and she has glimpses of a future that might be utopian or dystopian. Because all these conditions or awarenesses exist in the modern transitional woman, Russ creates four separate but interacting characters—Jeanette, Joanna, Janet, and Jael—as well as an "I" who occasionally pops into the text, each embodying one aspect of the female self. The text dazzles the reader with witty metafictional commentaries on society and the sexes, and finally on its own role in affecting social change. *The Female Man* cannot be adequately summed up (and thereby dismissed) as science fiction, although it is that. It is also among the most successful and enjoyable pieces of feminist metafictions.

Writers are drawn to speculative fiction and increasingly to fantasy because these forms are particularly amenable to exploration and experimentation. Realism, in the English-language novel, is essentially empiricism: reality is that which can be comprehended by the senses and explained in the language of logic and rationality. But many feminist writers draw on non-Western, nonempirical traditions in which what is real does not exclude what is magical or fanciful. As Ntozake Shange says, "Where there is woman there is magic" (p. 3). Black, Native American, Asian, and Jewish writers use legends, myths, and customs to redefine reality and fictional expectations. This style has been called magical or experimental realism; I prefer to call it expanded realism because it enlarges the reader's notion of what is real, and to whom. For example, E. M. Broner, in *A Weave of Women* (1978), incorporates female revisions of Jewish rituals, ceremonies, and tales to write "the story of sanity and madness in the house of women" (p. 9). Among contemporary black writers, Toni Morrison's* magical realism has been so thoroughly discussed that I will draw attention to the less celebrated but equally powerful Toni Cade Bambara. Her career began with exquisite short stories that are notable for their use of dreams, jazz language, and abrupt shifts in time and place. The real time of her first novel, *The Salt Eaters*, is a brief span of hours during which Velma Henry, a suicidal political organizer, undergoes a spiritual healing. But during this time, the novel flashes back and out to envelop the entire Southern town of Claybourne, including its spiritual and magical elements, and ends with

a mysterious, cataclysmic storm that is Bambers' gesture toward Morrison
and Gabriel García Márquez.* Maxine Hong Kingston, among the best
known of these writers, draws on the legends and myths of her native
China to juxtapose the Chinese reality given through her mother's "talk-
story" and the American reality lived by the protagonist. Neither reality—
neither that of the girl who gets straight As in school nor that of the girl
who lives with magicians and becomes an avenging warrior—is privileged
in the telling. Both achieve the same substantiality through the text's primary symbol of power— language. Like Kingston's protagonist, Ephanie,
in *The Woman Who Owned the Shadows* (Paula Gunn Allen), exists between the dominant American culture and that of her Guadalupe Indian
ancestors. As the novel progresses, she draws on their circular, nonlinear,
complicated language and myth. Because mythic time has no past or future,
but only an eternal present, Ephanie defines herself through the legendary
heroines of her culture: Spiderwoman, who weaves all life, and The Woman
Who Fell, who breaks through levels of reality. Absorbing the power of
the mystical, the magical, and the occult, Ephanie is reborn at the end.
At the conclusion of *The Woman Who Owned the Shadows*, Ephanie discovers the possibility of a world without men in which women can be sisters
to one another. This discovery of sisterhood, and what came to be called
woman-identification, led many feminists in the 1970s to become lesbians,
as it also led many lesbians to become part of the women's movement.
Many of the writers previously discussed belong to a consciously defined
school of lesbian writing. Some critics theorize that lesbian writing, because
it is particularly marginal to the reality of white men, is by its very essence
experimental.[7] As lesbians break the codes of sexuality, so lesbian writing
breaks the codes of textuality. There is certainly some suggestive evidence
in support of this position. Of the important early twentieth-century modernists, Woolf, Stein, Barnes, H.D., and Lowell were lesbians for part or
all of their lives. Furthermore, prominent expatriate lesbians like Margaret
Anderson and Sylvia Beach were instrumental in supporting and publishing
the work of male modernists. Many of the most radical experimental writers
of the 1970s, such as Millett, Wittig, Russ, Harris, and Jill Johnston, are
openly lesbian in some or all of their writing. The question is whether
marginality or superalienation can serve as an explanation for this trend.
To an extent, yes: it is even more difficult to write about lesbian life using
conventional realism than it is to write about heterosexual female life. One
may, however, point to two other factors at work in contemporary lesbian
literary culture. One factor is intertextuality: contemporary writers often
look back to the great modernists for literary role models. Thus, Johnston
is the heir of Stein, Arnold in some ways of Woolf, and Harris quite
deliberately of Barnes. The other factor concerns the material production
of literature. The most successful of the early feminist presses, Daughters
Inc., had as its agenda the publication of conspicuously literary, experi-

mental, and mostly lesbian novels. That lesbian writing (or reading) is not innately experimental can be demonstrated by observing the bulk of fiction published by other presses now that Daughters has disbanded. Naiad Press, the largest and most successful company, publishes traditional romantic fiction; The Crossing Press favors political realism. Both are in tune with their readership; the fact is that the lesbian public likes postmodern fiction no more than the public in general.

To begin a discussion of lesbian experimental, anti-realist fiction, we have to begin with French author Monique Wittig, who has recently adopted America as her home. *Les Guérillères*, part speculative fiction and part epic poem, imagines the war of women against men, male culture, male values, and male language. In its examination of female silence becoming female speech, *Les Guérillères* expresses what was to become a central concern of feminism in both the United States and France. The warriors of her not-quite-fantasy landscape dismantle society and speech as they exist, in order to rebuild both totally in the female mode. Female language, Wittig asserts, "can be found in the gaps, in all that which is not a continuation of their [men's] discourse, in the zero, the 0, the perfect circle that you invent to imprison them and to overthrow them" (p. 114). From this overthrow of male authority, Wittig moves on to the lesbian body, deconstructing the signs attached to it by patriarchy and reconstructing it according to a new logic by transforming metaphors, myths, symbols, even the female "I" itself. Because patriarchal language pits woman against herself (as in Chinese, Kingston tells us, the word for the female self means "slave"), Wittig breaks "je" ("I") into "j/e" ("i"). Only when a woman restructures language and the erotic can she speak a true self or name herself lesbian. Wittig's latest work, *Lesbian Peoples: Material for a Dictionary* (1979), is her most radical rejection of conventional realism. Through dictionary entries alone, the reader constructs a history of lesbian oppression, resistance, and survival. Wittig's concern with phallogocentric power leads her to a new beginning: the definition of words that create lesbian reality.

Wittig's counterpart in the United States is a writer who, like Norman Mailer and Tom Wolfe,* found in journalism an opportunity to explore the self and the political climate of her times. Beginning as a dance critic for *The Village Voice*, by 1970 Jill Johnston in her columns had broken with linearity, reality, and truth to journey instead into her growing lesbian and feminist identity, a journey expressed in the territorial metaphors of her book titles, *Lesbian Nation* (1973) and *Gullibles Travels* (1974). Her essays combine polemic, theory, reportage, autobiography, narrative, and poetry in varying proportions. Johnston, like her mentor Stein, is word-focused; her writing is full of allusion, puns, and sensible nonsense: "i know poets who list things and sometimes make a pretense of conjugating verbs and declining nouns. i accept nouns and i never conjugate. or rather except with women" (*GT*, p. 142). Widely considered unreadable and pretentious at the time, selections in *Lesbian Nation*, in particular, still have the audacity, wit, and linguistic brilliance that made Johnston the *enfant terrible* of the early 1970s.

The women's movement in New York City provided fertile material for the New Journalism/autobiography of Johnston and Millett, and for the second novel of Daughters publisher June Arnold. Her first novel, *Applesauce*, had modeled its exploration of the relation between gender and identity after Woolf's androgynous fantasy, *Orlando*. In *The Cook and the Carpenter* (1973), Arnold delved more deeply into the artificiality of gender construction by constructing a uniquely artificial text, its language being completely gender-free. *The Cook and the Carpenter* is even more uncompromising in its commitment to genderless language than is Piercy's *Woman on the Edge of Time* or LeGuin's *The Dispossessed*. Unmarked pronouns, ambiguous personal names, and occupational appellations (as in the title) disguise the sex of the characters. Only at the end are they revealed to be exclusively women, and the story is seen as that of a lesbian collective. In *Sister Gin* (1975), her final novel (she died prematurely in 1982), Arnold experimented with larger units of narrative structure. Her protagonist is split between Su, the balanced but repressed career woman, and her alter ego, Sister Gin, the angry, alcoholic, political lesbian who forces Su to come out and come of age. Su's relation to her community is then created through sections of conventional narrative, disruptive flashbacks, and glimpses into other minds, including a tour de force section in which Su's mother, under the influence of gas in the dentist's office, uncovers the deeply hidden lesbian in herself.

Another Daughters novel, *Riverfinger Women* (1974), by Elana Nachmann, is self-reflexive throughout, as the authorial persona, Inez Riverfinger, types herself and her friends into "identifiable shapes" (p. 7). One metafictional device Nachmann creates to comment on her text is a conglomerate FBI-CIA-DADDY called "The Committee" that dismisses her novel with a curt, "Who does she think is going to believe this garbage?" (p. 87). In response, Inez says simply, "I do not suggest that I am writing a complex anti-linear tract—far from it. All I have ever said was that I was writing the pornographic novel of my life." (p. 89). But, as Nachmann disingenuously suggests, to be a lesbian in America is indeed to be unbelievable, pornographic, and anti-linear.

Finally, Bertha Harris had written two literary, experimental novels, *Catching Saradove* (1970) and *Confessions of Cherubino* (1972), before publishing with Daughters. Like many male homosexual writers, Harris accepts and valorizes the unnaturalness, the unreality, of same-sex relationships. Lesbian love is a consciously created, chosen artifact, free from social and biological inevitability. Thus, in *Confessions of Cherubino* (which is a deliberate tribute to her mentor, Djuna Barnes) and in the more feminist and joyous *Lover*, Harris uses the artifice and transvestism of

opera to expose the paradoxes of sex roles and sexual identity. The protagonists of *Confessions* dress up as the characters from *The Marriage of
Figaro*, and *Lover* opens with a prologue that recounts the plot (as written
by Veronica, the "author" of *Lover*) of *Der Rosenkavalier*. Both operas
have as main characters boys played by women who dress up and masquerade as girls. As Harris reveals the false reality of Cherubino/Octavion,
she strips away the false reality of everyday lives.

The reality of everyday life is what Flynn, one of *Lover*'s main characters,
is searching for. Life and love are so shifty that Flynn tries to dig down to
the bedrock of self and locate "the truth of herself" in her disembodied
brain (p. 67). But her quest is undercut by her emotions and sexuality and
by the author. Flynn finds herself not as a mind-machine but as a "lover"—
the essential female identity that replaces "woman" (p. 103). And Flynn
can never get to the bedrock of reality because author Harris through
author-within-the-author Veronica keeps piling high the "fictional topsoil."
Lover is a classic self-reflexive novel, a novel about writing a novel, about
the fiction of fiction. Author-ego Veronica is a forger of paintings that are
celebrated as original Veronica-forgeries: "I am to invent origins. And
then to fake them" (p. 154). The effects of the novel are dazzling and
brilliant: characters are sometimes themselves and sometimes each other;
time past merges imperceptibly with time present; utterly improbable characters experience equally absurd events. Thus, *Lover* is among the few
feminist fictions thoroughly committed to the aesthetic aims of postmodernism.

When Daughters disbanded in the late 1970s, the main vehicle for experimental lesbian fiction disappeared. Occasionally, other nonrepresentational novels have been published or self-published, such as Sheila Ortiz
Taylor's *Faultline*, which dispenses with a single narrative voice in favor
of multiple voices offering partial perspectives on the heroine's life, and
Alesia Kunz's *Shangrila and Linda* (1980), which dispenses with linear
chronology altogether. But the locus of experimentation has shifted from
American lesbian fiction to French *écriture féminine*. Largely inspired by
the language-centered philosophies of Jacques Lacan* and Jacques Derrida*, French women writers posit a world in which language is privileged
as a source of meaning and change. Language is based on male presence
and female absence, a system named phallogocentrism, the discourse of
the Fathers. Woman cannot write herself in this discourse; she must create
a new women's language that will inscribe her/self. This controversial notion—that there is a Woman (what de Beauvoir and, later, Wittig disparage
as the Eternal Feminine) to be written—produces fiction and polemics that
are open, discursive, circular, fragmentary, punning, and neologistical (what
Russ earlier called the lyrical mode). To some this is feminist writing; to
others it is a parody of femininity. At present, only theoretical pieces such
as Hélène Cixous' "The Laughter of the Medusa" and short excerpts from

the works of Luce Irigaray have been published in the United States, so it is as yet unclear exactly what *écriture féminine* will be like.[8] No one in the United States is writing consciously in this style, and there is still considerable skepticism about its theoretical propositions. Nevertheless, the questioning of language and male-defined reality that is central to French feminism has already had a major influence on American literary critics. Some are even beginning to write criticism in a postmodern style. Inevitably, this work will expand the experimental, anti-realist element in American feminist fiction as has already happened with the Francophone literature being published in Quebec today.[9]

Despite the examples discussed throughout this chapter, more arguments exist for a postmodern feminist aesthetic than do examples of one. The writers discussed are, by and large, unfamiliar to the reading public and marginal to the literary world. Most fiction by women writers, either explicitly feminist or influenced by the larger aims of feminism (that is, comprehending the world through feminist consciousness, attending to the dailiness of female life, validating varieties of female experience), remains committed to realism, to creating an authentic female voice, and to portraying authentic female experience. Although some writers may push the limits of realism, the novels of Gail Godwin, Margaret Atwood, Mary Gordon, and Alice Walker,* to name but a few figures, at most adopt some techniques of experimentalism in the service of realism. For example, the epistolary style of *The Color Purple* (1982) is potentially metafictional, but Walker chooses it not to reflect on the inadequacies of realism but because it is the best way to let Celie write her own story. And even the most experimental of writers remain convinced that language—however variously used—represents something, something real and relational, and that that something is of vital importance to the women who read and write novels.[10] Perhaps women have been raised to see relations between things and people, perhaps we are not yet through with reality, perhaps the anti-realism of postmodernism is passé. For whatever reason or reasons, feminist fiction, from the late 1960s to the present, has maintained a tie to reality, however high it has soared above or beyond it.

NOTES

1. See Julia Penelope Stanley and Susan J. Wolfe, "Toward a Feminist Aesthetic," *Chrysalis* 6 (1978): 57–71; Rachel Blau DuPlessis and Members of Workshop 9, "For the Etruscans: Sexual Difference and Artistic Production—The Debate over a Female Aesthetic," in *The Future of Difference*, eds. Hester Eisenstein and Alice Jardine (Boston: G. K. Hall & Co., 1980), pp. 128–56. I am enormously indebted to these two essays.

2. See Cheri Register, "American Feminist Literary Criticism: A Bibliographical Introduction," in *Feminist Literary Criticism*, ed. Josephine Donovan (Lexington: University Press of Kentucky, 1975), pp. 1–28; Marcia Holly, "Consciousness

and Authenticity: Toward a Feminist Aesthetic," in Donovan, *Feminist Literary Criticism*, pp. 38–47; Evelyne Keitel, "Feminist Literature as a Theory of Feminism," translation by author of "Frauen, Texte, Theorie. Aspekte eines problematischen Verhältnisses," *Das Argument* 142 (1983): 830–41; Ann Barr Snitow, "Realist Women Novelists—1970–1980: The Fear of Naming and the Desire to Name," unpublished paper presented at the Modern Language Association (MLA) convention (1981).

3. Sandra Gilbert and Susan Gubar, *The Madwoman in the Attic* (New Haven, Conn. Yale University Press, 1979), p. 49.

4. Tom LeClair and Larry McCaffery, *Anything Can Happen: Interviews with Contemporary American Novelists* (Urbana: University of Illinois Press, 1983), p. 58.

5. This chapter examines *feminist* fiction, not all fiction by women. I have selected texts that are closely associated with the women's movement, late 1960s to the present, either because of the author or the content of the text itself. Feminist authors are those who have publicly identified themselves with an aspect of the movement; feminist texts are those in which gender and sex roles are central, not marginal, to its meaning.

6. Joanna Russ, "What Can a Heroine Do? or Why Women Can't Write," in *Images of Women in Fiction*, ed. Susan Koppelman Cornillon (Bowling Green: Bowling Green University Popular Press, 1972), pp. 3–20.

7. Bertha Harris, "*What we mean to say*: Notes Toward Defining the Nature of Lesbian Literature," *Heresies* 3 (Fall 1977): 7–8; Barbara Smith, "Toward a Black Feminist Criticism," *Conditions: Two* 1, no. 2 (October 1977): 25–44; Susan J. Wolfe, "Stylistic Experimentation in Millett, Johnston, and Wittig," unpublished paper presented at the MLA convention (1978).

8. See Elaine Marks and Isabel de Courtivon, *New French Feminisms* (Amherst: University of Massachusetts Press, 1980).

9. Karen Gould, "Setting Words Free: Feminist Writing in Quebec," *Signs* 6, no. 4 (Summer 1981): 617–42.

10. See the dialogue between Nathalie Sarraute and Alain Robbe-Grillet quoted in Roger Shattuck's review of *Childhood* in *The New York Times Book Review*, April 1, 1984, pp. 1 and 31. Sarraute states that, for her, the world of a novel is created out of something and "not completely out of language." Robbe-Grillet disagrees.

SELECTED BIBLIOGRAPHY

Primary Sources

Allen, Paula Gunn. *The Woman Who Owned the Shadows*. Argyle, N.Y. and San Francisco: Spinsters Ink, 1983.

Arnold, June. *Applesauce*. Plainfield, VT.: Daughters Inc., 1977 (1966).

———. *The Cook and the Carpenter*. Plainfield, VT.: Daughters Inc., 1973.

———. *Sister Gin*. Plainfield, VT.: Daughters Inc., 1975.

Ballantyne, Sheila. *Norma Jean the Termite Queen*. New York: Doubleday & Co., 1975.

Bambera, Toni Cade. *The Salt Eaters*. New York: Random House, 1980.

Bloch, Alice. *The Law of Return*. Boston: Alyson Publications, 1983.

Broner, E. M. *Her Mothers*. New York: Holt, Rinehart & Winston, 1975.

———. *A Weave of Women*. New York: Holt, Rinehart & Winston, 1978.

Brown, Rosellen. "Good Housekeeping." In *Bitches and Sad Ladies*. Ed. Pat Rotter. New York: Dell Books, 1975 (1973).

Cliff, Michelle. *Claiming an Identity They Taught Me to Despise*. Watertown, Mass.: Persephone Press, 1980.

Daly, Mary. *Gyn/Ecology*. Boston: Beacon Press, 1978.

Godwin, Gail. "Interstices." In *Bitches and Sad Ladies*. Ed. Pat Rotter. New York: Dell Books, 1975 (1972).

Gould, Lois. *A Sea Change*. New York: Avon Books, 1976.

Griffin, Susan. *Woman and Nature*. New York: Harper & Row, 1978.

Harris, Bertha. *Confessions of Cherubino*. New York: Harcourt, Brace Jovanovich, 1972.

———. *Lover*. Plainfield, Vt.: Daughters Inc., 1976.

Johnston, Jill. *Lesbian Nation*. New York: Simon & Schuster, 1973.

———. *Gullibles Travels*. New York: Links Books, 1974.

Jong, Erica. *Fear of Flying*. New York: New American Library, 1973.

———. *How to Save Your Own Life*. New York: New American Library, 1977.

———. *Fanny*. New York: New American Library, 1980.

Kingston, Maxine Hong. *The Woman Warrior*. New York: Vintage Books, 1976.

Kunz, Alesia. *Shangrila and Linda*. San Francisco: Prickley Pear Press, 1981.

Lessing, Doris. *The Golden Notebook*. New York: Ballantine Books, 1962.

Lorde, Audre. *Zami: A New Spelling of My Name*. Trumansburg, N.Y.: Crossing Press, 1982.

Millett, Kate. *Flying*. New York: Ballantine Books, 1974.

Nachmann, Elana. *Riverfinger Women*. Plainfield, VT.: Daughters, Inc., 1974.

Robinson, Marilynne. *Housekeeping*. New York: Bantam Books, 1981.

Russ, Joanna. *The Female Man*. New York: Bantam Books, 1975.

Shange, Ntozake. *Sassafrass, Cypress & Indigo*. New York: St. Martin's Press, 1982.

Taylor, Sheila Ortiz. *Faultline*. Tallahassee: Naiad Press, 1982.

Walker, Alice. *The Color Purple*. New York: Washington Square Press, 1982.

Wittig, Monique. *Les Guérillères*. New York: Viking Press, 1971.

———. *Le Corps lesbien*. New York: Avon Books, 1975.

———. *Lesbian Peoples: Materials for a Dictionary*. New York: Avon Books, 1979.

Zoline, Pamela. "The Heat Death of the Universe." In *The New Women of Wonder*. Ed. Pamela Sargent. New York: Vintage Books, 1977 (1967).

DORIS SOMMER AND GEORGE YUDICE

Latin American Literature from the "Boom" On

Contemporary writing in Latin America begins by being, if not post-modernist, then at least paramodernist, for it has never accommodated, feature for feature, the hegemonic Western modernist episteme from its inception in the early seventeenth century to its high modernist swan song in the first three decades of the twentieth century.[1] We could say that the 1960s "Boom" in Latin American literature takes its point of departure from the high modernists' (Joyce, Kafka, Faulkner) ambivalence (hostility, destruction, and nostalgia) toward a waning modernist discourse. This is true in part. But to favor such a criterion is mistakenly to recognize Latin American culture as the product of European (or Western) history, suffering by comparison in a kind of culturally unequal development.[2] Latin American literature, for example, may be seen as an echo of Western literature: Jorge Luis Borges "repeats" and even plagiarizes "our" Western heritage; Julio Cortázar* continues Kafka; Gabriel García Márquez* tropicalizes Faulkner; Guillermo Cabrera Infante Cubanizes Joyce. It can be read as an exercise in deference, although very often resulting in parody, whether by default or intentioned irreverence. In this spirit, Cortazar celebrated Lezama Lima's un-self-conscious borrowing and deformation of European texts which become mere raw material in the purposefully naive American hand.[3] Finally, Latin American literature has also been understood as an expression of national or regional identity that is discontinuous with foreign models.[4]

These views may not be mutually exclusive; rather, the Boom's combination of admiration for the First World masters and their parodic manipulation helps account for its enormous international success. A typical, and to a great degree justified, impression would read as follows: Latin American literature, especially narrative, hit the international literary scene like a tornado, leaving behind a path strewn with prestigious literary prizes and starry-eyed, awed, and even envious writers from the European and

North American centers of "World" culture. While the literary vanguard in these centers turned out grey experiments in technical minutiae (Robbe-Grillet, Sarraute, Sánchez Ferlosio), smoggy skyscapes of alienation (Butor, Updike), precious dry drolleries (Barthelme*, Pynchon*), humorless disquisitions on/of *écriture* (Sollers, Ricardou), Latin Americans dazzled the reader with crystalline lucidities (Borges), moving renderings of madness (Sabato, Cortázar) and violence (Vargas Llosa*), larger than life portrayals of power and corruption (Fuentes*, García Márquez), ebullient baroque recreations of tropical culture (Carpentier, Souza, Amado, Cabrera Infante, Sarduy).

But it was more than an explosion of narrative creativity; in fact, some observers are skeptical about the amount of work produced during that decade, pointing out that many of the books published then were formerly ignored works that represented a backlog for publishers to exploit once interest in Latin America had been established. The real explosion, then, may not be in the production of literature, but in its reception and market distribution. At home the process of modernization begun in the 1930s, and greatly enhanced by the period of import substitution industrialization of the 1940s and 1950s, was finally showing results in the field of mass communications. New consumer magazines such as *Primera plana* and *Siempre*, as well as major newspaper literary supplements, not only created a new reading public, but also provided the means (along with radio and TV variety shows) for transforming the writer into a superstar on a par with singers and movie celebrities.[5] And thanks to parallel advances in education, for the first time Latin American writers could count on a broad readership. At the same time, Spain's publishing capacities helped to launch the Boom by breaking the regional deadlock that often consigned novels to their national boundaries. On strictly commercial terms, the Boom may be said to begin with Seix Barral's publication and promotion of Mario Vargas Llosa's *The Time of the Hero* (1963), which coincided with Julio Cortázar's *Hopscotch*, published in Argentina. After this date printings of major authors' works jumped from the standard first edition of 3,000 copies to 25,000 in the case of Gabriel García Márquez's *One Hundred Years of Solitude* (1967). The masters of previous generations (Borges, Rulfo, Carpentier, and so on) rode these writers' coattails with equally sizable printings and reprintings.

It is important to bear in mind that subsequent reprintings of earlier works by Boom authors rose as well to 20,000 and upwards per year, not to mention 100,000 per year for García Márquez's blockbuster from 1968 on.[6] The phenomenal success of *One Hundred Years of Solitude* is something of an irony in the Boom canon. True, it has many of the experimental features of other new novels, principally a narrative line that manages to circle around to a dead end and a series of characters who are virtually forced into self-reflexivity. But this may be the only Boom novel consistently narrated in the third person, a strategy that seduces the reader into mistaking the discontinuity of the narrative line for a coherence associated with oral storytelling. Of course, it may be objected that given the multigenerational, epic quality of the book the omniscient voice is unavoidable. But this only begs the question of why García Márquez chose to write an epic. One possible reason is that, unlike its contemporaries, this novel prefigures a post-Boom concern with rewriting national history.

The appeal to foreign readers, no doubt, owed something to their degree of familiarity with or preparedness for the Latin American extensions of a European, sometimes called universal, literary tradition. That very familiarity allowed them to appreciate how the supplements to that tradition were unpredictable and refreshing. Spanish-Americans exploited the lessons of the modernists to their own ends, maintaining a tenuous or paradoxical balance between aesthetic experimentation and ethico-political motivation. While contemporary writers in France were cultivating the glossy stasis of the *nouveau roman*, Latin Americans offered something more dynamic and more ironic than despairing. This is one example of how a delayed and displaced response to First World intellectual trends results in the sophistication (without jadedness) of latecomers.

If the Boom is already post- or paramodern by definition, then the generation of the 1970s and 1980s cannot but be so. Yet the term may mislead us if we imagine the more recent literature to share the general obsession of Boom writers for ever more flashy technical displays. Nor do they share the earlier taste for a universal literature in which continental and regional peculiarities are crossed out under the marks of an international intellectual elite. We will refer below to some of the newer developments, especially to the efforts to renegotiate the balance between politics and experimental writing that went bust in the Boom.

LITERATURE EX NIHILO

Boom writers generally hated to admit any debt to earlier Latin American writers. If they had any "anxiety of influence," it was resolved by a round repudiation of local literary fathers. Their sudden burst onto the scene, with the freedom of orphanhood, was marked by a surge in regional euphoria, partly created and partly exploited by the mass consciousness industries. Add to this the liberatory possibilities and the attention provoked by the triumph of Castro in 1959, and you get an inflated belief in Latin America's final coming of age. It had finally begun to overcome economic dependency by naming it, and it had begun to formulate a cultural independence by cannibalizing European traditions. In the belief that the new literature had *invented* a truly proper language, it seemed that the Adamic dream had come true. Latin Americans could finally (re)name the world and, in doing so, name themselves. Caliban could finally possess his own kingdom.

For its authors and critical fellow travelers, the new literature was identified as revolutionary, no longer in simple metaphorical terms, but rather as a constitutive power. Unlike European writers who confronted their powerlessness (vis-à-vis the totalizing alienation and reification of the bourgeois order) precisely by cherishing, even savoring, their ennui (from Baudelaire to Butor, from Stendhal to Sollers), Latin American writers had reason to be euphoric regarding their praxis, which they undertook like a vindicating social cause:

...if we Hispano-Americans are capable of creating our own model of progress [as compared to Western technocratic models], then our language is the only vehicle that can give form, propose goals, establish priorities, elaborate critiques of a given way of life: of saying everything that cannot be said in any other way. I believe that in Spanish America there are novels being written and to be written which, when such a consciousness is attained, will provide the necessary instruments to drink the water and the fruits of our true identity.[7]

Despite, or perhaps because of, these protestations, the authors were in fact affirming their debts to a Latin American past. If the Boom novelists imagine themselves suddenly born into full maturity, like Athena from Zeus' head, this may indicate how secure their position is in an American tradition of writing. Similarly, other American writers of both the North and South have imagined that history begins anew with them. Perhaps this is only a radical formulation of an assumption in Western letters since the Middle Ages: that is, new texts mark new beginnings. Jorge Luis Borges' essay about "The Wall and the Books" jokes about the repetitive circularity and the impossible pride of starting anew; when the emperor of China orders the Great Wall to be built and all books before his reign to be burned, he already sensed that a future emperor would erase his epoch-founding work with another new beginning. Borges, the American writer, is evidently amused but fascinated with the paradox of a tradition built on disdain for the past. Like its political history, Latin America's paradoxical literary history is a series of efforts to catch up with the centers of power in order to achieve a real independence from them. It is significant that post-Boom writers are conscious that the First World has finally caught up with the dysfunctionality of modernism experienced by Latin Americans since their beginnings. This dysfunctionality, as Octavio Paz had already noted in 1950, made them "contemporaries of all mankind": "We Mexicans have always lived on the periphery of history. Now the center or nucleus of world society has disintegrated and everyone—including the European and the North American—is a peripheral being. We are all living on the margin because there is no longer any center."[8] Latin American authors, then, should no longer be preoccupied with this necessarily frustrating desire, just as they have also abandoned any belief in developmentalism.

In economic terms, the effort to emulate a putative center is called modernization, a process by which Latin American nations have come to participate directly in the capitalist world economy. The process has a specificity that cannot be thought of as a reflection of development in the metropolitan centers of Europe, the United States, and Japan. Rather, it accounts for the creation of social formations in which the modern and the traditional (or precapitalist) are progressively brought into contact, causing profound, often violent socioeconomic tensions. These tensions are expressed in the conflicts between elite and popular cultures as well as between universalizing and local or regional tendencies, so visibly manifested since Independence (early nineteenth century) and repeatedly coming to a head: at the turn of the century, during the Depression, and again since the 1960s. These periods also mark off successive literary movements whose goal it has been to produce a national or a continental literature on an equal footing with that of Europe and other metropolitan centers.

After Independence, and faced with the necessity to consolidate the newly formed nations, the writer-statesman strove to establish a new culture by, paradoxically, drawing on European progress (or civilization) against a native barbarism. The paradox is easily explained when we remember that Europe, especially England, was consolidating its mercantile interests in the New World under the mottos of freedom (of trade and from slavery) as against the self-defeating monopoly of Spain. The progressive Europeanizing fathers of the Latin American nations wanted to enter the international community by establishing harmony at home. First, they literally had to husband their Land, to domesticate and reproduce themselves on *her*, now that the usurping Spanish rivals for her love had been ousted. The challenge was not only to tame the Land, but to populate her; for in the absence of genealogical rights to America, the fathers had to legitimate their dominion through conjugal and then paternity rights. This brand of domestic heroism was plotted out in a series of sentimental novels that combined the personal and the political goals of establishing a legitimate family: for example, *Soledad* (1847; Solitude) by Bartolomé Mitre, *Amalia* (1855) by José Marmol, *Maria* (1867) by Jorge Isaacs, *Martin Rivas* (1862) by Alberto Blest Gana, and *Enriquillo* (1882) by Manuel de Jesus Galván. The national romance continued to be a model for the writer-statesman at least through the 1940s when populism adopted its gender-coded and rectilinear form. The best example is probably Rómulo Gallegos' *Doña Barbara* (1928). That the romance has a long afterlife is evident, for example, from the publishing success of Cuban Manuel Cofiño López's *The Last Woman and the Next Struggle* (1971).[9] When Carlos Fuentes* hastily celebrates its demise, he calls this heroic and self-confident narrative model populist. The new novel, by contrast, is marked by a circularity that doubts the relationship between history and progress (Fuentes, p. 12).

By the end of the nineteenth century, the rational patriarchal habit of combining literary and political responsibilities became somewhat outmoded, mostly because of the prosperity and political bureaucratization that capitalist progress had brought. This corresponds to the imperial phase of European capitalism which began to develop the infrastructure of Latin America, including industrialization and urbanization, channels of transport and communication, bringing Latin American intellectuals up to date with Europe. With the exception of José Martí and very few others, most writers felt that the fathers had already done their job and that now art could be free from instrumentality. They were the *modernistas*, led by Rubén Darío, and like the predecessors they repudiated, they availed themselves of the latest developments in European letters (i.e., Parnassianism, symbolism) in order to break with the colonialist legacy and enter modernity.

The avant-garde movements of the 1920s and 1930s, which also proclaimed a new culture that would supersede the past, were evenly split between those who, while not imitating nature, would parallel its processes, just as they would parallel and outdo Europe (the Ultraist Borges, Vicente Huidobro, and so on), and those who would recuperate and reconstitute a native culture (César Vallejo, Pablo Antonio Cuadra, Mario de Andrade, Miguel Ángel Asturias). That period corresponds to the boom and bust experienced between the two world wars. Economic prosperity after World War I intensified industrialization and urbanization, bringing to a head inherent contradictions. Greater industrial prosperity entailed greater proletarianization and a rise in worker consciousness; it also intensified the conflict between local metropolitan centers such as Buenos Aires, Lima, and Mexico, and the interior provinces where raw materials were produced under onerous conditions by peasants and Indians. This accounts, in part, for the conflict between cosmopolitan and regional/nativist vanguardists.

The literary Boom of the 1960s, then, is a break with the past in a tradition of similar breaks, to use Paz's phrase; it repeats the desire for autonomy through cultural production, paradoxically making use of its respective modernist legacy. Like the historical context of other avant-gardists, this one coincides with the rapid development of national economies under the tutelage of the post-World War II transnational economic order. The belief in cultural autonomy that characterizes Boom literature may be considered part of the *apertura* (openness) that takes place during the 1960s.[10] That is, the period spanning decolonization (the term Third World is coined at this time), the Cuban Revolution (1959), the civil rights movement in the United States, and the Cultural Revolution in China (1965–1969). Cuba acted as a catalyst for a tacit unity among Latin American writers of varied political sympathies; its revolution initiated a period of reflexivity when projects were rethought on every level—the economic, the political, the literary. The unity declines, however, with the imminent closure signaled by the Soviet invasion of Czechoslovakia (1968) and comes to its end with the overthrow of Allende (1973). Decolonization and the ultimate penetration of global industrialization go hand in hand such that the "last vestiges of nature"—the Third World and the unconscious—are transformed.[11] It could be said that the attention given Latin American literature during this period is, in part, due to this global transformation.

The *apertura* manifested itself as a series of contradictory experiences. On the one hand, most Latin American intellectuals and writers espoused a revolutionary discourse expressed either through the (Cuban) notion of praxis (armed struggle) or by the Boom's promulgation of liberation through language. On the other hand, their optimistic espousal of technological development (including the growth of an international publishing and promotion industry) was also, ironically, part of the global capitalization of all spheres of life; it not only made the explosion of subversive books possible, but also tended to neutralize their effect.

Like the *modernistas* who deplored the vulgarity of capitalism but profited from the freedom it brought, Boom writers enjoyed the double liberty of earning fame and often money, thanks to general modernization, especially in mass communications, while denigrating or, at least, ironizing modern times. Therefore, as regards literature, modernization made experimentation visible. The role of the mass media becomes crucial when one stops to consider the fact that, although the (mostly Southern Cone) *vanguardistas* (Borges, Macedonio Fernandez, Felisberto Hernandez, Juan Emar, Rosamel del Valle, Huidobro, and so on) had already effected a change in writing, by subverting narrative closure, deconstructing author and work, their texts were virtually unknown to the reading public precisely because there were no adequate means of circulation and publicity.

Clearly, many Boom writers condemn the advent of social technification:

We're running full speed in this rat race, we're subjected like any Frenchman or gringo to the world of competition and status symbols, the world of neon lights and Sears Roebuck and washing machines and James Bond movies and Campbell soup cans.[12]

The unreachable nature of the technological vanguard obliges us to revise our notions of "progress" and conclude that what today passes as such—the North American model—is not, can no longer be, will never be ours, like Tantalus' water and fruit. In the impossible race towards the impossible mirage even our own language becomes dispensable; Spanish will not be the language of that "progress"; before it, our language is but another junkyard on the side of the super highway, a cemetery of useless cars (Fuentes, p. 97) *La nueva novela*.

And yet his espousal of the *opera aperta* (Fuentes, p. 31), with all its attendant aesthetic techniques—ambiguity through polysemy, allusion, irony, shifting point of view, spatialization of time, exploration of different levels of consciousness—shows just the opposite. He not only revels in the margins to which technology has relegated his writing, but he also adopts the technocrat's skill at manipulating the unstable functions of modern society.

A TECHNICO-AESTHETIC CHECKLIST

Unlike the technocrats, however, Boom writers do not credit themselves with the right and rational answers. Instead, they make a point of undermining traditional authorial control, fragmenting it along with characterization, time, and language. As much as this tendency owes to the lessons of European high modernism, it owes to the sense of disappointment in the political and economic authors of Latin America with whom the novelists maintain, even against their will, a historical connection. Modernization had brought some prosperity, especially during the period of import substitution. But by the same capitalist logic it was reaching some deadends ever since the 1950s when imports began again to flood the Latin American markets. The evolutionary, rectilinear models of developmentalism, and their parallel national romances, simply were not going to deliver what the progressive fathers, or authors, of Latin American nationalism had promised. The Boom had benefited from modernization, but limits were already in view. One consequence was the high degree of writerly sophistication that questioned the author's or any one leader's (advis)ability to control narrative.[13]

Demoting, or defusing, the authorial voice was part of a general experimental strategy to break up the straight line of historical myths. Radical formal experimentation is, in fact, the Boom's most distinguishing feature. It can be understood as an aesthetic expression of the historical *apertura* of the 1960s in which mass culture played a major role. Indeed, as in a feedback circuit, mass culture and literature now interpenetrated each other, to the point that Cortázar's *Hopscotch* makes references to jazz, Eisenstein, Dos Passos, and so on; Fuentes mythifies the movie star in *Holy Place* (1967) and incorporates lists of favorite readings, movie and magazine photos in *A Change of Skin* (1967); and Cabrera Infante carnivalizes Western high and pop culture in *Three Trapped Tigers* (1967); while Vargas Llosa's personal romance gets contaminated with the clichés of radio melodrama in *Aunt Julia and the Scriptwriter* (1977). We could further characterize this *apertura* as expressing a period of radical change in which *heteroglossia* destabilized social and cultural formations.[14] Novelistic discourse, as Mikhail Bakhtin conceives it, is not a genre proper but precisely that which undermines stable formations. It is therefore particularly appropriate for the self-reflexivity that periods of change bring on and helps to explain why the Boom phenomenon has a narrative semblance.

By contrast with the novels of the 1960s, earlier and more predictable books about national identity form a genre that can be called romance. Of course, writers like Borges, Juan Rulfo, and Felisbento Hernandez, among others, fit neither category; they wrote essentially short fiction and helped to prepare the technical armory of the new generation. Its self-conscious experimentation challenges the institutionalized concept of the work of art as a coherent and perfected totality along with the program for a national self-improvement of the romances. With the exception of Borges (and his elitist circle organized around the journal *Sur*), the Boom writers were the first to challenge not so much the aestheticist view of art, but rather the diverse social realisms (e.g., *indigenismo*, *novela telurica*, subgenres of the national romance) which pretended to represent the social order or disorder. Instead, literature was now read as a series of fragments, reminiscent of Novalis' experiments in the early days of German Romanticism, acknowledging the disjuncture of perceptions and experience and rejecting the impulse to imprison narrative in neat and predictable plots and points of view.

Formal experimentation and self-consciousness go hand in hand with another dominant feature of Boom narrative; that is, self-reflexivity in relation to cultural and national identity. We have already quoted Fuentes regarding the exploration of Latin American identity, its national histories and myths, in order to construct a new literary language that can serve as a standard of value and the warrant for a proper identity. This may seem to be a contradiction, for one of the categories which the new narrative attempts to deconstruct is precisely that of established identities. How, then, can these writers reconcile myth and its deconstruction, especially in a mass culture that devalues particular national identities?

We can broach this contradiction by considering Severo Sarduy, the most radical of Latin American deconstructors of discursive authority.[15] According to him, Latin American literature tends toward the baroque because its language, its materiality (he might say corporeality) is an interplay of discourses that masks an absent or ever displaced warrant. Artificiality, resulting from the play of signifiers and erotic guises, becomes the revolutionary way of being of the marginal Latin American.[16] Sarduy draws on Lezama Lima's *Paradiso* (1966) and on Cabrera Infante's *Three Trapped Tigers* to illustrate his theory. His own *Where the Singers Come From* (1967) is an equally good example of the deconstruction of authorship, the fragmentation of character, and the dissemination of intertexts. What is most significant and goes beyond the simple echo of a nascent French post-structuralism, based on Roland Barthes,* Michel Foucault,* Jacques Lacan,* and Julia Kristeva's appropriation of Bakhtin, is Sarduy's insistence that such artificiality and superimposition of citations and discourses constitute an oblique representation of "Cubanness."

There is a stereophony in the Cuban language. I would even say that there is some sort of incapacity in the Cuban to deal with the national in a direct way. The topic is always broached indirectly, alluding to something else. Cuban literature, therefore, has taken shape as a superimposition of strata. And the Baroque is just that (...) I have converted the discourse on Cubanness into a true anamorphosis in which nothing is seen frontally, everything appears marginally, tangentially. We can't have direct access to representation, perception, the image. The only access is lateral, from the borders of representation.[17]

Sarduy's novel can be understood as a *Curriculum Cubense*, a (dis)course through "Three cultures—Spanish, African and Chinese—[which] have been superimposed to constitute the Cuban; the three fictions which allude to these cultures constitute this book."[18]

   The waning of Latin American authenticity which critics like Jean Franco attribute to the Boom turns out to be in writers like Sarduy, paradoxically, a greater form of authenticity because it recognizes the heterogeneous and constructed quality of Latin American identity. *Écriture* becomes identity. To this anti-bourgeois and utopian reversal of capitalist progress, Franco objects that it is a private utopia not only permissible within the world system but, even worse, also the expression of the logic of late capitalism.[19] Be that as it may, Sarduy's important contribution to the polemic between nativists (Americanists and so on) and cosmopolitans is that Latin American culture is always an interplay of heterogeneous discourses. Under another label, borrowed from another Cuban, Fernando Ortiz, Angel Rama characterizes this interplay as a transculturation: the mediation between two or more cultures from the perspective of one's native context.[20] Rama uses the concept to vindicate (and justly so) those writers like Brazilian João Guimarães Rosa, Mexican Juan Rulfo, and Peruvian José María Arguedas who, though widely published, were not canonized within the Boom pantheon precisely because of their adherence to indigenous (and oral) formations. They went beyond the mere reproduction of myth in their construal of "the mental operations that generate myth . . . by working on indigenous tradition and Western modernization," bringing them together "to the point of becoming indistinct, in an exercise of 'mythical thinking'."[21]

   The tension between modern and traditional claims on the authors, which characterizes regional (e.g., Arguedas) and urban (e.g., Cabrera Infante) transculturators alike can also be understood as a form of resistance. This is not to say that there are not different modes of expressing this resistance. There are, and they break down according to geocultural, gender, and class lines. Arguedas represents the solidarity of the Andean with his or her threatened peasant Indian heritage. Cabrera Infante represents the alienated tropical casino-consumer culture of a Cuban middle class intimately tied to U.S. interests. Luis Rafael Sanchez reworks this tension in *Macho Camacho's Beat* (1976) by making "Spanglish" not only the mark of Yankee corruption in Puerto Rico, but also the literary language in which Puerto Ricans sparkle.

The point is not so much that the canonical Boom reproduces the logic of late capitalism but rather that transculturation is experienced and expressed differentially in the texture of these authors' works. For example, the Quechua substratum endows the Spanish of Arguedas' *Deep Rivers* (1957) with a nominalist world view, not so much in a Whorfian or Sapirian sense (according to which language cuts the thought grooves of our imagination) but, rather, in a Vološinovian-Bakhtinian sense in which the word embodies *heteroglossia*, reverberates with the multiaccentuated tonalities of a changing social context.[22] Cabrera Infante's masterly pastiche and word-play also instantiate the texture of a changing social context (a decadent dependent culture on the eve of revolution) which is conceived as meaningless. Although Arguedas incarnates his language with a social sense rooted in the experience of the dominated classes, Cabrera Infante renders his senseless (in the experience of his alienated "bohemians"), though not without a palpable reference to a social situation. For Arguedas the word has social and ritual depth; for Cabrera Infante it weaves the surface texture poised over an exhilarating and nostalgic sense of loss. We dwell on the comparison between these two writers because it illustrates a major debate regarding the Boom's authenticity.[23] It also shows how the canonical writers, in conjunction with the mass media, managed to project their own literary project as the Latin American model, reducing and controlling the very *heteroglossia* that inheres in transculturation.

Latin American literature, then, does not fit comfortably into the category of postmodernism. On the one hand, it shares the postmodernist concern for the marginal, an ambiguous concept that has economic, sociological, and literary meanings. On the other, it is too concerned with its own identity to serve as the sheer surface on which a hegemonic postmodern culture mirrors itself. This was true of Latin American literature long before the Boom, despite the impression that the 1960s suddenly erupted with the work of the Canonical Four (Cortázar, Vargas Llosa, Fuentes, García Márquez). The fact that publishing enjoyed a boom during the 1960s is due just as much, if not more, to a 30- to 40-year backlog of important literary works that were reprinted in this period.[24] The presentation of several generations of writers under the hegemony of the Boom canceled out the chronology of Latin American literature, dehistoricizing it and projecting it as something new. This fact helps to explain why the literary market underwent a deflation during the 1970s and 1980s. The major publishing houses rode this wave of backlog reprintings until they ran out of a large enough supply of trademark authors to meet the demands of the public and of their own marketing schemes. Furthermore, by the mid-1970s the publishing business had changed such that the houses, having undergone the transformations required to compete in a climate of transnational economic rationality, began to produce fewer titles in ever larger printings hoping to score big with best-sellers. These changes had their repercussions on the writers who, like Cortázar, for example, rushed to get out as many titles as possible even if their books (e.g., *Octahedron*, 1974, *A Manual for Manuel*, 1973) had not been finished to their satisfaction.[25]

These strategies failed for reasons beyond the control of the publishing houses and the writers. We have already made reference to the political and economic closure that cut short the optimistic *apertura* enjoyed during the 1960s. The net result of this closure was the realization that the Boom, having proclaimed liberation and the end of ideology, was mostly an illusion. This is borne out by René Avilez Fabila's 1970 tongue-in-cheek recipe for writing Boom novels (i.e., make a collage of the quasi-pompous and pedantic references to literature, film, painting, and Pop culture endowed with a prestige of countercultural codes),[26] as well as José Donoso's *Personal History of the Boom* (1972), where the frustrated desire of celebrity transforms into the ironic realization that the Boom is nothing but a tinseled float on parade.

As for the effervescent reception of Latin American writers in Europe and North America, this also turns out to have been an inflationary illusion. To be sure, there is some interest in the literary quality and the cultural peculiarities of Latin American literary production. The majority of reviews, however, indicate that the dominant interest is otherwise: either a prurient fascination with the exotic or the confirmation of one's own discourse. Thus, one can read about Latin American "brutalities" and "intoxicated joy,"[27] and watch Sarduy strike a resonant chord in such enthusiasts of erotico-revolutionary *écriture* as Barthes and Cixous.[28] Similarly, Fuentes appeals to an Italian readership because his *A Change of Skin* (1974) deals with fascism.[29] The figures regarding translations are also misleading: "while there are numerous translations that signal a new distributionary phenomenon, the small printings and reprintings undo that impression."[30]

FRAGMENTATION OF THE CANON: THE DISSEMINATION OF MARGINALIA

With a kind of poetic justice, the fetishization of the privileged marginality of the canonical Boom soon gives way to other voices which the canon itself had marginalized. In fact, the differential nature of regions and cultures highlights the most significant feature of the many currents and tendencies characterizing Latin American literature since the Boom: the vindication of marginality and ex-centricity. The classics of the Boom are predominantly metropolitan. As the hegemony of the Boom begins to fade at the beginning of the 1970s, a cacophony of marginal voices can be heard. This is not to say that they didn't exist before and during the Boom, but, rather, that they were drowned out by its din.

To be sure, there are important exceptions such as the homoerotic *écriture* of Sarduy and Manuel Puig.* Héctor Libertella, following Emir Rodriguez Monegal, has attempted to privilege *écriture*, the *novela del lenguaje* (the novel of/about language), as the offspring of the *Aufhebung* or sublation of the Boom. In this view, language is foregrounded, banishing any notion of reference from the text in accordance with its semiotic autonomy.[31] Consequently, a writer cannot be assured that his or her intended meanings will be conveyed, making it impossible for literature to bear his or her social engagement. Novels such as José Donoso's *A House in the Country* (1977) and Enrique Lihn's *The Crystal Orchestra* (1968) and *The Art of Speech* (1980) construe Latin American reality as a *trompe l'oeil* (Donoso) or a phantasmal (Foucauldian) archive, conveying obliquely the hallucinatory terror of life in Pinochet's Chile. These works, however, continue to fit the canon because of their dependence on metropolitan phenomena: pop culture and Parisian theory.

By contrast, Central American writers, to give one example, are now cultivating a type of writing that incorporates the language and world view of the peasant (Claribel Alegria, Menlio Argueta, Alfonso Chase, Sergio Ramirez, and so on). This does not mean, however, that they necessarily revive "enterprises already mapped out in the social regionalism of the forties," as Angel Rama might have it.[32] Such an opinion would benefit a certain viewpoint in which the urban, the most modernized, sets the trend.

In some cases, the masters of the Boom themselves moved away from the canon. Both Cortázar and Vargas Llosa, for example, abandoned the extravagant formal experimentation of *Hopscotch* and *The Green House* and drifted toward certain modes of realism: *A Manual for Manuel* and *Captain Pantoja and the Special Service* (by Cortázar) and *Aunt Julia and the Scriptwriter* (by Vargas Llosa). García Márquez left behind the radical "marvelous realism" and self-referential *écriture* of *One Hundred Years of Solitude* and moved on to the overflowing orality of *The Autumn of the Patriarch* (1975) and the elaborate, yet stark, reportage of *Chronicle of a Death Foretold* (1981). Furthermore, the "dictator novels" that appeared in 1974–1975, García Márquez's *The Autumn*, Carpentier's *Reasons of State* (1974), Roa Bastos' *I the Supreme* (1975)—Donoso's *Casa de campo*, though later, could be included as well—focus on a representational topic that had a certain ascendancy much before the heyday of the Boom (e.g., Asturias' *El Señor Presidente*, 1946). But now they both deconstruct the centralizing power that underlies the concept of dictatorship, and suggest a relationship between dictators and those who dare to write after the Boom when writers worried collectively about the authoritarian traps set by narrative and representation.[33]

The remainder of this article outlines the diverse (mostly realist) literary currents that were overshadowed by or emerged after the Boom.

Regionalism. By this we do not refer to either realism à la the nineteenth-century bourgeois novel or to socialist realism. Rather than a rationalist analysis of society, we have a highly plastic linguistic representation of transculturation in regionalists such as the Peruvian José María Arguedas, the Mexican Juan Rulfo, and the Brazilian João Guimarães Rosa. This is a realism conditioned by traditional modes of thought and by the dynamism of the avant-garde. We might also mention the marvelous realism of the Cuban Alejo Carpentier and the magic realism of the Guatemalan Miguel-angel Asturias. Both directions of transculturation are at play in these writers: the penetration and transformation of Western discourse in the noncategorizable setting of America, in the case of Carpentier; the penetration of myth and Indian experience in narrative discourse in Asturias' case.

Women's Writing. Life at the margin of the Boom gave new space to women who would cultivate a variety of styles whose general hallmark was the combination of the intensely personal and sexual with what is a generally considered to be the political sphere. Clarice Lispector, doyenne of Latin American women writers, gives expression to the intimacies of a woman's life in *Near the Savage Heart* (1944); Rosario Ferré (Puerto Rico) explores the contradictions of class hegemony and gender subordination in *Pandora's Papers* (1976); Luisa Valenzuela (Argentina), author of *Strange Things Are Happening Here* (1975) and *The Lizard's Tail* (1983), has moved progressively to a condemnation of political repression through the subversive caricature of the sexual fantasies at the basis of tyrannical power; Fanny Buitrago (Colombia) is best known for her *Los Pañamanes* (1979); and there is the scandalously explicit sexuality of Reina Roffé (Argentina) and Ana Istaru (Costa Rica). Women have distinguished themselves as much in categories other than the predominantly personal-sexual: for example, Elena Poniatowska and Claribel Alegria in the politically motivated testimonial genre, as is noted below.

Jewish Cultural Regionalism. If marginality can be understood not only geographically, but also in cultural and linguistic terms, then Jewish writers also manifest the return of a repressed regionalism after the Boom. In Argentina, with the largest Jewish population in Latin America, the question of Jewishness had been given dramatic expression by German Rozenmacher contemporaneously with the Boom. As a critical category, however, Jewish writing does not emerge until the 1970s. It includes such writers as Mario Szichman (Argentina), whose novels, from *False Chronicle* (1969) to *At 8:25 pm the Woman Entered the Realm of Immortality* (1980), chronicle the life of the Pechofs, a family of Polish immigrants, in an elitist

Argentina; Isaac Goldemberg (Peru), who portrays the unusual social position of his half-Jewish, half-Indian protagonist in *The Fragmented Life of Don Jacobo* (1978); Isaac Chocrón and Elisa Lerner who deal with similar problems of accommodation in the Venezuelan context. This category could be considered as a subgenre of urban critical realism.

Urban Critical Realism. Still tied to the ethical concerns of existentialism, the critical realists trace the movements of modern Latin Americans in an alienating urban setting. This current runs the gamut from the highly imaginary representations of Juan Carlos Onetti (Uruguay), to the universal paranoia which Ernesto Sabato (Argentina) detects in the modern individual, the effects of political repression in Argentina in David Viñas's work, and the Marxist critique and commitment to revolution in José Revueltas (Mexico).

Whether regionalist, as in the case of Marcio Souza (Brazil), whom we have already mentioned, or urban, as in Ricardo Piglia (Argentina), more recent generations of writers are decidedly nationalist. Piglia's *Artificial Respiration* (1980), for example, is not an exercise in a translucent *écriture*. On the contrary, the novel is the inscription of the genealogy of oppositional Argentine writers, with the noted urban realist Roberto Arlt in the backround the whole time. Writing becomes the means to vindicate the marginal, the characters who comprise another Argentine history, not the abstract marginality of a Borges.

If the realism of Argentine writers expresses itself in relation to outward political repression, the younger generation of Mexican novelists attempts to capture the workings of an internalized system of repressive desublimation. In 1968 the Tlatelolco massacre became a dominant concern for Mexican writers. Representations of state power and repression were traditionally organized around images of the pyramid, the site of ritual sacrifice, as Octavio Paz explained in *Posdata*. Despite chronic economic crisis, after 1968 democratization permitted oppositional discourse. But with the shift from state order to a social order in which individuals respond to an invisible, dispersed control through the mass consciousness industries, it was no longer possible to represent and oppose power by "incorporating public discourse into the novel."[34] David Ojeda's *The Conditions of War* (1978), Guillermo Samperio's *Lenin in Soccer* (1977), and Jorge Aguilar Mora's *A Corpse Full of Earth* (1971) now represent this absence of the social.

The Return of History. With the revival of nationalist concerns there has been a renewed interest in national history. Although the majority of the dictator novels of the 1970s do not deal with specific dictators, it is Latin American history which motivates the composite wielders of power. It is also significant that this genre reemerges precisely when a new round of dictators has taken possession of the Southern Cone. In a sense, then, the representation of the dictator in Latin America's history is also a meditation and critique of this form of power in the present context. Written in the wake of poststructuralist critiques of power, these novels deconstruct the magic with which the dictator was traditionally thought to be invested.

The one exception to the composite figuration of power is Augusto Roa Bastos' *I the Supreme* (1974). Woven together from 20,000 documents which Roa Bastos researched over many years, the discourse deconstructs traditional notions of author and character in ways much more radical than any Boom text. *Écriture*, textuality, undoes the dictatorial (oral) power of Dr. Francia, whom Thomas Carlyle had characterized as the Dionysius of Paraguay, referring, no doubt, to the deity's mad display of power in Argos as an analogue for the dictator's Reign of Terror.[35] Like Borges, Roa Bastos constructs or compiles—the narrator is identified as a compiler—a utopian or heterotopian discursive space. Unlike the Argentine's *Absolute Book*, which contains endless repetitions of the same, Roa Bastos' compilation is a tribute to a history that had yet to be written, reproducing the weave of voices that had been left out in previous accounts. In other words, textuality here is the voice of the people, many people.

History has become the concern of so many writers since the Boom that there is not enough space here to mention all of them. A significant non-example, however, should be mentioned for the sake of contrast; it is Fuentes' *Terra Nostra* (1975) which proposes historical challenges and resorts to prescribed mythical resolutions. More open-ended structures of history are at the center of texts like *Palinurus of Mexico* (1977) by Fernando del Paso, *The Harp and the Shadow* (1978) by Alejo Carpentier (Cuba), *The Sea of Lentils* (1978) by Antonio Benítez Rojo (Cuba), *From April Onwards* (1975) by Marcio Veloz Maggiolo (Dominican Republic), *When They Loved the Communal Lands* (1978) by Pedro Mir (Dominican Republic), *Latin Homerica* (1979) by Marta Traba (Argentina), and *Memory of Fire* Vol. 1 (1982) by Eduardo Galeano. In the last work, for example, the Uruguayan journalist and novelist projects a monumental trilogy in which he pretends to rewrite the documents of Latin American cultural history from pre-Columbian times to the present.

Documentary and Testimonial Narrative. Interestingly enough, the concern with history evidently includes the desire to chronicle major social and political upheavals in the present. This is not to say that the testimonial is a new genre; personal accounts of historical events were written long before the 1960s. Rather, what is new is the literary and political attention given the testimonial. One important example is Rodolfo Walsh's *Operation Massacre* (1957) which, anticipating the documentary techniques used by Truman Capote, chronicles in literary fashion a 1956 massacre of a group of men who were thought to be Peronist sympathizers conspiring to overthrow the government. Perhaps the most important historical event of the twentieth century in our hemisphere, the Cuban Revolution, the "assault on the impossible," according to Mario Benedetti, begot myriad accounts from all sides of the struggle, and not least from the participants themselves, beginning with Fidel Castro and Ernesto "Che" Guevara. The very category of testimonial narrative was included by the Casa de las Américas editorial board among the other (traditional) genres in the journal's yearly prizes. Its ideological purpose was, no doubt, to portray the people as the agents of their own history. Whether or not the genre would have flourished without this stimulus is beside the point. The fact is that the testimonial narrative is now one of the most cultivated literary forms, by both sympathizers and critics of the revolution. Carlos Franqui's *Family Portrait with Fidel* (1981) is a good example of the latter camp.

One of the ways in which the people can participate in making their own history is to narrate it themselves. This is one of the functions of the testimonial, put to use by the anthropologist Miguel Barnet in his arrangement of the life story of a 105-year-old former slave, received piecemeal in several interviews. *The Autobiography of a Runaway Slave* (1966) radically blurs the distinctions between the literary and the ordinary. Women have also found their literary space in the testimonial. The Mexican Elena Poniatowska used a similar strategy of extended interview and first-person reconstruction in her stunning *Until I No Longer See You Dear Jesus* (1967), as did the Argentine Marta Traba in *Conversation in the South* (1981). *Let Me Speak* (1977) by Domitila Barrios de Chungara (written by Moema Viezzer), the wife of a Bolivian miner, is already a classic of testimonial literature. And the more recent *My Name is Rigoberta Menchu* (1983), the chronicle (recorded, transcribed, and arranged by anthropologist Elisabeth Burgos) of a Guatemalan Indian's use of religious community service as a weapon against oppression, promises to be one.

The decline of the Boom became evident in 1968, the year in which the Soviet Union occupied Czechoslovakia and Heberto Padilla's writing was first censured in Cuba. The same year saw the massacre at Tlatelolco, the highly symbolic Plaza of the Three Cultures, during the Olympic Games. In Mexico, at least, the social euphoria of the 1960s came to an abrupt end by 1968. Elena Poniatowska's *The Night of Tlatelolco* (1971), although a composite of reports and fragments of interviews dealing with the massacre, derives its literary specificity from the way in which the parts are brought together. Rather than present a particular point of view, Poniatowska's work, reminiscent of Roa Bastos' compilation, captures history as it is made (told, written, reported) by its agents.

Just as *Tlatelolco* moved many writers to account for the incredible event, Pinochet's 1973 coup and the murder of Allende generated numerous and generically diverse accounts: documentary accounts by Enrique Lafourcade (*Salvador Allende*, 1973) and Hernan Valdés (*Green Rooftiles*, 1974); impassioned denunciations by Antonio Skarmeta (*I Dreamt That The Snow Was Burning*, 1975) and Fernando Alegría (*Goose Step*, 1975); and a hallucinatory allegory of power relations by José Donoso (*A House in the*

Country, 1978). The case of Skarmeta is interesting in that, unable to fully give form to the plurality of voices and the epic nature of the Popular Front, thus producing a sense of failure, of lost opportunities under the Allende regime, he nonetheless achieves a triumphant documentary epic romance of the Nicaraguan Revolution in *The Insurrection* (1981).

Skarmeta's book and the objection he shares with many contemporary writers to what they call the hermeticism and elitism of the Boom lead us to the last historical event we will consider here: revolution in Central America. Unlike previous revolutions, numerous writers in both Nicaragua and El Salvador are on the front lines. Ernesto Cardenal, Rosario Murillo, Sergio Ramírez, Gioconda Belli, and Omar Cabezas Lacayo are, for example, all members of the Sandinista government. In addition, large numbers of "common" people participate in literary workshops to make writing a part of everyday life.

In literature, Central America has mostly generated poets. The greatest poet of the previous century was the Nicaraguan Rubén Darío. More recently, Salvadoran poets like Roque Dalton and Claribel Alegria have taken to writing novels and testimonial narratives. Dalton's *Poor Poet That I Was* . . . (1976) is the self-ironic account of a privileged poet in an oppressive society. Formally, it is a collage of diary, ethical, and aesthetic fragments concerning political activities and intellectual life. It is a kind of autobiographical *Libro de Manuel*. In Claribel Alegria's *No me agarran viva: La mujer salvadoreña en lucha* (1983), co-written with her husband D. J. Flakoll, she records the testimonies of Salvadoran revolutionaries regarding the death of a young bourgeois woman turned revolutionary, much like Alegria herself. Like Poniatowska and Roa Bastos, she becomes the medium through which others can tell their own and her history. *One Day of Life* (1980) by Salvadoran novelist Manlio Argueta, also a poet, is the almost impossible realization of a poetic rendering of the everyday life of a family of peasant women in a society beset by unrelenting state terror.

For all the shared features of Boom and later writing (specifically the multi-layered self-reflexivity), one major difference is already clear. Whereas the Boom writers tended to mine European and North American universal literature as well as the mass-produced and homogenizing culture of mass communications for their pastiches, assuming that a revolution in language would liberate Latin America at all other levels, their successors generally find this procedure to be frivolous. Instead, they compile and interpret the material of everyday history, not necessarily to reconstruct the populist romances of the pre-Boom—although this is certainly a temptation—but in the best cases to play the game of deconstructive self-reflexivity for the high stakes of constructing Latin America's future history.

NOTES

1. For a detailed account of the modernist episteme, see Timothy Reiss, *The Discourse of Modernism* (Ithaca, N.Y.: Cornell University Press, 1982), who re-names it analytico-referential discourse, which involves "such notions as those of truth and valid experiment (in science), of referential language and representation (in all types of discourse), of possessive individualism (in political and economic theory), of contract (in sociopolitical and legal history), of taste (in aesthetic theory), of commonsense and the corresponding notion of concept (in philosophy, all of which are "hypostatizations of a particular discursive system" (pp. 13–14).

2. Such a comparison, which has been effected on numerous discursive fronts, almost always in detriment of America and as a self-serving warrant of European superiority, can be discerned in philosophy, natural science, history, religion, lit-erature, and so on. Hegel, for example, explains that nature, in its extreme zones— intense cold or heat—is "too powerful to allow Spirit to build up a world for itself. ...The true theatre of History is therefore the temperate zone; or, rather, its northern half." This champion of universal history goes on to point out that "the Archipelago between South America and Asia shows a physical immaturity," a statement that leads to the conclusion that

America has always shown itself physically and psychically powerless, and still shows itself so.... A mild and passionless disposition, want of spirit, and a crouching submissiveness towards a Creole, and still more towards a European, are the chief characteristics of the native Americans; and it will be long before the Europeans succeed in producing any inde-pendence of feeling in them. The inferiority of these individuals in all respects, even in regard to size, is very manifest.

America is of no interest to Hegel because it "is only an echo of the Old World— the expression of a foreign Life," and as such it has no history. G.W.F. Hegel, *The Philosophy of History* (New York: Dover, 1956), pp. 90–97.

Similar statements can be found in other champions of disalienation such as Engels and Marx. Engels, for example, justifies Yankee aggression toward Mexico because it is in Mexico's interest to fall under the leadership of more advanced nations such as the United States (Friedrich Engels, *Los movimientos revolucion-arios de 1847*, included in the appendix to the *Manifiesto comunista* (Madrid: Cenit, 1932), p. 412. Marx, in his turn, berates Simón Bolívar as a bandit and explains that his early defeats in the War of Independence are due to his military incapacity, deriving no doubt from his general cognitive underdevelopment as a Latin Amer-ican, whereas his eventual victories are made possible by assistance from the British Legion. Karl Marx, *Simon Bolivar* (Buenos Aires: Ed. de Hoy, 1959), pp. 51 & ff.

Information regarding Engels' and Marx's views on America can be found in Jorge Abelardo Ramos, *Bolivarismo y marxismo* (Buenos Aires: A. Pena Lillo, Editor, 1969), pp. 26–29. For the denigration of America in natural history or science, see Antonello Gerbi, *The Dispute of the New World. The History of a Polemic, 1750–1900* (Pittsburgh: University of Pittsburgh Press, 1973).

3. See, for example, his "Approach to Lazama Lima," from *Vuelta al dia en*

ochenta mundos (Mexico: Siglo XXI, 1967), recently translated by Naomi Lind-strom in *The Review of Contemporary Literature* (Fall 1983).

4. Roberto Fernandez Retamar, in his *Caliban* (Mexico: Diogenes, 1972; trans-lated as "Caliban, Notes Towards a Discussion of Culture in Our America" in *The Massachusetts Review* (Winter-Spring 1974), verges on this latter view.

5. On this issue see Jean Franco, "Narrador, autor, superestrella: la narrative latinoamericana en la epoca de cultura de masas," in *Revista Iberoamericana* 47, nos. 114–115 (enero-junio 1981): 129–48, and Angel Rama, "El boom en per-spectivia," *La novela latinoamericana, 1920–1980* (Bogotá: Instituto Colombiano de Cultura—Procultura, 1982), pp. 235–93.

6. See Rama, "El boom en perspectiva."

7. Carlos Fuentes, *La nueva novela hispanoamericana* (Mexico: Joaquin Mor-tiz, 1969), p. 98.

8. Octavio Paz, *El laberinto de la soledad* (Mexico: Fondo de Cultura Econ-omica, 1959); originally 1960 in *Cuadernos americanos*: translated as *The Labyrinth of Solitude. Life and Thought in Mexico* (New York: Grove Press, 1961).

9. See Doris Sommer, "National Romances and Populist Rhetoric in Spanish America," *Europe and Its Others* (Essex: 1985).

10. The following account of 1960s periodization draws on Fredrick Jameson, "Periodizing the Sixties," in *The Sixties Without Apology*, eds. Sohnya Sayres, et al. (Minneapolis/New York: University of Minnesota Press/*Social Text*, 1984), pp. 178–209.

11. According to Ernest Mandel,

Far from representing a postindustrial society, late capitalism . . . constitutes generalized uni-versal industrialization for the first time in history. Mechanization, standardization, overspe-cialization and parcellization of labor, which in the past determined only the realm of commodity production in actual industry, now penetrate all sectors of social life. It is characteristic of late capitalism that agriculture is step by step becoming just as industrialized as industry, the sphere of circulation (e.g., credit cards and the like) just as much as the sphere of production, and recreation just as much as the organization of work.

Ernest Mandel, *Late Capitalism* (London: NLB-Verso Edition, 1978), quoted in Jameson, "Periodizing the Sixties," p. 207.

12. Carlos Fuentes, quoted in Emir Rodriquez Monegal, *El arte de narrar: dialogos* (Caracas: Monte Avila, 1977), p. 132.

13. In "Modernizacion, resistencia y revolucion. La produccion literaria de los sesenta," *Escritura* 2, no. 3 (January-June 1977) and "The Crisis of the Liberal Imagination," *Ideologies and Literature* 1, no. 1 (December 1976-January 1977), Jean Franco reduces the "new" *écriture*, whose *apertura* and play might have had subversive repercussions in a nineteenth-century setting, to a hypostatization of the technological society of late capitalism. In other words, she interprets the contradiction as a surface subversion with an accommodationist deep structure, not allowing for what seems to be, at least for us, a contradictory opposition, but opposition nonetheless.

14. For an explanation of the term *heteroglossia* as applied to literary and social discourses, see Mikhail Bakhtin, "From the Prehistory of Novelistic Discourse" and "Discourse in the Novel" in *The Dialogical Imagination. Four Essays by M.*

M. Bakhtin, ed. Michael Holquist (Austin: University of Texas Press, 1981), especially pp. 61–63, 75–77, 82–83, 284–85, 301–66.

15. He may seem, however, to subscribe completely to French poststructuralist discursive authority, quoting Roland Barthes, Jacques Lacan, Julia Kristeva, Philippe Sollers, Jacques Derrida,* and so on on almost every page of his essays. It is typical of the center-periphery dialectic that what subverts authority in the hegemonic center may surface in the periphery (ever eager for some form of "revolution" that will garner its self-determination) as an authoritative model.

16. Severo Sarduy, "El barroco y el neobarroco," in *America Latina en su literatura*, ed. Cesar Fernandez Moreno (Mexico: Siglo XXI, 1972), pp. 167–84.

17. From an interview—"Severo Sarduy. La serpiente en las singagoga," *Vuelta* 8, no. 89 (April 1984): 20—with Julia Kushingian.

18. Severo Sarduy, *De donde son los cantantes* (Mexico: Joaquin Mortiz, 1967), p. 151.

19. See Franco, "The Crisis of the Liberal Imagination," pp. 18–21.

20. Rama quotes Ortiz's definition of the concept: "We understand the word *transculturation* to better express the different phases of the transformation of one culture into another. This transformation is not so much the acquisition of another culture, which is what is strictly indicated by the Anglo-American term *acculturation*; rather, the process also necessarily implies the loss or uprooting of a previous culture, which might be called a partial deculturation. Furthermore, the process signifies the consequent creation of a new cultural phenomena which might be called *neoculturation*." Fernando Ortiz, *Contrapunteo cubano del tabaco y el azucar* (Caracas: Biblioteca Ayacucho, 1978), p. 86, quoted in Angel Rama, *Transculturacion narrative en America Latin* (Mexico: Siglo XXI, 1982), pp. 32–33.

21. Rama, *Transculturacion narrative*, p. 55.

22. Bakhtin's work is dedicated precisely to such changing social contexts in which "polyglossia flourishes," as in the Hellenic period which produced "Roman laughter" or as in the Middle Ages which saw the rise of parodic discourses in relation to the sacred Latin word. "From the Prehistory of Novelistic Discourse," pp. 61–64, 77.

23. According to Hernan Vidal, *Literatura hispanoamericana e ideologica liberal: surgimiento y crisis (Una problematic sobre la dependencia en torno a la narrativa del boom)* (Buenos Aires: Ediciones Hispamerica, 1976), the controversy hinges on the ability and desire of Boom writers to transcend a petty bourgeois liberal consciousness.

24. See Rama, "El boom en perspectiva," p. 270.

25. According to Rama, "The heteroclite completion of *Octaedro* by Cortazar or the faulty completion of *El libro de Manuel*, not very typical of his *oeuvre*, seem to respond to the demand of the period. And these demands, to be sure, are not merely economic as one might infer from the terms we use in describing the workings of the market, but rather may respond to multiple pressures: to be present in determined places, to respond to political problems, to participate in circumstantial struggles. "El boom en perspectiva," p. 275.

26. René Avilez Fabila, "Como escribir una novela y convertirla en un best-seller," in *Mundo nuevo*, 41–42 (October 1970).

27. "A squirming mass or tetterdemalion humanity emerges in these pages. . . . There are Amazonian river people and Amazonian women. There are missionary

nuns, lawless speculators in raw jungle rubber. Indian tribesmen who use blowguns and pilots on river boats in the amphibious world. . . . you get everything: the agony of a woman in childbirth, the brutalities of Indian torture, moments of intoxicated joy, a fatal game of Russian roulette, a provincial wedding. The catering is magnificent; every regional dish is served and savored . . . it is electrically alive." From a *New York Times* book review of Mario Vargas Llosa's *The Green House* (New York: Bard Books, 1973), reprinted on the back cover.

28. "Language reconstructs itself elsewhere under the teeming flux of every kind of linguistic pleasure. Where is this elsewhere. In the paradise of words. *Cobra* is in fact a paradisiac text, utopian (without site), a heterology by plenitude . . . ," in Roland Barthes, *The Pleasure of the Text* (New York: Hill & Wang, 1975), p. 8. See also Helen Cixous, " 'Ocobrabaroco.' A Text-Twister," *Review* (1974), p. 26. Both texts are quoted in Franco, "The Crisis of the Liberal Imagination," pp. 18–19.

29. Sara Castro Klaren and Hector Campos, "Tradduciones, tirajes, ventas y estrellas: el 'Boom'," *Ideologies and Literature* 4, no. 17 (September-October 1983), quote from an interview with Fuentes in which the interviewer insists that the European tradition is more evident than its "American roots" because the Mexican author's novel is concerned with "topics that until now we have considered to belong to us, such as war, fascism and concentration camps" (p. 320).

30. Klaren and Campos, "Tradduciones," p. 327.

31. See Hector Libertella, *Nueva escritura en Latinoamerica* (Caracas: Monte Avila, 1977) and Emir Rodriquez Monegal, *El Boom de la novela latinoamericana* (Caracas: Tiempo Nuevo, 1972).

32. Angel Rama, *Novisimos narradores hispanoamericanos en Marchas: 1964/ 1980* (Mexico: Marcha Editores, 1981), p. 43.

33. For a comprehensive analysis of the "dictator novels," see Angel Rama, *Los dictadores latinoamericanos* (Mexico: FCE, 1976), Domingo Miliani, "El Dictador: objeto narrativo en *Yo el Supremo*," *Revista de Critica Literaria Latinoamericana* 4 (1976): 103–19 and "El dictador: objeto narrativo en *El recurso del metodo*," *Revista Iberoamericana* 114–15 (January-June 1981): 189–225; Carlos Pacheco, *Narrativa de la dictadura y critica literaria* (Caracas: Celarg, 1983).

34. Jean Franco, "The Critique of the Pyramid and Mexican Narrative after 1968," in *Latin American Fiction Today* (Tacoma Park, Md.: Hispamérica, 1979), p. 79.

35. Thomas Carlyle, "Dr. Francia," in *Critical and Miscellaneous Essays*, Vol. 29 (New York: Scribner's, n.d.), p. 273.

SELECTED BIBLIOGRAPHY

Primary Sources

Aguilar Mora, Jorge. *Un cadaver lleno de mundo*. Mexico: Joaquin Mortiz, 1971.
Alegría, Claribel. *No me agarran viva: la mujer salvadoreña en lucha*. Mexico: Era, 1983. Transl. Robert L. Jones. New York: Tlön Editions, forthcoming.
Alegría, Fernando. *Paso de los gansos*. Barcelona: Editorial Laia, 1980.

Amado, Jorge. *Gabriela, Clove and Cinnamon*. Trans. James L. Taylor. New York: Alfred A. Knopf, 1962.

———. *Dona Flor and Her Two Husbands*. Trans. Harriet de Onis. New York: Alfred A. Knopf, 1969.

Arguedas, José María. *El zorro de arriba y el zorro de abajo*. Buenos Aires: Losada, 1971.

———. *Deep Rivers*. Trans. Frances Horning Barraclough. Austin: University of Texas Press, 1978.

———. "Focus on José María Arguedas." *Review* (1980): 25–26.

Argueta, Manlio. *One Day of Life*. Trans. Bill Browl. New York: Vintage, 1983.

Arlt, Roberto. *El juquete rabioso*. Buenos Aires: Losada, 1926.

Asturias, Miguel Ángel. *The President*. Trans. Frances Partridge. New York: Atheneum, 1964.

———. *Mulata*. New York: Delacorte Press, 1967.

———. *Strong Wind*. Trans. Gregory Rabassa. New York: Delacorte Press, 1968.

———. *The Green Pope*. Trans. Gregory Rabassa. New York: Delacorte Press, 1971.

Barnet, Miguel. *The Autobiography of a Runaway Slave*. Trans. Jacosta Innes. London: Bodly Head, 1966.

Benitez Rojo, Antonio. *El mar de las lentejas*. Havana: Editorial Letras Curbanas, 1979.

Borges, Jorge Luis. *Ficciones*. Ed. and introd. Anthony Kerrigan. New York: Grove Press, 1962.

———. *The Aleph and Other Stories, 1933–1969*. Ed. and trans. Norman Thomas di Giovanni. New York: E.P. Dutton, 1970.

Buitrago, Fanny. *Los Pañamanes*. Barcelona: Plaza & Janés, 1979.

Cabrera Infante, Guillermo. *Three Trapped Tigers*. Trans. D. Gardner and Suzanne Jill Levine. New York: 1971.

———. *Infante's Inferno*. Trans. Suzanne Jill Levine. New York: Harper & Row, 1984.

Carpentier, Alejo. "Manhunt." Trans. Harriet de Onis. *Noonday* 2 (1959): 109–80.

———. *Explosion in a Cathedral*. Trans. John Sturrock. Boston: Little, Brown, 1962.

———. *War of Time*. (Includes "The Highroad of Saint James," "Right of Sanctuary," "Journey Back to the Source," "Like the Night," and "The Chosen.") Trans. Frances Partridge. New York: Alfred A. Knopf, 1970.

———. *The Lost Steps*. 2d ed. Trans. Harriet de Onis. New York: Alfred A. Knopf, 1971.

———. *Reasons of State*. Trans. Frances Partridge. New York: Alfred A. Knopf, 1976.

———. *El arpa y la sombra*. Mexico: Siglo XXI, 1979.

Cofiño López, Manuel. *La última mujer y el próximo combate*. Havana: Casa de las Américas, 1971.

Cortázar, Julio. *Hopscotch*. Trans. Gregory Rabassa. New York: Random House, 1966.

———. *A Manual for Manuel*. Trans. Gregory Rabassa. New York: Pantheon, 1978.

Dalton, Roque. *Miguel Marmol. Los sucesos de 1932 en El Salvador*. 2d ed. Mexico: Ediciones Cuicuilco, 1982.

———. *Pobrecito poeta que era yo*. . . . 3d ed. San José: EDUCA, 1982.

Donoso, José. *The Obscene Bird of Night*. Trans. Hardie St. Martin and Leonard Mades. New York: Alfred A. Knopf, 1973.

———. *A House in the Country*. Trans. David Pritchard with Suzanne J. Levine. New York: Alfred A. Knopf, 1984.

Fernandez Moreno, César and Ivan Schulman. *Latin America in Its Literature*. Trans. Mary G. Berg. New York: Holmes & Meier, 1980.

Fernandez Retamar, Roberto. "Caliban. Notes Towards a Discussion of Culture in Our America." Trans. Roberto Marquez. *The Massachussetts Review* (Winter-Spring 1974): 7–72.

Ferré, Rosario. *Papeles de Pandora*. Mexico: Joaquin Mortiz, 1976.

Franqui, Carlos. *Family Portrait with Fidel*. New York: Random House, 1984.

Fuentes, Carlos. *The Death of Artemio Cruz*. Trans. Sam Hileman. New York: Farrar, Straus & Giroux, 1964.

———. *A Change of Skin*. Trans. Sam Hileman. New York: Farrar, Straus & Giroux, 1968.

———. *Terra Nostra*. Trans. Margaret Sayers Peden. New York: Farrar, Straus & Giroux, 1976.

Galeano, Eduardo. *Memoria del fuego*. Madrid: Siglo Veintiuno de España Editores, 1982.

———. *Days and Nights of Love and War*. Trans. Judith Brister. New York: Monthly Review Press, 1983.

García Márquez, Gabriel. *One Hundred Years of Solitude*. Trans. Gregory Rabassa. New York: Harper & Row, 1970.

———. *The Autumn of the Patriarch*. Trans. Gregory Rabassa. New York: Harper & Row, 1976.

Goldemberg, Isaac. *The Fragmented Life of Don Jacobo Lerner*. New York: Persea, 1976.

———. *Tiempo al tiempo*. Hanover, N.H.: Ediciones del Norte, 1984.

Guimarães Rosa, João. *Grande Sertao: Veredas*. Rio de Janeiro: J. Olympio, 1963.

Harss, Luis, and Barbara Dohmann. *Into the Mainstream: Conversations with Latin American Writers*. New York: Harper, 1969.

Lafourcade, Enrique. *Salvador Allende*. Barcelona: Ediciones Grijalbo, 1973.

Lezama Lima, José. *Paradiso*. Trans. Gregory Rabassa. New York: Farrar, Straus & Giroux, 1974.

Lihn, Enrique. *La orquesta de cristal*. Buenos Aires: Sudamericana, 1976.

———. *El arte de la palabra*. Barcelona: Pomaire, 1980.

Lispector, Clarice. *Perto do corasão*. . . . *Selvagem*. Rio de Janeiro: A Noite, 1944.

Mir, Pedro. *Cuando amaban las tierras comuneras*. Mexico: Siglo XXI, 1978.

Ojeda, David. *Las condiciones de la guerra*. Havana: Casa de las Américas, 1978.

Onetti, Juan Carlos. *The Shipyard*. Trans. Rachel Caffyn. New York: Scribner's, 1968.

———. *La vida breve*. 2d ed. Barcelona: Edhasa, 1980.

———. "The Pit." Trans. Hugo Verani. *Review* 29 (May/August 1981): 26–34.

Paso, Fernando del. *Palinuro de México*. Madrid: Ediciones Alfaguara, 1977. "The Voyage of Palinurus through the Advertising Agencies and Other Imaginary

Islands," excerpt trans. by Edith Grossman, in *Review* 28 (January-April 1981): 33–36.

Perus, Françoise. *Historia y critica literaria. El realismo social y la crisis de la dominación oligarquica.* Havana: Casa de las Américas, 1982.

Piglia, Ricardo. *Respiración artificial.* Buenos Aires: Pomaire, 1980.

Poniatowska, Elena. *Hasta no verte Jesús mio.* Mexico: Era, 1968.

———. *La noche de Tlatelolco.* Mexico: Era, 1971.

———. *Massacre in Mexico.* Trans. Helen R. Lane. New York: Viking Press, 1975.

Puig, Manuel. *Betrayed by Rita Hayworth.* Trans. Suzanne J. Levine. New York: E. P. Dutton, 1971.

———. *Heartbreak Tango.* Trans. Suzanne J. Levine. New York, E. P. Dutton, 1973.

———. *The Buenos Aires Affair. Detective Novel.* Trans. Suzanne J. Levine. New York: E. P. Dutton, 1976.

———. *The Kiss of the Spider Woman.* Trans. Thomas Colchie. New York: Alfred A. Knopf, 1979.

———. *Eternal Curse on the Reader of these Pages.* New York: Random House, 1982.

Ramirez, Sergio. *To Bury Our Fathers. A Novel of Nicaragua.* Trans. Nick Caistor. London: Readers International, 1984.

Revueltas, José. *The Stone Knife* ("El luto humano"). Trans. H. R. Hays. New York: Reynal & Hitchcock, 1947.

Roa Bastos, Augusto. *Yo el supremo.* Mexico: Siglo XXI, 1974.

Rodriguez Monegal, Emir, with the assistance of Thomas Colchie. *The Borzoi Anthology of Latin Am. Lit.* 2 vols. New York: Alfred A. Knopf, 1977.

Roffé, Reina. *Monte de Venus.* Buenos Aires: 1976.

Rulfo, Juan. *Pedro Paramo.* Mexico: FCE, 1955.

Sabato, Ernesto. *The Outsider.* Trans. Harriet de Onis. New York: Alfred A. Knopf, 1950.

———. *On Heroes and Tombs.* Trans. Helen Lane. New York: David R. Godine, 1981.

Samperio, Guillermo. *Lenin en el fútbol.* Mexico: Editorial Grijalbo, 1978.

Sanchez, Luis Rafael. *Macho Camacho's Beat.* Trans. Gregory Rabassa. New York: Pantheon, 1980.

Sarduy, Severo. *De dónde son los cantantes.* Mexico: Joaquin Mortiz, 1967.

———. *Cobra.* Trans. Suzanne Jill Levine. New York: E. P. Dutton, 1975.

Skarmeta, Antonio. *La insurrección.* Hanover, N.H.: Ediciones del Norte, 1982.

———. *Soñé que la nieve ardia.* Barcelona: Planeta, 1975.

Szichman, Mario. *At 8:25pm the Woman Enters the Realm of Immortality.* Hanover, N.H.: Ediciones del Norte, 1983.

Traba, Marta. *Homérica Latina.* Bogotá-C.: Valenclia Editores, 1979.

Valdés, Hernan. *Tejas verdes: Diario de un campo de concentración en Chile.* Barcelona: Ariel, 1974.

Valenzuela, Luisa. *Strange Things Happen Here.* Trans. Helen Lane. New York: Harcourt, Brace, Jovanovich, 1979.

———. *The Lizard's Tail.* Trans. Gregory Rabassa. New York: Farrar, Straus & Giroux, 1983.

Vargas Llosa, Mario. *The Time of the Hero*. Trans. Lysander Kemp. New York:
    Grove Press, 1966.
————. *Aunt Julia and the Scriptwriter*. Trans. Helen R. Lane. New York: Farrar,
    Straus & Giroux, 1982.
Veloz Maggiolo, Marcio. *De abril en adelante*. Santo Domingo: Editora Taller,
    1975.
Viñas, David. *Los hombres de a caballo*. Havana: Casa de las Américas, 1967.
Walsh, Rodolfo. *Operación masacre*. Buenos Aires: Jorge Alvarez, 1969.

Secondary Sources

Avilez Fabila, René. "Como escribir una novela y convertirla en un bestseller."
    Mundo nuevo (October 1970): 41–42.
Castro Klarén, Sara, and Héctor Campos. "Traducciones, tirajes, ventas y estrellas:
    el 'Boom'." *Ideologies and Literature* 4, No. 17 (September-October 1983).
Donoso, José. *The Boom in Spanish American Literature*. Trans. Gregory Kolo-
    vakos. New York: Columbia University Press, 1977.
Franco, Jean. "Narrator, Author, Superstar: Latin American Narrative in the Age
    of Mass Culture." *Revista Iberoamericana* 47, Nos. 114–115 (1981): 192–48.
————. "The Crisis of the Liberal Imagination and the Uptopia of Writing."
    Ideologies and Literature 1, No. 1 (December 1976-January 1977): 5–24.
————. "Criticism and Literature Within the Context of a Dependent Culture."
    In *The Uses of Criticism*. Ed. A. P. Foulkes. Frankfurt: Peter Lang, 1976,
    pp. 269–87.
————. "The Critique of the Pyramid and Mexican Narrative After 1968." In *Latin
    American Fiction Today*. Ed. Rose S. Minc. Tacoma Park, Md.: Hispa-
    mérica, 1979, pp. 49–60.
Fuentes, Carlos. *La nueva novela hispanoamericana*. Mexico: Joaquin Mortiz, 1969.
Libertella, Hector. *Nueva escritura en Latinoamérica*. Caracas: Monte Avila, 1977.
Paz, Octavio. *The Labyrinth of Solitude. Life and Thought in Mexico*. Trans.
    Lysander Kemp. New York: Grove Press, 1961.
Rama, Ángel. *La novela latinoamericana, 1920–1980*. Bogotá: Instituto Colom-
    biana de Cultura—Procultura, 1982.
————. *Los dictadores latinoamericanos*. Mexico: FCE, 1976.
————. *Novisimos narradores hispanoamericanos en marcha: 1964/1980*. Mexico:
    Marcha Editores, 1981.
————. *Transculturación narrativa en América Latina*. Mexico: Siglo XXI, 1982.
Rodriguez Monegal, Emir. *El arte de narrar: dialogos*. Caracas: Monte Avila, 1977.
————. *El Boom de la novela latinoamericana*, Caracas: Tiempo Nuevo, 1972.
Sommer, Doris. *One Master for Another. Populism as Patriarchal Rhetoric in
    Dominican Novels*. Lanham, Md.: University Press of America, 1983.
Vidal, Hernan. *Literatura hispanoamericana e ideologia liberal: surgimiento y crisis
    (Una problematica sobre la dependencia en torno a la narrativa del boom)*.
    Buenos Aires: Ediciones Hispamérica, 1976.

POSTMODERN CRITICISM

WILLIAM A. COVINO

Rhetoric Is Back:
The Old and New in Critical Theory

Critical theory, through the middle of this century, has been essentially a theory of reading that "locates" and "stabilizes" institutionally canonized literary works. From a modern vantage point, the critic of, say, Byron's *Don Juan*, examines the figurative and technical elements that Byron "put into" the poem (with reference to appropriate historical and biographical information), and synthesizes an "intention" or "theme" that describes the "meaning" of the work. The elaboration of a relatively stable intended meaning amounts to what has been called validity in interpretation.[1]

If a text resists this interpretive approach, if it escapes any reduction to critical generalization, the critic may become anxious. Motivated by what Jacques Derrida* calls "everything in us that desires a realm," and unable to locate the *sui generis* variegation of *Don Juan* comfortably within any critical realm, our critic might either banish the poem as bad literature (the practice of Byron's contemporaries), or place it with a handful of other "fascinating but inexplicable anomalies" that puzzle and upset modern literary studies.[2]

The professional criteria for what counts as literature and criticism have determined the nature of literacy as well. The virtues of unity and coherence determine the competency of student writers; academic essays replete with an identifiable thesis, and ordered into a beginning, middle, and end make the grade in modern writing classes. Altogether, the criteria for both effective rhetoric (understood as expository and persuasive prose) and significant belles lettres posit writing and reading as the creation and discovery of order and closure. And so literature and literacy, in modern terms, are wrapped in what Winston Weathers calls a "well-made box."[3]

The epistemological crisis of this century—the failure of objectivity, Cartesian rationality, and detachment to account for our complicated perception of a world in flux where matters are never settled—has called into question writing that tries to maintain unity, coherence, and certainty, writing that Edward Said has called preservative rather than investigative.[4] Postmodern critical theory celebrates uncertainty, upsetting the generic distinctions that tuck literature, science, and social science away from one another, blurring objectivity and subjectivity, fact and fiction, imagination and reality.

As Terry Eagleton demonstrates, what counts as a *literary* text, once one begins taking inventory, just cannot be determined.[5] All texts being equal, so to speak, any genre—a freshman essay, lyric poem, casual conversation, scientific treatise, lab report—is legitimate game for the critic, and each is potentially rich in symbolic action.

Just as the definition of a literary text has become a multiple choice, so has the nature of criticism. "The main ideal of criticism," to quote Kenneth Burke's longstanding but curiously postmodern proposition, "is to use all that is there to use."[6] Recognizing that no critical determination is either stable or limited, the postmodern critic acknowledges and plays with the psychological, cultural, political, epistemological, and linguistic variables that enrich and complicate meaning. Burke suggested almost 40 years ago that such variables increase the possibilities for textual richness, ambiguity, and complexity, proposing his now well-known pentad of Act—Agent—Scene—Agency—Purpose as a method for generating perspectives. Roman Jakobson schematizes "factors inalienably involved in verbal communication" by proposing an interplay among addresser, addressee, context, message, contact, and code. Most recently, Del Hymes has acknowledged both Jakobson and Burke as he presents an ethnographic inventory of discourse; Hymes would explicate relationships among participants, channels (media), codes, settings, genres, and attitudes.[7]

In sum, the recent theory and practice of criticism—that is, commentary about a text—has extended outside both traditionally literary disciplines and the established critical realm. One practices criticism not by positing meaning, but by demonstrating the possibilities for multiple perspectives. In this article I will sample those views and practices that illustrate postmodern critical theory, which encourage the ongoing invention of perspectives while they discourage certainty and closure, which hold that no interpretive statement offers more than a tentative and fragile viewpoint. By way of introducing current movements, let us first take up Terry Eagleton's recent suggestion that postmodern criticism is a return to rhetoric, in the richest classical sense of that term.[8] A survey of changes in the definition of rhetoric, and of the alliance between rhetoric and belles lettres, allows us to view recent changes in criticism as the revision of a tradition essentially forgotten since antiquity, and to sketch the historicity of attitudes toward language and literacy.

Aristotle's *Art of Rhetoric* (ca. 335 B.C.) has been the authoritative reference for centuries of rhetoricians, just as his *Poetics* remains a foundation of literary theory. Investigating what Aristotle means by art and rhetoric, we conclude that the principles of discourse are supple, inclusive, and finally indeterminate. For Aristotle, rhetoric functions "to find out in each case the existing means of persuasion" (1355b, 14). The art of rhetoric is an art of invention, of hypothesizing different variables informing a speech situation, and reflecting on how the situation is affected. The beliefs and presuppositions of the auditors, the character of the rhetor, the context and occasion for the speech, the prevailing conventions of language: these characteristics are always in flux, and Aristotle demonstrates the array of questions that a rhetor must consistently pose to himself or herself in order to invent possibilities for creating meaning, community, and goodwill. A rhetor's exploration is propelled by indeterminacy; the uncertainty of any speech situation makes truth a matter of probability.

Rhetoric is an art because, first of all, the rhetorical invention of perspectives can be pursued methodically; for Aristotle, the inventory of variables constitutes a systematic, thus artistic, investigation. Add to this idea of art another, quite appropriate one, from Aristotle's *Nichomachean Ethics*. There, art is "the coming into being of something which is capable of being different from what it is."[9] This definition both complements and complicates the investigative system offered in the *Rhetoric*. The art of rhetoric underlines the ambiguity of language; to practice the art, one remains mindful that all conclusions are provisional, tentative. The art lies not in the completion of a text, but in the transfiguration of one text—one system of possibilities—into another.

Although the art of rhetoric is inventing options, making a speech requires selecting from possibilities, trying to fit a text to a context of presentation. The context—those psychological, political, epistemological, and economic conditions, beliefs, and conventions in play—determines almost entirely what the text means. In effect, the context invents the text. And so it is with poetry as well. In his *Poetics* Aristotle identifies poetry (a term synonymous in ancient Greek with "making" in general) with the form or plot that appeals to the audience's expectations and sense of "general truths." The meaning of a poem is, in this sense, rhetorical; effective literature is convincing.

The history of rhetoric and poetics, after Aristotle, is a continually stronger refutation of the suppleness of discourse, a progressive denial of the ambiguity of language and literature, a more and more powerful repression of contextual variables by textual authority. The principles of literary criticism become even more explicitly aligned with the principles of rhetoric, but the study of discourse largely becomes formulary exercises in terminology. In ancient Rome, criticism and oratory were ossified into stock recitations and formulas; training in these subjects both maintained an elite class and contained the imaginative power that could threaten imperial rule. In the Middle Ages God replaced the emperor; both rhetoric and criticism largely consisted of the correct, established interpretation of scrip-

ture. Encyclopedic catalogues of tropes and figures had grown ever larger
from Roman antiquity onward, and in the Renaissance style alone became
the substance of rhetoric; questions about the invention and arrangement
of discourse became the province of logic. One learned rhetoric and criticism by recognizing and manipulating the ornaments of language.[10] But
with the Cartesian reduction of knowledge to "plain" observation from
the seventeenth century onward, approved style became plain style, and
the primary virtue in both exposition and literature was perspicuity. The
Royal Society of London for Improving Natural Knowledge moved to
"reject all amplifications, digressions, and swellings of style; to return back
to the primitive purity, and shortness, when men delivered so many *things*,
in almost an equal number of words."[11] In 1840 Thomas DeQuincey explicitly leagued himself with Aristotle as he called for a return to rhetoric
and criticism that exploit uncertainty, the play of "inversions, evolutions,
and harlequin changes" that "eddy about a truth"; but, DeQuincey concludes, "the age of rhetoric has passed among forgotten things."[12]

Postmodern criticism is the reinvention of a forgotten rhetoric, of the
antique sophistry possible before the state and God and science took their
turns at checking the play of discourse. Kenneth Burke is perhaps the first
postmodern of this century. In 1931 he wrote *Counterstatement* in response
to positivistic movements in both science and the arts; there, in his "*Lexicon
Rhetoricae*," Burke proposes that form and meaning in literature are entirely ambiguous phenomena. The critic's task is the exploitation of that
ambiguity; toward that end, as Burke writes later, we need "*terms that
clearly reveal the strategic spots at which ambiguities necessarily arise.*"[13]
He stands alone, through the New Critical middle of this century, as the
great complicator of positivistic and logocentric criticism, and as the proponent of a "new" rhetoric (which some have recognized as an Aristotelian
retread).[14]

With a survey of views and problems in postmodern critical theory, I
wish to reinforce the alliance of criticism and rhetoric. Postmodern critical
theory recognizes that texts are rhetorical, in the oldest and richest sense
of that term. Both more celebrated and infamous than Kenneth Burke,
Jacques Derrida reigns as the more recent proponent of textual
indeterminacy.

Derrida recognizes the tendency of all discourse systems to circumscribe
thought, noting that the Western practice has been, always and everywhere,
to *structure* experience, and "above all to make sure that the organizing
principle of the structure would limit what we might call the *play* of the
structure."[15] In line with Derrida's proposal, we can regard the dominant
mode of communicating literary experience, the critical essay, as one type
of limited structure. As Keith Fort argues, "In general, we cannot have
attitudes toward reality that cannot be expressed in available forms. If, for
example, we can only express our relation to literature in the form of the

standard critical essay, we can only have an attitude that would result in the proper form."[16] Derrida believes that resisting enclosure by institutionalized structures requires intellectual play by writers who recognize the limitations of their discourse clearly enough to push against them: "In effect, what appears most fascinating in this critical search for a new status of discourse is the stated abandonment of all reference to a *center*, to a *subject*, to a privileged *reference*, to an origin, or to an absolute *archia* (p. 286).[17]

As Derrida explains, however, complete "decentering," free play equivalent to total anarchy, can never occur. All play begins with "the means at hand" and entails to some extent "the necessity of borrowing one's concepts from the text of a heritage" (pp. 282–85). By concluding that all play cannot escape "the culture of reference," Derrida counters any misconception of play as solipsistic meandering with his implication that members of a culture can play *together*, able to share new conceptions because they share the received tradition against which the innovator struggles. But Derrida holds little hope for shared play; what prevails are "dreams of deciphering a truth or an origin which escapes play," dreams of achieving certainty. Those who idealize certainty and conviction "turn their eyes away when faced by the as yet unnameable which is proclaiming itself," blind to departures from received ways of knowing and naming (pp. 292–93).

The controversy over textual authority has emerged in the philosophy of science, which also opposes the rhetoric of free play to the valorization of truth. Both Thomas Kuhn and Paul Feyerabend have dethroned logical positivism and empiricism. Kuhn's position, that scientific progress always results from a paradigm shift that discards theories and methods no longer applicable to new problems, has been adapted by historians, sociologists, and educators, among others, as they recognize that what counts as research or discovery or progress in any discipline depends on the paradigm implicitly espoused by its practitioners. Kuhn has provoked interest in how the virtues and values of any profession are relative, or we might say, rhetorical.[18]

More interesting, more radical, and less well known than Kuhn, Paul Feyerabend disrupts the philosophy of science with the same advocacy of play as methodology that distinguishes Derrida's work. Feyerabend summarizes his argument "Against Method" with the following advice:

Do not work with stable concepts. Do not eliminate counterinduction. Do not be seduced into thinking that you have at last found the correct description of "the facts" when all that has happened is that some new categories have been adapted to some older forms of thought, which are so familiar that we take their outlines to be the outlines of the world itself.[19]

This advice means to correct the tendency in scientific education to kill the ability of students to think for themselves and make discoveries: "An essential part of the [scientific] training is the inhibition of intuitions that might lead to a blurring of boundaries. A person's religion, for example, or his metaphysics, or his sense of humor must not have the slightest connection with his scientific activity. His imagination is restrained and even his language will cease to be his own" (p. 20). Shackled by a "professional conscience," students and scientists alike proceed by ignoring any variables that upset the uniformity and objectivity of their investigation. In uncompromising opposition to a fixed method or fixed theory, whose fixity "arises from too naive a view of man and of his social surroundings," Feyerabend proposes *counterinduction*: "Introducing, elaborating, and propagating hypotheses whch are inconsistent either with well-established theories or well-established facts" (p. 26). Explaining that the proliferation of alternative views coincides with a pluralistic society whose people share their unique talents and predispositions, and that such pluralism flourishes only in the absense of constraints, Feyerabend offers a single maxim: "Anything goes" (p. 26).

Feyerabend's professed anarchistic theory does not lead to chaos; he deflects the fear that "anything goes" will promote the erosion of all community by stressing the essentially constructive nature of play. With repeated references to the "aimless wandering" of young children engaged in intuitive exploration, he notes that the absence of some predetermined goal or purpose makes possible "accidental solutions to unrealized problems" while the investigator pursues unsanctioned lines of research. And he adds that "we need not fear that the diminished concern for law and order in science and society that is entailed by the anarchistic philosophies will lead to chaos. The human nervous system is too well-organized for that" (p. 21). Even the most "unreasonable, nonsensical, unmethodical" play will tend toward a resolution because each of us cannot tolerate a suspended conclusion for very long. Wondering does lead to a determination, whose consequences need not remain strictly private:

It is possible to *retain* what one might call the freedom of artistic creation *and to use it to the full*, not just as a road of escape, but as a necessary means for discovering and perhaps even changing the properties of the world we live in. For me this coincidence of the part (individual man) with the whole (the world we live in), of the purely subjective and arbitrary with the objective and lawful, is one of the most important arguments in favor of a pluralistic methodology. (p. 27)

But while recognizing the potential usefulness of the determinations we create, we must not resist their undoing: "Whatever we accept we should trust only tentatively, always remembering that we are in possession, at best, of partial truth (or rightness)" (p. 79). Temporary clarity yields to a fresh start.

One's capacity for innovation varies with the "observation language" one chooses; this major point merges Feyerabend's reflections on science with a theory of the origins and uses of discourse in general, and highlights Feyerabend's thinking as a rhetorical theory. He insists that the rhetoric of innovation cannot find voice in the normalized lexicon of old ideas: "We are of course obliged to appeal to the existing forms of speech that do not take [counterinductive speculation] into account and which must be distorted, misused, and beaten into new patterns in order to fit unforeseen situations (without a constant misuse of language there cannot be any discovery and any progress)" (p. 25). Both Derrida and Feyerabend admit the danger of thinking with language that embodies rationalistic, positivistic biases, and thus delimits what we are capable of observing, feeling, knowing, changing. They also charge that *any* language, any style of investigation, embodies some bias. Such biases are not strictly personal; we carry with us all the cultural and academic baggage that necessarily informs our learning, and comprises the context within which we perceive anything. So even deconstructing one's heritage begins with "borrowing" and working with "the means at hand," those very concepts, that very language, one aims to obliterate. Derrida maintains that "no one can escape this necessity," and he shares Feyerabend's belief that "experience arises *together with* theoretical assumptions, *not* before them" (Feyerabend, p. 292; Derrida, p. 93).[20]

A certain security comes from the fact that one always begins within a context of received assumptions, the security that every counterinduction derives somehow from "the culture of reference." For this reason the innovator sustains a dialogue as well as a tension with that culture, never cut loose altogether from communal exchange, never isolated in an entirely private subjective world. But also, never capable of pure observation, only of seeing things in some measure as others have seen them.

Acknowledging the fraudulence of neutral perspectives in social anthropology, Clifford Geertz joins forces with Derrida and Feyerabend as he advocates "thick description," an approach set against the practices of universalizing the concept of culture, practices that ignore the "piled up structures of inference and implication" that complicate social life. Seeking to "limit, specify, focus, and contain" the concept of culture, modern anthropology has created a "conceptual morass" of vague definitions that "obscures a good deal more than it reveals." Geertz sets out "in search of meaning" rather than "in search of law," with the assumption that meaningful generalizations come from analyzing a very specific situation on a number of levels. "Thick description" means "doing ethnography," which means doing whatever multiplies the available perspectives: "establishing rapport, selecting informants, transcribing texts, taking genealogies, mapping fields, keeping a diary, and so on."[21] Ethnographic research views each culture as a context of interrelationships that can be explicated with the help of heuristic inventories. The inventory proposed by Del Hymes was mentioned briefly above; a fuller explanation is in order here:

For what has to be inventoried and related in an ethnographic account, a somewhat elaborated version of factors identified in communication theory, and adapted to linguistics by Roman Jakobson (1953;1960), can serve. Briefly put, (1) the various kinds of participants in communicative events—senders and receivers, addressors and addressees, interpreters and spokesmen, and the like; (2) the various available channels, and their modes of use, speaking, writing, printing, drumming, blowing, whistling, singing, face and body motion as visually perceived, smelling, tasting, and tactile sensation; (3) the various codes shared by various participants, linguistic, paralinguistic, kinesic, musical, interpretative, interactional, and other; (4) the settings (including other communication) in which communication is permitted, enjoined, encouraged, abridged; (5) the forms of messages, and their genres, ranging verbally from single-morpheme sentences to the patterns and diacritics of sonnets, sermons, salesmen's pitches, and any other organized routines and styles; (6) the attitudes and contents that a message may convey and be about; (7) the events themselves, their kinds and characters as wholes—all these must be identified in an adequate way (Hymes, "Toward Ethnographies of Communication," p. 10).

The spirit of free play informs the ethnographic process, insofar as ethnographers deliberately resist "the study of abstracted categories" and counter an ossified observation language with a generative one.

Geertz encourages ethnography while also warning that the fullness, or thickness, of an ethnographic account does not safeguard its accuracy. Because anthropologists always begin observation with conscious and unconscious assumptions and presuppositions, always detached from the native experience itself, "anthropological writings are themselves interpretations, and second and third order ones to boot" (p. 15). To say that all writing interprets rather than re-presents experience threatens "the objective status of anthropological knowledge," as long as we believe that the goal of the process is closure, "discovering the continent of meaning and mapping out its bodiless landscape" (p. 20). But Geertz desires that cultural knowledge become a much more tentative and lively enterprise: "Guessing at meanings, assessing the guesses, and drawing explanatory conclusions from the better guesses" (p. 20). The resulting science draws its life from intellectual free play, "marked less by a perfection of consensus than by refinement of debate. What gets better is the precision with which we vex each other" (p. 29).

With summary attention to Derrida, Kuhn, Feyerabend, and Geertz, I have tried to portray an emergent, interdisciplinary critical theory, fundamentally a theory of discourse that devalues certainty and closure while it celebrates the generative power of the imagination. Kenneth Burke reminds us that the proponents and practitioners of postmodern critical theory, with their acute sense of the relativism and ambiguity of every statement, are our rhetoricians:

A rhetorician, I take it, is like one voice in a dialogue. Put several such voices together, with each voicing its own special assertion, let them act upon one another in co-operative competition, and you get a dialectic that, properly developed, can lead to views transcending the limitations of each.[22]

Burke recognizes that "new" rhetoric partakes from and contributes to the many voices of social inquiry, and equates rhetoric with identification, social cohesion that results when a multiplicity of views interact. Intellectual movements that follow Burke's conception of rhetoric validate it; postmodernism leaves the suasory dominion of truth for the variegated mindscape of tentative speculation.

NOTES

1. I allude to E. D. Hirsch's *Validity in Interpretation* (New Haven, Conn.: Yale University Press, 1967).
2. Throughout this article I will distinguish modern from postmodern criticism, conceiving the former as an appreciation of objective interpretation, and the latter as a movement against objectivity and intellectual stability.
3. Winston Weathers offers alternatives to the "well-made box" of academic writing in *An Alternate Style* (Rochelle Park, N.J.: Hayden Book Co., 1980).
4. Said distinguished preservative and investigative writing in his talk, "The Future of Criticism," delivered at the MLA Convention, New York, December 29, 1983.
5. Terry Eagleton, *Literary Theory* (Minneapolis: University of Minnesota Press, 1983), pp. 1–16.
6. Kenneth Burke, *The Philosophy of Literary Form* (1941; 3d ed. rev., Berkeley: University of California Press, 1973), p. 23.
7. Kenneth Burke, *A Grammar of Motives* (1945; 3d ed., Berkeley: University of California Press, 1969), pp. xv–xxiii. Roman Jakobson, "Linguistics and Poetics," in *Style and Language*, ed. Thomas Sebeok (Cambridge, Mass.: Massachusetts Institute of Technology Press, 1960), p. 353. Del Hymes, "Toward Ethnographies of Communication," in *Foundations in Sociolinguistics* (Philadelphia: University of Pennsylvania Press, 1974), p. 10.
8. See Eagleton, *Literary Theory*, pp. 205ff., and "A Small History of Rhetoric," in *Walter Benjamin, or Towards a Revolutionary Criticism* (London: NLB, 1981), pp. 101–113.
9. This is George Kennedy's paraphrase/translation of 1140a, 10–15; see *Classical Rhetoric* (Chapel Hill: University of North Carolina Press, 1980), p. 62. In recent correspondence, Professor Kennedy has explained his translation as an acknowledgment of an earlier proposition in the *Ethics*, that the poetic and the practic (i.e., art) belong in the category of that which is capable of being other than (or different from) what it is.
10. Definitions and illustrations of well over 100 tropes and figures take up most

of George Puttenham's 1589 *Art of English Poesie*, the first full-scale English work of poetic criticism.

11. A concise discussion of the Royal Society appears in W. Ross Winterowd, *Rhetoric: A Synthesis* (New York: Holt, Rinehart & Winston, 1968), pp. 64–68.

12. Thomas DeQuincy, *Selected Essays on Rhetoric*, ed. Frederick Burwick (Carbondale: Southern Illinois University Press, 1967), p. 97 and passim.

13. Burke, *A Grammar of Motives*, p. xviii.

14. See especially Laura Holland, *Counterpoint: Kenneth Burke and Aristotle's Theories of Rhetoric* (New York: Philosophical Library, 1959).

15. "Structure, Sign, and Play in the Discourse of the Human Sciences," in *Writing and Difference*, trans. Alan Bass (Chicago: University of Chicago Press, 1978), p. 278.

16. Keith Fort, "Form, Authority, and the Critical Essay," in W. Ross Winterowd's *Contemporary Rhetoric* (New York: Harcourt, Brace Jovanovich, 1975), p. 174.

17. The particular critical search to which Derrida refers is that of Levi-Strauss in *The Raw and the Cooked*, whose method Derrida admires and engages in himself, with differences.

18. Kuhn advances his theory in *The Structure of Scientific Revolutions*, 2d ed. (Chicago: University of Chicago Press, 1970). For the application of Kuhn's work to other disciplines, see *Paradigms and Revolutions*, ed. Gary Gutting (Notre Dame, Ind.: University of Notre Dame Press, 1980).

19. Paul Feyerabend, "Against Method: Outline of an Anarchistic Theory of Knowledge," *Minnesota Studies in the Philosophy of Science* 4 (1960): 36. Feyerabend has enlarged this monograph for paperback publication, making no substantial changes (New York: Schocken Books, 1978).

20. Stanley Fish makes a convincing argument for the influence of interpretive assumptions in *Is There a Text in this Class* (Cambridge, Mass.: Harvard University Press, 1980), passim. Fish explicates Derrida's views on this matter in "With the Compliments of the Author: Reflections on Austin and Derrida," *Critical Inquiry* 8 (Summer 1982): 693–721.

21. Clifford Geertz, "Thick Description: Toward an Interpretive Theory of Culture," in *The Interpretation of Cultures* (New York: Basic Books, 1973), pp. 4–5. Geertz further illustrates and explains thick description in *Local Knowledge* (New York: Basic Books, 1983).

22. From "Rhetoric—Old and New," in *New Rhetorics*, ed. Martin Steinmann, Jr. (New York: Scribner's, 1967), p. 63. This essay was adapted from a 1950 address to the College Conference on Composition and Communication.

SELECTED BIBLIOGRAPHY

Primary Sources

Aristotle. *Art of Rhetoric*. Trans. John Henry Freese. Cambridge, Mass.: Harvard
     University Press, 1925.
———. *Poetics*. Trans. W. Hamilton Fyfe. Cambridge, Mass.: Harvard University
     Press, 1932.

Burke, Kenneth. *Permanence and Change*. 2d ed. Los Altos, Calif.: Hermes Publishers, 1959.

――. *Attitudes Toward History*. 2d ed. Los Altos, Calif.: Hermes Publishers, 1959.

――. *Counterstatement*. 2d ed. 1953; rpt. Berkeley: University of California Press, 1968.

――. *A Grammar of Motives*. New York, 1945; rpt. Berkeley: University of California Press, 1969.

――. *A Rhetoric of Motives*. New York, 1950; rpt. Berkeley: University of California Press, 1969.

――. *Dramatism and Development*. Barre, Mass.: Clark University Press with Barre Publishers, 1972.

――. *The Philosophy of Literary Form*. 3d ed. Berkeley: University of California Press, 1973.

DeQuincey, Thomas. *Selected Essays on Rhetoric*. Ed. Frederick Burwick. Carbondale: Southern Illinois University Press, 1967.

Derrida, Jacques. *Of Grammatology*. Trans. Gayatri Chakrovorty Spivak. Baltimore: Johns Hopkins University Press, 1974.

――. *Writing and Difference*. Trans. Alan Bass. Chicago: University of Chicago Press, 1978.

Eagleton, Terry. *Walter Benjamin, or Towards a Revolutionary Criticism*. London: NLB, 1981.

――. *Literary Theory*. Minneapolis: University of Minnesota Press, 1983.

Feyerabend, Paul. *Against Method: Outline of an Anarchistic Theory of Knowledge*. New York: Schocken Books, 1978.

Fish, Stanley. *Is There a Text in This Class?* Cambridge, Mass.: Harvard University Press, 1980.

Geertz, Clifford. *The Interpretation of Cultures*. New York: Basic Books, 1973.

――. *Local Knowledge*. New York: Basic Books, 1983.

Gutting, Gary, ed. *Paradigms and Revolutions*. Notre Dame, Ind.: University of Notre Dame Press, 1980.

Hirsch, E. D. *Validity in Interpretation*. New Haven, Conn.: Yale University Press, 1967.

Holland, Laura. *Counterpoint: Kenneth Burke and Aristotle's Theories of Rhetoric*. New York: Philosophical Library, 1959.

Howell, Wilbur S. *Eighteenth-Century British Logic and Rhetoric*. Princeton University Press, 1971.

Hymes, Del. *Foundations in Sociolinguistics*. Philadelphia: University of Pennsylvania Press, 1974.

Kennedy, George. *Classical Rhetoric and its Christian and Secular Tradition from Ancient to Modern Times*. Chapel Hill: University of North Carolina Press, 1980.

Kuhn, Thomas. *The Structure of Scientific Revolutions*. 2d ed. Chicago: University of Chicago Press, 1970.

Lévi–Strauss, Claude. *The Raw and the Cooked*. Trans. John and Doreen Weightman. New York: Harper & Row, 1969.

Murphy, James J., ed. *Medieval Eloquence: Studies in the Theory and Practice of Medieval Rhetoric*. Berkeley: University of California Press, 1978.

————. *Renaissance Eloquence: Studies in the Theory and Practice of Renaissance Rhetoric*. Berkeley: University of California Press, 1983.

Pattison, Robert. *On Literacy: The Politics of the Word From Homer to the Age of Rock*. New York: Oxford University Press, 1982.

Puttenham, George. *The Arte of English Poesie*. 1589; facsimile reproduction. Kent, Ohio: Kent State University Press, 1970.

Sebeok, Thomas, ed. *Style and Language*. Cambridge, Mass.: Massachusetts Institute of Technology Press, 1960.

Sprat, Thomas. *History of the Royal Society*. Eds. Jackson Cope and Harold Jones. St. Louis: Washington University, 1958.

Steinmann, Martin, ed. *New Rhetorics*. New York: Scribner's, 1967.

Weathers, Winston. *An Alternate Style*. Rochelle Park, N.J.: Hayden Book Co., 1980.

Wellek, René. *A History of Modern Criticism*. 4 vols. New Haven, Conn.: Yale University Press, 1955.

Winterowd, W. Ross. *Rhetoric: A Synthesis*. New York: Holt, Rinehart & Winston, 1968.

R. RADHAKRISHNAN

Reality, the Text, and Postmodern Representation:
A Question in Theory, or
Theory in Question

What would you call a person who demonstrates the architectonic inevitability of say, a Miltonic text, or establishes a theory of language and reality based on the poetry of a particular period? Or who conducts polemical maneuvers arguing that literary works are immaculate systems whose plenitude rules out possibilities of reference to "a world outside," or contends authoritatively that literary discourse is a superstructure symptomatic of a mode of cultural production enabled by a determinate sociopolitical and economic conjuncture? Is such a person a literary critic, a literary theorist, a critical theorist, or a theoretical critic? Is literary criticism a consensually established domain characterized by a uniform methodology or even shared substantive or thematic concerns? What are the intentions of the critic, and how do these intentions and the methods they entail make a difference in determining the meaning and the significance of literature?

This article examines the many singular features of postmodern criticism and suggests how the postmodern critical episteme inaugurates a definitive break from traditional modes of critical representation. We begin with a synoptic recapitulation of the traditional relationship of literature to criticism and then proceed to elaborate a few of those postmodern practices that interrogate the many received structures that constitute traditional criticism. As suggested here, issues are still being contested, and postmodernism is by no means a taxonomic rubric representing a single essence.

What is critical theory and what is the function of the critical theorist? It is interesting to note that critical theory came of age only recently, that is, within the institution of university departments of English. Schools of criticism and theory and job descriptions in critical theory are also of recent origin. There have always been practical as well as literary critics, but no literary or critical theorists. The conscious and thematic invocation of theory in the critical area poses a number of interesting questions: What is it that theorists are doing now that has not already been accomplished by conventional critics? Is it the case that earlier critics lack in theory, and if so, what is the nature of theory when applied to literary studies? How is critical theory different from any other kind of theory, and finally, how does the emergence of critical theory into epistemological autonomy alter canonical perceptions of the literature-criticism nexus?

We are all familiar with the cliché that a critic is a failed author. Implicit in this statement is the valorization that literature is original, primary, expressive, creative, and autonomous, whereas criticism is derived, secondary and parasitic, repetitive, and heteronomous. To use a dynastic as well as genetic-structuralist metaphor, literature fathers criticism; literature is the donor-progenitor and criticism the beneficiary-offspring. Within such a framework, there develops a relationship of complicity determined by the sacred primacy of literature. The critic genuflects to the original text and attaches his or her text subserviently to the timeless truth of literature. The critic becomes the ideal commentator, the faithful apologist who, while seemingly taking up a position outside the original text, is in fact well entrenched within the putative structure of the literary classic or masterpiece, and executes the task of re-presenting, celebrating, legitimizing, and vindicating the essence of literature. The critical exegete is in fact a votary, a devout worshipper incapable of questioning the authority of the literary text. It is quite obvious that this model of criticism is both logocentric and theophanic; for the words elaborated by the critic in secular and historical time are empowered only to validate endlessly the rectitude of the primordial Word. The duplicity of this model lies in the fact that on the one hand the Word/literature seems to be in need of critical representation and yet, on the other, is entirely invulnerable to it. The full presence or identity of the literary masterpiece engenders and anticipates criticism, thus rendering it tame and redundant.

That precisely is why literature has continued to be "understood," "appreciated," "adulated," "emulated," and "glorified," but never "diagnosed." There was no need for an independent theory of criticism *qua* criticism; what theory there was took the form of validation and prescription. Literature was naturalized and thus placed beyond active, perspectival scrutiny and analysis. Because literature and the cultural exellence it exemplified were assumed to be axiomatic, there seemed to be no reason for the development of a theory that could be diagnostic and adversarial in intent. Literature was closed off as the domain of perfection, epiphanic truths, and timeless verities. The very performance of language in literature was contra-distinguished from the social and quotidian aspects of language-in-the-world. It was perfectly admissible for teachers and professors of English to be blissfully oblivious of developments in sociology, linguistics, ethnology, political science, philosophy, psychology, and any form of social epistemology. It was even considered the unique privilege of literature to continue its timeless, preordained, teleological path in the face of all sorts of upheavals, ruptures, and revolutions in the social sciences. The conviction was that great literature did not need to be self-referential in any problematic or critical manner. Indeed, it was considered a sign of enervation when postmodern writers such as Samuel Beckett, Thomas Pynchon,* John Barth,* and Donald Barthelme* began writing highly complex, un-innocent, nonspontaneous, metafictional works that debunked the privileged aplomb of literature. How is one to understand the intentions of these authors who produce attenuated texts in gesture after gesture of authorial anxiety and representational crisis? How are we to make sense of works that explicitly distrust language and authors who "can't but must go on?"

It is in response to some of these crises that contemporary critical theory emerged, as theory of-and-in-crisis, and not as theory of acquiescence. Thus, to understand some of these issues we turn not to a literary critic but to an unclassifiable intellectual, Michel Foucault,* philosopher, historian, archaeologist of ideas, social scientist, and political activist. Foucault's notion of language as discourse has revolutionized the meaning of critical scholarship in the context of textual interpretation. In *The Order of Things*, Foucault accounts for the historical materiality of language by noting:

Having become a dense and consistent historical reality, language forms the locus of tradition, of the unspoken habits of thought, of what lies hidden in a people's mind; it accumulates an ineluctable memory which does not even know itself as memory. Expressing their thoughts in words of which they are not the masters, enclosing them in verbal forms whose historical dimensions they are unaware of, men believe that their speech is their servant and do not realize that they are submitting themselves to its demands. The grammatical arrangements of a language are the *a priori* of what can be expressed in it. The truth of discourse is caught in the trap of philology.[1]

Foucault's interrogation of man's anthropocentric mastery of language is actually part of a larger project of demystification. Foucault's attack is aimed at the very core of humanistic thought: the concept of the natural man, sovereign subject blessed with a trans-historical essence. When we consider how literature has been enshrined as a core value within humanistic modes of thought, and how aggressively co-axial such an idea of literature has been with the notion of the central man as inculcated and naturalized by Western civilization, we can understand the full significance of the Foucauldian critique. Foucault historicizes not just some aspect of the human endeavor, but the very concept of man:

When natural history becomes biology, when the analysis of wealth becomes economics, when, above all, reflection upon language becomes philology, and Classical *discourse*, in which being and representation found their common locus, is eclipsed,

then, in the profound upheaval of such an archaeological mutation, man appears
in his ambiguous position as an object of knowledge and as a subject that knows:
enslaved sovereign, observed spectator, . . . [2]

While elaborating the necessary recursivity of the knowledge of man, Foucault also problematizes that infinite solidarity accorded to the human
subject by metaphysical, humanistic, and logocentric systems of thought.

. . . it is possible to have access to him (man) only through his words, his organism,
the objects he makes—as though it is they who possess the truth in the first place
(and they alone perhaps); and he, as soon as he thinks, merely unveils to himself
to his own eyes in the form of a being who is already, in a necessarily subjacent
destiny, in an irreducible anteriority, a living being, an instrument of production,
a vehicle for words which exist before him. All these contents that his knowledge
reveals to him as exterior to himself, and older than his own birth, anticipate him,
overhang him with all their solidity, and traverse him as though he were merely
an object of nature, a face doomed to be erased in the course of history. Man's
finitude is heralded—and imperiously so—in the positivity of knowledge; we know
that man is finite, as we know the anatomy of the brain, the mechanics of production
costs, or the system of Indo-European conjugation. [3]

    Foucault's thematization of man as a necessary and plenary subject into
a contingent and finite epistemological object immediately threatens the
notion of authorial control/mastery that effects the formal perfection of
the literary text. In the light of the Foucauldian thesis, the literary text is
perceived not as the celebration of the author's unquestioned dominion
over language, but as a system that subjects the author's intention to the
antecedent historical density of language. And so, in an essay entitled not
"Who," but "What Is an Author?," Foucault proposes a series of questions
that seek to redefine the meaning of the human subject and the authoritative text.

We should suspend the typical questions: how does a free subject penetrate the
density of things and endow them with meaning; how does it accomplish its design
by animating the rules of discourse from within? Rather, we should ask: under
what conditions and through what forms can an entity like the subject appear in
the order of discourse; what position does it occupy; what functions does it exhibit;
and what rules does it follow in each type of discourse? In short, the subject (and
its substitutes) must be stripped of its creative role and analysed as a complex and
variable function of discourse. [4]

Foucault is quoted extensively here, even though he is not a literary critic,
because he provides the most formidable oppositional model for literary
and critical scholarship. His notion of discourse and its entrapment in
worldly circumstantiality shatters the very identity of literature. Literary
texts are seen no more as originary sources of authority to be propagated

and institutionalized but rather as determinate forms and structures of cultural production that are susceptible to historical and ideological con- tamination. As cultural mediations in discourse, literary texts are to be read and studied not as ends in themselves but as symptomatic texts in- dicative of sociopolitical-economic-and cultural reality. And because dis- course, as Foucault demonstrates in his *The Archaeology of Knowledge* (1972), is expressive precisely to the extent to which it is exclusionary, the so called well-rounded structure or identity of the well-made literary text is necessarily incomplete and intentionally repressive.

And now, to sum up the revolutionary impact of Foucault's anti-hu- manistic thought on the institution of literary criticism: (1) Meaning and identity do not inhere in a literary text as metaphysical theories of language would have us believe; (2) the so-called dispassionate, value-free truths of literature are indeed hegemonic representations projected from a specific point of view, and thus it is possible and desirable for a critic to read any text "against its grain" by asserting his or her historical perspectivity (a decidedly Nietzschean aperçu); (3) language in literature is a mediation or a signifier, and not a transparent mystique that is in numinous touch with truth or reality or the primordial Signified; (4) the notion of representation as internalized in literary mimesis is duplicitous and in need of ideological deconstruction or demystification (Foucault argues, first, that the body or the materiality of representation is always subjected to an anterior spiritual presence, and second, that representation as the mode of speaking for or on behalf of the Other is by definition repressive); and (5) the intention of the author, or analogously, the subject of the literary text does not command the unfolding of the text as process from a panoptic distance, but is in fact the micrological outcome of the process whereby in a sense, the author is authored by the medium.

These postmodern impulses in critical theory tend, in one sense or an- other, to be critical in the strong sense of the term: that is, as attitudes or perspectives they are strong enough not to allow the fetishization of the text. On the contrary, the tendency is to use the literary text as a pre-text for provocative philosophic speculation. The literary work is deconstructed, and its putative unitary meaning is either suspended in the abyss of an aporia or aggravated into a kind of schizophrenic battle with itself. At any rate, the literary work is destabilized and "terrorized" into a state of anomie and indeterminancy. The father of this school of deconstruction is, of course, Jacques Derrida,* the French philosopher. Within the scope of this essay it is not possible to do justice to the rich and sophisticated complexity of Derrida's deconstruction of Western metaphysics, onto-theo- logy, and logocentrism, or to delineate the definitive resemblances and the subtle differences among Derridian deconstruction, Foucauldian analysis, and Marxist theories of ideology and culture-production. Rather, the intent here is to locate Derrida and his brand of textual deconstruction in the context of literary studies and describe briefly some of the patterns taken by deconstruction in American literary criticism.

Grammatology as invoked by Derrida is the science of writing, of *écriture* in its broadest sense of cultural inscription. Consequently, Derrida studies texts and textuality, terms that by now have become habitual expressions in contemporary critical theory. Derrida argues that Western systems of thought have consistently valorized speech to the detriment of writing. The full and undivided presence of the speaker, his or her demonstrable proximity with the speech, makes possible a theory of meaning and referentiality-as-immediacy that in Derrida's reading renders secondary the process of writing. Whereas in speech language and meaning find voice (phonocentrism) unmediatedly (for the voice is considered not so much a medium or process but a direct human function), in writing language encounters a slippage, a remove from the origin, and a material density that often proves impervious and resistant to phonocentric inculcation. Derrida claims that cultural texts in the Western tradition display such oppositional and grammatological dimensions, but traditional exegesis has smothered or neutralized these possibilities. Derrida's intention when he reads these canonical texts is to make them stutter, and this he does by carefully locating those details and trajectories within the text that are recalcitrant to unitary resolution. He deconstructs the macrology (i.e., the predetermined, centralized semantic core) of the text into adversarial micrologies (i.e., syntactic or processual energies that resist totalization and semantic closure). He enables the written text to rebel against an all too easy paraphrase and semantic determination. In the following passage, we find Derrida attributing to writing a status of orphanhood—a status that empowers the orphan to go beyond filial and dynastic allegiances:

The status of this orphan, whose welfare cannot be assured by any attendance or assistance, coincides with that of a *graphein* which, being nobody's son at the instant it reaches inscription, scarcely remains a son at all and no longer *recognizes* its origins, whether legally or morally. In contrast to writing, living *logos* is alive in that it has a living father (whereas the orphan is already half-dead), a father that is *present*, *standing* near it, behind it, within it, sustaining it with his rectitude, attending it in person in his own name. Living *logos*, for its part, recognizes its debt, lives off that recognition, and forbids itself, thinks it can forbid itself patricide.[5]

The metaphor of patricide enables Derrida to articulate a theory of history that, while acknowledging the brute reality of antecedents and origins, is not committed to the consecration of these very origins and antecedents. Instead, the movement is toward a rejection and, if possible, a disinheritance of origins, or to put it in Nietzschean terms, the objective is to remember in such a way that a creative and powerful forgetting becomes possible. Thus, in his various deconstructive readings, Derrida employs what he calls the double session or the double seance, whereby he uses the very instruments and the apparatus of metaphysics and philosophy to repudiate the validity of metaphysics and philosophy. Deconstruction then can be seen simultaneously as an exercise in insurrection and liberation. Structurally speaking, it is an attempt to decentralize the equilibrium of the monolithic text.

Derrida is relentless in his critique of the center, a concept that has become synonymous with the meaning of structure. Rather than accept the axiology of the center, Derrida problematizes the efficacy of the center by bringing out a contradiction:

The center is at the center of the totality, and yet, since the center does not belong to the totality (it is not part of the totality), the totality *has its center elsewhere*. The center is not the center. The concept of centered structure although it represents coherence itself, the condition of the *episteme* as philosophy or science—is contradictorily coherent.[6]

It is not coincidental that William Butler Yeats had resorted to the metaphor of the center while lamenting the loss of meaning, significance, and order. The poet assumed that when "the center cannot hold, Mere anarchy is loosed upon the world": an assumption exemplary in its commitment to metaphysical (and, analogously, positivistic and representational) epistemology. For by the laws of binarity and noncontradiction, the situation has to be read either as centered structure or as mere, undifferentiated anarchy. Thus, the loss of the center is immediately interpreted as the advent of anarchy. Similarly, Derrida questions the center's monopolistic hold over the very meaning of "meaning," and its right to represent the meaning of all structure. To bring this discussion closer to issues in literary criticism, let us take a quick look at Derrida's subversion of the title of a work or text, for the title is that official (I am thinking of the entitlement that the title entails) semantic core or center that dominates and monitors the elaboration of the text. For example, Derrida radicalizes the crisis of the title in Mallarmé by stating:

Mallarmé prescribes a *suspension* of the title, which like the head, or capital—or the oracle—carries its head high, speaks in too high a voice, both because it raises its voice and drowns out the ensuing text, and because it is found high up on the page, the top of the page becoming the eminent center, the beginning, the command station, the chief, the archon. Mallarmé thus urges the title to be stilled.[7]

It is obvious that Derrida effectively sabotages the authority of the text, but a number of critics are wary of Derrida's text-centeredness; claiming that Derrida's obsession with textuality is little different from the new critical approach to close textual reading. Apart from the fact that Derrida's texts are dense with interdisciplinary erudition, what else is there to differentiate his engagement with texts from that of the New Critics, or the Formalists in general? Hasn't Derrida himself proclaimed in his *Grammatology* that "there is nothing outside the text?" These tough questions have been made even more difficult by two factors: (1) there is no apparent consensus on the exact meaning of a text, and (2) Derrida has repeatedly been identified with his American counterparts, many of whom have modified and recontextualized Derrida in ways that are not necessarily Derridian.

So, what is a text? One critic who answers this question formally and immaculately is the late Paul de Man,* in many ways the founder of American deconstruction and of the Yale School (a term I am using contingently) of deconstructionists. In essay after essay characterized by exegetical virtuosity and formidable scholarship, de Man formalizes and vindicates the identical relationship of a text to itself and brings home to the critic the chastening realization that a great literary text is always already demystified about itself and that, indeed, it is the pretentious critic who is in a state of mystification. Both in *Blindness and Insight* (1971) and in *Allegories of Reading* (1979) de Man is interested in complex texts to the extent to which they engender strings of formalization, and his preoccupation with texts is figural, discursive, and tropological. In the context of Paul de Man, even the most exiguous invocation of reality or truth, or the world outside the text would constitute a solecism. All that we have to work with is language, its figurality and rhetoricity; any references to what language might represent or refer to are in themselves further linguistic/discursive deployments. Thus, in a paradoxical way, de Man finds absolute aesthetic freedom within "the prison-house" of language. It is not that he denies the reality of time or history, but he merely reminds us that even time and history, and their primordiality if you will, are but epistemological constructs and as such are none other than texts. It would not be an exaggeration to say that de Man, almost singlehandedly, has established the ontology of the text. Even when he is reading a text virulently and adversarially, he concedes to the original text (whether it be Nietzsche, Hegel, or Heidegger) the vatic capacity to proliferate, diversify, and even deconstruct, but in the ultimate analysis, indubitably preserve its charmed and privileged identity. In other words, when the critic arduously deconstructs a text, she or he is unconsciously in the service of the powerful text that coopts the independent and diachronic agency of the critic; hence, while seeming to succumb to external pressures he or she is in fact consolidating and aggrandizing its own identity. It is a telling example of sublation whereby the self continues to master itself in ever-increasing narcissistic complexity. There is and there can be no real other; there is and can be no space outside the text.

De Man's most significant contribution to critical theory is his restoration of rhetoric to a position of centrality in the area of literary scholarship. He has insistently admonished gnostic literary theorists for their naiveté in assuming that a hermeneutic hunt for the meaning of a text somehow transcends discursive and linguistic operations. He also dismisses as simplistic the quest for verifiable pre-linguistic meaning. The only way to disagree effectively with de Man's discourse is to quarrel with his basic assumptions and show up the constitutive selectiveness and the inadequacy of his apodictic premises. And no other critic has taken this path with more conviction and success than Edward Said.

Edward Said's career as an intellectual brilliantly exemplifies the crises and complexities that constitute critical theory. Starting out as a philosophic interpreter of narrative, Said developed into a proto-Foucauldian archaeologist of ideas, but only to reject the avant-gardism of some crucial aspects of Foucauldian thought in favor of a more explicit sociopolitical perspective. With the publication of *Orientalism* (1978), *The Question of Palestine* (1980), *Covering Islam* (1981), and, most recently, *The World, The Text, The Critic* (1983), Said has emerged as a secular, exilic, and oppositional critic who in his avowed intention to work between system and culture would like to avoid on the one hand the lack of worldliness of textual criticism that ignores sociopolitical circumstances, and on the other, the professional and ideological rigidity brought about by affiliation to narrow academic isms and schools of thought. What Said cherishes most for the critic is the capacity to intervene critically and conscientiously in sociopolitical reality, a capacity that is often eschewed by academic intellectualism. What Said is concerned with is reality in its diverse textual structurations and representations, and he is anathema to the notion of textuality as an end in itself. Although Said has no difficulty in agreeing with the formulation that there are only representations and signifiers and that there is no immediate presence or signified to which we may have direct access, he is irreconcilably opposed to those theorists who use this theory to suggest the notion that terms such as history, intention, and reality are but philosophic misnomers. On the contrary, Said proves powerfully in his *Orientalism* that history as willed narrative has always been a matter of representation and textual production, but the fact that it is a text or a representation does not make it any less worldly or real. Said's hermeneutic move is into a text, but always with the intention of forcing the identity of the text out of its self and bringing out the complicity of the text with the larger sociopolitical situation. There are texts and texts, and representations and representations; there are those who represent and those that are represented, there are those whom the text serves and those whom the text imprisons or exiles. Just as *Orientalism* has functioned as a political-epistemological text subjecting the indigenous history of the East to the imperialist will of the West, literary texts too (whether it is narrative in Conrad or social representation in Flaubert) have been used hegemonically to preserve and legitimate a certain notion of culture at the expense of a vital and adversarial sense of reality and history.

In such a conjuncture, Said exhorts the critic to read texts diagnostically and symptomatically as well as secularly and oppositionally. In other words, the critic does more than render appreciatively the formal and epistemological self-consistency of the text; he or she unmasks the interests and the will to power that underlie and enable every instance of text production. As a secular and oppositional intellectual, the critic (1) interprets a text not with the intention of unearthing a transhistorical essence, meaning, or interiority that is coeval with the identity of the text, but implicates the text in its own determinate historical contingency; and (2) functions in vigilant opposition to the complacency as well as the insensitivity of cultural orthodoxy. Said thus brings back ethics into the field of theory and epistemology. The critic as an agent has to intend and make a choice about his or her role.

Though profoundly appreciative of the impact of Foucault and Derrida on the critical consciousness, Said is wary of Derridian textuality and Foucauldian notions of time, change, and history. Said himself has sensitively appropriated many strategies of deconstruction, but what he disapproves of is the hypostasis of deconstruction into an ahistorical philosophy: Derridian deconstruction is just not specific enough when it deals with history and the intentionality of human agency. Although Foucauldian analysis, from Said's point of view, is effective in laying bare the many connections of complicity between knowledge and power, it is incapable of committing itself to different political choices. In other words, Foucault leaves no room for hope or for progressive intervention. His massive and trenchant archaeologies in the final analysis take the form of a secular but totalized theodicy, for Foucault foresees no escape from the closure of discourse as power, nor does he project any goal (based on ideals such as liberty, freedom, and justice) for the human endeavor. As for Marxism and Marxists, Said is in sympathy with many of their historically sensitive interpretations of culture but is skeptical of their intrinsic commitment to academicism and professionalism. As the following passage clearly illustrates, Said is not a debunker of theory, but a critic who would like to see theory work as praxis in a troubled world:

I do not wish to be misunderstood as saying that the flight into method and system on the part of critics who wish to avoid the ideology of humanism is altogether a bad thing. Far from it. Yet the dangers of method and system are worth noting. Insofar as they become sovereign and as their practitioners lose touch with the resistance and the heterogeneity of civil society, they risk becoming wall-to-wall discourses, blithely predetermining what they discuss, heedlessly converting everything into evidence for the efficacy of the method, carelessly ignoring the circumstances out of which all theory, system and method ultimately derive.[8]

Said is not alone in vigorously opposing the reification of the text. There are four other theorists who offer battle (each from his own different point of view) with the authority of the isolated text: Pierre Macherey, Terry Eagleton, Fredric Jameson,* and William Spanos. The first three are, broadly speaking, Marxist critics, and Spanos is a destructionist who selectively appropriates Heidegger, Nietzsche, Foucault, and Derrida to call into question the anthropocentric will to power that informs the reality of texts.

In his book *A Theory of Literary Production* (1978), Macherey accounts for the significance of the text in terms of both its substantive concerns and its formal qualities. He locates the text as work in the context of the ideology of culture and goes on to analyze the genesis as well as the aetiology of specific texts. His most telling contribution to critical theory is his definition of a text not as the plenitude of identity, but as a system of determinate absences, as a system whose consciousness of itself is powerfully circumscribed and even deterred by an ideology that, while concretizing itself as text, also exhibits the repressive pattern or structure that constitutes it as text. It is up to the critic to "question the work as to what it does not and cannot say, in those silences for which it has been made."[9] For, to Macherey, "the work exists above all by its determinate absences, by what it does not say, in its relation to what it is not."[10] The critic then unmasks the falsity of the ideological order of the text and shows that the text is not the resolution of a conflict, but is in fact the very body of that conflict. By interpreting the text counter-identically, the critic discovers that "in the defect of the work is articulated a new truth."[11] Waxing almost visionary, Macherey concludes that "for those who seek to know this truth it establishes an original relation to the real, it establishes the revealing form of a knowledge."[12]

Terry Eagleton, who conceives of critical theory as revolutionary praxis, endorses a similar project for the critic:

The task of criticism, then, is not to situate itself within the same space as the text, allowing it to speak or completing what it necessarily leaves unsaid. On the contrary, its function is to install itself in the very incompleteness of the work in order to *theorise* it—to explain the ideological necessity of those "*not-saids*" which constitute the very principle of its identity. Its object is the *unconsciousness* of the work—that of which it is not, and cannot, be aware.[13]

The critic thus interprets the text in violation of its original identity; the critic can know more than the original text, and so the critical consciousness is free, independent, and original. Eagleton employs Marxist strategies of ideology-critique in conjunction with a few deconstructionist ploys, and like Said, he finds fault with Derrida for his insensitivity to history. Despite their many modal and epistemological differences, Said and Eagleton entertain a common hope: the hope to change reality progressively through the application of critical intelligence.

Fredric Jameson is even more explicit than Eagleton in his desire to conduct the human enterprise toward a happy and just resolution. Candidly utopian and redemptive in intention, Jameson asserts that "the primary energy of revolutionary activity derives from this memory of a prehistoric happiness which the individual can gain only through its externalization, through its reestablishment for society as a whole."[14] To Jameson, history as the narrativization of reality has a plot; and there are desirable plots and undesirable plots, plots that project a good *telos* and those that inaugurate a bad *telos*. The choice of telos is not formal or epistemological, but intensely moral. And as a committed Marxist, Jameson makes the following programmatic affirmation:

Only Marxism can give us an adequate account of the essential *mystery* of the cultural past, which, like Tiresias drinking blood, is momentarily returned to life and warmth and allowed once more to speak, and to deliver its long-forgotten message in surroundings utterly alien to it. This mystery can be reenacted only if the human adventure is one. . . . These matters can recover their original urgency for us only if they are retold within the unity of a single great collective story; only if, in however disguised and symbolic form, they are seen as sharing a single fundamental theme—for Marxism, the collective struggle to wrest a realm of Freedom from a realm of Necessity; only if they are grasped as vital episodes in a single vast unfinished plot.[15]

Indubitably, Jameson's rhetoric is oracular to the extent to which it is also recuperative, and totalizing in the name of a moral end (for, surely, the "single vast unfinished plot" in Jameson's context does not solicit some arbitrary or aleatory denouement) whose rectitude is guaranteed by the apodictic rectitude of Marxism itself. Jameson is aware that a value-free and open-ended attitude to epistemology may lead to "polymorphous perversity" and even to moral, political, and social decadence, whereas, on the other hand, a prescriptive or didactic morality might preempt that very freedom it aims to effect. In other words, Jameson's problem is to reconcile revolution-as-process or micrology with revolution-as-end or meaning or macrology—a problem particularly difficult for Jameson to whom the notion of a perennial revolution is almost synonymous with anomie. He solves this problem by grounding revolution-as-process in Marxist macrology. In his own words,

One of the essential themes of this book [*The Political Unconscious*] will be the contention that Marxism subsumes other interpretive modes or systems; or, to put it in methodological terms, that the limits of the latter can always be overcome, and their more positive findings retained, by a radical historicizing of their mental operations, such that not only the context of the analysis, but the very method itself, along with the analyst, then comes to be reckoned into the "text" or phenomenon to be explained.[16]

The challenge for Jameson is to combine the constructive aspects of cultural criticism with rigorous historicizing, to use Marxism productively while at the same time submit Marxism itself to self-critique.

The work of William Spanos derives strongly from Heidegger's de-struction of metaphysics and Western onto-theology. Spanos takes special care to differentiate his version of de-struction (1) from Derridian deconstruction which he finds unsituated and ahistorical; and (2) from those readings of Heidegger that seek to reinscribe him within the metaphysical fold rather than valorize him as the philosopher who transgresses metaphysics definitively. Spanos appropriates Heidegger's radical Dasein-analysis to *disclose* (as in Heidegger's own *a-letheia*) errant, iconoclastic, antinomian, and differential meanings of texts, meanings that have been closed over by a sclerotic tradition. Spanos takes traditional criticism to task for adopting panoptic (Spanos makes brilliant use of Foucault's analysis in *Discipline & Punish* of Jeremy Bentham's *Panopticon*), ironic, spatial as well as specular strategies in the interpretation of texts. As he puts it:

In privileging a visually oriented epistemology that perceives *meta-ta-physica*, from after or above things-as-they-are, this tradition spatializes or reifies and re-presents the radical temporality of being by "over-looking" the differences that time disseminates. In other words, it transforms a primordially temporal mode of enquiry— a mode of enquiry as *dis-covering* or *dis-closing*—into a secondary or derivative theoretical method, that is, a distanced, authoritative, and supervisory instrument of confirmation that "deprives Dasein of its leadership in questioning and choosing." To appropriate Foucault's archaeological rhetoric, the tradition becomes an *archive* that exists, as the etymology suggests, to re-form Dasein's essentially errant being-in-the-world in the glaring light emanating from a hidden absolute origin, a first (and last) Word *Aarché logos*), beyond the reach of free play.[17]

Spanos' de-structive analysis sets itself the following tasks: (1) to situate itself interestedly (*inter esse*) in relation to the text (as against the canonical method of establishing aesthetic distance); (2) to call into question the authorial as well as anthropocentric will to power that coerces texts into the architectronics of *entelechy*, and *telos*; (3) to discredit spatial modes of critical perception by releasing the disruptive dehiscence of time or temporality (and thereby dis-close the *anxiety* that informs the constitution of texts) that is incarcerated within the timeless structures of literary texts; (4) to revise and reread the masterpieces in the tradition from the point of view of *difference*, and not *identity*; and (5) to combat the indifference of solipsistic scholarship with the difference and *care* (the Heideggerian *Sorge*) of a critical engagement that is to operate on what Spanos calls "the many different sites of Being."

All these different critics and theorists inhabit the postmodern episteme not in the way of members who share unshakable familial bonds, but rather as diverse trajectories or impulses of energy that traverse a common space.

Among these forces we have identities (homologous and isomorphic), differences, shared axes, and absolute differences. What is common to the
entire group is a sophisticated awareness of the reality and the problematics
of the text, textuality, ideology, meaning, and representation. The time
has probably come to make further differentiations and identify each critic
not by the conceptual/epistemological rigor or the formal/stylistic elegance
of his or her method, but rather by the often undeclared perspectival
investment of interests that underlie and motivate the elaboration of that
system. For what can be more intellectually depressing and politically de-
ceitful than the degeneration of the critical *agon* into the academic cloister
of textual resolution?

NOTES

1. Michel Foucault, *The Order of Things*, a translation of *Les Mots et les choses*
(New York: Random House, 1970), p. 297.
2. Ibid., p. 312.
3. Ibid., pp. 313–14.
4. Michel Foucault, "What Is an Author?" in *Language, Counter-Memory,
Practice*, trans. Donald F. Bouchard and Sherry Simon (Ithaca, N.Y.: Cornell
University Press, 1977), pp. 137–38.
5. Jacques Derrida, *Dissemination*, trans. Barbara Johnson (Chicago: University of Chicago Press, 1981), p. 77.
6. Jacques Derrida, "Structure, Sign, and Play," in *Writing and Difference*,
trans. Alan Bass (Chicago: University of Chicago Press, 1978), p. 279.
7. Derrida, *Dissemination*, pp. 177–78.
8. Edward W. Said, "Secular Oppositional Criticism," Paper presented at The
School of Theory and Criticism, Northwestern University, Evanston, Illinois, Summer 1982.
9. Pierre Macherey, "Literary Analysis: The Tomb of Structures," in *A Theory
of Literary Production*, trans. Geoffrey Wall (London: Routledge & Kegan Paul,
1978), pp. 155–56.
10. Ibid., p. 155.
11. Ibid., pp. 155–56.
12. Ibid.
13. Terry Eagleton, *Criticism and Ideology*, London: NLB, Humanities Press,
1976), pp. 89–90.
14. Fredric Jameson, *Marxism and Form: Twentieth-Century Dialectical Theories
of Literature* (Princeton, N.J.: Princeton University Press, 1971), pp. 113–14.
15. Fredric Jameson, *The Political Unconscious: Narrative As a Socially Symbolic
Act* (Ithaca, N.Y.: Cornell University Press, 1981), pp. 19–20.
16. Ibid., p. 13.
17. William V. Spanos, "The Indifference of *Différance*: Retrieving Heidegger's
Destruction," in *Annals of Scholarship: Metastudies of the Humanities and Social
Sciences* 2, no. 3 (1981): 112.

SELECTED BIBLIOGRAPHY

Primary Sources

Barthes, Roland. *Elements of Semiology*. Trans. Annette Lavers and Colin Smith. New York: Hill & Wang, 1968.

———. *Writing Degree Zero*. Trans. Annette Lavers and Colin Smith. New York: Hill & Wang, 1968.

———. *Mythologies*. Trans. Annette Lavers. New York: Hill & Wang, 1973.

———. *The Pleasure of the Text*. Trans. Richard Miller. New York: Hill & Wang, 1975.

———. *S/Z*. Trans. Richard Miller. New York: Hill & Wang, 1977.

———. *The Fashion System*. Trans. Matthew Ward and Richard Howard. New York: Hill & Wang, 1982.

———. *Empire of Signs*. Trans. Richard Howard. New York: Hill & Wang, 1982.

Bloom, Harold. *The Ringers in the Tower: Studies in Romantic Tradition*. Chicago: University of Chicago Press, 1971.

———. *The Anxiety of Influence*. New York: Oxford University Press, 1973.

———. *A Map of Misreading*. New York: Oxford University Press, 1975.

———. *Poetry and Repression: Revisionism from Blake to Stevens*. New Haven, Conn.: Yale University Press, 1976.

Culler, Jonathan. *Saussure*. Hassucks, England: Harvester Press, 1971.

———. *Structuralist Poets*. Ithaca, N.Y.: Cornell University Press, 1975.

Eagleton, Terry. *Criticism and Ideology*. London: NLB, Humanities Press, 1976.

———. *Literary Theory: An Introduction*. Minneapolis: University of Minnesota Press, 1983.

———. *The Function of Criticism*. London: Verso Press, 1984.

Eco, Umberto. *A Theory of Semiotics*. Bloomington: Indiana University Press, 1976.

———. *The Role of the Reader*. Bloomington: Indiana University Press, 1978.

Foucault, Michel. *Madness and Civilization*. Trans. Richard Howard. New York: Pantheon, 1965.

———. *The Order of Things*. Trans. Alan Sheridan. New York: Pantheon, 1970.

———. *The Archaelogy of Knowledge*. Trans. A. M. Sheridan Smith. New York: Random House, 1972.

Hartman, Geoffrey. *Beyond Formalism*. New Haven, Conn.: Yale University Press, 1970.

———. *Deconstruction and Criticism*. London: Routledge & Kegan Paul, 1979.

Hawkes, Terence. *Structuralism and Semiotics*. London: Methuen, 1977.

Jameson, Fredric. *Marxism and Form: Twentieth-Century Dialectical Theories of Literature*. Princeton, N.J.: Princeton University Press, 1971.

———. *The Prison House of Language*. Princeton, N.J.: Princeton University Press, 1972.

———. *The Political Unconscious: Narrative As a Socially Symbolic Act*. Ithaca, N.Y.: Cornell University Press, 1981.

Kristeva, Julia. *About Chinese Women*. New York: Columbia University Press, 1977.

————. *Desire in Language*. Oxford: Oxford University Press, 1980.

————. *Revolution in Poetic Language*. New York: Columbia University Press, 1984.

————. *Revolution in Poetic Language*. New York: Columbia University Press, 1984.

Macherey, Pierre. *A Theory of Literary Production*. London: Routledge & Kegan Paul, 1978.

————, and Eugenio, Donato, eds. *The Structuralist Controversy: The Language of Criticism and the Sciences of Man*. Baltimore: Johns Hopkins University Press, 1972.

Miller, J. Hillis. *The Disappearance of God*. Cambridge, Mass.: Harvard University Press, 1963.

————. *Thomas Hardy: Distance and Desire*. Cambridge, Mass.: Harvard University Press, 1970.

————. *Fiction and Repetition*. Cambridge, Mass.: Harvard University Press, 1982.

Norris, Christopher. *The Deconstructive Turn*. New York: Methuen, 1984.

Said, Edward. *Beginnings: Intention and Method*. Baltimore: Johns Hopkins University Press, 1975.

————. *Orientalism*. New York: Pantheon, 1978.

————. *Covering Islam*. New York: Pantheon, 1981.

————. *The Question of Palestine*. New York: Random House, 1980.

————. *The World, the Text, and the Critic*. Cambridge, Mass.: Harvard University Press, 1983.

Todorov, Tzvetan. *The Fantastic: A Structural Approach to a Literary Genre*. Cleveland: Press of Case Western Reserve University, 1973.

————. *The Poetics of Prose*. Trans. Richard Howard. Ithaca, N.Y.: Cornell University Press, 1977.

————. *Symbolism and Interpretation*. Trans. Catherine Porter. Ithaca, N.Y.: Cornell University Press, 1982.

————. *Introduction to Poetics*. Trans. Richard Howard. Minneapolis: University of Minnesota Press, 1981.

————. *Theories of the Symbol*. Trans. Catherine Porter. Ithaca, N.Y.: Cornell University Press, 1982.

Williams, Raymond. *Politics and Letters*. New York: Schocken, 1979.

————. *Problems in Culture and Materialism*. London: NLB, 1980.

————. *The Sociology of Culture*. New York: Schocken, 1982.

PART II

AUTHORS AND
CRITICS OF
POSTMODERN FICTION

A

ABISH, WALTER (1931–   )

This is an introduction to the unreliability of the first name. In this instance the first name is Walter. It is the first name of the writer, Walter Abish, whose fiction undermines the seamless continuity of the familiar world—the obvious, the self-evident, the axiomatic. Abish takes a perverse pleasure in pulverizing the patho-logics of the familiar world into its alphabetical bits, or in assembling those bits into alliterative sequences of words. For Abish, words are slippery and unstable agglutinations of one or more of 26 letters, at least in English. Communication is therefore often slippery and unstable, and narrators in Abish's fiction are as unreliable as the language they use.

Abish's writing calls into question the reliability of previous knowledge, of what we see/what we know. In its place is the dubiousness of the familiar world where nothing can be taken for granted. Abish's language is accessible and apparently neutral, but becomes provocative and disturbing when handled with his flat, playful, and ironic style, where what is unsaid seems to take on a greater import than what is said.

Abish was born in Vienna in 1931, a Vienna that was soon to "embrace the new emblems, the paraphernalia of Nazism . . . to absorb with a shudder of ecstasy the aesthetic of the swastika" (*Antaeus*, 52 [Spring 1984]). At the age of five he wanted to be a mailman, because "mailmen wore uniforms, but unlike soldiers, they were able to eat at home." His family left Austria and in 1940 arrived in Shanghai, a place he writes about in "Self-Portrait" (published in Alan Sondheim, ed. *Individuals* [New York: E. P. Dutton, 1977]). Later he lived in Israel for eight years where he served in the tank corps of the Israeli Army. He came to the United States in 1960 and worked as an urban planner. His first published book, *Duel Site* (1970), is a collection of poetry.

Abish began publishing fiction in 1970–1971, first in *Confrontation* and in the New Directions anthologies, where he has published work nearly every year since anthology #23 (1971). His stories have appeared in numerous literary magazines—*Paris Review, TriQuarterly, Fiction, Extensions, Fiction International, Seems,* and *Antaeus.* New Directions also published his first novel, *Alphabetical Africa* (1974), as well as his story collections, *Minds Meet* (1975) and *In the Future Perfect* (1977). His latest novel, *How German Is It* (1980), also published by New Directions, was awarded the PEN-Faulkner Prize in 1981. As of this writing, *How German Is It* has been translated into nine languages and has received strong critical acclaim internationally.

Alphabetical Africa is Abish's most arbitrarily constructed fiction. The first chapter uses words beginning with the letter "a," the second with "a" and "b," the third with "a," "b," and "c," and so forth. Like the waxing and waning of the moon, the alphabet first expands to a full orchestration of 26 letters, and then diminishes letter by letter until we are left again in the final chapter with words beginning only with the letter a . . . "Another abbreviation another abdomen another abduction another aberration . . . " This obviously artificial structure that Abish imposes on his prose draws attention to its construction as fiction. Here Abish deconventionalizes plot and character, pointing to the seemingly natural way these literary conventions are taken for granted in the ways they are commonly used.

In *Minds Meet*, as in *Alphabetical Africa*, arbitrary external constraints again give Abish the freedom to generate his text. His fiction works over the meaning of signs, usually familiar and reassuring, that become ominous in their implications. In "How the Comb Gives a Fresh Meaning to the Hair," the retarded children, like all children, have names, but theirs are "Harry, John, Dwight, Lyndon, Dick, Frank, Bess, Jackie, Minnie, Lady, Pat, and Eleanor." Abish is interested in neither authenticating nor duplicating the familiar world and the signs that constitute it, but in undermining habitual modes of perception by constantly displacing the reader's preset, Pavlovian responses to these signs.

Abish continues to undermine the order and equilibrium of the familiar world in his second collection, *In the Future Perfect*. In "The English Garden," the first story of the collection, the narrator purchases a coloring book of the new Germany. The images in the coloring book function as both a complement and a contrast to the Germany the narrator encounters. The contrast is rendered through Abish's stark prose style that resembles the two-dimensional reality of the coloring book, a world where perspective is flattened, a world without shadow, shading, nuance, or depth. But unlike the coloring book, Abish's language resonates with a disquieting and disturbing irony. Language for Abish often functions as a barrier, a boundary, like the black lines circumscribing the coloring book images. But Abish creates a more complex understanding beyond the circumscriptions and outlines of a world that cannot be quantified, explicated, and sewn up in its entirety.

What is familiar and reassuring in *How German Is It*, Abish's latest novel, is the American "idea" of Germany and those signs that constitute that reality. This "idea" of Germany is again pictured in a coloring book, but in *How German Is It*, the usual visual repertoire of the coloring book has been "manipulated" to include images of terrorists and their ambiguous activities. Just as the coloring book has been manipulated, so too the smooth and sanitized surfaces of the new Germany show signs of stress. Here, abundance is stark, ambience is ordered, and characters change sexual partners like they change their clothes, but not quite; one partner, Vin, the Mayor's wife, is always to be found crouching in the corner. And when a sewer line erupts, the old Germany covered over by the town of Brumholdstein seeps through as all-pervasive stench from the remains of a mass grave. Abish is careful not to create a certain identity for these skeletons, but rather engages the reader in the task of filling in the inde-terminacies and gaps in the text.

The world for Abish is always more than a sum of our explanations for it. The potential expressivity of Abish's language is disciplined and carefully constrained, but its force that much more potentially explosive as it fissures the hegemonic seamlessness of the familiar world.

Selected Bibliography

Primary Sources

Duel Site. New York: Tibor de Nagy editions, 1971.
Alphabetical Africa. New York: New Directions, 1974.
Minds Meet. New York: New Directions, 1975.
In the Future Perfect. New York: New Directions, 1977.
How German Is It. New York: New Directions, 1980.

Secondary Sources

Baker, Kenneth. "Restrictive Fiction: The Writing of Walter Abish." *New Directions: An International Anthology of Prose and Poetry*. New York: New Directions, 1977, pp. 48–56.
Durand, Regis. "The Disposition of the Familiar." In Maurice Couturier, ed., *Representation and Performance in Postmodern Fiction*. Montpelier, France: Delta, 1983, pp. 73–83.
Kearns, George. "Fiction Chronicle': *How German Is It*." *The Hudson Review* 34 (Summer 1981): 303–306.
Klinkowitz, Jerome. "Walter Abish: An Interview." *Fiction International* 4/5 (1975): 93–100.
———. "Walter Abish and the Surfaces of Life." *The Georgia Review* 35 (Summer 1981): 416–20.
Lotringer, Sylvere. "Wie deutsch ist es" (interview). *Semiotext(e)* 4, no. 2 (1982): 160–78.

McCaffery, Larry, and Sinda Gregory. "An Interview with Walter Abish." *Fiction International* 17, no. 1 (1986).

Misson, Arias. "New Novel and TV Culture." *Fiction International* 17, no. 1 (1986).

Tanner, Tony. "Present Imperfect: A Note on the Work of Walter Abish." *Granta*, September 1979, pp. 65–71.

DEBORAH SMALL

ACKER, KATHY (1947–   )

Kathy had long hair once, and another last name. She seems to have been born on April 18, 1947, to have grown up in New York, to have attended Brandeis, to have passed through San Diego in 1970 on her way to San Francisco, perhaps Seattle, and back to New York where, as everyone wants to know, she performed sex acts on stage and screen. Somewhere she began to write.

Acker's early books were published by small presses and featured an abrupt and sensationalistic prose style that, a bit anachronistically, led to her identification as a "punk writer" in reviews of her recent books, *Great Expectations* (1982) and *Blood and Guts in High School* (1984). Her early books even more than the later feature graphic and desperate sex fantasies, images of sadism, masochism, masturbation, and death or, in one reviewer's words, "far-flung visions of sex and violence, of time-travel and gender-bender identities, splattered on the page with willful lack of control." When Acker says "I want to become famous so I can get fucked" she doesn't mean "fucked over." "Time travel" is a misreading—these texts have no real "narrative present" anymore than William Burroughs' *Cities of the Red Night*, for example—and Acker's seeming lack of narrative control, such as it is, has the same sort of significance as early punk rockers' rejection of melody, musical tradition, and musicianship in favor of a home-made artistry—and, like punk musicians' technique, her "control" gets tighter in her later works.

Toughness and desperation are (on) the surface of the work; beneath are other things, formally more interesting: writing as role-playing, plagiarism, and a kind of literal referentiality. The first section of her first available book—*The Childlike Life of the Black Tarantula by the Black Tarantula* (1973), apparently a compilation of other, shorter, books—begins with this prospectus: "Intention: I become a murderess by repeating in words the lives of other murderesses." Later in the same book, "I move to San Francisco. I begin to copy my favorite pornography books and become the main person in each of them." Acker's *Great Expectations* begins, "My father's name being Pirrip, and my Christian name Philip, my infant tongue could make of both names nothing longer or more explicit than Peter. . . . "

There is nothing surreptitious about any of this. Some of her early books contain something like footnotes or credits at the ends of the sections. Later she drops this device but calls the first section of *Great Expectations* "Plagiarism." The reader gets the uneasy feeling, recognizing some passages, that the passages he or she doesn't recognize might just be from books he or she hasn't read. But who writes anything anyway? Surely what these texts force us to remember is that everything anyone ever writes is informed by everything one has read. Who is writing this, for example? Yet the third paragraph of *Great Expectations* (in that section called "Plagiarism") begins, "On Christmas Eve 1978 my mother committed suicide. ..." Kathy's mother, one reviewer wrote, thus it must be true, "was a Park Avenue suicide." *Great Expectations* is not "the story" of this—what is the story of anything?—but is it perhaps a story of coming to terms with it? Can real writing be done this way?

Plagiarism is a kind of role-playing, getting inside the other writer's life by copying his or her words, or trying to, but Acker plays roles in other ways too. In two of her books (*Tarantula*, *Toulouse Lautrec*), even the author wears a pseudonym; in another (*Kathy Goes to Haiti*) the author is in the title. One thinks of Jorge Luis Borges' Pierre Menard who (re)wrote *Don Quixote*. Is all writing role-playing? Writers sometimes say they "get inside the character" in order to tell a better story; Acker claims other motives.

In *The Adult Life of Toulouse Lautrec* (1975) Acker's narrator plays the role of Toulouse Lautrec as a woman, with interesting results. This book is full of names of painters and of fictional characters like Agatha Christie's Hercule Poirot. In *Blood and Guts* the narrator, Janey, ends the book in conversation with Jean Genet (the homophony of the names is interesting). These things are not too unusual: "real people" crop up in other writers' books. Naming your friends is something else. What about that scene on a bus with Ron Silliman* in *Toulouse Lautrec*? Did that "really happen"? The presence of the name, at least for those who know it's a "real name"— who know, perhaps, the "real Ron Silliman," language poet named for an actor who would be President, rider of busses—drives a nail through the text, pinning it, if not to real life, at least to a reference to that life, another part of the story found, not invented. Writers always draw from their own lives—what else do they have?—describing real events while hiding their friends (and enemies) behind aliases. Acker has this backwards too: Melvyn Freilicher dies in *Toulouse Lautrec*, but I saw him last week.

Plagiarism, role-playing, nomination: the making explicit of some things always already there in writing. Therefore—a syllogism—this is postmodern narrative all right. Traditional narrative, despite its theoretical referentiality, is ideally a horizontal product, connecting events in a formal illusion apparently parallel to real life. Acker's texts, on the other hand, are rent by verticality, scenes and events interrupted by other scenes and events, names from real life, authorial asides, passages from Keats, de Sade, Poe, cheap pornography. The result is not stories but structures, something like poetry, something like collage, something like rant. Laminated and bristling. Inside, always, are tender moments: "I'm going to tell you something. The author of the work you are now reading is a scared little shit. She's frightened, forget what her life's like, scared out of her wits, she doesn't believe what she believes so she follows anyone. A dog." (*Great Expectations*, pp. 70–71).

The image is sweet and tough, terrifying and pervasive. Don't tell her I said "sweet." Someone is writing *Fear of Kathy Acker*; another, *My Life as Kathy Acker*. Is all this to be taken seriously? Yes.

Selected Bibliography

Primary Sources

Politics. Papyrus Press, 1972.

The Childlike Life of the Black Tarantula, by the Black Tarantula. 5 parts. Various presses, 1973. Reprinted: Viper's Tongue Books, 1978.

I Don't Expect You'll Do the Same, by Clay Fear. San Francisco: Musicmusic Corp., 1974.

I Dreamt I Became a Nymphomaniac!: Imagining. San Francisco: Empty Elevator Shaft Poetry Press, 1974.

The Adult Life of Toulouse Lautrec, by Henri Toulouse Lautrec. 6 volumes. New York: TVRT Press, 1975–1976.

Blood and Guts in High School. New York: Grove Press, 1984. Copyright 1978 by Kathy Acker.

Kathy Goes to Haiti. Toronto: Rumour Publications, 1978.

Great Expectations. Barrytown, N.Y.: Open Book/Station Hill Press, 1982. Also Grove Press, 1983.

Hello, I'm Erica Jong. Hello, I'm Erica Jong. New York: Contact II, 1982.

Secondary Sources

Crichton, Jennifer. "Who Is Kathy Acker? And Why Does She Write So Dirty?" *Ms.* (March 1985): 86–87.

RICHARD ASTLE

APPLE, MAX (1942–   )

If artifice has been a chief characteristic of postmodern fiction, then Max Apple certainly fits into this tradition. Apple's stories are, at first glance, much too odd, the situations too allegorical and unlikely, the characters too mythic and one-dimensional, to bear much direct relationship with reality. And yet, despite their improbability, there is also an uncanny perception of American life within Apple's fiction. This perception has been knocked askew by the circumstances of his birth—Apple was born into an Orthodox Jewish family in a Polish-English speaking Protestant neighborhood—which has given him insights into the everyday world of America that most natives are blinded to due to overfamiliarity and sensory overload. Gas stations, healthfood fanatics, Disneyland, real estate brokers, game show hosts, boxers—these ordinary elements become not mundane but fantastic elements that Apple shows to be truly wondrous. From his perspective as both a cultural outsider and a Midwestern native, he is able to see through the neon glare to the essence that is America. Thus, with his ability to render appreciatively the contradictory results of the American dream, Apple is able to convey a sense of the marvelous-within-the-ordinary that realism could never render.

Born in 1942, Max Apple was raised in a Jewish family (indeed, Yiddish was his first language) in Grand Rapids, Michigan. Growing up, Apple was influenced by his father, with whom he shared a great interest in sports, especially boxing (which was to be the central metaphor in his first novel, *Zip*). But it was his grandmother, with her marvelous tales of the old country and her quirky insights into the mysteries of American life, who inspired his desire to be a fiction writer. Even at an early age, Apple was able to appreciate the craft and the fluid movement from dailiness to fantasy and allegory that went into his grandmother's stories. He decided to be a writer and subsequently attended the University of Michigan, where he received his B.A. and Ph.D. in English literature (his dissertation examined Burton's *Anatomy of Melancholy*). He also briefly attended Stanford's writing program during the early 1960's.

Apple's first novel, *Zip: A Novel of the Left and Right*, was published in 1978, and predictably various autobiographical features are found here, from the focus on boxing to the use of a character—a Jewish grandmother—that combined features of various members of Apple's family. The book follows the rise of a young Puerto Rican fighter, Jesus Goldstein (a Marxist), who blackmails the United States into a heavily promoted fight in Cuba. Although the novel's allegorical structure makes it obvious that the fight is ultimately a clash between capitalism and Marxism, Apple, who was politically active during the 1960s, does not wave a flag for either side. Instead, he is able to look, with sympathy, understanding, and irony, at the solutions offered by both the left and the right. Thus, in the final contest, both fighters are ambiguously victorious—an open-ended conclusion that is found in many of Apple's fictions. Apple sees the world too clearly to give most of his stories pat endings, so instead he usually provides conclusions that provide pregnant complexities that cannot be defined in black and white.

Toward the end of *Zip* a cast of "ready-made" characters begin to appear, including Jane Fonda, J. Edgar Hoover, and Fidel Castro. The use of such ready-mades, which is one of Apple's most distinguishing trademarks, is essentially a technical device that allows him to present instantly recognizable mythic types without having to clutter his narratives with traditional means of character development, description, action, or dialogue. This short cut allows Apple to tap the reader's store of characters and move on more directly to other concerns. Thus, Apple doesn't spend his time developing the character of a Marxist leader of a Latin American nation; instead he gives us "Fidel Castro."

Apple's use of ready-made characters is the strongest in *The Oranging of America and Other Stories* (1976). The title story takes the reader on a journey through America with Howard Johnson and his associate Mildred. Apple, however, hasn't researched the real Howard Johnson, but has instead given us a character more akin to the image in our minds—the "real" Howard Johnson, who sensed America's need for comfort and shelter, and, Godlike, made monuments to these needs appear all over this nation.

Apple's stories are woven on the loom of the unconscious, pulling together the oddities that everyday life joins. Manifest destiny, free competition, and death are joined in a tale that defies unraveling. The title story ends with the blending of these threads.

The California sun was on her back, but her cold breath hovered visibly within the U-Haul. No tears came to Mildred now; she felt relief much as she had felt it that afternoon near ancient Jericho. On Santa Monica Boulevard, in front of Lawrence Welk's apartment building, Mildred Bryce confronted her immortality, a gift from the ice-cream king, another companion for the remainder of her travels.

In addition to his novel and short stories, Apple has edited an anthology titled *Southwest Fiction*, contributed to *Esquire* magazine, and a collection of short stories titled *Free Agents*. Max Apple teaches at Rice University in Texas.

Selected Bibliography

Primary Sources

The Oranging of America and Other Stories. New York: Grossman Publishers, 1976.
Zip: A Novel of the Left and Right. New York: Viking Press, 1978.
Free Agents. New York: Alfred A. Knopf, 1984.

Secondary Sources

McCaffery, Larry, and Sinda Gregory, "An Interview with Max Apple." *Mississippi Review* 13 (Fall 1984): 9–32.
Wilde, Alan, *Horizons of Assent*. Baltimore: Johns Hopkins University Press, 1981, pp. 132–33, 161–67.

DOUGLAS CAPPS

B

BALLARD, J. G. (1930–)

Throughout his career as a writer of novels and short stories, J. G. Ballard has tread the line between science fiction and the avant-garde. Veterans of the British New Wave regard him as a founder of their movement, which brought to the science fiction of the 1960s and early 1970s a set of literary values the genre had not previously demonstrated, a turning away from pure scientific speculation to the probing of the human soul. Ballard's fiction is dominated by tortured but terrestrial settings and the tormented people who inhabit them, characters confronting and in general yielding to their own atavistic compulsions. In Ballard's work, Earth itself is, in his words, "the only truly alien planet," and its human inhabitants much stranger than any extraterrestrial being.

James Graham Ballard knew alienation first hand at an early age. Born of English parents in Shanghai on November 15, 1930, he spent his first 15 years of life in China. Interned by the Japanese in 1945, he was repatriated in 1946. He made up his mind to become a professional writer while studying pre-med at King's College, Cambridge. He dropped out of school and joined the Royal Air Force; while stationed in Canada he discovered American science fiction. His own SF career began in 1956 with several short stories in British magazines. Even then his fiction showed the influence of literary figures like Joseph Conrad, Franz Kafka, Herman Melville, and Graham Greene as much as that of science fiction favorites such as Ray Bradbury, William Kuttner, Richard Matheson, and Robert Sheckley. Ranging from psychological horror stories and chilling intimations of the future to Kafkaesque fables and whimsical fantasies, many of these pieces were brought together into collections.

Ballard became a novelist in 1962 with the American publication of *The Wind from Nowhere*, his most commercial and least interesting work of long fiction. He quickly followed this disaster novel with three others of greater value: *The Drowned World* (1962), *The Burning World* (1964; British title—*The Drought*), and *The Crystal World* (1966). Each presents a different scenario for the destruction of Earth as we know it—the first by a heating of the atmosphere and the melting of the ice caps, the second by a form of pollution that prevents evaporation from the oceans and thus precipitation, and the third by a bizarre space-time process that causes all matter to crystallize. Against these backdrops of irreversible catastrophe, the characters pursue various paths toward epiphany via self-destruction. This pursuit appears in its most atavistic form in *The Drowned World*, where the protagonist rejects all possibilities of saving himself from the encroaching reptile-infested, paleozoic swamp and heads south, even deeper into the superheated tropics and certain death. *The Crystal World* is the best novel of the three, with its stunning, surreal images of jeweled jungle and gem-bedecked birds, crocodiles, and humans freezing solid in patterns of glass and ice. Here the main character, a psychically exhausted physician, seeks illumination amid the external stasis of the crystallizing jungle while a battle between human evils reminiscent of Conrad rages around him.

For the rest of the decade, Ballard published little but more story collections and pieces in British literary magazines. In 1970 he began the second stage of his career with the non-SF volume *The Atrocity Exhibition*, later published in America as *Love and Napalm: Export USA* (1972). It is a series of semifictional commentaries on the violence of the 1960s, culminating in "The Assassination of John Fitzgerald Kennedy Considered as a Downhill Motor Race." A different sort of commentary on the psychopathology of contemporary violence appears in his 1973 novel *Crash*. Some view this narrative of automotive sadomasochism as the first of another disaster trilogy, the other volumes being *Concrete Island* (1974) and *High-Rise* (1975). Again Ballard makes familiar landscapes unfamiliar, though this time the landscapes of contemporary urban life; again he leads the reader through one exercise after another in entropy and degeneration. *Concrete Island* depicts a man marooned as certainly as Robinson Crusoe in the abandoned triangle between freeway ramps. In *High-Rise*, tribal warfare breaks out between the floors of a modern multistory condominium building. This later group of works has made Ballard especially popular in France.

If Ballard's novels seem, despite their overt differences, to be variations on a single theme, his shorter fiction has continued to show considerable diversity, from the droll scenes of decadent luxury in *Vermillion Sands* (1971) to the nightmare and transcendent visions collected in *Low-Flying Aircraft* (1976). A recent novel, *The Unlimited Dream Company* (1979), though it also treats entropic devolution, marks a return to fantasy: one man's mind transforms an English suburb into a jungle and the townspeople into sex-crazed savages. Though occasionally criticized for this thematic redundancy and certain lapses in style, Ballard merits reading for his brilliant dreamlike images and his relentless portrayal of the beast in people.

Selected Bibliography

Primary Sources

The Drowned World. New York: Berkeley, 1962.
The Crystal World. London: Jonathan/Cape, 1966.
Chronopolis and Other Stories. New York: G.A. Putnam, 1971.
Love and Napalm: Export USA. New York: Grove Press, 1972.
Crash. London: Jonathan/Cape, 1973.
Concrete Island. London: Jonathan/Cape, 1974.
High-Rise. London: Jonathan/Cape, 1975.
Low-Flying Aircraft. London: Jonathan/Cape, 1976.
The Unlimited Dream Company. London: Jonathan/Cape, 1979.
Empire of the Sun. London: Jonathan/Cape, 1983.

Secondary Sources

Aldiss, Brian. "The Wounded Land: J. G. Ballard." *SF: The Other Side of Realism*. Ed. Thomas D. Clareson. Bowling Green, Ohio: Bowling Green Popular Press, 1971.
Franklin, H. Bruce. "What Are We to Make of J. G. Ballard's Apocalypse?" *Voices for the Future*, Vol. 2. Ed. Thomas Clareson. Bowling Green, Ohio: Bowling Green Popular Press, 1979.
Goddard, James, and David Pringle, eds. *J. G. Ballard: The First Twenty Years*. Hayes, Middlesex: Bran's Head Books, 1976.
Nicol, Charles. "J. G. Ballard and the Limits of Mainstream SF." *Science Fiction Studies* 3, no. 2 (July 1976): 150–57.
Pringle, David. *Earth Is the Alien Planet: J. G. Ballard's Four-Dimensional Nightmare*. San Bernardino, Calif.: Borgo Press, 1979.
Stableford, Brian. "Short Fiction: J. G. Ballard." *Survey of Science Fiction*. Ed. Keith Neilson. Englewood Cliffs, N.J.: Salem Press, 1979.

STEPHEN W. POTTS

BARTH, JOHN (1930–)

For many readers, John Barth, is the central spokesperson for postmodernism. Unlike a large number of other postmodern novelists, Barth—at least since the publication of *Giles Goat-Boy* (1966)—has been able to place his fictions before a mass audience. His visibility and importance as a spokesperson have been increased by the awards he has won, the reviews he has received in first-rate periodicals, and the essays he has written about the state of fiction. The titles of two of these essays, "The Literature of Exhaustion" (1967) and "The Literature of Replenishment" (1980), sum up his attitudes toward fiction and reality. In these essays and in his fiction he suggests that traditional concepts of the self, truth, reality, and literature are somehow exhausted. They have lost whatever power and value they may have had. Barth's role, as he sees it, is to replenish, re-energize, these concepts by examining them and positing alternatives to them. The fictions that result from this program are highly experimental, intellectually ambitious, and wildly comic.

Born a twin on May 27, 1930 in Cambridge, Maryland, John Simmons Barth, Jr., has spent most of his adult life in university settings. Since receiving his master's degree in creative writing from Johns Hopkins in 1952, he has taught at a number of universities and since 1973 has been at Hopkins. This academic career allows him the time he needs for his fiction; it figures in the settings of some of his works and results, some critics feel, in the eruditeness of all his fictions. His concern with ideas has led one critic to describe him as a "perpetual-notion machine."

Barth's eight long fictions can be divided into four couplets. His first two novels, *The Floating Opera* (1956) and *End of the Road* (1958), are largely realistic and more traditional than his later works. The former is the story of protagonist-narrator, Todd Andrews, who is writing about the day on which he decided not to commit suicide. By the end of the day he describes, he realizes that just as there is no reason to live, there is no reason to end one's life. On his way to this epiphany, Andrews reveals a number of Barth's major concerns. This hero is a shapeshifter without a stable identity. Reality is similarly elusive. Andrews' attempt to explain why he does not kill himself leads to a series of digressions that lead him to suspect that nothing can be explained. Finally, these digressions and Andrews' self-conscious manipulation of them point to Barth's own playing with the narrative form that he has labeled exhausted.

Although less metafictional, Barth's *End of the Road* continues his discussion of the nature of the self. The novel's protagonist, Jake Horner, suffers from "cosmopsis." Bereft of any consistent identity, his inner self is a realm of unpredictable moods, and he is incapable of action. He temporarily overcomes this languor by assuming a series of masks, by practicing "mythotherapy." However, it fails him. After arranging for an abortion that ends in a woman's death, Jake falls into cosmopsis again.

Abandoning the realistic novel, Barth turns away from the contemporary scene in his next couplet: while *The Sot-Weed Factor* (1960) is set in the seventeenth century, *Giles Goat-Boy* (1966) takes place in the future. Both works, however, continue Barth's concern with cosmopsis. The protagonists of these novels lack consistent identities until they practice a form of mythotherapy. These novels also display Barth's return to the self-conscious play with narrative form that characterized *Floating Opera*. In *Sot-Weed* the reader encounters the parodic reworking of eighteenth-century fictional themes and techniques, the incorporation of digressions and non-existent historical documents, and an excessiveness in action and dialogue that suggests that they are included in the novel more for their own sake than for what they reveal about the main character. Likewise, in *Giles*, Barth presents a farcical reworking of mythic elements and a series of frames for his narrative that continually point to its artificiality.

His next couplet, *Lost in the Funhouse* (1968) and *Chimera* (1974), reveals Barth's deepening exploration of narrative form and language. *Funhouse* is a series of 14 short fictions that include a three-dimensional, Moebius-strip story, a story in which the story is the narrator, a fiction about writing fictions, and a story embedded in a story embedded in a story embedded in a story. *Chimera*, a National Book Award winner, consists of three novellas in which narrators discourse on the nature and function of fiction while acting within their own fictions. In both collections, Barth also reveals his continuing concern with mythology. To understand and revivify narrative, he returns to its Greco-Roman roots.

The most recent couplet, *Letters* (1979) and *Sabbatical* (1982), signals Barth's return to the novel after more than a decade. It also signals his attempt to bring together the various themes of his previous fiction. His examination of self, his experiments with form, his involvement with the contemporary scene, history, and myth—all come together in these two novels. It is as if he himself is like the heroes of *Letters* and *Sabbatical* looking back on his accomplishments at mid-career before setting off in a new direction. Reviewing Barth's career to this point, we can assume that this direction will be as innovative, interesting, and intellectually challenging as his earlier turnings.

Selected Bibliography

Primary Sources

The Floating Opera. New York: Appleton-Century-Crofts, 1956; rev. ed., Garden City: N.Y.: Doubleday, 1967.
End of the Road. Garden City: N.Y.: Doubleday, 1958; rev. ed., 1967.
The Sot-Weed Factor. Garden City: N.Y.: Doubleday, 1960.
Giles Goat-Boy or The Revised New Syllabus. Garden City: N.Y.: Doubleday, 1966.
Lost in the Funhouse. Garden City: N.Y.: Doubleday, 1968.
Chimera. New York: Random House, 1972.
Letters. New York: Random House, 1979.
Sabbatical. New York: G. P. Putnam, 1982.
The Friday Book. New York: G. P. Putnam, 1984.

Secondary Sources

Harris, Charles B. *Passionate Virtuosity: The Fiction of John Barth*. Urbana: University of Illinois Press, 1983.

Lemon, Lee. *Portraits of the Artist in Contemporary Fiction.* Lincoln University of
Nebraska Press, 1985, pp. 148–210.
McConnell, Frank D. *Four Postwar American Novelists: Bellow, Mailer, Barth,
and Pynchon.* Chicago: University of Chicago Press, 1978.
Morell, David. *John Barth: An Introduction.* University Park: Pennsylvania University Press, 1976.
Tanner, Tony. *City of Words: American Fiction, 1950–1970.* New York: Harper
& Row, 1971, pp. 230–59.
Tharpe, Jack. *John Barth: The Comic Sublimity of Paradox.* Carbondale: Southern
Illinois University Press, 1974.
Waldmier, Joseph J., ed. *Critical Essays on John Barth.* Boston: G. K. Hall, 1980.
Weixlmann, Joseph N. *John Barth: A Bibliography.* New York: Garland, 1976.

JOHN Z. GUZLOWSKI

BARTHELME, DONALD (1931–   )

Only occasionally does experimentation in literature bring immediate
success to a writer. Barthelme, who has done as much, and sometimes
more, than his fellow postmodernists to revolutionize fiction, has achieved
this extraordinary feat. The lasting popularity of his short fictions in the
New Yorker quickly made him a prosperous full-time writer. This success
may have been based partly on a providential misunderstanding: Barthelme's fictions, which are sometimes difficult to distinguish from his satirical vignettes (in *Guilty Pleasures*), can be read as a good-humored
criticism of urban life in America, and Barthelme himself tends to encourage this approach. But to the aficionados of modernist and postmodern
literature, they appear as highly sophisticated constructs and surrealistic
compositions that expand the capacities of language, produce unprecedented images, and obscure the differences between literary genres.

Donald Barthelme was born in Philadelphia on April 7, 1931. His family
soon moved to Houston where his father rose to prominence as an architect.
Emulating the "great paradigmatic writer" (Barthelme's own words) of
the time, Hemingway, he started his literary career working on a newspaper, the *Post*, while he was only a sophomore in the journalism department at the University of Houston. After his undergraduate years,
which were interrupted by two years in Korea, he worked as editor of the
Forum and as temporary director of the Contemporary Arts Museum of
Houston, a job for which, as he admits, his qualifications were meager.
This experience was to prove highly valuable to him as a writer; it also
earned him a job as managing editor of the shortlived *Location*, the art
and literary magazine started by Harold Rosenberg and Thomas B. Hess
in New York in 1962. It is around that time that he mailed his first fiction
to the *New Yorker* where it was immediately accepted. It was "agented by

probably a nine-cent stamp," as he once put it. This easy beginning was to make him a full-time writer and a resident of New York.

The first collection of his *New Yorker* fictions, *Come Back, Dr. Caligari,* appeared in 1964. It was followed by *Unspeakable Practices, Unnatural Acts* (1968), *City Life* (1970), his best works perhaps, and, later, by *Sadness* (1972), *Amateurs* (1976), *Great Days* (1979), and *Sixty Stories* (1981), a selection from his earlier books. Besides these fictions, Barthelme has published a children's book, *The Slightly Irregular Fire Engine* (1971), a book of satirical vignettes, *Guilty Pleasures* (1974), and two novels, *Snow White* (1967) and *The Dead Father* (1976), parts of which had previously appeared in the *New Yorker* also.

Although many critics, like Charles Newman, have claimed that Barthelme was no realist, it is hard to imagine how he could have been so popular with the readers of the *New Yorker* if they had not found in his works an echo of their preoccupations or a projection of their dreams. Like a good journalist, Barthelme seems to have covered all the important subjects of his time: consumerism ("To London and Rome," *Guilty Pleasures,* "Concerning the Bodyguard"), politics ("Robert Kennedy Saved from Drowning", "The President," "The Rise of Capitalism," "The Royal Treatment," "Belief"), and war ("A Picture History of the War," "Engineer-Private Paul Klee"). But the theme that reappears the most regularly in his fictions is no doubt sexual war ("Will you Tell Me," "City Life," "Perpetua," and, of course, *Snow White*) and fatherhood ("A Shower of Gold," "The Agreement," and *The Dead Father*). The theme permeates practically each of his fictions under one form or another, but it is treated with less complacency than in the novels of Philip Roth, for example. Barthelme never gives the impression of working out his own psychological problems or of fighting his private wars against society. Whatever theme or object he tackles, he submits it to his subtle irony which is capable of "depriving the object of its reality in order that the subject may feel free" ("Kierkegaard Unfair to Schlegel").

This irony is in fact a new species of art that is neither systematically iconoclastic or purely surrealistic. Barthelme points toward a world that is somehow easily recognizable, but he does so in a language that is so remote from daily language (which, however, it sometimes parodies), that the reader feels as if he or she had landed in another "universe of discourse"(*Snow White*). "Reality," which is none other than a body of verbalized or contractual representations, no longer seems to impose words on the writer; it appears rather as a fathomless source of incredible images and of unruly games. These images, which are as surrealistic as the paintings of Magritte or Delvaux, or the lithographs of Escher, have little of the oneiric quality of those deposited on the page by Desnos or Breton. They are elaborate compositions that depend for their success on the blessed polysemy of words and the amusing arbitrariness of discursive rules. Traditionally, such linguistic manipulations were more or less restricted to poetry whose image-making capacity has always been acknowledged. Barthelme, who always wanted to be a painter, though he "can't draw a lick," has considerably developed the image-making capacities of prose. In some cases, especially in *City Life* and *Sadness*, he has also inserted drawings (not his own, of course) and collages in his fictions, producing a strange dialogue between images and words.

His novels, *Snow White* and *The Dead Father*, share many of the characteristics of the shorter fictions; they are collections of short, uncanny pieces in which a comparatively small number of characters and stereotypes are made to perform. The plots, which are extremely thin, constantly fork out into whimsical digressions, as in *Tristram Shandy*.

One has the feeling, reading Barthelme, that modern fiction, after more than two centuries of verbal inflation, has talked itself dumb, but also that language has recaptured some of its old-time iconicity.

Selected Bibliography

Primary Sources

Come Back, Dr. Caligari. Boston: Little, Brown, 1964.
Snow White. New York: Atheneum, 1967.
Unspeakable Practices, Unnatural Acts. New York: Farrar, Straus & Giroux, 1968.
City Life. New York: Farrar, Straus & Giroux, 1970.
The Slightly Irregular Fire Engine. New York: Farrar, Straus & Giroux, 1971.
Sadness. New York: Farrar, Straus & Giroux, 1972.
Guilty Pleasures. New York: Farrar, Straus & Giroux, 1974.
Amateurs. New York: Farrar, Straus & Giroux, 1976.
The Dead Father. New York: Farrar, Straus & Giroux, 1976.
Great Days. New York: Farrar, Straus & Giroux, 1979.
Sixty Stories. New York: Farrar, Straus & Giroux, 1981.
Overnight to Many Distant Cities. G. P. Putnam's, 1983.

Secondary Sources

Clark, Beverly Lyn. "In Search of Barthelme's Weeping Father: *Philological Quarterly* 62, No. 4 (1983): 419–33.
Couturier, Maurice. "Barthelme's Uppity Bubble: 'The Balloon'." *Revue Française d'Etudes Americaines* 9 (October 1979): 183–201.
————,and Regis Durand. *Barthelme*. New York: Methuen, 1982.
Critique 16, no. 3 (1975). Special Barthelme issue.
Dervin, Daniel A. "Breast Fantasy in Barthelme, Swift and Philip Roth: Creativity and Psychoanalytic Structure." *American Imago* 33 (1976): 102–22.
McCaffery, Larry. "Donald Barthelme and the Metafictional Muse." *Sub-Stance* 28 (1980): 75–88.
————. "An Interview with Donald Barthelme." *Anything Can Happen: Interviews with Contemporary American Novelists*. Urbana: University of Illinois Press, 1983, pp. 32–44.
————. "Meaning and Non-Meaning in Barthelme's Fiction." *Journal of Aesthetic Education* 13 (January 1979): 69–80.

————. *The Metafictional Muse: The Works of Coover, Barthelme and Gass*. Pittsburgh: University of Pittsburgh Press, 1982.

Molesworth, Charles. *Donald Barthelme's Fiction: The Ironist Saved from Drowning*. Columbia: University of Missouri Press, 1982.

O'Hara, J. D. "Donald Barthelme: The Act of Fiction LXVI." *Paris Review* 80 (1981): 180–201.

Stott, William. "Donald Barthelme and the Death of Fiction." *Prospects* 1 (1975): 369–86.

Wilde, Alan. "Barthelme Unfair to Kierkegaard: Some Thoughts on Modern and Postmodern Irony." *boundary 2* 5 (Fall 1976): 45–70.

MAURICE COUTURIER

BARTHES, ROLAND (1915–1980)

On February 25, 1980, the French critic Roland Barthes had lunch with Michel Foucault* and François Mitterand; crossing the street near the Collège de France after lunch, he was hit by a laundry truck. He died on March 26, 1980, the same month in which *Camera Lucida: Reflections on Photography* was published. *Camera Lucida* is Barthes' book of the dead: he had earlier proclaimed the death of the author and now announced the death of the world of photographable physical objects, where "death" is the failure of authors to be present to readers of their words and objects to be present to observers of their images.

Born in Cherbourg on November 12, 1915, Barthes moved with his mother and brother to her parents' home in Bayonne after his father, Louis, was killed in a naval battle in 1916. They moved to Paris when he was nine, and when he was nineteen, he received the baccalaureate and contracted tuberculosis, which stayed with him through his twenties, exempting him from the military and preventing him from competing for entrance to the Ecole Normale Supérieure. Having spent 1934–1935 in a sanatorium, Barthes studied at the Sorbonne for four years—he earned a license in classics, and a final license in grammar and philology in 1943—and taught in lycées for two years. The result of a relapse in 1941 was that he was in and out of sanatoria until a final convalescence in Paris in 1946–1947. Cured, Barthes taught for two years abroad (Rumania and Egypt) and spent the decade 1950–1960 at various posts in Paris. Only when he was 45, in 1960, did he assume a stable position, at the Ecole Pratique des Hautes Etudes of which he was the director of studies from 1962. In 1963, *On Racine* appeared; it elicited a response from Raymond Picard, *Nouvelle critique ou nouvelle imposture?*, which attacked the New Criticism exemplified by *On Racine*, sparking a new quarrel between the ancients and moderns and catapulting Barthes to prominence. Barthes was elected to the Chair of Literary Semiology at the Collège de France in 1977, and on October 26 of that year his mother, Henriette Binger, died. Not only a theory of photography and perception and time, *Camera Lucida* is Barthes writing his love for his mother: since he is the only one left of their line and he will not procreate, when he dies there will be no one to remember her and, since she is now dead, no one to remember him and his love for her. Therefore, he writes, "in her death my death is inscribed." Barthes, writer above all, writes even his death.

In his first book, *Writing Degree Zero* (1953), Barthes identified the appearance in French literature after 1848 of a writing that was instrumental, was not a vehicle for the expression of an author's mind and representation of an already present world or prevailing ideology: a writing that was about nothing other than itself. After 1975 Barthes examined such writing in light of what at first glance is utterly different from it: autobiographies and personal diaries, the discourse of lovers, and photographic images—to find the differences between them vanish as the same division within writing and its apparent others opens up. The final division is between what is and what is not mediated by culture, and freedom is the freedom to think against the stereotypes celebrated by a culture.

In the middle of his working years Barthes studied the life of signs in society and showed that much of what is taken to be natural is the product of human beings' performing the *structuralist activity*, fragmenting the given into units unmeaning in themselves and relating them to each other according to codes which are, then, the principles of intelligibility. The resulting structures have the form of the linguistic model developed by Saussure, who had also posited the existence of the science of semiology of which linguistics would be a part, words simply being one kind of sign whose meaning lies in relations of difference from others of its kind. With *The Elements of Semiology* (1965) Barthes introduced structural linguistics to the French world and inverted the relation between the two sciences on the ground that all sign systems have a verbal element, and no system of images or objects signifies anything not individuated by language. Semiology is part of linguistics, the part "covering the *great signifying unities of discourse*" (p. 11).

Barthes' views on how the world is made intelligible had not, however, taken into account the structuring subject, and in 1970 he published *S/Z*, in which reading, and the role of the subject in reading, comes center stage. It is Barthes' structuring of a Balzac story: the story is broken into 561 units that are related to each other and, in principle, to all else that has been written, by five codes; interspersed are 93 tiny essays in which the distinction between the readerly and writerly appears. This is elaborated in *The Pleasure of the Text* (1973) and adumbrated in *Writing Degree Zero* in the break between traditional literature transparent to the author's mind and world and modern literature, opaque, signifying itself, "pointing to its mask." The readerly is the comfortable, the writerly what "unsettles the reader's . . . assumptions, the consistency of his tastes, values, memories, brings to a crisis his relation with language.'' The writerly is not only a kind of text but also a way to read, a way that does not consume the already written but produces the text that is read: the price of production is the reader's surrender of assigned meanings and fixed values and, hence, of his or her self, constituted as it is by memory and desire for what lasts. The strings of randomly ordered fragments that comprise *The Pleasure of the Text, Roland Barthes by Roland Barthes* (1975), and *A Lover's Discourse* (1977) mime the shattering of concepts accomplished in Barthes' books.

Barthes charts a path from structuralist activity to structuring subject to subject's body to physical objects in general, whose presence gives way in *Camera Lucida* to the imprint, on camera or eye, of the light rays the object configure. Because light takes time to travel, what is imprinted is always a past state of the object, with the photographed object usually being further removed from its image than the seen object is. The photograph bears perfect witness to the *past reality* of its object: it is as transparent as language is opaque. Just as one may read a text as its consumer or producer, so one may view a photograph as an image, significant through its relation with other images, or a record of the real, that is, semiotically or referentially. To regard it as referential, however, is to court madness, for now to be touched by what does not exist is to surrender one's commitment to the irreversibility of time and the presence of the present, as the writerly reader surrenders commitment to stable meanings and a subject to which they could be present. The ecstatic "dissolve" of viewer and reader into image and text is possible only because subjects and time are encoded: what is unmediated is the result of disruption of what is mediated, including any subject that might restructure the disrupted and any time in which the restructuring might occur. The unmediated is the *intractable*; between it and the civilized code of perfect illusions, "the choice," Barthes writes in the last sentence of the last book, "is mine."

Selected Bibliography

Primary Sources

Le Degré zéro de l'écriture (1953), with *Nouveaux essais critiques* Paris: Seuil, 1972. *Writing Degree Zero* trans. Annette Lavers and Colin Smith. New York: Hill & Wang, 1968. *New Critical Essays*. Trans. Richard Howard. New York: Hill & Wang, 1980.
Mythologies (1957). Paris: Seuil, 1970. Partial translation: *Mythologies* trans. Annette Lavers. New York: Hill & Wang, 1973. Translation of remaining essays: *The Eiffel Tower and Other Mythologies*. Trans. Richard Howard. New York Hill & Wang, 1979.

Sur Racine Paris: Seuil, 1963. *On Racine*. Trans. Richard Howard. New York: Hill
    & Wang, 1964.

Eléments de sémiologie (1964). In *Le Degré zéro de l'écitiure, suivi de Eléments de
    sémiologie*. Paris: Seuil, 1965. *The Elements of Semiology*. Trans. Annette
    Lavers and Colin Smith. New York: Hill & Wang, 1968.

Essais critiques. Paris: Seuil, 1964. *Critical Essays*. Trans. Richard Howard. Ev-
    anston: Northwestern University Press, 1972.

Système de la mode Paris: Seuil, 1967. *The Fashion System*. Trans. Matthew Ward
    and Richard Howard. New York: Hill & Wang, 1982.

S/Z. Paris: Seuil, 1970. *S/Z*. Trans. Richard Miller. New York: Hill & Wang, 1977.

L'Empire des signes. Geneva: Skira, 1970. *Empire of Signs*. Trans. Richard How-
    ard. New York: Hill & Wang, 1982.

Sade/Fourier/Loyola. Paris: Seuil, 1971. *Sade/Fourier/Loyola*. Trans. Richard Miller.
    New York: Hill & Wang, 1976.

Le Plaisir du texte. Paris: Seuil, 1973. The Pleasure of the Text. Trans. Richard
    Miller. New York: Hill & Wang, 1975.

Roland Barthes par Roland Barthes. Paris: Seuil, 1975. *Roland Barthes by Roland
    Barthes*. Trans. Richard Howard. New York: Hill & Wang, 1977.

Fragments d'un discours amoureux. Paris: Seuil, 1977. *A Lover's Discourse: Frag-
    ments*. Trans. Richard Howard. New York: Hill & Wang, 1978.

Image-Music-Text. Essays selected and trans. by Stephen Heath. New York: Hill
    & Wang, 1977.

*Leçon: Leçon inaugurale de la chaire de sémiologie littéraire du Collège de France,
    prononcé le 7 janvier 1977*. Paris: Séuil, 1977. "Inaugural Lecture." Trans.
    Richard Howard. In *A Barthes Reader*. Ed. Susan Sontag. New York: Hill
    & Wang, 1982.

La Chambre clair: note sur la photographie. Paris: Gallimard & Seuil, 1980. *Camera
    Lucida: Reflections on Photography*. Trans. Richard Howard. New York:
    Hill & Wang, 1981.

Le Grain de la voix: Entretiens. 1962–1980. Paris: Seuil, 1981. *The Grain of the
    Voice*. Trans. Linda Coverdale New York: Hill & Wang, 1985.

A Barthes Reader. Ed. Susan Sontag. New York: Hill & Wang, 1982.

L'Obvie et l'obtus: Essais critiques III. Paris: Seuil, 1982. *The Responsibility of
    Forms*. Trans. Richard Howard. New York: Hill & Wang, 1985.

Secondary Sources

Culler, Jonathan. *Barthes*. New York: Oxford University Press, 1983.

Lavers, Annette. *Roland Barthes: Structuralism and After*. Cambridge, Mass.: Har-
    vard University Press, 1982.

Studies in Twentieth Century Literature. Spring 1981. Special issue on Barthes.

Thody, Philip. *Roland Barthes: A Conservative Estimate*. Chicago: University of
    Chicago Press, 1983.

Ungar, Steven. *Roland Barthes: The Professor of Desire*. Lincoln: University of
    Nebraska Press, 1983.

Visible Language. Autumn 1977. Special issue on Barthes.

MARY BITTNER WISEMAN

BATCHELOR, JOHN CALVIN (1948–)

John Calvin Batchelor has written two diverse and entertaining novels, *The Further Adventures of Halley's Comet* (1980) and *The Birth of the People's Republic of Antarctica* (1983). Both are long, ambitious works which blend philosophical, religious, and political discussion within the framework of a romance or sea-adventure tale. Batchelor's fiction reflects the political and cultural ferment of the Vietnam Era in its diversity, imagination, and concern with issues; his novels refer specifically to events and public figures of that period.

Batchelor was born in Bryn Mawr, Pennsylvania on April 29, 1948 and graduated from Princeton University in 1970. Six years later, having studied in Scotland (1973–74), Batchelor graduated from the Union Theological Seminary in New York. Citing his literary influences in *Contemporary Authors*, Batchelor lists the Gospel of Matthew, Augustine's *Confessions*, Rabelais, Martin Luther, and Lawrence Sterne as the first five. It is significant that three are religious influences, and the other two are irreverently comic writers. It is just this unsettling mixture of serious moral issues and the wildly comic that Batchelor presents in his fiction.

Halley's Comet contains aspects of the romance novel of Walter Scott (complete with a quest for a new Grail) and is also a comic exploration of the corporatization of America and the world; Proto Industrial Trust (PIT), of which the Means Corporation is a part, attempts to stake a claim to Halley's Comet as a stepping stone to the economic development of the Solar System. The novel is fast-paced concoction of puns and wordplay with allusions to rock and roll and the pop culture of the 1960s. The appearances of the comet throughout history are catalogued at the beginning of the novel in the Cometological Calendar, an extended prayer to the comet, who appears in human form in the novel and is variously called the Comet Incarnate, Voluntas Hallei, Freewill, or just Majesty. Having guessed the existence of such a being, Rufus Broadsword has sent his nephew, Effert, in search of physical evidence of the comet's previous presences on earth; he has also chronicled the last four "apparitions" of Freewill to ancestors of the Means and Broadsword families, which involve such figures as John D. Rockefeller, Natty Bumpo, and Isaac Newton. With the aid of Freewill, the Broadswords attempt to defeat the Means Corporation's plot against the comet, code-named "Harold Starr." On a more serious level, the novel is pointing out the corruption of values in the twentieth century by the corporate forces that control the world, while humorously undercutting Rufus and Effert's naive search for faith, fulfilled in the appearance of the Comet Incarnate.

Reviewers and critics of Batchelor's second novel have noted its ancestry in *Moby Dick* and *The Narrative of A. Gordon Pym*, as well as *Beowulf* and Norse legends. *People's Republic* is a futuristic fantasy of an apocalyptic collapse of world order out of which a permanent population of international exiles, The Fleet of the Damned, emerges, preyed upon by plague and pirates, while defended by an International Ice Cross. The novel is presented as a first-person confession, written in an Antarctic prison in 2037 A.D., in which the narrator, Grim Fiddle, tells of his flight from political upheaval in Sweden with a band of outcasts and his Savonarola-like grandfather, Mord Fiddle. Torn between the influence of his grandfather and his sybil mother, Lamba Time-Thief, he unwillingly retraces the path of the legendary Norseman, Skallagrim Strider, his namesake, becoming involved in a war in the Falkland Islands and eventually forced to seek refuge in Antarctica. Countering comparisons with Jesus, David and Moses that others have made of him, Grim presents himself as a vengeance-seeking mass-murderer, repenting for the crimes he has committed. Batchelor beautifully and vividly recreates the imagery and style of *Beowulf* in a portion of Grim's final confession.

Though a more mature and controlled work than the first novel, *People's Republic* suffers the defect of being overlong and sometimes tedious in the philosophical, religious, and political digressions on issues such as republicanism versus a dictatorship of personality and ultilitarianism. This wordiness, however, is probably intentional and illustrates Grim's attempt to navigate the morally murky seas of his past with his faulty memory, sorting fact from imagined fact, truth from lie, reality from illusion, ultimately revealing a distrust of any truth as merely one version or vision of an ever-shifting reality.

In the epic scope of his novels, in his use of bizarre names, and in the broad range of his knowledge, Batchelor resembles Pynchon*, whom he mentions twice in *Halley's Comet* and includes in his list of influences. In his synthesis of fantasy and philosophy within traditional forms of narrative, Batchelor is experimenting with the form of the novel. His work is memorable for its inventiveness, though at times, the narrative loses focus and become bogged down in theoretical or metaphysical digressions. In both novels, there is a sense of a talent slightly out of control, but showing great promise. Though flawed, Batchelor's novels are word feasts not easily forgotten.

Selected Bibliography

Primary Sources

The Further Adventures of Halley's Comet. New York: Congdon & Lattes, 1980.
The Birth of the People's Republic of Antarctica. New York: Dial Press, 1983.

Secondary Sources

Edwards, Thomas R. *New York Times Book Review* (May 9, 1983).
Park, Clara Clairborne. *Commonweal* 110 (May 20, 1983): 307–8.
Prescott, Peter S. *Newsweek* 101 (May 9, 1983): 80.

DAVID W. COVEY

BEATTIE, ANN (1947–   )

To some Ann Beattie is a chronicler of life after the 1960s; to others she is a "major new voice" in American fiction, both a popular and a critical success. Certainly she is mistress of the story story and an accomplished novelist. Admired by John Updike, Margaret Atwood, and other contemporaries, and compared to such diverse talents as J. D. Salinger, Samuel Beckett, and Thomas Pynchon,* Ann Beattie has developed a style immediately recognizable—short flat sentences, often non-sequiturs, matter of factly illuminating the banal details of contemporary popular culture, its fads and fantasies, quirks and pitfalls. In all her work, she combines deadpan dialogue, humor, and trivia to expose the disorder in her characters' lives, their states of flux, and their desire to establish some pattern to their randomness. Her writing then explores our need to resolve contradictions in our lives—to resolve order with chaos, action with inaction, the concrete with the abstract, being with nothing. Through the behavior of her characters, she suggests the problems facing postmodern writers as well, the dilemma of reconciling the past with the present, the antiquated with the avant-garde.

In Beattie's world, men and women are often adrift or immobile, dropped out or barely making it in some dully conventional job, escaping through grass, rock music, or Red Mountain wine. In mostly Eastern landscapes— New York, Connecticut, New Hampshire, Virginia—her shoe and suit salesmen, accountants and ad men, and Bloomingdale clerks seek meaning in their dismal surroundings; they grasp at details, attaching importance to anything concrete, as to a lifeline that will anchor them to a purpose or rescue them from their individual quagmires of confusion.

Unlike her characters, Ann Beattie seems neither adrift nor immobile. At 38—she was born September 8, 1947, in Washington, D.C.—a prolific writer who may complete a draft in an hour or two, she has found one outlet through *The New Yorker*, which has first reading rights to her stories, and another through various literary journals and magazines such as *Atlantic Monthly, Antaeus, Virginia Quarterly*, and *Mississippi Review*. Growing up in Chevy Chase, a suburb of Washington, she received a B.A. from American University in 1967 and an M.A. in 1970 from the University of Connecticut, where she completed further graduate study from 1970 to

1972. She has taught both at Harvard and at the University of Virginia, and has received several honors: a Guggenheim in 1977; an award in literature from the American Academy and Institute of Arts and Letters in 1980; and, most recently, an honorary degree of Doctor of Humane Letters from American University in 1983. Presently, Beattie lives in New York, writing and traveling throughout the United States to give readings at college campuses.

Her first two major publications appeared in 1976: *Chilly Scenes of Winter*, a novel, and *Distortions*, a collection of stories, many of which first appeared in *The New Yorker*. These quickly established her as a major new talent and attached to her the label of post-1960s' chronicler. *Chilly Scenes of Winter* (made into the film *Head Over Heels*) especially evokes the 1960s' nostalgia: its protagonist transforms a memory—a chocolate-orange soufflé—into an absolute standard by which he can measure current inscrutable events, and by which he hopes to recapture a past relationship. Here, with wit and compassion, Beattie examines our need for stability and the ways we seek it—psychologically, emotionally, or physically, through obsession, hope, or inaction.

Distortions, as the title implies, also concerns itself with our reluctance to accept reality, and the way it slides from our grasp to become as distorted as our responses to it. From this collection comes the quintessential distortion, the popular and surprising "Dwarf House," anthologized recently in college literature texts. In such stories as "Gaps" and "Marshall's Dog," Beattie's interest in form becomes apparent as, reminiscent of Donald Barthelme* and Robert Coover,* she manipulates time and perspective so that we must establish meaning through our own ordering of the text.

Although some critics appraised Beattie's next collection of stories, *Secrets and Surprises* (1978), as a distillation of content and style—similar settings, themes, character types, and sentence structures—others admired the increased complexity of its material and its longer, more sustained stories. In several—"A Clever-Kids Story," "Shifting," and "Octascope"—Beattie further explores our responses to fictive and actual reality, and the relationship of storyteller to audience, to self, and to reality.

The form of her second novel, *Falling in Place* (1980), shifts from the straightforward narrative of *Chilly Scenes of Winter* to multiple perspectives and alternating plot lines, while it paints a typically offbeat Beattie tableau—a missing lover, a collapsed marriage, a sibling assault. Here again, employing her infallible gauge for measuring contemporary values and responses, Beattie demonstrates her skill at capturing the nuances of educated middle and upper-middle class over-30 Eastern America.

Beattie's most recent collection of stories, *The Burning House* (1982), continues to examine the effects of the past on the present and the relationship between art and reality, as in "Jacklighting" (also published separately in 1981 as a limited edition by Metacom Press) and "Winter: 1978," through the perceptions and reactions of her characters. Since the appearance of this collection, Beattie has produced a wealth of new stories, many already published by *The New Yorker* ("Television," "One Day," "Heaven on a Summer Night," and "Lofty"). Shorter than many of her earlier pieces—Beattie calls them "drawing room dramas"—these are less speculative and more pronounced in their resolutions, which are often epiphanies.

Primarily as a realist—though not only as a post-1960s' chronicler (while Beattie admits to an earlier interest in the period and in her friends' nostalgia, she asserts her interest is more psychological than sociological)—or as a compiler of trivia, Ann Beattie has crafted a distinct place in postmodern fiction. Her prose captures the mundane rhythms of a select, peculiarly American pulse and has established her voice as a refrain for the 1980s.

Selected Bibliography

Primary Sources

Chilly Scenes of Winter. New York: Random House, 1976.
Distortions. New York: Random House, 1976.
Secrets and Surprises. New York: Random House, 1978.
Falling in Place. New York: Random House, 1980.
The Burning House. New York: Random House, 1982.
Love Always. New York: Random House, 1985.

Secondary Sources

Atwood, Margaret. "Stories from the American Front." Rev. of *The Burning House*. *New York Times Book Review*, September 26, 1982, pp. 1, 34.
Epstein, Joseph. "Ann Beattie and the Hipposisie." *Commentary*, March 1983, pp. 54–58.
Gelfant, Blanche H. "Ann Beattie's Magic Slate or the End of the Sixties." *New England Review* 1 (1979): 374–84.
Gregory, Sinda, and Larry McCaffery. "A Conversation with Ann Beattie." *The Literary Review* 27 (1984): 165–77.

SUE SANDERA RUMMEL

BENFORD, GREGORY (1941–   )

The science fiction of Gregory Benford raises the problem of the postmodernist label, and at the same time offers perhaps a way of resolving tensions inherent in it. As used here, it would define sci-fi as the extension of, and departure from, what sort of literature? For some, modernism is Joyce, texts where the primary narrative dwindles to "a day in the life" while an abyss of parallel subnarratives opens out underneath, mythic plots themselves overlaid with multiple strands of linguistic/stylistic arabesque. And if it is Joyce's Bloom who calls for "new worlds for old," the author, however, explores the depth of myth, old worlds for new. Is sci-fi then, by virtue of its future orientation, its pretense to extrapolate new worlds, postmodernist? If so, we see why many more traditional critics consider sci-fi, in its adherence to the horizontal time line, a literature of rupture. Indeed, it is often faulted, on the assumption that stylistic and narrative complexity somehow bestows mythic depth, for the thinness of its constructs. A dilemma gapes here: modernism becomes an iceberg without a tip, sci-fi a tip without an iceberg. This gap, however, is in many ways an artificial one, and Gregory Benford is a writer who is breaching it. Scientist *and* stylist, he seeks in his fictions to examine that interaction of progressive and regressive tendencies—of extraterrestrial visions and terrestrial longings—which he feels defines the condition of contemporary man, modern or postmodern.

Born in 1941 in Mobile, Alabama, Benford grew up "among uneducated, near-illiterate people" in a strongly regional, oral culture. This upbringing explains his lifelong fascination with the storytelling rhythms of Faulkner and other Southern writers, and his feeling of being rooted in this tradition. In fact, the narrative voice of his recent novel, *Against Infinity* (1983), skillfully blends these primal rhythms of Southern storytelling with sophisticated speculation on the nature of a future alien encounter. At the same time, however, Benford's upbringing has been intensely international. His father being a military officer, he has lived for extended periods in both Europe and Japan, and he openly claims that Japanese culture influenced his world view. Indeed, like Japan, Benford is dynamically poised between past and future, between tradition and exploration, the old earth and the new "ocean" of the stars.

The same dynamic tension is seen in Benford's career pattern. Benford considers his decision to study science a practical one; "joining the Sputnik sendup," he took a B.A. in physics from the University of Oklahoma in 1963. Yet he had been an avid sci-fi fan in his teens and editor of the "fanzine" *Void*, whose title hints at the deep mystical strain in this avowedly pragmatic person, and in a sense reveals the single theme—the attraction of that alien unknown—that will motivate his future speculations, both in physics and in fiction. While a graduate student in physics at the University of California at San Diego, he published his first story, "Stand In" (1965). Again, while claiming he wrote this and other stories for recreation, Benford in a sense established a pattern here—a need to move back and forth between analagous physical and fictional models, letting the acts of doing physics and writing about doing it interpenetrate—that has continued to mark his work and life. After taking his Ph.D. in 1967, he embarked on a successful scientific career. Characteristically, however, his domain of investigation has shifted from solid state physics to relativistic astrophysics, a field that allows scientific speculation once again to run parallel to that single growing theme in Benford's fiction—the alien encounter.

This full-time science career is often seen as the reason why his literary output, measured against that of other sci-fi professionals, is restricted. In terms of quality, however, it is an enviable output. Benford himself uses Graham Greene's division of works into "entertainments" and "novels." There are very few of the former, for Benford constantly reworks and reshapes, over and over probing the deeper implications of a story whose beginnings seemed unabashed formula. The early "Deeper Than the Darkness"(1967), for example, was novelized in 1970, then rewritten as *The Stars in Shroud* (1978). His *Jupiter Project*, a consciously written tribute to the Heinlein juvenile, serialized in 1972 and rewritten for book publication in 1975, is now being rewritten, retitled, retransformed. This restless return to written texts is, more than traditional literary experimentation, the mark of the scientist for whom the act of writing is an experiment which, for the sake of truth to a changing self and world, must be continuously redone, expanded, and redirected.

Benford, then, views fiction, more than a self-reflexive act, as an ongoing process wherein forms and structures, always tentative, are at the service of that pursuit which is that of modern science and should be that of modern humanism as well—the possibility of communication with the truly alien at the "growing edge" of our quest for knowledge. An example of the shaping power of this vision is his excellent *In the Ocean of Night* (1977). This novel shapes several separately published episodes into an epic of first contact. In the place of the classic space opera hero, however, his Nigel Walmsley is presented in detail as a living and working scientist, as a being for whom living and working cannot be separated from his search for the alien unknown. A central scene in the novel has Nigel, arguing with a priest of the New Sons cult, reject his view that physical laws are a mind cage, a set of bars we need only transcend. For Benford, these material bars are real; and if the individual cannot get out, he or she must continue to reach out but always through bars. For if Nigel's quest dissolves barriers, at the same time it generates involvements and mysteries that create new ones.

Benford has written a continuation of *Ocean, Across the Sea of Suns* (1983), and he plans to write more sequels, with each expanding the space/time perspectives surrounding his hero. At the same time he is expanding his use of stylistic devices and modes. To Benford, many of the mannerisms of modernist prose have served as bars to the fictional process, making the act of narration a series of idiosyncratic explorations of individuals that, in the end, offer no unified field or "consensus worldview." But, again, these bars are not to be abandoned so much as explored. And in *Sea of Suns* Benford plays these otherwise isolating modes of "talk" against each other to reveal their incommunicability, their mutual alienness. It is over such a landscape of different styles and typefaces that his fiction, in its relativizing explorations, seeks to build an integrated net of communication.

Benford has won a number of awards within the sci-fi community (Nebulas for "If the Stars Are God" and *In the Ocean of Night*, and a Nebula and a Campbell for *Timescape*). His fiction continues to evolve and grow, and deserves a wider audience, however. A powerful fusion of conventions and world views from both mainstream and science fiction, his recent work offers a way of synthesizing those scientific and literary methods which modern culture elsewhere seems so intent on keeping apart. An example is *Timescape*. One of the finest novels about scientists doing science, it is much more than well-written C. P. Snow. For here, in the alternating yet converging narratives of two temporal worlds, Benford mixes a detailed account of the travails of everyday research with fantastic occurrences at the edge of human knowledge. The crux is the tachyon, the postulated faster-than-light particle that allows a dying future world to communicate with its past, to plant mysterious data for its scientists to pursue, in hopes of leading them to understand physical processes which in turn will alter the course of things and "save" their world. This slow quest opens out, in a magnificent conclusion, onto the new, fantastic narrative landscape of time paradox.

Benford has described his art of fiction as "enlisting the devices of realism in the cause of the fantastic." And his most recent novel, like *Timescape*, does just that. *Artifact: A Scientific Romance* (1984) sets two distinct cultural lines of investigation, physics and archaeology, converging toward the mystery of a cube sculpture discovered in a Mycenaean tomb. What unfolds here, again in what the author calls "slow revelation," is the fragility of traditional systems of explanation, and the necessity of seeking, through further investigation, new models of order. This, it seems, is the major task for fiction today, if it is to survive. And a writer like Benford is pointing the way to renewal.

Selected Bibliography

Primary Sources

Deeper Than the Darkness. New York: Ace Publishing Corp., 1970.
Jupiter Project. New York: Thomas Nelson, 1975.
If the Stars Are Gods (with Gordon Eklund). New York: Berkley Publishing Corp., 1977.
In the Ocean of Night. New York: Dial Press/James Wade, 1977.
The Stars in Shroud. New York: Berkley Publishing Corp., 1978.
Find the Changeling (with Gordon Eklund). New York: Dell Publishing Co., 1980.
Shiva Descending (with William Rotsler). New York: Avon Books, 1980.
Timescape. New York: Simon & Schuster, 1980.
Against Infinity. New York: Simon & Schuster, 1983.
Across the Sea of Suns. New York: Pocket Books, 1983.

Artifact: A Scientific Romance. New York: Simon & Schuster, 1984.
Of Space-Time and the River. New Castle, Va.: Cheap St., 1985.

GEORGE SLUSSER

BERGER, THOMAS (1924–   )

For more than 25 years, Thomas Berger has been one of America's most prolific and consistently entertaining comic novelists. Berger is endowed with a zest for comic invention in a wide variety of forms, from parody and farce to social satire and domestic comedy, and he engages an equally broad range of subject matter. As one might expect of a consummate ironist, he has explored in depth the many permutations of appearance and reality, especially those deriving from the problematic causal connections of human existence. In addition, Berger's comic vision encompasses such classic themes as the variety of love and its responsibilities, the possibility of acting with decency in an indifferent world, and the limitations of time and change. Although his concerns are traditional, Berger's novels are very contemporary, if not postmodern, in their comic acceptance of the fictive nature of reality, in their reliance on the power of language to create alternative worlds, and in their exploitation of various generic possibilities.

Born July 20, 1924, in Cincinnati, Ohio, Thomas [Louis] Berger attended local schools and was graduated with a B.A. (honors) from the University of Cincinnati in 1948. Like the hero of his novels, Carlo Reinhart, he had earlier served in the Army Medical Corps during the Berlin occupation. In the early 1950s Berger attended Columbia University graduate school, married artist Jeanne Redpath, and worked as a librarian, *New York Times* indexer, and magazine editor. Primarily known as a novelist, Berger has, over the years, published numerous short stories, been a film critic for *Esquire*, and written a play. Although in recent years Berger has steadfastly avoided publicity, rarely giving interviews, he has made forays into academia from his residence in the New York City area.

Berger's first two novels, *Crazy in Berlin* (1958) and *Reinhart in Love* (1962), depict the life and times of Carlo Reinhart, whose sometimes bizarre, always humorous, encounters with the incongruities inherent in America's history and culture, from the occupation Army and postwar Vetville to the revolutionary 1960s and today's ubiquitous shopping mall, are further developed in the subsequent novels, *Vital Parts* (1970) and *Reinhart's Women* (1981). Although the Reinhart novels vary in tone and substance, they are consistent in their exuberant comedy and in a comic hero who is large in body and spirit, a latter-day American Adam, daunted but not defeated by a world that is not what it seems. Beset by hoaxes, fraud, and all manner of apparent contradictions, Reinhart's passive but persistent humanity survives intact.

Little Big Man (1964) was both a popular and critical success. Again, he created a memorable comic hero in Jack Crabb, who, as a 111-year-old survivor of the battle of the Little Big Horn, recounts his unlikely adventures into a tape recorder in 1953. The novel, however, is more than a parody of the Western and our received notions about the West; it profoundly challenges some of America's most cherished myths and radically undermines the credibility of written history itself. Along the way, both the white and Indian worlds are sharply satirized, and such figures as General Custer, Bill Hickok, Wyatt Earp, and Kit Carson are irretrievably deflated in comedy. In his use of the conventions of traditional picaresque narrative and in his comic subversion of the Western and historical novel, Berger also displays a willingness to explore generic possibilities that is evidenced in later works.

Since the success of *Little Big Man*, Berger has shown no sign of repeating himself and has consistently taken creative risks. Often, his novels have attempted to reinvent, or reinvigorate, traditional literary forms. In rather different ways, *Killing Time* (1967) and *Who Is Teddy Villanova?* (1977) depart from but do not finally depend on the conventions of crime and detective fiction. Typically, both novels achieve their effects through the use of a language wholly and appropriately developed for their needs. In *Regiment of Women* (1973) Berger chooses science fiction as the mode most useful in conveying his satiric vision of the perennial struggle between the sexes, especially as complicated by the tendency toward role reversal. *Arthur Rex* (1978), yet another abrupt formal and linguistic departure, is Berger's re-imagining and retelling of the Arthurian romances for the contemporary reader. Berger returns to today's world but not to the conventional realistic novel in *Neighbors* (1980), a stringent moral parable, whose nightmarish vision owes much to Kafka. Like the earlier *Sneaky People* (1975), *The Feud* (1983), Berger's twelfth novel, is set in a small, Midwestern town in the 1930s. But although the setting allows Berger to indulge his sensitive ear for the idiosyncrasies of American speech, the world is rendered more in terms of moral fable than social history or even satire.

Sympathetic book reviewers frequently remark on the fact that Berger's work remains relatively underestimated and critically neglected. Why this should be is puzzling in view of the consistently high level of his achievements. His fiction displays a rich and versatile comic vision, manifested in a variety of forms and engaged with American life and society from the quotidian to the most central myths and dreams. His use of language is attuned to his imaginative needs; his comedy is at home in many modes; and his sense of the absurd is subordinate to a generous spirit.

Selected Bibliography

Primary Sources

Crazy in Berlin. New York: Scribner's, 1958.
Reinhart in Love. New York: Scribner's, 1962.
Little Big Man. New York: Dial Press, 1964.
Killing Time. New York: Dial Press, 1967.
Vital Parts. New York: Baron, 1970.
Regiment of Women. New York: Simon & Schuster, 1973.
Sneaky People. New York: Simon & Schuster, 1975.
Who Is Teddy Villanova? New York: Delacorte Press, 1977
Arthur Rex. New York: Delacorte Press, 1978
Neighbors. New York: Delacorte Press, 1980.
Reinhart's Women. New York: Delacorte Press, 1981
The Feud. New York: Delacorte Press, 1983.

Secondary Sources

Betts, Richard A. "Thomas Berger's *Little Big Man*: Contemporary Picaresque."
    Critique 23 (1981–1982): 85–96.
Gurian, Jay. "Style in the Literary Desert: *Little Big Man*." *Western American*
    Literature 3 (1969): 285–96.
Hassan, Ihab. "Conscience and Incongruity: The Fiction of Thomas Berger." *Cri-*
    tique 5 (1962): 4–15.
Hughes, Douglas A. "The Schlemiel as Humanist: Thomas Berger's Carlo Rein-
    hart." Cithara 15 (1975): 3–21.
Lee, L. L. "American, Western, Picaresque: Thomas Berger's *Little Big Man*."
    South Dakota Review 4 (1966): 35–42.
Wilde, Alan. "Acts of Definition, or Who Is Thomas Berger?" *Arizona Quarterly*
    39, no. 4 (Winter 1983): 312–50.

RICHARD A. BETTS

BERNHARD, THOMAS (1931–   )

Thomas Bernhard ranks among Austria's most widely discussed and controversial contemporary writers. If one is to believe a popular Vienna newspaper, Bernhard is even among those authors who are most frequently read in German classes in the United States. Little evidence can be found for this, however, and the Austrians, most of whom prefer not to read Bernhard themselves, need not worry that the image of their country might get tarnished from too much exposure to a writer for whom they show little affection. Certainly, however, Bernhard knows how to capture the attention of his countrymen. His entire *oeuvre* reflects his obsession, his love-hate relationship with his homeland. Moreover, with his extraordinary sense of the theatrical, Bernhard, the recluse, has managed to provoke many a scandal at his not-too-frequent public appearances. In the speech he gave in 1967 when he was awarded the Great Austrian State Prize for Literature, Bernhard first irritated his audience by insisting that all thinking was second hand. His subsequent statement that the Austrians, being apathetic and contemptible, were doomed to failure and deserved no less than chaos did not endear him to the nation or its political representatives. Bewildered and professing his pride in being an Austrian, the minister of education left the ceremony. No wonder then that Bernhard, in order to avoid such incidents, was asked to refrain from making speeches at other similar festive occasions. All the same, this virtuoso of insults made headlines again some ten years later when, in a letter to the prestigious Hamburg weekly, *Die Zeit*, he called then Austrian chancellor Bruno Kreisky an aging clown and a *Salzkammergut- und Walzertito* (a lake district and waltz-time Tito).

Born in Holland in 1931 of Austrian parents, Bernhard spent his early childhood in Vienna, in a town near Salzburg and in Bavaria. He experienced the last few years of the war with its air raids and bombings in a Salzburg boarding school. In 1947 he dropped out of the *Gymnasium* he hated so much to become an apprentice in a grocery store. A serious illness, the death of his grandfather, a writer of some renown to whom Bernhard had been very close, and the passing of his mother only a year later were serious blows to the troubled young man, who, in the 1950s, studied music and drama, worked as a courtroom reporter, and traveled extensively. Finally, in 1965, Bernhard settled on a farm in Upper Austria where he has lived ever since.

In the five volumes of his autobiography, (*The Cause, The Cellar, The Breath, The Cold, A Child*), Bernhard describes his childhood and his formative years as a cold and lonely world, as one endless path of suffering. In particular, he attacks Salzburg, known to the world as the gentle city of Mozart and music, as a repressive "death museum" that has suffocated its inhabitants.

All of Bernhard's novels basically are variations of the themes to be found in the autobiographies: not only his own but all human existence as such is an agony, and personal communication is impossible. The protagonists of Bernhard's novels live in a world that is doomed to stupidity, brutality, disease and decay, and, in the final analysis, death. Not only are they themselves victims of this "sinister tragicomedy of human existence" (Peter Spycher); they also constitute a counterforce which, in vain, tries to find some meaning behind the terror and horror of everyday reality. But the world of Bernhard is a world beyond hope. There exists only one vantage point: the finality of death. Viewed from this perspective, Bernhard (here possibly inspired by Schopenhauer or Sartre) shows the world as meaningless and with only one creative possibility. One must establish a new artificial universality devoid of the vestiges of one's heritage. Not surprisingly then, Bernhard's characters are degenerating individuals, be they aristocrats or scholars, who live in isolation on rundown properties, remote from civilization. They are psychopaths who, by resorting to philosophical speculation and introspection, end in madness and suicide. In *The Lime Works* (1973), a brilliant but unbalanced scientist-philosopher living in a building of an abandoned limestone quarry kills his wife in despair over his failure to write a scholarly book. *Gargoyles* (1970) is about the deranged mind of an Austrian prince, and in *Correction* (1979), the hero, an eccentric also, having once designed a cone-shaped building for his sister, takes his own life.

Bernhard's existential pain is reflected in his style. As his characters contemplate and get lost in their thoughts, long, continuous, spiral-like monologues dominate much of his prose. His diction is marked by endless sentences that have become a trademark and are dreaded by many readers. Sentences are repeated relentlessly numerous times; long passages are written in the subjunctive, and monologues are recorded in indirect discourse. Bernhard's style has rightly been called awkward, monotonous, and tedious. In fact, Bernhard's entire work has been called monotonous, dreary, deadening. Reading Bernhard can become emotionally trying, even a torture as some critics have claimed. Nevertheless, paradoxical as it may seem, Thomas Bernhard has succeeded in attracting and fascinating a growing readership worldwide.

Selected Bibliography

Primary Sources

Frost. Frankfurt: Insel Verlag, 1963.
Verstörung (*Disturbance*). Frankfurt: Insel Verlag, 1967. (*Gargoyles*. Trans. Richard and Clara Winston. New York: Alfred A. Knopf, 1970.)
Das Kalkwerk. Frankfurt: Suhrkamp, 1970. (*The Lime Works*. Trans. Sophie Wilkins. New York: Alfred A. Knopf, 1973.)
Korrektur. Frankfurt: Suhrkamp, 1975. (*Correction*. Trans. David McLintock. New York: Alfred A. Knopf, 1979.)
Die Ursache (The Cause). Salzburg: Residenz Verlag, 1975.
Der Keller (The Cellar). Salzburg: Residenz Verlag, 1976.
Der Atem (The Breath). Salzburg: Residenz Verlag, 1978.
Der Stimmenimitator (The Mimic). Frankfurt: Suhrkamp, 1978.
Die Kälte (The Cold). Salzburg: Residenz Verlag, 1981.
Ein Kind (A Child). Salzburg: Residenz Verlag, 1982.
Benton. Frankfurt: Suhrkamp, 1982. (*Concrete*. Trans. David McLintock. New York: Alfred A. Knopf, 1984.)

Secondary Sources

Arnold, Heinz Ludwig, ed. *Text + Kritik 43. Thomas Bernhard*. 2d ed. Munich: edition text + kritik, 1982.

Bartsch, Kurt, Dietmar Goltschnigg, and Gerhard Melzer, eds. *In Sachen Thomas Bernhard*. Königstein/Ts.: Atheneum, 1983).

Dierick, A. P. "Thomas Bernhard's Austria: Neurosis, Symbol or Expedient?" *Modern Austrian Literature* 12, no. 1 (1979): 73–93.

Mauch, Gudrun. "Thomas Bernhard. Eine Einführung in sein Werk," *Modern Austrian Literature* 12, no. 2 (1979): 113–27.

Sorg, Bernhard. *Thomas Bernhard*. Munich: Beck; edition text + kritik, 1977.

Van Ingen, Ferdinand. "Denk-Übungen. Zum Prosawerk Thomas Bernhards." In *Studien zur österreichischen Erzählliteratur der Gegenwart*. Ed. Herbert Zeman. Amsterdam: Rodopi, 1982, pp. 37–86.

Wolfschütz, Hans. "Thomas Bernhard: The Mask of Death." In *Modern Austrian Writing. Literature and Society After 1945*. Eds. Alan Best and Hans Wolfschütz. London: Oswald Wolff; Totowa, N.J.: Barnes & Noble, 1980, pp. 214–35.

JÜRGEN KOPPENSTEINER

BERNSTEIN, CHARLES (1950–   )

To a much greater degree than most of his contemporaries, the writings of Charles Bernstein adopt and adapt a wide range of forms, of which prose is but one possibility. Because his books are thematic and formal in their construction, carefully avoiding the emphasis on self, a sort of personism, implicit in any chronological (autobiographical) composition, the bulk of his prose is concentrated in just three of his twelve books: *Poetic Justice* (1979), *Controlling Interests* (1980), and *The Occurrence of Tune* (1981), a book-length work written in 1977 and published as a collaboration with painter-photographer Susan B. Laufer. Yet, although only a fraction of his output has been in paragraph/sentence format, many of his best known pieces are in prose, such as *Occurrence*, "Palukaville," "The Taste Is What Counts," and "The Italian Border of the Alps."

Although there is a formal element in Bernstein's writing, it has little of the symmetry or balance which the term *formalism* is often thought to imply. In contrast (and far exceeding the uses of asymmetry employed by Charles Olson), Bernstein is the poet of awkwardness, hesitation, the step back, decenteredness, doubt. Yet, whereas in this epoch of poststructuralism and deconstruction some authors, such as the Canadian Steve McCaffery, take the diaspora of significations in their work as an end in itself, Bernstein alternates imbalance with elegance and continually returns the reader to the origin of such "dysraphisms" (a term for mis-seaming Bernstein, a free-lance medical writer, expropriated from the theory of congenital disease), the social context of language itself.

The emotional impact of such works on a reader can be unsettling, both for the normative presumptions of literature which they disrupt and the world thus characterized. If, for example, literary coherence requires both continuity and closure, a text that reveals such effects to be no more (or other) than the consequence of a series of rhetorical and syntactic devices insinuates a bleak universe—what little that seems whole, rooted, connected, or intelligible in our personal lives may equally be a delusion. Such is the thrust of the final passage of "The Italian Border of the Alps" in *Controlling Interests*:

That's just the way it. In our studious, the shape of, everybody grouped, along the shore, clammy, pleasure and an, at approaches attended to, towards. I like hard work and I don't care how long my hours are. I have an inquisitive and analytical mind, make a good appearance and get along well with others. Gives way to. A reality continually demanded of, give up, renovated. Or else the hygenics of personal encounter are bowled over by autodidactic posturings in the name of space. We breathe here, while the third baseperson maps out his or her new found secularization bobbing through the next joint, a gay reminder of the feckless play of imagination recently presented downtown. The aerial bombardment lasted several weeks, with intermittent disruption, but life went on much as usual, the shop steward noting several irregularities.

Coherence here is feigned, countered, parodied. That which is most continuous is "aerial bombardment," and the moment of completion falls on the word "irregularities." Readers of contemporary verse will, of course, recognize the presence of Charles Olson in the terms *space* and *breathe*, the passage being an explicit rejection of the neo-romantic individualism of the New American poetry.

Even couched in a pervasive irony, Bernstein's cynicism is not that of "The Waste Land," that nihilism so characteristic of a narcissistic modernism. In fact, Bernstein goes so far as to reject romantic love (intersubjectivity, that love of self reflected from the eyes of an Other) as anything more than a further delusion. But it is not a failing of people. Language and social relationships, particularly those that take place on the job or in bed, are mutually constitutive. Read from the perspective of "Alps" or *The Occurrence of Tune*, modernism (be it that of Eliot or the postmodernism of Olson) can be seen as a writing that dealt only with the linguistic half of this complex equation, while the social realism of writers such as the 1930s novelist Michael Gold just reversed the problem.

Like Gold and Louis Zukofsky, the Objectivist poet who combined the development of new forms with progressive politics, Charles Bernstein is a product of the Jewish experience in Manhattan. Born in 1950 and raised on the Upper West Side by a family that had found some success in the garment industry, he attended the Bronx High School of Science before studying philosophy at Harvard. There, he worked with Stanley Cavell (whose famous essay "Must We Mean What We Say?" can be read as a call for a contextual theory of language) and wrote a lengthy paper on Ludwig Wittgenstein, the most "poetic" of modern philosophers, and on

Gertrude Stein, a poet, prose poet, and novelist who had studied with William James. After Harvard, he moved to Santa Barbara, California, where he worked for a community-based health program, before returning to the Upper West Side.

In 1978, with only two self-published collections, *Asylums* and *Parsing*, but a rapidly growing collection of magazine credits, Bernstein joined with Fordham political scientist and poet Bruce Andrews to edit and publish $L=A=N=G=U=A=G=E$, a journal explicitly focused on the poetics of current writing. The magazine quickly became the hub of new critical thought on the East Coast, an in-print counterpoint to the San Francisco Talk Series begun by Bob Perelman the year before. Although the publication lasted for only four volumes, the writers whose work most often appeared there became known, if not stereotyped, as the language poets.

Shade, the first really extensive collection of Bernstein's work, was published by Sun & Moon Press in 1978, but it wasn't until the rapid-fire sequence of *Poetic Justice, Controlling Interests,* and *The Occurrence of Tune* that his own writing reached a national audience. Since then he has published one large collection, *Islets/Irritations* (1983), and several smaller ones. With Andrews, he edited *The $L=A=N=G=U=A=G=E$ Book*, an anthology of pieces from the magazine. He also edited *Content's Dream*, a selection of his critical writing, due out from Sun & Moon Press in 1985. The Fall 1982 issue of *The Difficulties* was devoted to Bernstein's work— only four years after the publication of *Shade*—and included several critical pieces on his work and an interview, as well as a fairly complete bibliography.

Selected Bibliography

Primary Sources

Asylums. New York: Asylums, no date listed.
Parsing. New York: Asylums, 1976.
Shade. College Park, Md.: Sun & Moon Press, 1978.
Poetic Justice, Baltimore: Pod Books, 1979.
Senses of Responsibility. Berkeley, Calif.: Tuumba 20, 1979.
Controlling Interests. New York: Roof, 1980.
Legend (with Bruce Andrews, Ray DiPalma, Steven McCaffery, and Ron Silliman). New York: $L=A=N=G=U=A=G=E$/Segue, 1980.
The Occurrence of Tune. New York: Segue, 1981.
Stigma. Watertown, N.Y.: Station Hill, 1981.
Resistance. Windsor, Vt.: Awede, 1983.
Islets/Irritations. N.Y.: Jordan Davies Books, 1983.

RON SILLIMAN

BLOOM, HAROLD (1930–)

Born in New York City in 1930, Harold Bloom belongs to an intellectual generation of literary critics whose primary practical concern has been with revising the low modernist estimate of romantic poetry by offering a tough-minded and anti-idealist version of its poetics. After earning his B.A. from Cornell University in 1951, Bloom moved on to Yale, first as student (gaining his doctorate in 1955) and then as teacher (he is currently professor of English and of Humanities). His primary companions in the effort to reinterpret and perhaps revalorize romanticism have been his Yale colleagues: Paul de Man,* Geoffrey Hartman,* and J. Hillis Miller.* Along with Bloom, in many minds, these are the four horsemen of the past decade's literary critical apocalypse. That the relations among these four have frequently taken on an oppositional cast disturbs none of them—and perhaps least of all Bloom, whose work has been a continuing promotion of literary and critical agonism.

Bloom's early work must have looked very much of a piece with other contemporary or slightly earlier efforts to reestablish the value and interest of romantic poetry and poetics—work by, for example, Northrop Frye or M. H. Abrams or Earl Wasserman. *The Visionary Company* (1960) is dedicated to Abrams and seems to share Frye's interest in myth and his insistence on the centrality of Blake. It is with his study of Yeats (1970) that Bloom first really opens his distinctive problematic, and it is one that places him in inevitable conflict with such figures as Abrams and Wasserman. *Poetry and Repression: Revisionism from Blake to Stevens* (1976) offers the following Arnoldian gloss on Bloom's activity: "The function of criticism at the present time, as I conceive it, is to find a middle way between the paths of demystification of meaning, and of recollection or restoration of meaning, or between limitation and representation" (p. 68). Elsewhere he casts his contrast in terms of de-idealization and re-imagination. In each instance Bloom sets himself off from the modernist debunkers of romanticism on the one hand, and, on the other, from those who would simply reassert the romantic self-image and valorization in the face of that critique—T. S. Eliot or T. E. Hulme on the one side, M. H. Abrams or Wasserman on the other. (Hulme and Abrams meet in describing romanticism as "spilt religion"—they disagree about the value of that thing: Bloom rejects the description.)

It is not accidental that Bloom borrows Arnold's title to lay out his own ambition. Eliot attempted to dismiss Arnold as a propagandist rather than a critic—and from a Bloomean angle that attempt to separate *polemos* and creation is continuous with Eliot's ("weak") idealization of influence into the "simultaneous order" of "Tradition and the Individual Talent." If, as Eliot would have it, the existing order of art is complete before each new work arrives and must be altered to accommodate it, this must mean that each new work actively struggles against its precursors in order to forge for itself a place at their expense. This is the fact about poetry that romanticism makes crucially visible for Bloom (so that his theory and criticism are both bound to and continually surpass the particular ground of romantic poetry—*The Anxiety of Influence* [1973] is uneasily subtitled *A Theory of Poetry*).

Every (romantic) poem *is* its struggle to displace its precursors. W. J. Bate sounded the first notes of Bloom's theme with his *The Burden of The Past and the English Poet* (1970)—but Bloom radicalized that book's thesis (beyond Bate's recognition) by passing it through Nietzsche and Freud and their French readers and revisers, Jacques Lacan* and Jacques Derrida* above all. This theoretical smorgasbord allowed Bloom to construct the "map of misreading" that organizes his readings and writing from the early 1970s on. This map charts the abstract progress of any poetic struggle for imaginative space and priority—that is, it charts the structure of the romantic poem. It does so in terms simultaneously of imagery, rhetorical tropes, Freudian defense mechanisms (a poem is, then, like a person, fighting for selfhood), and what Bloom calls "revisionary ratios," whose names are drawn from a variety of more or less classical, more or less religious, sources: clinamen, kenosis, tessera, daemonization, askesis, apophrades.

The last of these names the return of the dead and represents in miniature the achievement of the poem: a reversal of the relation between priority and belatedness so that the poem, rather than seeming to have fought its way into an already full and closed universe of poetry, claims to have been there all along and relegates its precursors to the position of the late, derivative, and secondary. The success of this claim is the measure of poetic strength.

The writing of a poem is then the reading of another poem, and this is always an active, transforming reading, attempting to undo its knowledge of that poem's priority and establish its own lie against time. A poem is the misprision of another poem, and such polemic reading must also be called misreading. The question of interpretation is not one that criticism brings to the poem, but one that is internal to it and is continued—for the most part weakly—in criticism: "There are," Bloom writes in *The Anxiety of Influence*, "no interpretations, but only misinterpretations, and so all criticism is prose poetry." This continuity of poetry and criticism sounds another Arnoldian note, but it is here worked by a sense of contestation and struggle foreign to Arnold's "disinterested endeavour to learn and propagate the best that is known and thought in the world." Bloom recognizes no such disinterest, and so it is inevitable that what might once have looked like an application of Freud to literature has become also a reading, and revising, of Freud—"wrestling Sigmund" in the title of a 1981 lecture.

If Bloom rejects all descriptions of romanticism as "spilt religion," it is perhaps because for him it remains religion—albeit a peculiar, antithetical religion (gnostic, Jewish, Kaballistic) concerned above all with history, our condemnation to it and our struggle against it. Our condition—poetic, critical, real—allows neither of serene timeless orders nor any secure aesthetic or moral sublimity. In seeking to "raise the rhetoricity of the reader's stance" (*Kaballah and Criticism*, 1975), Bloom would enforce on us the full weight of our historicity. This is a peculiarly American ambition, as it is a peculiarly American accomplishment to have found in contemporary French theory a means to the recovery of history.

Bloom's extraordinary rate of production through the 1970s and into the current decade have combined with his equally extraordinary and bewildering multiplication of theoretical terms and resources and his encyclopedic grasp of poetic texts to make his work appear both overwhelming and idiosyncratic in the extreme. In this he means perhaps to be an inheritor—or displacer—of Emerson. Certainly, it is in such company he would have his work judged, and by such strength he would have it tested. Such testing itself will be the work above all of strength and not—not simply—theoretical abstraction: reading poetry as poetry, criticism as criticism.

Selected Bibliography

Primary Sources

Shelley's Mythmaking. New Haven, Conn.: Yale University Press, 1959.

The Visionary Company: A Reading of English Romantic Poetry. Garden City, N.Y.: Doubleday, 1960. Revised and enlarged ed., Ithaca, N.Y.: Cornell University Press, 1971.

Blake's Apocalypse: A Study of Poetic Argument. Garden City, N.Y.: Doubleday, 1963.

Yeats. New York: Oxford University Press, 1970.

The Ringers in the Tower: Studies in Romantic Tradition. Chicago: University of Chicago Press, 1971.

The Anxiety of Influence: A Theory of Poetry. New York: Oxford University Press, 1973.

Kaballah and Criticism. New York: Seabury Press, 1975.

A Map of Misreading. New York: Oxford University Press, 1975.

Figures of Capable Imagination. New York: Seabury Press, 1976.

Poetry and Repression: Revisionism from Blake to Stevens. New Haven, Conn.: Yale University Press, 1976.

Wallace Stevens: The Poems of Our Climate. Ithaca, N.Y.: Cornell University Press, 1977.

"The Breaking of Form" In *Deconstruction and Criticism*. New York: Seabury Press, 1979, pp. 1–37.

The Flight to Lucifer. New York: Farrar, Straus & Giroux, 1979.

Agon: Towards a Theory of Revisionism. New York: Oxford University Press, 1982.

The Breaking of the Vessels. Chicago: University of Chicago Press, 1982.

Secondary Sources

Arac, Jonathan. *The Yale Critics: Deconstruction in America*. Minneapolis: University of Minnesota Press, 1983.

Bruss, Elizabeth. *Beautiful Theories: The Spectacle of Discourse in Contemporary Criticism*. Baltimore: Johns Hopkins University Press, 1982, pp. 288–362.

Handelman, Susan. *The Slayers of Moses: The Emergence of Rabbinic Interpretation in Modern Literary Theory*. Albany, N.Y.: SUNY Press, 1982, pp. 179–223.

Lentricchia, Frank. *After the New Criticism*. Chicago: University of Chicago Press, 1980, pp. 318–46.

Miller, J. Hillis. "Stevens' Rock and Criticism as Cure." *Georgia Review* 30 (1976): 330–48.

STEPHEN MELVILLE

BRAUTIGAN, RICHARD (1935–1984)

In the 1960s Richard Brautigan became one of America's most widely read experimental authors. Following the publication of *Trout Fishing in America* (1967), his importance to the counterculture, particularly in San Francisco, rivaled that of Carlos Castañeda* and Alvin Toffler. "The greening of America" provided fertile ground for an author with a cynical view of American values and an antipathy for literary traditions. As that era passed, however, Brautigan's popularity faded, and many critics who admired his early works began to dismiss him as a relic of the "hippie" generation. At the same time, some critics have come to look past the apparent thematic thinness and have found deeper motives and complexities in his work. The metafictional aspects of his books are more than a whimsical trick; they are the products of Brautigan's aesthetic concern for the spontaneous and immediate, and his rejection of fixed forms.

Born in Tacoma, Washington, on January 30, 1935, Richard Gary Brautigan was the oldest child of Bernard and Lula Mary Keho Brautigan. In 1954 he moved to San Francisco where, at one time, he shared an apartment with Philip Whalen. He married Virginia Dionne Adler in 1957, and their daughter Ianthe was born in 1960. The Brautigans were divorced in 1970. He maintained homes in both Montana and Bolinas, California, while often traveling to Japan. It was at his cabin in Bolinas that Brautigan committed suicide in October 1984.

In 1954 San Francisco was about to become the literary center of the Beat Generation. Besides Whalen, Brautigan became friends and was influenced by Gary Snyder, Lawrence Ferlinghetti, and Michael McClure. It was in San Francisco that Brautigan was first exposed to Zen Buddhism. His first three books, *A Confederate General from Big Sur* (1964), *Trout Fishing in America*, and *In Watermelon Sugar* (1968), all echo the Zen aversion to fixity and intellectual reflection. It was with these books that Brautigan, for the most part, earned his critical reputation.

A Confederate General from Big Sur, although written after *Trout Fishing in America*, was Brautigan's first published book of fiction. The general is

Lee Mellon, a friend of the narrator (Jesse) who establishes his own "country" in Big Sur. It is a community that, like the Confederacy, is antithetical to mainstream America. Although the book proceeds in a fairly straightforward narrative, a military tale of the Civil War is inserted into the text more and more obtrusively. In the final three chapters the primary discourse seems to be moving toward a conventional resolution, but this possibility is exploded with an ending that produces an infinite number of futures: "endings going faster and faster, more and more endings, faster and faster until this book is having 186,000 endings per second" (p. 159). This conclusion—endings occurring at the speed of light—denies the book's ability to create a closed reality and is linked to Jesse's pondering of nature, a contemplation that has left him "distracted" and impotent.

The book that brought nationwide popularity to Brautigan was *Trout Fishing in America*. Eschewing intellectual reflection, the text moves along the surface of reality, from image to image, usually offering scenes from two very different Americas. "The Cover for Trout Fishing in America" contrasts the America of Benjamin Franklin (a statue of whom is on the cover) and Adlai Stevenson to an America where "people gather in the park across the street from the church and they are hungry" (p. 2). It is through the accumulation of images that the text resonates, not through referential discourse. Brautigan's rejection of fixity is reflected through his use of a verbal phrase as the book's title and central metaphor. In addition, it is never determined just what *Trout Fishing in America* is. At different times it is a person, place, hotel, adjective, author, sport, and the book itself.

Brautigan's reluctance to employ stable signifiers is also an important part of *In Watermelon Sugar*: "my name depends on you. Just call me whatever is in your mind" (p. 4). The narrator's anonymity, along with a nearby community called iDEATH, suggests the death of the individual ego. As in his two previous books, Brautigan uses statues to suggest permanence. Of his experience as a sculptor, the narrator can only say, "the statue did not go well and pretty soon I was only going down to iDEATH and staring at the statue. . . . I had never had much luck at statues" (p. 75). Nearly everything in iDEATH is made of watermelon sugar, suggesting fluidity and change.

In each of these books, Brautigan rejected the notion that traditional texts can truly reflect reality. Jesse attempts to find enlightenment in Ecclesiastes and ends up concentrating entirely on the punctuation marks. In *Trout Fishing in America* the reader is told that "the bookstore was a parking lot for used graveyards. Thousands of graveyards were parked in rows like cars" (p. 32). All the books in *In Watermelon Sugar* have either been burned or relegated to Forgotten Works, the land of fixed ideas.

With *The Abortion: An Historical Romance 1966* (1971) Brautigan began a series of books in which, by mixing genres, he attempted to break down traditional literary definitions. *The Abortion* begins in a bizarre library where authors go and place their books wherever they want, thus denying categorization. When the librarian's girlfriend Vida (life) becomes pregnant, they travel to Mexico for an abortion and the book becomes a realistic love story. Brautigan also employs multiple genres in *The Hawkline Monster: A Gothic Western* (1974), *Willard and His Bowling Trophies: A Perverse Mystery* (1975), *Sombrero Fallout: A Japanese Novel* (1976), and *Dreaming of Babylon: A Private Eye Novel 1942* (1977). By mocking and subverting genre categories, Brautigan was trying to free literature from its own world of predetermined definitions—fixed definitions that he felt are both a distortion and a limit to creativity.

Brautigan's final books, *The Tokyo-Montana Express* (1980) and *So the Wind Won't Blow It All Away* (1982), seem to return to earlier techniques and themes. Many critics applauded this move, particularly in the case of *The Tokyo-Montana Express*. The structure is reminiscent of *Trout Fishing in America*, with each chapter an apparently autonomous vignette. He again presented images of two very different cultures, this time East and West.

Even though these last books received a more favorable critical response, Brautigan was still widely viewed as a writer whom time and events had passed by. In *The Tokyo-Montana Express*, he fueled this sentiment with melancholy themes of nostalgia and aging: "What makes you older is when your bones, muscles and blood wear out, when the heart sinks into oblivion and all the houses you ever lived in are gone and people are not really certain that your civilization ever existed" (p. 162). Although Brautigan's themes may never again be as appealing to readers as they were in the 1960s, his attempts to move beyond traditional genres and narrative styles still deserve attention from critics and readers interested in metafictional texts.

Selected Bibliography

Primary Sources

The Galilee Hitch-Hiker. San Francisco: White Rabbit Press, 1958.
Lay the Marble Tea. San Francisco: Carp Press, 1959.
The Octopus Frontier. San Francisco: Carp Press, 1960.
A Confederate General from Big Sur. New York: Grove Press, 1964.
Trout Fishing in America. San Francisco: Four Seasons Foundation, 1967.
All Watched Over by Machines of Loving Grace. San Francisco: Communication Co., 1967.
Please Plant This Book. San Francisco: Graham Mackintosh, 1968.
In Watermelon Sugar. San Francisco: Four Seasons Foundation, 1968.
The Pill Versus the Springhill Mine Disaster. San Francisco: Four Seasons Foundation, 1968.
Rommel Drives on Deep into Egypt. New York: Delacorte Press/Seymour Lawrence, 1970.

Revenge of the Lawn: Stories 1962–1970. New York: Simon & Schuster, 1971.
The Abortion: An Historical Romance 1966. New York: Simon & Schuster, 1971.
The Hawkline Monster: A Gothic Western. New York: Simon & Schuster, 1974.
Willard and His Bowling Trophies: A Perverse Mystery. New York: Simon & Schuster, 1975.
Sombrero Fallout: A Japanese Novel. New York: Simon & Schuster, 1976.
Loading Mercury with a Pitchfork. New York: Simon & Schuster/Touchstone, 1976.
Dreaming of Babylon: A Private Eye Novel 1942. New York: Delacorte Press/ Seymour Lawrence, 1977.
June 30th–June 30th. New York: Dell/Delta, 1978.
The Tokyo-Montana Express. New York: Delacorte Press/Seymour Lawrence, 1980.
So the Wind Won't Blow It All Away. New York: Delacorte Press/Seymour Lawrence, 1982.

Secondary Sources

Chenetier, Marc. *Richard Brautigan*. New York: Methuen, 1983.
Critique: Studies in Modern Fiction 16, no. 1 (1974). Special Brautigan issue.
Foster, Edward Halsey. *Richard Brautigan*. Boston: Twayne Publishers, 1983.
Loewinsohn, Ron. "After the Mimeograph Revolution." *Tri-Quarterly* 18 (1970): 221–36.
Malley, Terence. *Richard Brautigan*. New York: Warner Paperback Library, 1972.
Tanner, Tony. In *City of Words*. New York: Harper & Row, 1971. pp. 393, 406–15.

                                                            CRAIG THOMPSON

BRUNNER, JOHN (1934–   )

First and foremost, John Brunner is a professional writer. In the course of his 30-year career, he has published an incredible 70 novels and over 200 pieces in periodicals, including short stories, articles, and verse. His works have spanned contemporary genres from mainstream to mystery; the vast majority, however, have been science fiction or marketed as such. Not surprisingly, only a small percentage of this huge canon merits serious critical attention. Of this, the best known and most-successful novels are those concerned with humanity's immediate future. In what Brunner calls his social-science fiction, he delineates the dangers we face if certain modern trends are not reversed. He does so with great force, using a vivid style characterized by Joycean word-play and other techniques borrowed from the literary experiments of modernism and postmodernism.

John Kilian Houston Brunner was born on September 24, 1934, in rural Oxfordshire, England. Isolated and perennially invalided as a child, he sought company in reading and imagination. Having digested novels like *Robinson Crusoe*, *War of the Worlds*, and the entire opus of Kipling, Brunner began writing his own fiction at the age of nine. His determination to become a professional writer survived prep school and his parents' plans to put him to work in the family chemical company. He sold his first novel, a piece of pulp science fiction, at 17 and soon after emerged into the better paying American magazine market. Following a dreadful two years as a draftee with the Royal Air Force, Brunner plunged off on his own, starving during most of the rest of the decade even as he continued to sell several sci-fi stories and novels. The next quantum leap in his career came with his signing as a writer for Ace Books, a mass paperback sci-fi line. From 1958 to 1963, he wrote 20 novels in the subliterary subgenre known as space opera. Even in some of these, however, the social and moral issues that would dominate his later and better fiction are apparent, if only subtly. During his Ace period, Brunner was actively involved in the British nuclear disarmament movement and traveled widely in the East and West.

Although his Ace fiction is critically negligible, much of his shorter work of that period shows marks of genuine literary talent. One group of stories was brought together into the novel *The Whole Man*, first published in 1964, a sensitive tale of a badly crippled telepath who, Christ-like, finds his fulfillment in healing others. More suggestive of the experimentation to come is *The Squares of the City*, written in 1960 but not published until 1965. It takes place in the ultramodern capital of a South American dictatorship, where the conflict between the authoritarian ruler and his political opponent unfolds following the moves of a classic chess game.

It was not easy for a pulp writer to convince potential publishers that his more innovative work had a market, even when both *The Whole Man* and *The Squares of the City* were nominated for the Hugo, one of sci-fi's highest awards. Brunner followed these triumphs with *The Productions of Time* (1966) and *Quicksand* (1967). The latter in particular, which focuses on the relationship between a burnt-out psychiatrist and a strange, powerful young woman who claims to be from the future, reflects a seamless conjunction of science fiction and the contemporary mainstream.

It was in 1968, however, that Brunner rocked the sci-fi community with the first of three ambitious novels that brought together scientific speculation, experimental technique, and the author's deep involvement in political issues. *Stand on Zanzibar* depicts a near-future Earth strangled by overpopulation and the resultant social problems: worldwide violence, international intrigue and neocolonial exploitation, and the misuse of technology. The novel is nothing less than encyclopedic; using methods pioneered by an earlier political novelist, John Dos Passos, *Zanzibar*'s far-flung plot weaves together such fragments as fictional news clippings and official reports, sociological observations, and condensed overviews of individual lives. The whole presents a complete and convincing picture of this world. Not only did the novel impress the science fiction establishment, but it also received much favorable attention in the mainstream literary press.

Less experimental but equally hard-hitting are the subsequent novels *The Jagged Orbit* (1969), concerning racial violence, and the relentless *The Sheep Look Up* (1972), about the ecological destruction of the United States. Brunner wrote other novels in various genres circa 1970—suspense, mainstream, adult fantasy, and, of course, sci-fi—though none as successful as these. His last novel in the dystopian mode, *The Shockwave Rider* (1975), again extrapolates from present trends, this time investigating the social and political consequences of future shock in a computer-controlled America.

Brunner has turned increasingly in the past decade to nonfiction and verse to expand the themes closest to his heart. His most recent fiction remains varied, though less cleverly innovative. He continues to be active in international campaigns for nuclear disarmament, environmentalism, and similar progressive causes. Prolific professional, literary experimenter, social activist—John Brunner deserves an audience beyond the confines of science fiction, an audience willing to accept the challenge of his blending of genres and styles and his passionate concern for humankind's future.

Selected Bibliography

Primary Sources

The Whole Man. New York: Ballantine, 1964.
The Squares of the City. New York: Ballantine, 1965.
The Productions of Time. New York: Signet, 1966.
Quicksand. Garden City, N.Y.: Doubleday, 1967.
Stand on Zanzibar. Garden City, N.Y.: Doubleday, 1968.
The Jagged Orbit. New York: Ace, 1969.
The Sheep Look Up. New York: Harper & Row, 1972.
The Shockwave Rider. New York: Harper & Row, 1975.
The Book of Brunner. New York: DAW, 1975.
Players at the Game of People. New York: Ballantine, 1980.
Intersteller Empire. New York: DAW Books, 1981.
Catch a Falling Star. New York: Ballantine, 1982.
Badlam Planet. New York: Ballantine, 1982.
The Crucible of Time. New York: Ballantine, 1983.
The Great Steamboat Race. New York: Ballantine, 1983.
Total Eclipse. New York: DAW Books, 1984.

Secondary Sources

DeBolt, Joe, ed. *The Happening Worlds of John Brunner: Critical Explorations in Science Fiction*. Port Washington, N.Y.: Kennikat Press, 1975.
Samuelson, David. "New Wave, Old Ocean." *Extrapolation* (December 1973): 75–96.

Spinrad, Norman. "*Stand on Zanzibar*: The Novel as Film." *SF: The Other Side of Realism*. Ed. Thomas Clareson. Bowling Green, Ohio: Popular Press, 1971.
Watson, Ian. "Rading the Whirlwind." *Foundation 7 and 8* (March 1975): 55–59.
                                                              STEPHEN W. POTTS

BUMPUS, JERRY (1937–   )

Jerry Bumpus is known as the Clark Kent of contemporary American fiction by his scattered, often secretive groups of fans throughout the world. His fictions operate in a place outside the veneer of civilized human constructs where characters seem to be more quadruped than biped, or else eerie clones of what humans think themselves to be in their foolish personal and metaphysical quests. The tyrannies of conventional psychology are never allowed to exist in Bumpus' fiction. His writing methods range from naturalism (in *Anaconda*, 1967) to highly innovative and chaotic renderings (especially in *Special Offer*, 1981) as he attacks the interface between notions of normality and the "other" in the human personality. He brings the reader to a little explored world where dream and reality often merge— a strange world full of terror and humor which reveals the animal within us all.

Bumpus' literary career spans more than 20 years and includes six books of fiction and over 100 stories published in magazines and anthologies. He was born in 1937 in Mount Vernon, Illinois, a rural farming community in the southcentral part of the state. His father ran the family-owned grocery store until he was drafted at age 40 and was killed in the battle of the Bulge—an early and tragic experience for Bumpus in the irrationality and indifference of events. Bumpus began writing early, completing a novel in his senior year of high school. His family talked him out of an army career and encouraged his writing activities as Bumpus worked in canning plants, on a psychiatric ward as an orderly, and in bean fields as a flagman for a cropduster.

Bumpus enrolled at the University of Missouri and received his B.A. degree in 1958. He then studied creative writing with Vance Bourjaily at the University of Iowa, earning his MFA in 1960. Throughout the 1960s Bumpus traveled extensively, first to Spain where he witnessed the repression of the Franco regime firsthand, and then to Japan. When he returned to the United States, he traveled in Arizona, Colorado, and Washington as he worked on at least a dozen novels along with a prolific outpouring of short fiction.

Anaconda (1967), his only published novel, details the last days of an anguished old man as he returns home to the Midwest to die. Amidst the conventional plot, *Anaconda* is filled with motifs that will become central in Bumpus' later fiction: states of delirium, self-imposed isolation, and a terror-filled mix of self-awareness and hallucination. Bumpus' relentless evocation of anguish and depression was so effective in *Anaconda* that many editors and critics saw the novel as too grim for the publishing industry.

In the 1970s Bumpus became known primarily as a writer of experimental short fiction, and his pieces appeared in *The Best American Short Stories 1974, 1975*, and the O'Henry Award collection of 1976. His eclectic collection of short fiction, *Things in Place*, appeared in 1975 and included several pieces of startling originality, including the title story, "Things in Place," a bizarre encounter between an old man and bikers, and "The Heart of Lovingkind," the story of a man who falls in love with a kangaroo.

Jerry Bumpus eventually settled in San Diego after nearly ten years of travel and visiting lectureships to work on stories that resonate with an unsettling mixture of the fantastic and the commonplace. Several of these pieces appear in his second and most experimental collection, *Special Offer* (1981). Bumpus' most recent novel, *The Happy Convent*, and another collection of short fiction, *Heroes and Villains*, were published in 1985. An intensely private and committed writer, Bumpus makes public appearances only rarely and always in disguise.

Selected Bibliography

Primary Sources

Anaconda. Western Springs, Ill.: December Press, 1967.
Things in Place. New York: Fiction Collective, 1975.
The Worms Are Singing. Ellensburg, Wash.: Vagabond Press, 1979.
Special Offer. Pomeroy, Ohio: Carpenter Press, 1981.
Heroes and Villains. New York: Fiction Collective, forthcoming in 1985.
The Happy Convent. La Jolla, Calif.: Canard Foundation, 1986.

Secondary Sources

McCaffery, Larry. "The Fiction Collective." *Contemporary Literature* 19 (Winter 1978): 106–107.
———. "The Fiction Collective: An Innovative Alternative." *Chicago Review* 30 (Autumn 1978): 107–26.
———, and Sinda Gregory. "Jerry Bumpus." *The Dictionary of Literary Biography: Yearbook, 1981*. Detroit: Gale Research Co., 1981, pp. 168–75.
Murray, G. E. "Unmapped Places." *Fiction International* 6, no. 7 (1978): 140–46.

MICHAEL KREKORIAN

BUSCH, FREDERICK (1941–)

Never an author to elevate pyrotechnical display over the concerns for character and story, Frederick Busch has achieved a reputation as a writer's writer, as an artist whose fiction requires close reading if one hopes to see how the tricks of style and structure support the nuances of characterization and plot. Refusing to settle for the safeties of a single style and voice, Busch has told his tales from the points of view of despairing parents, troubled children, harried doctors, and even Charles Dickens. Through all the experimentation with various voices, however, he has kept a steady eye on the realistic tradition. The result is a series of novels that demand the attention given to more obviously experimental fiction but that also keep the reader in touch with the requirements of the daily routine: the crush of domestic commitment, the necessity of holding on, and the imperative for talking to each other, though uncertainty owns the mortgage.

Frederick Busch was born in the Millwood section of Brooklyn on August 1, 1941. After his primary and secondary education, he left Brooklyn to earn his A.B. degree in English at Muhlenberg College (Allentown, Pennsylvania) in 1962. He returned to New York as a Woodrow Wilson Fellow to study seventeenth-century English literature at Columbia University, but he did not complete the program. Married to Judith Burroughs in November 1963, Busch began his professional writing career while sitting on the business side of the desk: from 1963 through 1965 he was first a clerk in marketing research firms and then a writer and editor for a feature-article syndicate and for *School Management*. In 1966 he was hired by Colgate University to teach while working on his graduate degrees, and though he stopped short of the Ph.D., he did earn the M.A. degree in 1967 by writing a thesis on John Hawkes. Since then, Busch's academic home base has been Colgate, although he has taught at such universities as Iowa and Columbia.

A London firm published his first novel, the now hard-to-find *I Wanted a Year Without Fall* (1971). Busch had written two novels before *Fall* which he says will never be printed, and he has also scrapped a novel he wrote immediately after *Fall*. Seeking an opinion of *I Wanted a Year Without Fall*, he sent it to a friend living in Wales. Without telling Busch, the friend submitted the manuscript to his own publisher in London, Calder and Boyars, who in turn cabled Busch an offer to publish.

Calder and Boyars also published Busch's second book, a collection of short stories titled *Breathing Trouble* (1973), but *I Wanted a Year Without Fall* is clearly the primary starting point of his career. The novel has obvious weaknesses: the pacing is slow in the first movement, and the subtle characterization that is the hallmark of Busch's mature fiction is missing. But in structuring the novel according to the classic form of the quest, and by setting up allusions to Bunyan's *Pilgrim's Progress* and *Beowulf*, Busch takes his first steps toward the considerations of domestic heroism that have earned acclaim for his later work. The two young men on the lam in this novel may joust with unexpected enemies in a manner both comic and violent, but the frame of the tale is that of a father singing a lay to his sleeping son.

From the advantage of hindsight, one sees that *Fall*, with all its literary allusions and highjinks, is the work of a young man with an academic background. Such is not the case with *Manual Labor* (1974) and *Domestic Particulars: A Family Chronicle* (1976). These novels are the true beginnings of the kind of fiction readers expect when picking up a book by Frederick Busch: tales of marital pain and domestic crisis that jerk the reader into a minute, harrowing, and finally loving examination of common people heroically hanging on through the unspectacular dismantling of their dreams. These two novels are unusual as well as moving because Busch uses nontraditional techniques to tell traditional tales. Excerpts from diaries and letters, long interior monologues, and cross-cutting through multiple points of view and narrative voices frame the fleshing out of rounded characters that supporters of more conventional fiction expect. Metaphors of renovating crumbling houses and rebuilding shattered lives mix with closely observed domestic details, and the reader is treated to realistic characters whose discovery that language is inadequate to pain is couched in a relatively unrealistic manner.

With the publication of *The Mutual Friend* (1978), perhaps his finest novel to date, Busch surprised those who keep up with contemporary novels, stepped outside the houses of his fictional domestic crises, and turned to Victorian England to write a novel about a master writer of novels, Charles Dickens. Named by the *Manchester Guardian* as one of the ten best novels of 1978, *The Mutual Friend* is Busch's most experimental book. On the surface it is a testimony to the force of Dickens' personality, complete with details that can be gathered only by meticulous research, but beneath these inquiries into the nature of fame and the contradictions of the Victorian Age rests Busch's experiment with the fictitiousness of fiction, his own as well as Dickens'. A series of voices certified by history— Dickens, George Dolby, Ellen Ternan, Kate—lures the reader into accepting the reliability of the tale, but the introduction of an imaginary character in the final chapter, a character who plans to rewrite all that the reader has been told, undercuts the impact of history. History and fiction, Busch suggests, are made up.

Following a collection of stories, *Hardwater Country* (1979), Busch returned to domestic particulars with two novels about grace in the face of loss, dignity with the loss of love: *Rounds* (1979), and *Take This Man* (1981). The triumph of these novels is characterization. More ambitious than his early work, less experimental than *The Mutual Friend*, *Rounds* and *Take This Man* focus on voices circling around one another, grasping amid pain for the commitment of hope, until the characters' realizations of themselves offer the reader the pleasure of fictional people fully developed. Tenses shift between past and present, and action darts from then to now, but the seam between technical display and conventional story-telling is all but hidden: Dr. Silver (*Rounds*) and Anthony Prioleau (*Take This Man*) finally accept the consequences of love.

Although Busch's fiction reflects the postmodernist interest in technique, it is equally concerned with such traditional staples of the novel as round character and recognizable plot. One expects an extension of this mixture in his latest published works, *Invisible Mending* and *Too Late American Boyhood Blues*.

Selected Bibliography

Primary Sources

I Wanted a Year Without Fall. London: Calder & Boyars, 1971.
Hawkes: A Guide to His Fictions. Syracuse, N.Y.: Syracuse University Press, 1973.
Breathing Trouble. London: Calder & Boyars, 1973.
Manual Labor. New York: New Directions, 1974.
Domestic Particulars: A Family Chronicle. New York: New Directions, 1976.
The Mutual Friend. New York: Harper & Row, 1978.
Hardwater Country. New York: Alfred A. Knopf, 1979.
Rounds. New York: Farrar, Straus & Giroux, 1979.
Take This Man. New York: Farrar, Straus & Giroux, 1981.
Invisible Mending. Boston: Godine, 1984.
Too Late American Boyhood Blues: Godine, 1984.

Secondary Sources

Ellman, Richard. "Specific Instances of Pain." *Nation* 6 (November 1976): 468–69.
Greiner, Donald J. "After Great Pain: The Fiction of Frederick Busch." *Critique* 19 (August 1977): 101–11.
———. "Frederick Busch." *Dictionary of Literary Biography: American Novelists Since World War II*. Detroit: Gale Research Co., 1980, pp. 25—33.

DONALD J. GREINER

C

CALVINO, ITALO (1923–1985)

Italo Calvino is one of the most radically innovative writers of the postwar era, and yet it is only in recent years that his fiction has begun to receive the serious critical attention it deserves. Curiously, although his works are sophisticated language structures of incredible complexity, many readers think of him as a writer of children's stories. Like so many Italian authors of his generation, Calvino was part of the Italian post-war neo-realist movement. Then, in the 1950s, he seemed to reject his early works in favor of wildly fantastic fictions. At the time, many critics and writers accused him of betraying his earlier neo-realist political and social convictions. Today, however, it is clear that in his folktales, his fantasies, and his realistic works, Calvino has been pursuing a single theoretical course for nearly 40 years.

Calvino was born on October 5, 1923, in Santiago de Las Vegas, a small village near Havana, Cuba, where his Italian parents were doing field studies, and he grew up in San Remo on the Riviera. During the war, he fought with the Italian partisans of the Garibaldi Brigade against the German occupation forces. Later, he studied English literature at the University of Turin where he wrote his thesis on Joseph Conrad. But Calvino was not particularly interested in the academic life. In Turin, he continued his involvement in politics and contributed to a number of left-wing journals. Then, while he was still in his early twenties, he joined the Turin publishing house of Giulio Einaudi Editore, first as a salesman, then as an editor, and his work in publishing proved to be a lifetime commitment. Calvino spent most of his adult life in Paris, but he returned to Italy in 1980 to settle with his family in Rome.

In his essay "Myth in the Narrative"—the clearest statement of Calvino's literary theories—he writes: "Literature is a combinatorial game which plays on the possibilities intrinsic to its own material, independently of the personality of the author." The implication here is that every possible story is already implicit in the rules of literature, just as any possible game of chess is implicit in the rules of chess. In this sense, the writer writes only what has already been written.

The folktale is the oldest and most basic example of this literary game, as Calvino shows in his *Italian Folktales* (1980), his own rewriting of many traditional stories that have had a profound influence on his work. Genre fiction, which also combines established elements according to established rules, is in many ways the contemporary equivalent of the folktale, and so Calvino has chosen to examine the origins of literary games by exploring a variety of genres in his own work—the historical romance in *The Baron in the Trees* (1977), *The Cloven Viscount* (1977), and *The Nonexistent Knight* (1977), science fiction in *Cosmicomics* (1970) and *t zero* (1969), the boy-adventure tale in *The Path to the Nest of Spiders* (1976), the travelogue in *Invisible Cities* (1974), the mystery in *If on a winter's night a traveler* (1981). In short, like the ancient teller of folktales, Calvino generates his fictions by accepting or creating a system of rules and playing out his literary game within that system. He is fascinated by word games, and he is the only Italian member of the French Oulipo (Ouvroir de littérature poten-tielle/Workshop of Potential Literature), an organization of writers, phi-losophers, and mathematicians dedicated to exploring the literary possibilities of verbal play.

But if literature is only a game, it is also serious as only games can be. Again, in "Myth in the Narrative," Calvino argues: "The whole struggle of literature is in fact an effort to escape from the confines of language." According to Calvino, the goal of the literary game is to transcend literature and to transform the writer's culture and the language that first gave birth to the story itself. In essence, literature is always a potentially revolutionary act, and the successful tale transcends itself and the language that made it possible.

Calvino attempts to transcend his chosen forms by parodying them and betraying the rules that made them possible. Thus, whereas most works of genre fiction are simply examples of what is implicit within a given system of rules, Calvino's tales are both examples of the genre and recap-itulations of the generic structure, like a perfectly crafted sonnet that ex-plains the rules by which a sonnet is written. Thus, each Calvino fiction is what it is and something more; it is both particular and universal, a simple rewriting and yet somehow all possible writing.

For Calvino, literature is always and only a language game, a system of signs. And yet it is also by such sign systems that we attempt to define ourselves and our world. Calvino's self-reflexive language games urge us to explore the games of reality, to juggle the familiar in unfamiliar ways, and, perhaps, to come a bit closer to something we might call truth.

Selected Bibliography

Primary Sources

Il sentiero dei nidi di ragno, 1947. (*The Path to the Nest of Spiders*. Trans. William Weaver. New York: Ecco Press, 1976.)

Il visconte dimezzato, 1952. (*The Cloven Viscount*. Trans. Archibald Colquhoun. New York: Harcourt Brace Jovanovich, 1977.)

Fiable italiane, 1956. (*Italian Folktales*. Trans. George Martin. New York: Harcourt Brace Jovanovich, 1980.)

Il barone rampante, 1957. (*The Baron in the Trees*. Trans. Archibald Colquhoun. New York: Harcourt Brace Jovanovich, 1977.)

Il cavaliere inesistente, 1959. (*The Nonexistent Knight*. Trans. Archibald Colquhoun. New York: Harcourt Brace Jovanovich, 1977.)

Le cosmicomiche, 1965. (*Cosmicomics*. Trans. William Weaver. New York: Collier Books, 1970.)

Ti con zero, 1967. (*t zero*. Trans. William Weaver. New York: Harcourt Brace & World, 1969.)

Le citta invisibili, 1972. (*Invisible Cities*. Trans. William Weaver. New York: Harcourt Brace Jovanovich, 1974.)

Il castello dei destini incrociati, 1973. (*The Castle of Crossed Destinies*. Trans. William Weaver. New York: Harcourt Brace Jovanovich, 1981.)

"Myth in the Narrative." In *Surfiction: Fiction Now and Tomorrow*. Ed. Raymond Federman. Chicago: Sparrow Press, 1975.

Se una notte d'inverno un viaggiatore, 1979. (*If on a winter's night a traveler*. Trans. William Weaver. New York: Harcourt Brace Jovanovich, 1981.)

Marcovaldo, or, The Seasons in the City. Trans. William Weaver. London: Secker and Warburg, 1983.

Different Loves. Trans. William Weaver and Archibald Colquhoun and Peggy Wright. San Diego: Harcourt Brace Jovanovich, 1984.

Secondary Sources

Cannon, JoAnn. "The Image of the City in the Novels of Italo Calvino." *Modern Fiction Studies* 24 (1977): 83–90.

———. *Italo Calvino: Writer and Critic*. Ravenna: Longo, 1981.

Heiney, Donald. "Calvinismo." *Iowa Review* 2 (1971): 80–88.

Hume, Kathryn. "Science and Imagination in Calvino's Cosmicomics." *Mosaic* 15, no. 4 (December 1982): 47–58.

James, Carol P. "Seriality and Narrativity in Calvino's *Le citta invisibili*." *Modern Language Notes* 97, no. 1 (January 1982): 144–61.

McCaffery, Larry. "Form, Formula and Fantasy: Generative Structures in Postmodern Fiction." In *Bridges to Fantasy*. Eds. George Slusser, Eric Rabkin, and Robert Scholes. Carbondale: Southern Illinois University Press, 1982.

Ragusa, Olga. "Italo Calvino: The Repeated Conquest of Contemporaneity." *World Literature Today* 57, no. 2 (Spring 1983): 195–201.

Schneider, Marilyn. "Calvino's Erotic Metaphor and the Hermaphroditic Solution." *Stanford Italian Review* 2, no. 1 (Spring 1981): 93–118.

Tani, Stefano. *The Doomed Detective: The Contribution of the Detective Novel to Postmodern American and Italian Fiction*. Carbondale: Southern Illinois University Press, 1985.

WELCH D. EVERMAN

CARVER, RAYMOND (1938–)

In his essay "On Writing," Raymond Carver says that, "A writer sometimes needs to . . . just stand and gape at this or that thing—a sunset or an old shoe—in absolute and simple amazement." In writing his stories, Carver himself gapes at infidelity, alcoholism (he has acknowledged that he had a major drinking problem until the late 1970s), birthday cakes, automobile accidents, door-to-door salesmen, and ordinary people in luckless or boring lives; what he discovers in these lives are unarticulated tensions, repressed violence, people's overwhelming confusion in facing their own lives and their own weaknesses. What seems especially distinctive about his work, however, is the way he creates a significant, serious, even terrifying picture of these nonspectacular lives: with an unerring feel for structure and nuance and a poet's ear for language, Carver finds complexity in simplicity and volume in silence.

Carver's style doesn't presume to add any tone of terror through stagey melodrama or through ornamental writing. His clear prose gives the reader no assistance in terms of providing explanations within the narrative of motive or emotion. Yet in his precisely controlled choice of description of scene and action, and carefully rendered dialogue, all the complexities of his situations are implied (more effectively for their subtlety), and the repressed violence, perhaps only suggested in the casual snuffing out of a cigarette, seems more menacing than an actual description of bloodshed would.

It is the quality of actually being brought close to a rendering of certain features of reality usually unobserved by writers that makes Carver's work nontraditional; his contribution to contemporary literature is not to denounce realism in fiction but to charge further into it. He doesn't create the condensed and sensationalized reality of popular fiction or the exaggerated nonreality of experimental fiction. Geoffrey Wolff, in his March 7, 1976 review of *Will You Please Be Quiet, Please?* in the *New York Times Book Review*, noted that Carver does not rely on the surreal; he uses no "psychedelic effects . . . no anti-gravitational hocus-pocus, but rather a clean shearing off of sequence." The experimentation that Carver's fiction *does* offer is not in the area of plot or experience, but in a new way to use dramatic urgency and structure. This effect is especially characteristic in Carver's use of an uncomfortable, familiar, but rarely dramatized, part of life—a stagnant but tension-filled lull—which is apparent from the first sentence to the last in nearly every story without being changed by the standard attempts to order and explain experience: rising action, climax, and resolution. Most of the stories are open-ended, starting after the traditional "inciting incident" and ending before a resolution. What will eventually happen to the characters—the crisis point—is often just beyond the final words of the fiction. The drama exists in suggested possibilities under the surface of what should be simple or harmless situations: a child playing hooky, a marital reconciliation, four people sitting at a table talking about love, the arrival of a houseguest, or a caller who has dialed the wrong number.

Raymond Carver was born in 1938 in Clatskanie, Oregon. He graduated from California State University at Humbolt in 1963 and did further study at the University of Iowa. Later, after a short career as an editor for Science Research Associates, Inc., he taught fiction-writing at the University of Iowa, the University of Texas, the University of California (Santa Cruz and Berkeley), and Syracuse University where he became the English Department chairman. Carver was twice a recipient of a grant from the National Endowment for the Arts, a Guggenheim Fellow in 1979, and received the Mildred and Harold Strauss Living Award in 1983. He had collections of poetry published in 1968, 1970, and 1976. The remainder of his books are story collections, one of which (*Fires*, 1983) is a combination of stories, essays and poetry. Carver gained national attention after 1976 with *Will You Please Be Quiet, Please?* which was nominated for the National Book Award. Following that work, he published *What We Talk About When We Talk About Love* (1981), *Fires*, and *Cathedral* (1983), which contains the first place story for 1983 from *Prize Stories: The O'Henry Awards*. As yet Carver has not written a novel, he says he is (so far) not interested in writing longer works because he feels the most effective way for him to work is to "Get in, get out. Don't linger."

As precise in talking about his stories as he is in their construction, Carver himself seems to have best solved the minimalist problem of describing his work: "It is possible . . . in a short story, to write about commonplace things . . . using commonplace but precise language, and to endow those things—a chair, a window curtain, a fork . . . a woman's earring—with immense, even startling power. It is possible to write a line of seemingly innocuous dialogue and have it send a chill along the reader's spine."

Selected Bibliography

Primary Sources

Near Klamath. Sacramento: Sacramento State College, 1968.
Winter Insomnia. Chico, Calif.: Kayak, 1970.
Will You Please Be Quiet, Please? New York: McGraw-Hill, 1976.
At Night the Salmon Move. Santa Barbara, Calif.: Capra, 1976.
Furious Seasons. Santa Barbara, Calif.: Capra, 1977.

What We Talk About When We Talk About Love. New York: Vintage, 1981.
Fires. Santa Barbara, Calif.: Capra, 1983.
Cathedral. New York: Alfred A. Knopf, 1983.

Secondary Sources

Boxer, David, and Cassandra Phillips. "*Will You Please Be Quiet, Please?* Voyeurism, Dissociation, and the Art of Raymond Carver." *Iowa Review* 10, no. 3 (1980): 75–90.
Simpson, Mona. "The Art of Fiction LXXVI" (interview). *Paris Review* 38 (Winter 1983): 193–221.

CRIS MAZZA

CASTAÑEDA, CARLOS (1925–   )

Since the publication of his first book, Carlos Castañeda's work has stirred endless controversy and debate, primarily over the issue as to whether his books are to be perceived as fictions or as the records of actual experiences. Castañeda continues to maintain that in 1960, while he was an anthropology student at the University of California at Los Angeles (UCLA), he had made several trips to Arizona to collect information on the medicinal plants used by the Indians. There he was introduced to the Yaqui *brujo* (sorcerer), whom he calls don Juan, and who became the central figure in his books. Castañeda underwent an unusual apprenticeship with don Juan for the next ten years in order to become "a man of knowledge," a process that initially entailed the specialized use of a variety of hallucinogenic plants found in the deserts of Sonora and various other areas throughout Mexico. The use of drugs, however, was gradually supplanted by a diversity of ways by which a sorcerer must live in the world. Throughout Castañeda's books, the most important feature of his apprenticeship involves the use of the body in exploring alternative perceptions of reality, and the power of controlled dreaming.

The controversy over the reality of Castañeda's work has also been applied to his life. We know little more about Castañeda's background and origins than about the life of Thomas Pynchon.* Most sources agree that Castañeda was born in Sao Paulo, Brazil, sometime between 1925 and the early to mid-1930s. On the other hand, immigration records, which may be regarded as being the most accurate, show that he was born on Christmas Day, 1925, in the ancient Inca town of Cajamarca, Peru. His father was a goldsmith named Cesar Arana Burungaray, and his mother, Susana Castañeda Novoa, died when he was 24. The young Castañeda attended high school in Cajamarca, and in 1948 his family moved to Lima where he graduated from the Colegio Nacional de Nuestra Señora de Guadalupe. He then studied painting and sculpture at the National Fine Arts School of Peru. He was said to have developed an obsession there with cards, horses, and dice, and one classmate characterized him as "witty, imaginative, cheerful—a big liar and a real friend."

After moving to the United States in 1951, Castañeda was enrolled as a pre-psychology major at Los Angeles City College. His liberal arts studies included, in his first two years, two courses in creative writing and one in journalism. Letters to his sister show that he served in the U.S. Army and left it after suffering a slight wound or "nervous shock," but the Defense Department has no record of Castañeda's service. Little is known about Castañeda because, as don Juan taught him, a "warrior" must divorce himself from his past, and "to weasel in and out of different worlds you have to remain inconspicuous."

His first book, *The Teachings of Don Juan: A Yaqui Way of Knowledge* (1969), which later became the initial part of a tetralogy, was written while Castañeda was still a graduate student at UCLA. Adopting a modified form of the journal, the book is divided into two sections. The first half recounts the series of events that led to meeting don Juan and the initiation Castañeda experienced in order to gain power over the demonic world through the ritualized ingestion of peyote and other hallucinogenic plants. The second half of the book, now widely considered to be a type of metafiction, is called "A Structural Analysis," in which the author attempts to analyze his experiences in the language of the social sciences.

In *A Separate Reality: Further Conversations with Don Juan* (1971), the social setting of Indian sorcery emerges more clearly. The instructions of don Juan occur through a dialogue with him, and also by way of physical acts: lying down in a specific way, gazing fixedly at one object or nothing, immersion in water, and, significantly, the smoking of a mixture that consists of peyote, dried mushrooms, and other hallucinogenic plants. Like the first book, there is "A Structural Analysis" at the end.

When Castañeda wrote *Journey to Ixtlan* (1972) as his Ph.D. doctoral thesis, UCLA's Department of Anthropology became involved in scandal for accepting a work it apparently knew to be a fiction. *Journey* shows the reader the means by which a "man of power" sees, as opposed to merely looking, and how by his concentrated "seeing" he can "stop the world." Castañeda describes the exercises of the will and body, the visions and experiences by which don Juan prepares the author for the task of perceiving "things as they are."

With the publication of *Tales of Power* (1974), which forms the capstone of the tetralogy, there were very few reviewers left who believed in the reality of don Juan. Consequently, these books are widely valued for the meticulously crafted dialogues and for the element of fictive power, particularly by writers like Ronald Sukenick* and Joyce Carol Oates. By now drugs are no longer a part of the story, and most of the book engages don Juan in dialogue for the purpose of explaining the experiences that have been encountered in the previous books.

The Second Ring of Power (1977) signals a major change in Castañeda's work because of the absence of don Juan and because of the introduction of significant women. In this book Castañeda does deadly battle with some female apprentices, who, under don Juan's "absentee direction," make a "final assault" on his reason. Castañeda is saved by his "awesome side," his "nagual." He receives from the women powerful demonstrations in the art of dreaming, and after he has been initiated into the mastery of the "second attention"—with don Juan gone—he is henceforth in charge of the women's welfare.

The Eagle's Gift (1981) returns to the apprentice sorcerers introduced in *The Second Ring of Power* and concerns the art of retaining the awareness that is normally lost at death, a gift of the eagle, "that power that governs the destinies of all living things." This theme is further developed in *The Fire from Within* (1984) in which the author, through experiences involving the nonrational left side of the mind, attains an awareness that produces the total freedom to escape beyond death.

These last "novels" have received mixed reviews from critics, many dismissing them as regressive for a man of Castañeda's age; other praise them as significant achievements of the imagination and as unique novels that require more serious attention. Castañeda's fictions have been compared with those of Jorge Luis Borges, Sukenick, and even J. D. Salinger. He has incorporated ideas from Zen Buddhism in addition to those described by split brain researchers, and many other ideas both fashionable and abstruse. An important view of his work posits the modern writer in the role of sorcerer and the controller of dreams; it is this authorial role which, for Castañeda, moves the writer beyond fiction and into the world, where the distinctions between fiction and reality become tentative, if not ambiguous.

Selected Bibliography

Primary Sources

The Teaching of Don Juan: A Yaqui Way of Knowledge. New York: Ballantine, 1969.
A Separate Reality: Further Conversations with Don Juan. New York: Simon & Schuster, 1971.
Journey to Ixtlan. New York: Simon & Schuster, 1972.
Tales of Power. New York: Simon & Schuster, 1974.
The Second Ring of Power. New York: Simon & Schuster, 1977.
The Eagle's Gift. New York: Simon & Schuster, 1981.
The Fire from Within. New York: Simon & Schuster, 1984.

Secondary Sources

de Mille, Richard. *Castañeda's Journey.* Santa Barbara, Calif.: Capra, 1976.
———. *The Don Juan Papers: Further Castañeda Controversies.* Santa Barbara, Calif.: Ross-Erickson, n.d.

Faber, M. D. "Castañeda and Don Juan: An Unconscious Dimension of the Master-Pupil Relationship." *Psycul R* 1 (1977): 399–34.

Gorman, Michael. " A. J. Korzybski, J. Krishnamurti, and Carlos Castañeda: A Modest Comparison." *ETC* 35 (1977): 162–74.

Noel, Daniel C. *Seeing Castañeda*. New York: G. P. Putnam's, 1976.

————. "Tales of Fiction Power: Dreaming and Imagination in Ronald Sukenick's Postmodern Fiction." *boundary 2* 5 (Fall 1976): 117–35.

Radin, Sharon Lee. "Spirit Warriors: The Samurai Figure in Current American Fiction." *DAI* 40 (1979): 2682A–83.

                                                                    CHRIS CECIL

COETZEE, J. M. (1940–   )

J. M. Coetzee is a South African novelist who is rapidly gaining international repute. However, his innovative work is clearly in the tradition of Western literature rather than that of African writing; the latter is usually more didactic and less formally experimental than Coetzee's fiction, and tends to see "the people" as hero, rather than specific individuals. Coetzee's books are characterized by their stylized treatments of South African politics (oblique metaphors often provide the only connections), and they are always narrated in the present tense. Thus, they move us quickly from moments in history and the specifics of South Africa to explorations of the timeless human condition.

The author's trials are of individuals isolated in "the heart of the country"; hence, sanity and survival become obsessive themes as the "heart of darkness" of various oppressors is unlayered. Predictably, the books are powerful and harrowing for the reader, for they invite a sharing in cruelty's bloodtaste. Coetzee displays great dexterity in employing different narrative modes and styles, but his verbal and contextual mise-en-scène is always remarkably stark. The precision with words is hardly surprising, given Coetzee's interest in linguistics, which he teaches, together with literature, at the University of Cape Town. Born in 1940, Coetzee was educated in South Africa and Texas, and has published translations and criticisms, besides his four novels.

The first work of fiction, *Dusklands*, was published in South Africa in 1974. It is made up of two parts, "The Vietnam Project" and "The Narrative of Jacobus Coetzee." The latter originally appeared in Afrikaans, but was translated into English when the book was released in the United Kingdom in 1983; it is a spoof documentary, complete with footnotes and afterword, re-creating the savagely racist vendetta of one of Coetzee's ancestors in eighteenth-century Namaqualand. The author's ties to Jacobus Coetzee prefigure his concern with notions of guilt and complicity in the books that follow. *Dusklands* also anticipates Coetzee's other work in its delineation of the barbaric soul and in the writer's experimentation with neurotic narrative voices, but the prose is not as tight as it would become later, and the correlation between Jacobus Coetzee and the United States in Vietnam is a tenuous one.

In 1980 Coetzee's award-winning *Waiting for the Barbarians* was published. Narrated by a middle-aged anti-hero, the magistrate of an unspecified colonial outpost, the novel is a poetic chronicle of his conscience, as well as a forceful allegory of imperialism. As the magistrate's affair with an injured "barbarian" girl progresses, so the officials of the Third Bureau become more ruthless in their search for enemies. The magistrate finally finds himself speaking out against injustice and suffering the expected punitive humiliation. Coetzee shows that we all need enemies and chastisers, and that the dividing line between the lover's touch and that of the torturer is fine indeed.

Coetzee's latest novel, *Life and Times of Michael K* (1983), won the prestigious Booker-McConnel Prize. Coetzee, typically avoiding the spotlight, refused to fly to London to collect the award, claiming that his teaching duties could not be neglected. The novel, which takes us with Michael K on a flight through a South Africa in the throes of civil war, perfects Coetzee's ascetic manner, which here underpins the protagonist's enduring understanding of and intimacy with the land.

Despite Nadine Gordimer's efforts to politicize *Michael K*, Coetzee has been criticized in South Africa for his novels' lack of political commitment. The focus on the characterization of an alienated individual in *Michael K*, as well as the use of a dream landscape and a fictitious empire and time frame in *Waiting for the Barbarians*, does suggest that Coetzee is perhaps striving too much for universal relevance.

But his most interesting novel is undoubtedly the neglected *From the Heart of the Country* (U.S. publication: 1977), which was written before *Waiting*. By its detail, this book is inextricably rooted in South Africa, yet one in which farmtime smoothly becomes the time of the heart and the world, too. Here Coetzee, like Faulkner before him, digs at history and politics through the personal. And whereas *From the Heart of the Country* is far from being an obvious political diatribe, it is reflexive enough to preclude the writer from any easy evasion of social responsibility.

The work's title was originally *In the Heart of the Country* (maybe the change reflects the novel's movement from South Africa to the "outside world"?), which might be an allusion to William H. Gass'* story, "In the Heart of the Heart of the Country," where "there were a few wasps, several sorts of bees and butterflies—checkers, sulphurs, monarchs, commas, question marks. . . . They loved the pears. Inside, they fed. If you picked up a pear, they flew, and the pear became skin and stem."

Like Gass' solipsistic narrator, Magda (O Magda, wie is jy?), a lonely spinster on a Godforsaken farm near Armode (poverty)—this is the stone land—also suspires by means of language alone ("I am a hole"). The dialogue sections of the book were originally written in Afrikaans, clearly establishing *Heart* as an examination of and insight into the Afrikaner's mentality via her or his language. Speech defines position and interaction— the primal "aaaa" must be nuanced—so it is language that is subverted when Magda's father takes Anna, his Hottentot servant's wife, for his concubine: "The violation of the old language, the correct language . . . takes place when he exchanges kisses and the pronouns of intimacy with a girl who yesterday scrubbed the floors and today ought to be cleaning the windows." The commerce of words is needed to forestall a descent into animalism, yet words are stultifiers as they are saviors. Self-consciousness is seen equally as ambiguously; Magda's sky voices tell her, "When we dream that we are dreaming, the moment of awakening is at hand." Yet she wallows in her creations. In fact, her melodrama of bloodily hatcheting a white stepmother or murdering her father for his miscegenation might as easily be what we call fantasy, as it might be reality. The doubts, the "perhaps's," the "or's," which so overwhelm the story, not only show how Magda's monologue of projections gives life to herself and her surroundings (the "heart of nowhere"), but also suggest the speculative nature of history itself. Is apartheid then just a vicious circle of make-up? "Hendrik may take me, but it is I holding him holding I." What is profoundly pessimistic about *From the Heart of the Country* is the hint that even those least capable of racism are unable to contemplate a future of happy integration. This seems to be a trend in "white" South African writing, as Sheila Roberts notes in her article, "Character and Meaning in Four Contemporary South African Novels" (1980). Emptiness and degradation thus become Magda's insistent vision of the intercourse between Hendrik (the "black" servant) and herself. Here Coetzee's analysis of sexual politics is cynical, but it also borders dangerously on chauvinist myth-reinforcement (all white spinsters dream of being schticked by a long black dong . . .). However, the bleakness is what makes Magda's search for voice and home, for other voices and love, so moving and sad.

More disturbing in *Heart* (and also in *Michael K* and *Waiting*) is Coetzee's intimation that his victims are party to their oppression. This thesis does not seem to reflect the turbulence of present-day South Africa, as Gordimer points out. Not only does Magda, lover of "the gloomy, the hideous, the doom-ridden," have to ask herself, "Do I truly wish to get beyond myself?" but the masochism motif is extended to include the servants, who, it is suggested, are as involved in the power games as master and madam, and who perpetuate their subservience to taunt their oppressors. Prisoner and guest become one. The mood of *From the Heart of the Country* is thus one of inexorable night. Our rituals, both linguistic and cultural, have so entrenched division that reconciliation is literally unthinkable. Coetzee's is a terrible indictment of the irreparable mind-set spawned by apartheid's dehumanizing structures.

Despite the book's repetitiveness and overstatement (a fault *Michael K* shares), its patterns are not advanced in the bland and abstract terms that are implied here. Rather, they dawn on us gradually as Magda's convolutions "(weave, weave!)" uncover the ambiguities of her consciousness and persona. We may be alarmed by her pleasure in action of any nature; we may find her as dry and youthless as a withered root, as self-centered as Miss Rosa; but Magda never fails to engage our outrage and pity as her Dickinsonian imaginative sensibility and artist's pen transform mundanity. She is Coetzee's triumph. The horror and beauty of South Africa, and of our lives, and of Coetzee's work, come together in her.

Selected Bibliography

Primary Sources

From the Heart of the Country. New York: Harper & Row, 1977.
Waiting for the Barbarians. New York: Penguin, 1980.
Dusklands. London: Secker & Warburg, 1983.
Life and Times of Michael K. New York: Viking Press, 1983.

Secondary Sources

Coetzee, J. M. "How I Learned About America—And Africa—in Texas." *New York Times Book Review*, July 15, 1984, p. 9.
Du Plessis, Menan. "Towards a True Materialism" (*Waiting*). *Contrast*, December 1981, pp. 77–87.
Gordimer, Nadine. "The Idea of Gardening" (*Michael K*). *New York Review of Books*, February 2, 1984, pp. 3, 6.
Harvey, C.J.D. "Waiting for the Barbarians." *Standpunte*, August 1981, pp. 3–8.
Knox-Shaw, Peter. "*Dusklands*: A Metaphysics of Violence." *Contrast*, September 1982, pp. 26–38.
Kramer, Jane. "In the Garrison" (*Waiting*). *New York Review of Books*, December 2, 1982, pp. 8–12.
Roberts, Sheila. "Character and Meaning in Four Contemporary South African Novels" (*Heart*). *World Literature Written in English*, 1980, pp. 19–36.

IAN BERNARD

COOVER, ROBERT (1932–   )

Although never a mass-market success, Robert Coover has gradually achieved a recognition among college and academic audiences as one of postmodern fiction's most versatile and distinctive voices. Mixing elements of popular culture, myth, fairy tales, historical recreations, metafiction, and various other experimental forms of discourse, Coover's work typically forces a confrontation between the sources and structures of our most deeply cherished beliefs and his own lexical structures. His multi-leveled fictions are nearly all concerned with the most fundamental issues: the nature of change and death, the way the mind subjectively imposes its forms on experience, the perils and attractions of the imagination, the means by which institutions manipulate our desire for stability and order. But it is Coover's brilliant recreation of a wide range of voices and styles that is his fiction's most distinctive feature.

Robert Lowell Coover was born in Charles City, Iowa, on February 4, 1932, but his family settled after World War II in Herrin, Illinois, where Coover's father became the managing editor of the *Herrin Daily Journal*. His father's newspaper work and a mining disaster that took place in Herrin in the early 1950s became source materials for Coover's first novel, *The Origin of the Brunists* (1966). In 1953, Coover received his B.A. from Indiana University, after which he joined the Navy, spending most of his four-year stint in Europe. By the time he was released from the Navy in 1957, he was considering writing as a career and spent a fruitful month in a cabin on Rainy Lake, Wisconsin, writing his first serious pieces, including "Panel Game." (This stay hovers in the background of other stories, such as "The Magic Poker" and "Beginnings.")

During the 1950s and early 1960s, Coover continued to write experimental fiction, including nearly all of the "Exemplary Fictions" that were eventually included in *Pricksongs and Descants* (1969), attended art school at Chicago's Art Institute, and went to graduate school at the University of Chicago (M.A., 1965), where he did a thesis on the fiction of Asturias. His first publications were various stories, poems, and translations that appeared in journals like *The Evergreen Review, Cavalier*, and *Noble Savage*. His work on *The Origin of the Brunists* evolved, in part, from his desire to try his hand at traditional, realistic forms before continuing his exploration of experimentalism. The novel, which won the prestigious Faulkner Award, explores the origins of a modern religion, based on obvious Christian analogues. Constructed out of multiple perspectives and literary forms, *The Brunists* immediately demonstrates Coover's sure handling of a wide range of discourses and his concern for disarming myth on its own grounds by manipulating familiar patterns into new narrative structures.

Coover's next novel, *The Universal Baseball Association* (1968), was initially dismissed by most critics as being a "mere" sports novel; but in fact the novel is a complex, multi-layered investigation into myth, religion, history, politics, and the way our imaginative constructions can work their way into our lives so as to dominate them eventually. It also provides a good example of Coover's interest in the structures of popular culture and of the way Coover opens up complex metaphors—here, the God-like role of a man who has become obsessed with a table-top baseball game he has invented—and explores their implications exhaustively.

From the mid-1960s until the mid-1970s, Coover spent most of his time in England and Spain, only occasionally returning to the United States to lecture or teach when his finances ran low. Although he published a number of stories and plays during this period (including a collection of plays, *A Theological Position*, in 1972), his main energies were devoted to work on a massive novel dealing with the Rosenberg case of the 1950s. This novel, *The Public Burning* (1977), created complex legal problems for Coover: publishers were unwilling to print the book because its principal narrator was "Richard Nixon," and because the book used the actual names of various other participants in the Rosenberg drama. As a result, publication of the book was delayed for several years. Although the novel recasts a variety of Coover's favorite themes about the dangers of dogmatic thinking and the enormously complex operations of history and myth, it is altogether a broader and more ambitious novel than anything he had previously published. A number of critics noted a comparison with Joyce's *Ulysses*: both novels meticulously re-create the details of a given period, both construct a virtual compendium of literary styles and forms, both display a remarkable ear for the sources of voice that make up a country's lingo, both rely on a complex interaction of realism, myth, and fabulism to achieve their results. Although critical opinion about the book remains divided, *The Public Burning* is clearly a book of fiercely held moral conviction, full of memorable voices and characters and scenes of remarkable invention. It is also a bawdy, obscene, devastating portrayal of America's political psyche, here embodied in the figures of Nixon (a brilliant, almost sympathetic portrayal) and Uncle Sam.

Since 1976 Coover has lived in Providence, Rhode Island, where he occasionally teaches courses at Brown University. During this period he has published a number of short works: *Hair O' the Chine* (1979), *After Lazarus* (1980), *A Political Fable* (1980), *Charlie in the House of Rue* (1980), *Spanking the Maid* (1981), and *In Bed One Night* (1983). These works extend Coover's interest in experimental forms (the use of cinematic structures is especially noticeable). *Spanking the Maid* is an especially rich, tightly controlled story in which Coover uses a theme-and-variation approach to a central image (a maid enters a room, attempts to fulfill her duties, fails, is spanked by her master) to explore the relationship between order and disorder, the writer and the text, life and death, and other issues.

Although Coover's fiction has certain affinities with other postmodern abulists and metafictionists (e.g., Donald Barthelme,* John Barth,* Jorge Luis Borges, Vladimir Nabokov, Italo Calvino,* Thomas Pynchon*), his work is also solidly grounded in the language and experience of American daily life. His structures emphasize a fluid movement between private and public experience, memory, imagination, and the collectively perceived archetypes of myth, literature, and pop culture. Emphasizing process and multiple possibilities instead of stable patterns, his works demonstrate the beauty and appeal of fictional constructions even as they reveal the passions, subjectivity, and needs involved in their creation.

Selected Bibliography

Primary Sources

The Origin of the Brunists. New York: G. P. Putnam's, 1966.
The Universal Baseball Association, J. Henry Waugh, Prop,. New York: Random House, 1968.
Pricksongs and Descants. New York: E. P. Dutton, 1969.
A Theological Position. New York: E. P. Dutton, 1972.
The Public Burning. New York: Viking Press, 1977.
A Political Fable. New York: Viking Press, 1980.
Spanking the Maid. New York: Grove Press, 1981.
In Bed One Night and Other Brief Encounters. Providence, R. I.: Burning Deck Press, 1983.
Gerald's Party. New York: Simon and Schuster, 1986.

Secondary Sources

Anderson, Richard. *Robert Coover*. Boston: Twayne, 1981.
Berman, Neil. "Coover's *The Universal Baseball Association*: Play as Personalized Myth." *Modern Fiction Studies* 24 (1978): 209–22.
Cope, Jackson I. "Robert Coover's Fictions" *Iowa Review* 2 (Fall 1971): 94–110.
Gordon, Lois. *Robert Coover: The Universal Fictionmaking Process*. Carbondale: Southern Illinois University Press, 1984.
Gregory, Sinda, and Larry McCaffery. "Robert Coover." *Dictionary of Literary Biography Yearbook, 1981*. Detroit: Gale Research Co., 1982, pp. 34–43.
Hume, Kathryn. "Robert Coover's Fiction: The Naked and the Mythic." *Novel* 12 (1978): 127–48.
McCaffery, Larry. "An Interview with Robert Coover." *Anything Can Happen: Interviews with Contemporary American Novelists*. Urbana: University of Illinois Press, 1983, pp. 63–78.
———. *The Metafictional Muse: The Works of Robert Coover, Donald Barthelme and William H. Gass*. Pittsburgh: University of Pittsburgh Press, 1982.
———. "Robert Coover." *The Dictionary of Literary Biography: American Novelists Since World War II*. Detroit: Gale Research Co., 1978, pp. 106–21.
Schmitz, Neil. "Robert Coover and the Hazards of Metafiction." *Novel* 7 (Spring 1974): 210–19.
Shelton, Frank. "Humor and Balance in *The Universal Baseball Association*." *Critique* 15 (1975): 78–90.

LARRY McCAFFERY

CORTÁZAR, JULIO (1914–1984)

What is an author to do when he becomes increasingly aware that the language at his imperfect command keeps slipping away from him, that referents cannot be authentic because the very words that point to them wither away their reality? In some ways, Cortázar's career gives a series of possible answers to this issue of the slippage of personalities, of character referents, and in general of all referents from a language that reveals itself to be merely allegorical. These answers can be read in a general periodization of his aesthetic and intellectual experiments. Cortázar's geographic displacements, along with his literary replacements of one pronominal narrator for others, made him feel the problem keenly, first as rather tragic and then as both tragic and liberating. Born of Argentine parents in Brussels in 1914, voluntarily exiled from Argentina in 1951 during the Perón regime, and writing mostly from Paris until his death in 1984, Cortázar's historical "disencounters" with himself helped to provide the slippery ground for his always evolving style. His writing moves from (1) a surrealism that invited irrational desire to break through a brittle veneer of language (*Bestiario*, 1951; *End of the Game*, 1956; *The Winners* 1959; *Cronopios and Famas*, 1963); toward (2) a kind of existentialist masochism that understood linguistic structures as traps or no-win games (*Hopscotch*, 1963; *All Fires the Fire*, 1966; and *Octaedro*, 1974); to (3) an imaginary postmodern utopia produced by willfully shifting some pronouns (*Alguien que anda por ahi*, 1977; *Libro de Manuel*, 1973) and finally to (4) a poststructuralist acknowledgment of the ways in which language can and cannot coincide with the desire for utopia (*We Love Glenda So Much*, 1981; *Deshoras*, 1983).

Cortázar's worry over the incommensurability between grammatical shifters–pronouns, that is—and human subjects first produces disdain for a world that language covers over and perverts. Then the worry intensifies around the body of the particular subject who becomes both the site of oozing meaning and the source of universal confusions. The reasoning at this stage is that if one is not a unique and fixable identity, then one is nothing. This is the way Carlos Fuentes* frames the problem of Cortázar's 1963 novel, *Hopscotch*. When its protagonist confronts his double, the only possible responses are madness or death. But later Cortázar will learn to experiment with the slippage when he discovers that this very problem may be an opportunity for intersubjective intimacy and the kind of imaginary harmony that the linguistic order seemed to rule out. Still later, he will qualify his hope about the ways in which language can empower us, because fixing any image, shooting a picture, for example, will be seen as a violence against the desire that makes us human.

In Cortázar's last period, his early concept of harmony, the "kibbutz of desire" as he called it in *Hopscotch*, is colored by Lacanian irony. Harmony belongs to the imaginary realm, where the child perceives its mother as an extension of itself, so there is no contradiction between self-love and love for the other. Language, or the symbolic order, breaks that dyadic relationship and dooms the child to frustrating attempts to recover the paradise of being at one with the other. Cortázar may always have had his doubts about the human capacity to attain harmony, but he understood that desiring and striving after it were constitutive of the human condition. So instead of calling off the search, he developed strategies that responded to the waves of his own cynicism. Did language make unity impossible? Well, rather than recover a happiness, Cortázar would experiment with language to construct a slippery paradise akin to the Moebius Strip which defies the dichotomies of inside and outside, origin and *telos*.

We can therefore think of his utopia as the site of construction, the very space in language that divides desire from realization and that provides the possibilities for happy slippages, for example, from the alienating singular pronoun "I" to the coalescence of the plural "we." (See the stories in *Change of Light*, 1977). In *We Love Glenda So Much*, utopia gets reformulated as a dynamic shifting from place to place, as a nowhere in the sense of no one place. This should give us a hint about how his worry over shifty pronouns resolved itself. But even before this, while Cortázar still contemplates the possibility of encoding a harmonious situation in language, his utopia is internally dynamic. It is not the undifferentiated and boring model that some anti-utopians sneer at; but a space in language and in human relationships for desire to act itself out through the play of differences. Fixity, a static harmony, is therefore a grim parody of paradise.

As two consequences of this dynamism, or perhaps two causes, Cortázar moves beyond a cavalier sexism that, for example, characterized passive readers as female, his *lectores hembras* in *Hopscotch*, and also beyond the political pessimism and fatalism that his radical friends objected to. *A Manual for Manuel* was one result. Another was to shift from considering women to be predictable and increasingly allowing himself to be surprised by them and to narrate through their personae. And rather than opposing art to politics as he used to, he came to see them as parallel and mutually empowering vehicles for freeing desire from the mire of habit.

Selected Bibliography

Primary Sources

Bestiario. Buenos Aires: Ed. Sudamericana, 1951.

Final del juego. Mexico: Los Presentes, 1956. (*End of the Game, and Other Stories*. Trans. Paul Blackburn. New York: Random House, 1967.)

Los premios. Buenos Aires: Ed. Sudamericana, 1959. (*The Winners*. Trans. Elaine Merrigan. New York: Random House, 1965).

Historia de cronopios y de famas. Buenos Aires: Ed. Minotauro, 1962. (*Cronopios and Famas*. Trans. Paul Blackburn. New York: Random House, 1969.)

Rayuela. Buenos Aires: Ed. Sudamericana, 1963. (*Hopscotch*. Trans. Gregory Rabassa. New York: Random House, 1966.)

62/Modelo para armar. Buenos Aires: Ed. Sudamericana, 1968. (*62: A Model Kit*. Trans. Gregory Rabassa. New York: Random House, 1972.)

Ultimo Round. Mexico: Siglo Veintiuno, 1969.

Literatura en la revolución y revolución en la literatura. Mexico: Siglo Veintiuno, 1970.

Todos los fuegos el fuego. Buenos Aires: Ed. Sudamericana, 1966. (*All Fires the Fire*. Trans. Suzanne Jill Levine. New York: Alfred A. Knopf, 1973.)

Un tal Lucas. Buenos Aires: Ed. Sudamericana, 1977. *A Certain Lucas*. Trans.
Gregory Rabassa. New York: Alfred A. Knopf, 1984.)
Queremos tanto a Glenda. Madrid: Ediciones Alfaguara, 1981. (*We Love Glenda
So Much*. Trans Gregory Rabassa. New York: Alfred A. Knopf, 1983.)

Secondary Sources

Note: Given the proliferation of books and articles on Cortázar, a selective list
would be sorely unrepresentative. Instead, we note the following publication containing some of the most advanced work on Cortázar.

O'Brien, John, ed. *The Review of Contemporary Fiction* 3, no. 3 (Fall 1983), Special
issue dedicated to Cortázar and John Hawkes. Essays by Cortazar himself,
Sara Castro-Klarén, Carlos Fuentes, Saul Sosnowski, Jaime Alazraki, and
others.

DORIS SOMMER

CREWS, HARRY (1935–)

Between 1968 and 1982 Harry Crews published eleven books—eight
novels, an autobiography, and two collections of nonfiction pieces. He
remains one of the most original, prolific, uneven, and compelling of the
post-Styron Southern generation. In whatever form it is manifest, his vision
is powerful and idiosyncratic, not in the service of any conventional moral
message, social insight, or economic imperative. Although bemused reviewers, after an exclamatory plot summary, continue to compare him to
such diverse notables as Barry Hannah,* Jim Harrison, Flannery O'Connor, and William Faulkner, Crews is very much his own man. The essence
of Crews' art and vision is experiential and aesthetic risk-taking: excess is
his mean. His fiction is fast, mean, extraordinarily violent, and often horrifyingly funny, altogether an unsettling combination. The books—most of
them—bear rereading well, but the intensity of his characters' resistance
to the brutal stringencies of their lives makes an engaged reading of Crews'
fiction painful work.

Things relentlessly go wrong, yet self-discipline and craftsmanship do
not altogether fail; people suffer and die after struggling to make their
lives mean something. The body, however powerful, finally gives out; the
spirit, bereft of wholeness, hungers. Religion does not yield meaning (thus
the first three novels). *The Gospel Singer* (1968), for instance, reaches its
climax with the title character's lynching. Physical ritual or performance
is ultimately unsatisfying (thus the next four novels). *Karate Is a Thing of
the Spirit* (1971), for example, ends with its battered young hero driving
an old VW off to domesticity. *A Feast of Snakes* (1976), Crews' most recent
novel, delivers an agonizing company of ex-high school football All-Amer-

icans, a rattlesnake-handling preacher, and a pack of pit bulldogs merci-
lessly trained and eagerly waiting to kill each other. The novel's hero finally,
mercifully, inevitably, goes berserk, killing four people before himself disappearing into the snake-collecting pit. Only in such violence does he
achieve what he has never had: the power to decide, a sense of being at
last, however briefly, in control.

Crews came from a family of Georgia tenant farmers; their lives, as he
describes it in his best book, *A Childhood: The Biography of a Place* (1978),
were often hard, even nightmarish. The restrictive realities of his early
years figure prominently in his fiction; indeed, Crews could almost be a
character in one of his novels. As a child, he recalls, he fell into a vat of
boiling water, had infantile paralysis, moved practically every year, and
believed his uncle was his father. Crews (born June 6, 1935) left his birthplace of Alma, Georgia, in 1953 for the U.S. Marine Corps, was discharged
as a sergeant in 1956, received B.A. (1960) and M.S. Ed. (1962) degrees
from the University of Florida, and, largely by accident, he says, began
teaching English, first at a junior college in Fort Lauderdale in 1962, and
more recently at the University of Florida, Gainesville. He has found his
largest audience as an *Esquire* columnist and *Playboy* contributor; these
essays are collected in *Blood and Grits* (1979) and *Florida Frenzy* (1982),
the latter easily the least distinguished of his works. He has been married
and has one son.

In terms of fictional techniques, Crews is a traditional storyteller, raised
in a society of storytelling people, among whom all the good and the bad
are carted up and brought along from one generation to another. Unlikely
as it seems, Crews learned how to fashion a story, discovered what would
work on the page, by sedulous analytical study of Graham Greene's fiction.
Crews most often writes about present-day, small-town, blue-collar Geor-
gians and Floridians, some of whom have escaped their godforsaken homes,
more of whom die trying. The rural life has few charms; an anti-Disney
savagery usually obtains. Personal rather than regional history is what
counts, and the afflicted—dwarfs, mutes, giants, no- and one-legged people—are numerous. Crews, who himself as a child felt like a freak, creates
characters with limited options for self-concealment, men and women who
are true by and to nature.

The work is strikingly uneven. If *Car* (1972) is a remarkable, gruesomely
funny tour de force and *The Hawk Is Dying* (1973) a beautifully lucid,
tightly controlled tragicomedy, neither novel prepares one for the rather
disconnected and gratuitous horrors of *This Thing Don't Lead to Heaven*
(1970) or the circling redundancies of *Naked In Garden Hills* (1969). Nor
can the reader take consistent comfort in chronology, as witnessed by *The
Gypsy's Curse* (1974), in which a freaky sensationalism is preeminent. *A
Feast of Snakes* is Crews in good form; he may make us gag, but he holds
us, in awe and admiration, to the sickening end.

As Crews approaches 50, what may his readers anticipate? The signs seem mixed. After eight novels in as many years (half of those novels first class), there have been no more for almost a decade. The best volume, *A Childhood*, was fresh, beautifully crafted, very touching, and admiringly reviewed, yet its nonfiction successors have been uninspired. We wait in hope.

Selected Bibliography

Primary Sources

The Gospel Singer. New York: William Morrow, 1968.
Naked in Garden Hills. New York: William Morrow, 1969.
This Thing Don't Lead to Heaven. New York: William Morrow, 1970.
Karate Is a Thing of the Spirit. New York: William Morrow, 1971.
Car. New York: William Morrow, 1972.
The Hawk Is Dying. New York: Alfred A. Knopf, 1973.
The Gypsy's Curse. New York: Alfred A. Knopf, 1974.
A Feast of Snakes. New York: Atheneum, 1976.
A Childhood: The Biography of a Place. New York: Harper & Row, 1978.
Blood and Grits. New York: Harper & Row, 1979.
Florida Frenzy. Gainesville: University Presses of Florida, 1982.

Secondary Sources

Bellamy, Joe David. "Harry Crews: An Interview." *Fiction International* 6, no. 7 (1976): 83–93.
Bonetti, Kay. "An Interview with Harry Crews." *The Missouri Review* 6 (Winter 1983): 145–64.
Jeffrey, David H. *A Grit's Triumph: Essays on the Works of Harry Crews*. New York: Associated Faculty Press, 1983.
Long, Gary L. and Larry W. Debord. "Literary Criticism and the Fate of Ideas: The Case of Harry Crews." *The Texas Review* 4 (Fall-Winter 1983): 69–91.
Shelton, Frank. "Harry Crews: Man's Search for Perfection." *The Southern Literary Journal* 12 (Spring 1980): 97–113.
Shepherd, Allen. "Matters of Life and Death: The Novels of Harry Crews." *Critique* 20 (September 1978): 53–62.

ALLEN SHEPHERD

D

DAVENPORT, GUY (1927–)

Guy Davenport's imaginative writings cannot accurately be called stories at all; they are, rather, literary collages or, to use the author's own phrase "assemblages of fact and necessary fiction." A mingling of the factual and the fantastic, his works seem to resemble, in miniature, the better known historical fabulations of Robert Coover,* E. L. Doctorow,* and Thomas Pynchon*. The verbal play, occasional self-reflexiveness, and emphasis on the artifice of order further evidence his affinity to literary postmodernism. Yet in other ways, the assemblages are distinctly modernist: erudite, allusive, intricately structured, and richly, alluringly textured. Against the apparent randomness and disrupted surfaces of Davenport's works (there are no connectives or visible transitions between sentences, paragraphs, or even narrative lines), one finds an imaginative vision of wholeness. This vision is clearly reflected in what John Gardner* called the "sheer precision and uncompromising artistry" of Davenport's sentences: "What works in the angle succeeds in the arc and holds in the chord." Chiefly an art of modernist concealments rather than of postmodernist cancellations, Davenport's daedalian assemblages serve to awaken the reader from a drugged acceptance of the world and the language conventionally used to define it.

Guy Mattison Davenport, Jr., was born on November 23, 1927, in Anderson, South Carolina. He was educated at Duke University (B.A., 1948), at Merton College, Oxford (B. Litt., 1950), and, after a tour of duty in the Army and a faculty appointment at Washington University in St. Louis, he completed his formal schooling at Harvard (Ph.D., 1961), where he wrote a dissertation on Pound's *Cantos*. After teaching for two years at Haverford College in Pennsylvania, Davenport joined the English faculty at the University of Kentucky where he continues to teach, to write reviews, essays, libretti, poems, and assemblages, to illustrate his works and those of friends, and to edit and translate the neglected works of Agassiz, Alkman, Archilochus, and others. Until the publication of *Da Vinci's Bicycle* in 1979, Davenport lived in scholarly obscurity, better known as a translator than as the author of *Tatlin!* (1974). Since then, he has received the Academy and Institute of Arts and Letters Morton Dauwen Zabel Award for fiction and the admiration of a small band of discerning readers.

The major reason Davenport will never appeal to a large audience is that his assemblages tell no clear story. The densely textured prose, cubistlike structure, and tendency toward multiple plots overshadow and obscure the tenuous narrative thread. "Au Tombeau de Charles Fourier," for example, interweaves anecdotes and reports about Gertrude Stein, Picasso, the Dogon creation myth, wasps, early aviation history, da Vinci, the boyhood of the French photographer Lartigue, a pilgrimage to the grave of the utopian socialist Fourier, and Samuel Beckett chatting about James Joyce. Davenport's illustrations introduce additional, yet subtly related, subjects. The narrative fragmentation is partly intended as a reflection of twentieth-century chaos. More importantly, by juxtaposing the fragments, Davenport is able to generate meaning synergistically. The technique of plotting by means of justaposition (rather than by the more conventional means of chronological order or cause and effect) derives, Davenport has said, less from Pound than from the avant-garde filmmaker Stan Brakhage, who substituted "an architectonic arrangement of images" for conventional plot. Thus, in Davenport's assemblages a page is a metaphoric picture, "essentially a texture of images." Understood in this way, the seeming disunity of an assemblage gives way to the reader's deeper understanding of the discrete order underlying not only individual works but each of Davenport's three collections as well. Disparate characters and plots merge into Davenport's single hero—the searching imagination—and overriding "plot"—the quest for order and continuity.

Davenport draws his heroes from the past, rescuing them from the obscurity to which history and the modern age have assigned them: the skeptic, Pyrrhon of Elis, for example; the Stoic, C. Musonius Rufus; the inventorartist, da Vinci; the Japanese poet of linked verses, Basho; the Russian sculptor and engineer, Vladimir Tatlin; and the proto-Kafka, Robert Walser. As distinct in character and as separate in time as they are, all are alike in one important respect: they are "foragers" in search of the values, meanings, and connections that others have neither the imagination nor the inclination to seek. Their task is, in fact, the reader's as well: to discover correspondences in the chaos of the apparently dissimilar, to imagine or to invent (which Davenport uses in its earlier meaning of "to find") the pattern concealed in the randomness. For Davenport, the world can only be imagined, rather than analytically known: because reality is fluid, not fixed, meaning is mysterious and therefore elusive. That the search is endless does not lead to despair, however. Instead, it leads to those possibilities for imagining and thereby redeeming a world flattened and dulled by the shallow deceptions of a modern age that has unwisely cut itself off from it archaic roots.

In all his assemblages and especially in his best—Tatlin!, "The Aeroplanes at Brescia," "A Field of Snow on the Slope of the Rosenberg," "On Some Lines of Virgil," and "Fifty-Seven Views of Fujiyama"—Davenport defeats the notion of linear time and indeed of linear reading as well and proves, more convincingly than Pound or Eliot ever did, the aliveness of the past. Rescuing the past from the ravages of the present, he reinvests reality as well as literary modernism with mystery and new-found meaning.

Selected Bibliography

Primary Sources

The Intelligence of Louis Agassiz: A Specimen Book of Scientific Writings. Boston: Beacon, 1963.
Carmina Archilochi: The Fragments of Archilochus. Berkeley: University of California Press, 1964.
Sappho: Songs and Fragments. Ann Arbor: University of Michigan Press, 1965.
Flowers and Leaves. Highlands, N.C.: Nantahala Foundation, J. Williams, Publisher, 1966.
Tatlin! New York: Scribner's, 1974.
Da Vinci's Bicycle. Baltimore: Johns Hopkins University Press, 1979.
Herakleitos of Ephesius and Diogenes the Cynic. San Francisco: Grey Fox, 1979.
Archilochus, Sappho and Alkman: Three Lyric Poets of the Late Greek Bronze Age. Berkeley: University of California Press, 1980.
The Geography of the Imagination. San Francisco: North Point Press, 1981.
Eclogues. San Francisco: North Point Press, 1981.
Trois Caprices. Louisville, Ky.: Pace Trust, 1981.
The Mimes of Herondas. San Francisco: Grey Fox, 1981.
"Fifty-Seven Views of Fujiyama." *Granta*, 4 (1981): 5–62. *Cities on Hills: A Study of I-XXX of Ezra Pound's Cantos*. Ann Arbor: UMI Research Press, 1983.
Apples and Peas & Other Stories. San Francisco: North Point Press, 1984.

Secondary Sources

Morace, Robert A. "Davenport, Guy." *Critical Survey of Short Fiction*. Englewood Cliffs, N.J.: Salem Press, 1981.
———. "Invention in Guy Davenport's *Da Vinci's Bicycle*." *Critique* 22 (April 1981): 71–87.
Pevear, Richard. "*Tatlin!*, or the Limits of Fiction." *Hudson Review* 23 (Spring 1975): 141–46.
Wertime, Richard. Review of *Tatlin! Georgia Review* 29 (Winter 1975): 948–57.

Wilson, John. "*Tatlin!*: The Renaissance of the Archaic." M.A. Thesis, California State University 1975.

ROBERT A. MORACE

DELANY, SAMUEL R. (1942–   )

Samuel R. Delany is a writer at the second degree, and his choice of science fiction as *textus*, as system of themes and formulas within which the individual writer chooses to construct his texts, makes us wonder whether unreflexive, first-degree writing, once considered the purview and strength of this genre, is really possible anymore. From the beginning of his precocious career, Delany has embraced science fiction, not for its themes per se nor for its scientific vision, but for its linguistic potentialities, as what he calls a "powerful trajectory" for the creation of word-worlds. His sense of language has moved consistently on a symbolist-Saussurian axis: narrative does not imitate, it constructs artifacts, models that do not require our naive belief in their possibility (as with science fictional "anticipation") so much as an ever more sophisticated suspension of disbelief. Science Fiction thus becomes for Delany essentially a language vector that allows the writer to reach beyond "mundane" realism—belief in a concurrence between world and word that permits language to serve as the technology by which science can be said to write the fiction—to new forms of fantasy and, perhaps ultimately, of mystical horror.

Delany was born on April 1, 1942, in Harlem, and attended the Bronx High School of Science, a public school for the mentally gifted. In the vanguard of the coming 1960s "revolution," he dropped out of City College of New York after two years to explore new cultures and social milieus, and to pursue a career as a writer. Delany's first novel, *The Jewels of Aptor*, appeared in 1962. Other novels followed in rapid succession: *The Fall of the Towers* trilogy (1963–1965), *The Ballad of Beta–2* (1965), *Empire Star* (1966). Then came two Nebula award-winning works: *Babel–17* (1966) and *The Einstein Intersection* (1967). With these novels Delany, the writer on the metafictional edge of science fiction, was accepted by the genre at its center.

Much has been made of Delany being a black science fiction writer. But this combination seems paradoxical, for science fiction in itself has traditionally tended to look away from, or leap over, pressing social problems of the here and now, as if Rip Van Winkle had gone to sleep and wakened in a world where such problems, as if by magic, were simply gone. In fact, to Delany, it is this avoidance, these magical leaps, that seem to give sf its uniqueness. In fact, for this black, middle-class polymath, science fiction has acted as a conduit away from Harlem and Africa, and increasingly toward the structuralist views of thinkers like Michel Foucault* and Claude Lévi-Strauss, for whom matters of violence and race have become questions of cultural code—metaproblems in relation to the real cities, the real unrest and starvation that so stubbornly returns to haunt our future predictions today.

Delany's first set of major novels—beginning with *Babel-17*, running through *Empire Star* to what may be his masterpiece to date, *Nova* (1968)—are sophisticated reworkings of the pulp conventions of space opera. Delany looks on this form as a potentially potent one for generating word worlds and word quests. In reworking these formulas, which he treats as a system of signs emptied of all hegemonic belief in the event as a real or fixed point in time and space, as a nexus where the word is linked in some determined, nonarbitrary way to phenomena it signifies, Delany draws inspiration from the symbolist aesthetic, again a source foreign to science fiction. To the symbolist the word is revered for its incantatory power. Thus, in an exotic space opera name like Aptor lies, in the manner of Baudelaire's *sorcellerie evocatoire*, a world. And if time (as in the title of a Delany story) can be a helix of semiprecious stones, so mere words can function like jewels, symbolic counters all the more powerful in that their referential aspect is unclear. And in Delany's novels the traditional space opera hero has been transposed into a symbolist artist-criminal, one whose crime is linguistic subversion, the creation of "wordviews." Babel–17, as a speakerless language, one without a word for "I," is perfect for such linguistic criminality, for each user weaves a web of words that seems absolute, which cannot be traced back to a speaker, a point of view.

Delany's space operas, as the struggle of individuals within systems rather than the classic science fictional battle with nature, are eventless as well. He describes his *Fall of the Towers* series as based on a series of drawings "depicting different groups of people reacting to some catastrophic incident never shown." Those reactions, in the incident-vectored world of the traditional space opera, are wordviews, the substitution (as Roland Barthes* says) of the instance of discourse for the instance of reality. In *Babel-17* language functions as a reflexive mirror that cancels the events of our formula expectations. The setting in this novel is one of intergalactic war, between the typically named Alliance and the Invader. Yet as soon as the former renames itself, in *Babel-17*, as the "one-who-has-invaded," this struggle of empires is reduced to one vast tautology. And in *Nova* hero Lorq von Ray's quest for the element Illyrium (echoing Faustus' "topless towers of Illium"?) leads him away from the stars toward the systemic space of language, of all human patterns of order. This element is at once heterotropic and psychomorphic—an entity that simultaneously takes its existence from the speaker and denies all attachment to that speaker, declares itself speakerless, change per se.

A key recurring object in Delany's fiction is the city, and it throws its persistent shadow over a long series of works from the early *Towers* trilogy, through *The Einstein Intersection* (1967) and *Dhalgren* (1975), to *Triton*

(1976) and, most recently, the "tale of signs and cities," *Neveryòna* (1983). In all these fictions the modern city is dealt with less on a primary level—as interface between human order and chaos—than on a secondary one as matrix for the creation of models that express changing relationships and modes of social behavior. *The Einstein Intersection* tells of the questing voyage of some alien "users" of the human cultural system—fragmented by what are again unnamed wars—back to the city as place of maximum intersection of competing cultural systems. On his journey the hero Lobey passes through the different forms of societal organization we recognize as village, tribe, town, city. In *Dhalgren*, another hero in search of names enters and leaves a city recognized—in this notebook diary as novel—as the mirror of his looping search through a multiplicity of verbal and social systems, a search that begins and ends in the fractured symmetry of a name: Grendal-Dhalgren. Following this golden braid, the urban realities of violence and murder are transposed (as they were in the earlier piece of linguistic pornography *The Tides of Lust*) to a secondary level where rape has become a pun and weapons "brass orchids," new flowers of evil.

Dhalgren's Bellona is a shadow city of the present, minimally science fictional. The future moon city of *Triton*, however, is no more a construct of solid materials. Delany calls it, using Foucault's term, a heterotopia, a place nested in language and, unlike utopia, moving against its grain, "contesting the possibility of language at its very source." Indeed, in *Triton* and the works that follow, Delany is openly questioning everything at its source, that source being the set of cultural codes implicit in such science fiction formulas as the good or bad city. The structure of *Neveryòna*, Delany tells us, was suggested by Frank Romeo's film *Bye Bye Love*, "about two small-town adolescents who journey to New York City and return." This is transposed, though, into Nevèrÿon, the old sword and sorcery land of never-yon given new linguistic coinage by a couple of diacritical marks. And its city, Neveryòna, is a heterotopia, dissolving the myths and sterilizing the lyricism of the formula quest and its fabulous actors.

The power that has moved Delany across what is now a 16-year career is a fascination with the world view behind structuralist linguistics. In this fascination Delany, a talented critic who has published two formidable sets of essays, *The Jewel-Hinged Jaw* (1977) and *The American Shore* (1978), has followed the academic path into deconstructionism, a trend increasingly evident from the epigraphs that adorn his recent fictions. Speaking of the structuralist vision, Robert Scholes finds "a move away from adversary relationships in political processes . . . away from combat between countries, between parties, between factions, and above all between man and nature." But if the central concern of science fiction in general is this struggle between humankind and nature, that of the sword and sorcery subgenre Delany has recently turned to in works like *Tales of Nevèrÿon* (1979) and *Neveryòna* is precisely combat between societies and cultures. In these works

Delany has radically subverted these conflicts, emptied the formulas until they emerge as pure models, devices for organizing and examining not the dynamics of society but the problems posed by those dynamics. These latest fictions, including his most recent return to space opera, *Stars in My Pocket Like Grains of Sand*, are metastructures at their most ornate.

Selected Bibliography

Primary Sources

The Jewels of Aptor. New York: Ace Books, 1962.
Captives of the Flame. New York: Ace Books, 1963.
The Towers of Toron. New York: Ace Books, 1964.
Empire Star. New York: Ace Books, 1966.
Babel-17. New York: Ace Books, 1966.
The Einstein Intersection. New York: Ace Books, 1967.
Nova. Garden City, N.Y.: Doubleday, 1968.
Driftglass. Garden City, N.Y.: Nelson Doubleday, 1971.
The Tides of Lust. New York: Lancer, 1973.
Dhalgren. New York: Bantam, 1975.
Triton. New York: Bantam, 1976.
The Jewel-Hinged Jaw: Notes on the Language of Science Fiction. Elizabethtown, NY: Dragon Press, 1977.
The American Shore: Meditations on a Tale of Science Fiction by Thomas Disch—Angouleme. Elizabethtown, NY: Dragon Press, 1978.
Heavenly Breakfast: An Essay on the Winter of Love. New York: Bantam, 1979.
Tales of Nevéryon. New York: Bantam, 1979.
Neveryòna. New York: Bantam, 1983.
Stars in My Pocket Like Grains of Sand. New York: Bantam, 1984.

Secondary Sources

Barbour, Douglas. *Worlds out of Words: The SF Novels of Samuel R. Delany*. Summerset, Great Britain: Brans Head Books, Ltd., 1979.
McEvoy, Seth. *Samuel R. Delany*. New York: Frederick Unger, 1985.
Nichols, Peter, ed. "Samuel R. Delany" in *The Science Fiction Encyclopedia*. New York: Doubleday, 1979.
Peplow, Michael W. and Robert S. Brevard. *Samuel R. Delany: A Primary and Secondary Bibliography, 1962–1979*. Boston: G. K. Hall, 1980.
Slusser, George. *The Delany Intersection: Samuel R. Delany Considered as a Writer of Semi-Precious Words*. San Bernadino: The Borgo Press, 1977.
Weedman, Jan. *Samuel R. Delany*. Mercer Island: Starmont House, 1982.
Weixlmann, Joe, ed. *Black American Literature Forum* 18, 2 (Summer 1984). Special issue devoted primarily to Delany.

GEORGE SLUSSER

DeLILLO, DON (1936–   )

In eight novels over a 13-year span, Don DeLillo has established himself as a distinctive voice in contemporary fiction, with affinities to other innovative writers, particularly Thomas Pynchon,* but with qualities uniquely his own. His novels reveal less a variety of technical experiments than a single voice and intelligence brought to bear on a panorama of contemporary obsessions, anxieties, and cultural phenomena. His subjects have ranged from filmmaking, football, the drug culture, and theoretical mathematics, to terrorism, espionage, and fanatical cults. Yet all eight novels are of a piece. DeLillo decodes or deconstructs popular mythologies and other systems of imposing order on chaos. He is less a physician than a metaphysician of society's ills. He self-consciously deals in ultimacies: life and death, reason and irrationality, appearance and reality, order and randomness, violence, language. Having stripped his protagonist of illusion and unmade the world, DeLillo typically concludes, ambiguously, with the possibility of a remaking based on reconstituted language.

Like a number of other contemporary writers, DeLillo has been protective of his private life and history. Born in 1936 in the Bronx and graduated from Fordham University in 1958, DeLillo has lived with his wife in New York and Canada, and for three years in Greece and the Middle East while researching the novel *The Names*, (1982), with the aid of a Guggenheim Fellowship in 1979–1980. Raised a Catholic, he has retained in his fiction an interest in religion as ritual and system, as a discipline that drives people to extreme behavior. The asceticism of the Jesuits he encountered at Fordham is reflected in several of his novels as a necessary prelude to illusionless living. More specifically, artistic influences have been both literary and nonliterary: the risk-taking inventiveness of Stein, Pound, Joyce, Faulkner, Nabokov, Lowry; the paintings at the Museum of Modern Art in New York; the music at the Jazz Gallery and Village Vanguard; the films of Howard Hawks, Fellini, and particularly Godard. In his construction of scenes and the rhythms of his language, these nonliterary influences seem the most significant.

DeLillo began publishing short fiction in 1960, through that decade placing stories in *Epoch*, the *Kenyon Review*, and the *Carolina Quarterly*. With the publication of his first novel, *Americana*, in 1971, more popular magazines such as *Esquire, Sports Illustrated*, the *New Yorker*, and the *Atlantic* have published his short fiction, often excerpts from forthcoming novels. But he is primarily a novelist. Following *Americana*, he has averaged a novel every year or two: *End Zone* (1972), *Great Jones Street* (1973), *Ratner's Star* (1976), *Players* (1977), *Running Dog* (1978), *The Names* (1982), and *White Noise* (1984). The period between them reflects the length and complexity of the novel in progress; one senses in DeLillo a highly disciplined commitment to his craft. He has managed to support himself with his writing, despite a lack of mass-market success, without teaching, reviewing, talk-show appearances, or any of the other activities often required for literary survival.

The eight novels reveal distinctive subjects but an overriding consistency of vision and technique. The influence of the visual arts, both photo-realist painting and contemporary film, is always apparent. His novels are series of scenes: two-dimensional, often baroque, characters set against elaborately detailed backdrops, speaking dialogue that is sometimes brilliantly mimetic of popular jargons, other times stunningly poetic. Scenes do not dissolve but jump-cut to the next, creating an impression of discontinuity rather than logical causation. Texture and density are created with language itself rather than exposition. Characters lack history and background, are defined by gesture and particularly speech. Character does not determine action; action determines character. The mere juxtaposition of two persons in a room precipitates events that one neither intended nor foresaw. Technique creates the angle of vision, an emphasis on randomness in human lives. Characters are players, both of games and of roles; reality exists only on the surface, beneath which lies ultimate mystery.

Above all, language is central to DeLillo's fiction, as both subject and instrument. He shares other metafictionists' self-consciousness about language but exceeds them all in giving language a voluptuous, nearly physical presence in his novels. DeLillo's wit is extraordinary. He recreates the jargons and specialized languages, whether of football players or of mathematicians, with an unfailing ear for sound and rhythm, yet the words themselves are wholly original. Most importantly, for DeLillo language is the ultimate system. Games are systems of rules and meaning; mathematics is a system of rational explanations. Language is the ur-system. All systems fail by their very nature as systems. DeLillo repeatedly pushes reason to its limits until it bursts through to unreason. *Great Jones Street* ends in babbling, *The Names* in the near-babble of a nine-year-old's writing. Language continually remakes itself, however, through a kind of primal violence. DeLillo moves beyond the superficial manifestations of social and political violence, whether in football or terrorism, to a sense of the more fundamental violence out of which life emerges and language is created anew—a sort of little bang, endlessly repeated.

DeLillo has been widely praised by critics but little read by the public. He is most admired for his verbal inventiveness and most criticized for his authorial detachment which, to some, tends to noncommitment or even cynicism. His primary commitment is an aesthetic one. *End Zone* has received the most critical attention because it lends itself to treatment within a familiar subgenre, the sports level. *Ratner's Star*, his most ambitious, is DeLillo's own choice as his best, but he has not yet written that breakthrough novel that assures a consensus among critics of his major stature. He is a disturbing and elusive writer who seems to have decided not to court popular success, sharing with many other modernists and postmodernists a resistance to being fully understood. He admires other risk-takers, such as William Gaddis* and Pynchon, who extend fiction's possibilities. In his case, it is that sense of ultimate mystery that leads him, in his own words, to wish not to be "diminished by his audience."

Selected Bibliography

Primary Sources

Americana. Boston: Houghton Mifflin, 1971.
End Zone. Boston: Houghton Mifflin, 1972.
Great Jones Street. Boston: Houghton Mifflin, 1973.
Ratner's Star. New York: Alfred A. Knopf, 1976.
Players. New York: Alfred A. Knopf, 1977.
Running Dog. New York: Alfred A. Knopf, 1978.
The Names. New York: Alfred A. Knopf, 1982.
White Noise. New York: Alfred A. Knopf, 1984.

Secondary Sources

Berman, Neil David. "*End Zone*: Play at the Brink." Chapter Four of *Playful Fictions and Fictional Players: Game, Sport and Survival in Contemporary American Fiction*. Port Washington, N.Y.: Kennikat, 1981, pp. 47–71.
Bryson, Norman. "City of Dis: The Fiction of Don DeLillo." *Granta* 2 n.s. (1980): 145–57.
Burke, William. "Football, Literature, Culture." *Southwest Review* 60 (Autumn 1975): 391–98.
LeClair, Tom. "An Interview with Don DeLillo." *Anything Can Happen: Interviews with Contemporary American Novelists*. Eds. Tom LeClair and Larry McCaffery. Urbana: University of Illinois Press, 1983, pp. 79–90.
Oriard, Michael. "Don DeLillo's Search for Walden Pond." *Critique* 20 (August 1978): 5–24.

MICHAEL ORIARD

DE MAN, PAUL (1919–   )

According to Paul de Man, resistance to the possibility of critical theory has traditionally entailed a methodological flight from the semantic and semiological elements of somewhat chaotic structures of meaning, a reluctance to analyze the rhetorical dimensions of its own text. De Man's endeavor has been to articulate the complexities of *reading* through writing analyses that are inscribed and circumvented by the necessity of misreading they engender and advocate. This has been performed while practicing a tropological mode of reading, which is simultaneously being disfigured by a deconstructive rhetoricity he claims constitutes and saturates all texts. In "Semiology and Rhetoric" he writes: "a literary text simultaneously asserts and denies the authority of its own rhetorical mode." Hence, for de Man, critical writing, as the récit of this demystified reading experience, potentially offers resistance to instituted cognitive or referential restraints by attempting to reinscribe the power of performative linguistic figuration in the textual field of tropes. Rhetoric is language as well as the ground of the analysis of language.

Paul de Man was born in Antwerp, Belgium, in December 1919, and educated in philosophical thought in Europe and at Harvard in techniques of attentive reading. After teaching at the University of Zurich, Cornell, and Johns Hopkins, he became Sterling Professor of the Humanities at Yale University. If we consider the number of distinguished critics who have worked with him, we may assume his teaching in the United States has been as decisive in shaping contemporary American criticism as have his publications. Recently, de Man has contrasted his teaching career in Europe and America, claiming the contractual relationship between professors and students possible in the United States allowed a predominantly political and positive collegiality. Furthermore, according to de Man, political problems are radically transposed in this context, hence his strategy of approaching these concerns by means of a critico-linguistic analysis, or practicing a critique of ideology issuing from the study of philology.

His first book, *Blindness and Insight,* initially published in 1971, explores the rhetoric of interpretive reading procedures in American New Criticism and in the writings of Ludwig Binswanger, Georg Lukács, Maurice Blanchot, Georges Poulet, Stéphane Mallarmé, Jacques Rousseau, and Jacques Derrida.* The second, revised and augmented edition, released in 1983, includes the renowned "Rhetoric of Temporality," two pieces previously published in French, "The Dead-End of Formalist Criticism," and "Heidegger's Exegeses of Hölderlin," a review and a commentary. In these early essays, de Man reviews the conceptual contradictions in critical reading(s) by concentrating on *the* deconstructive object: the unexamined confidence bestowed on and invested in critico-linguistic analysis. He cogently argues how certain exegetical principles, presupposed by both Continental and American criticism, may illuminate explicit degrees of insight only because methodologies are always already oblivious to an itinerant "peculiar blindness." Reading may recognize moments when the rhetorical resonances and properties of language disguise and distort a writer's apparent commitment to a specific poetics or philosophy, and it must respond to the figural complexities of a perhaps contrasting desire.

Allegories of Reading, published in 1979, suggests a disruptive theory of reading at the impasse of the "impossibility of reading" and at the expense of an envisioned "historical study." It offers a kind of reading along tropological lines, which maintains that every interpretation registers a perceptible double bind for meticulous readers, with regard to the intricate relationship between an alleged literal and figural dichotomy within the linguistic sign. Again, from "Semiology and Rhetoric," de Man remarks: "Rhetoric radically suspends logic and opens up vertiginous possibilities of referential aberration." Rigorous readings of Rilke, Proust, Nietzsche, and Rousseau figure in the strategic reversal between grammar and rhetoric, as well as the refiguring of such authoritative notions as referentiality, genetic history, and "the autonomous power to will of the self." De Man asserts that the undoing of the relationship between grammar and trope demonstrates, in Nietzschean fashion, that rhetorical deconstruction is not something added to or subtracted from textuality. Rather, this duplicity and displacement of grammatical ground and its presumed authority of meaning is the truest nature of language.

Allegories of Reading, as *Blindness and Insight*, is as fundamentally contradictory, dissimulating, and unreadable as all other texts. Hence, critics of de Man's rhetorical strategies forget to read the linguistic predicament of a writing that is playfully aware of its deceptively tropological and desperately ideological quest for ligature. Their misreadings of de Man's work, their allegorical narratives, tell the familiar story of how grammar and rhetoric deconstruct their own performances, rather than accomplish any privileged metametaphorics. De Man writes in relation to this curious reversal: "For this deconstruction *seems* to end in a reassertion of the active performance function of language and it rehabilitates persuasion as the final outcome of the deconstruction of figural speech."

In the future, several additional texts by Paul de Man will be published. These texts appear to include one tentatively titled *The Resistance to Theory*, another which collects fugitive essays composed in the 1960s, a third oriented around romanticism, and a fourth which may encompass the essays de Man delivered in the spring of 1983 during the Messenger Lectures at Cornell University. These readings of Jauss, Riffaterre, Kleist, Schelling, Kant, Hegel, Kierkegaard, Benjamin, and Friedrich Schlegel, among others, will no doubt proceed from a philological, rather than philosophical, reading practice in pursuit of the limits of the field of tropological saturation. It will be reading informed by the concept of rhetoric and its relationship to other modes of language and from "the perspective of a critical-linguistic analysis to which these texts have not been submitted," as well as *inaugural* writing, in the Derridean sense, of not knowing its destination.

Selected Bibliography

Primary Sources

Blindness and Insight: Essays in the Rhetoric of Contemporary Criticism. New York: Oxford University Press, 1971.
Allegories of Reading: Figural Language in Rousseau, Nietzsche, Rilke and Proust. New Haven, Conn.: Yale University Press, 1979.

Secondary Sources

Corngold, Stanley. "Error in Paul de Man," in *The Yale Critics: Deconstruction in America.* Minneapolis: University of Minnesota Press, 1983, pp. 90–108.

Fletcher, Angus. "The Perpetual Error." Review of *Blindness and Insight*. *Diacritics* (Winter 1972): 14–20.

Klein, Richard. "The Blindness of Hyperboles: The Ellipses of Insight." *Diacritics* (Summer 1973): 33–44.

Leitch, Vincent B. "Allegory and (Mis)Reading." In *Deconstructive Criticism, An Advanced Introduction*. New York: Columbia University Press, 1983, pp. 183–90.

Lentricchia, Frank. "Paul de Man: The Rhetoric of Authority." In *After the New Criticism*. Chicago: University of Chicago Press, 1980, pp. 282–317.

DAVID RANDALL

DERRIDA, JACQUES (1930–   )

By carefully working out the consequences of a new way to grasp the meaning of meaning, the work of Jacques Derrida aims to overturn a millennium-long tradition of Western knowledge.

Derrida was born in 1930 into an assimilated middle-class Jewish family of El-Biar, a suburb of Algiers, Algeria. At the age of 19 he went to Paris to study philosophy at the celebrated École Normale Supérieure, where he returned two decades later to teach philosophy until 1983. In 1984 he became professor of philosophy at the École des Hautes Études, Paris, as well as assuming the directorship of the newly formed Collège International de Philosophie, which he was instrumental in establishing. In addition to his more traditional academic activities, Derrida contributed regularly to the avant-garde journal *Tel Quel* in the 1960s; in the 1970s he was associated with GREPH, a research group concerned with the teaching of philosophy in France, and more recently has been involved with human rights activists in Prague, Czechoslovakia.

Derrida burst onto the French intellectual scene as a major force in 1967 with the publication of three philosophical works: *Speech and Phenomena*, a critical study of Husserl's theory of meaning and evidence; *Of Grammatology*, an examination of Rousseau presenting an innovative theory of language based on writing rather than speech; and *Writing and Difference*, a collection of articles written between 1959 and 1967 on Antonin Artaud, George Bataille, Michel Foucault,* Sigmund Freud, G.W.F. Hegel, Edward Jabès, Emmanuel Levinas, and Claude Lévi-Strauss, centered primarily on language and meaning. These three works shape Derrida's subsequent thought. Although they deal with diverse philosophical and nonphilosophical figures, they are united by a central concern, the fundamental theme of Derrida's entire philosophical enterprise: textuality.

Textuality, in Derrida's hands, means not merely an attentiveness to a work's literary qualities, but also and primarily a fundamental critique of the entire Western intellectual and cultural tradition. Oddly enough, the latter comes from the former. For Derrida the Western tradition, in one form or another, comes down to the "metaphysics of presence": the attempt to articulate—in books, in speech, in politics, and so on—signifiers that refer beyond themselves to a hierarchic signified, which, because the signifier is meant to be discarded, can be made definitively present. Through close textual analyses of Plato, Rousseau, and other philosophers, especially Husserl, Derrida shows how the intended discarding of signifiers is in fact never realized but always deferred. By giving greater weight to this deferral rather than to the promise of its transcendence, Derrida may be said to be original.

To clip the wings of the flight from signifier to signified, Derrida deconstructs the disguises of this conceit. To do so without being deceived himself, he shifts his critical discourse, as well as the discourse criticized, from the plane of semantics to the groundless ground of semiotics, to a differential theory of meaning. According to this view, meaning depends not on the premature exclamations of an always incompleted reference (to God, to truth, to justice, and so on), but on the unsettled play of *différance*, that is, the inner and multiple movement of differences between signifiers, which as such can never be brought to presence. The remarkable penetration, subtlety, and delightful irony of Derrida's textual analyses come from bringing this play onto stage where it is least expected—Plato's "pharmakon," Rousseau's "supplement," Nietzsche's "hymen"—and keeping the play playing without reducing it to a theme, that is, to metaphysics pure and simple.

Having established the anti-metaphysical play of *différance* as a necessary moment of meaning formation, Derrida proceeds to deconstruct the epistemological hubris of numerous texts unaware of their own textuality. The success and sophistication of the analyses, however, do not come from a more original or creative final word, which would merely install yet another presence, raising the naiveté of the same stakes. Rather, because the metaphysics of presence cannot be eradicated but, like difference itself, is an ineluctable moment of meaning formation, deconstruction is self-referential and hence an essentially unending task. Despite much noisy saber rattling against Derrida's procedures, then, deconstruction and grammatology in fact only claim a relatively stricter enlightenment and a greater modesty than their predecessors. By heightening the awareness of language's essential contribution to meaning, metaphysics cannot be overcome once and for all, but it can be made to dance to a new nonmetaphysical tune.

In 1972 Derrida published three more books: *Dissemination*, a deconstruction of Plato, playing on the ambiguity of the term "pharmakon," which means both cure and poison; *Margins of Philosophy*, "marginal" essays where the notions of center and margin have both been displaced; and *Positions*, wide-ranging interviews with Derrida on his own work. *Glas* (1974) compares Hegel and Genet in a multiplicity of more or less trivial and/or significant ways; its pages are printed in parallel columns. *Spurs: Nietzsche's Styles* (1976) is a short but penetrating look at Nietzsche's use of female metaphors in relation to truth. *The Postal Card: From Socrates to Freud and Beyond* (1980) is a collection of articles on Freud and Jacques Lacan.* These works continue the grammatology whose theoretical base was worked out in the texts of 1967.

Selected Bibliography

Primary Sources

Translation and Introduction to Edmund Husserl, *L'Origine de la geometrie*. Paris: Presses Universitaires de France, 1967. (*Edmund Husserl's Origin of Geometry: An Introduction*. Trans. John R. Leavey. New York: Nicolas Hays, 1977.)

De la Grammatologie. Paris: Minuit, 1967. (*Of Grammatology*. Trans. Gayatri Chakravorty. Baltimore: Johns Hopkins University Press, 1976.)

La Voix et le phenomène. Paris: Presses Universitaire de France, 1967. (*Speech and Phenomena*. Trans. David B. Allison. Evanston, Ill.: Northwestern University Press, 1973.)

L'Écriture et la différence. Paris: Seuil, 1967. (*Writing and Difference*. Trans. Alan Bass. Chicago: University of Chicago Press; 1978.)

La Dissemination. Paris: Seuil, 1972. (*Dissemination*. Trans. Barbara Johnson. Chicago: University of Chicago Press, 1981.)

Marges de la philosophie. Paris: Minuit, 1972. (*Margins of Philosophy*. Chicago: University of Chicago Press, 1981.)

Positions. Paris: Minuit, 1972. (*Positions*. Trans. Alan Bass. Chicago: University of Chicago Press, 1981.)

Glas. Paris: Galilee, 1974.

Spurs: Nietzsche's Styles/Éperons: les styles de Nietzsche. Bilingual edition. Chicago: University of Chicago Press, 1976.

La Carte postale de Socrates a Freud et au-dela (*The Postal Card: From Socrates to Freud and Beyond.*). Paris: Flammarion, 1980.

Signeponge-Signsponge. Trans. Richard Rand. New York: Columbia University Press, 1984.

Secondary Sources

Culler, Jonathan. *On Deconstruction: Criticism after Structuralism*. Ithaca, N.Y.: Cornell University Press, 1982.

Harvey, Irene. *Derrida and the Economy of Difference*. Bloomington: Indiana University Press, 1985.

Krupnik, Mark, ed. *Displacement: Derrida and After*. Bloomington: Indiana University Press, 1983.

Leitch, Vincent. *Deconstructive Criticism: An Advanced Introduction and Survey*. New York: Columbia University Press, 1982.

Magliola, Robert R. *Derrida on the Mend*. West Lafayette: Purdue University Press, 1984.

Megill, Allan. *Prophets of Extremity: Nietzsche, Heidegger, Foucault, Derrida*. Berkeley: University of California Press, 1985.

Norris, Christopher. *Deconstruction: Theory and Practice.* New York: Methuen, 1982.
Spivak, Gayatri. Translator's "Preface" to Derrida's *Of Grammatology.* Baltimore: Johns Hopkins University Press, 1976, pp. ix-lxxxvii.

RICHARD A. COHEN

DICK, PHILIP K. (1928–1982)

By the time of his death, at the age of 53, on March 2, 1982, Philip K. Dick had established himself as one of the most important writers of modern fiction. Although he was categorized as a science fiction writer, the scope of his work was actually somewhat broader than the work conventionally contained by the genre. One of the major themes in his work is the effect on the human existential situation of the gradual mechanization of the environment. Thus, a great many of his stories are set in hypothetical futures inhabited by sophisticated machines, especially the humanoid machines that he usually calls androids. His other major concerns, however, are less manifestly science fictional. Almost all of his novels reflect a curious, quasi-paranoid sensitivity to the question of whether the world is really *real*, or whether it might instead be an artifact or an illusion. His characters are perennially tearing away veils of illusion in which they have found themselves wrapped, mostly to find that there is nothing beyond but more tantalizing illusions. Often, when they make that profound discovery, Dick's heroes are deflected from their initial search for ontological solidity into an equally frustrating quest for moral and metaphysical meaning.

Philip Kendred Dick was born on December 16, 1928, in Chicago but was brought up and spent most of his life in California. He attended college for one year but then left and held various odd jobs before deciding to make a career as a writer in 1951. In the following year his stories began to appear in science fiction magazines in some profusion. His characteristic preoccupations show up even in these early works: in "Second Variety" (1953), machines built to fight wars evolve of their own accord and produce pathetic android figures to lure real humans into traps; in "Impostor" (1953) the protagonist's life becomes a nightmare when his friends become convinced that he is an android time-bomb.

In the mid-1950s the magazine market went into decline, and the principal market for science fiction became paperback books. Dick began to produce novels (most of which were published as halves of Ace Doubles) with the same impressive fluency that he had shown as a short story writer. His work of this period was striking in its originality, though sometimes lacking in structure. Not all his experiments were successful, but *The World Jones Made* (1956) is an impressive story of a man dislocated in time, who is (from his own point of view) living in a world that lies a year in his past, and which he must try to guide through a time of great crisis. *Eye in the Sky* (1957) is equally impressive, describing the experiences of a group of people thrust by a freak accident into a series of alternate worlds, each reflecting the neurotically confused beliefs of one of their number. In this and the novel that followed it, *Time Out of Joint* (1959), Dick's characters can still find their way back from false realities to the dubious comfort of the true one, but Dick was fast losing faith in that kind of resolution.

Although he expanded a couple of early magazine stories to novel length at about the same time that he published *Time Out of Joint*, there was a pronounced hiatus in Dick's career as science fiction writer between 1957 and 1962. He was still writing novel after novel, but without science fictional apparatus. None of these experimental fictions was published at the time, but two have subsequently been rescued from obscurity: *Confessions of a Crap Artist* (1975) and *The Man Whose Teeth Were All Exactly Alike* (1984). Both are stories of innocent protagonists brutally ill-used by circumstance, victims of the unfeeling carelessness of those around them. Dick, now living in abject poverty and embarked on what was to be a long series of unsuccessful marriages, clearly saw himself in much the same way. Indeed, his later work, for all its bizarrerie, retains an intensely introspective quality. He drew on and exaggerated his own experiences in remarkable fashion. His rather tentative experiments with drugs led to a dramatic series of novels featuring powerful psychotropic substances, and the echoes of the mental illness that led to his temporary hospitalization in a later phase of his career also resonate through his fictions.

His first step on the road to success came with his return to science fiction with the brilliant novel of alternate realities, *The Man in the High Castle* (1962). The book was plotted with the aid of the *I Ching*, which plays a crucial role in the story by informing the characters that their world (in which the allies lost World War II) is not the real one—but neither, it is implied, is ours. This was soon followed by *Martian Time-Slip* (1964), *The Three Stigmata of Palmer Eldritch* (1964), and *Now Wait for Last Year* (1966)—the best of a second flood of genre novels. All of them feature characters who are gradually enveloped by and absorbed into distorted realities from which there is no escape. In the first, the distortions emanate from the time-bending perceptions of a schizophrenic child; in the other two hallucinogenic drugs are the agents of dislocation. It was in this phase of his career that Dick gradually set to one side as unsolvable the question of discriminating between the real and the unreal, and forced his characters to seek an existential anchorage instead in the question of what is good (truly human) and what is evil (androidal). This is the central concern of two of his finest novels: *Do Androids Dream of Electric Sheep?* (1968; perverted into a mere adventure story by the film *Blade Runner*) and *We Can Build You* (1972). Other novels of the period pose more abstract questions about the essence of moral order, frequently dealing explicitly with theological issues. Examples include *Ubik* (1969), *Our Friends from Frolix-8* (1970), and *A Maze of Death* (1970).

After a further hiatus in his work in the early 1970s Dick began publishing again, though on a more modest scale; this was the period when reevaluation of his early works began to boost his reputation. He produced two new psychotropic novels in *Flow My Tears, the Policeman Said* (1974) and *A Scanner Darkly* (1977), the latter an intensely tragic story of the destruction of identity, and then two more quasi-theological stories, *Valis* (1981) and *The Divine Invasion* (1981). The last novel completed before his death was a fictionalized biography of Bishop Pike, *The Transmigration of Timothy Archer* (1982), which suggests that he may have been making another attempt to move into the literary mainstream when he fell victim to the series of strokes that finally killed him.

Many of Dick's lesser novels peter out into a tangle of loose ends, but in those works where his frenetic creativity sustained him through to the end he shows great imaginative power and considerable narrative skill. He can make readers *feel*, intensely, the pressure of moral and metaphysical questions which, in his view, are attaining new relevance because of the advancement of science and technology. Although there are many writers whose work dramatizes the sense of existential insecurity that one can easily feel in today's world, there is no one else who combines his imaginative richness with his special *caritas*.

Selected Bibliography

Primary Sources

The World Jones Made. New York: Ace, 1956.
Eye in the Sky. New York: Ace, 1957.
The Man in the High Castle. New York: G. P. Putnam's, 1962.
Martian Time-Slip. New York: Ballantine, 1964.
Do Androids Dream of Electric Sheep? New York: Doubleday, 1968.
The Preserving Machine and Other Stories. New York: Ace, 1969.
We Can Build You. New York: Daw, 1972.
A Scanner Darkly. New York: Doubleday, 1977.
The Divine Invasion. New York: Timescape, 1981.
Valis. New York: Bantam, 1981.
The Transmigration of Timothy Archer. New York: Bantam, 1982.

Secondary Sources

Fitting, Peter. "Reality as Ideological Construct: A Reading of Five Novels by Philip K. Dick." *Science Fiction Studies* 10 (1983): 219–236.
Foundation 26 (October 1982). Special issue containing memoirs of and essays on Dick.
Gillespie, Bruce, ed. *Philip K. Dick: Electric Shepherd.* Melbourne: Norstrilia Press, 1975.
Greenberg, Martin Harry, and Josephy Olander, eds. *Philip K. Dick.* New York: Taplinger, 1983.

Pierce, Hazel. *Philip K. Dick.* Mercer I., Washington, D.C.: Starmont House, 1982.

Science Fiction Studies. Vol. 2, part 1 (March 1975). Special issue containing essays on Dick.

Robinson, Kim Stanley. *The Novels of Philip K. Dick.* Ann Arbor, Mich.: UMI Research Press, 1985.

BRIAN STABLEFORD

DIDION, JOAN (1934–   )

Joan Didion was born in 1934 to a family that had resided for several generations in California. She graduated from the University of California at Berkeley in 1956 and shortly thereafter moved to New York to take up a position at *Vogue* magazine. Although she has subsequently become a highly regarded novelist, over the years Didion has continued to work as a journalist, contributing essays and columns to the *Saturday Evening Post,* the *National Review, Harper's,* and *New West,* among others. In 1964 she married John Gregory Dunne (author of *Vegas, True Confessions, Dutch Shea, Jr.,* and so on). The couple soon settled in southern California, where they continue to live, write, and occasionally collaborate on screenplays.

Didion has published seven books to date, including four novels. *Slouching Towards Bethlehem* (1968) and *The White Album* (1979) are collections of her journalistic writings. *Salvador* (1983) recounts her impressions of that troubled country gathered during a visit the previous year. Her first novel, *Run River* (1963), concerned old California families and originally received little attention; but her subsequent works of fiction—*Play It as It Lays* (1970), *A Book of Common Prayer* (1977), and *Democracy* (1984)— have been widely and, in the main, quite favorably received.

It is her sensibility that gives distinction to Joan Didion's prose. She has said that she first learned how sentences, commas, and paragraphs worked in her teens, when she would type over pages by Hemingway and Conrad. The practice obviously worked, for her prose possesses the tautness of Hemingway in "Big Two-Hearted River," and conveys a comparable anxiety over what might exist just out of sight. Readers of her novels immediately recognize the voice, rhythms, and preoccupations of her occasional prose, and must be forgiven if they come to disregard the distance usually assumed to exist between writer and work. In *Play It as It Lays,* Maria Wyeth is drawn to Hoover Dam only to be temporarily overcome by the power concentrated there. In "At the Dam," a short piece originally published the same year and later collected in *The White Album,* Didion records her own similar reactions. In the essay as in the novel, one feels that the ominous power of the dam is being held at bay by little more than the strictness of Didion's prose.

Didion's characters find the world a decidedly unfriendly place. It showers loss and aimless violence upon them, thereby resisting all efforts to create stable, meaningful lives. They seem particularly vulnerable to the upheaval about them, as though their nerves can register even the slightest tremors. By and large, this world quickly disabuses Didion's characters of large expectations; instead, they seem bent on suing for some personal accommodation within a most unaccommodating world. Didion is a moralist who apparently believes that morality is finally a matter of character, of old and unfashionable virtues. The character who embodies these virtues most completely is Jack Lovett, in *Democracy*, who remains loyal to old ties and old values.

If the characters in Didion's earlier fiction are unconcerned about matters of state or justice except as their own lives are affected, as an essayist Didion has long been an alert observer of the social scene. Her investigations of the seedier and more violent sides of the 1960s, the title essays in *Slouching Towards Bethlehem* and *The White Album*, are justly famous. More recently, her interests have extended into the realm of politics proper. Neither *Salvador* nor *Democracy*, however, grapples with politics in its institutional and historical dimensions. *Salvador* records the feel of terror, not the possible reasons for its existence; and *Democracy* suggests the personal costs of the political life, not the possible reasons for its shallowness. Didion's strengths are as an observer and stylist, and one should not read her in search of telling analyses of what she sees.

Selected Bibliography

Primary Sources

Run River. New York: Obolensky, 1963.
Slouching Towards Bethlehem. New York: Farrar, Straus & Giroux, 1968.
Play It as It Lays. New York: Farrar, Straus & Giroux, 1970.
A Book of Common Prayer. New York: Simon & Schuster, 1977.
The White Album. New York: Simon & Schuster, 1979.
Salvador. New York: Simon & Schuster, 1983.
Democracy. New York: Simon & Schuster, 1984.

Secondary Sources

Friedman, Ellen G., ed. *Joan Didion: Essays and Conversations*. Princeton, N.J.: Ontario Review Press, 1984.
Hanley, Lynne T. "To El Salvador." *Massachusetts Review* 24 (Spring 1983): 13–29.
Harrison, Barbara Grizzuti. "Joan Didion: Only Disconnect," *Off Center*. New York: Dial Press, 1980, pp. 113–37.
Henderson, Katherine Usher. *Joan Didion*. New York: Frederick Ungar, 1981.
Jacobs, Fred Rue. *Joan Didion—A Bibliography*. Keene, Calif.: Loop Press, 1977.
Lahr, John. "Joan Didion and John Gregory Dunne." *Automatic Vaudeville: Essays on Star Turns*. New York: Alfred A. Knopf, 1984, pp. 205–16.
Winchell, Mark Royden. *Joan Didion*. Boston: Twayne Publishers, 1980.

Wolff, Cynthia Griffin. "Play It as It Lays: Didion and the Diver Heroine." *Contemporary Literature* 24 (Winter 1983): 480–95.

C. BARRY CHABOT

DIXON, STEPHEN (1936–   )

Stephen Dixon is one of the most prolific writers of the 1970s and 1980s, and it should not be surprising that a man who has published four novels, four collections of fiction, and more than 150 short stories in a decade is obsessed by the idea of storiness. In fact, much of Dixon's work is rooted in his ongoing attempt to answer the question: What makes a story?

He was born in 1936 in New York City, where he spent most of his life. With a degree in international relations from City College, Dixon went on to a variety of jobs as newsman, technical writer, magazine editor, radio producer, bartender, waiter, and substitute teacher. His fiction began to appear in the mid–1960s, but his first book was not published until he was 40 years old. Since then, Dixon has received many awards, including the Award in Literature from the American Academy and Institute of Arts and Letters in 1983. At present, he teaches in the Writing Seminars at Johns Hopkins University. His wife is translator Anne Frydman, and they have one daughter, Sophia.

Dixon is a writer of urban tales—often bizarre and darkly humorous stories about characters who are themselves full of stories. The novel *Too Late* (1978) is such a story. Art, the narrator, and Donna are at the theater. She doesn't like the movie and decides to return to the apartment they share, where Art will join her later. But when he goes home, she is not there. And she never returns. For the rest of the work, Art searches for her, attempts to interest the police in her case by forging a kidnapper's ransom note, and tries to explain to others and to himself—with story after story, most of them pure fictions—what happened to her. In the end, after Art has told all his stories, neither he nor the reader knows the truth of Donna or of their relationship. There are only the stories and stories-within-stories, told in a marvelously elliptical style that attempts to explain everything while in fact explaining nothing.

Dixon is a masterful stylist. His long sentences—most of them in the first person, many in dialogue—full of twistings and turnings and digressions, seem designed to speak the whole of any situation, to exhaust all possibilities. His characters continually weave words into patterns intended to explain everything, but the "true story" always seems to outrun the possibilities of speech.

In some works, Dixon's characters invent their own languages in hopes of speaking beyond speaking. "Milk Is Very Good for You" is a wild parody of a pornographic story, but the four-letter words are so badly misspelled that the reader must "translate" continually to know what is going on. ("We were in red, Jane heated on top of me, my sock deep in her funt and linger up her masspole.") And the protagonist of the novel *Fall and Rise* (1984) makes notes for himself in his own shorthand that the reader learns as he reads. ("Oh so thas wha happed & I rly felt that partic nit so memobl becaus so many eventfl events & all t dif things I fel, I remem now.") But regardless of the style, Dixon's fictions remain fictions—not truth but stories and often stories about storiness.

The title work in the collection *14 Stories* (1980) is a convoluted maze of tales centered on a shocking suicide, but the play of the stories goes beyond this tragic death to the very idea of what it means to explain an event in a story. As the title suggests, the story "14 Stories" is many stories, but the title also marks the setting for the central event of the tale—the fourteenth floor of a midtown hotel. And yet even so many stories do not and cannot reach the true story. A 14-story building has in truth only 13 stories (the thirteenth floor is traditionally numbered "14"), just as there are only 13 stories collected in *14 Stories*. As a nameless character and fellow storyteller in "14 Stories" asks: "Now what kind of story is that?"

It is, of course, the kind of story that questions the very nature of all stories. In *Movies*, the story "Small Bear" is about a bear, or rather it is a story about bear stories. Some of these bear stories are or seem to be true (the narrator sees what seems to be a dead bear in the woods), though they could be fictions (a game warden cannot find the dead bear), and still others are complete fictions (a newspaper report of this nonevent says the narrator fought off a wounded bear with an axe). In "The Barbecue," Ron tries to tell a true story he has heard from Jack, but his listeners keep interrupting and questioning the facts until the storiness of the story, the very structure that makes the tale a tale, begins to collapse. "It really all happened," a friend of Ron's says at last, "though maybe some parts of it are a little changed in passing from Jack and Ron to us." And, of course, the story is changed again in passing through the narrator who retells Ron's telling. Ron's story is questionable, but Dixon's story *of* Ron's story opens storiness itself to question.

In "Magda . . . Reading," Willy writes a story that comments on the story he is writing about Magda, who sits out on the porch reading some stories he has written.

I try to write another story so she'll have a fifth one of mine to read . . . if I finish it on time written the same day I finished the last page of the fourth story, and now of a length where I can at least say—well, maybe I could have said it two or three pages back—that if I have to stop because she's opening the screen door to come upstairs to tell me what she thinks of my four stories, it'll at least be, if not finished, then long enough to be considered in some circles a story . . .

But "Magda . . . Reading" fails to capture itself as a story and finally stop.

In trying to tell the true story of a story, this story collapses in on itself and grinds to a halt in mid-sentence.

For Dixon, the "true story" never appears. And yet he, and everyone else, must keep telling them, because such stories—such convoluted and obvious fictions—give us our lives and ourselves. Stories are what we live by, and so we must know what they are and how they work. Stephen Dixon's stories remind us to keep questioning the stories we tell and the stories we are.

Selected Bibliography

Primary Sources

No Relief. Ann Arbor, Mich.: Street Fiction Press, 1976.
Work. Ann Arbor, Mich.: Street Fiction Press, 1977.
Too Late. New York: Harper & Row, 1978.
Quite Contrary. New York: Harper & Row, 1979.
14 Stories. Baltimore: Johns Hopkins University Press, 1980.
Movies. Berkeley, Calif.: North Point Press, 1983.
Time to Go. Baltimore: Johns Hopkins University Press, 1984.
Fall and Rise. Berkeley, Calif.: North Point Press, 1984.

Secondary Sources

Klinkowitz, Jerome. *The Self Apparent Word.* Carbondale: Southern Illinois University Press, 1984, pp. 95–108, 122–127.

WELCH D. EVERMAN

DOCTOROW, E. L. (1931–)

E. L. Doctorow's chief significance in the context of postmodern fiction is in his invention of a certain form of the historical novel, where, through his eccentric *bricolage*—patching together, tinkering—with fragments, images of our real and imagined past, he compels our recognition of aspects of both American history and our accounts of it. This is normally the function of much of the popular culture he evokes for our examination to conceal, through the ideological practices at work whenever language writes, thought thinks. His evident awareness that such strategies, with inevitable attendant mystifications, must needs inhabit his own prose is typical of the ironic, self-conscious, dialectical perspective that informs the work of our most important historical novelist since World War II.

Edgar Lawrence Doctorow was born in New York City on January 6, 1931. He graduated with honors in philosophy from Kenyon College in 1952. Largely on the basis of *The Book of Daniel* (1971), Doctorow was already well known among those interested in American fiction's relation to politics and to history before the publication of the phenomenally successful *Ragtime* (1974), which received the National Book Critics Circle Award for Fiction and brought to this novelist the attention both in the mass market and in the academy which he has continued to merit and to receive. Since that time, *Loon Lake* (1979) has also attained best-seller status, and both *Daniel* and *Ragtime* have been made into big-budget, major studio movies, bringing further attention to Doctorow's work.

It is in terms of its relations to American history that Doctorow's fiction is most significant. In *Ragtime*, through the popular culture lenses implied by the title, we see a crazy, kitsch, storybook version of that history, with a cast that includes Emma Goldman and Houdini, Henry Ford and J. P. Morgan, during the first three decades of this century. *The Book of Daniel,* in its complex representation of the Rosenberg case and the Cold War through the eyes of an imagined son of the executed couple caught up in the Vietnam era world of Yippies, SDS, and even the very march on Washington of Mailer's *Armies of the Night,* seeks to illuminate our history from the late 1940s until the recent past. Meanwhile, *Loon Lake* fills the gap between the other two, with a haunting rendering of the 1930s and the Depression.

Even Doctorow's first novel, the anti-Western, *Welcome to Hard Times* (1960), can be seen as part of this historical sequence, set as it is on the turn-of-the-century frontier, on an unspecified barren waste somewhere in some place like Nebraska. The novel is an unrelievedly ironic and devastating overture to Doctorow's dissonant and polyphonic representation of twentieth-century America. In this popular culture subgenre piece, the conventions of the Western are used to expose at once the barrenness of the culture, of those conventions and of the American Dream mythos at the heart of what our culture thinks are its own deep structures, and to reveal the cruel and predatory material practice of capitalism which it is the function of "straight" uses of forms like the Western to mystify and conceal.

In its laconic, elliptical, and understated way, *Welcome to Hard Times* announces all the themes of Doctorow's subsequent fiction, as well as his primary concerns with modes of representation themselves as objects of scrutiny. Thus, our discursive practices and strategies themselves, from the comic books and advertisements of mass culture through the sophisticated discourse of academic and political intellectual culture, remain at the center of Doctorow's attention throughout all the novels.

This highly reflexive, ironic self-consciousness in and of his fictions is a key to Doctorow's significance. The historical and political concerns that have fueled Doctorow's imagination and have been the subjects of his artistic rendering have normally been the province of literary realism. Doctorow engages and represents the stuff of history as seriously and intensely as any realist. But his obsessive awareness and concern with the fictions of history, seeing all history as narrative, as discourse, place him in the forefront of postmodernism, a movement preoccupied since Nietzsche and especially now, since Jacques Derrida,* with the deconstruction of all historical narrative claiming any direct, naive relationship to truth.

The dialectic in all Doctorow's fiction is that between a powerful sense of the often tragic weight of historical events, in the economy and in politics and culture, and a contradictory sense of the unreality of it all, of the inevitable distortions of history through "History," through our accounts of it, which are our only ways of seeing and knowing it. This powerful contradiction is embodied in Doctorow's best work: the distancing devices of irony seem necessary to protect someone—Doctorow or us—from the pain and moral revulsion over the historical material he works with and represents. Even though some Marxists find his use of historical matters crucially important, they argue that his use is so pessimistic and ironic as to negate the value of Doctorow's fiction. Others, purists of the modernist avant-garde, criticize him for being too much concerned with both history (or "reality") and politics.

A complete account of Doctorow's career to date also includes *Big as Life* (1966), the science fiction novel he will reportedly not allow to be republished; his play, *Drinks Before Dinner* (1978), which was produced by Joseph Papp at the New York Shakespeare Festival in 1978, under the direction of Mike Nichols; and his years in publishing during the 1960s, both with New American Library and Dial Press, where he served as editor-in-chief and then publisher. He has also contributed often brilliant interventions in the form of serious journalism, like his piece on Orwell's *1984*, which appeared in the February 1983 *Playboy*.

Selected Bibliography

Primary Sources

Welcome to Hard Times. New York: Random House, 1960.
Big as Life. New York: Simon & Schuster, 1966.
The Book of Daniel. New York: Random House, 1971.
Ragtime. New York: Random House, 1974.
Drinks Before Dinner. New York: Random House, 1979.
Loon Lake. New York: Random House, 1979.
Lives of the Poets: Six Stories and a Novella. New York: Random House, 1984.
Worlds Fair. New York: Random House, 1985.

Secondary Sources

Cooper, Barbara. "The Artist as Historian in the Novels of E. L. Doctorow." *Emporia State Research Studies* 29, no. 2 (1980): 5–44.
Emblidge, David. "Marching Backward into the Future: Progress as Illusion in Doctorow's Novels." *Southwest Review* 62 (1979): 397–409.
Foley, Barbara. "From *U.S.A.* to *Ragtime*: Notes on the Forms of Historical Consciousness in Modern Fiction." *American Literature* 50 (1978): 85–105.

Gross, David S. "Tales of Obscene Power: Money and Culture, Modernism and History in the Fiction of E. L. Doctorow." *Genre* 13 (1980): 71–92.

Hague, Angela. "*Ragtime* and the Movies." *North Dakota Quarterly* 50 (Summer 1982): 101–12.

Stark, John. "Alienation and Analysis in Doctorow's *The Book of Daniel.*" *Critique* 26 (1982): 101–10.

Trenner, Richard, ed. *E. L. Doctorow: Essays and Conversations.* Princeton, N.J.: Ontario Review Press, 1983. Trenner has collected in this volume many of the best articles on Doctorow, as well as interviews conducted by Larry McCaffery, Paul Levine, and Trenner.

                                                                    DAVID S. GROSS

DOWELL, COLEMAN (1925–1985)

Upon first encountering Coleman Dowell's works, an image creeps into our minds which is certain to become definitely fixed after a close reading of his novels: the image of Narcissus, in its primeval, original sense. The *narcissistic* definition is not adopted to link Dowell's case to the postmodern "Culture of Narcissism" (as defined in Christopher Lasch's work) nor to any self-contained or self-conscious type of metafiction ("The Novel as Narcissus," John Aldridge called it, rather contemptuously). The fact that Coleman Dowell generally writes about people who write, or about creative people in some sense, might easily lead us to place him among the pure metafictionists, but his evocation of the spirit of the beautiful youth and of his myth happens in a deeper and more direct sense.

In Dowell's fictional country, at least two themes and *loci* of the Narcissus story are strikingly present: a recurrent, allusive play with mirrors, reflections, transparencies, present both at the thematic and at the technical level; and a peculiar aesthetic intercourse between creator and creation, in which—as for Narcissus and his reflected image—Beauty is primarily implied.

The artful, superbly crafted fiction of Coleman Dowell shows how deeply beauty and the search for aesthetic achievement may affect a narrative body and tilt its balance. His writing is expressed through a highly sophisticated style and structure, in a language that is not only sensuous, dense, and lyrical, but also very supple in all thematic needs, so that it can be constricted to amusing funambolisms of transcription when necessary, or at other times, unpredictably ridden with scholarship. But Dowell's beautiful language is also functional because it reveals itself as a crucial means, essential to soften the disturbance of his central themes: eroticism and its powerful relation to human existence; intimacy between victimizer and victim, or the peculiar complicity between disgust and desire; sexual ambivalence and the isolation of the "fragmented man"; the evaluation of the darker side of Eros, at times envisioned as in the celebrated formula by Georges Bataille: eroticism "as an affirmation of life reaching into death."

Dowell often presents extreme situations, shifting toward the end of the social spectrum, sometimes to the verge of virulence or obsession. These situations, however, are never vulgar or outrageous; rather, their obscenity is proposed as a basic component of our psyche. Their crudity is thus filtered through feelings of compassion, through tonal devices of mystery or ambiguous irony, or through refined technicalities, such as a calculated reticence or understatement.

Undoubtedly, these textual strategies are connected with Coleman Dowell's cult of lifestyle, with his innate elegance, with his irreducible attachment to a supreme discipline of civilities. In brief, they would stem from his Southern culture and upbringing. (It is no mere chance that in his *Island People* a character says: "In my South the only things it is alright to display are manners.") Born in Adairville, Kentucky, on May 29, 1925, Coleman Dowell reports to have spent an intellectually exciting life there. One of six children, Dowell was the son of Morda Wilson, a farmer and a collector of folk songs (Dowell acknowledges an influence from folk music in his works), and of Beulah Dowell. He left Kentucky in 1950 and moved to New York, where he has lived ever since.

Also a composer-lyricist and a playwright, Dowell worked for TV and theater before dedicating himself to fiction writing. (His many plays include: *Gentle Laurel*, 1957; *The Indian Giver*, 1959; *The Tattooed Countess*, 1961; and *Eve of the Green Grass*, 1963.) A rich series of his rather surrealistic short stories appeared in various anthologies, including those of New Directions, the publishing house that has also issued three of his five novels: *Mrs. October Was Here* (1974), *Island People* (1976), and *Too Much Flesh and Jabez* (1977).

Although his first novel, *One of the Children Is Crying* (1968), is generally considered as standing apart from the others because of its rather realistic, conventional plot, it is linked to his other work by being placed in a Southern setting which works as a veritable resonance chamber for human feelings and passions. In his first novel, a family gathering back home after the father's death is an occasion to the members for painful psychological revelations about homosexuality, incest, and parental abuse. In *Too Much Flesh,* it is the beautiful and gentle Jabez who acts as a catalyst in the process. A gay intellectual, Jabez fulfills the expectations of a trio of characters: a sexually overgifted male, his delicate, poetry-loving wife, and the husband's former schoolteacher, who, we eventually discover, by inventing Jabez in this fiction is also able to invent a sexual intercourse with her longed-for pupil. This well-crafted innovative structure, with its framing of the story within the story, is employed basically as a means of psychological unveiling of the characters and not as a sterile metafictional play per se.

In his experimental masterpiece *Island People*, this kind of formal economy reaches its highest achievement. Here interrelation and juxtaposition of stories of different characters are gradually revealed to be the masked embodiments of a single persona's split personality. The acrobatic interplay of these selves and mysterious transfigurations (male/female), and the alteration of the multiple points of view and voices is stunning. But again in this complex mosaic, Dowell pulls the narrative strings perfectly in sealing up his resolution.

This rigorous formal control is equally evident in the complex *Mrs. October Was Here*, a cryptic and radical satire on the American bourgeoisie and creativity, as well as in the more linear *White on Black on White* (1983), his latest novel, which may be assumed to represent a compendium of Dowell's work to date. This layered story, which focuses on interracialism in America, points out the universality of Dowell's moral landscape. It is that common territory in which our individual topography may find familiar landmarks, the reverberations of its own fires. To emphasize how sex, violence, and suffering may constitute those common territories and to discover the cathartic function of eroticism as a longing for death, Dowell penetrates the heart of Harlem and of black America in much the same way that Georges Bataille did, when he penetrated the almost inaccessible pit of the Lascaux cave, where the upsetting unity of death and eroticism in the prehistoric graffiti let him discover *la naissance de l'art*.

Selected Bibliography

Primary Sources

One of the Children Is Crying. New York: Random House, 1968. (British ed.: *The Grass Dies*. London: Cassell, 1968.)
Mrs. October Was Here. New York: New Directions, 1974.
Island People. New York: New Directions, 1976.
Too Much Flesh and Jabez. New York: New Directions, 1977.
White on Black on White. Woodstock, Vt.: Countryman Press, 1983.
The Silver Swanne. New York: Grenfell Press, 1983.

Secondary Sources

Martin, Stephen-Paul. "White on Black on White." *The Review of Contemporary Fiction* 4, 1 (1984): 162–67.
O'Brien, John, ed. *The Review of Contemporary Fiction* 2, 3 (1982). Special issue on Dowell.

MARIA VITTORIA D'AMICO

E

EASTLAKE, WILLIAM (1917–   )

Of the numerous authors writing today of the ills wearing away at contemporary society, few do so with the imagination, humor, and understanding of William Eastlake. Although Eastlake has displayed his literary gifts in novels dealing with World War II, Vietnam, and the American Revolution, his most successful and entertaining treatments of society are set in the American West. It is here that Eastlake's range of thought, imagination, and mysticism blend to form his most significant literary statements. In his Western novels he has erected a wacky and absurd civilized world contrasted by Indian Country, an ideal landscape peopled by sophisticated and enlightened Indians. With these oppositions, Eastlake has been able both to debunk the myth of the West and to identify the evils that the civilized world perpetuates.

Eastlake was born on July 14, 1917, in Brooklyn. At an early age he was sent to the Bonnie Brae Boarding school in New Jersey, which he attended through high school under the discipline of his Episcopalian masters. Eastlake himself has said that this background is the source of his fondest childhood memories as well as the inspiration for "Little Joe," his first short story to be published in an American magazine. Eastlake left Bonnie Brae at the height of the Depression and, with no clear career goals, chose the life of the hobo. This marked the beginning of his literary apprenticeship. Working his way West, he earned a living by an assortment of pick-up jobs until finally he found himself employed as a clerk in Stanley Rose's bookshop in Los Angeles. Experiences at this shop, which happened to be a gathering place for artists and writers such as Theodore Dreiser, Nathanael West, and William Saroyan, had a catalytic impact on Eastlake and his career: from that point Eastlake's energies were directed toward writing. While at the bookshop Eastlake also met Martha Simpson, whom he married; her brother would later lead him to New Mexico and Indian Country.

During World War II, Eastlake joined the Army and was wounded in the battle of the Bulge. Twenty years later, this episode would become the basis for his surrealist World War II novel, *Castle Keep* (1965). After the war, Eastlake unsuccessfully attempted to start a European literary magazine and after similar failures eventually returned to Los Angeles. There, in the early 1950s, Eastlake and Martha earned their living by selling houses which Martha designed. In the summers they would visit Martha's brother who lived on a ranch in the Jemez Mountains of New Mexico, a land to which they were drawn both physically and spiritually and to which they eventually moved in 1955. This land became the foundation for Eastlake's finest novels—*Go in Beauty* (1956), *The Bronc People* (1958), *Portrait of an Artist with Twenty-six Horses* (1963), and *Dancers in the Scalp House* (1975). During the 1960s and the Vietnam War, Eastlake served as a correspondent for *Nation*, journalistic experience that provided material for two later works about this era—a novel, *The Bamboo Bed* (1969), and a collection of poems and essays, *A Child's Garden of Verses for the Revolution* (1970). Eastlake is now living in Bisbe, Arizona, and is at work on a new novel about the Southwest.

Eastlake's works may be divided by subject into two groups, the war novels and his Southwestern series. Despite this division, certain characteristics are common to all of his stories. These trademarks include a style that is sometimes compared to that of Hemingway, the use of absurdity and black humor, frequent structural reliance on oppositions, and a strong undercurrent of didacticism. Above all, Eastlake is a storyteller. He began his career by writing short stories, and it is this form that seems to come most naturally to him. Both *Portrait of an Artist with Twenty-six Horses* and *Castle Keep* are built around an accumulation of self-contained episodes, and some of the most interesting moments in his other works occur in anecdotal digressions.

Castle Keep is the first of Eastlake's novels to deal with war. It is a kind of fantasy, each chapter describing the events that occur in a castle in France from the point of view of different characters. The next two war novels, *Bamboo Bed* and *The Long Naked Descent into Boston* (1977), a parody of the American Revolution written as an ironic accompaniment to America's bicentennial celebration, demonstrate Eastlake's artistic evolution. They show an increasing reliance on surrealism and reveal more extensive use of absurdity and black, bitter humor to criticize contemporary society.

Eastlake's artistic refinement and his tendency to criticize the modern world similarly evolve in his Southwestern works. Of particular note are his manipulation of more traditional literary themes, such as the initiation story, the journey, and the stereotypes of the American West. *Go in Beauty* is concerned with the growth and decline of an artist. Set in the Checkerboard area of New Mexico, a land of rugged and sublime natural beauty that forms the backdrop dominating all of the Southwestern novels, the story is about two brothers and the conflicts that separate them. The brothers have allowed the world of the artificial to interfere with their natural ability to communicate both artistically and personally, introducing a pattern of opposition found throughout the remaining Southwestern novels. In *The Bronc People,* one again sees the use of characters entangled with the opposing realms and their struggle as they journey toward identity. Likewise, *Portrait of an Artist* tells of an individual's attempt to sort out meaning amidst the forces of the artificial and the natural. Finally, *Dancers in the Scalp House,* while dominated by the absurdity and black humor characteristic of Eastlake's later works, also depends on this opposition as it describes civilization's attempts to build a dam in Indian Country.

In these works Eastlake gives the reader one of his most memorable inventions, his Indians. These Indians completely shatter the stereotypical image of the Indian created by traditional Westerns. Eastlake's Indian possesses the wisdom of nature, sufficient wit to triumph verbally over non-Indians, and a sense of humor that usually allows him to cope with the moral outrages imposed on him by the civilized, white world.

In all of Eastlake's works a fundamental sense of moral responsibility emerges. This responsibility is most successfully expressed in his Southwestern novels where he has drawn from standard motifs in American literature—the pastoral theme and the journey—to create an Indian Country that represents the ideal, a considerably less than perfect civilized world, and characters who must decide which world they wish to join. In the end, after the imaginative digressions and the clash of opposing realms, Eastlake assigns true value to only one world, that of the natural which for him is the repository for all that is of spiritual and moral worth.

Selected Bibliography

Primary Sources

Go in Beauty. New York: Harper, 1956.
The Bronc People. New York: Harcourt, Brace, 1958.
Portrait of an Artist with Twenty-six Horses. New York: Simon & Schuster, 1963.
Castle Keep. New York: Simon & Schuster, 1965.
The Bamboo Bed. New York: Simon & Schuster, 1969.
A Child's Garden of Verses for the Revolution. New York: Grove Press, 1970.
Dancers in the Scalp House. New York: Viking Press, 1975.
The Long Naked Descent into Boston. New York: Viking Press, 1977.
Jack Armstrong in Tangiers and Other Escapes. Flint, Mich.: Bamberger Books, 1984.

Secondary Sources

Graham, Don. "William Eastlake's First Novel: An Account of the Making of *Go in Beauty.*" *Western American Literature* 16 (Spring 1981): 27–37.

Haslam, Gerald. "William Eastlake: Portrait of the Artist as Shaman." *Western Review* 8 (1971): 2–12.

McCaffery, Larry. "Absurdity and Oppositions in William Eastlake's Southwestern Novels." *Critique* 29 (1977): 62–76.

————, and Sinda Gregory. "An Interview with William Eastlake." *South Shore: An International Review of the Arts* 1, No. 2 (1978): 41–65.

The Review of Contemporary Fiction 3 (Spring 1983). Special Issue on Eastlake.

Wylder, Delbert E. "The Novels of William Eastlake." *New Mexico Quarterly* 34 (Summer 1964): 188–203.

BARBARA BARNES

ELKIN, STANLEY (1930–   )

Stanley Elkin's literary career delineates, more clearly than anything else, one writer's love-hate relationship with the ordinary. With one terrible exception, his life appears to have been ordinary enough: born in New York in 1930 and raised in Chicago, Elkin received his B.A. from the University of Illinois, served in the Army during the mid–1950s, and returned to Urbana, where he earned an M.A. and (after a year "spent in bed, reading") a Ph.D. in English in 1961. He had by then accepted a faculty appointment at Washington University in St. Louis, where he has lived with his wife and three children ever since and where he is currently Merle King Professor of Modern Letters. If his life seems ordinary, however, his fiction, from the very beginning, has betrayed a marked ambivalence toward what it projects as ordinary life.

In the title piece of Elkin's first story collection, *Criers & Kibitzers, Kibitzers & Criers* (1965), Jake Greenspahn's son has died, and the grocer finds the indifferent survival of the ordinary world with its mercantile concerns and trivial preoccupations an unforgivable insult, an obscenity. Bertie, the garrulous beatnik protagonist of "The Guest," briefly inhabits the middle-class digs of a vacationing couple of his acquaintance, hilariously reducing the place to a shambles as his not completely intentional critique of the life quotidian. James Boswell, the protagonist of Elkin's first novel, *Boswell* (1964), imitates his namesake's means of raising himself above the ordinary by attaching himself to the famous, only to discover that that route necessarily culminates not in the exultation of the self but in its betrayal. Still more emphatic is Elkin's treatment of this theme in *A Bad Man* (1967), the novel clearly identifying the ordinary with a prison warden whose self-professed values of order, conformity, and accommodation are opposed by the willfulness, irascibility, and contentiousness of the novel's protagonist, Leo Feldman. The ordinary, Feldman sees, is the cell in which the world would imprison his impulses, the leverage it applies to impose guilt and exact a compensatory sublimation of his needs. He comes to recognize the conflict between himself and the warden as a cultural clash between Jewish and WASP perceptions of reality. The relative ease with which Elkin was able to relegate the ordinary to the status of simple antagonist in *A Bad Man* reflects the extent to which the novel was written under the influence of Saul Bellow and the American-Jewish novel tradition, in which the comic identification of Jews with an un-WASPish spontaneity, impropriety, and dedication to extreme positions and behavior was not untypical. Although the accumulation of ideas and associations around the central Jew/WASP antinomy in *A Bad Man* distinctly anticipated Elkin's subsequently realized mastery of the art of elaborating metaphor and of creating palimpsests of intricately related images, the novel's effectiveness was nonetheless compromised by the diagrammatic nature of its central conflict.

The Dick Gibson Show (1971) and *The Franchiser* (1976) reflect a markedly more ambivalent perception of the ordinary; Elkin's shift in attitude, however, arguably has both artistic and biographical sources. In the mid–1960s, Elkin learned that he had multiple sclerosis, a disease which, as he defined it, "kills you by inches, but you suffer by yards"; in 1968 he suffered a nearly fatal heart attack. These afflictions apparently had two effects on Elkin: first, they confirmed him in certain aesthetic prejudices; thus, the reservations he felt about a novel he had been reading prior to the heart attack multiplied in its aftermath, the book's casual satire seeming that much more insubstantial to this self-proclaimed "dying man of changed tastes and raised expectations". Second, they simultaneously increased his regard for the ordinary. Accordingly, the most moving scene in *The Franchiser* dramatizes an exultant reconciliation with the routine and the daily, Ben Flesh, the novel's multiple sclerotic protagonist, ecstatically living out the remission of his illness as a restoration of his ability to tactilely experience the fabrics and textures of the ordinary world to which his askew nervous system had deadened him. Neither Dick Gibson nor Flesh identifies himself with the American ordinary for its own sake; each of them has his own self-seeking (or even self-fleeing) reasons for casting his lot with the winsome sounds and facades of commercial America. But Dick Gibson's desire to become the broadcast voice of the American ordinary, the very intonation of reassurance and optimism, and Flesh's efforts at "costuming his country," dotting its landscape with indistinguishable franchises so that he might become "the man who made America look like America," are not merely ludicrously quixotic enterprises. Elkin treats his protagonists' attempts to patch the rents in the national consciousness with talk shows and HoJos with a bemused and palpable sympathy. Why? Because one side of Elkin is delighted by that enchantedly comic realm of commercial America with all its "mansard roofs and golden arches and false belfries, all its ubiquitous, familiar neon signatures and logos, all its *things,* all its *crap,* the true American graffiti, the perfect queer calligraphy of American signature, what gave it meaning and made it fun." And, because the alternative is insupportably grim: as Flesh laments in an un-franchiserian funk, " 'Nothing happens but disease. Nothing.' " The thematic tension sustained throughout these two novels between the ordinary and the extraordinary, between normalcy and extremity, is arguably their most fully achieved literary effect. The resultant mood of these books recalls that of Emerson's "Experience," with its acknowledgment that "We live amid surfaces, and the true art of life is to skate well on them." It is frequently the Elkin protagonist's fate to plunge haplessly through that ice and sometimes his luck to find a kind of redemption in the pratfall.

The ordinary is more negatively depicted in the novellas of *Searches & Seizures* (1973) and *The Living End* (1979), both of which contain protagonists reminiscent of Leo Feldman and Push the Bully, the central figure of the early story, "A Poetics for Bullies." Push (whom Elkin has designated a sort of ur-protagonist in his fiction) could be speaking for Feldman or for Alexander Main of "The Bailbondsman" in his prideful declaration that he is an "incarnation of envy and jealousy and need," in his insistence on the efficacy of "the cabala of my hate, of my irreconcilableness." Although Main is older, more weary, and less confident than Push, he nonetheless similarly affirms the cutting, biting edge of the individual's passion and life, that ferocious, unaccommodating desire that refuses to let him submit to the domestication of the real, to the reduction of its opportunities for resistance, opposition, and tension. This idea not only represents a pervading ethic of Elkin's fiction, but also provides its actuating aesthetic, the elaborately rhetorical style which is his trademark, enacting what he has termed "the aggression of syntax and metaphor," the literary bully's means of bearing down on the world. That style—an eruption of puns, violent yokings of disparate idioms, solecisms, apostrophes, metaphors, crazily portmanteau'd verbs, similes (*especially* similes), harangues, catalogues, plays on familiar slogans and song lyrics—plunges ahead in a breathless rush calculated above all to keep the energy level up and the linguistic possibilities open. Such is the language with which the uplifted find themselves invested in the Heaven of *The Living End,* but at least one of them is finally satisfied to take his heightened rhetorical capacity to Hell, where he can use it not to serve the almighty conventional wisdom, but to resist it and the God who is its source. Such, too, is the language of *George Mills* (1982), Elkin's most ambitious attempt to re-create the universe in his own idiom.

Spanning ten centuries and four different generations of Millses, this densely poetic novel is held together by Elkin's style (which evokes Faulknerian cadences more insistently than any but the earliest of Elkin's work, without seeming in the least derivative of the writer on whom Elkin wrote his Ph.D. thesis) and by the unchangingness of the Millses' second-fiddle fate, their compulsively repeated failure to rise above blue-collar meniality.

It is the Millses' lot forever to inhabit the stagnant, undynamic ordinary, and it is obvious that Elkin identifies with this composite character whose life is stuck in neutral, who believes himself so secure against change or consequence that he declares that he's "saved, in a state of grace." Elkin has confessed to feeling similarly about his own condition, and his *Esquire* essay on living in University City, Missouri (where he is professor of English at Washington University) reflects the same basically conciliatory attitude toward the place and toward the life he lives there: "I live where I live . . . because I feel no need." None, save for that of producing aggressively poetic, defiantly rhetorical, endlessly imaginative, and relentlessly energetic works of fiction which are Stanley Elkin's best response to the ordinary.

Selected Bibliography

Primary Sources

Boswell. New York: Random House, 1964.
Criers & Kibitzers, Kibitzers & Criers. New York: Random House, 1965.
A Bad Man. New York: Random House, 1967.
The Dick Gibson Show. New York: Random House, 1971.
Searches & Seizures. New York: Random House, 1973.
The Franchiser. New York: Farrar, Straus & Giroux, 1976.
The Living End. New York: E. P. Dutton, 1979.
Stanley Elkin's Greatest Hits. New York: E. P. Dutton, 1980.
George Mills. New York: E. P. Dutton, 1982.

Secondary Sources

Bailey, Peter. *Reading Stanley Elkin*. Urbana: University of Illinois Press, 1985.
Chenetier, Marc, ed. *Homage to Stanley Elkin: A Collection of Essays. Delta: A Journal of American Literature*, Spring 1984.
Clayton, Jay. "An Interview with Stanley Elkin." *Contemporary Literature* 24 (Spring 1983): 1–12.
Duncan, Jeffrey L. "A Conversation with Stanley Elkin and William H. Gass." *The Iowa Review* 7, no. 1 (Winter 1976): 48–76.
Gass, William H. "Foreword" to *The Franchiser*. Boston: Nonpareil Books, 1980, pp. vii–xv.
LeClair, Thomas. "An Interview with Stanley Elkin." *Anything Can Happen: Interviews with Contemporary American Novelists*. Urbana: University of Illinois Press, 1983, pp. 106–25.
McCaffery, Larry. "Stanley Elkin: A Bibliography, 1957–1977." *Bulletin of Bibliography* 34, no. 2 (1978): 73–76.
———. "Stanley Elkin's Recovery of the Ordinary." *Critique* 21, no. 2 (1979): 39–51.
Olderman, Raymond. "The Six Crises of Dick Gibson." *The Iowa Review* 7, no. 1 (Winter 1976): 127–39.

Wilde, Alan. " 'Strange Displacements of the Ordinary': Apple, Elkin, Barthelme
    and the Problem of the Excluded Middle." *boundary 2,* no. 9 (Fall 1981):
    177–98.

PETER J. BAILEY

EXLEY, FREDERICK (1929–   )

It is difficult to separate with any confidence Frederick Exley's life from
his work. The wonderful opening scene in *A Fan's Notes* (1968) takes place
in the New Parrot Restaurant, just outside Watertown, New York. The
central character, also named Fred Exley, seemingly suffers a heart attack
when the bartender refuses to believe that the young boys in the photograph
he has been shown are in fact Exley's children. So far as I can tell, the
bartender is correct: author Exley has imagined for character Exley a family
situation different from his own. *A Fan's Notes* bears the subtitle "a fictional
memoir," and an introductory note to the reader asks that he be judged
as a "writer of fantasy," even though the pattern of events depicted resembles Exley's life.

The facts about Exley's life seem to be the following: born in 1929, he
was raised in Watertown. Like the Exley in *A Fan's Notes,* he briefly
attended Hobart College in upstate New York and subsequently graduated
from the University of Southern California in 1953, the same year as Frank
Gifford. He has been married and divorced twice, and he has a daughter
by each marriage. He won a measure of the fame the character Exley
covets with the publication of *A Fan's Notes.* It was nominated for a
National Book Award, and it received both the William Faulkner Award
for a first novel and the National Institute of Arts and Letters' Rosenthal
Award. *Pages from a Cold Island* (1975), the second volume in his projected
autobiographical trilogy, was not as well received; but he has recently won
a Guggenheim Fellowship to work on the final volume. Portions of *Last
Notes from Home* have appeared in *Rolling Stone,* where for several years
Exley served in an editorial capacity.

A Fan's Notes suggests that Exley developed a virtually unappeasable
appetite for fame as a young boy eager for a share of his father's attention.
He eventually determined to achieve his ends through writing rather than,
like his father, athletics, but initially he had little appreciation of the pain
and anguish such ambitions would cost himself and others. For a long time
it appeared that his only fame would be as his father's son, or as the New
York Giants' most fanatical follower. Both *A Fan's Notes* and *Pages from
a Cold Island* demonstrate Exley's frustration and anger at a culture seemingly unwilling and unable to give him a proper hearing. What finally saves
his writing from falling into mere self-pity, however, is the emotional distance Exley achieves between himself as a character and as the writer. He

can be as unsparing of his own callow ambitions and behavior as he is of those exemplified by American culture at large.

Exley freely introduces public figures (the Frank Gifford of *A Fan's Notes*, Gloria Steinem, Norman Mailer, and Edmund Wilson of *Pages from a Cold Island*) into the otherwise fabricated accounts of his life. They are invariably individuals who have achieved the visibility Exley would like for himself, and their presence in his novels testifies to both the steadiness of his ambitions and the continuing need to fulfill them via reflection from others—he is still his father's son. Exley is at his best when retailing his own and others' shortcomings, but is not so good when expressing admiration. One of the very few false notes in his remarkable first novel, for instance, concerns his renewed admiration for Hawthorne (" . . . and since so many better qualified to judge him than I esteemed him a writer of the very highest order . . . "). His respect for Edmund Wilson keeps *Pages from a Cold Island* from acquiring the power of the earlier book. It obviously costs something in terms of time and psychic energy for Exley to sustain the angle of vision that makes his work so uniquely rewarding. The sections of the final volume of his autobiographical trilogy published in *Rolling Stone* are promising, and it is to be hoped that he manages to bring *Last Notes from Home* to completion in the near future. I, at least, await it eagerly.

Selected Bibliography

(*Exley's papers are in the collection of the University of Rochester.*)

Primary Sources

A Fan's Notes. New York: Harper & Row, 1968.
Pages from a Cold Island. New York: Random House, 1975.
"Last Notes from Home," *Rolling Stone*, June 30, 1977, pp. 79–84.
"James Seamus Finbarr O'Twoomey," *Rolling Stone*, October 5, 1977, pp. 58–61, 63–64, 67–68.
"Ms Robin Glenn," *Rolling Stone*, February 22, 1979, pp. 44–49, 93.

Secondary Sources

Bailey, Peter. "Notes on the Novel-as-Autobiography." *Genre* 14, no. 1 (1981): 79–92.
Chabot, C. Barry. "The Alternative Vision of Frederick Exley's *A Fan's Notes*," *Critique* 19, no. 1 (1977): 87–100.
Johnson, Donald R. "The Hero in Sports Literature and Exley's *A Fan's Notes*." *Southern Humanities Review* 13 (1979): 233–44.
Sterling, Phillip. "Frederick Exley's *A Fan's Notes:* Football as Metaphor," *Critique* 22, no. 1 (1980): 39–46.

C. BARRY CHABOT

F

FEDERMAN, RAYMOND (1928–   )

As a writer of both fiction and criticism, Raymond Federman has been one of the most important voices in contemporary American fiction. His work has consistently challenged conventional attitudes toward plot, character, and narration; yet, while he is often viewed as an experimental writer, he is also one of the best storytellers writing today. An exuberant writer, he plays with language and narrative conventions to expose the illusions of our fictions, at the same time revelling in those illusions. In his varied and complex way, his work has circled back to a central theme: what it means to survive and write in a post-Holocaust world. In addressing this as a central problem, he also confronts the relationship between fiction and autobiography, storytelling and the story, calling into question these very differences.

Raymond Federman was born in Paris, France, on May 15, 1928, the son of Simon (a painter) and Marguerite. When the Germans came to take his parents and two sisters away in July of 1942, his mother hid him in a closet; his family died in concentration camps. From 1942 to 1945, he worked on a farm in southern France, returning to Paris just after the liberation. Federman came to the United States in 1947, living first in Detroit where he attended high school, worked at the Chrysler plant, and started playing jazz saxophone. Later (1950) he moved to New York, where he held a series of jobs—in a cafeteria as a dishwasher and in a lampshade factory. Inducted into the U.S. Army in 1951, he served in the 82nd Airborne Division in both Japan and Korea. Federman's writing draws extensively from this period of his life, though the reader should be careful not to confuse life and art; as Federman is fond of saying (citing Céline), "I suppose a man's biography is always something one invents afterwards, after the facts."

Federman began to be interested in writing when he enrolled at Columbia University, where he received his B.A. in 1957. There he began studying literature and writing seriously for the first time. From this time until 1966, when he began work on his first novel, Federman actually thought of himself as a poet, eventually publishing a collection of poems, *Among the Beasts/Parmi les monstres* (1967). But his first major publication would be a work of criticism, *Journey to Chaos: Samuel Beckett's Early Fiction* (1965), a work that grew out of his graduate studies at the University of California, Los Angeles, where he received his Ph.D. in French in 1963. This is the first of an extended corpus of writings on Beckett. *Journey to Chaos* represents more than Federman's almost filial interest in Beckett; it also provides an index of Federman's own aesthetic concerns. His thesis—that Beckett's work progressively disintegrates realist conventions of language, form, character, and social reality—could be seen as the seed for the later flowering of *Surfiction: Fiction Now and Tomorrow* (1975, 1981), a collection of essays edited and introduced by Federman defining the broad areas of experimentation mapped by current and future fiction.

Federman's first published novel, *Double or Nothing* (1971), winner of the Frances Steloff Fiction Prize and the Panache Experimental Fiction Prize, inaugurates many of Federman's enduring concerns. A novel about the process of writing a novel, it is also about the process of finding and defining our own experience. Its narrative play, matched by typographical experimentation, is generated by the interplay among the four voices that frame the novel: a narrator-recorder who is transcribing the story of a novelist-inventor who invents the story of a protagonist, all finally overlaid by the author's own voice. That voice is also plural, speaking in at least two languages: Federman's next novels, *Amer Eldorado* (1974) and *Take It or Leave It* (1976), grow out of his bilingual, bicultural experience. He began the two novels, one in French and one in English, simultaneously, working on them on alternate days; eventually, he set aside the English and worked on the French novel exclusively, returning later to finish the English. Like *Double or Nothing,* these two novels foreground the problems of telling a story; working with a somewhat autobiographical quest motif, both novels promise to show the protagonist on a journey across America to discover self. The journey is forever delayed in a Don Quixote-like series of adventures, the exaggerated second-hand tales Federman is master of. In the process of inventing and reinventing his life, he must also renew the language he uses. In the spirit of play, he frequently borrows phrases from other writers and from his own previous work, elaborating and exaggerating until he makes that language his own.

Whereas *Take It or Leave It* takes Federman's poetics in the direction of exaggeration—on the model of jazz improvisation—his next novel, *The Voice in the Closet/La Voix dans le cabinet de debarras* (1979) moves toward condensation. The very material form of the book, with its textual parts arranged in symmetrical blocks of writing, is a sign of the book's subject, a literal *emboitement* of the voice in the closet of language. Here Federman attempts to confront more directly the central act around which his previous novels have circled: the extermination of his family. And he does so in two languages and multiple voices—adding to his own the voice of Maurice Roche, whose text *Echos* occupies the center of this book.

Coming after this highly condensed work, Federman's most recent work, *The Twofold Vibration* (1982), strikes a balance between the exuberance of the early work and the extreme control of *The Voice*. Its subject—the "central unspeakable event" of the twentieth century—is the Holocaust; in it, Federman investigates specifically the "insult of survival," as he continues his aesthetic struggle with the truth and lie of fiction. As if to underscore the provisional status of our quest for self-definition, Federman begins here, as in previous novels, in the conditional tense, a tense that speaks to the provisional tense of the writer as Jew, as survivor. He has just finished a new novel, *Smiles on Washington Square* (1985).

Since 1964, Federman has been a professor at State University of New York at Buffalo. He travels frequently to France and recently spent time in Israel. Federman's work, in both fiction and criticism, has consistently struggled with the paradoxes of postmodern aesthetics, with the boundaries between life and art. In questioning those boundaries, he shows us both the pleasure of play—of humor and storytelling—and the very serious purpose of art as a frame for understanding our selves and our history.

Selected Bibliography

Primary Sources

Journey to Chaos: Samuel Beckett's Early Fiction. Berkeley: University of California Press, 1965.
Among the Beasts/Parmi les monstres. Paris: Editions Millas-Martin, 1967.
Double or Nothing. Chicago: Swallow Press, 1971.
Amer Eldorado. Paris: Editions Stock, 1974.
Surfiction: Fiction Now and Tomorrow. Chicago: Swallow Press, 1975; revised edition, 1981.
Take It or Leave It. New York: Fiction Collective, 1976.
The Voice in the Closet/La Voix dans le cabinet de debarras. Madison, Wis.: Coda, 1979.
The Twofold Vibration. Bloomington: Indiana University Press, 1982.
Smiles on Washington Square. New York: Thunder's Mouth Press, 1985.

Secondary Sources

Caramello, Charles. "Flushing Out 'The Voice in the Closet.' " *Sub-Stance* 20 (1978): 101–13.
Chamberlain, Lori. "Raymond Federman's *The Twofold Vibration*." *Chicago Review* 34, no. 1 (1983): 117–23.
Klinkowitz, Jerome. *Literary Disruptions: The Making of a Post-Contemporary American Fiction*. Urbana: University of Illinois Press, 1980, pp. 119–53.

Kutnik, Jerzy. *The Novel As Performance: Ronald Sukenick and Raymond Federman*. Carbondale: Southern Illinois University Press, 1985.

McCaffery, Larry. "An Interview with Raymond Federman." *Anything Can Happen: Interviews with Contemporary American Novelists*. Urbana: University of Illinois Press, 1983.

————. "An Interview with Raymond Federman." *Contemporary Literature* 24 (1983): 285–306.

LORI CHAMBERLAIN

FISH, STANLEY (1938–   )

"In April 1489 Henry Percy, fourth earl of Northumberland, was slain near Thirsk as he attempted to reconcile an insurgent mob to an unpopular tax." With this fact Stanley Fish opened his first book, *John Skelton's Poetry* (1965). His own career since then has been composed of ever more vigorous attempts to reconcile an unruly profession to his own unpopular text and, by doing so, to reconcile it to itself as well. The Skelton book finds the "keystone" of its subject's poetic universe to lie in the intimate connection of temporal and eternal hierarchies in which "a challenge to one is a challenge to the other." The result of such intimate connection, which Fish claims as the novelty of his reading, is the recognition of a Skelton poem as "the psychological (spiritual) history of its protagonist." It is not unfair to say that the progress of Fish's work, from the Skelton book to *Is There a Text in This Class?* (1980), has been from reading such histories to writing them—his own at least. At every step along this way Fish has been concerned with the dual interplay of text and community and of the temporal and atemporal.

Stanley Eugene Fish was born on April 19, 1938, in Providence, Rhode Island. After graduating from the University of Pennsylvania in 1959, he went on to Yale University for the M.A. (1960) and Ph.D. (1962). His doctoral dissertation was subsequently revised to become *John Skelton's Poetry*. He began his teaching career in 1962 at the University of California, Berkeley, and stayed there until 1974 when he became Kenan Professor of English at Johns Hopkins University.

In 1967 Fish brought out his second book, *Surprised by Sin: The Reader in Paradise Lost*. The title is a succinct abbreviation of the book's argument: Fish's reading of Milton's poem is a reading of its effect—an effect of repeated entrapment and surprising in sin—upon its reader. As such, its critical assumptions are a direct attack on one of the central tenets of American New Criticism. As Fish put it for the paperback edition:

It is obvious that in saying this, I am courting the "affective fallacy." Indeed I am embracing it and going beyond it. The fear expressed by Wimsatt and Beardsley—that by focussing on the "psychological effects" of a work, there is a danger "that

the poem itself as an object of specifically critical judgment tends to disappear"—
exactly defines my intention. That is, making the work disappear into the reader's
experience of it is precisely what should happen in our criticism, because it is what
happens when we read.

The stance thus taken toward Milton as a Christian poet with particular
designs on his audience becomes ever more general in the works that follow.
*Self-Consuming Artifacts: The Experience of Seventeenth-Century Litera-
ture* (1972) offers (behind its cover illustration of Tinguely's 1960 *Homage
to New York*) treatments of Francis Bacon, George Herbert (also the object
of Fish's 1978 study *The Living Temple: George Herbert and Catechizing*),
John Bunyan, Richard Hooker, Richard Burton, and Sir Thomas Browne,
as well as shorter considerations of Plato, Augustine, and John Donne. *Is
There a Text in This Class? The Authority of Interpretive Communities*
offers a general theory of literary criticism and interpretation. It may be
that by the close of *Is There a Text . . . ?* Fish has succeeded in fulfilling
the intention defined in *Surprised By Sin*. The movement away from New
Critical formalisms proved considerably more difficult in the event than in
the proclamation, and the essays gathered together in *Is There a Text . . . ?*,
along with the retrospective commentary Fish offers on them, detail the
stages of his passage from the "reader-response" manifesto of "Literature
in the Reader: Affective Stylistics" to a suite of concluding essays in which
it becomes clear that for Fish making the work disappear into the reader's
experience of it entails making the reader disappear as well—the two vanish
together into the radical and constitutive priority of professional, institutional practice over both. His distance from New Critical scruples about
what is intrinsic or extrinsic to a text and from the whole array of loosely
liberal and formalist worries about imposing on the work is clearly evident
in his assertion that "the practice of literary criticism is not something one
must apologize for; it is absolutely essential not only to the maintenance
of, but to the very production of, the objects of its attention." This implies
the further conclusions that "off-the-wallness is not inimical to the system
but essential to it and its operation," drawing Fish close to a range of
theories developed in the plastic arts in the wake of Duchamp and his
Ready-mades (George Dickie, Arthur Danto). Recently, Walter Benn
Michaels and Steven Knapp, both of Berkeley, have given this argument
a further, "conceptualist" twist, arguing that it follows from Fish's theory
that theory should end.

The resulting small uproar is, in Fish's view, empty; there is no room
for real outrage within the institution of literature—until there is, and then
that outrage is internal to the institution, structured and perhaps even
demanded by it. People don't get slain reconciling other people to unpopular texts; our tempests are invariably shaped to our teapots. It is an odd
and ironic consequence of Fish's most recent views that what began as an

attempt to return us, readers and critics, to our experience may now look to deprive us of it—peculiarly, by confining us within it. This can seem a solution to the problem of joining temporal experience and atemporal sense which so exercised the writers Fish began by reading, or it can seem the most radical sundering of the two terms yet. Whichever way we take it, it seems to represent a weakening of the dialectical tension and energy that drives the best of Fish's reading and writing.

Since the publication of *Is There a Text in This Class?*, this tension has been most visible in a series of polemics Fish has engaged in with, among others, Wayne Booth, Ronald Dworkin, and Wolfgang Iser. In these debates as well as in his ongoing efforts to unfold the inner structure and constraints of the institution of literature, Stanley Fish continues to show himself as one of the most forceful, pointed, and combative enthusiasts of criticism, in all its forms, on the current scene.

Selected Bibliography

Primary Sources

John Skelton's Poetry. New Haven, Conn.: Yale University Press, 1965.
Surprised by Sin: The Reader in Paradise Lost. Berkeley: University of California Press, 1967.
Seventeenth Century Prose: Modern Essays in Criticism. New York: Oxford University Press, 1971.
Self-Consuming Artifacts: The Experience of Seventeenth-Century Literature. Berkeley: University of California Press, 1972.
The Living Temple: George Herbert and Catechizing. Berkeley: University of California Press, 1978.
Is There a Text in This Class? The Authority of Interpretative Communities. Cambridge, Mass.: Harvard University Press, 1980.

Secondary Sources

Iser, Wolfgang. "Talking Like Whales: A Reply to Stanley Fish." *Diacritics* 11, no. 3 (Fall 1981): 82–87.
Knapp, Steven, and Walter Benn Michaels. "Against Theory." *Critical Inquiry* 8, no. 4 (Summer 1982): 723–42.

STEPHEN MELVILLE

FOUCAULT, MICHEL (1926–1984)

Michel Foucault called himself an historian of systems of thought. Through the detailed analysis of a multitude of documents—police reports, novels, hospital records, confessions, technical journals, works of art, and philosophy—whose interrelationships he often evoked by means of an intentionally excessive and paradoxical rhetoric, Foucault sought to reveal how intellectual systems, materialized in disciplines, institutions, and our own bodies, have been used as instruments of classification and control. He distinguished himself from others who have addressed similar themes, such as the deconstructionists and members of the Frankfurt School, by the originality, even eccentricity, of his formulations and the relentlessness with which he pursued the theme of Western humankind's self-subjugation. History for Foucault comprised systems at once homogeneous and dispersed, types of discourse which we create but which are prior to our intentions, selves split by impossible polarities, and, above all, a power which, because it works by incitement rather than repression, has been able to penetrate everything, everywhere.

Foucault was born in 1926 in Poitiers, France, studied at the Ecole Normale Supérieure, and received a degree in philosophy from the Sorbonne in 1948. He was influenced by Jean Hyppolite, who, Foucault said, transformed the study of philosophy into a "continually recurring question in life, death and memory" ("Discourse on Language"). Briefly a member of the Communist party, he broke with it in 1951; from 1952 to 1954 he studied psychopathology, in which he earned an advanced degree. In 1954 he published *Mental Illness and Personality*. After a brief lectureship at the Ecole Normale, Foucault wandered on the "margins" of French academic life: he spent four years at Uppsala University in Sweden, one year as director of the French Institute in Warsaw, and the next in the same position in Hamburg. During this time he wrote *Madness and Civilization: A History of Insanity in the Age of Reason,* which was published in Paris in 1961. Although concerned mainly with extralinguistic systems of order, these early works introduce the dominant theme of Foucault's career: how we have become the victims of our desire for rationality. *Madness and Civilization* deals with the extension of reason over that which defies reason: it tells how in the late eighteenth century a medical model was applied to the insane and they were confined in asylums, an historical innovation that resulted not in their cure but in their subjection to an increasingly irresistible, because "scientific" and "therapeutic," form of control.

In 1960 Foucault became head of the Philosophy Department at the University of Clermont-Ferrand, where he stayed for six years. During this time he practiced what he called archaeology: the effort to uncover the "general archive system" of a given epoch, the set of rules determining which statements may emerge into the discourse of the social sciences. *The Birth of the Clinic* (1963) traces the development of anatomical knowledge as a science organized under the power of the gaze. *The Order of Things* (1966), his most difficult and perhaps most important book, applies a Kantian analytic of finitude to modern social science as a whole, which emerges as a disturbing, volatile mix of empiricist humility and transcendentalist pretension, both disguising a will to infinite power/knowledge. Foucault expressed his longstanding aversion to anthropocentric and totalizing ways of thinking in his 1969 *Archaeology of Knowledge*: here society's sole organizing principle is discontinuity, and historical periods succeed one another in a series of "breaks," without development or direction. Within this fractured universe the human agent is unable to control even his or her own language, which is prior to any act of meaning.

After Clermont-Ferrand, Foucault became head of the Philosophy Department at the Vincennes campus of the University of Paris, and in 1970 he was elected to the Collège de France. By the end of the 1960s he had begun to move away from the formulations of his "archaeological" period, discarding signifier/signified and other expressions to use a less specialized vocabulary. After the disruptions created by the student/worker demonstrations in Paris in May 1968, he embraced a new method, "genealogy," which once again emphasized extralinguistic systems, but with an increasing focus on the ways subjects "subject" themselves. In *Discipline and Punish: The Birth of the Prison* (1975), Foucault analyzed "a new way of administering time and making it useful, by segmentation, seriation, synthesis, and totalization" (p. 160). In *The History of Sexuality*, Foucault began what was to be a six-volume study of power as manifested in sexual practices. The introductory volume, *The Will to Know* (1976), presents sexuality as having been incited, rather than repressed, by the modern family, state, and school system.

In these works power, like language, is transubjective and indivisible from human existence: it is impossible to conceive of a point of reconciliation, within or outside history, where we would be free from the necessity of constituting ourselves as the simultaneous subjects and objects of power. In his last project, a genealogical investigation of ethical codes, Foucault argued that power inhabits even our relation to ourselves. More than that: power is directly inscribed in our bodies, for as Foucault emphasizes throughout *Power/Knowledge*, power relations can deeply penetrate the material body even without depending upon the mediation of the subject's own representations. Foucault died in Paris in 1984, leaving his Genealogy of Ethics incomplete. He was never able to satisfy those critics who charged him with denying the possibility of liberation. Yet his writings have been instrumental in giving contemporary social history a new orientation toward the victimized and the dispossessed, and have made us aware of the real complexity of our aspiration to freedom.

Selected Bibliography

Primary Sources

Folie et déraison: historie de la folie à l'age classique. Paris: Librairie Plon, 1961. (*Madness and Civilization: A History of Insanity in the Age of Reason*. Trans. Richard Howard. New York, 1965.)
Maladie mentale et psychologie. 2d ed. Paris: Presses Universitaires de France, 1962. (Title of 1st ed.: *Maladie mentale et personnalité*.) (*Mental Illness and Psychology*. Trans. Alan Sheridan. New York, 1976.)

Naissance de la clinique: une archéologie du regard médical. Paris: Presses Univer-
  sitaires de France, 1963. (*The Birth of the Clinic: An Archaeology of Medical
  Perception.* Trans. A. M. Sheridan Smith. New York, 1973.)
Les Mots et les choses: une archéologie des sciences humaines. Paris: Gallimard,
  1966. (*The Order of Things: An Archaeology of the Human Sciences.* Trans.
  Alan Sheridan. New York, 1973.)
L'Archéologie du savoir. Paris: Gallimard, 1969. (*The Archaeology of Knowledge.*
  Trans. A. M. Sheridan Smith. New York, 1972.)
Moi, Pierre Rivière, ayant égorgé ma mère, ma soeur et mon frère . . . Paris: Gal-
  limard, 1973. (*I, Pierre Riviere, Having Slaughtered My Mother, My Sister,
  and My Brother* . . . Trans. Frank Jellinek. Lincoln, Nebr., 1982.)
Surveiller et punir: naissance de la prison. Paris: Gallimard, 1975. (*Discipline and
  Punish: The Birth of the Prison.* Trans. Alan Sheridan. New York, 1978.)
Histoire de la sexualité: la volonté du savoir. Paris: Gallimard, 1976. (*The History
  of Sexuality: The Will to Know.* Trans. Robert Hurley. New York: Pantheon,
  1978.)
Language, Counter-Memory, Practice: Selected Essays and Interviews. Ed. Donald
  F. Bouchard, Trans. Sherry Simon. Ithaca, N.Y.: Cornell University Press,
  1977.
Power, Truth, Strategy. M. Morris and P. Patton, eds. Atlantic Highlands, N.J..
  Humanities, 1979.
Power/Knowledge: Selected Interviews and Other Writings, 1972–1977. New York:
  Pantheon, 1980.
This Is Not a Pipe: With Illustrations and Letters by René Magritte. Trans. James
  Harkness. Berkeley: University of California Press, 1982.

   Secondary Sources

Lemert, Charles, and Garth Gillan. *Michel Foucault: Social Theory and Transgres-
  sion.* New York: Columbia University Press, 1982.
Major-Poetzl, Pamela. *Michel Foucault's Archaeology of Western Culture: Toward
  a New Science of History.* Chapel Hill: University of North Carolina Press,
  1983.
Megill, Allan. *Prophets of Extremity: Nietzsche, Heidegger, Foucault, Derrida.*
  Berkeley: University of California Press, 1985.
Sheridan, Alan. *Michel Foucault: The Will to Truth.* New York: Tavistock, 1980.

STEVEN CRESAP

FOWLES, JOHN (1926–   )

   John Fowles is a writer attracted to paradox, primarily because he believes that growth comes dialectically from a web of contradictions. Like
Nicholas Urfe, the protagonist of *The Magus* (1965), Fowles sees "That
reality [is] endless interaction. . . . The endless solitude of the one . . . seem[s]
the same thing as the total interrelationship of the all. All opposite seem[s]
one, because each [is] indispensable to each." Like the romantics, Fowles
concerns himself with process and wholeness. He understands the ability

to see two sides, to perceive alternatives as parts of a whole, as necessary for attaining a balanced vision. The tension in these perceived alternatives forms the liberating energy in Fowles' work, and, when confronted by his protagonists, it allows their growth, freedom, and involvement in love. Those critical moments, when the tension is greatest and when choices must be made, form the core of his narratives. He invites the reader to participate in these moments of choice, most famously in the ambiguous ending to *The Magus* and the several endings to *The French Lieutenant's Woman* (1969): his open endings are not so much attempts to confuse the reader as they are intended to force the reader to choose. Although his characters are often coerced into becoming free—imprisoned in order to be liberated—so are his occasionally manipulated readers part of what one critic calls "the liberating possibilities . . . of fiction itself." In creating test situations for his characters, he lures readers to undergo similar tests, hoping that both will develop increased vision and balance.

Born March 31, 1926, in Leigh-on-Sea, Essex (a suburb of London, to which his father, Robert, a cigar importer, commuted), John Robert Fowles felt "dominated by conformism" as a child. He attended Bedford School from 1939 to 1944 and, as a senior, was head boy with disciplinary power over more than 600 others. From 1944 to 1947 he served in the Royal Marines, where he trained commando recruits. During these eight years he developed his hatred of "anyone who thinks it good to . . . have arbitrary power over other people." After escaping what appear in retrospect to be two hells, he spent "three years of heaven" at New College, Oxford, reading French, developing a passion for his most-admired novelist, Flaubert, and dabbling in the existentialism that strongly influenced his early work. Fowles began to write a series of gnomic pronouncements, later published as *The Aristos* (1965; revised, 1968), which contains many of his themes: the need to live without absolute assurance and with tension, mystery, hazard. Graduating in 1950, Fowles spent the next 14 years teaching English in France, Greece (where he gathered much background material for *The Magus*), and England; he also began to write poetry (*Poems*, 1973) and fiction. After the publication of *The Collector* (1963), he quit teaching to devote full time to writing and, with his wife Elizabeth (whom he married in 1954), moved from London to Underhill Farm (the Dairy in *Lieutenant*), near Lyme Regis, in 1966 and then, in 1968, into Lyme itself—and into the house where he still lives and writes.

The Collector, the first published of Fowles' six books of fiction, is a relatively traditional work. Yet perhaps because it is such a gripping story, many readers failed to see the complexity of the two-part narrative, the importance of paradox, and the method by which the superficial black-white antithesis is undercut by a tentative moral vision. In many ways, however, *The Magus*, which he began writing in 1953, is—in its emphasis on beginnings rather than endings—more representative of Fowles. Nevertheless, even after its 1978 revision—where the excessive ambiguity and reader manipulation are both moderated and freedom of choice is made more central—it is an immature, albeit a fascinating, novel. *The French Lieutenant's Woman* is his most popular novel and the one that most successfully combines experimental features—the self-consciousness and reflexiveness of postmodernism, for example, are both employed and parodied—with realistic character and description. The novel also contains Fowles' clearest and fullest treatment of feminism—both radical and domestic—a concern in all his work, especially his nonfiction.

Fowles' next book, *The Ebony Tower* (1974), contains the title story, as well as three other stories and a translation of "Eliduc." Although the tales generally mirror themes and narrative modes used earlier, the characters, more established in their lives than Fowles' previous protagonists, face more complex choices. This is especially true regarding the question of freedom within relationships. Except for "The Cloud," however, the stories are told quite traditionally, reflecting Fowles' admission in 1976 that "Realism interests me increasingly in fiction." In *Daniel Martin* (1977), Fowles creates his most believable characters, problems, and situations. He drops his earlier fictional masks and moves away from some of the more facile tricks of his early work. Although some critics charged he had ceased taking risks, others argued that he had taken a large one by casting aside the popular narrative sleight-of-hand and storytelling ability shown in his first novels. For all that, the book is less traditional than it seems: Fowles skillfully juxtaposes chapters that counterpoint one another, and he juggles both time sequences and narrative perspectives to mirror his protagonist's fragmentation. His latest and most joyful novel, *Mantissa* (1982), in many ways parodies writers, critics, and readers of serious contemporary fiction. And the most parodied is Fowles himself.

Fowles—as the last two works suggest—is a difficult writer to label. He seems to prefer it that way. His work is never static; the focus is always on process, on the possibilities for growth and vision. Each of his novels subsumes the last; no work "dies," but, always in process, it moves toward the next. Perhaps Dan Martin best characterizes Fowles' stylistic and moral emphases when, thinking of his proposed novel, he says: "To hell with cultural fashion; . . . and above all, to hell with the imagined that does not say, not only in, but behind the images, the real."

Selected Bibliography

Primary Sources

The Collector. Boston: Little, Brown, 1963.
The Aristos: A Self-Portrait in Ideas. Boston: Little, Brown, 1964.
The Magus. Boston: Little, Brown, 1965. (*The Magus: A Revised Version,* 1978.)
The French Lieutenant's Woman. Boston: Little, Brown, 1969.
The Ebony Tower. Boston: Little, Brown, 1974.

Daniel Martin. Boston: Little, Brown, 1977.
Mantissa. Boston: Little, Brown, 1982.
Shipwreck. Boston: Little, Brown, 1983.
A Short History of Lyme Regis. Boston: Little, Brown, 1983.
A Maggot. Boston: Little, Brown, 1985.

Secondary Sources

Binns, Ronald. "John Fowles: Radical Romancer." *Critical Inquiry* 15, no. 4 (Winter 1973): 317–44.
Campbell, James. "An Interview with John Fowles." *Contemporary Literature* 17, no. 4 (Autumn 1976): 455–69.
Conradi, Peter. *John Fowles.* New York: Methuen, 1982.
Huffaker, Robert. *John Fowles.* Boston: Twayne Publishers, 1980.
Klemtner, Susan Strehle. "The Counterpoles of John Fowles' *Daniel Martin.*" *Critique* 21, no. 2 (1979): 59–71.
Lemon, Lee T. Portraits of the Artist in Contemporary Fiction. Lincoln: University of Nebraska Press, 1985, pp. 109–47.
Olshen, Barry. *John Fowles.* New York: Frederick Ungar, 1980.
Palmer, William J. *The Fiction of John Fowles: Tradition, Art and the Loneliness of Selfhood.* Columbia: University of Missouri Press, 1974.
Wolfe, Peter. *John Fowles: Magus and Moralist.* Lewisburg, Pa.: Bucknell University Press, 1976.

RONALD C. DIXON

FRISCH, MAX (1911–   )

There is general consensus that, next to Friedrich Dürrenmatt, Max Frisch is the most outstanding representative of contemporary Swiss literature. Primarily known for his plays (*Biedermann und die Brandstifter* [*The Firebugs*]; *Andorra*), Frisch has also written a number of novels that have won both critical acclaim and popular success. It is not easy to define what is particularly Swiss about Frisch. His ethnic background, after all, shows that his Swiss roots are not that deep. His paternal grandfather came from Austria, his maternal grandfather from Württemberg. Frisch's attitude toward Switzerland and the Swiss has always been ambivalent at best. He has been a critic of his native country and, much to their chagrin, has attacked his compatriots for their alleged self-righteousness, complacency, and quietism on numerous occasions. In many ways Frisch has deliberately chosen to assume the position of an emigrant, absenting himself from his native country frequently and taking up lengthy residences abroad (New York, Rome). At the same time, however, Frisch has never cut himself off completely from his roots.

Frisch readily admits that, as a writer, he has been influenced by Gottfried Keller, the great nineteenth-century Swiss novelist, and by the lesser known Albin Zollinger (1895–1941). Although Zollinger, in his novels, had consciously limited himself to issues of local concern, Frisch, from the outset, tried to reach an audience beyond the narrow confines of Switzerland. For this reason he has also rejected the use of dialect, always popular and even on the increase in modern Swiss literature. Topics, themes, and characters in Frisch's work, on the other hand, frequently have a distinct Swiss flavor. Stiller, for example, the hero of the novel that bears his name, reminds the reader of Wenzel Strapinski, the melancholy, adventurous, out-of-work tailor in Keller's popular story, *Kleider machen Leute* [*Clothes Make the Man*]. Both, in their own way and in their own time, want to escape their reality and are at odds with society. By refusing to submit to the forces of convention, traditionally extremely strong in Switzerland, both Keller's and Frisch's lives are extraordinary by Swiss standards. Their heroes, striving for self-fulfillment, frequently clash with society's demands for conformity, thus reflecting the authors' personal situation. Nothing could be more Swiss, of course, than the William Tell subject. Convinced that it has turned into a neurotic complex for the Swiss, Frisch, in his 1971 prose text, *William Tell for School Instruction*, takes up his country's most ancient and sacrosanct myth. Obviously, this was no easy task for him. Otherwise, it would not have taken him almost 25 years to complete the new *Wilhelm Tell*. Frisch's *Tell* has little in common with the idealized portrait of the Swiss as it has become known mostly through Schiller's drama. On the contrary, Frisch shows the Swiss, of many centuries ago to be sure, as narrow-minded reactionaries, lacking any vision. The message was not lost on his contemporaries, who, understandably, did not extend a warm welcome to the new *Wilhelm Tell*.

A glimpse at the author's biography reveals that Frisch is a highly unconventional individual. Ironically, his early years appear unconventional simply because they took such a conventional course. As a youngster he neither rebelled against the established order, nor did he drop out of school. Born in Zurich in 1911, the son of a self-made architect, he attended the *Gymnasium*, and, more importantly, he passed his final examinations so that he could study German language and literature at the university as he had wanted. But after some dissatisfaction with what he, most pointedly, called the university's warehouse approach to haphazardly stored knowledge, he became a journalist. In 1936, however, he abandoned his short journalistic career and decided to take up architecture. He earned his degree in 1941 and worked as an architect until 1954, when his literary success had made him financially independent. Frisch's service in the Swiss Army resulted in a well-received diary of army life, *Blätter aus dem Brotsack* (1940; *Leaves from a Knapsack*). It reveals traces of the author's humanism that is evidenced throughout his later work. Little as he sympathized with Nazi Germany, he sees in a German soldier a fellow human being and speaks out courageously against any form of nationalism.

Among the events that had considerable impact on Frisch's literary career were his frequent travels to all parts of the world, in particular to the United States. America, above all, made him conscious of his own relationship to Switzerland and expanded his awareness of his identity. Frisch, incidentally, is one of the few writers from the German-speaking countries to have developed an overall positive attitude toward the United States. Although he is not blind to the deficiencies of American institutions and the American way of life, he sees in individual Americans a positive element of cosmopolitanism and rejects the cultural arrogance many Europeans have displayed toward the United States. Many of Frisch's novels are set in America.

The dominant theme in Frisch's fiction is the search for identity. In *I'm Not Stiller* (1954), a man wants to escape from his own self. Only after being arrested and put on trial does he learn to accept himself with both the positive and negative characteristics he had been trying to shed. A variation of this theme can be found in Frisch's two other major novels, *Homo faber* (1957) and *A Wilderness of Mirrors* (1964). *Homo faber* is the story of a highly successful executive who realizes the fallacy of his belief in technology and rationalism when it is already too late. In *A Wilderness of Mirrors* a character plays a role that corresponds to his self-image, but he does not find self-fulfillment either.

Montauk (1975), a fictional diary centering around the aging narrator's love affair with a young woman, continues the autobiographical works that have become an integral part of Frisch's *oeuvre*. *Man in the Holocene* (1979) describes the struggle of an old man against the limitations of old age.

In his novels, written over a time span of 40 years, Frisch has shown that modern humankind suffers from alienation in a characterless, indifferent society. Although his answers do not reflect much optimism, Frisch must be given credit as being one of the first writers of the postwar period to treat such significant issues as the problem of identity in fiction and subsequently bringing Switzerland into the mainstream of European literature.

Selected Bibliography

Primary Sources

Tagebuch 1946–1949. Frankfurt: Suhrkamp, 1950. (*Sketchbook 1946–1949*. Trans. Geoffrey Skelton. New York: Harcourt Brace Jovanovich, 1977.)
Stiller. Frankfurt: Suhrkamp, 1954. (*I'm Not Stiller*. Trans. Michael Bullock. London: Abelard-Schumann, 1958.)
Homo faber. Frankfurt: Suhrkamp, 1957. (*Homo faber*. Trans. Michael Bullock. London: Abelard-Schumann, 1959.)
Mein Name sei Gantenbein. Frankfurt: Suhrkamp, 1964. (*A Wilderness of Mirrors*. Trans. Michael Bullock. London: Methuen, 1965.)

Wilhelm Tell für die Schule (William Tell for school instruction). Frankfurt: Suhr-
    kamp, 1971.
Tagebuch 1966–1971. Frankfurt: Suhrkamp, 1972. (*Sketchbook 1966–1971*. Trans.
    Geoffrey Skelton. New York: Harcourt Brace Jovanovich, 1974.)
Montauk. Frankfurt: Suhrkamp, 1975. (*Montauk*. Trans. Geoffrey Skelton. New
    York: Harcourt Brace Jovanovich, 1976.)
Der Mensch erscheint im Holozän. Frankfurt: Suhrkamp, 1979. (*Man in the Hol-
    ocene*. Trans. Geoffrey Skelton. New York: Harcourt Brace Jovanovich,
    1980.)
Triptychon. Frankfurt: Suhrkamp, 1980. (*Triptych*. New York: Harcourt Brace
    Jovanovich, 1981.)
Bluebeard. Trans. Geoffrey Skelton. San Diego: Harcourt Brace Jovanovich, 1984.

Secondary Sources

Butler, Michael. *The Novels of Max Frisch*. London: Oswald Wolff, 1976.
Jurgensen, Manfred. *Max Frisch. Die Romane. Interpretationen*. Bern: Francke,
    1972.
Petersen, Carol. *Max Frisch*. New York: Frederick Ungar, 1972.
Probst, Gerhard F., and Jay F. Bodine, eds. *Perspectives on Max Frisch*. Lexington,
    Ky.: University Press of Kentucky, 1982.
Weisstein, Ulrich. *Max Frisch*. New York: Twayne Publishers, 1967.
                                                                 JÜRGEN KOPPENSTEINER

FUENTES, CARLOS (1928–   )

Although known mainly as a novelist, the Mexican Carlos Fuentes has
at different times distinguished himself as an essayist, journalist, dramatist,
short story writer, filmmaker, lecturer, and diplomat. He is considered by
many to be the most versatile living Spanish-American person of letters.

The trilingual son of a diplomat, Fuentes spent his youth in such diverse
cities as Panama City, Quito, Montevideo, Rio de Janeiro, Washington,
D.C., Santiago, Buenos Aires, Geneva, and London. His first novel, *Where
the Air Is Clear* (1958), an exuberant critical portrait of Mexico City, bears
two traits that are characteristic of almost all of Fuentes' fiction: a global
perspective on local phenomena and daring stylistic innovation. Other
important elements in this work include the search for a Mexican national
identity—which entails the recognition of a pervasive indigenous, mythic
presence as well as a reinterpretation of modern Mexican history—and a
confrontation with the dual insatiable desires of humankind: power and
love. Absent from the curiously parochial *The Good Conscience* (1959),
these themes return as fundamental to *The Death of Artemio Cruz* (1962),
which focuses on an individual rather than a collective subject. Through
a series of rotating first-, second-, and third-person narrations, the character
Artemio Cruz, a former revolutionary who abandoned his cause in order
to become the country's leading capitalist power broker, reviews his life

from the telling angle of his deathbed. Largely inspired by Octavio Paz's essay *El laberinto de la soledad (The Labyrinth of Solitude*, 1950), Cruz's (auto)biography is recounted with admirable restraint; the protagonist's basest impulses are revealed with the same force as his joys and achievements. Both in commercial terms and in the sense of wedding a particular theme to a most efficacious form, *The Death of Artemio Cruz* is Fuentes' most successful novel to date.

In *Holy Place* (1967) and *A Change of Skin* (1967), Fuentes continues to investigate the origins and present state of the Mexican psyche. The former novel presents the case study of a young man neurotically infatuated with his movie-star mother, or perhaps with her image. The latter work, which won the Biblioteca Breve Prize of 1967, is narrated by an inmate of a sanatorium. It treats of four tourists who, because of a mechanical breakdown, must spend a night in Toluca where, in at least one version of the story, some of them perish in the cave-in of a Mesoamerican pyramid. The plot, however, is a mere pretext for a baroque game of betrayal and self-betrayal among the characters, whose personal identities are subjected to an implacable questioning. These are Fuentes' most experimentally symbolic novels, for they defy the expectations of even seasoned readers. *Holy Place*, for instance, ends with the narrator transformed into a dog, while *A Change of Skin*, in addition to revealing the narrator's insanity, concludes with a parody of the foregoing fiction performed by a cast of roving bohemians.

Terra nostra (1975) is a vast literary rewriting of the conquest of New Spain, from the refreshing viewpoint of the conquered. This mammoth novel, which ranges from imperial Roman times to Paris at the end of the present millennium, but focuses chiefly on the court of the Spanish counter-reformist Philip II, shows history and literature to consist in a dizzying series of repetitions and transformations. One finds Fuentes at his most unabashedly grandiloquent, raising questions of intertextuality, multivocity, and the dynamics of reading and writing. Although at times unwieldy, *Terra nostra* is nonetheless a mature, visionary tour de force, for which Fuentes has received the Javier Villarutia Prize in Mexico City and the Rómulo Gallegos Award in Caracas.

After a brief period as the Mexican ambassador to France, Fuentes wrote the relatively facile but engaging *The Hydra Head* (1978), an international spy thriller reminiscent of the works of Dashiell Hammett and Raymond Chandler. *Distant Relations* (1980), a gothic-fantastic novel which in many ways is generically allied with Fuentes' novellas *Aura* (1962) and *Birthday* (1969), again raises the issue of a stable personal identity as it flirts with the beauty of the horrible in a charged autumnal atmosphere.

In addition to these novels, all of which have been widely translated, Fuentes has to his credit the short story collections *Los días enmascarados (The Masked Days,* 1954) and *Cantar de ciegos (Songs of the Blind,* 1964) and the dramas *El tuerto es rey (The One-eyed Man Is King,* 1970), *Todos los gatos son pardos (All Cats Are Gray,* 1970), and *Orquídeas a la luz de la luna (Orchids in the Moonlight,* 1982). His most influential essays are *La nueva novela hispanoamericana (The New Spanish-American Novel,* 1969), in which he combines a linguistic and sociological approach to the fiction of his peers, and *Cervantes, o la crítica de la lectura (Cervantes, or The Critique of Reading,* 1975), a companion volume to *Terra nostra,* which advocates a Derridian free play of signifiers for the interpretation of literary texts.

Once denied entry into the United States for his political views on Cuba, Fuentes has since 1978 been a resident of Princeton, New Jersey, and he is now a familiar figure on American university campuses. Recent accomplishments include winning the University of Oklahoma's Neustadt Prize in 1983 and receiving in 1984 a five-year appointment to the faculty of Harvard University. A voracious reader and gifted performer, Fuentes continues to embody the Nietzschean dialectical principle of reconciling opposites (the Western and the indigenous, myth and history, the unconscious and the purposive, the popular and the erudite, the erotic and the political, tragedy and reform, and so on) which has permitted him to practice the self-transcendence of which he writes.

Selected Bibliography

Primary Sources

La región más transparente. Mexico: Fondo de Cultura Económica, 1958. (*Where the Air Is Clear.* Trans. Sam Hileman. New York: Ivan Obolensky, 1960.)

Las buenas conciencias. Mexico: Fondo de Cultura Económica, 1959. (*The Good Conscience.* Trans. Sam Hileman. New York: Ivan Obolensky, Inc. 1961.)

La muerte de Artemio Cruz. Mexico: Fondo de Cultura Económica, 1962. (*The Death of Artemio Cruz.* Trans. Sam Hileman. New York: Farrar, Straus & Giroux, 1964.)

Aura. Mexico: Biblioteca Eva, 1962. (*Aura.* Trans. Lysander Kemp. New York: Farrar, Straus & Giroux, 1965.)

Zona sagrada. Mexico: Siglo Veintiuno Editores, 1967. (*Holy Place.* Trans. Suzanne Jill Levine. New York: E. P. Dutton, 1972.)

Cambio de piel. Mexico: Joaquín Mortiz, 1967. (*A Change of Skin.* Trans. Sam Hileman. New York: Farrar, Straus & Giroux, 1968.)

Cumpleaños. Mexico: Joaquín Mortiz, 1969. (*Birthday.* Trans. Lysander Kemp. New York: Farrar, Straus & Giroux, 1975.

Terra nostra. Mexico: Joaquín Mortiz, 1975. (*Terra Nostra.* Trans. Margaret Sayers Peden. New York: Farrar, Straus & Giroux, 1976.)

La cabeza de la hidra. Barcelona: Librería Editorial Argos, 1978. (*The Hydra Head.* Trans. Margaret Sayers Peden. New York: Farrar, Straus & Giroux, 1978.)

Una familia lejana. Mexico: Joaquín Mortiz, 1980. (*Distant Relations.* Trans. Margaret Sayers Peden. New York: Farrar, Straus & Giroux, 1982.)

Burnt Water. Trans. Margaret Peden. New York: Farrar, Straus & Giroux, 1980.

Secondary Sources

Bifumo Boshi, Liliana, and Calabrese, Elisa. *Nostalgia del futuro en la obra de Carlos Fuentes.* Buenos Aires: Fernando García Cambeiro, 1974.
Brody, Robert, and Charles Rossman, eds. *Carlos Fuentes: A Critical View.* Austin: University of Texas Press, 1982.
Faris, Wendy B. *Carlos Fuentes.* New York: Frederick Ungar, 1983.
Guzmán, Daniel de. *Carlos Fuentes.* New York: Twayne Publishers, 1972.
Reeve, Richard. "Carlos Fuentes." *Narrativa y crítica de nuestra América.* Ed. Joaquín Roy. Madrid: Castalia, 1978, pp. 287–316.
Tittler, Jonathan. "*Cambio de zona, Piel sagrada:* Transfiguration in Carlos Fuentes." *World Literature Today* 57, no. 4 (1983): 585–90.
Weiss, Jason. "An Interview with Carlos Fuentes." *The Kenyon Review* 5 (Fall 1983): 105–118.

JONATHAN TITTLER

G

GADDIS, WILLIAM (1922–   )

"What is it they want from a man that they didn't get from his work? What do they expect? What is there left of him when he's done his work? What's any artist, but the dregs of his work?" (*The Recognitions,* pp. 95–96). Until publication of his most recent novel, William Gaddis granted only one interview in English—and that only 2 1/2 pages long. In the few available quotations, he reiterates his distaste for the tendency today "to turn the creative artist into a performing one, to find what a writer says about writing somehow more valid, or more real, than the writing itself." Yet this reticent man is the author of fiction that is as absorbing in its detail as it is exhilarating in its recognitions—which go much deeper than those of any other twentieth-century American writer. Still largely unacknowledged, his work stands above the general triviality of most contemporary postmodern fiction.

Little is known: that he was born William Thomas Gaddis on December 29, 1922, and lived in New York City and on Long Island until the age of five. That he was educated in Connecticut and on Long Island. That he grew up without a father. That he entered Harvard in 1941, where he edited the *Lampoon*, developing a reputation as a humorist, but left in 1945 without a degree. That he was then employed by *The New Yorker* as a facts checker before beginning five years of international travel, first to Mexico City, then to Panama, where he intended to launch a news career but settled for work on the Canal as a machinist's assistant. That his travels continued through other Central American countries, the Caribbean, Spain, North Africa, and Paris. It was during this time—Madrid, 1948—that serious writing on his first novel, *The Recognitions,* began and continued up through his return to the United States and its publication in 1955. Additional miscellaneous: grants from the National Endowment for the Arts and Letters and the American Academy and Institute of Arts and Letters in 1963, and the National Endowment for the Arts in 1966; Guggenheim Fellowship in 1981; two grown children from a previous marriage.

The Recognitions (1955) is a self-conscious satire about the dubious possibility of attaining personal salvation in a world corrupted with hypocrisy, heresy, and deceit. It is a quest novel, a grand, queasily comic voyage through spiritual squalor propelled by "the sense of something lost." It is about originality and imitation, those great siamese twins of Western civilization. About the parody inherent in both art and religion and the proliferation of frauds in both. An intensely moral book, *The Recognitions* attacks the problem of separateness in the modern world where people hold too desperately onto the singleness of identity. By its very existence it asks whether "a work of art redeems time."

In a complex series of plots delightfully complicated through indirection, this encyclopedic novel of 956 pages ranges through New England, Greenwich Village, Paris, Spain, Central America, and Eastern Europe. It begins with the two people who raise Wyatt Gwyon, the central figure of *The Recognitions:* his Great Aunt May, a pillar of the Calvinist community and his father, Reverend Gwyon, a New England Congregational preacher who explores the rites of non-Christian faiths, finally discovering Mithraism and an asylum called Happymount. As an emerging artist, Wyatt's ability to forge "undiscovered" Flemish masterpieces of the fifteenth and early sixteenth centuries attracts the attentions of Basil Valentine, an ex-Jesuit art critic and authenticator of fakes, and Recktall Brown, the wealthy demon of the book who commissions the fakes for his international forgery ring. Meanwhile, Stanley, an intensely devout Catholic, composes religious organ music. Agnes Deigh is a literary agent who prefers the company of gay men. Mr. Pivner, an everyman figure, stumbles his way through the proliferation of commercial messages advertising products that are certain to win him friends and influence people. Esther, a long-suffering aspiring writer with a promiscuous "village past," convinces Wyatt to marry her. Frank Sinisterra is a professional counterfeiter and impersonator who considers himself an artist. Esme, a heroin addict, a poetess with "manic depressive, schizoid tendencies," is the artist's model for Wyatt's madonnas. Otto, a would-be playwright, is a parody of Wyatt, transcribing Wyatt's conversation to attribute to his own alter ego in his play. All of these, plus assorted homosexuals and pseudo-intellectuals, writers, painters, and critics, advertising hacks and media men, wander through a world of misplaced faiths and fakes where the boundaries between hallucination and reality are constantly reset.

Although Gaddis' work is not experimental in the usual sense, there is something unique about his style and techniques. In *The Recognitions,* a baroque style is fortified by tone and motivic repetition. The use of cinematic cross-cuts and montage produces a sense of simultaneity: mystics and alchemists from the Middle Ages mingle freely with Greenwich Village artists and swindlers. *J R* (1975), Gaddis' second novel, is known for its overpoweringly accurate colloquial dialogue/monologue and the dominance of that dialogue over the few scraps of narration. This chapterless, sectionless flow of 726 pages exposes "what America's all about, waste disposal and all." Characters are identifiable by speech patterns, linguistic ticks, coughs, stutters, smells, clothing. Transitions occur mouth to mouth: via telephone lines, chance meetings on the street, in conference rooms.

Out of a Long Island elementary school comes J R Vansant, an 11-year-old turned tycoon. When his sixth grade class goes on a field trip to Wall Street, he uses their one common share of stock as his entry into corporate finance. Eventually, the perpetually runny-nosed, torn-sneakered JR, muffling his voice in a dirty handkerchief while making deals from a phone booth he's had installed in the school corridor, becomes the head of a massive conglomerate. J R emerges out of the corporate Babel as a normal, relatively well-adjusted kid—adjusted to this world whose mores of money, fame, and power he's absorbed without a second thought because "that's what you do." The absurd logic of free enterprise breeds excess as educational and domestic systems fail. Communication deteriorates to the self-parody of jargon.

Although much of the surface of *J R* is devoted to the business antics of the child-tycoon, and much of its satiric bite is directed there, the real heart of the novel lies in the stories of three adult characters—the moral centers of the book: Edward Bast, a young composer; Amy or Emily Joubert, one of JR's teachers; and Jack Gibbs, a somewhat older man currently teaching science at the same school. Midway through the novel, JR tells Mrs. Joubert that for "everything you see someplace there's this millionaire for it," and she points to the evening sky and asks "Is there a millionaire for that?" It is then that we realize that JR is lost and landed for good on the side of Mammon, and, despite the title, it isn't really JR's story after all.

In 1985, both *The Recognitions* and *J R* were reissued in the Viking/Penguin Contemporary American Fiction Series along with the publication of *Carpenter's Gothic,* Gaddis' "first and last attempt to reach the man at the airport." Written in much the same style as *J R*—almost entirely dialogue and monologues—*Carpenter's Gothic* is both shorter (only 262 pages) and less ambitious in scope: the entire novel takes place within a single house: "—it's a classic piece of Hudson river carpenter gothic. . . . All designed from the outside . . . they drew a picture of it and squeezed the rooms in later."

Paul and Elizabeth Booth have rented the house from a Mr. McCandless. The main onstage character, Elizabeth (a.k.a. "Bibbs"), an heiress and an aspiring writer, is married to Paul, a "media consultant," who is promoting a Southern evangelist called Reverend Elton Ude. (Paul turns the mishap of one of Ude's baptisms, during which the child is drowned, into an opportunity to praise—and sell—the Lord.) Reverend Ude is the "dynamic leader of Christian Recovery for America's People" who broadcasts over his own "Voice of Salvation" radio station and campaigns against "the atheist doctrine of evolution." McCandless is a geologist, an authority on the age of the Earth who testifies in a creationism trial. He is also a published novelist who's written at least one book with a few lines from *The Recognitions.*

In this house, the door is always left ajar and the phone is always ringing, but the company and communication are negligible. Liz herself is an innocent abused by the constant cacophony of America selling America. There is little concern for her sanity and sense of self, let alone her soul. When McCandless suggests that people write novels out of outrage, Liz counters "No or maybe just boredom." Literature has become "What's here today and you wrap the fish in tomorrow."

The Recognitions appeared to hostile and ignorant reviews, but during the next decade became an underground classic. It wasn't until *J R* was published 20 years later that some restitution was made: Gaddis won the 1976 National Book Award. In the midst of the slowly developing Gaddis scholarship, many critics claim that in order to read his work, it is necessary to identify sources, allusions, historical references, and so on. Although Gaddis may have earned his reputation as a "difficult" novelist, the point rarely made is that he is enjoyable to read. Having received the MacArthur Fellows Award in 1982, William Gaddis continues to live in and around New York where he continues (presumably) to write books "for people who [don't] read with the surface of their minds" . . . not like "most writing now . . . [which] never takes your breath away, telling you things you already know."

Selected Bibliography

Primary Sources

The Recognitions. Harcourt, Brace & Co., 1955; World, Meridian Fiction, 1962; Harcourt, Brace & World, Inc., 1970, Harvest paperback; Avon, 1974, mass market paperback. New York: Viking/Penguin Contemporary American Fiction Series, 1985 (corrected ed.).
J R. New York: Alfred A. Knopf, 1975; New York: Viking/Penguin, Contemporary American Fiction Series, 1985.
Carpenter's Gothic. New York: Elisabeth Sifton Books, Viking/Penguin, 1985.

Secondary Sources

Aldridge, John W. *The American Novel and the Way We Live Now.* New York and London: Oxford University Press, 1983, pp. 46–52, 148. Revision of review of *J R* in the *Saturday Review,* October 4, 1975, pp. 27–30.
Karl, Frederick R. *American Fictions: 1940–1980.* New York: Harper & Row: 1983, pp. 176–190.

Kuehl, John, and Steven Moore. *In Recognition of William Gaddis*. Syracuse, N.Y.: Syracuse University Press, 1984.

LeClair, Thomas. "William Gaddis, *J R* & the Art of Excess." *Modern Fiction Studies* 27 (Winter 1981–1982): 587–600.

Moore, Steven. *A Reader's Guide to William Gaddis's The Recognitions*. Lincoln and London: University of Nebraska Press, 1982. See also: "Additional Sources for William Gaddis's *The Recognitions*." *American Notes & Queries* 22 (March/April 1984): 111–14.

O'Brien, John, ed. *The Review of Contemporary Fiction* 2, No. 2 (Summer 1982): 4–56. Special section on WG, including interview.

Tanner, Tony. *City of Words: American Fiction 1950–1970*. New York: Harper & Row, 1971, pp. 393–400.

SARAH E. LAUZEN

GARCÍA MÁRQUEZ, GABRIEL (1928–   )

One of the most gifted storytellers of the "Boom" of Latin American literature, Gabriel García Márquez gained international recognition when he was awarded the Nobel Prize for Literature in 1982. His major novel, the stunning *One Hundred Years of Solitude* (1967), translated into over 20 languages by the early 1970s, had established his international reputation as a major novelist. The humor, sense of history, spontaneous imagination, and mythical overtones of this novel are its most outstanding features. Although *One Hundred Years of Solitude* seems quite traditional in many respects, García Márquez's total fiction reveals a sophisticated master of a panoply of narrative techniques.

García Márquez was born in a small town on Colombia's Caribbean coast, Aracataca, on March 6, 1928. He lived with his grandparents until he was eight years old. García Márquez has claimed that nothing interesting has happened to him since his grandfather's death when he was eight. In those early years he heard the legends and tales of the region from his grandparents, who apparently were very good storytellers. Many of these tales, such as those about the War of a Thousand Days (1899–1902), would appear later in his fiction.

García Márquez's parents sent him to Bogotá for high school, where he graduated in 1946. In April 1948 a populist candidate for the presidency was assassinated in Bogotá, and the ensuing violence in the capital and civil war resulted in García Márquez's move back to the Caribbean coast. He began working as a journalist and published his initial stories in newspapers. He and his friends of the "Group of Barranquilla" also read the novels of writers such as Faulkner, Virginia Woolf, and Kafka.

In 1955 García Márquez published his first novel, *Leafstorm*. Soon thereafter he went to Europe as a newspaper correspondent, and he lived in Paris until 1958. During those years he worked on the manuscripts for *No*

One Writes to the Colonel (1961) and *In Evil Hour* (1962). After moving to Caracas in 1958 and New York in 1961 to work as a correspondent for Cuba's Prensa Latina, he lived in Mexico during several years of literary silence. In 1965 the pieces of his culminating work began to fall into place for the creation of *One Hundred Years of Solitude*. García Márquez had found the key to the creation of the magical reality of a town called Macondo which had been portrayed only partially in his previous fiction. After its completion and resulting success, García Márquez began to enjoy economic stability, living comfortably in Spain, Mexico, and Colombia, and continued writing.

The setting for his first novel, *Leafstorm*, is Macondo during approximately the first quarter of the twentieth century. The action centers on an unnamed doctor, believed to be from France, who had lived in Macondo during this 25-year period and ultimately committed suicide. This story is revealed through narrators who attend the doctor's wake: a nine-year-old boy, his mother, and his grandfather. The effect of this structure is to penetrate more deeply into the reality of Macondo than either a personal or historical version could have allowed.

The next steps in García Márquez's apprenticeship for the creation of *One Hundred Years of Solitude* were two short novels, *No One Writes to the Colonel* and *In Evil Hour*. Both are more firmly based on Colombia's historical reality than most of the writer's later work. This reality is *la violencia*, the period of civil war during the late 1940s and 1950s. *No One Writes to the Colonel* is a psychological portrayal of a retired colonel. The novel also deals with an entire town's suffering from corruption and repression.

In Evil Hour also features a basically linear development of the story, but García Márquez now employs the juxtaposition of different scenes to create a montage effect. Someone puts up placards that undermine the town's stability. These anonymous notes contain personal accusations that lead to conflicts—fights, persons moving from the town, and deaths. The mayor, who had been proud of the control he had established in the town before the appearance of the placards, is forced to repress the town's inhabitants in order to maintain order. García Márquez captures the essence of the fear and distrust that pervaded the national consciousness in Colombia at the time.

One Hundred Years of Solitude is a family saga that tells the story of five generations of the Buendías. It begins with the foundation of Macondo. Initially, Macondo's only contact with the outside world is provided by gypsies who bring items such as ice and magnets, which the inhabitants find amazing. Civilization slowly penetrates into Macondo along with its numerous institutions. With the arrival of the national political parties come civil wars. The Americans bring economic prosperity, exploiting workers on banana plantations. These intrusions of foreigners and modernity are eliminated by a flood that washes them away and returns Macondo to a state similar to its original paradise. In the end Macondo is not a paradise, however, but a fiction: a member of the Buendía family deciphers a parchment written in Sanscrit which had told the entire story of the family and Macondo. History was the completion of a fiction.

Since *One Hundred Years of Solitude* García Márquez has published a volume of short stories and two novels. The stories included in *Innocent Erendira* (1972) feature the playful invention and fantasy of *One Hundred Years of Solitude*. His complex novel *The Autumn of the Patriarch* (1975) is about an archetypal Latin American dictator. In García Márquez's most recent novel, *Chronicle of a Death Foretold* (1981), he has penned a tour de force that tells the story of a vendetta. The assassination of the protagonist is announced on the first page, but the author masterfully holds the reader's attention until the end.

García Márquez's fiction transcends its regional base, creating what one critic has identified as "transcendent regionalism." García Márquez has been a self-proclaimed admirer of Faulkner and strives toward a transcendent regionalism in nearly all his writing. This transcendent regionalism, in addition to the constant presence of the anti-rational and myth, is key to the aesthetics and universality of García Márquez's fiction.

Selected Bibliography

Primary Sources

La hojarasca. Bogotá: Ediciones Sipa, 1955, 1960. (*Leafstorm and Other Stories*. Trans. Gregory Rabassa. New York: Harper & Row, 1972.)

El coronel no tiene quien le escriba. Medellín, Colombia: Aguirre Editor, 1961. (*No One Writes to the Colonel and Other Stories*. Trans. J.S. Bernstein. New York: Harper & Row, 1968.)

La mala hora. Madrid: Talleres de Gráficas "Luis Pérez," 1962. (*In Evil Hour*. Trans. Gregory Rabassa. New York: Avon Bard, 1979.)

Cien años de soledad. Buenos Aires: Editorial Sudamericana, 1967. (*One Hundred Years of Solitude*. Trans. Gregory Rabassa. New York: Harper & Row, 1970.)

La increíble y triste historia de la cándida Eréndira y de su abuela desalmada. Barcelona: Barral Editores, 1972. (*Innocent Erendira and Other Stories*. Trans. Gregory Rabassa. New York: Harper Colophon Books, 1979).

El otoño del patriarca. Barcelona: Plaza & Janés Editores, 1975. (*The Autumn of the Patriarch*. Trans. Gregory Rabassa. New York: Harper & Row, 1976.)

Crónica de una muerte anunciada. Buenos Aires: Editorial Sudamericana, 1980. (*Chronicle of a Death Foretold*. Trans. Gregory Rabassa. New York: Alfred A. Knopf, 1982.)

Collected Stories. New York: Harper & Row, 1984.

Secondary Sources

Brushwood, John S. *The Spanish-American Novel: A Twentieth Century Survey*. Austin and London: University of Texas Press, 1975.

Earl, Peter, ed. *García Márquez*. Madrid: Taurus, 1981.

Janes, Regina. *Gabriel García Márquez: Revolutions in Wonderland*. Columbia: University of Missouri Press, 1981.

McMurray, George. *Gabriel García Márquez*. New York: Frederick Ungar, 1977.

Williams, Raymond L. *Gabriel García Márquez*. Boston: G. K. Hall, Twayne's World Author Series, 1984.

RAYMOND L. WILLIAMS

GARDNER, JOHN (1933–1982)

Believing that art should create myths that help us to live, John Gardner revitalizes the "eternal verities" for postmodern fiction. He experiments with fable, myth, and re-creating traditional literary forms as he confronts basic thematic and narrative concerns: the boundaries of storyteller and story told; the relationship of language and reality; the nature of love, death, and religion. At the center of his fictions—about half of which are set in ancient or medieval times, while the other half occur in contemporary middle America—is the merging of contradictions, the fusion of apparent opposites. Through this merger comes Gardner's myth: there is an oxymoronic reality that resurrects our belief in love, holiness, and heroism, even as these virtues are voiced by the mad, the disfigured, or the purely ordinary.

His interest in myth and storytelling came from both his family and his academic studies. Born in 1933, John Champlin Gardner grew up on a farm in Batavia, New York (the setting for some of his fiction) where his father was famous for his orations from the Bible and Shakespeare and his mother, an English teacher, for her singing. From them he learned the power of story and song, a lesson translated into all of his fictions. Gardner attended DePauw University for two years and then transferred to Washington University in St. Louis, where he received his B.A. in 1955. At Washington he was introduced to medieval literature, an interest he continued at the State University of Iowa, where he received his M.A. (1956) and Ph.D. (1958). His dissertation was a novel, *The Old Men*.

During the 1960s, while teaching medieval literature at Oberlin College, California State, San Francisco State, and then Southern Illinois University, Gardner published numerous poems in journals like *The Southern Review, Perspective* and *The Kenyon Review*. He also published one novel, *The Resurrection* (1966), in which James Chandler goes home to Batavia to face his death. To understand his present, Chandler returns to ancient philosophy; as he resurrects ancient texts, he resurrects his life. Gardner continues to experiment with the conflation of past and present in *The Wreckage of Agathon* (1970), an historical re-creation of Ancient Greece. These novels received positive but limited critical notice.

With the publication of *Grendel* (1971) Gardner achieved a wide audience and critical acclaim. Retelling the Beowulf legend from the monster's point of view, Gardner explores the many layers of myth and language. An apparent representative of order (Beowulf) and one of disorder (Grendel) confront each other only to discover that each is part of the other. Gardner both re-creates and preserves myth: Grendel's language changes the myth, and yet the myth remains the same—Grendel dies.

The Sunlight Dialogues (1972) continues Gardner's interest in the mythic confrontation of apparent opposites, this time in the Middle American setting of Batavia. Another disfigured, monstrous anarchist meets an advocate of order; this duality quickly gives way, however, as Gardner insists that our lexical divisions, as necessary as they may be, belie multiple reality. In this novel Gardner also explores exhaustively the power of myth: it can kill you as well as help you live.

During the 1970s, Gardner published works, some of which had been written previously, in rapid succession. *Nickel Mountain* (1973) reworks the middle-aged American's quest for myth, for heroic possibility amid common, domestic life. Here Gardner returns to the pastoral novel, while in *Jason and Medeia* (1973) he rewrites an epic poem. Not simply using an ancient setting but also re-creating traditional forms, Gardner works with expanding the limits of narrative. The narrator is spectator to the myth, but at points the line between storyteller and story told dissolves: the narrator is wounded by the story he tells. *The King's Indian* (1974), a collection of stories set in both the past and present, demonstrates Gardner's fusion of myth and quotidian reality.

In *October Light* (1976) he experiments with a novel within a novel. Although it was awarded the National Book Critics Circle Award, its metafictional mode confused a number of critics. By using the double narrative of story told and story read, Gardner explores further the nature of order and disorder and the relationship among the reader, the writer, and the text.

Gardner's interests are crystallized in "Redemption" (1977), a short story in which he transforms into art a tragic incident from his childhood when his brother was killed in a tractor accident on the farm in Batavia. Here we see an excellent example of Gardner's insistence that art can redeem, that language can resurrect love, compassion, and dignity amid the violent chaos of the universe. This story was included in *The Art of Living and Other Stories* (1981) whose title indicates an attempt to conflate art and life as he probes deeply into the connection between language and reality. His theory about the nature of art appears in *On Moral Fiction* (1978), a controversial work that articulates his belief in the responsibility of art to create didactic myths.

During this prolific period, Gardner taught at Bennington College and then at SUNY/Binghamton, where he was head of the creative writing program. *Freddy's Book* (1980) creates a fabulous reality of kings, knights, and the Devil. His last published novel, *Mickelsson's Ghosts* (1982), is a return, in a sense, to *The Resurrection* and *Nickel Mountain*: Gardner creates a mythic hero out of the language of everyday America. This novel was published just months before his death, at the age of 49, in a motorcycle accident in September 1982.

Gardner's fiction shares an affinity with that of other postmodern fabulists, but it is also firmly based in quotidian reality. Returning to traditional forms, Gardner celebrates the need for conventional order at the same time he subverts that order by his use of mythic disorder and experimental form. This is the power of his fiction: at the intersections of these ordered distinctions lies his belief that we ourselves are the myth that can help us to live.

Selected Bibliography

Primary Sources

The Resurrection. New York: Alfred A. Knopf, 1966.
The Wreckage of Agathon. New York: Harper & Row, 1970.
Grendel. New York: Alfred A. Knopf, 1971.
The Sunlight Dialogues. New York: Alfred A. Knopf, 1972.
Nickel Mountain: A Pastoral Novel. New York: Alfred A. Knopf, 1973.
Jason and Medeia. New York: Alfred A. Knopf, 1973.
The King's Indian. New York: Alfred A. Knopf, 1974.
October Light. New York: Alfred A. Knopf, 1976.
On Moral Fiction. New York: Basic Books, 1978.
The Art of Living and Other Stories. New York: Alfred A. Knopf, 1981.
Mickelsson's Ghosts. New York: Alfred A. Knopf, 1982.
On Becoming a Novelist. New York: Harper & Row, 1983.

Secondary Sources

Arnold, Marilyn. "*Nickel Mountain*: John Gardner's Testament of Redemption." *Renascence* 30 (1978): 59–68.
Butts, Leonard C. "Locking and Unlocking: Nature as Moral Center in John Gardner's *October Light*." Critique 22 (1980): 47–60.
Cowart, David. *Arches and Light: The Fiction of John Gardner.* Carbondale: Southern Illinois University Press, 1983.
Henderson, Jeff. "The Avenues of Mundane Salvation: Time and Change in the Fiction of John Gardner." *American Literature* 55 (December 1983): 611–33.
Howell, John H. *John Gardner: A Bibliographical Profile.* Carbondale: Southern Illinois University Press, 1980.
Mendez-Egle, Beatrice, ed. *John Gardner: True Art, Moral Art.* Edinburg, TX.: Pan American University School of Humanities, 1983.
Murr, Judy Smith. "John Gardner's Order and Disorder: *Grendel* and *The Sunlight* Dialogues." *Critique* 18 (1976): 97–101.
McCaffery, Larry. "Showdown on Mainstreet: The Gass-Gardner Debate." *The Literary Review* 23, no. 1 (Fall 1979): 134–44.

Strehle, Susan. "John Gardner's Novels: Affirmation and the Alien." *Critique* 18 (1976): 86–96.

JUDY R. SMITH

GASS, WILLIAM H. (1924–   )

As both a professor of philosophy and a writer of fiction, William Gass brings a unique combination of talents to postmodern fiction. In both vocations, he is necessarily concerned above all else with language, with the way in which it literally creates concepts in philosophy and people and things in fiction. Probably more than any other living writer, Gass firmly believes that words are our ultimate reality and that they ought not to be required merely to mimic external reality. In his insistence on the primacy of the "world within the word," he has become both the leading theoretician of metafiction and one of contemporary fiction's most meticulous craftsmen.

William Howard Gass was born in Fargo, North Dakota, on July 30, 1924, but the family moved shortly thereafter to Warren, Ohio, where he spent a childhood troubled by his mother's alcoholism and his father's crippling arthritis. His reaction to his troubled relationship with his parents was introversion and eventually a retreat into writing formalist fiction. Although his college studies were interrupted by service in the Navy during World War II, he received his B.A. degree in philosophy from Kenyon College in 1947. He went on to do graduate work under Max Black at Cornell University, where he also heard Ludwig Wittgenstein speak on several occasions. His study of metaphor under Black became the basis for much of his own literary practice, and Wittgenstein led him to realize both the astounding possibilities and limitations of language. While working on his doctoral dissertation, he taught philosophy at the College of Wooster (1950–1954). He received his Ph.D. in philosophy from Cornell in 1954 and accepted a teaching position at Purdue University, where he taught philosophy until 1969. Since 1969 he has taught at Washington University in St. Louis.

Gass' writing career began in the 1950s with the publication of short stories in *Accent* magazine. His first novel, *Omensetter's Luck*, was published in 1966 to critical acclaim but little popular interest. The novel is set in rural Ohio in the 1890s and uses the Faulknerian technique of presenting a touchstone character through the eyes of three other characters. The central character is Omensetter—a happy, Adamic character who, in his harmony with nature and his self-sufficiency, represents the American romantic ideal. He is presented first through the eyes of Israbestis Tott, the town historian who lives wholly within the past and his own imagination; then through Henry Pimber, Omensetter's landlord, who envies him but who kills himself when he finds that he is incapable of Omensetter's natural freedom; and finally through Jethro Furber, a minister who sees Omensetter's delight in the physical as a threat to the Christian doctrines of asceticism which he preaches in public but ignores in private. These three characters are typical of Gass' fiction in being essentially lonely, physically weak characters who seek refuge from the problems of life by immersing themselves in language. Even Omensetter, with all of his natural confidence, cannot solve their problems and leaves town a disillusioned man. The power of this novel, however, is not in the characters as much as in Gass' painstaking attention to the language itself—to individual sounds, words, and sentences. It is perhaps the first American novel written as carefully as if it were a poem.

Gass' second major work, *In the Heart of the Heart of the Country* (1968), is a collection of five short stories, each of which focuses on yet other disembodied characters attempting to create themselves through language. The first story, "The Pederson Kid," seems at first to be a Hemingway gangster story amid snow, but it concludes as an ironic initiation story affirming the youthful central character's psychological independence from his just-murdered father. Each of the middle three stories presents a different isolated character—an unemployed neighbor, a real estate salesman, and a frustrated housewife—in their private attempts to compensate for their failed lives by organizing their thoughts. The best and most well known of the stories is the title story. Constructed of 36 brief and individually titled sections, the story reveals the central character's attempts to find order in his muddled life through language, the only aspect of his life he can still control. In its lack of traditional plot structure and its collection of miniature essays, it also represents another major thrust of Gass' career: his attempt to explore and break down the restrictive limits of traditional genres.

Similar experimentation with the limits of genre occurs in his other works. *Willie Masters' Lonesome Wife* (1968) is both a fiction about a promiscuous wife attempting to coax an unenthusiastic lover into sharing her pleasure in the senses and an essay about how language seduces the reader into the very real sensuous pleasures of its own imaginative world. *On Being Blue* (1976) is an intriguing mixture of philosophical inquiry and a prose poem exploring the various levels of meaning in the single word "blue."

In recent years Gass' aesthetic theories have attracted more attention than his fiction, primarily because of a series of debates with John Gardner,* the standard-bearer of moral fiction. Gass' controversial assertion that the purpose of fiction is not primarily moral truth, but rather the creation of a verbal world is eloquently conveyed in three collections of theoretical and critical essays, *Fiction and the Figures of Life* (1970) and *The World Within the Word* (1978), and *Habitations of the Word* (1985).

The dense texture of Gass' language and the unsavory qualities of many of his characters have continued to keep his fiction from popular success, a situation he seems to accept and even to encourage. The eventual publication of his novel-in-progress, *The Tunnel*, seems likely to attract further critical acclaim but not a wider audience. It promises, however, to reaffirm Gass' uncompromising commitment to the reality of language and its use as the main human defense against psychological and spiritual chaos.

Selected Bibliography

Primary Sources

Omensetter's Luck. New York: New American Library, 1966.

In the Heart of the Heart of the Country. New York: Harper & Row, 1968.

Willie Masters' Lonesome Wife. Evanston, Ill.: Northwestern University Press, 1968.

Fiction and the Figures of Life. New York: Alfred A. Knopf, 1970.

The World Within the Word. New York: Alfred A. Knopf, 1978.

The First Winter of My Married Life (a portion of *The Tunnel*). Northridge, Calif.: Lord John Press, 1979.

Habitations of the Word. New York: Simon & Schuster, 1985.

Secondary Sources

Busch, Frederick. "But This Is What It Is Like to Live in Hell: William Gass's *In the Heart of the Heart of the Country*." *Modern Fiction Studies* 20 (1973): 97–103.

French, Ned. "Against the Grain: Theory and Practice in the Work of William H. Gass." *Iowa Review* 7 (Winter 1976): 96–106.

Gilman, Richard. "William H. Gass." In *The Confusion of Realms*. New York: Random House, 1969, pp. 69–81.

McCaffery, Larry. "The Art of Metafiction: William Gass's *Willie Masters' Lonesome Wife*." *Critique* 18 (Summer 1976): 21–35.

———. *The Metafictional Muse: The Works of Robert Coover, Donald Barthelme, and William H. Gass*. Pittsburgh: University of Pittsburgh Press, 1982.

———. "William H. Gass." *Dictionary of Literary Bibliography: American Novelists Since World War II*. Detroit: Gale Research Co., 1978, pp. 190–95.

———, and Tom LeClair, eds. "A Debate: William Gass and John Gardner" and "An Interview with William Gass." *Anything Can Happen: Interviews with Contemporary American Novelists*. Urbana: University of Illinois Press, 1983, pp. 20–31, 153–75.

Schneider, Richard J. "The Fortunate Fall in William Gass's *Omensetter's Luck*." *Critique* 18 (Summer 1976): 5–20.

Tanner, Tony. *City of Words*. New York: Harper & Row, 1971, pp. 269–72.

RICHARD J. SCHNEIDER

GRASS, GÜNTER (1927–   )

Although his prestige may have declined in the 1980s, Günter Grass is still regarded as the most prominent representative of post-World War II

German literature. More than any of his writer colleagues, he deserves credit for reestablishing the reputation of the German novel internationally.

Since the publication of his first novel, *The Tin Drum,* in 1959, Grass has enjoyed international fame and notoriety. Equally, Oskar Mazerath, the dwarfish narrator-hero of *The Tin Drum,* has joined the ranks of great, unforgettable characters in world literature.

Originally decried as a pornographer ("Pornograss") and a pervert in his own country, Grass is now widely read in German schools, and he has traveled extensively as an unofficial ambassador of German culture. Most of his writings have been translated into all major languages. Even in the United States, the name Günter Grass has, at least among literati, become a household word. *The Tin Drum* was on the American best-seller list for several months in 1963. Ironically, his novel *Local Anaesthetic* (1969), considered secondary by most critics, was highly successful in the United States and brought Grass to the attention of a wider American reading public. It was praised by *Time* magazine, which has featured Grass prominently and sympathetically, even having his portrait on the cover of the April 13, 1970, issue. The author did not, however, repeat his American success of *The Tin Drum* or *Local Anaesthetic* with his 1977 novel, *The Flounder.* Whereas in Germany *The Flounder* was again hailed as a major artistic accomplishment and achieved sales records, its American reception was rather cool. The book was primarily identified as a work by the author of *The Tin Drum.*

Grass was born in Danzig (now the Polish city of Gdańsk) in 1927. While still in his teens, he served briefly as an anti-aircraft auxiliary. After being wounded on the day of Hitler's last birthday, he was taken into an American prisoners' camp in Bavaria. When he was discharged two months later, he deliberately chose not to resume the traditional middle-class education expected of him. Instead of attending the *Gymnasium,* he became an apprentice to a tombstone cutter in Düsseldorf. Subsequently, he studied painting and sculpture at the Düsseldorf Academy of Art, played in a local jazz band, and began to write poetry. In 1958 he read before the Group 47, an influential literary forum where young German writers could read works-in-progress and have them criticized. Grass won the Group's coveted prize for what was to become *The Tin Drum.* This book catapulted its author from obscurity to instant celebrity status. It also marked the beginning of what, in retrospect, appears to have been Grass' most productive phase. In the late 1950s and early 1960s, in addition to *The Tin Drum,* a few plays, and some poetry and prose, Grass published two more novels, *Cat and Mouse* (1961) and *Dog Years* (1963). Those three books became known as "The Danzig Trilogy" even before they were reissued under that title much later.

Grass' talents are not limited to writing; in fact, he is an artist of stunning versatility. A graphic artist of international renown, he has illustrated his books with his own drawings and designed dust-jackets. In addition, he has produced some 150 etchings, which are considered works of fine art in their own right.

Not surprisingly, in a country that still reveres specialization, Grass' branching out into so many areas has aroused some suspicion among his fellow Germans. Especially when, in addition to his artistic endeavors, he became heavily involved in politics, campaigning actively for the Social Democrats in the 1960s and 1970s, many thought his literary career would be shortlived. Grass proved them wrong, however. His 700-page novel, *The Flounder*, was ample evidence that he had lost none of his epic talent. His most recent novel to date, *Headbirths* (1980) seems to have further strengthened Grass' reputation as Germany's most original and versatile writer.

The novels of "The Danzig Trilogy" have many important features in common. Not only is the city of Danzig a unifying subject; characters, themes, and events constantly overlap. They all contain a wealth of adventures and episodes, ideas and fantasies, which are, however, not ends in themselves. They reflect the savagery of Germany's Nazi period while, at the same time, satirizing the self-righteous, affluent society of the Adenauer era. Oskar's postwar Düsseldorf resembles in many ways Nazi Danzig. The ending of *Cat and Mouse*, a meeting of former war heroes, expresses Grass' concern that militarism, coupled with empty traditionalism, might be on the rise again in Germany. *Dog Years* is not only a satire of the economic miracle, but it also exposes former Nazis who are back in leading positions.

"The Danzig Trilogy" (particularly *The Tin Drum*) established Grass' reputation as a linguistic virtuoso. Indeed, in his fiction, Grass has employed all aspects of language, including colloquial speech, children's talk, dialect, as well as military and technical jargon. He has formed new words latent in the language and given old ones a new meaning. All this he blends into an iridescent, highly idiosyncratic style that has fascinated his readers and made extraordinary demands on his translators.

Grass' 1980 novel *Headbirths or The Germans Are Dying Out*, together with its immediate predecessors, *The Flounder* and *The Meeting at Telgte* (1979), in many ways constitute his second trilogy. Shifting the focus to Germany's future, Grass, no less politically engaged in the 1980s, has now taken up concerns such as women's liberation and its implications for men (*The Flounder*), environmentalism, rearmament, consumerism, overindustrialization, and the fear of world overpopulation (*Headbirths*), as well as the role of literature in a divided Germany (*The Meeting at Telgte*). Whether Grass will become equally successful as a literary chronicler of the Orwell decade remains to be seen.

Selected Bibliography

Primary Sources

Die Blechtrommel. Neuwied: Luchterhand, 1959. (*The Tin Drum.* Trans. Ralph
  Manheim. New York: Pantheon Books, 1963.)
Katz und Maus. Neuwied: Luchterhand, 1961. (*Cat and Mouse.* Trans. Ralph
  Manheim. New York: Harcourt, Brace & World, 1963.)
Hundejahre. Neuwied: Luchterhand, 1963. (*Dog Years.* Trans. Ralph Manheim.
  New York: Harcourt, Brace & World, 1965.)
Örtlich betäubt. Neuwied: Luchterhand, 1969. (*Local Anaesthetic.* Trans. Ralph
  Manheim. New York: Harcourt, Brace & World, 1969.)
Der Butt. Neuwied: Luchterhand, 1977. (*The Flounder.* Trans. Ralph Manheim.
  New York: Harcourt Brace Jovanovich, 1978.)
Das Treffen in Telgte. Neuwied: Luchterhand, 1979. (*The Meeting at Telgte.* Trans.
  Ralph Manheim. New York: Harcourt Brace Jovanovich, 1981.)
Kopfgeburten oder Die Deutschen sterben aus. Neuwied: Luchterhand, 1980.
  (*Headbirths or The Germans Are Dying Out.* Trans. Ralph Manheim. New
  York: Harcourt Brace Jovanovich, 1982.)

Secondary Sources

Brode, Hanspeter. *Günter Grass.* Munich: Beck; edition text + kritik, 1979.
Cunliffe, W. Gordon. *Günter Grass.* New York: Twayne Publishers, 1969.
Hollington, Michael. *Günter Grass. The Writer in a Pluralist Society.* London,
  Boston: Marion Boyars, 1980.
Mews, Siegfried, ed. *"The Fisherman and His Wife," Günter Grass's The Flounder
  in Critical Perspective.* New York: AMS Press, 1983.
Miles, Keith. *Günter Grass.* New York: Barnes & Noble, 1975.
Reddick, John. *The "Danzig Trilogy" of Günter Grass. A Study of The Tin Drum,
  Cat and Mouse and Dog Years.* New York: Harcourt Brace Jovanovich,
  1975.
Ryan, Judith. " 'Into the Orwell Decade': Günter Grass's Dystopian Trilogy,"
  World Literature Today 55, No. 4 (1981): 564–67.
Tank, Kurt Lothar. *Günter Grass.* New York: Frederick Ungar, 1969.

JÜRGEN KOPPENSTEINER

H

HANDKE, PETER (1942–   )

Peter Handke is a young Austrian author whose widely translated novels, plays, and poems have been hailed as a major contribution to the contemporary style known as postmodernism. Like many of his fellow postmodernists, Handke has rejected the traditional modernist aim of totalizing human experience through literature in favor of a new and self-apparent type of writing that steadfastly refuses to point to referents outside of itself, insisting that literature represent only itself and the language from which it derives. Handke's writing, largely devoid of the metaphors and comparisons that convey the implicit notion of a prestabilized connectedness of things, casts a skeptical glance at the function of language in contemporary society. Handke sees modern individuals imprisoned in a rigid semiotic system that has broken loose from its signified reality, thus ensnaring them in the fateful conviction that the signifiers surrounding them accurately reflect and make knowable the factual world. Handke's work, particularly his early novels and plays, deconstructs this erroneous notion by operating largely on the signifier level without referring to an omnipresent signified. Handke's novels and plays are not *about* something; they *are* that something.

Born in 1942 in the small Austrian village of Griffen, Handke, whose father was a German and a *Wehrmacht* paymaster, spent his early years growing up in his home town and with his father's family in Berlin, surrounded by the ever-present destruction of war. His earliest memories are of leaving the Soviet Zone of a divided postwar Berlin to return to the backwardness of his natal village. After attending a cloister school (he was headed for the priesthood), where he read widely and experimented with fiction, he attended Graz University, where he majored in law. In Graz he spent more time with that city's literary avant-gardists—now known as the Graz Group—than with his books. His first stories were published in the Group's journal, *manuskripte*. Handke's first novels, published by the prestigious German house of Suhrkamp, brought instant success with the critics, if not with the reading public. The largely experimental novels *The Hornets* (1966) and *The Peddler* (1967) and the parallel plays *Offending the Audience* (1966) and *Kaspar* (1968) received a good deal of attention from critics and intellectuals, but Handke wasn't able to reach a wider readership until the early 1970s, when he published *The Goalie's Anxiety at the Penalty Kick* (1970), *Short Letter, Long Farewell* (1972), and *A Sorrow Beyond Dreams* (1972). By the mid-1970s, Handke's international reputation was established.

Handke's journey from the brash young rebel of the 1960s to the mature spokesman of the new-subjective literature of the late 1970s and early 1980s brought him to the United States, where on several occasions he lectured, traveled, and read from his books. His startling appearance at the Princeton meeting of Germany's respected Group 47 is today legend; he upbraided these established representatives of postwar social realism for misunderstanding the function and effect of literature, for the mistaken belief that literature, a creation of words, dealt with the factual world instead of its representation in language. He accused the writers present of believing that in manipulating words they were changing the world.

Handke's experiences in America found their expression in *Short Letter, Long Farewell*, a novel based on a journey through the United States, and *Slow Journey Home* (1979), in which the protagonist is a geologist working in Alaska and California. Handke has also lived in Paris (*The Weight of the World*, 1977; *The Lesson of Sainte Victoire*, 1980; *Children's Story*, 1981) and in several German cities. Today he resides with his teenage daughter in a suburb of Salzburg, Austria.

Handke's obsession with the notion that language stands as a barrier, a prefixed, falsified system of signifiers no longer representing a coherent world, occupied his early work, from the densely complex *Hornets* through the playful but obtuse *Peddler* to *The Goalie's Anxiety at the Penalty Kick*. *The Goalie's Anxiety* marks a turning point in Handke's work, a new direction in which more directly human concerns begin to supplant the rather abstract view of humankind found in his earlier work. In these novels of the middle period, real, living human beings suffer in the semiotic process; their alienation often stems from their inability to break through the language structures surrounding them to reach the world. The protagonists of *Short Letter, Long Farewell*, *A Sorrow Beyond Dreams* (in this case the narrator himself), *A Moment of True Feeling* (1975), and *The Left-Handed Woman* (1976) all suffer because they are unable to impose a meaningful order on the world around them—an order that might re-establish a link between themselves and their fellow humans.

The Weight of the World, Handke's Paris journal, announces another shift in his view of art and life, initiating a third phase in his writing. The hopelessness and dread his characters experience, Handke now believes, lies in their rootlessness, in the lack of a transcendent signifier in their lives, a signifier that can only be rooted in myth. Thus, a concern with myth and meaning dominates Handke's latest work, from *Slow Journey Home* through *The Lesson of Sainte Victoire* and *Children's Story* to *Through the Villages* (1981) and *A Chinese of Pain* (1983). Each of these works portrays the pressing need, often expressed by a protagonist in quest of meaning, to discover myths that might provide a sense-giving link between threatened human existence and a meaningless world.

Handke's most recent writing, though unconventional as always, shares many concerns with West Germany's literature of New Subjectivity, a movement largely inspired by young leftists of the 1960s and early 1970s who have now withdrawn from activism in a world of reified and estranged human relationships and turned inward in an attempt to establish an inner, personal authenticity. In a very important sense, Handke, never one to jump on bandwagons, presaged this movement with his work of the early 1970s.

Thus, Handke's literature has progressed from the pessimistic skepticism and rebellious flippancy of the 1960s to a more mature conviction that art and the artist can play a vital role in human society.

Selected Bibliography

Primary Sources

Die Hornissen (The Hornets). Frankfurt: Suhrkamp, 1966.

Die Angst des Tormanns beim Elfmeter. Frankfurt: Suhrkamp, 1970. (*The Goalie's Anxiety at the Penalty Kick*. Trans. Michael Roloff. New York: Farrar, Straus & Giroux, 1972.)

Der kurze Brief zum langen Abschied. Frankfurt: Suhrkamp, 1972. (*Short Letter, Long Farewell*. Trans. Ralph Manheim. New York: Farrar, Straus & Giroux, 1974.)

Wunschloses Unglück. Salzburg: Residenz, 1972. (*A Sorrow Beyond Dreams*. Trans. Ralph Manheim. New York: Farrar, Straus & Giroux, 1975.)

Die Stunde der wahren Empfindung. Frankfurt: Suhrkamp, 1975. (*A Moment of True Feeling*. Trans. Ralph Manheim. New York: Farrar, Straus & Giroux, 1977.)

Die linkshändige Frau. Frankfurt: Suhrkamp, 1976. (*The Left-Handed Woman*. Trans. Ralph Manheim. New York: Farrar, Straus & Giroux, 1978.)

Das Gewicht der Welt: Ein Journal (November 1975-März 1977). Salzburg: Residenz, 1977. (*The Weight of the World*. Trans. Ralph Manheim. New York: Farrar, Straus & Giroux, 1983.)

Slow Homecoming. Trans. Ralph Manheim. New York: Farrar, Straus & Giroux, 1985.

Secondary Sources

Hern, Nicholas. *Peter Handke.* New York: Frederick Ungar, 1972.
Kermode, Frank. "The Model of the Modernist." *New York Review of Books,*
     May 1, 1975, 20–22.
Klinkowitz, Jerome. "Aspects of Handke: The Fiction." *Partisan Review* 43 (1978):
     416–25.
————, and James Knowlton. *Peter Handke and the Postmodern Transformation:
     The Goalie's Journey Home.* Columbia: University of Missouri Press, 1983.
Schlueter, June. "An Interview with Peter Handke." *Studies in Twentieth Century
     Literature* 24 (1979): 63–73.
————. *The Plays and Novels of Peter Handke.* Pittsburgh: University of Pittsburgh
     Press, 1981.
————, and Ellis Finger. *Peter Handke: An Annotated Bibliography.* New York:
     Garland Publishing, 1982.

                                                              JAMES KNOWLTON

HANNAH, BARRY (1942–   )

Since 1972 Barry Hannah has published five novels and a prize-winning collection of short stories. The setting of most of his fiction is the contemporary South. Hannah's prose is characterized by lyricism, zany humor, and violence, as he uses the South as microcosm of the universal human condition.

Hannah was born in Clinton, Mississippi, on April 23, 1942. He received his B.A. degree from Mississippi College in Clinton and his M.A. and M.F.A. degrees from the University of Arkansas. He has taught literature and fiction writing at Clemson University, the University of Alabama, the University of Montana, and the University of Mississippi. He has also been writer-in-residence at Middlebury College. He has received a Bellaman Foundation Fellowship, a Bread Loaf Fellowship, the first Arnold Gingrich Short Fiction Award for *Airships,* and a Guggenheim Fellowship. He has been married twice and is the father of three children.

Hannah began *Geronimo Rex* (1972) while he was a student at the University of Arkansas. It is a wild, energetic initiation novel that tells the story of Harry Monroe, the novel's protagonist and narrator, as he grows up in Dream of Pines, Louisiana, a squalid paper-mill town. Harry's life as a high school and college student constitutes a comic quest, a search for certitude, symbolized by his longings for the bright world outside the boundaries of the provinces. It is a story of the South caught up in the turmoil of the civil rights movement, a story told with surreal humor and characterized by violent incident. *Geronimo Rex* was received by the majority of its reviewers as a brilliant first novel, and it was nominated for a National Book Award.

In Hannah's second novel, *Nightwatchmen* (1973), Harry Monroe reappears, this time as one of the narrators of this arcane and outrageous murder mystery. The setting is a sleepy Southern college campus which is beset by the "Knocker," an unknown assailant who clubs graduate students and faculty. *Nightwatchmen* is pervaded by violence: in the midst of beheadings, rapes, and shootings, there is also death and mutilation from hurricane "Camille." Hannah molds this violence around a core of humor that in its irony is reminiscent of Nabokov and Celine.

Hannah's *Airships* (1978) is composed of 20 stories, nine of which first appeared in *Esquire*. Most of these stories are told by physically wounded and handicapped narrators, and their subjects range from the Civil War to an American apocalypse in the future. Several of the stories were gleaned from two of Hannah's aborted novels, one about the exploits of Confederate General Jeb Stuart and the other about the lives of professional tennis players. The masterful story "Mother Rooney Unscrolls the Hurt" is an expanded version of an episode in *Geronimo Rex*. The short stories of *Airships* display Hannah's development of new narrative voices and his increased exploration of surreal humor and action. Also noteworthy here are his experiments with use of time and place in several stories, which are set in fantasylands of no determinable era.

In *Ray* (1980) the title hero is a medical doctor, ex-fighter pilot, and budding poet. In some ways, Dr. Ray is Harry Monroe at middle age, a man daffy about music and poetry, a man troubled by the vagaries of love and marriage. With a sometimes misdirected idealism, Ray wants to protect the good necessary things: motherhood, innocent children, good poetry, the hapless victims of the world, but he often botches the work and becomes a victim himself. His second wife tells it this way: "There is something about you, Ray, that wants to set yourself deliberately in peril and in trash."

Ray's life is plagued by his alcoholism and the dissolution of his marriages. In the larger world of the novel, the Vietnam War becomes symbolic of a universal malaise. Despite all these troubles, *Ray* ends with an optimistic speech by Ray: "And you can see that my poetry is improving. Hoo! Ray! Ray, yes, Ray! Doctor Ray is okay!"

The first two chapters of *The Tennis Handsome* (1983) are expanded versions of two of the *Airships* stories. This novel tells the story of Dr. Baby Levaster and French Edward, the handsome pro tennis player of the title. Levaster forsakes his medical career to become sidekick and protector of the brain-damaged French Edward. A Vietnam veteran named Bobby Smith, a man with a very peculiar concept of history, is added to the duo. These three men are haunted by the ubiquitous Dr. Word, bisexual English professor and tennis coach. As French Edward's tennis career crumbles before the juggernaut of middle age, he develops a new occupation—he becomes a poet who gains inspiration from being struck by a lightning bolt and from orthodox electric shock treatment. The novel ends with the violent deaths of Drs. Levaster and Word. French Edward goes forward, trying to find Tennessee Williams, so that the playwright can help with Edward's new career.

In several ways, *Ray* and *The Tennis Handsome* mark a change in direction for Hannah's fiction. These two recent novels are shorter than the early novels and have fewer characters and less plot complication. To this point, in a recent interview Hannah said, "What I'm after now in my work is to make it short, clean, interesting. I want to let my readers enjoy the book without my having to tie everything together in a conventional plot."

Much of Barry Hannah's fiction is experimental and belongs to the category of dark comedy. All of it presents a highly original portrait of American life, both past and present, particularly American life in the South. It is a fiction that is consistently poetic, with a language and style both dazzling and believable.

Selected Bibliography

Primary Sources

Geronimo Rex. New York: Viking Press, 1972.
Nightwatchmen. New York: Viking Press, 1973.
Airships. New York: Alfred A. Knopf, 1978.
Ray. New York: Alfred A. Knopf, 1980.
The Tennis Handsome. New York: Alfred A. Knopf, 1983.
Captain Maximus. New York: Alfred A. Knopf, 1985.

Secondary Sources

Demott, Benjamin. "Rudeness Is Our Only Hope." *The New York Times Book Review*, November 16, 1980, pp. 7, 26.
Gregory, Sinda, and Larry McCaffery. "An Interview with Barry Hannah." *Conjunctions* 5 (1983): 193–205.
Israel, Charles. "Barry Hannah." *Dictionary of Literary Biography: American Novelists Since World War II*. Vol. 6. Detroit: Gale Research Co.: 1980.
Vandarsdall, R. "The Spirits Will Not Win Through: An Interview with Barry Hannah." *The Southern Review* 19 (Spring 1983): 317–341.

CHARLES ISRAEL

HARTMAN, GEOFFREY (1929–)

Geoffrey Hartman, professor of English and comparative literature at Yale University, has distinguished himself as one of the most prolific, freewheeling, and playful of American critics. Along with J. Hillis Miller* and Paul de Man,* Hartman has pushed hermeneutics to the point of deconstruction, and like his colleagues he cites Jacques Derrida* as one of his main guides in this endeavor. In books such as *The Fate of Reading* (1975) and *Criticism in the Wilderness* (1980), Hartman breaks down the barriers between commentary and text, criticism and philosophy, explication and confession. In a loose-ended, conversational style that rarely presents a definite argument and never expresses a single point of view, Hartman relies on the Derridean concept of textuality as a liberating force, freeing criticism to penetrate all dimensions of writing, from the most personal to the most theoretical.

Born in Germany in 1929, Hartman attended school in the United States, receiving his doctorate from Yale in 1953. His doctoral dissertation, which became his first book, *The Unmediated Vision* (1954), was composed under the direction of René Wellek. Hartman cites such figures as Ludwig Lewisohn and Randolph Bourne as distant precursors, insofar as they called for a new American classicism that was to be Continental in inspiration rather than English. Indeed, the ideal of a nonparochial American criticism has been evident in all his work. He names Northrop Frye and Harold Bloom* as influences, and Kenneth Burke, because of Burke's emphasis on politics entering into art and criticism. But Hartman's characteristic points of reference have been the phenomenological and hermeneutic traditions of France and Germany, especially in their hyperstructuralist extremes.

Hartman's early work took the form of a direct, unmediated communing with the text. This approach allowed him to take criticism beyond what he saw as the formalism of the New Critics, and in *The Unmediated Vision* and *Wordsworth's Poetry* (1964) we can detect the sure sign of Continental hermeneutics at work. *The Unmediated Vision* presents a narrative of desecularization, whereby the removal of the authority of sacred texts in the modern period opened artists to nature, the body, and consciousness. The Wordsworth study describes that poet's development as a dialectic of nature and consciousness, whose mediation lies in imagination. This theme is repeated in "Romanticism and Anti-Self-Consciousness" in *Beyond Formalism* (1970), in which the "fixated self-consciousness" of a J. S. Mill is seen as a fall from nature, to be cured by romantic imagination. Elements of deconstruction—"doublings, circlings, the generation of personae, metaphorical transference, and syntactical distribution" ("Retrospect 1971" to *Wordsworth's Poetry*)—are present but subordinated to the critic's direct description of the artist's intentions and the clear presentation of his development, which never fails to find some satisfying point of resolution, no matter how complicated.

In the 1970s Hartman's vocabulary changed, so that "proliferating texts" became as important in the liberation of the modern artist as those solid entities, nature, self, and imagination. The ideal of unmediated vision, which underlay the early direct communing with texts, was now considered to lie beyond the reach of language because of the thoroughly mediating character of language itself. Accuracy of description began to look less and less feasible, in the face of what Hartman calls "the scandalous figure."

In *The Fate of Reading*, Hartman launches into a confessional mode in the opening essay, "The Interpreter: A Self-Analysis." He admits to an inferiority complex vis-à-vis art and a superiority complex vis-à-vis other critics; and then he proceeds to deconstruct both complexes, with the result that criticism is freed to explore all possibilities of style and is made equal to the text criticized. This theme is broadened in *Criticism in the Wilderness*, in which the critic achieves parity with the creator, partly because of the indeterminacy of language, which implies for Hartman the impossibility of complete closure or sure communication, even in the works of the masters.

Hartman, however, cannot be reduced to deconstructionist orthodoxy. Just as *Criticism in the Wilderness* contains a muted apology for Hegel's teleological rationalism, so too his latest work, *Saving the Text* (1981), a commentary-cum-confession based on Jacques Derrida's* *Glas*, reinstates the *bête noir* of the deconstructionists, closure or unified meaning. Without denying the slippery quality of linguistic (and critical) reference, Hartman can justify closure, albeit with characteristic paradoxicality, as "positive negation" (pp. 148–50).

Selected Bibliography

Primary Sources

The Unmediated Vision. New Haven, Conn.: Yale University Press, 1954.
Wordsworth's Poetry 1787–1814. New Haven, Conn.: Yale University Press, 1964.
Beyond Formalism. New Haven, Conn.: Yale University Press, 1970.
The Fate of Reading and Other Essays. Chicago: University of Chicago Press, 1975.
"The Recognition Scene of Criticism." *Critical Inquiry* 4 (1978): 407–16.
Psychoanalysis and the Question of the Text. Baltimore: Johns Hopkins University Press, 1978.
Deconstruction and Criticism. London: Routledge & Kegan Paul, 1979.
"Hermeneutic Hesitation: A Dialogue Between Geoffrey Hartman and Julian Moynahan." Ed. Edward Bloom. *Novel* 12 (1979): 101–12.
Criticism in the Wilderness. New Haven, Conn.: Yale University Press, 1980.
Saving the Text: Literature/Derrida/Philosophy. Baltimore: Johns Hopkins University Press, 1981.

Secondary Sources

Culler, Jonathan. *On Deconstruction: Theory and Criticism After Structuralism*. Ithaca, N.Y.: Cornell University Press, 1982.
Hughes, Daniel. "Geoffrey Hartman, Geoffrey Hartman." *MLN* 96 (1981): 1134–48.
Martin, Wallace. "Literary Critics and Their Discontents: A Response to Geoffrey Hartman." *Critical Inquiry* 4 (1977): 397–406.

Norris, Christopher. *Deconstruction: Theory and Practice*. New York: Methuen, 1982.

STEVEN CRESAP

HASSAN, IHAB (1925–   )

The critic perhaps most responsible for the currency of postmodernism as a literary concept, Ihab Hassan remains the critic perhaps most responsive to the varieties of postmodern experience. He has evolved from postformalist critic of American and comparative literature to paracritic of posthumanist thought and postmodern society and increasingly has forgone literary analysis in order to promulgate his often idiosyncratic cultural theories. He has essayed the new in literature, ideas, and social formations and has shaped novel discursive forms for its expression, but he has increasingly tempered his zeal for contemporaneity and for experimentalism with esteem for the values of the liberal humanist tradition and for the true expression salient among them. As a result of Hassan's focal shift, his work has come to resist assessment as literary criticism; as a result of his humoral shift, it has become anomalous within the postmodern critical discourse its author helped to found.

Born in Cairo, Egypt, on October 17, 1925, and naturalized as a U.S. citizen in 1956, Ihab Hassan was graduated with highest honors from the University of Cairo in 1946 and took his doctorate in English at the University of Pennsylvania in 1953. Following an instructorship at Rensselaer Polytechnic Institute, Hassan taught for 16 years at Wesleyan University, whose Benjamin L. Waite Professorship in English he assumed in 1964. Since 1970, he has held the Vilas Research Professorship in English and Comparative Literature at the University of Wisconsin at Milwaukee. Hassan has received two Guggenheim Fellowships, three Fulbright Lectureships, and appointments to the School of Letters of Indiana University, the Salzburg Seminars in American Studies, the Woodrow Wilson International Center for Scholars, the Camargo Foundation, and the Rockefeller Study Center; he has delivered in some 25 countries over 300 lectures on modern literature and culture; and he has published over 125 scholarly articles and reviews, seven books, and two editions.

Although his doctoral dissertation formed a comparative study of French symbolist and British modernist poetry, Hassan won national attention as a specialist in contemporary American fiction. Informed by existentialist thought, his *Radical Innocence: Studies in the Contemporary American Novel* (1961) displayed an urgent prose that corresponded to Hassan's then emergent apocalyptism and a tripartite division that signaled his abiding prepossession with heroism, formalism, and individualism. Hassan found that the postwar American novel focused on its protagonist's need for self-invention when faced with oppressive social and cultural norms and for self-transcendence when those norms were internalized. He found, however, that this novel figured the redemptive act of rebellion in an ambiguous quixotic gesture that left the protagonist both rebel and victim. Having followed this pioneering study with *Crise du héros américain contemporain* (1964), Hassan revamped its thesis a decade later in *Contemporary American Literature, 1945–1972: An Introduction* (1973). Its prose again urgent and its text again divided between assessments of individual talents and reports on types and trends of writing, this mass-market survey reflected the influence of the 1960s no less on the sensibility of the critics than on the literature they addressed. Hassan now found that "the opposing Self pursues beyond disaffiliation a new concept of love or of freedom," a pursuit in which "saintliness and crime violently merge in quest of a new consciousness."

In the intervening years, Hassan had written two comparative studies that traced literary origins of the apocalyptic quest for new consciousness increasingly central to Hassan's reading of modern literature. In *The Literature of Silence: Henry Miller and Samuel Beckett* (1967), Hassan postulated for literature the alterity of positive and negative silence while he transposed from characters to authors the alterity of hero and anti-hero. Borrowing his concept from Elizabeth Sewell, Hassan placed Stéphane Mallarmé and Arthur Rimbaud at the poles of language aspiring to Nothing and language aspiring to All—to number and to dream—and advanced Beckett and Miller as their counterparts in modern prose. Concluding that "the polarities of creation and destruction no longer exclude one another; they exclude the middle," Hassan laid the groundwork for his seminal *Dismemberment of Orpheus: Toward a Postmodern Literature* (1971). Interleaving chapters on individual authors with two interludes on literary trends, Hassan here focused on the former of "two accents of silence" in modern literature: "the negative echo of language, autodestructive, demonic, nihilist"; and "its positive stillness, self-transcendent, sacramental, plenary." But the more preoccupied with this accent Hassan's work had become, the stronger had become his call for the visionary imagination signaled by the latter accent. Concluding here with the hope that "art may move toward a redeemed imagination, commensurate with the full mystery of human consciousness," Hassan had pressed literature to its vanishing point so that it might rediscover itself, as he soon would argue, "at some future point" where "a new form of art, of consciousness, may lie."

Hassan's subsequent two books charted that consciousness in its cultural variousness. *Paracriticisms: Seven Speculations of the Times* (1975) comprised seven essays on criticism and literature and on syncretisms of myth and science, ideology, and technology; *The Right Promethean Fire: Imagination, Science, and Cultural Change* (1980) interwove its five essays on criticism, literature, the arts, the sciences, and planetary society with four extended autobiographical extracts. In these books, Hassan developed his paracriticism, his "attempt to recover the art of multivocation." Its visual surface distinguished by experimental typography and by such devices as the mosaic and the catalogue, its prose texture by aphorism and by a complex patterning of allusions, images, and ideas, paracriticism was meant to fuse the analytical and the intuitive, the ideational and the experiential, the objectively verifiable and the subjectively testifiable. In *Paracriticisms,* Hassan introduced the "new gnosticism" that he would define as "that tendency of mind to dematerialize reality, to gather more and more mind in itself, to turn nature into culture, culture into language, language into immediate consciousness," a tendency he saw manifested in and acceler- ated by such phenomena as the ephemeralization of technology and the revolution in electronic communications media. His *Right Promethean Fire* informed by an abiding desire to reconcile transcendentalist and post- structuralist thought, Hassan there absorbed his new gnosticism into a posthumanism that would entail a re-vision of the human form and a re- vision of human destiny; but he also contended that corporeality and mor- tality would remain the human reality that brakes the drive of the human imagination through language to pure mind.

Hassan's project displays a marked continuity: the elegant, if urgent, prose became epigram and aphorism, the symmetrical structures became elaborate architectonics; the characters and authors needing to self-invent and self-transcend became the paracritic testifying in an existential act of vatic imagination; the literature of silence, straining in the alterity of num- ber and dream, became modern society, straining between the two cultures, and paracritical discourse, straining within its own aporia; postmodernism as "a contemporary artistic movement" became absorbed into postmo- dernity in its current macrohistorical and metahistorical acceptations; and the apocalyptic soundings, the probes for new consciousness, quit epilogues and postludes to become the body of the text. Having reached this high pitch of mannerism, personalism, reflexivity, and speculativeness, Hassan since has returned to more traditional forms of exposition and to more discretely delineated, if not quite discreet, subject matters: he has replaced his new gnosticism with a new pragmatism informed by his reading of William James and Richard Rorty and advanced in such essays as "Plu- ralism in Postmodern Perspective"; he has reprised his study of heroism, its anti-heroic component now absent, in a work-in-progress on American quest literature; and he has reinstated the individual subject to centrality in his autobiography-in-progress, *Passage from Egypt.* But Hassan's ad- venturousness also remains continuous; he has evolved from literary critic to paracritic to yet something else, not in order to shift from critical to imaginative literature but precisely in order to confute that tawdry opposition.

Selected Bibliography

Primary Sources

Radical Innocence: Studies in the Contemporary American Novel. Princeton, N.J.:
    Princeton University Press, 1961.
Crise du héros américain contemporain. Paris: Lettres Modernes, 1964.
The Literature of Silence: Henry Miller and Samuel Beckett. New York: Alfred A.
    Knopf, 1967.
The Dismemberment of Orpheus: Toward a Postmodern Literature. New York:
    Oxford University Press, 1971.
Contemporary American Literature, 1945–1972: An Introduction. New York: Fred-
    erick Ungar, 1973.
Paracriticisms: Seven Speculations of the Times. Urbana: University of Illinois Press,
    1975.
The Right Promethean Fire: Imagination, Science, and Cultural Change. Urbana:
    University of Illinois Press, 1980.

Secondary Sources

Blinde, Patricia. "Avant-Garde Criticism: The Criticism of Exhaustion." *DAI* (May
    1978) 38, no. 11: 6694A–95A.
Caramello, Charles. "On Ihab Hassan." *Chicago Review* 33, no. 3 (1983): 78–81.
————. "Returning in *The Right Promethean Fire*." *Silverless Mirrors: Book, Self
    and Postmodern American Fiction.* Tallahassee: Florida State University
    Press, 1983, pp. 174–210.
Klinkowitz, Jerome, and Loree Rackstraw. "The American 1970's: Recent Intel-
    lectual Trends." *Revue Francaise d'Etudes Americaines* 8 (1979): 243–54.
Scheer-Schazler, Brigette. "From New Criticism to Paracriticism: Some Comments
    on the Work of Ihab Hassan." *Americana-Austriaca.* Wien and Stuttgart:
    Wilhelm Braumuller, 1980, pp. 117–32.

                                                                        CHARLES CARAMELLO

HEJINIAN, LYN (1941–   )

No writer of her generation has provided as much in the way of meticulously recorded biographical detail as has Lyn Hejinian in her monumental
"prose poem novel" *My Life* (1980). This information, however, is not
presented as subservient to (evidence for) a dominant narrative line, a
teleological exposition of one's events and their consequences, the self
viewed as an externalized public fact. More typical is this account of her
earliest memory, in which memory itself, that universal mode of editing,
is the pertinent issue: "A moment yellow, just as four years later, when
my father returned home from the war, the moment of greeting him, as
he stood at the bottom of the stairs, younger, thinner than when he had
left, was purple—though moments are no longer so colored." This sentence, which begins *My Life*, seemingly might initiate any autobiography.
In addition to the color-coded meditation on memory, this is a tale complete

within itself, with two characters who undergo transformations. This containment is subtly emphasized, beyond the reiteration of the word "moment," by Hejinian's use of vowels: the same long *o* which dominates the first clause likewise dominates the last, a bracketing index of closure.

This sense of completeness, of the self-valuable local unit of writing in all its presentness and presence, is an essential element in Hejinian's mature work. The reader who (perhaps not noting the deviant nature of that first sentence, whose independent clause lacks a verb and is constructed around a most arch inversion, the adjective "yellow" trailing its noun) anticipates an easy glide into the transparent plenitude of referential meanings coordinated about a never-present abstraction, such as character or plot, might not make it through the next five sentences: "Somewhere, in the background, rooms share a pattern of small roses. Pretty is as pretty does. The better things were gathered in a pen. The windows were narrowed by white gauze curtains which were never loosened. Hence, repetitions, free from all ambition." Another reader, conditioned by modernism, might expect these separate statements to gather themselves together at some deferred moment into distinct narrative and/or thematic lines. They do and they don't. They do only insofar as the work is, as it professes to be, autobiographical. As the source for most, although not all, of the sentences, the events and configurations of Hejinian's own existence pattern the content of the book's 37 paragraphs of 37 sentences each (composed in 1978, when Hejinian was herself 37). A careful reading will yield signs of occasions both public (the race riots of the 1960s) and personal (the death of her father, the birth of her children).

Yet, although these occurrences are often organized approximately around a paragraph equivalent in its sequence to her age at the time of the event (thus, the first memory in the first sentence, or the recurrence of sentences in the twenty-first paragraph concerning setting up housekeeping in an apartment, presumably in Boston), this principle never dominates the writing: a discussion with her youngest child is reported on page 63, while an image of pregnancy follows in the next paragraph. Themes do accumulate, but—in that optical sense which the referential dimension of language so often suggests—they never resolve.

Thirty-seven crystalline structures, *My Life* reaches an equilibrium at no less than three levels: at the level of the individual unit, in this instance the sentence, to a degree that is rare even in the best poetry; at the level of the paragraph, each of which is a work unto itself—the twenty-first is just as much "about" naming and metaphor—something Hejinian emphasizes in endowing these small chapters with titles, phrases that often recur elsewhere in the book; and at the level of the whole, nothing less than a vision of what it means, individually, to be human. Critical to the success of this volume is Hejinian's ability to keep all three levels perceptibly present and active: the work never flattens toward a single effect. As rich in nuance as it is simple in plan, as intimate as it is formally stunning, *My Life* has had an enormous impact on writers who would stake out a territory between the arbitrary domains of poetry and fiction.

The desire for a writing or language whose meaning is not merely instrumental, slavish to some exterior intent, and whose value and integrity must be located within the terms of its own existence, perceiving itself more as process than product, can be seen in "Mythopoesis." This work appeared in *Epoch*, the Cornell literary magazine, in 1964, the first publication of a recent Radcliffe graduate, C. H. Hejinian. A canto in a sense far more literal than ever envisioned by Pound, the 29-page poem is openly derivative of Joyce's *Finnegans Wake*, convoluted with the rush of sea sounds and neologisms ("wakelyn" "poetide"), tending toward glossalalia.

Married at the time to novelist/physician John Hejinian, she adopted the initials of her maiden name, Carolyn Hall, in publishing works in university and small press journals throughout the remainder of the 1960s because, she discovered, male editors and poets immediately stopped taking her seriously as a writer and thinker once they discovered she was a woman. She and her husband separated after their return to the Bay Area, where she, as the daughter of a Cal professor, had in part grown up and where her brother, installation and performance artist Doug Hall, was establishing himself as a member of the West Coast visual arts scene.

After the breakup, she, her two children and saxophonist Larry Ochs moved onto a piece of land near Willits, California, where they built a house, sans electricity, owned a horse named Tuumba, and remained for several years. The relative solitude of the Willits period seems to have been critical in Hejinian's development as a writer. Her one self-published pamphlet prior to the move, *the gRReat adventure* (1970), reflects an author still working through the many possibilities of influence, notably that of Philip Whalen. *A Thought Is the Bride of What Thinking* (1976), the first publication of her own Tuumba Press, is the work of a seasoned and confident artist. Already the three essays of that text *are* poems and have moved beyond the constraints of both influence and genre.

Tuumba Press would eventually publish 50 books by such writers as Barrett Watten,* Rae Armantrout, Charles Bernstein,* Lynne Dreyer, Kit Robinson, and Jean Day, an accomplishment that caused Don Byrd in *Sulfur 8* to say, "She alone manages to bring us more 'nutrition of impluse,' . . . than the National Poetry Series and the university presses combined."

After her return to Berkeley in 1977, Hejinian saw her work reach a broader audience for the first time. A major text that preceded *My Life* was the serial poem *Writing Is an Aid to Memory* (1978). She has served on the literature panel of the National Endowment for the Arts, has had her works translated into several languages, and has traveled in Europe and the Soviet Union with her husband's Rova Saxophone Quartet, a post-jazz new music ensemble. $L=A=N=G=U=A=G=E$ magazine published a critical feature on her work in June 1979. She is presently working on a series of prose pieces entitled *The Green*, scheduled for publication by This Press.

Selected Bibliography

Primary Sources

the gRReat adventure. Self-published, no date listed but 1970 (includes a collaboration with Doug Hall).
A Thought Is the Bride of What Thinking. Berkeley, Calif.: Tuumba Press, 1976.
A Mask of Motion. Providence, R.I.: Burning Deck Press, 1977.
Writing Is an Aid to Memory. Berkeley, Calif.: The Figures, 1978.
Gesualdo. Berkeley, Calif.: Tuumba Press, 1978.
My Life. Providence, R.I.: Burning Deck Press, 1980.

RON SILLIMAN

HOBAN, RUSSELL (1925–)

How many children's stories contain parodies of Samuel Beckett's dramaturgy? Exactly one, I would guess: Russell Hoban's *The Mouse and His Child*, and that fact shows the sophistication that sets this novel apart from most other children's books and signals Hoban's transition to writing some of the most interesting adult novels being written anywhere by anybody right now. Although the identity quest of the mouse and his child is geared to the development of children and is quite conventional as plot, Hoban manages to invest his children's-book imagery with metaphysical complexity and psychological insight. It's as if the simplicity and openness of the symbolic processes characteristic of children's literature allow Hoban to be ostensibly metaphysical in a way that would be too obvious in a normal adult book. And yet he succeeds in carrying this metaphysical directness, in one way or another, into his adult novels, making each of them (with one possible exception) a fresh, original essay into novelistic form.

Born on February 4, 1925, in Lansdale, Pennsylvania (near Philadelphia), to Russian-Jewish immigrant parents, Russell Hoban grew up in the verbally fertile world of a journalist father who produced and performed in plays in the Yiddish theaters of the time. He began his career as a visual artist, attending the Philadelphia Museum School of Industrial Art (1941–1943), where he met his first wife, Lilian. He was married and off to World War II at the early age of 19. After the war he settled in New York City, curiously unaffected by his military experience, at least insofar as his writing is concerned (until his most recent novel, *Pilgermann*). After a hodgepodge of miscellaneous jobs and free-lance illustrating in the immediate postwar years, he worked in advertising as TV art director and copywriter in the 1950s and 1960s. Combining his interests in the verbal and the visual arts, he had begun to do children's books as early as 1959 (soon yielding the illustration of them to his wife and others), producing about 40 of them over the years. The most substantial of them, *Mouse*, was published in 1967.

Mouse marked a change not only in Hoban's writing, but also in his whole life. His marriage broke up, estranging him from his children, and in 1969 he moved to England where he has since resided and worked, though he maintains his American citizenship. His first adult novel, *The Lion of Boaz-Jachin and Jachin-Boaz* (1973), as might be expected, contains more vestiges of his children's work than any of his other adult novels. Although basically naturalistic, the story has its metaphysical elements of fantasy mysticism. Jachin-Boaz is a mapmaker, making and selling maps that "showed [poets] where thoughts of power and clarity had come to other poets." The primary metaphysical motif, however, is the title's lion, which appears to the reciprocally named father and son, representing both their estrangement and their reciprocal need for reconciliation and atonement.

Kleinzeit's (1974) experimentalism is less child-like (though some reviewers have found it child*ish*): it's loaded with word-play, ranging from subtle to sublime to outrageous to ridiculous. Kleinzeit is an advertising copywriter; his illness symbolizes a nearly total breakdown of the language system, the tyranny of words over people represented by a peculiar sort of allegory whereby words take on an ominous reality, becoming actual characters in the novel. References to the Orpheus myth point to Kleinzeit's possible redemption from his mouse-like predicament.

Hoban's fourth novel, *Turtle Diary* (1975), is his most conventional. Yet it, too, has originality in its format of alternating diary entries by its nebbishy two main characters, who simultaneously get the urge to free the turtles, and in the female character's dissatisfaction with her career of writing children's books about "furry-animal picnic[s] or birthday part[ies]. . . . My next book will be about a predator." Perhaps the most original thing about the novel is that, contrary to all reader expectations, the two characters do not pair off at the end.

Although the narrator-hero of Hoban's next book, *Riddley Walker* (1980), is only 12 years old, the book is no more a children's story than would be *Huckleberry Finn* rewritten by James Joyce. A tightly woven chronicle of life in post-nuclear holocaust England, it is Hoban's masterpiece, already acknowledged by many as a cult-classic but destined perhaps to become a classic in the fullest sense of the word. For its greatest achievement is its language. Hoban embodies the decay of human society into almost Stone Age savagery in a crudely degenerated language almost entirely purged of humankind's cultural heritage. And yet, paradoxically, he makes of this brute English a surprisingly flexible instrument as its stripped-down physicality removes layers of metaphoric abstraction and takes us closer to the physical origins of language's meaning. Strange, sometimes comic and sometimes sinister folk etymologies are a vital part of this effect—the chief government officer, for example, is the "Pry Mincer."

The characters try desperately to understand just what it was that happened back then, on the basis of painfully few and badly distorted pre-holocaust memories and one fragment of text which they have developed into a sort of folk mythology manifested in traveling Punch-and-Judy shows. And despite their technological, historical, and linguistic deficiencies (or precisely *because* of them), they are on their way to repeating the mistakes of the past.

Pilgermann (1983) is a phantasmagoric rhapsody on the meaning (or lack thereof) of history and humankind's cruelties and kindnesses to one another, narrated from a vaguely present (or timeless) viewpoint by a disembodied soul remembering his existence in the eleventh-century Europe of the Crusades. The book has a rudimentary plot, as Pilgermann tries to redeem his castration by a pilgrimage to Jerusalem, but as he himself says, "I can't tell this as a story because it isn't a story; a story is what remains when you leave out most of the action; a story is a coherent sequence of picture cards." No "coherent sequence," perhaps, but the novel has a wealth of "picture cards," the verbal equivalent of a Hieronymous Bosch painting (a comparison Hoban himself hints at), full of overt but mysterious symbols, allegorical figures, and such grotesqueries as human heads being used as cannon balls.

In each of Hoban's novels there's a sense of something, not *hidden* exactly, but submerged, in the depths of the mythic unconscious. He uses this image directly sometimes—in *Mouse*, in *Turtle*, and in his essays, as in this image of the womb of time, "where moments followed one by one in an unbroken flow from ocean and the primal salt, from far back, far down where the light was dim and green through ancient reeds" ("Thoughts on Being and Writing," p. 70).

Often these depths suggest an inexpressible sense of loss—of lions, of freedom, of civilization itself—but also a yearning, a striving for redemption. Even the conclusions of his novels leave us with this sense of elusiveness, with something unresolved: at the end of *Lion* Boaz-Jachin and Jachin-Boaz have begun to be reconciled, but there's no sense that the process is complete or that it will be easy; Riddley goes back out to confront his world—to possible success, or inevitable failure? Hoban offers no easy answers, no easy stories, as Pilgermann makes clear. But he offers a constantly inventive vision throughout his challenging and original approaches to fiction-writing.

Selected Bibliography

Primary Sources

Approximately 60 children's books, 1959–present.

The Mouse and His Child. New York: Harper & Row, 1967.
The Lion of Boaz-Jachin and Jachin-Boaz. New York: Stein & Day, 1973.
Kleinzeit. New York: Viking Press, 1974.
Turtle Diary. New York: Random House, 1975.
Riddley Walker. New York: Summit Books, 1980.
Pilgermann. New York: Summit Books, 1983.

Secondary Sources

Bannon, Barbara. "Rusell Hoban" (interview). *Publisher's Weekly* 219 (May 15, 1981), pp. 10–11.
Hauptfuhrer, Fred. "After the Apocalypse the Language Is the Riddle in the Bleak New World of Russell Hoban (interview)." *People* 16 (August 10, 1981): 81–82.
McMahon-Hill, Gillian. "A Narrow Pavement Says 'Walk Alone': The Books of Russell Hoban" *Children's Literature in Education* 29 (Spring 1976): 41–55.
                                                                                                                ALFRED F. BOE

I

IRVING, JOHN (1942–)

What primarily distinguishes John Irving's fiction from that of the American writers (Robert Coover,* E. L. Doctorow,* Stanley Elkin,* John Gardner*) to whom he is most often compared are two things: first, his work has come progressively to strive for accessibility, for simplicity of texture, and for a coherent, linear narrative surface. And, second, it sells. Some have seen fit (frequently to Irving's discredit) to correlate the first characteristic with the second, but rather than seeing this as a flaw in his work, Irving perceives the coincidence of directness of presentation with popular success as a consciously sought achievement of his fiction. That coincidence was effectuated by *The World According to Garp*, the book in which Irving found the form, the voice, and the popular audience that had eluded him through three previous technically sophisticated and largely unnoticed novels.

Irving was born in 1942 in Exeter, New Hampshire, where his father was teaching at Exeter Academy, the prep school setting that would be dimly figured in the academic landscapes of much of Irving's fiction. While enrolled at Exeter, Irving developed the two talents that would become, respectively, his favorite avocation and his chosen vocation, as well as prime subjects in his fiction—wrestling and writing. A trip to Austria in 1963–1964 introduced him to his third great subject: Vienna, "a place," as he later described it, "I could make up." He returned to the United States to complete work on his B.A. at the University of New Hampshire, after which he attended the Iowa Writers Workshop, earning an M.F.A. while working with instructors Vance Bourjaily and Kurt Vonnegut, Jr.* and completing a draft of his first novel, *Setting Free the Bears*. He has taught at Mount Holyoke and the Iowa Writers Workshop, and has collaborated in the scripting and filming of one of his novels, *The Hotel New*

Hampshire (1984), in which Colin Irving, one of his two sons, has a small part.

Irving's first novel, *Setting Free the Bears* (1968), begins conventionally enough. The narrator, Hannes Graff, meets Sigfried Javotnick—Siggy— and the two mildly madcap bohemians set off on a freewheeling tour of Austria on a motorcycle, discussing, as they travel, the implementation of Siggy's lifelong ambition: springing the animals in Vienna's Hietzinger Zoo. Part One's cheerfully picaresque narrative sobers precipitously upon the gratuitously accidental death of Siggy (the first of many such deaths in Irving's fiction). That tone continues into Part Two, which reproduces two narratives culled from the pages of Siggy's surviving notebook. Graff presents the notebook's two narratives (that of Siggy's Austrian Resistance ancestors and that of his casing the zoo in preparation for the break) contrapuntally, the two interweaving with each other to give dramatic substance and an appropriate ironic edge to Siggy's ponderous concluding disclosure that he was born on the day that Drazha Mihailovich—"the last honest and stupid liberator or revolutionary left in the world"—died. (Irving has rightly termed this chapter "the most interesting thing I've ever published" in its alternation between compelling historical narrative and the dramatic rendering of the zoo, its ex-Nazi zookeeper, and Siggy's plans for them.) Siggy's death leaves Graff with the obligation of seeing through the would-be liberator's scheme. If it at first seems to fail in accomplishing its end ("Things didn't piece together any different than before," Graff complains upon perceiving the brutal confusion he has unleashed), his subsequent sighting of the Rare Spectacled Bears entering a deep Austrian wood convinces him that he has achieved the "harmless disruption" of order to which Siggy had aspired. This disruption, ironically, reconciles Graff to the customs, names, and conventions of the orderly world from which the bears are escaping. The inordinately optimistic note on which *Setting Free the Bears* concludes is considerably qualified by Irving's later novels, in which he, by his own admission, "continued to write new versions of that zoo bust story, the escape becoming more and more disastrous and fewer and fewer animals getting away."

Fred "Bogus" Trumper, the protagonist of *The Water-Method Man* (1972), doesn't get away, but he gets away with a lot. Irving's most generically pure central character, Trumper recalls protagonists of black humor novels of the 1950s and 1960s (*The Adventures of Augie March*, *The Ginger Man*, *A Bad Man*) who mean well but have an irrepressible tropism toward disorder, an instinct for freedom that prompts them habitually to trample on the feelings of others. Nor is a libertine spirit Trumper's only liability: he is trying (and failing) to translate an old Norse epic as a Ph.D. thesis, and he also has a urinary tract deviation that interferes with his sex life and obliges him to adopt the water-method treatment of his symptoms. Finally, he has a serious uncertainty about his possession of a self. " 'No one knows you, Trumper,' " his lover charges, " 'You don't *convey* any-thing. . . . Things just sort of happen to you, and they don't even add up to anything. You don't make anything of what happens to you.' " Her characterization of Trumper is formally approximated by the confusion of voices, tenses, forms, flashbacks and -forwards, and other devices through which the novel is narrated, their accumulation mimicking his lack of di-rection, the adevelopmentality that is his life. That he is a surface without substance is confirmed by a film a friend shoots about him, a *Life* magazine reviewer remarking on the movie's "surfacy, vignette approach," which "almost demands a nonending sort of ending." The reviewer's contention that the film is marked by "a progression which fails to develop in depth," "simply showing more facets on the surface," leaves little doubt that not only the film or the man are being characterized, but the novel as well. Indeed, the passage articulates explicitly one of the givens of Irving's fic-tional universe: its insistence on settling for surfaces, its refusal to evoke depths or to invite excavatory critical analysis. For all the plethora of narrative perspectives, modes, and tenses in *The Water-Method Man*, Trumper remains very much a surface of a man; for all the obstacles opposed to his success, he (and the fiction for which he represents a kind of emblem) figuratively and literally straightens himself out and comes to a distinctly comic "nonending of an ending."

The narrative indirections of Irving's first two novels are reduced to a relatively straightforward first-person narrative in *The 158-Pound Marriage* (1974), although the narrator's consistent interweaving of flashbacks into his story creates some density of chronological layering. A terse cautionary fable presented by an unreliable narrator, the novel deals with two uni-versity couples involved in a *ménage a quatre*, the ultimate cost of their adulteries anticipating the stiffer penalties exacted of the Garps for their infidelities. Irving's least flamboyant novel, *The 158-Pound Marriage* in-dicates his mastery over certain favorite motifs and recurring symbols. (The university's wrestling room, for instance, proves as pivotal and significant a site in this book as the scaffold is in *The Scarlet Letter*.) Beyond everything else, however, *The 158-Pound Marriage* proves that when Irving wants to write a highly literary, tightly structured, serious plot free of digressive extravagances and boffo comic scenes, he is more than equal to the task.

In writing *The World According to Garp* (1978), Irving was acting on two realizations which, in concert with effective promotion by E. P. Dut-ton, culminated in his coming suddenly to rival Kurt Vonnegut as America's most popular serious writer. First, he saw that the quality of his imagination was best conveyed through an uncomplicatedly linear, stable, and chron-ologically progressive narrative voice. Hence, he told *Garp*, from concep-tion to assassination, from one static third-person stance, allowing only Garp's own stories, "The Pension Grillparzer," "Vigilance," and "The World According to Bensenhaver," to interrupt that voice. Second, Irving decided that his first three novels had suffered from his lack of admiration for and enthusiasm about his characters; he compensated for this in *Garp* by "creating characters I really admired and cared for," which was "a real breakthrough for me." The general readability, humor, and accessibility of *Garp* are in part responsible for its extraordinary popular success, but perhaps as significant was the choice of a narrator so obviously engaged with and delighted by what he's narrating. There's no trace of Joycean detachment here: the narrator of *Garp* is very much at home in the magic circle of Garp, his family and friends, evoking the spirit of their pleasures and suffering stylistic deflation upon their reversals, quoting Garp's work with ill-concealed approbation, and appropriating for his own narrative purposes Garp's best witticisms. This narrator is not above Garp's sphere but in it, never once suggesting that "the world according to Garp" isn't world enough for him. But for all his benignity of attitude toward Garp and company, there is one thing this sympathetic narrator cannot do for them, and herein lies the source of the novel's most crucial tension: he can't protect them from their (usually violent) fates. Even in *The World According to Garp* a good guy narrator is no match for the undertoad.

The same basic tension underlies *The Hotel New Hampshire* (1981), the deliberate fairy tale quality of the novel heightening the disparity between the goodness of (at least some) human beings and the badness of what happens to them. The sympathetic narrator here is John Berry, son of an idealistic father who buys and moves his family into one hotel after another in hopes not merely of succeeding financially but of creating what he calls a "sympathy space," hotels seeming to him places that provide "space and light" for the world's maimed (everyone, in other words) to recuperate in. The Hotel New Hampshire (the novel's generic label for this sense of sanctuary, as well as a literal place) cannot save the elder Berry's father from a fatal heart attack, his wife and son from a plane crash, one daughter from rape and another from suicide, or himself from blindness, but it is nonetheless a self-contained, independent, "happily fatalistic" little world of shelter, succor, and encouragement. Which is also what *The Hotel New Hampshire* is. For, as Irving has explained, "Something is not comic as *opposed* to serious; something is comic as a form of consolation. Comedy, it seems to me, is simply a mode of sympathy taken toward an unhappy ending. I'm a comic novelist, and I also write unhappy endings. I write sad stories and the comedy in my fiction really serves as a kind of relief." Irving's latest novel, *The Cider House Rules* (1985), extends his concern with developing serious modes of comedy and fable; despite mixed reviews, its long run near the top of the best-seller list reinforces Irving's position as perhaps the most popular "serious" novelist writing today in the United States.

Selected Bibliography

Primary Sources

Setting Free the Bears. New York: Random House, 1968.
The Water-Method Man. New York: Random House, 1972.
The 158-Pound Marriage. New York: Random House, 1974.
The World According to Garp. New York: E. P. Dutton, 1978.
The Hotel New Hampshire. New York: E. P. Dutton, 1981.
The Cider House Rules. New York: E. P. Dutton, 1985.

Secondary Sources

Drabble, Margaret. "Muck, Memory and Imagination." *Harper's*, July 1978, pp. 82–84.
McCaffery, Larry. "Interview with John Irving." *Anything Can Happen: Interviews with Contemporary American Novelists*. Eds. Tom LeClair and Larry McCaffery. Urbana: University of Illinois Press, 1983, pp. 176–98.
Marcus, Greil. "*Garp*: Death in the Family, I and II." *Rolling Stone*, August 24, 1978, pp. 60, 62, and September 21, 1978, pp. 76, 79.
Miller, Gabriel. *John Irving*. New York: Frederick Ungar, 1982.
Priestly, Michael. "Structure in the Worlds of John Irving." *Critique: Studies in Modern Literature* 23, no. 1 (1981), pp. 82–96.
Renwick, Joyce. "Interview with John Irving." *Fiction International* 14 (1982): 5–18.

PETER J. BAILEY

J

JAFFE, HAROLD (1940–)

Harold Jaffe's highly experimental, socially-committed fiction simultaneously seeks to ensnare and estrange the reader in the underbelly of Western culture. Jaffe rejects the prevailing canons of plot and character to render the voices of people commonly relegated to the margins. His fictions are energized by his outrage at the savage and prevailing political, cultural, and linguistic forces that serve to uphold the dominant ideology that subjugate the oppressed. The tone in his work is a complex mix of rage and humor as his disaffiliated characters attempt to unwrap themselves from insidious and often tentacular forms of power and oppression. His writing utilizes stylistic and atonal collisions of words, ideas, images, and histories to draw the reader into an uncomfortable and disquieting world. The reader cannot help but embrace the challenge which the intricate surface of the prose presents—a visionary fiction as original as Nathanael West's departure from dreary social realism generations before.

Harold Jaffe was born in 1940 in New York City where he became a star basketball player, a fast-moving power forward and a not so passive observer of the everyday atrocities in the urban war zone of race and class struggle. Jaffe attended Grinnell College in Iowa on a basketball scholarship, then returned to New York for graduate work at New York University. He taught literature at Long Island University in the late 1960s and early 1970s.

Between 1965 and 1973, Jaffe published poetry and an eclectic series of scholarly articles on subjects ranging from Walt Whitman to Diane Arbus to contemporary film; he coedited two innovative reading anthologies, edited an early biography on Whitman, and wrote numerous book reviews.

Jaffe resigned from his tenured associate professorship at Long Island University in 1976 in order to write fiction full-time. He began work on

Mole's Pity (1979), his first published novel, and traveled extensively in India, Nepal, Guatemala, Ecuador, Peru, Bolivia, and the Caribbean. He lived in India, Guatemala, and Ecuador for about three and a half years, recording with an ornithologist's precision his intimately engaged, yet unsentimental vision of the effects of political repression and poverty. During this time Jaffe completed two other as yet unpublished novels—one a species of sleuth tale set in India, the other about the Cakchiquel Indians of the Guatemalan highlands.

When Jaffe returned to the States in the late 1970s, he settled in Sag Harbor, Long Island, where he completed a collection of twenty intricate, overlapping fictions, *Mourning Crazy Horse* (1982) published by the Fiction Collective. Here, the reader is led on a Dantesque excursion through the circular substrata of the American underbelly, a textual journey cleansed of romanticism, yet poetic and charged with a biting humor. Since these sociopolitical fictions contain neither ideas for social amelioration nor a specific radical agenda for the disaffiliated, Jaffe takes an approach that is deliberately problematic. His multi-layered prose is as complex as the injustices his work embraces: a counterhegemonic writing in response to the imposition of a cultural homogeneity that renders invisible those people relegated to the margins.

Mourning Crazy Horse contains an impressive range of innovations. Characters reappear with different characteristics. The fiction itself is deployed in stunning unlinear patterns so that the political writing therein is mediated. Fictional discourse and "real" discourse constantly overlap, and much of the fiction is deliberately unresolved. And yet the effect is that of a brilliant and compassionate political intervention on behalf of the oppressed.

A year later Jaffe's unusual novel, *Dos Indios* (1983), was published. Begun while living in Peru, *Dos Indios* is an evocative portrayal of a crippled Peruvian Indian flute player. Unlike the multilayered discourses of *Mourning Crazy Horse*, the language in *Dos Indios* is relentlessly stripped and pared. The novel's principal innovation derives from the strange meld of realism and allegory that dominates the physical details of the modern Peruvian landscape, where the Indians are encompassed by poverty, empty political rhetoric, and the evangelistic religion of their conquerors. But the Peruvian highlands are as they have always been. This dialectic between Peru-now and Peru-immemorial is among the subjects that this deceptively powerful lyric novel addresses.

Beasts (1986) appears to combine aspects of the two preceding volumes. It consists of ten fictions modeled on the medieval Bestiary. Each fiction has a beast as its title, and in each instance the particular beast, whether Sheep, Monkey, Salamander, Sidewinder, is employed variably as the name of a parlor game, as the name of a prison, or as a title without any apparent reference. Yet Jaffe has devised his fiction so that the predominant resonance of every beast is potently allegorical. The allegory always has to do with the socially dispossessed, such as the out-of-work Blacks, adolescent heroin addicts, or other miscellaneous social rejects. As in his previous fiction, these are Jaffe's subjects and his portrayal of them, always from one oblique angle or another, is both mysterious and moving.

Language is always a critical feature of Jaffe's fiction, and in *Beasts*, one finds everything from political newspeak to prison lingo to Caribbean pidgin to post-structuralist theory. The effect is virtuosic and often hilarious, but as with Brecht, Jaffe's intention, finally, is to stun into alertness and outrage rather than to amuse.

Currently, Jaffe teaches creative writing at San Diego State University and is coeditor, with Larry McCaffery, of *Fiction International*, a journal of politically committed and postmodernist fiction.

Selected Bibliography

Primary Sources

Walt Whitman. (Facsimile edition of the 1883 biography by Richard Maurice Bucke; edited and with an introduction by Harold Jaffe.) New York: Johnson Reprint Corporation, 1970.
The American Experience: A Radical Reader. Coeditor. New York: Harper and Row, 1970.
Mole's Pity. New York: Fiction Collective, 1979.
Mourning Crazy Horse. New York: Fiction Collective, 1982.
Dos Indios. New York: Thunder's Mouth Press, 1983.
Beasts. New York: Curbstone, 1986.

Secondary Sources

Koning, Hans. "Our Literary Siberias." *The Fairfield Advocate*, June 12, 1984, pp. 84–85.
Krekorian, Michael. "*Mourning Crazy Horse* and *Dos Indios*." *The American Book Review* (Fall 1984), 12.
Moramarco, Fred. "The Education of Manco." *The San Diego Reader*, December 16, 1983, p. 22.
Nietzel, Nancy. *Mourning Crazy Horse*. *The Minnesota Review*, 20 (Spring 1983).

MICHAEL KREKORIAN

JAMESON, FREDRIC (1934–   )

Jameson is the most important Marxist literary critic in this country since World War II; only Raymond Williams in Britain has produced a body of work as substantial and significant. Jameson's primary significance as a critic and theorist of literature and culture lies in three areas. First, his work (especially his early work) had the immense political significance of reinserting the Marxist concerns and problematic into the discourse of literary studies—from which it had been almost entirely eliminated by Cold

War and McCarthyite pressures—in a very sophisticated and persuasive form, remarkably free of economic determinism and other reductive pseudo-simplicities of the so-called vulgar Marxists. Second, he has done an enormous amount to bring into the discourse of American scholarly and academic practice the (broadly political) concerns of important European thinkers of this century—a partial list would include Georg Lukács, T. W. Adorno, Fred Bloch, Walter Benjamin, Bertolt Brecht, Herbert Marcuse, Jean-Paul Sartre, Vladimir Propp, Ferdinand de Saussure, Claude Lévi-Strauss, Roland Barthes,* Louis Althusser, Jacques Derrida,* Michel Foucault,* Jacques Lacan,* Jurgen Habermas, and Max Weber—in ways that illuminate the most important questions in the areas of literature, culture generally, and society. Third, from "Metacommentary" through his most recent works, Jameson has continued to foreground the act of criticism itself, to question the bases of what it is to think and write about literature, even as he calls into question the purposes and function of culture as a whole.

Educated at Haverford College, Yale University, and the universities of Aix, Munich, and Berlin, Fredric Jameson has taught at Harvard University, the University of California (UC) at San Diego, Yale, and, currently, UC Santa Cruz. His major works are *Marxism and Form: Twentieth-Century Dialectical Theories of Literature* (1971), *The Prison House of Language: A Critical Account of Structuralism and Russian Formalism* (1972), and *The Political Unconscious: Narrative as a Socially Symbolic Act* (1981). He is the author as well of two more focused studies of individual authors, *Sartre: The Origins of a Style* (1961), and *Fables of Aggression: Wyndham Lewis, the Modernist as Fascist* (1979). Major, as yet uncollected, essays have appeared in a wide variety of scholarly, political, and theoretical journals—notably PMLA, which awarded the prize for its best essay of the year to "Metacommentary" in 1971, *Yale French Studies*, where the influential "Imaginary and Symbolic in Lacan: Marxism, Psychoanalytical Criticism and the Problem of the Subject" appeared in 1977, *Salmagundi*, *New Literary History*, *Minnesota Review*, *Diacritics* (which devoted a special issue to his work, with an interview, in 1982), *Social Text*, of which he was a founding editor in 1979, and many others.

Jameson's work is not without its detractors. In addition to the expected hostility or willed ignorance toward his position from the Right, from formalists, from old-fashioned historicists, Leavisites and the like, he has also been subject to criticism from other Marxists, who see in his writing a most significant and extreme example of texts that cannot be considered Marxist at all. They consider his writing to be rarified and abstract, inaccessible to all but a few academic intellectuals. Although his writing does sometimes get very complex and abstract, a passage such as the following, which articulates his strong moral concerns in the interpretation of literary, social, and historical matters, is certainly a text firmly grounded in human practice:

No, the ultimate form of the "nightmare of history" is rather the fact of labor itself, and the intolerable spectacle of the backbreaking millennial toil of millions of people from the earliest moment of human history. The more existential versions of this dizzying and probably unthinkable, unimaginable spectacle . . . are themselves only disguises for this ultimately scandalous fact of mindless alienated work and of the irremedial loss and waste of human energies, a scandal to which no metaphysical categories can give a meaning. This scandal is everywhere known, everywhere repressed—*un secret de tous connus*. (From "Marxism and Historicism, *New Literary History* 11, no. 1, Autumn 1979.)

Like the great Continental thinkers with whom and against whom he works, Jameson's texts constantly seek to reshape, extend, and alter ways of thinking and knowing, modes of perception and understanding of the most important aspects of our social existence, of both material and intellectual production, of our insertion into history—to "recuperate" such matters from their repressed position in the dominant discourse, from our political unconscious. His contributions to our understanding of literary history especially concerns the periodization implicit in the use of such terms as high modernism, postmodernism, and modernism *tout court*, all three of which Jameson uses frequently and carefully, with precise definitions and distinctions. He discusses modernism at considerable length in *The Political Unconscious*, where he proffers a balanced, dialectical insertion of modernist practice into history. In that view modernism is seen, on the one hand, as "an ideological expression of capitalism," of the reification of everyday life, a symptomatic response to "a distressingly alienating reality":

Yet modernism can at one and the same time be read as a Utopian compensation for everything reification brings with it. . . . The increasing abstraction of visual art thus proves not only to express the abstraction of daily life and to presuppose fragmentation and reification; it also constitutes a Utopian compensation for everything lost in the process of development of capitalism—the place of quality in an increasingly quantified world, the place of the archaic and of feeling amid the desacralization of the market system, the place of sheer color and intensity within the grayness of measurable extension and geometrical abstraction.

Jameson sees modernist practice generally in terms of "the vocation of the perceptual, its Utopian mission as the libidinal transformation of an increasingly dessicated and repressive reality." Most recently, he has phrased similar views in Marcusean terms, seeing modernist literary practice as first affirmative, as a semi-autonomous realm, self-defined as separate from the economic, political, or social realms. In that autonomy, he states that it constitutes a powerful negation, a critique of our "time of the now" by implicit comparison to the properly Utopian urges given powerful libidinal investment and embodiment in modernist cultural practice.

Whether he is presenting critical theory or practical criticism on writers as different as Norman Mailer, Raymond Chandler, James Dickey, Ursula LeGuin,* Conrad, and Balzac, Jameson's concern is always to extend our understanding of the complexly overdetermined situations of the novelist, scholar, critic, or teacher in the modern era, to illuminate the relations among the most abstract or formal literary qualities and the most urgent political, social, and economic forces. In this passage from Jameson's latest writing ("Periodizing the 60s," in *The Sixties Without Apology*, 1984), we see the sort of concerns he would have, questions he would raise about the very enterprise of assembling a text such as this one. He is addressing the question of "the historical specificity of postmodernism . . . in terms of the social functionality of culture itself":

In effect, with the canonization of a hitherto scandalous, ugly, dissonant, amoral, anti-social, bohemian high modernism, offensive to the middle classes, its promotion of the very figure of high culture generally, and perhaps most important, its enshrinement in the academic institution, postmodernism emerges as a way of making creative space for artists now oppressed by those henceforth hegemonic modernist categories of irony, complexity, dense temporality, and particularly, aesthetic and utopian monumentality. In some analagous way . . . high modernism itself won its autonomy from the preceding hegemonic realism (the symbolic language or mode of representation of classical or market capitalism). But there is a difference in that realism itself underwent a significant mutation: it became *naturalism* and at once generated the representational forms of mass culture (the narrative apparatus of the contemporary bestseller is an invention of naturalism and one of the most stunningly successful of French cultural exports). High modernism and mass culture then develop in dialectical opposition and interrelationship with one another. It is precisely the waning of their opposition, and some new conflation of the forms of high and mass culture, which characterizes postmodernism itself.

Such thought-provoking readings of the shapes and forces of literary history have marked Jameson's work throughout his career and continue to influence critical discussion. Any thorough understanding of what is meant by a term like postmodernism must take serious account of Jameson's work.

Selected Bibliography

Primary Sources

Sartre: The Origins of a Style. New Haven, Conn.: Yale University Press, 1961.
Marxism and Form: Twentieth-Century Dialectical Theories of Literature. Princeton, N.J.: Princeton University Press, 1971.
The Prison House of Language: A Critical Account of Structuralism and Russian Formalism. Princeton, N.J.: Princeton University Press, 1972.
Fables of Aggression: Wyndham Lewis, the Modernist as Fascist. Berkeley: University of California Press, 1979.

The Political Unconscious: Narrative as a Socially Symbolic Act. Ithaca, N.Y.:
Cornell University Press, 1981.

Secondary Sources

Green, Leonard, ed. "A Special Issue on Fredric Jameson: *The Political Unconscious.*" *Diacritics* 12, no. 3 (Fall 1982).

DAVID S. GROSS

K

KATZ, STEVE (1935–   )

Steve Katz has said that he wants his books to look different, to "look like another context than a novel." A cursory glance at one of them proves that he has succeeded. And yet, while Katz's versions of radical postmodernist strategies are undoubtedly there, waiting to be seized upon and advanced as the defining elements of his art, Katz is not merely an iconoclast. He is, above all, an explorer, seeking out authentic configurations for his fictions amidst the many possibilities and impossibilities present in contemporary life, and seeking also to discover where the writer can find his or her footing on that slippery ground where fact and fiction meet.

Katz's explorations began in the Bronx on May 14, 1935, and were continued in the schoolyards, movie theaters, and museums of Manhattan. Among his early discoveries Katz has listed Rousseau's *Sleeping Gypsy*, Nancy and Sluggo, Bela Bartok, Mel Allen, Hieronymous Bosch, the right hand of Joe Louis, Charlie Parker, Captain Marvel . . . memories of art seen and felt in a uniquely American context. Katz knows a thing or two about quicksilver, and the forests of certain parts of Idaho, about Tennessee and South Dakota, about Hollywood and its scenarios. He knows about Kafka, Flaubert, Tolstoy, Massaccio, and Pisanello. He knows Salerno and Istanbul, and he can tell the difference between Swisher, Iowa, and midtown Manhattan. He knows, too, about places that do not appear on any maps, like all the true places of the American imagination. He has talked to others about his discoveries—at Cornell, at Notre Dame, at the University of Colorado.

What Katz has to share with his readers is a double fascination, with what he has called "the shape of American experience, the discontinuous drama, all climax, all boring intermissions," and with himself as a writer, seeking to record the experience in appropriate forms. *The Exagggerations of Peter Prince* (1968) bears witness to the complexity of vision born of this double focus. Too casually dismissed by some reviewers as little more than a kind of typographical circus performance, the novel invites the reader into an unsettling world in which fact and fiction blend and separate as Katz's own experiences are forced up against overtly imagined, and occasionally parodied, fragments of narrative. The resonances of that confrontation are heard most clearly in the characteristic appearances of the author himself on page after page of the novel. Katz lays bare the anxieties of the writer struggling toward coherence who discovers that the world he or she inhabits, in both its real and its imagined configurations, has an inherent tendency to resist the authority of the artist. The very shape of the book, and the protean characteristics of its pages, increase our awareness of the variety of forms that human experience can generate, and remind us that no single form will prove adequate as a container for the multiple perspectives demanded by the relativistic bias of contemporary culture.

More overtly formal concerns surface in the "Mythologies" that dominate *Creamy and Delicious* (1970). Here Katz subjects the idea of myth to an arbitrary constraint (each of the pieces was written in two hours), subverting its potential for fixing human experience in a timeless narrative. The characters of myth, too, are wrenched out of context—Danae meets Bad Company, Apollo visits a brothel, Achilles rides the subway—and even the quasi-mythic figures of an American childhood are revealed in new guises. Nancy is a transvestite cowboy and Sluggo her gunslinging nemesis; Wonderwoman is a lesbian. The figures of Gandhi, Nasser, and Dickens complete the spectrum of devalued possibilities. Historical figures, fictional characters, and mythic archetypes (ambiguously situated in a realm between the real and the imagined) are all re-created temporarily in Katz's uniquely American idiom, their actions as inconsequential as the forms that contain them, their power to define our human predicament sufficient only for the time it takes to "read" them.

In *Saw* (1972), Katz again appears as explorer, identifying himself as The Astronaut, an amorphous extraterrestrial being, temporarily incarnated on planet Earth. Katz's claim that the novel is autobiographical, therefore, clashes deliberately with the extravagant fantasy of the plot, suggesting the writer's somewhat perilously maintained equilibrium between the worlds of imagination and reality. The artist-as-alien perspective from which much of the world of the novel is observed generates an uncharacteristically somber vision. Urban America is a battleground, a monstrous trash heap, a world that is helpless in the face of the apocalypse that finally comes. The Astronaut blasts off, leaving behind a landscape that is gradually being flattened by a huge, insouciant cylinder—the embodiment, perhaps, of a purity of form that Katz regards with suspicion.

Moving Parts (1977) finds Katz on the road again, once more examining the relationship between fact and fiction, and once more discovering the appropriateness of a means of expression that refuses to grant greater authority to either. The photographs, diagrams, and blank or black pages that accompany the text are the now familiar trademarks of Katz's cartography. They are landmarks on his journey in search of his identity as a writer, reminders that, in his own words, "truth is everything included," and that the writer who would tell the truth about himself, about the world he lives in and experiences, must find an authentic voice somewhere beyond the confines of traditional literary signs.

Rather than reading Katz as an experimental novelist, then, we should read him as a mapmaker, charting the progress of a sometimes hesitant, sometimes exuberant one-person expedition into unknown territory. The journey is one that is undertaken by most writers, of course, but not many writers have decided with such certainty that the record of that journey should be the basis for his or her fictions. Katz has shown himself willing to share with his readers the frustrations and delights of his explorations, leaving in the wrong turnings, the fatal lapses of concentration, as well as the moments of triumph, those "most informed and exhilarating moments [that] occur when quotidian reality and [his] inventions intersect or have a mutual resonance."

Selected Bibliography

Primary Sources

The Lestriad. Milan: Edizioni Milella, 1962.
The Weight of Antony. Ithaca, N.Y.: Eibe Press, 1964.
The Exagggerations of Peter Prince. New York: Holt, Rinehart & Winston, 1968.
Creamy and Delicious. New York: Random House, 1970.
Posh (Stephanie Gatos, pseud.). New York: Grove Press, 1971.
Saw. New York: Alfred A. Knopf, 1972.
Cheyenne River Wild Track. Ithaca, N.Y.: Ithaca House, 1973.
Moving Parts. New York: Fiction Collective, 1977.
Stolen Stories. New York: Fiction Collective, 1984.
Wier & Pouce. New York: Sun & Moon Press, 1984.

Secondary Sources

Grant, J. Kerry. "Fiction and the Facts of Life: Steve Katz's *Moving Parts*." *Critique* 24, no. 4 (1983): 206–14.
Gregory, Sinda, and Larry McCaffery. "Steve Katz." *Dictionary of Literary Biography Yearbook, 1982*. Detroit: Gale Research Co., 1983, pp. 271–78.
Klinkowitz, Jerome. "Steve Katz." *The Life of Fiction*. Urbana: University of Illinois Press, 1977, pp. 105–15.

McCaffery, Larry. "An Interview with Steve Katz." *Anything Can Happen: Interviews with Contemporary American Novelists*. Urbana: University of Illinois Press, pp. 219–34.

J. KERRY GRANT

KENNEDY, WILLIAM (1928–   )

Although his early novels attracted little immediate attention, William Kennedy's Albany trilogy received national recognition and critical acclaim when Kennedy was awarded the Pulitzer Prize for fiction in 1984 for his novel *Ironweed*. Kennedy's emergence as a major figure in contemporary fiction has injected a fresh and lively Irish-American voice and a tough, yet mellifluous, style into American fiction's bloodstream. Combining history, legend, myth, politics, and sport, Kennedy's novels invite readers into a highly personal vision of life that springs up in an urban microcosm populated by mythical gangsters, gamblers, bums, prostitutes, scabs, and Irish-American families.

William Kennedy was born into an Irish-Catholic, working-class family in 1928 in Albany, New York, the city that would become the nexus of his fictions. After finishing college, Kennedy became a sports writer, but this apprenticeship in journalism was interrupted when the U.S. Army sent him to Europe during the Korean War. Kennedy later returned to Albany for a stint as a general assignment reporter, but, eager for change, he moved to Puerto Rico, where he married, worked as a journalist, and, in 1959, co-founded *The San Juan Star*. Although he wrote some short stories based on his expatriate life, Kennedy found himself writing about Albany and creating a fictional family, the Phelans, in an early unpublished novel, *The Angels and the Sparrows*. Having discovered the richness that Albany offered his work, Kennedy left San Juan and went home, where he has lived ever since. "I write," Kennedy has said, " . . . as a person whose imagination has become fused with a single place, and in that place finds all the elements that a man ever needs for the life of the soul" (*O Albany*, p. 3). Indeed, Kennedy's Albany, the Albany of the 1930s, where *Legs*, *Billy Phelan's Greatest Game*, and *Ironweed* are set, is imbued with a fictive opulence reminiscent of Kafka or Faulkner or even Gabriel García Márquez.*

Yet Kennedy's first published novel, *The Ink Truck* (1969), is not set in post-Depression Albany. Rather, this experimental novel, based loosely on an Albany newspaper strike, surrealistically meshes the radical political spirit of the 1960s with the comic intensity of the sex and drug experimentation of that era. Kennedy's reporter hero, Bailey, the last hold-out in a strike that is about to be administered last rites, plots to pull the plug on the ink supplier's truck, but his quixotic attempts lead finally to the letting of only a few drops of black blood. As the union chapter is dissolved by the national, Bailey, who has a "long time ago contracted the disease of the open mind," finds himself wielding a pistol at the victory party thrown by management, a fête that evolves into a grotesque, drug-induced orgy. While painting a political theme with Fellini-esque imagery (Kennedy has called Fellini's *8 1/2* the greatest movie ever made), Kennedy eschews didacticism and realism, and he establishes what will come to be recognized as his hallmark: an energetic, lush, and highly appealing prose style.

The first of Kennedy's "Albany novels," *Legs*, appeared in 1975. Based on the real-life exploits of Irish-American gangster Jack "Legs" Diamond, this novel explores the American mythmaking process as much as it celebrates the violent life and times of its legendary hero. Narrated by Diamond's attorney, Marcus Gorman, a man entranced with Legs' "luminosity" and energy and eventually corrupted by his affiliation with his client, the novel is set in Albany in the 1930s, and, though fictionally re-created, is steeped in thorough biographical research. Through Kennedy's fictionalization, Legs—bootlegger, thief, drug dealer, murderer, lover—emerges as a peculiarly American and almost lovable gangster, one who, like Gatsby, has willed himself into being but is doomed to lose his empire. As does Gorman, we come to see Diamond as a "venal man of integrity for he never ceased to renew his vulnerability to punishment, death, and damnation," and to salute Jack's talent for making virtue seem unwholesome. In exploring the myth of Legs, Kennedy inflates it until, paradoxically, it nearly implodes when Diamond, finally, is shot full of bullets in a threadbare rooming house.

Yet it is the language, more than the richness of plot and character, that sets *Legs* apart from the traditional historical-biographical novel, for just as Jack is "a moving glob of electricity, a live wire," so Kennedy's prose twitches, jitterbugs, pulsates with the energy of the Jazz Age and the giddiness that informs Jack's quest. And the density of the novel—the levels of history, biography, and legend that are carried along by forceful and funny dialogue, lyrical musings, and rapid-fire action—belies analysis. Kennedy's delight in telling a story becomes our delight in listening.

We meet Kennedy's fictional Phelan family for the first time in *Billy Phelan's Greatest Game* (1978), yet the spotlight here is not so much on Billy as it is on Albany. It's 1938, and the city is run by an omnipotent Democratic party machine. When Charlie Boy McCall, nephew and sole heir of the city's boss, is kidnapped, Billy Phelan—bookie, pool-shark, bowler of 299—is ordered by the McCalls to inform on a suspect, a fellow gamester. Playing by the rules—of politicians, priests, hustlers, pimps—is the name of the game in Albany, but Billy doesn't rat on anyone, so he's marked lousy and can't get a drink—let alone a game—in his own territory. Much of the action is seen through the eyes of Martin Daugherty, a journalist who, on orders from the McCalls, hushes the news of the kidnapping, and once Charlie Boy is safe, writes a column vindicating and praising Billy whom he has come to see as magical. Although some reviewers charged that the novel's core was weak, its plot too digressive, it is Kennedy's digressions—into Albany's history, Daugherty's disappointment with his seminarian son, Billy's reunion with his long-lost wino father, Francis— which turn a newspaper story into a memorable multi-layered fiction.

If *Ironweed* (1983) is Kennedy's most ambitious novel to date, it is also his richest, his most provocative. Tinged with the surrealism of *The Ink Truck*, haunted by history as are *Legs* and *Billy Phelan*, *Ironweed* is rooted in human realities and frailties. Francis Phelan, introduced in *Billy Phelan* as a "razzmatazz third baseman, maestro of the hidden ball trick," on the bum for 22 years, returns to Albany in the company of Helen, another wino, and, amidst ghosts and derelicts, they wander the streets on Halloween, 1938.

Francis has been on the lam out of guilt, but also out of laziness. The guilt—well, he's killed a few: first, by letting a stone fly with his third baseman's instincts at a scab conductor during a trolley strike; then, by accidentally letting his infant son Gerald slip to his death from a diaper; later, by violently refusing to let a bum steal his shoes off him. Now Francis makes no excuses for his violence or his running: "I ain't worth a goddam in the world and I never was."

Through Francis' stream-of-consciousness ramblings and the tragicomic dialogue of the down and out, we watch Francis roam about his old Albany haunts, working first as a gravedigger with his 'bo pal Rudy, then as a ragman. When Francis finally meets up with the family he's left behind, having already learned that his wife Annie has never divulged the true cause of Gerald's death, reconciliation seems at once imminent and impossible. So Francis returns to his world, to a good cheap drunk, and winds up confronting a gang of legionnaires out to raze the local hobo camp. Francis takes a baseball bat to the raider who brutally assaults Rudy, and having deposited Rudy, dead, in the hospital, and discovered Helen, dead, in a cheap hotel, he once again jumps a train. But no. Not this time. Francis opts to hide out at Annie's.

Ironweed is saturated with time and place but goes far beyond its setting to probe the center of Francis Phelan's being, of his spirit. With ironic self-awareness that borders on the mystical, Francis—tough as the stem of ironweed—is determined to live life as he sees fit, whether in flight, on the streets, or in hiding. Once more, Kennedy presents us with a man who creates his own moral code and then surpasses it. Francis has nothing except a vague memory of his baseball career and a family he feels he doesn't deserve, yet he can do a day's work, stay sober for a while, protect the likes of Helen or Rudy. The past beyond forgetting, Francis lingers in the present with his ghosts, no slave to the future. Never a victim, rather a warrior, Francis is, in other words, a real loser's loser.

Selected Bibliography

Primary Sources

The Ink Truck. New York: Dial Press, 1969.
Legs. New York: Coward, McCann, & Geoghegan, 1975.
Billy Phelan's Greatest Game. New York: Viking Press, 1978.
Ironweed. New York: Viking Press, 1983.
O Albany! New York: Viking Press, 1983.

Secondary Sources

Gregory, Sinda, and Larry McCaffery. "Interview with William Kennedy." *Fiction International* 15, no. 1 (1984): 157–79.
Pritchard, William H. "The Spirits of Albany." *The New Republic*, February 14, 1983, pp. 37–38.
Stade, George. "Life on the Lam." *The New York Times Book Review*, January 23, 1983, p. 1.

ELISE MILLER

KINGSTON, MAXINE HONG (1940–   )

The first American child born into a Chinese family whose members' lives read more like Old Testament legends than they do modern biographies, Maxine Hong Kingston weaves myth, history, fantasy, and autobiography in two extended prose poems attempting to reconcile a Chinese past and an American present. The first, *The Woman Warrior: Memoirs of a Girlhood Among Ghosts* (1976), records Kingston's efforts to forge a female identity by confronting the lessons of her female family members in China during the generation directly preceding her own. Its companion volume, *China Men* (1980), extends across two continents and four generations in a general "claiming of America" for all her male ancestors who sojourned and labored in America, numbering among its unsung pioneers. *The Woman Warrior* was awarded a 1976 National Book Critics Circle Award for nonfiction, and *China Men*, a 1981 American Book Award for nonfiction. In both instances the term *nonfiction* seems inadequate and inaccurate, for Kingston merges nonfiction and fiction to approach more essential truths. In *Woman Warrior* and *China Men* it is neither possible nor desirable to determine where fact leaves off and fantasy begins.

Like many of her sojourner ancestors, Maxine Hong Kingston belongs equally to the East and West. She was conceived in New York where her mother joined her father in 1939 after a 15-year separation during which their first two children, born in China, died; he became a partner in a Manhattan laundry, and she earned a degree at the To Keung School of Midwifery in Kwangtung. Kingston was born and grew up in Stockton, California, where her parents worked for a wealthy emigrant villager from home until they secured their own laundry and where her mother bore four additional children after Maxine. As a child, Kingston attended both Chinese and American schools, sorting and interpreting for herself their conflicting demands on her feelings, intelligence, behavior, and beliefs. She graduated from Berkeley in 1962, married Earl Kingston the same year, and returned to Berkeley for a teaching certificate in 1964–1965. In 1967, after teaching English and mathematics in Hayward, California, she moved with her husband and son, Joseph, to Hawaii, where two of her greatgrandfathers cleared sugar cane plantations out of wilderness over a century before. Shortly before the publication of *China Men*, a Honolulu Buddhist sect claimed her as an official "living Treasure of Hawaii." Shortly after the publication of *China Men*, Stockton recalled her for an awards ceremony that included a proposal to rechristen her birthplace "Kingston-town." Since then she has journeyed to the Far East, stopping short, however, of New Society Village, the China of her family's roots. But there can be little doubt of that China's tug on her spirit, for the legends of the woman warrior, Fa Mu Lan, and the woman poet, Ts'ai Yen, which unify her first book, both resolve into messages for the Han people back in the China that might have been her home.

The sources for the Chinese material in both of Kingston's books are the women story-talkers of Stockton's Chinatown, not least among them Kingston's own mother, Brave Orchid. Her tales of peasant prejudices and Communist brutalities made bare and enigmatic lessons "to grow up on," lessons onto which Kingston embroidered her own fantasies and interpretations. About these women Kingston concludes "I would never be able to talk with them; I have no stories of equal pain." Nevertheless, from the village women and her champion story-talker mother, Kingston also heard myths of warrior women who escaped the prosy destinies of slave girls and wives. From the same sources she absorbed the story-talker's power to transform words into weapons and private tragedy into public art.

Both *Woman Warrior* and *China Men* are plotless in the traditional sense. They are structured instead into patterned sequences alternating fiction-alized biographies of family members with passages of straight myth, leg-end, autobiography, and, in *China Men*, history. Within the biographies the same people and events are transformed in multiple variations. "No Name Aunt" who commits spite suicide with her illegitimate baby in the family well appears as rape victim, romantic, bawd, and spoiled only daugh-ter before Kingston abandons her tale in *Woman Warrior*. And Kingston's father's entry into the United States is retold five ways in *China Men*. The repetitions and transformations reveal a daughter attempting against im-possible odds to capture truth by cataloguing its possible forms. What emerges in the process is an imaginative vision so compelling that it tran-scends the quest from which it springs.

The critics agree that Kingston's first two books are extraordinary triumphs. But conclusions about her career are premature. Its focus on

Chinese consciousness will soon shift, for Kingston is at work on a novel set in California and peopled with characters who have forgotten their pasts. This third book will also represent a break in style and structure, for in it she will attempt to create a novel without the aid of Chinese metaphors.

Selected Bibliography

Primary Sources

The Woman Warrior: Memoirs of a Girlhood Among Ghosts. New York: Alfred A. Knopf, 1976.

"Duck Boy." *New York Times,* June 12, 1977, VII, 54–58.

"Reservations About China." *Ms.* 7 (October 1978), pp. 67–68.

"San Francisco's Chinatown." *American Heritage* 30 (December 1978), pp. 35–47.

China Men. New York: Alfred A. Knopf, 1980.

"The Making of More Americans." *New Yorker* 55 (February 11, 1980), pp. 34–58.

"China Men." *Redbook* 155 (July 1980), pp. 161–76.

"The Coming Book." *The Writer on Her Work.* Ed. Janet Sternburg. New York: W. W. Norton, 1980.

"A Writer's Notebook from the Far East." *Ms.* 11 (January 1983), pp. 85–86.

Secondary Sources

Brownmiller, Susan. "Susan Brownmiller Talks with Maxine Hong Kingston." *Mademoiselle* 83 (March 1977), 148ff.

Currier, Susan. "Maxine Hong Kingston." *Dictionary of Literary Biography Supplement.* Detroit: Gale Research Co., 1980.

Gordon, Mary. "Mythic History." *New York Times Book Review,* June 15, 1980, p. 1ff.

Kramer, Jane. "The Woman Warrior." *New York Times Book Review,* November 7, 1976, p. 1ff.

Miller, Margaret. "Threads of Identity in Maxine Hong Kingston's *Woman Warrior.*" *Biography* 6 (Winter 1983): 13–33.

Pfaff, Timothy. "Talk with Mrs. Kingston." *New York Times Book Review,* June 15, 1980, p. 1ff.

———. "Whispers of a Literary Explorer." *Horizon* 23 (July 1980), pp. 58–63.

Thompson, Phyllis Hoge. "This Is the Story I Heard: A Conversation with Maxine Hong Kingston and Earl Kingston." *Biography* 6 (Winter 1983):1–12.

SUSAN CURRIER

KLINKOWITZ, JEROME (1943–)

Jerome Klinkowitz has been described by the *New York Times* as "a John the Baptist, crying in the wilderness for what he describes as a new fiction." His advocacy of writers who challenge the familiar conventions of the novel and short story has made him controversial; in *American Fictions, 1940–1980* (New York: Harper & Row, 1983), Frederick R. Karl quotes a Klinkowitz assessment of Kurt Vonnegut* and complains that "Academic criticism here becomes indistinguishable from media hype; this could have come from *Time*, *Newsweek*, *People* magazine or a CBS television commentator." Karl then weighs the alternative, that "The opposite of such hyperbole comes from *Commentary* mercenaries who, as the result of conservative political allegiances and/or toadying to the editor, feel obliged to denigrate what are often solid literary impulses" (p. xii). Klinkowitz's combative sense of advocacy, then, does not originate in his own critical temperament, but is instead a defensive reaction to the academic and cultural establishment prejudice against nonmimetic fiction.

Born in Milwaukee, Wisconsin, on December 24, 1943, Klinkowitz was educated in the area's Catholic school system and went on to Marquette University for his B.A. and M.A., studying with Gerard Manley Hopkins scholar John Pick, British novel specialist Jerome Thale, and the New Criticism theorist Joseph Schwartz. His first courses in American literature were taken for doctoral study at the University of Wisconsin, where he specialized in historical method and devised a structural approach to Hawthorn's fiction under Harry Hayden Clark. Completing his studies at age 24, he took his first appointment as assistant professor of English at Northern Illinois University, teaching his initial courses on contemporary literature when additional staffing was needed in that area. His graduate seminars introduced him to two Northern Illinois doctoral candidates—Jack O'Brien and John Somer—with whom he began collaborating on projects concerning innovative black American writers such as Imamu Amiri Baraka and Clarence Major, and such newly mainstream fictionists as Kurt Vonnegut, Richard Brautigan,* and Donald Barthelme.*

In 1971 Klinkowitz and Somer prepared three collaborative anthologies, all subsequently published by Dell: *Innovative Fiction* (1972), *The Vonnegut Statement* (1973), and *Writing Under Fire: Stories of the Vietnam War* (1978). In these introductory works may be found the roots of Klinkowitz's aesthetic: that the innovative writers of the American 1960s had rejected the Aristotelian notion that fiction should represent (or imitate) an action, in favor of being an action itself; that such a transformation should not take place within the stolid phenomenology of the French *noveau roman* but rather with a more characteristically American sense of comic exuberance; and that the social and political disruptions of these same years were directly indexed in fiction's aesthetic radicalization.

In 1972 Klinkowitz accepted an associate professorship at the University of Northern Iowa and was promoted to full professor in 1976. By then he had begun his critical trilogy: a literary history of the contemporary period, *Literary Disruptions* (1975); a broadly cultural commentary on the roots of this transformation in politics, social history, and the popular and sophisticated arts, *The American 1960s* (1980); and a literary theory for this phenomenon, *The Self-Apparent Word* (1984). In the first of these studies, he describes his group of authors as being of "a definite style and school: given to formal experimentation, a thematic interest in the imaginative transformation of reality, and a sometimes painful but often hilarious self-conscious artistry, they stand apart from the Updike group, and especially from John Barth* and his circle, as clearly as do Hemingway and Fitzgerald from their two generations of elders writing as they began their own careers" (p. x).

With John Somer, Klinkowitz was the first critic to publish a volume on Kurt Vonnegut; in his own books appeared the first chapters on Donald Barthelme, Clarence Major, Jerzy Kosinski,* Gilbert Sorrentino,* Ronald Sukenick,* Grace Paley, Ishmael Reed,* Walter Abish,* and Raymond Federman,* all of whom have subsequently received wide treatment. The clearest insights into Klinkowitz's working methods, however, come from studying his three collections of essays. The most radical of these is *The Life of Fiction* (1977); organized along visual and spatial, rather than discursive and linear, principles, its intention is one of compositional honesty and of confidence in the reader's ability to complete the critical act by juxtaposing the various evidences of phone calls, interviews, letters, quotations, and bits of analysis laid out on the page. Responding to interviewer Gérard-Georges Lemaire on the French national radio show "France-Culture," Klinkowitz described any page of this book as resembling "a photograph of my desk top on the day I was writing that page." The book also spoke to his intensely personal involvement with the authors of his study, encompassing worldwide travel and collaborative projects for the past 15 years. His sense of the continuity of experiment in American fiction dating back to Hawthorn's day is demonstrated in his collection *The Practice of Fiction in America* (1980), whereas his book in progress (*Literary Subversions*) proposes new critical forms in response to innovations in fiction: the essay as polemic, as lyric, as meditation, and as witness.

Since 1978 Klinkowitz's critical interests have taken him to twice-annual month-long residencies at the Sorbonne's Centre de Recherche sur la Littérature Américaine Contemporaine. His association with the "Tri-Lateral" group of young Americanists at the Université de Paris-III, the University of East Anglia, and the Universität Würzburg led to his publication of *Kurt Vonnegut* (1982) in the Contemporary Writers series written and edited by this group, and to his study completed with James Knowlton, *Peter Handke and the Postmodern Transformation* (1983). Nevertheless, Klinkowitz prides himself on being "an unreconstructed American, a true barbarian in the sense of being innocent of the higher principles of colonial culture," admiring most the multi-cultural aesthetic of Ishmael Reed, who celebrates the artifacts native to American shores: blues, jazz, rock and roll, commercial TV, comic books, detective novels, and the like. Keeping these interests alive, he has worked regularly as a saxophonist in rhythm and blues bands and is an executive director of the minor league baseball club in his neighboring city of Waterloo, Iowa.

Selected Bibliography

Primary Sources

The Vonnegut Statement (with John Somer). New York: Dell, 1973; London: Panther Books, 1975.

Literary Disruptions: The Making of a Post-Contemporary American Fiction. Urbana: University of Illinois Press, 1975; revised and expanded, 1980.

The Life of Fiction. Urbana: University of Illinois Press, 1977.

Vonnegut in America (with Donald Lawler). New York: Dell, 1977.

Writing Under Fire: Stories of the Vietnam War (with John Somer). New York: Dell, 1978.

The American 1960s: Imaginative Acts in a Decade of Change. Ames: Iowa State University Press, 1980.

The Practice of Fiction in America: Writers from Hawthorne to the Present. Ames: Iowa State University Press, 1980.

Kurt Vonnegut. London: Methuen, 1982.

Peter Handke and the Postmodern Transformation (with James Knowlton). Columbia: University of Missouri Press, 1983.

The Self-Apparent Word: Fiction as Language/Language as Fiction. Carbondale: Southern Illinois University Press, 1984.

LYNN McKEAN

KONRAD, GEORGE (1933–   )

If history is a force that happens to us—behind our backs—how can we be considered the makers of our own history? An examination of this paradox underlies some of the finest Eastern European fiction being written today. A man whose work typifies this perspective is an experimental writer from Hungary, the novelist George Konrad. Konrad has written three novels since 1974, each of which is a dense, multi-layered examination of the human relationship to history. For Konrad, that relationship is an ethos of violence and desperation. His books are concerned not merely with personal acts of brutality but with a much more imposing form of violence: the violence of human history. Konrad's narrative voices—at times clinically controlled, at times disembodied and maniacal, but always raging—are the realization that, like murder, we keep committing history.

Konrad himself grew up in that ethos of violence he so effectively portrays in his novels. Born in 1933 of Jewish ancestry, Konrad grew up in a small village in eastern Hungary and, while still a boy, witnessed the arrest and deportation of his parents during the Nazi occupation of 1944. He fled the village to Budapest by bribing a local police official; the next day the women and children were sent to Auschwitz. Few survived. Konrad shares with Polish novelist Jerzy Kosinski* a profound understanding of flight, of escape—a prominent idea in both men's work.

Konrad has worked in Budapest as a social worker, a sociologist, and a novelist. He once described himself as a "planner who worked for the state." His only major work of nonfiction demonstrates his commitment to political philosophy; it is a Marxist critique of Eastern European socialism co-authored with an Economics professor, Ivan Szelenyi, and entitled *The Intellectuals on the Road to Class Power* (1974). The book was seized by local police for being subversive, and both Szelenyi and Konrad were arrested and then released because, according to Hungarian law, one can only be convicted of subversion if there is proof that someone else has read it. The two men's habit of burying their manuscript in a garden after each day's work proved crucial to their defense; the state could find no readers who were familiar with the political philosophies of the book and who also had dirt under their fingernails. After spending one week in jail, they were released in May of 1975. Szelenyi emigrated to London but Konrad stayed on in Budapest, only to emigrate later himself. Upon leaving Hungary he moved to an area just outside of Berlin, near the Schlachtensee, which translates—appropriately—into the "Lake of Battles." After more than two years in exile, he recently returned to Hungary to live and write.

Konrad's first novel, *The Case Worker* (1974), received favorable critical reviews from the press, but failed to reach a widespread audience. On one hand, it is a harrowing look at a carefully regulated and oppressive state bureaucracy; on the other, it is a kind of verbal "Guernica," with images of violence and chaos exploding throughout. The narrator is a social worker whose lyrical, Joycean ruminations are in stark contrast to the brutalized lives of his clients on caseload. He saves no one; the pages of suicides and compulsive acts of violence seem the only remedy for people hoping to escape their loveless, dehumanized lives.

The City Builder (1977) explores endemic despair—endemic because we plan for it, nurture it, develop it on drawing boards, and then label it with vapid titles like "progress" and "environmental planning." Konrad the social critic is apparent here, relentless in his investigation of the structures of socialism. From a complex historical perspective, weaving images of apocalyptic floods, outmoded factories, and sterile cities whose underpinnings are centuries of murder and senselessness, Konrad indicts all the social planners of his society. Why nations continue to structure themselves using blueprints for folly is one of the central issues of *The City Builder*.

The Loser (1982) is George Konrad's latest and most ambitious novel, numbering more than 300 pages, which is twice as long as either of his previous two novels. The loser is a man hounded by his own consciousness. After the revolutions, the insane asylums, family squabbles and hatreds, after all the writing and political machinations, he is still left with it: consciousness. He remembers the concepts and colors and logics of an insane world. Konrad's voices experiment with language in an attempt to reach some a priori state of clarity, a place beyond the tormenting effect of words and memory, a place that Nathalie Sarraute calls "before language." The intensity of *The Loser* comes from a narrator who attempts to reach this hallowed place and who understands he will fail from the start: Sisyphus and the loser, sharing the same senseless push on the stone.

The narrator of *The City Builder* comments that he is "surrounded by the dripstones of a historical slaughterhouse." This metaphor is an apt one; reading George Konrad's compelling prose is like watching a hammer fall on the heads of stunned cattle. The terror and the awe we feel are because we never cease the slaughter. George Konrad's courageous work reminds us that we know this, have known it all along, and still, we have never ceased the slaughter.

Selected Bibliography

Primary Sources

Az ertelmiseg utja as osztalyhatalomhoz (with Ivan Szelengi). Budapest: Magreto, 1974. (*The Intellectuals on the Road to Class Power*. Trans. Andrew Arato and Richard E. Arlen. New York: Harcourt Brace Jovanovich, 1979.)
A varosalapito. Budapest: Magreto, 1974. (*The Case Worker*. Trans. Paul Aston. New York: Harcourt Brace Jovanovich, 1974.)
The City Builder. Trans. Ivan Sanders. New York: Harcourt Brace Jovanovich, 1977.
The Loser. Trans. Richard E. Arlen. New York: Harcourt Brace Jovanovich, 1982.
Antipolitics. Trans. Richard E. Arlen. San Diego: Harcourt Brace Jovanovich, 1984.

Secondary Sources

Bryfonski, Dedria, ed. "George Konrad." *Contemporary Literary Criticism* 10. Detroit: Gale Research Co., 1979, pp. 304–305.
Howe, Irving. "The Case Worker." *New York Times Book Review*, January 27, 1974, p. 1.
Kauffmann, Stanley. "George Konrad." *Salmagundi* 57 (Summer 1982): 87–91.
Locher, Francis Carol, ed. "George Konrad." *Contemporary Authors* 85–88. Detroit: Gale Research Company, 1980, pp. 319–20.

BRUCE KUTNEY

KOSINSKI, JERZY (1933–   )

With the publication of *The Painted Bird* in 1965, Jerzy Kosinski emerged as a powerful voice in the literature of postmodernism. Readers were shocked by this violent story of a young boy's nightmarish adventures in Eastern Europe during World War II. In subsequent novels Kosinski has continued to develop the original themes of his literature of violation—a literature that depicts scenes of cruelty and violence in the fictive realm while simultaneously violating the traditional form of the novel and forcing the reader to violate his or her own beliefs about the nonfictive world in which he or she lives.

Jerzy Kosinski was born in Poland in 1933. Like the unnamed boy in *The Painted Bird*, he was separated from his family in the early days of the Second World War and wandered alone through the German-held countryside for four years. As a result of his wartime experiences, he was mute well into his teens. Kosinski studied at the Polish Academy of Sciences in Warsaw until 1957 when he escaped from behind the Iron Curtain and arrived in New York, again on his own.

His first book, *The Future Is Ours, Comrade*, was written in English and published in 1960 under the pen-name Joseph Novak. This study of life in collective society and a second volume, *No Third Path* (1962), were well received, and Kosinski had launched his writing career, though he had not yet published under his own name.

By the late 1960s, Kosinski had become internationally famous. During his marriage to the late Mary Tenet Weir, the widow of a billionaire Pittsburgh steel tycoon, he became something of a jetsetter and moved in the international circles of big business and high society. Since the publication of *The Painted Bird*, he has appeared often on television talkshows, and in 1981 he made his debut as an actor in Warren Beatty's Academy Award-winning film, *Reds*. In fact, Kosinski has lived almost every life imaginable: polo player and boat painter, student and restaurant worker, photographer and chauffeur, university professor and truck driver, parking lot attendant and novelist. Today he lives in New York City and travels widely.

Like Samuel Beckett, Raymond Federman,* Andrei Codrescu, and a number of other postmodernists, Kosinski has chosen to write in an adopted tongue. By establishing a distance between himself and his second language, he has developed a cool, detached style that presents even the most horrifying events as basic facts within his violent, sexually charged fictional world.

Kosinski's world is a world of victims and victimizers who in turn are victimized. The boy in *The Painted Bird* is brutalized and tortured, almost killed, by superstitious peasants who think he has the evil eye and by German soldiers who think he is a Jew, and he strikes back in kind whenever he can. The nameless narrator of *Steps* (1968) dominates others, even commits murder, but also works to free a retarded woman who is being held prisoner by villagers who use her for their sexual pleasure. Even Jonathan Whalen, the wealthy protagonist of *The Devil Tree* (1973), is the victim of his own privilege, and he murders his godparents in the hope of freeing himself from his past. In Kosinski's world—and by implication in our world as well—everyone is both violator and violated, and in the end everyone is the victim of time. The radical individual has the best chance of surviving through strength, cunning, and luck, but in time even the survivor's luck runs out. The blind date in the title of the Kosinski novel is with death.

Kosinski pits the individual with all his or her strengths and weaknesses against mass society and its ideologies—religion, morality, politics. In the collective world, the individual abdicates the self in favor of the group and the protection it offers. The individual rejects all questions to accept the answers proposed by Christianity, Marxism, capitalism, and so on. But ideologies cannot save mass humanity from becoming victims; in fact, by abdicating one's individuality, one victimizes oneself. And, of course, no ideology can protect a person from the radical individuality of his or her own death. Ideologies exist to convince people that there is a "plot" to existence and that they are in control. But in Kosinski's plotless novels, the protagonists recognize that risk is the only reality, and they become themselves most certainly in boundary situations that force them to succeed or fail, live or die, as individuals. As George Levanter says in *Blind Date* (1977): "I'm myself—it's the ultimate risk."

Kosinski responds to this ultimate risk by writing novels that call on readers to respond as well, each in their own way.

Selected Bibliography

Primary Sources

The Future Is Ours, Comrade (as Joseph Novak). Garden City, N.Y.: Doubleday, 1960.
No Third Path (as Joseph Novak). Garden City, N.Y.: Doubleday, 1962.
The Painted Bird. Boston: Houghton Mifflin, 1965.
Notes of the Author on The Painted Bird. New York: Scientia-Factum, Inc., 1967.
Steps. New York: Random House, 1968.
The Art of the Self: Essays a propos Steps. New York: Scientia-Factum, Inc., 1968.
Being There. New York: Harcourt Brace Jovanovich, 1971.
The Devil Tree. New York: Harcourt Brace Jovanovich, 1973.
Cockpit. Boston: Houghton Mifflin, 1975.
Blind Date. Boston: Houghton Mifflin, 1977.
Passion Play. New York: St. Martin's Press, 1979.
The Devil Tree: Newly Revised and Expanded Edition. New York: St. Martin's Press, 1981.
Pinball. New York: Bantam Books, 1982.

Secondary Sources

Cahill, Daniel J. "*The Devil Tree*: An Interview with Jerzy Kosinski." *The North American Review* 61 (Spring 1973): 56–66.
———. "An Interview with Jerzy Kosinski on *Blind Date*." *Contemporary Literature* 19 (Winter 1977): 133–42.
Green, Geoffrey. "The Nightmarish Quest of Jerzy Kosinski." In *The Anxious Subject: Nightmare and Daydreams in Literature and Film*, Moshe Lazar, ed. Malibu: Undena Press, 1983.

Harpham, Geoffrey Galt. "Survival in and of *The Painted Bird*: The Career of Jerzy Kosinski." *The Georgia Review* 35 (Spring 1981): 142–57.

Klinkowitz, Jerome. "Betrayed by Jerzy Kosinski." *The Missouri Review* 6 (Summer 1983): 157–75.

———. "Jerzy Kosinski: An Interview," *Fiction International* 1 (Fall 1973): 31–48.

Mortimer, Gail L. "Fear Death by Water: The Boundaries of the Self in Jerzy Kosinski's *The Painted Bird*." *Psychoanalytic Review* 63 (1976–1977): 511–528.

Plimpton, George A., and Rocco Landesman. "The Art of Fiction, XLVI: Jerzy Kosinski." *The Paris Review* 54 (Winter 1969): 183–207.

Richter, David H. "The Three Denouements of Jerzy Kosinski's *The Painted Bird*." *Contemporary Literature* 15 (Winter 1973): 370–85.

WELCH D. EVERMAN

KOSTELANETZ, RICHARD (1940–   )

Although perhaps best known as a prolific anthologist whose books cover the avant-garde of many of the new arts and cultural thought, and as a critic whose profiles, for example, of John Cage and other major figures are still sought after, Richard Kostelanetz has also staked out for himself a particularly original kind of fiction which is expressed not only through literary means, but also through other arts. This province is the area of pure sequence (or sometimes counter-sequence, if the ordering of the materials defies any logical trajectory). A fiction, as we see it in his work, is any sort of natural sequence or counter-sequence, be it numbers, autobiography, biography, visual progression, or even found materials (the *Epiphanies* film, 1981–   , and the *Invocations* text sound tape, the latter based on "The Lord's Prayer"). In such pieces as *Invocations* the sequence of the fragments is so well known that the work develops a logic of its own which plays off the traditional sequences by scrambling them or permuting them in a sort of fugal manner; the development of such logic into new forms of expression is the quintessence of Kostelanetz's art. Although Kostelanetz himself insists on the distinction between poetry and prose, and would not himself list a number of the works mentioned here as fiction, this distinction seems artificial in the context of his work.

On first encounter, a typical Kostelanetz work is apt to strike the listener (or viewer or reader) as excessively cold and rationalistic, but with familiarity this breaks down and the work assumes an unusual lyrical quality as the listener (or reader) experiences a dichotomy between the expected trajectory of the piece and its actual one. The result is not unlike a Bach fugue, although music remains virtually the only art which Kostelanetz has not systematically attempted. (He has, however, written extensively about music in such works as the brilliant *John Cage* monograph [New York:

Praeger, 1970], and such taped pieces as *Invocations* are essentially musical approaches to their materials.)

Kostelanetz's personal biography seems almost irrelevant to his fictions even when, in a highly factual way, he uses materials from it, as in "Relationships" in *Autobiographies* (Santa Barbara and New York: Mudborn & Future Presses, 1981), a listing of women he slept with and why. The facts and his speculations on the unnamed women, given only as disguised initials, are at the core of the piece, not the psychological or situational sharing of the experience as in the normative autobiographical mode. His biography thus becomes almost a sequence of abstractions.

Kostelanetz was born in New York City in 1940, educated (together with a surprising number of other artists) at Scarsdale High School, New York State, received an A.B. with honors in American Civilization from Brown University, an M.A. in American History from Columbia University in 1966, and attended King's College (London) in 1964–1965 as a Fulbright scholar. His first books were in the fields of modern thought and literature (e.g., *Master Minds* [New York: Macmillan, 1969] and *On Contemporary Literature* [New York: Avon, 1964 and two subsequent editions]) but with *The Theater of Mixed Means* (New York: Dial, 1968) he began the series of authored and edited books and anthologies which explore the new arts, especially the minimalism and intermedia of the 1960s and since. By 1983 he was already responsible for around 43 books, depending on how one chooses to count their various incarnations. A significant biographical fact which does not appear in his many biographical listings is that he speaks only English, in spite of a year's residence, off and on (1981–1983) in Berlin as a guest of the Deutscher Akademischer Austauschdienst. Hence, the influences on his thinking and art have tended to come mainly from his American contemporaries, despite the breadth of his interests. He himself lists Moholy-Nagy, on whom he has written a monograph (not listed in the Selected Bibliography below, since it is not fiction), as one of his main influences, perhaps his only European one.

Divorced, he has lived in New York City continuously since 1965, refers to it in his writings and interviews as "our town," and, though by no means a "New York Provincial" as outsiders tend to call them, he has tended to share the concerns of the New York cultural communities.

"Sequence" and "counter-sequence" are the key words explaining the nature of Kostelanetz's creative works, most of which are, in his term, "fictions," that is, the art of sequence. (He would probably add, "in prose," but we do not.) In fact, ever since his anthology *Breakthrough Fictioneers* (Barton, Vt.: Something Else Press, 1973), an international anthology of innovative fictions, he has tended to use the term "fictioner" (his preferred form) as more inclusive than such terms as "novelist" or "short story writer," since it includes the abstract numerical, stylistic, or even visual sequences that he and many others of our contemporaries have found necessary to express their experience and concerns. In approaching a Kostelanetz work, no matter how unorthodox it seems, the reader should look for this sequence or counter-sequence, imagine its possible trajectories, and compare what Kostelanetz presents to this—that is, the entry into the "pleasure of the text" in Roland Barthes'* phrase.

Selected Bibliography

A normal bibliography, listing all of Kostelanetz's anthologies, criticism, polemics, monographs, and so on, would lose focus on and misrepresent his fictions, for many are not in book form but are films, videotapes, audiotapes, graphic works, and the like. It would also be extremely lengthy, beyond the scope of the present volume. We therefore present the following listing of what strike us as fictions, whatever their form, alphabetical within each year. Presented in this way, one can see the sequence of his concerns, and can also see, in such cases as *Epiphanies* or *Openings & Closings*, how the idea for some works interpenetrates with several distinct media.

1970: *Visible Language* (poetry book/Brooklyn, N.Y.: Assembling Press). 1971: *In the Beginning* (book/Somerville, Mass. and Brooklyn, N.Y.: Abyss and Assembling Press). 1973: *Accounting* (booklet/Sacramento: Poetry Newsletter Books), *Ad Infinitum* (booklet/Friedrichsfehn, BRD: International Artists Cooperation). 1974: *Articulations/Short Fictions* (2 books bound as 1/New York: Kulchur Foundation), *Recyclings: Volume One* (book/Brooklyn: Assembling). 1975: *Constructs: Stories* (book/Reno, Nev.: West Coast Poetry Review), *Extrapolate* (booklet/Des Moines, Iowa and Brooklyn, N.Y.: Cookie and Assembling Presses), *Modulations* (booklet/Brooklyn: Assembling), *Numbers One* (portfolio/New York: RK Editions), *Numbers: Poems and Stories* (tabloid format/Brooklyn, N.Y.: Assembling), *Openings & Closings* (book/New York: D'Arc and RK Editions), *Openings & Closings* (videotape/New York: RK Editions), *Portraits from Memory* (book/n.p.: Ardis), *Three Prose Pieces* (videotape/New York: RK Editions). 1976: *Experimental Prose (1)* (audiocassette/New York: RK Editions), *Openings & Closings* (film made with Bart Weiss/New York: RK Editions, completed 1978), *Openings & Closings* (audiotape/New York: RK Editions), *Rain Rains Rain* (book/Brooklyn, N.Y.: Assembling), *Word Prints* (portfolio/New York: RK Editions), *Constructivist Fictions* (film made with Peter Longauer/New York: RK Editions, completed 1977). 1977: *Foreshortenings & Other Stories* (audiocassette/New York: RK Editions), *Illuminations* (poetry book/Woodinville, Wash. and New York: Laughing Bear and Future Press), *Numbers Two* (booklet/Columbus, Ohio: Luna Bisonte), *One Night Stood* (book/New York: Future Press, 2 eds.), *Praying to the Lord* (audiocassette/New York: RK Editions), *Prunings/Accruings* (booklet/Genève: Écart). 1978: *Audio Art* (audiocassette/New York: RK Editions), *Constructs Two* (book/Milwaukee: Membrane), *Foreshortenings and Other Stories* (book/Berkeley, Calif.: Tuuma Press), *Inex-

istencies (book/New York: RK Editions), *Tabula Rasa* (book/New York: RK Editions), *Wordsand* (book/Vancouver, B.C.: Simon Fraser University Gallery and New York: RK Editions). 1979: *And So Forth* (book/New York: Future Press), *Declaration of Independence* (videotape/New York: RK Editions), *Exhaustive Parallel Intervals* (book/New York: Future Press). 1980: *More Short Fictions* (book/Brooklyn, N.Y.: Assembling). 1981: *Autobiographies* (book/Santa Barbara, Calif. and New York: Mudborn and Future Presses), *Ein Verlorenes Berlin* (film made with Martin Kroeber/ New York: RK Editions), *Epiphanies* (film being completed in Berlin, Germany [1983]), *Invocations* (radio play/Berlin: Sender Freies Berlin), *Reincarnations* (book/New York: Future Press). 1982: *Arenas/Fields/Pitches/ Turfs* (poetry book/"BkMk Series." Kansas City, Mo.: University of Missouri at Kansas City), *The Gospels/Die Evangelien* (radio play/Köln: Westdeutscher Rundfunk).

DICK HIGGINS

KOSTER, R. M. (1934–   )

Although they have attracted little critical attention, R. M. Koster's three novels about the imaginary Central American republic of Tinieblas are both highly satisfying and unusually representative of postmodernism. *The Prince* (1971), *The Dissertation* (1975), and *Mandragon* (1979) deal with such postmodernist concerns as the transformation of reality by consciousness, the relation of fiction to history and to the temporal world, the influence of popular culture clichés on behavior, the importance of dreaming, myth, and the unconscious, art as a shaper of perception, and the autonomy of language. Koster's juxtaposition of fantasy with historical materials (a technique he shares with John Barth,* Thomas Pynchon,* Kurt Vonnegut,* and Robert Coover*) reflects two major traits of postmodernism—its assumption that all views of reality are fictional in the sense of being subjective and its consequent tendency to blur once axiomatic distinctions between the realms of reality and imagination.

Richard Morton Koster was born in Brooklyn on March 1, 1934. He received his B.A. from Yale in 1955 and his M.A. from New York University in 1962. He taught English at the National University of Panama in 1960–1961 and in 1964 became a lecturer at the Canal Zone Branch of Florida State University. Koster's experience, however, has not been solely academic: he worked as a free-lance correspondent for Copley News Service from 1964 to 1967 and has served as a Democratic national committeeman and delegate to several Democratic National Conventions from the Canal Zone. The dichotomy in Koster's life between the academic and the political points toward the most striking characteristics of his work— the fascination with reflective artists and scholars on the one hand and with forceful adventurers on the other, and his repeated attempts to reconcile these two types.

In a sense Koster's novels have grown out of the clash between the man of thought and the man of action. He had six full-length manuscripts rejected before his first novel, *The Prince*, was accepted, and it began as a few paragraphs about Kiki Sancudo, once a virile adventurer and now an introspective quadriplegic. *The Prince* covers one day in Kiki's life, as he imaginatively reconstructs the checkered history of Tinieblas, particularly the career of his father, a werewolf and presidential aspirant, and his own former exploits as a gunrunner, pimp, wrestler, politician, and lover. The structure enables Koster to contrast the paralyzed Kiki, all thought, sensibility, understanding, and shaping imagination, with the past Kiki, an amoral, insensitive, and essentially unthinking picaro. The novel suggests that the raw experience of Kiki's past, no matter how exciting it is, has no human reality until it has been "invented," been given order and meaning in his reflections. Thus, Kiki is an artist whose masterpiece is his imaginative reconstruction of his life.

Cast in the form of a doctoral dissertation in history, *The Dissertation* once more examines the conflict between the man of action, here the subject of the dissertation, León Fuertes, former war hero and Tinieblan president, and the man of thought, the author of the dissertation, León's son Camilo. *The Dissertation* demonstrates how Camilo's private obsessions color his allegedly factual biography of his father, but more interesting is the contrapuntal structure balancing dissertation and notes, experience and the interpretation of experience, the temporal world of history and a timeless afterlife, and political commitment and scholarship. Camilo's symbolic reunion with his father's ghost reflects a deeper effort by Koster to reconcile the imperative of action to make public and private life tolerable in the real world and the imperative of imagination to process experience and make it "real" to human understanding.

Action and imagination are most successfully reconciled in the hero of Koster's third novel, the hermaphrodite and shaman Mandragon. Whereas *The Prince* contains the reflections of a single day, *Mandragon* consists of the hero's memories on a single night. There is thus a sense of derangement. Places and events are distorted and dreamlike, somewhat in the manner of Nabokov's *Ada* or Vonnegut's *Slapstick*, but the distortion is not in the narrator's consciousness. The action of the novel is truly mythic, employing wasteland motifs and the folklore of shamanism. As a mythic projection of the romantic concept of the artist as seer, *Mandragon* unites action and imagination: he literally shapes the dream world of the novel through the divine light of inspiration which fills him with the power to perform his magic. His magical feats (animating a corpse, causing a typewriter to predict the future, ending a drought by curing a dictator's impotence, and hypnotizing an entire nation) testify to Koster's own inventive power and give the novel its rich texture and imaginative force.

Koster admits to having been influenced by Nabokov, and in notes to his novels he has explicitly affirmed the superiority of art to life and made light of the novel's mimetic function. Nevertheless, he has never sacrificed characters and setting to symbolism, imagery, and language, as Nabokov, Barth,* Pynchon,* and others sometimes have. Koster's attraction to picaresque heroes has no parallel in Nabokov, and his books take the kind of genuine interest in the domestic instability of Central America and in U.S. colonialism in the region that can be found in Joseph Conrad's *Nostromo* and Gabriel García Márquez'* *One Hundred Years of Solitude* (both alluded to in *The Prince*). In the foreground of Koster's fiction is a riveting drama of imagination; in the background, he constructs a world like Costaguana, Macondo, Faulkner's Yoknapatawpha, or even Dickens' London. Densely populated, rich in historical and geographical detail, this fictional universe forms a morally significant metaphorical model of our own.

Selected Bibliography

Primary Sources

The Prince. New York: William Morrow, 1971.
The Dissertation. New York: Harper's Magazine Press, 1975.
Mandragon. New York: William Morrow, 1979.

Secondary Sources

Crump, G. B. "Transformations of Reality in R. M. Koster's Tinieblan Novels." *Critique* 26 (1983): 241–52.
Rand, Peter. "Review of *The Prince*." *New York Times Book Review*, March 5, 1972, pp. 6, 18.

G. B. CRUMP

KUNDERA, MILAN (1929–   )

Although he has been translated into some twenty languages, earning international critical acclaim, Milan Kundera is no longer published in his native Czechoslovakia. His books—banned for more than fifteen years—examine the effects of political oppression on individual lives. Structurally inventive, Kundera often achieves artistic unity through thematic unity, using humor and irony to explore memory, politics, sex, and art. The effect is an erotic, surreal fiction, both playful and pessimistic, which depicts culturally fragmented, psychically confused humans groping for personal validation in a world that ignores individual worth.

Milan Kundera was born April 1, 1929 in Brno, the son of a famous concert pianist and musicologist. A student when the Communist party took power in 1948, Kundera studied piano and composing, then film directing and screen writing. He joined the party in 1947, but his early criticisms resulted in his being dropped in 1950. Dismissed from his studies, he worked for a time as a mine laborer, an experience reflected in his first novel, *The Joke* (1967). Though he was reinstated in 1956, Kundera's early political conflicts prefigured later confrontations.

During the 1950s and early 1960s, Kundera taught literature and published a variety of works, including literary criticism, three volumes of poetry (which won governmental criticism for "deviationism"), and *The Keepers of the Keys* (1962), a play which became an immediate success. In 1963, Kundera published *Laughable Loves*, a collection of short stories exploring the dichotomy between love and sex, intimacy and the erotic.

In 1967, after a four month delay, the government finally allowed publication of *The Joke*. As Kundera has said, this first novel prefigures many formal and thematic considerations of his later works. Written in seven sections with four different narrators, *The Joke* illuminates Kundera's musical background in its theme-and-variation structure; shifting perspectives inform the story, and unity develops from the reverberations of key words and themes. Concerned with a man whose ruined life results from an offhand political joke, Kundera explores the troublesome rift between human intentions and the cruel joke's circumstance, the eroding relationship between past and present, and the relativity of truth, especially in the face of self-deception and political manipulation. The biggest joke forms what might be termed a core motivation for all of Kundera's art: the political utopia promised by socialist idealism that evolves into a repressive, opportunistic nightmare.

Retrospectively, *The Joke* seems prophetic. Czechoslovakia enjoyed a brief cultural and political renaissance during 1967 and 1968 with President Dubček's attempt to present Communism "with a human face." During the Prague Spring, Kundera delivered a keynote address at a meeting of the Writers' Union, blasting political oppression and warning of its negative effects on Czech literature. But the liberal atmosphere vanished when Soviet forces invaded Prague on August 20, 1968. With government restrictions newly tightened on the press, Kundera's second novel, *Life is Elsewhere*, was refused publication. Depicting the life of a young poet, the book criticizes the notion shared by some revolutionaries and poet-dreamers that total harmony is attainable and that truth is fixed and absolute. Blinded by his idealistic vision, Jaromil becomes an informer, dooming his girlfriend's innocent brother to a concentration camp. Because he condemned its politics fearlessly, Kundera was expelled from the Communist Party in 1970, stripped of his teaching position, forbidden to travel, his work proscribed. Though *Life is Elsewhere* was published in France in 1973 (winning the Prix Médicis award), his work would never again be published in Czechoslovakia.

In 1975, Kundera was permitted to accept a teaching position in France. He wrote *The Farewell Party* (1976), a farcical comedy set in a fertility spa, which explores serious issues such as self-deception and awareness, and the personal annihilation suffered by many who find their cultural ties severed by politics. Meanwhile, Kundera's personal ties were severed by politics: in 1979, in reaction to the publication of *The Book of Laughter and Forgetting*, the Czechoslovakian government revoked his citizenship.

An enchanting weave of literary criticism, fantasy, erotica, and musicology, many critics consider *The Book of Laughter and Forgetting* Kundera's masterpiece. Though not united by traditional novelistic conventions, such as the considerations of plot, narrator, and linear time sequences, Kundera argues that his seven-part work is a novel in which coherence emerges with his theme-and-variation approach to structure. Memory, for example, becomes a central focus for all the pieces. Individuals struggle to remember personal details, thus retaining some measure of private continuity in the face of national amnesia and cultural fragmentation. (Gustav Husak, Dubček's successor, is called the "president of forgetting.") The sections telling Tamina's story, which Kundera considered to be the main focus of the work, are especially poignant. Laughter provides another unifying motif, a metaphor for both the healing potential of humans and their potential for maniacal political tyranny.

In his next novel, *The Unbearable Lightness of Being* (1984), Kundera traces the overlapping lives of two couples. All are victims of some type of betrayal, sexual or political, or both. Kundera again explores the seeming impotence of individual efforts in an environment where homogenized human concerns become superficial and trivialized kitsch. Sincere goodness is rewarded by death, and the only arena where people retain power is the sexual one. A playful blend of styles and subjects, *Unbearable Lightness* is disturbingly cynical—all the more so for its international setting.

The problems envisioned throughout Kundera's work literally hit home in *Unbearable Lightness*, to all of us, to all political systems. As some critics argue, one of Kundera's greatest gifts is his ability to communicate his vision to readers who do not share his particular experience—a small consolation to a writer who must compose, from far away, love songs to a lost Prague.

Selected Bibliography

Primary Sources

Směšné lásky. Prague: Ceskoslovensky spisovatel, 1963. (*Laughable Loves*. Trans., Suzanne Rappaport. New York: Alfred A. Knopf, 1974.)

Žert. Prague: Ceskoslovensky spisovatel, 1967. (*The Joke*. Trans., Michael Heim. New York: Harper and Row, 1982.)

Život je jinde (No Czech edition published). *La Vie est ailleurs*. Trans., Francois Kerel. Paris: Gallimard, 1973. (*Life is Elsewhere*. Trans., Peter Kuzzi. New York: Alfred A. Knopf, 1974.)

Valčík na rozloučenou (No Czech edition published). (*The Farewell Party*. Trans.,
   Peter Kussi. New York: Alfred A. Knopf, 1976.)
Kniha smíchu a zapomnění (No Czech edition published). (*The Book of Laughter
   and Forgetting*. Trans., Michael Heim. New York: Alfred A. Knopf, 1980.)
Nesnesitelná lehkost bytí (No Czech edition published). (*The Unbearable Lightness
   of Being*. Trans., Michael Heim. New York: Harper and Row, 1984.)

   Secondary Sources

Fuentes, Carlos. "The other K." *TriQuarterly* (Spring 1981): 256–75.
Harkins, William E., ed. *Czech Literature Since 1956: A Symposium*. New York:
   Bohemica, 1980.
Porter, Robert C., *Milan Kundera: A Voice from Central Europe*. Arhus: Arkona,
   1981.
Kussi, Peter. "Milan Kundera: Dialogues with Fiction." *World Literature Today:
   A Literary Quarterly of the University of Oklahoma*. 56, 2, (1978), 206–9.
Salmon, C., "The Art of Fiction LXXXI; Milan Kundera" [interview]. *Paris Review*
   26 (1984), 107–23.

PENELOPE RITHNER

L

LACAN, JACQUES (1901–1981)

Jacques Lacan was born in Paris in 1901 and died there in 1981. After taking his degree in medicine at the Sorbonne, he founded and assumed the directorship of the Ecole Freudienne de Paris, where he soon established himself as the reigning figure and *enfant terrible* of modern French psychoanalysis. During his long tenure at the Ecole Freudienne and at the Ecole Normale Supérieure, he produced a large corpus of theoretical and technical writings, most of which were published in a multi-volume collection entitled *Ecrits* (1966). These works and Lacan's rather baroque personal style became the subjects of enormous controversy. Those in his camp lauded his work and style as the products of a largely misunderstood but highly creative genius, second, perhaps, only to Freud himself. His detractors, on the other hand, found his theories intentionally obscure and his professional conduct (five-minute therapy sessions, for example) outright scandalous. This personal and often political controversy does not, however, diminish Lacan's substantial contribution to modern psychoanalytic theory.

Singular among his innovations is the recognition of the confluence of language and psychoanalysis. This abiding interest in the linguistic side of the discipline arose from Lacan's more general need to reevaluate and recover the entire Freudian psychoanalytic project. In this connection Lacan argued that modern psychoanalysis had lost touch with its original *raison d'être*. In Freud's hands, psychoanalysis centered around a single, crucial observation: the neurotic suffered from memories and discourses which were deeply buried in the unconscious and accessible only through regenerative speech, that is, the so-called talking cure. Lacan's course correction of psychoanalysis, then, consisted largely in rediscovering, in his own terms, this fragile, now overlooked language of the unconscious.

Simply put, this rediscovery proceeds on the supposition that there is an absolute identity between language and the unconscious; that the unconscious is, in effect, structured like a language. Basic to this insight is the idea that a full understanding of the subject can only be accomplished in terms of a schema composed of several layers of structures, which, incidentally, correspond to the topological distinctions developed by Freud in *The Ego and the Id* (1923) between conscious, unconscious, and preconscious psychic layers. For Lacan, as for Freud, the unconscious layer is distinct and summable but masked by a conscious lucidity. But, unlike Freud, Lacan tries to overcome this screening lucidity by claiming that the unconscious consists of a "chain of signifiers"—a sequence of discrete linguistic elements—and is structured in such a way that the elements are articulated in categories and subsets in accordance with strict laws of organization. The interpretation of these enchained signifiers would, then, proceed in precisely the same way as any structural analysis of language: what does each element mean differentially? in isolation? in relation to the whole? and so on. The conclusions drawn from this kind of analysis could then be applied to a therapeutic model, involving the key signifiers that disrupt the patient's mental life.

Lacan's stress on an unconscious language, its metaphorical and metonymical content, and its role in the development of the self was naturally of considerable interest to writers and literary theorists. Authors of the stature of Alain Robbe-Grillet and Maurice Blanchot can be counted among his admirers. Literary critics of no less eminence than Roland Barthes* and Gérard Genette were also struck by his innovative theories. What seems to captivate both types of literary practitioners is Lacan's stress on both the development of self through the Other and language and textuality as constituted by "floating signifiers." In the former, Lacan proposes that the self passes through a mirror stage. This stage, occurring sometime between six and eighteen months of age, involves the child recognizing his image in the mirror and taking that image to be an "Ideal I" or fictional ego. This "I" exists prior to any form of social determination, since the child has not entered into language, nor has he encountered the Other or society. Eventually, however, this "Ideal I" does come into contact with the mediated, less than ideal world of socially and linguistically determined reality. And according to Lacan, it is the constant interplay and struggle between these two realms—the real and the imaginary—which eventually constitutes the self. Lacan's stress on the textuality of floating signifiers was important to literary practice because it confirmed the entire postwar structuralist enterprise. By suggesting that the psychic text was constituted by signifiers, he further exposed the mimetic fallacy, subverting any naive belief in the referential function of language. This insight also helped nurture the growing belief in the importance of linguistic determinism.

It may not be correct to state, as many of his followers do, that Lacan was Freud's equal in all things. But it is safe to say that he was the master's equal in ability to synthesize extremely diverse material. Lacan borrowed his ideas from many, often disparate fields, including neurophysiology, mathematics, and poetics. He was alternately linked with the structuralists, surrealists, existentialists, and French neo-Hegelians. His psychoanalytic theories, though seeming wildly speculative at times, were actually derived from an extraordinarily close reading of Freud's texts (the connection between Freud's theory of narcissism and the mirror stage, for example). Thus, we could say that, if nothing else, Lacan pulled together virtually all the important strands of twentieth-century thought, albeit in an imaginative, poetic, convoluted, and highly personal way.

Selected Bibliography

Primary Sources

Ecrits. Paris: Seuil, 1966. (*Ecrits: A Selection*. Trans. Alan Sheridan. London: Tavistock; New York: W. W. Norton, 1977.)
Fonction et champ de la parole et du langage en psychanalyse in *La Psychanalyse*, Vol. 1 (Paris 1956) and in *Ecrits*. (*The Language of the Self*. Trans. Alan Sheridan. New York: Delta, 1968.)
The Four Fundamental Concepts of Psychoanalysis. Trans. Alan Sheridan. London: Hogarth Press; New York: W. W. Norton, 1977.
Speech and Language in Psychoanalysis. Trans. Anthony Wilden. Baltimore: Johns Hopkins University Press, 1981.

Secondary Sources

Bowiek, M. "Jacques Lacan." In *Structuralism and Since*. Ed. J. Suttock. Oxford: Oxford University Press, 1979.
Clement, Catherine. *The Lives and Legends of Jacques Lacan*. Trans. Arthur Goldhammer. New York: Columbia University Press, 1983.
Lamire, A. *Jacques Lacan*. London and Boston: Routledge & Kegan Paul, 1977.
Laplanche, J. and J. B. Pontalis. *The Language of Psychoanalysis*. London: Hogarth Press, 1973.
Muller, John P., and W. Richardson. *Lacan and Language: A Reader's Guide to the Ecrits*. New York: International Universities Press, 1982.

MARK S. ROBERTS

LeGUIN, URSULA (1929–   )

Ursula LeGuin's novels have taken her to the forefront of the fields of science fiction, fantasy, and children's literature, winning her nearly a dozen literary awards. Her wide appeal to both the general reader and the critical establishment stems not from adherence to any specific ideology, but from a wide-ranging humanism that incorporates anthropological knowledge, Taoist theology, anarchist politics, and Jungian psychology under the aegis of a pellucid and lyrical style.

She was born in California in 1929, the daughter of anthropologist Alfred Kroeber and writer Theodora Kroeber (author of *Ishi of Two Worlds*). In this highly intellectual environment she started young as a writer, submitting a science fiction story to *Amazing* at around age ten. She graduated from Radcliffe, got her Master's in French literature from Columbia, and went to France on a Fulbright scholarship. It was there that she met her future husband, historian Charles LeGuin. They have lived for many years now in Portland, Oregon, raising three now-grown children.

LeGuin's professional career began in the early 1960s with short stories, mostly in the science fiction magazines. Her first three novels, *Rocannon's World* (1966), *Planet of Exile* (also 1966), and *City of Illusions* (1967), were all colorful mixtures of standard science fiction and fantasy elements, much in the vein of that finest of science fiction juvenile writers, André Norton. Many of the themes and techniques she later mastered are present in these early works in embryo, and would be further honed with each book. The last of the three, though LeGuin herself regards it as a failure, attains a high level of poetic prose right from its memorable first line, "Imagine darkness."

In 1967 Parnassus Press, publisher of picture books for young children, asked LeGuin to write a book for older children. Searching for a subject, she hit upon the world of many small islands she had discovered and briefly touched on in two early short stories, "The Word of Unbinding" and "The Rule of Names." She wondered how the aged wizards of so many fantasies learned their lore; the result was the first volume of the Earthsea trilogy, *A Wizard of Earthsea* (1968).

LeGuin realized at this point that one sign of her artistic immaturity was the mixing of science fiction and fantasy elements; Earthsea separated out the fantasy elements, and her next project isolated the science fictional ones. Again, the source was a short story, "Winter's King," which speculated on the effect of faster-than-light travel (people using such travel do not age) on the succession of a medieval-style kingdom on a planet called Winter. Interestingly enough, LeGuin did not realize until the story was already in print that the planet's inhabitants were androgynous. The ruminations this engendered turned out to be her masterpiece, *The Left Hand of Darkness* (1969).

Seldom has a science fiction novel established itself so quickly as a classic. *The Left Hand of Darkness* represents an ideal combination of an interesting plot of adventure and intrigue, a solidly imagined ecology and several cultures (lacking only the larger scope of Tolkien or *Dune*), and fascinating philosophical and psychological speculations on the nature of gender, implicitly presented in contrast with a race where gender distinctions do not exist. It won LeGuin, deservedly. both the Hugo and Nebula awards for best science fiction novel of the year. With subsequent changes in ways of thinking, it has become fashionable to criticize the work's social and political shortcomings, but for the pre-consciousness-raised era in which it was written it was truly innovative. Furthermore, its Orient-influenced anti-dualism steers a refreshing middle course between both extremes of sexual politics.

Over the next several years LeGuin wrote various other science fictional short works using the same future-history framework as her novels: "Vaster Than Empires and More Slow," concerning a forest group-mind; "Nine Lives," exploring the social and psychological implications of cloning; and her other masterpiece of the period, "The Word for World Is Forest." It is true, as LeGuin herself admits, that she "succumbed to the lure of the pulpit," and that the story can be read—and dismissed—as a shallow allegory of American cultural imperialism in Vietnam; but the real center of the story is the contrast between the nonviolent, dream-adept Athsheans (modeled loosely on various Earth tribal groups) and the technologically adept, militaristic Ekumen. Read this way the implications are broader and the conclusion is far more poignant.

LeGuin's next novel, *The Lathe of Heaven* (1971; later made into a successful television movie), an homage to the "what is reality" novels of Philip K. Dick,* is the clearest expression of her Taoist leanings (where a man with the power to change the world with his dreams constantly seeks to redress the balance), but it so limits itself to a small compass of time and space that it lacks the scope of her other works.

In the next two years LeGuin completed her Earthsea trilogy with *The Tombs of Atuan* (1971) and *The Farthest Shore* (1972), the latter winning her the National Book Award for Children's Literature. The series, as completed, is probably the most outstanding example of post-Tolkien fantasy. Self-consistent in its worldbuilding and rigorously scientific in its magic, it is also psychologically convincing in its use of Jungian archetypes to demonstrate three differing aspects of coming of age: the training of the adept and the acceptance of self in the first; a more specifically feminine coming of age and acceptance of sex in the second; and acceptance of death in the last.

LeGuin's long interest in anarchist politics led her inexorably to the culmination and terminus of her Ekumen future history, *The Dispossessed* (1974; again a double award winner). This novel also was criticized as naive and oversimplified in its portrait of twin planets, one much like Earth, the other an exile colony that had built an anarchist utopia. But the strength of the book lies in its portrayal of the physicist Shevek and his personal reaction to a journey from anarchy to capitalism and back, and the way his mathematical/philosophical theory of Sequence and Simultaneity pervades both the imagery and the very structure of the book itself.

LeGuin's next work, a sequence called *Orsinian Tales*, appeared two years later (1976). These brief vignettes about a mythical Eastern European country extend back to her first published story, "An die Musik" (1961), which is perhaps the strongest in the book, with its evocation of the dilemma of a musician tied to a responsibility-ridden life that won't allow him to compose. His acceptance at the end is presented as a Joycean epiphany— and, indeed, the whole book becomes clear if one compares it, not to LeGuin's science fiction, but to *Dubliners*. The revelatory psychological possibilities of the quotidian can be as fascinating a theme as far-flung anthropological adventures.

In the end, *Orsinian Tales* is the key to LeGuin's other area of endeavor, the short story or (as she sometimes calls it) the psychomyth. In examining the 1975 collection *The Wind's Twelve Quarters* and the recent collection *The Compass Rose* (1982), one finds distributed throughout her work a whole body of highly sophisticated pieces like the surrealistic identity-crisis "A Trip to the Head," the subtle dystopia "The Ones Who Walk Away from Omelas," the linguistic speculation of "The Author of the Acacia Seeds," the nonthreatening feminism of "Sur," and the latest and most formally brilliant Orsinian tale, "Two Delays on the Northern Line" (which gained her entry into *The New Yorker*). These stories belong more to the tradition of James Joyce, Franz Kafka, Jorge Luis Borges, and Italo Calvino* than to any narrowly conceived tradition of science fiction and fantasy. As much as any other contemporary writer, LeGuin has expanded and changed the science fiction field so that it can never again be conceived in such narrow limits.

Selected Bibliography

Primary Sources

Rocannon's World. New York: Ace Books, 1966.
Planet of Exile. New York: Ace Books, 1966.
City of Illusions. New York: Ace Books, 1967.
A Wizard of Earthsea. Berkeley: Parnassus Press, 1968.
The Left Hand of Darkness. New York: Ace Books, 1969.
The Lathe of Heaven. New York: Scribner's, 1971.
The Tombs of Atuan. New York: Atheneum, 1971.
The Farthest Shore. New York: Atheneum, 1972.
The Dispossessed. New York: Harper & Row, 1974.
The Wind's Twelve Quarters. New York: Harper & Row, 1975.
The Word for World Is Forest. New York: Harper & Row, 1976.
Orsinian Tales. New York: Harper & Row, 1976.
The Language of the Night. Ed. Susan Wood. New York: G. P. Putnam's, 1979.
The Compass Rose. New York: Harper & Row, 1982.

Secondary Sources

Bucknall, Barbara J. *Ursula K. LeGuin*. New York: Frederick Ungar, 1981.

DeBolt, Joe, ed. *Ursula K. LeGuin: Voyager to Inner Lands and to Outer Space*. Port Washington, N.Y.: Kennikat Press, 1979.

Delany, Samuel R. "To Read *The Dispossessed*," In *The Jewel-Hinged Jaw: Notes on the Language of Science Fiction*. New York: Berkley Publishing Corp., 1977.

Gregory, Sinda, and Larry McCaffery. "An Interview with Ursula LeGuin." *Missouri Review* 7, no. 2 (1984): 64–85.

Olander, Joseph D., and Martin Harry Greenberg, eds. *Ursula K. LeGuin*. New York: Taplinger Publishing Co., 1979.

Science Fiction Studies 2, No. 3 (1975). Special LeGuin issue.

Slusser, George E. *The Farthest Shores of Ursula K. LeGuin*. The Milford Series: Popular Writers of Today, vol. 3. San Bernardino, Calif.: Borgo Press, 1976.

DONALD G. KELLER

LEM, STANISŁAW (1921–   )

Author of over 35 books representing the most diverse kinds of creative writing and nonfiction, Stanisław Lem is unquestionably one of the most versatile and expansive writers working today. A man of insatiable desire for knowledge and exuberant imagination, he has been moving with unrelenting fervor into areas of thought and creativity largely unexplored by others, claiming for himself even the tiniest gaps between science, philosophy, and literature and filling them with original ideas about such fundamental issues as the place of humanity in the universe, the limits of knowledge and understanding, or the implications of scientific and technological progress for nature and humankind, issues that, he believes, must be raised today if humankind is to maintain the faintest hope of ever solving them in the future. His works, which include novels, short stories, fables, dialogues, autobiography, poetry, plays, television scripts, scientific, philosophical, and journalistic essays, literary criticism and theory, and innumerable hybrid pieces that are several or all of these at the same time, have been translated into 35 languages and are available to millions of readers throughout the world.

Stanisław Lem was born in Lvov, formerly Poland, on September 12, 1921, in a doctor's family. In 1940 he entered Lvov's Medical Institute, but the outbreak of the war soon disrupted his newly begun studies. During the occupation years, he worked as a car mechanic and then had to go into hiding for almost a year under an assumed name. Immediately after the liberation of Lvov in 1944, he resumed his medical studies, which he completed in 1948 in Cracow, where his family had moved in the meantime following the shifting of the Polish-Soviet frontier west of Lvov. By the time he graduated from Jagiellonian University's Medical School, he was publishing scholarly articles and reviews of scientific books in the areas of medicine, philosophy, and methodology of science. His first novel, *Czło-*

wiek z Marsa (*A Man from Mars*), was serialized in 1946 in an adventure story magazine, and within the next two years more reviews, short stories, and poems appeared in several magazines published across the country.

Lem's first novel to appear in book form was *Astronauci* (1951, *The Astronauts*), a conventional story of an expedition to Venus which, though dismissed by the critics, brought its author immediate success with popular audiences. Despite its numerous imperfections as a literary work, it already demonstrated Lem's commitment to scientific credibility and imaginative buoyancy in the kind of fiction which, he says, will not save humanity but can at least keep humankind alert in anticipation of the not-yet-known. Three years after his debut as a novelist, his first story collection, *Sezam* (1954, *Sesame*), came out which brought out the first five of the Ijon Tichy stories, a cycle continued in *The Star Diaries* (1957) and some later collections published in the 1960s and 1970s. In 1955, another utopian novel of interplanetary travel, *Obłok Magellana* (*Magellan's Cloud*), was published along with the trilogy *Czas nieutracony* (*Time Not Wasted*), Lem's only work so far dealing with contemporary Polish reality, specifically with the moral impact of the war and its political aftermath on a young doctor.

The following decade marked a great acceleration in the writer's productivity as well as an important shift in his approach to and treatment of science fiction's standard subjects and strategies. Between 1957 and 1966, Lem published 18 books, which included most of his best-selling sci-fi novels and stories as well as his autobiography, *Wysoki zamek* (*The High Castle*, 1966), and his first important quasi-philosophical work, *Summa technologiae* (1964). Two tendencies in this second phase of Lem's career are particularly noteworthy: one, a steady movement away from the adventure-type story and toward the problem-type story and, two, the growth of the writer's awareness of and interest in the general problems involved in the making of fiction itself. Thus, on the one hand, the motif of the exploration of outer space, while it continued to be the primary vehicle by which the novel's action was carried forward, gradually gave way to the exploration of the mind's inner space. In novels such as *Eden* (1959), *The Investigation* (1959), *Return from the Stars* (1961), *Solaris* (1961), *The Invincible* (1964), *His Master's Voice* (1968) and the Pilot Pirx cycle begun in *Inwazja z Aldebarana* (*The Invasion from Aldebaran*, 1959) and continued in later collections, Lem shows that the true barrier to humankind's future conquest of the cosmos may prove to be not technological but psychological, that humanity's defeat may come not from people's inability to escape the prison house of space and time but from their failure to understand, and articulate their understanding of, the phenomena that they may encounter in other worlds as well as in their own—phenomena that include their own mental operations. On the other hand, realizing that the cognitive limits of the mind are determined by the individual's ability to create formal systems describing real or hypothetical phenomena, Lem expands the possibilities of literature, which is just such a system, by inventing new combinations of and applications for established literary conventions. The result can be very comical, as Lem's science fiction grotesques such as *Bajki robotów* (*Robot Fables*, 1964), *The Cyberiad* (1965) and, to a lesser degree, *The Star Diaries* (1957) and *Memoirs Found in a Bathtub* (1961) demonstrate.

Lem's growing dismay at the pathetic ignorance and incompetence of most contemporary science fiction writers, in matters of both science and fiction, and his ambivalence about the ability of literature to respond adequately to the challenge that scientific discovery in areas such as cybernetics and biology poses to humankind today have been reflected in a succession of works published since the late 1960s in which he progressively dissociates himself from science fiction in favor of philosophic speculation and literary criticism. These critical works—*Dialogi* (*Dialogues*, 1957) and *Summa technologiae, Filozofia przypadku* (*The Philosophy of Chance*, 1968), and *Fantastyka i futurologia* (*Science Fiction and Futurology*, 1971)— continue Lem's ambitious project to present a synthetic overview of the possible directions of postmodern science and literature in view of the present state of humankind's empirical knowledge about the world. In fiction, his innovative thought is expressed in innovative forms, such as the fictitious reviews of and introductions to nonexistent books collected in *A Perfect Vacuum* (1971) and *Imaginary Magnitude* (1973).

Over the past decade, Lem has published only two new novels, *Katar* (*Catarrh*, 1976), a detective story that makes the cognitive value of scientific experiment a function of experience as opposed to rationalization, and *Wizja lokalna* (*Inspection of the Scene of Action*, 1982), a Borgesian story of a man studying the history of a fictitious civilization, one collection of essays in literary criticism and futurology, *Rozprawy i szkice* (*Treatises and Sketches*, 1975), and several short stories. These more recent works are much less accessible to popular audiences than his more conventional novels and stories written in the 1950s and 1960s, but the loss of readership will hardly be a problem for Lem in the forseeable future. Quite the contrary, as the current vogue of Lem's writing among academic audiences in the United States and elsewhere shows, new, and more serious, readers will continue to be attracted to his mind-boggling fictions and essays which prove that imagination is the individual's most precious instrument of cognition. Not being bound by the exigencies of empirical veracity and understanding, Lem's work guarantees that the human mind will always remain open to innovation, whose occurrence somewhere in the universe, he suggests, can never be excluded as a possibility in an a priori manner, even though reason may tell us otherwise.

Selected Bibliography

Primary Sources

Solaris. New York: Walker & Co., 1970. (Trans. of *Solaris*, 1961)

Memoirs Found in a Bathtub. New York: Seabury Press, 1973. (Trans. of *Pamiętnik znaleziony w wannie*, 1961.)

The Invincible. New York: Seabury Press, 1973. (Trans. of *Niezwyciężony i inne opowiadania*, 1964.)

The Investigation. New York: Seabury Press, 1974. (Trans. of *Śledztwo*, 1959.)

The Cyberiad: Fables for the Cybernetic Age. New York: Seabury Press, 1974. (Trans. of *Cyberiada*, 1965.)

The Futurological Congress. New York: Seabury Press, 1974. (Trans. of *Kongres futurologiczy*, 1971.)

The Star Diaries. New York: Seabury Press, 1976. (Trans. of *Dzienniki gwiazdowe*, 1957.)

Tales of Pirx the Pilot. New York: Harcourt, 1979. (Trans. of *Opowieści o pilocie Pirxie*, 1968.)

A Perfect Vacuum. New York: Harcourt, 1979. (Trans. of *Doskonała próżnia*, 1971.)

Return from the Stars. New York: Harcourt, 1980. (Trans. of *Powrót z gwiazd*, 1961.)

Memoirs of a Space Traveler. New York: Harcourt, 1981. (Trans. of the second part of *The Star Diaries*, 1971, above.)

Imaginary Magnitude. New York: Harcourt, 1984. (Trans. of *Wielkość urojona*, 1973.)

Secondary Sources

Barnouw, Dagmar. "Science Fiction as a Model for Probabilistic Worlds: Stanislaw Lem's Fantastic Empiricism." *Science Fiction Studies* 6 (1979): 153–63.

Guffey, George R. "The Unconscious, Fantasy, and Science Fiction: Transformation in Bradbury's *Martian Chronicles* and Lem's *Solaris*." In George E. Slusser, ed. *Bridges to Fantasy*. Carbondale: Southern Illinois University Press, 1982, pp. 142–59.

Jarzebski, Jerzy. "Stanislaw Lem, Rationalist and Visionary." *Science Fiction Studies* 4 (1977): 110–26.

Olander, Joseph D., and Martin Greenberg, eds. *Stanislaw Lem*. New York: Taplinger, 1984.

Rose, Mark. "Filling the Void: Verne, Wells, and Lem." *Science Fiction Studies* 8 (1981): 121–42.

Rothfork, John. "Having Everything in Having Nothing: Stanislaw Lem vs. Utilitarianism." *Southwest Review* 66 (Summer 1981): 293–306.

Ziefeld, Richard. *Stanislaw Lem*. New York: Frederick Ungar, 1984.

JERZY KUTNIK

M

McELROY, JOSEPH (1930–   )

If modernism was the high craft of genius, and if postmodernism is the beginning of collaboration—the artist collecting and arranging mutating disciplines and proliferating languages, as in Thomas Pynchon,* William Gaddis,* Robert Coover,* and John Barth*—then Joseph McElroy belongs on the short list of postmodern achievement. The self-reflexive negations, the notes on fictional futility, of much postmodern fiction come from a refusal to collaborate with—to know and use—the ideas and metaphors offered by extraliterary realities, especially science and technology. By extending his attention to the microscopic and macroscopic, McElroy shows that familiar novelistic situations, even the power of the familial past, can still be represented with far-ranging language. Authoritative in the knowledge they contain, inventive in their use of formal principles from nonliterary sources, McElroy's five novels are also stroked with postmodern uncertainties: about the limits of language, the gaps in the best of explanatory networks, the distortions of history, the Gödelian infinity of frames. "Knowing and Not Knowing," as McElroy described the conceit of *Lookout Cartridge*, is the central concern of his fiction—the extension of knowledge and the extension of uncertainty. When more readers come to understand that they live in the Age of Information and that fiction lives there too, McElroy's work will be recognized as the leading edge of postmodern fiction.

Born in 1930, McElroy grew up in Brooklyn Heights, the setting of his first three novels. After graduating from Williams College, McElroy served in the Coast Guard and earned a Ph.D. in English from Columbia in 1961. Now a professor at Queens College, he has taught at the University of New Hampshire, Johns Hopkins, and the Sorbonne. During the early 1970s, McElroy reviewed books on a wide variety of subjects, published essays on art and literature, and covered several early Apollo launches. He describes these and other influences in his remarkable autobiographical and critical essay "Neural Neighborhoods and Other Concrete Abstracts" which documents his turning away from the "regular, sensitive American novel" to a fiction "dense in the fullness of attention given to a mass of life," to a kind of work with an old American impulse "to set out to do more than can be done." These early intentions, though reformulated from one novel to the next, mark each of his books: ambitious, large, overloaded, verging on chaos, moving in their testing of limits—McElroy's, his characters', and his readers'.

McElroy's first two novels, *A Smuggler's Bible* (1966) and *Hind's Kidnap* (1969), can most quickly be described as experiments with the fictional energies in their respective models, Gaddis' *The Recognitions* and Nabokov's best acrostics. The writer-hero of *A Smuggler's Bible* attempts to smuggle himself across boundaries of time and temperament to his dead father. Like the Bible and *The Recognitions*, the novel is composed of different books and styles, unified in inspiration but discontinuous in its eight points of view. It was meant, says McElroy, "to fracture." *Hind's Kidnap* is also about a search for a person, a young boy who has been kidnapped, and a past, what is left of pastoral values in an urban culture. Here the quest is foiled by a Nabokovian duplicity of language, which both enriches and confounds the reader.

It's in *Ancient History* (1971) that McElroy abandons the mostly "literary" language of the first two novels and establishes his own voice with his anthropologist narrator Cy—a cybernetic voice as his name suggests. Meditating on his relation with the polymath Dom, a compound of Buckminster Fuller and Norman Mailer, Cy also measures his attachment to and distance from childhood friends Al and Bob. These A, B, C, D characters are presented as points in space, figures in a field composition influenced by physics. The languages of space—historical, mathematical, astronomical—that McElroy employs give vitality to the familiar materials of childhood and friendship.

Lookout Cartridge (1974) is McElroy's best book, the present summary of his humane concern with family connection, bringing together the detecting impulse (a search for a stolen film), metaphors from technology for "Knowing and Not Knowing" (Stonehenge, cartography, cartridges, liquid crystals), and McElroy's own widening experience (living and traveling abroad, covering the Apollo program). The novel's hero, Cartwright, doesn't find his film, but he and the reader are ushered by McElroy into a network of correspondences and information loops that form a new intellectual map of the postmodern world. Like *Gravity's Rainbow*, *Lookout Cartridge* is about power and control, their institutions and conditions, but McElroy replaces Pynchon's paranoia with an appreciation of plenitude because, as a character says, the collaborative process leads to "new modes of mind."

Plus (1977) is both a sport—McElroy's single work of science fiction—and his most radical experiment with nonliterary language. Imp Plus is a disembodied brain launched into space in a rocket. As Plus grows, he develops a singular consciousness, a hybrid language of neurophysiology and Gertrude Stein. A moving story about recovery of the human, *Plus* is also a coda to McElroy's fiction, for this orbiting consciousness Plus, like McElroy, sends back to earth original and large visions of human possibility. Plus means positive and plus means more, two of the prime qualities of McElroy's art present in his nearly completed "monsoon of a book" *Women and Men*, parts of which have been appearing for the past few years. Set in a realistic New York City, gathering its metaphors from economics, geology, and parapsychology, *Women and Men* promises to further extend the planetary realism of *Lookout Cartridge* and dramatize once again that postmodern fiction—at least McElroy's—can combine large-minded invention with wide-minded observation and learning.

Selected Bibliography

Primary Sources

A Smuggler's Bible. New York: Harcourt, 1966.
Hind's Kidnap: A Pastoral on Familiar Airs. New York: Harper & Row, 1969.
Ancient History: A Paraphase. New York: Alfred A. Knopf, 1971.
Lookout Cartridge. New York: Alfred A. Knopf, 1974.
"Neural Neighborhoods and Other Concrete Abstracts." *TriQuarterly* 34 (1975): 201–17.
Plus. New York: Alfred A. Knopf, 1977.

Secondary Sources

Brooke-Rose, Christine. *A Rhetoric of the Unreal*. Cambridge: Cambridge University Press, 1981, pp. 268–88.
LeClair, Thomas. "An Interview with Joseph McElroy." *Anything Can Happen: Interviews with Contemporary American Novelists*. Urbana: University of Illinois Press, 1983, pp. 235–51.
———. "Joseph McElroy and the Art of Excess." *Contemporary Literature* 21 (1980): 15–37.
Tanner, Tony. "Toward an Ultimate Topography: The Work of Joseph McElroy." *TriQuarterly* 36 (1976): 214–52.

THOMAS LeCLAIR

McEWAN, IAN (1948–   )

Ian McEwan writes dark comedies of manners about murder, insanity, sexual perversion—especially incest—and all the sick games people play in the modern wasteland. His characters have lost their sense of purpose, search desperately for an identity, any identity, try to escape into fantasy existences that often are more boring or more horrifying than the real world. McEwan takes a tired cliché such as the decline of England and breathes new decay into it. Few contemporary writers in England (or anywhere else) create such beautiful prose about such repulsive subjects.

Ian Russell McEwan was born on June 21, 1948, in Aldershot where his father was stationed in the Army. During his childhood, he lived in Singapore and Libya and, like many children of military personnel serving overseas, attended a state-run boarding school in England. He received an honors degree in English from the University of Sussex in 1970 and an M.A. in 1972 from the University of East Anglia, where he studied creative writing under Malcolm Bradbury. The stories in *First Love, Last Rites* (1975) were submitted for his master's degree, and the collection won the 1976 Somerset Maugham Award.

McEwan's stories deal either with unusual people doing what they consider to be normal or apparently normal people doing the unusual: murdering children, simulating intercourse in a nude play, living in a cupboard, keeping a nineteenth-century criminal's penis preserved in formaldehyde, committing incest, castrating a man for spreading venereal disease. The latter is one of the few instances in McEwan's fiction in which a wrongdoer is punished: usually, only the innocent suffer. Typical is "Solid Geometry," in which a man uses a bizarre geometrical theory to make his wife or girl friend disappear. McEwan can make the irrational seem commonplace, as in "Reflections of a Kept Ape," in which a very sophisticated ape recounts his brief love affair with a woman novelist. As at least one critic has noted, McEwan is constitutionally incapable of being appalled.

The four children in *The Cement Garden* (1978) realize the limitations of freedom after their parents die. Released from the restrictions of adult authority, free to act out their fantasies or luxuriate in inertia, the children enjoy their freedom at first, but as they drift gradually into a fantasy world of role-playing, sexual confusion, and incest, a return to reality is almost welcomed. They want to be freed from a burden of responsibility they do not want or understand. McEwan avoids sentimental clichés about the innocence of childhood; for all the children in his fiction, this period is filled with loneliness, boredom, and frustration.

McEwan uses the relations between two brothers and two sisters to satirize the male tendency to make women into mothers to get attention from them. (A subtle feminism runs throughout his work.) His point seems to be that the family roles people assume are simply that: roles. He also satirizes the rebellious generation of the 1960s and early 1970s who broke away from conventional behavior only to search aimlessly for some new role to play. In delineating what society considers to be abnormal behavior, McEwan brings normality into question. Incest becomes little more than a desperate need to share an experience, any experience, with someone.

The children in *The Cement Garden* are both drifting from order into chaos and establishing a special order of their own. Many McEwan characters do this only to meet disaster since their idea of order may be logical only to them.

The adult protagonists of *The Comfort of Strangers* (1981) are even more aimless, and their disorder leads to murder. The something-terrible-about-to-happen which never occurs in *The Cement Garden* explodes obscenely in McEwan's second novel. The couple visiting Venice mistakenly try to remodel their decaying lives in a decaying city. Their aimlessness makes them susceptible to a helpful stranger who turns out to be a sadomasochist. Ironically, the couple can communicate only sexually, and sex becomes the instrument of their destruction. In McEwan's world, fantasies can turn into nightmares. Sex can be an escape but also a means of drowning in harsh reality.

Time after time, McEwan shows how people develop strange ways of dealing with loneliness and confusion, creating even more desperation and chaos. Their conviction that they are doing something positive with their lives provides McEwan's distinctively dark irony and humor. His more rational characters merely evolve ineffectual theories of human behavior. He writes in his introduction to *The Imitation Game* (1981), a collection of three television plays, that he attempted to experiment with the conventions of television naturalism so that "by calling into question the rules of the common language the viewers could be disoriented and tempted to regard the world afresh." Such experimentation, disorientation, and temptation are also the essence of his fiction.

Selected Bibliography

Primary Sources

First Love, Last Rites. London: Jonathan Cape, 1975; New York: Random House, 1975.

In Between the Sheets. London: Jonathan Cape, 1978; New York: Simon & Schuster, 1978.

The Cement Garden. London: Jonathan Cape, 1978; New York: Simon & Schuster, 1978.

The Comfort of Strangers. London: Jonathan Cape, 1981; New York: Simon & Schuster, 1981.

The Imitation Game: Three Plays for Television. London: Jonathan Cape, 1981; Boston: Houghton Mifflin, 1982.

Secondary Sources

Fletcher, John. "Ian McEwan." *Dictionary of Literary Biography: British Novelists Since 1960*. Detroit: Gale Research Co., 1983, pp. 495–500.

Forbes, Jill. "Crossover: McEwan and Eyre." *Sight and Sound* 52 (Autumn 1983):
    232–36.
Hamilton, Ian. "Points of Departure." *New Review* 5 (Autumn 1978): 9–21.
                                                                MICHAEL J. ADAMS

McGUANE, THOMAS (1939–   )

Perhaps no other writer in recent memory has so captured the strangeness
and sadness of being an American as Thomas McGuane. Because many
of his books use sports and Western motifs, many critics mistakenly refer
to McGuane as a "Western writer," but his work clearly transcends such
categories. Although some postmodernists are distinctive for their pursuit
of innovative structures, McGuane's uniqueness results from his rendering
of a highly personalized vision of America which he presents through an
idiomatic style that is instantly recognizable. Typically, McGuane's characters confront the absurd American world (which seems to extend infinitely) and attempt desperately to find something redeeming within it.
Critic Larry McCaffery states in an article for *Fiction International* that,
"McGuane's novels depict an America which seems determined to cut
itself off from all sense of beauty, morality, and proportion. *Ninety-Two
in the Shade* begins with the words, 'Nobody knows from sea to shining
sea, why we are having all this trouble with our Republic,' and in a sense
all of McGuane's books form a single allegory about this trouble"(p. 129).

Thomas Francis McGuane III, born on December 11, 1939, in Wyan-
dotte, Michigan, grew up enjoying the exigencies of his rural environment.
Fishing, sailing, hunting, hiking, and stealing golf balls (an experience he
recounts in a book of essays entitled *An Outside Chance*) occupied much
of his time as a youth. Although the idea of becoming a writer appealed
to him early on in high school, it was the adventurous lifestyle of the writer
(not the writing) that appealed to him most. As he has stated in his *Paris
Review* interview, "As a kid I always associated being a writer with leading
an adventurous life. I associated a life of action and a life of thought as
being the writer's life." In college, where he married his first wife, Becky
Crockett, he earned himself a reputation as a relentless bookworm. "I was
a pain in the ass," he admits. "But I desperately wanted to be a good
writer. My friends seem to think that an hour and a half effort a day is all
they need to bring to the altar. I couldn't do that. I thought if you didn't
work at least as hard as the guy running a gas-station, you had no right to
hope for any kind of achievement." With the publication of his first novel,
The Sporting Club (1969), McGuane achieved critical (but not commercial)
success. The story of two men who return to the sporting club of their
youth only to renew a destructive rivalry, the novel develops a mood that
evolves steadily from one of craziness to one of apocalyptic doom. The

book (which can be read as a political allegory about the logical outcome of anarchy) immediately demonstrates the gifted talents of the young author with language (especially dialogue, character, and humor).

Following that success, McGuane, who had been diligent in his clean living approach to writing, entered a strange period that included the birth of his son and a divorce from his wife. The drugs, partying and silliness that he had avoided in college began to interest him. While residing in both Florida (he owned a sailing yacht) and Montana (where he was able to pursue his passion for horsemanship and ranching), he published *The Bushwacked Piano* (1971), a zany, picaresque novel that chronicles the lunatic escapades of the rootless Nick Payne as he makes tracks across America. Along the way he thinks of his estranged girl like a "lovely decal on the rigid Ptolemaic dome," and runs into a less-than-average citizen named C. J. Clovis who enlists him in a bat-tower scheme.

McGuane's third novel, *Ninety-Two in the Shade* (1973), recounts the life of Thomas Skelton, a "practicing Christian . . . a little gone in the faith," and his struggles to become a fishing guide off the Florida Keys. The book revolves around a series of relationships between Skelton and his father (the father-son relationship is important in all of McGuane's fiction), mother, his lover Miranda, and in particular a "private legislator" named Nichol Dance (a fellow guide, owner of a used Bisley Colt with Mexican ivory grips) who forbids Skelton to guide. Relying heavily on tragic structure, the book achieves stunning force and in 1974 was nominated for the National Book Award.

Following a brief marriage to actress Margot Kidder, McGuane married Laurie Buffett (sister of singer Jimmy Buffett) and wrote his only first-person narrative to date, *Panama* (1978), a novel that partly exorcizes the excesses of McGuane's own recent life. Chet Pomeroy, a declining star, tells of his return to Key West and his desperate hope that he might rekindle his love with his ex-wife and halt the evaporation of his life. Highly elliptical, relentless, the book reverberates with a stark pain that is obviously genuine. Many critics misunderstand the book, however, interpreting it narrowly as McGuane's account of his own life, when in fact the book contains some of his most inventive and compelling writing.

Fully recovered from the excesses of the previous period, McGuane lives presently a relatively calm life with wife Laurie, raising cutting horses on their Montana ranch. His recent novel, *Nobody's Angel* (1983), represents a refinement in his art, successfully unifying many of his earlier thematic pursuits. In the novel, Patrick Fitzpatrick, a "fourth generation cowboy outsider, an educated man, a whiskey addict and until recently a professional soldier," comes home from Germany to his family's failing Montana ranch, inhabited now by his lonely grandfather. As Fitzpatrick attempts to resume the rituals of his previous life (raising cutting horses, hunting, blackout drinking), he falls in love and suffers bouts of sadness for no reason. With brilliant imagery and deftly conceived dialogue (characteristic of all McGuane's books), the novel details Fitzpatrick's futile and tragic attempt to detour the collapse of love.

Throughout his career McGuane has pursued many interests related to writing. His screenplays include *Rancho Deluxe* (1975), *Ninety-Two in the Shade* (1975—which he also directed), *The Missouri Breaks* (1976—with Bud Shrake), and *Tom Horn* (1980). He has worked as a special contributor to *Sports Illustrated Magazine*, and a book of essays entitled *An Outside Chance* (1980) recounts and examines some of McGuane's sports adventures.

Despite his present day-to-day duties as a rancher, McGuane still seeks to write fiction from a seeming crisis mode. Asked by McCaffery and Gregory if in fact the storm had passed (a reference to McGuane's turbulent personal history and the dedication in *Nobody's Angel*, which reads: "This book is for my beloved Laurie, still there when the storm passed"), McGuane replied: "The storm has passed in the sense that the steering linkage has been restored. I think the storm system is still in effect. In fact if it weren't I would reconstitute it, because you get to the point, and I've been to that point a couple of times, where the risk factor has been over-regulated. And that's an alarming feeling for me."

Selected Bibliography

Primary Sources

The Sporting Club. New York: Simon & Schuster, 1969.

The Bushwacked Piano. New York: Simon & Schuster, 1971.

Ninety-Two in the Shade. New York: Farrar, Straus & Giroux, 1973.

Panama. New York: Farrar, Straus & Giroux, 1978.

An Outside Chance. New York: Farrar, Straus & Giroux, 1980.

Something to Be Desired. New York: Random House, 1982.

Nobody's Angel. New York: Farrar, Straus & Giroux, 1983.

Secondary Sources

Carney, Thomas. "McGuane's Game." *Esquire*, June 6, 1978, pp. 44–53.

Carter, Albert Howard, III. "McGuane's First Three Novels: Games, Fun, Nemesis." *Critique* 17, No. 1 (1975): 91–104; 17, No. 1 (1975): 91–104.

———. "An Interview with Thomas McGuane." *Fiction International* 4, No. 5 (1975): 50–62.

McCaffery, Larry. "On Turning Nothing into Something." *Fiction International* 4, No. 5 (1975): 123–29.

———, and Sinda Gregory. "Thomas McGuane: The Art of Fiction LXXXIX." *Paris Review*, Fall 1985: 50–72.

CARLTON SMITH

MATHEWS, HARRY (1930–   )

Although much postmodern fiction is wildly innovative, sometimes bizarre, even raucous, the novels and stories of Harry Mathews are mysterious, delicately humorous, profoundly subtle. Mathews' works are ingeniously crafted language games, played out within carefully defined limits. For him, literature is a way of using words according to strict rules, and once those rules are set, the tales almost seem to write themselves.

Harry Mathews was born in New York City in 1930 and studied music at Harvard and at the Ecole Normale de Musique in Paris. For the past 30 years, he has spent most of his time in Europe, chiefly in France. He is the only American member of Oulipo (Ouvroir de littérature potentielle, a group of mathematicians, philosophers, and writers who use language games to extend the possibilities of literature). Along with his own fiction and poetry, Mathews has translated the works of Georges Perec, Maurice Roche, Raymond Roussel, Giuseppe Ungaretti, Hugo von Hofmannstahl, and others.

Each of Mathews' three novels documents an elaborate quest for an elusive goal. In *The Conversions* (1962), a nameless narrator's search for a treasure leads him to the documents of an esoteric religious cult that seems to offer the answers he seeks. But in the end, the cult's secrets are as difficult to uncover as the treasure itself, even though it seems the narrator could well be the rightful heir to the leadership of the group. *The Sinking of the Odradek Stadium* (1975) is an exchange of letters between Zachary McCaltex and his Asian wife Twang as they, too, seek a lost treasure that, like the treasure in *The Conversions*, is concealed beneath layers of texts and documents, of language, including the idiosyncratic English of Twang's letters. In this later novel, Twang succeeds in finding the treasure, and she writes to her husband that "the chest was . . . sunk in to the hold of the *Odradek Stadium*," a ship that will take it from Italy to Rangoon. The novel ends here, but the title suggests that the treasure will never arrive.

The narrator of *Tlooth* (1966) is also on a quest, this time for revenge, and again the goal remains beyond reach. *Tlooth* is something of a science fiction novel, and the science that is fictionalized is dentistry (T . . . ooth). In fact, the title of the novel comes from the advice an oracle offers the dental assistant/narrator—it is the sound made by the mud in an ancient bog when one puts a foot beneath the surface, then pulls it out again. And the oracle is right. The narrator is on a quest for the "t(r)ooth," as is the reader who, again, must sift through esoteric texts and documents to discover the whereabouts of Evelyn Roak, the object of the quest, and the name and sex of the narrator, both concealed until the end.

In each novel, the reader follows the protagonist through a maze of language, discovering a chain of linguistic clues that eventually reach a point of complete stasis. In the end, the words are simply there on the page, pointing toward nothing beyond themselves. Like Mathews' heroes, the reader searches through a textual world, looking for a single phrase or word that will provide the metaphysical "answer to everything." But the answer is not there. In each case, the play of/with language in the telling of the story is both the beginning and the end of the quest.

The title story of the collection *Country Cooking* (1980) is an elaborate recipe for a traditional French dish called "farce double." The name is apt, for the meal would be impossible to prepare. Like the novels, the text of "Country Cooking" points to other nonexistent texts—at one point the reader is asked to refer to page 888 of this 88-page book. But at the center of the recipe, Mathews does provide a real story—the tale of a blacksmith's son that is sung during the ritual preparation of "farce double" in the old country. In fact, the preparation of the meal, like the goals of *The Conversions*, *Tlooth*, and *The Sinking of the Odradek Stadium*, is the excuse for telling the tale. As Mathews explains: "Your satisfaction will have been in the doing, not in the thing done." The various goals are only fictions, words that generate stories. And it is the telling of the stories that counts.

Like the texts of the novels and stories, the texts of *Selected Declarations of Dependence* (1977) are dependent on elaborate language games that generate tales. In this case, Mathews has set incredibly strict rules for his games. The opening piece, "Their Words, For You," answers the question: "What can you do with the language of proverbs? Here 46 proverbs have been broken down into a vocabulary (of about 185 words) and these words alone have been used to tell a story." Other texts are based on hybrid proverbs Mathews calls "preverbs"—A rolling stone leads to Rome; too many cooks from little acorns grow. Mathews writes preverb poems and stories that paraphrase these bizarre sentences. In *Selected Declarations*, as in all of Mathews' fictions, it is not life or reality or experience but language that creates the stories.

Literature is a way of using words—not a product but a process of writing and reading. The literature of Harry Mathews is an ongoing quest for a writing that, in the process, becomes that which it seeks.

Selected Bibliography

Primary Sources

The Conversions. New York: Random House, 1962.
Tlooth. New York: Doubleday—Paris Review Editions. 1966.
The Ring. New York: Juillard, 1970.
The Planisphere. Providence, R.I.: Burning Deck Press, 1974.
The Sinking of the Odradek Stadium and Other Novels. New York: Harper & Row, 1975. (Includes *The Conversions* and *Tlooth*.)
Le Savoir de rois. Paris: Bibliothèque oulipienne, 1976.
Trial Impressions. Providence, R.I.: Burning Deck Press, 1977.

Selected Declarations of Dependence. Calais, Vt.: Z Press, 1977.
Country Cooking and Other Stories. Providence, R.I.: Burning Deck Press, 1980.

Secondary Sources

Stonehill, Brian. "On Harry Mathews." *Chicago Review* 33 (1982): 107–11.

WELCH D. EVERMAN

MILLER, J. HILLIS (1928–   )

J. Hillis Miller has defined a kind of criticism that credits literary texts with an inherent capacity to defy criticism itself. Throughout his prolific writings on romantic and post-romantic fiction and poetry, Hillis Miller has looked to Continental thinkers for insights only hinted at by American New Critics and other formalists. Yet his spiritual roots are rural America (upstate New York). Miller is the most Protestant of the "new" New Critics. He himself connects Protestantism with Derridean deconstruction: the main impulse behind both is "a dubeity about the mediating power of anything or anyone, even Christ." Indeed, Miller's brand of deconstruction is almost frankly Presbyterian in its relentless suspicion of the "graven images" of the literary marketplace, such as narrative forms, a suspicion based on the dark premonition that truth and morality are in original conflict (Moynihan, pp. 103–104 and 117).

Joseph Hillis Miller was born in 1928 near Albany, New York. He was an undergraduate at Oberlin and received an M.A. and Ph.D. from Harvard; from 1953 to 1972 he taught at Johns Hopkins, and he has been at Yale since then. He is often linked to two other Yale critics, Paul de Man* and Geoffrey Hartman.* Miller is famous for hunting down and exposing narrative forms in Victorian literature. In his view, the Victorian period (specifically, varieties of Victorian Platonism and romanticism) is continuous with modernity, loosely conceived. From *The Disappearance of God* (1963) to *Fiction and Repetition* (1982), Miller revels in every case of disarticulation or self-defeating contradiction he can find in narrative forms or philosophical problems. Miller has distinguished himself as a playful, yet sober, cadre in the Roundhead wing of the poststructuralist rebellion, akin to Hartman and de Man in mastery of the daring game of irreverence and the self-reflective squelch. His guides in his projects of disassembly have always been Continental (although he has been willing to credit Kenneth Burke with some influence). Nietzsche, the Geneva School of criticism, and Jacques Derrida* have all coached him in the by now common technique of close reading and artful paradox.

In the 1960s and early 1970s, Miller allied himself with the Geneva School, whose phenomenological approach to literary texts appeared to him to go beyond structuralism to reveal states of consciousness. In his

1966 essay "The Geneva School," Miller identified the aim of criticism as re-creating the exact tone of the writer in question. The operative critical mechanism here was sympathetic (or empathetic, or synthetic) transference: language was a transparent medium for an intuitive melding of minds. His move away from the Geneva School was a move away from such basic categories as consciousness, the literal, mimesis, and space. It was also a move away from a monological, progressive theory of literary history (although not from theory itself). Now Miller emphasizes language, figures, the intraliterary generation of meaning, time, and dialogical or permutative theories of literary history. Time or temporality carries the weight of discontinuity—such as is found in the relation of sign to sign across the gap of time, as opposed to the "spacial" relation of reflector and reflected inside a mirroring mind (1975 Preface to *Disappearance of God*, p. xi).

Yet Miller's gradual move to deconstruction reveals an underlying continuity. Deviations have always seemed to him to be an objective feature of the literary universe: for him we must always be caught in the impossible task of searching for warps, gaps, and self-defeating ploys that defy our powers to elicit them, but they are always *out there*. It follows that our most appropriate stance toward the literary universe is to make criticism itself reflect, as transparently as language allows (which is not much), the inherent abnormality of the text. Miller may well be fundamentally Protestant in his mature criticism, but it might be said, on his own showing, that he is a sort of literary positivist as well. "Why do poets write things which are so strange from the point of view of scientific language?" Miller asks. Most criticism covers over the strangeness of literature, and especially poetry. So the task of the critic is to do a job of translation, into the rigor and clarity of ordinary normal-scientific English—"something a physicist might understand" (Moynihan, pp. 108–109). Surely this attitude, approaching positivism, accounts for the apparent dryness of Miller's prose, a commonsensicality that casts a veil of domestication over the deeply bizarre games Miller plays with literary comprehension.

Selected Bibliography

Primary Sources

The Disappearance of God. Cambridge, Mass.: Harvard University Press, 1963.
Thomas Hardy: Distance and Desire. Cambridge, Mass.: Harvard University Press, 1970.
Fiction and Repetition: Seven English Novels. Cambridge, Mass.: Harvard University Press, 1982.

Secondary Sources

Abrams, M. H. "The Limits of Pluralism: The Deconstructive Angel." *Critical Inquiry* 3 (1977): 424–38.
Cain, William E. "Deconstruction in America: The Recent Literary Criticism of J. Hillis Miller." *College English* 41 (1979): 367–82.

Leitch, Vincent B. "The Lateral Dance: The Deconstructive Criticism of J. Hillis Miller." *Critical Inquiry* 6 (1980): 593–607.
Moynihan, Robert. "Interview with J. Hillis Miller" (Yale, Fall 1979). *Criticism* 24 (1982): 99–125.

STEVEN CRESAP

MILLHAUSER, STEVEN (1943–   )

Steven Millhauser's first novel, *Edwin Mullhouse: The Life and Death of an American Writer, 1943–1954, by Jeffrey Cartwright* (1972), received the kind of reviews first novelists dream about, won the Prix Medicis Etranger, France's prestigious literary award, and developed a small but passionate cult following. In *The New York Times Book Review*, George Stade called it "probably the best Nabokovian novel not written by the master himself" (17 September 1972, p. 2). In *Edwin Mullhouse* and his second novel, *Portrait of a Romantic* (1977), Millhauser writes about childhood and adolescence with unique insight and style, exploring the banality, strangeness, and violence of ordinary life.

Millhauser was born in New York City on August 3, 1943, and grew up in Connecticut. Milton Millhauser, his father, was an English professor at the University of Bridgeport. Millhauser graduated from Columbia University in 1965, worked as a copy editor and rewrite man in New York, and studied medieval and Renaissance English literature at Brown University from 1968 to 1971. This is all the available public information about Millhauser, who does not grant interviews or allow his photograph to be published. He believes that a writer's work should speak for itself and that the reader's experience of it should not be colored by autobiography.

Edwin Mullhouse is a satire of literary biographies, a detective story parody, and an examination of growing up in America. Millhauser clearly intends to have fun with every literary biography from Boswell's *Life of Johnson* to Leon Edel's five-volume analysis of Henry James. Jeffrey Cartwright's obsessive listing of all the minutiae of Edwin's rather ordinary childhood recalls Carlos Baker's biography of Hemingway. But the major influence on this aspect of *Edwin Mullhouse* is obviously Nabokov's *Pale Fire* (1962). Jeffrey Cartwright is a pedantic, humorless biographer, a wonderfully unreliable narrator. Jeffrey is jealous of his subject, misses the point of *Cartoons*, Edwin's novel, and is self-congratulatory, describing one of his terms, "the obscenity of maturity," as a "memorable phrase."

Millhauser's playful wit can also be seen in his detective story parody, another Nabokovian influence. The reader knows from the beginning that Edwin dies on his eleventh birthday but not how or why. Jeffrey plants clues, some unintentional, throughout the book, beginning with his praise for himself in his preface "for doing all the dirty work." He is also like a plodding, obtuse Dr. Watson to Edwin's Sherlock Holmes.

More significant than any satire and games-playing in *Edwin Mullhouse* is its depiction of a typical mid-twentieth-century middle-class American childhood. Many reviewers have compared the novel to J. D. Salinger's Glass family stories, but while Salinger emphasizes atypical children, Millhauser is interested in the ordinary. Edwin Mullhouse is no genius; he simply has the "capacity to be obsessed" which all children possess. Millhauser, who seems to have total recall of childhood, does not romanticize growing up but shows how there is more variety to life during this period, doing so without condescension, sentimentality, or nostalgia.

The sometimes deadly games of childhood receive further attention in *Portrait of a Romantic* which depicts the gothic gloom of adolescence. Twenty-nine-year-old Arthur Grumm narrates the events taking place between his twelfth and fifteenth years in an overblown romantic style. These events center around Arthur's friendships with his "double," William Mainwaring, a Huck Finn-like realistic; his "triple," Philip Schoolcraft, who is more than half in love with easeful death; and Eleanor Schumann, a 13-year-old enchantress. Again, there are echoes of Nabokov with the doppelgangers battling for Arthur's soul and the constant allusions to Humbert Humbert's beloved E. A. Poe. Instead of the detail-filled realistic world of Edwin and Jeffrey's childhood, *Portrait of a Romantic* offers a dream world of adolescent agony and ecstasy. Arthur becomes increasingly restless with the boredom of growing up, longing for "dangerous and unknown realms of freedom at the opposite end of so-called life," becoming a "connoisseur of decay," until death shocks him back to a reality of sorts. Millhauser unveils the darker world that would have awaited Edwin Mullhouse but presents it humorously through the excesses of Arthur's romantic fantasies.

Reviewers of these novels have attacked Millhauser for an absence of emotion and an overdose of cleverness, for being too literary, too allusive, too self-conscious, for overwriting, for creating beautifully pointless prose. He has perhaps paid too much attention to such criticism because his output since *Portrait of a Romantic* has been two rather conventional stories in the *New Yorker*. Such a distinctive stylist should continue to extend himself until he becomes the complete original he promises to be.

Selected Bibliography

Primary Sources

Edwin Mullhouse: The Life and Death of an American Writer, 1943–1954, by Jeffrey Cartwright. New York: Alfred A. Knopf, 1972.
Portrait of a Romantic. New York: Alfred A. Knopf, 1977.
"Protest Against the Sun." *New Yorker* 57 (August 31, 1981): 35–41.
"The Sledding Party." *New Yorker* 58 (December 13, 1982): 47–54.

Secondary Sources

Adams, Michael. "Steven Millhauser." *Dictionary of Literary Biography: American Novelists Since WWII*. Detroit: Gale Research Co., pp. 337–39.
Petrie, Dennis. *Ultimately Fiction: Design in Modern American Literary Biography*. West Lafayette, Ind.: Purdue University Press, 1981.

MICHAEL J. ADAMS

MOONEY, TED (1951–)

With the publication of *Easy Travel to Other Planets* in 1981, Ted Mooney, not yet 30, was established as a major literary talent. Dubbed a New Wave novel by one reviewer, *Easy Travel* combines an unconventional content—the book opens with the seduction of Melissa, a marine biologist, by Peter, the dolphin-subject of her study—with a sharp-edged, cinematic style. In this book as well as in his two earlier published stories, Mooney explores what he has described as a Western, and particularly American, ambivalence about boundaries, a wish for freedom from responsibility mingled with a fear of losing oneself.

Edward Mooney was born in Dallas, Texas, on October 19, 1951. In 1953 his family moved to Washington, D.C., where his father worked for then Democratic Senator Lyndon Johnson. Both parents, Booth and Elizabeth, were writers, and Mooney made his decision to follow their path early on. He began writing "seriously" in the tenth grade (at Exeter) and continued to pursue creative writing programs in college, first at Columbia (1969–1971) and then at Bennington, where he received a B.A. in 1973.

During his undergraduate years, Mooney spent two summers in Oregon fighting fires for the U.S. Forest Service and a third one as a reporter for the Portland *Oregon Journal*. He moved to New York City, where he still lives, in 1973. A job as managing editor of City College's *Fiction* magazine in 1975 provided partial payment in the form of tuition, and Mooney took the opportunity to take writing classes with Susan Sontag and Donald Barthelme.* In 1977 he began working for *Art in America* magazine, where he is now a senior editor.

Recognition of Mooney's talents also began early: he was awarded residences at the Breadloaf (1976) and McDowell (1979) writers' colonies, as well as two Ingraham Merrill Foundation grants (1977, 1978) and a CAPS grant for fiction (1977)—all before the publication of his first novel. Since then, he has received a Guggenheim Foundation fellowship (1983) and another Ingraham Merrill grant (1985) to pursue his writing. *Easy Travel to Other Planets* was nominated for an American Book Award in 1982 and in that year received the Sue Kaufman Award for First Fiction from the American Academy and Institute of Arts and Letters. Moreover, if Mooney's output has thus far been relatively small, what he has written has been well showcased. His first short story, "The Interpretation of Dreams," appeared in the *American Review* (1975), and his second, "The Salt Wife," was published in *Esquire* (1979).

"The Interpretation of Dreams," originally part of an abandoned first novel, is a fabulist tale of a child who develops an olfactory rather than a verbal vocabulary. "The Salt Wife" is a more realistic story of nuclear isotopes and contemporary Los Angeles. The lyrical, mythic qualities of the former and the cool irony of the latter combine in *Easy Travel* to produce an unsettling, poetic narrative. Mooney is currently finishing a novel titled *Traffic and Laughter*, set in Los Angeles and South Africa. He describes it as "taking account of history" where *Easy Travel* did not, and as being even more formally experimental than his first novel.

Easy Travel to Other Planets is not an easy book to categorize. Its events take place in a not very distant future: familiar details of contemporary life in New York, Connecticut, and St. Thomas, Virgin Islands, are mixed with unfamiliar ones, such as a "new emotion" people are experiencing, a new disease they are suffering—"information sickness"—and an impending worldwide conflict over energy resources in Antarctica. The novel has been described as a scientific romance, as an eco-fi novel, and as more akin to murder mystery than science fiction, while Mooney has been compared to Thomas Pynchon,* John Hawkes, Gabriel García Márquez,* Donald Barthelme,* and Jorge Luis Borges for his strange, imaginative constructs—and to Ann Beattie* and Raymond Carver* for his cool, realistic rendition of the manners and practices of the post-World War II generation. Based on the evidence of this innovative first novel, Ted Mooney's work promises a continuing interest in the formal as well as thematic probing of boundaries.

Selected Bibliography

Primary Sources

"The Interpretation of Dreams." *American Review* 23 (1975): 116–41.
"The Salt Wife." *Esquire* 92 (August 1979), pp. 72–79.
Easy Travel to Other Planets. New York: Farrar, Straus & Giroux, 1981.
"A Culture Ends Not with a Bang, But with the Gurgle of a Nightmare." *Los Angeles Times*, February 5, 1982, Sec. II, p. 7.

Secondary Sources

Haas, Scott. "Easy Travel to Other Pages" (interview). *Detroit Metro Times* 2, No. 10 (March 4–18, 1982), pp. 1, 5–6.
Schott, Webster. "Love in the Shallows." *Washington Post Book World*, October 4, 1981, pp. 1, 7.
See, Carolyn, "A Girl, a Dolphin, and a Book to Flip Over." *Los Angeles Times Book Review*, October 5, 1981, p. 10.

Welcott, James. "Brave New World." *New York Review of Books*, November 19, 1981, p. 27.

EDITH JAROLIM

MORRISON, TONI (1931–   )

With four critically acclaimed novels, Toni Morrison has become recognized not only as one of the preeminent voices of the black experience in America but also as an important innovator of fictional techniques. Richly varied in subject, setting, and structure, the novels have in common narrative and thematic strength, comic realism, and myth. The result is an exciting melange of grotesque characters and situations made the more ironic as they are presented straightforwardly and with a matter-of-fact tone. Morrison's success with both the satirical and symbolic modes allows her an effective moral stance that rarely sinks to didacticism.

Chloe Anthony Wofford was born in 1931 in Lorain, Ohio, an industrial town where her parents settled after having been raised in the South. Unlike her parents, she grew up relatively unaffected by discrimination. She told an interviewer from *Newsweek* that when she was in the first grade she was "the only black in the class and the only child who could read." In 1953 she graduated from Howard University in Washington, D.C., and went on to do graduate work at Cornell University, where she received a master's degree in English literature in 1955. She spent nine years teaching college English, first at Texas Southern University and later at Howard. While she was working in Washington she met and married Harold Morrison, a Jamaican architect.

In 1964 Morrison and her husband were separated, and she moved with her two sons to Syracuse, New York, where she secured a job with a subsidiary of Random House. Four years later she was transferred to Manhattan and a senior editorship, a position she currently holds.

While she was on the faculty at Howard, Morrison joined a creative writers group whose rule was that each participant bring something to read at every meeting. Once she brought a short story about a black girl who wanted blue eyes. That story eventually became her first novel, *The Bluest Eye* (1970). Set in a small Northern town, the novel deals with the relationships among a group of black residents. The central character is Pecola Breedlove, who prays every night for blue eyes like Shirley Temple's. After a series of devastating events, Pecola is finally driven mad and believes herself to have the bluest eyes of all. Although all the major characters in *The Bluest Eye* are black, the theme of the struggle of blacks in a racist society is indicated by the unusual framework of the narrative, a reading primer. A "Dick and Jane" passage at the outset, repeated without punctuation, becomes the organizing principle of the book in that parts of it provide chapter headings for the rest of the novel.

Morrison's second novel, *Sula* (1973), chronicles the friendship between Nel Wright and Sula Mae Peace from 1919 to 1965. The two black girls from markedly different environments share adventures as they grow up in Medallion, Ohio. More conventional in form but more complex in theme than its predecessor, *Sula* is marked by casual violence and unnatural phenomena. The heavy symbolism of the novel is concentrated in the depiction of the two chief characters, who variously represent order and disorder, rationality and emotion, conventionality and eccentricity, good and evil. *Sula* was nominated for the National Book Award in 1975 and was selected as a Book-of-the-Month Club alternate.

Song of Solomon (1977) is Morrison's most successful novel so far. Twice as lengthy as either of the other two, it deals with the search for identity of the male protagonist, Milkman Dead. (In this novel Morrison maintains her practice of using inspired names.) Son of a prominent businessman in a Northern town and grandson of the only black doctor there, Milkman seeks his roots from his father and his father's estranged sister, Pilate, who stands out in a gallery of bizarre characters because of her lack of a navel. Milkman's ostensible search for the family gold takes him from his Northern home to a remote section of Virginia, where he learns through a children's game the secrets of his family. This novel is distinguished by the use of folklore as well as myth. The symbolism and taut structure of the preceding novels is present, but the book's superior power derives from the amplification of characters and elaboration of plot.

Tar Baby (1981) is less realistic and more satiric than its predecessors. In this fable the beautiful black princess (in this case a Paris fashion model with a Ph.D.), visiting her extremely wealthy white benefactors in their tropical island retreat, falls in love with the handsome black commoner who has taken secret refuge there. After intrusions from the real world, represented by their stay in New York City and rural Florida, the couple separates. Here the conclusion and the use of the title are reminiscent of *Song of Solomon*, but the themes of mutual guilt and isolation, not to mention the exotic setting, are new.

Toni Morrison, combining the magical and the mundane and creating a rich if uneven panoply of action, character, and myth, has become a major voice in American fiction.

Selected Bibliography

Primary Sources

The Bluest Eye. New York: Holt, Rinehart & Winston, 1970.
Sula. New York: Alfred A. Knopf, 1973.
Song of Solomon. New York: Alfred A. Knopf, 1977.
Tar Baby. New York: Alfred A. Knopf, 1981.

Secondary Sources

Bakerman, Jane S. "Failure of Love: Female Intuition in the Novels of Toni Morrison." *American Literature* 52 (1981): 541–63.

Christian, Barbara. "Community and Nature: The Novels of Toni Morrison." *Journal of Ethnic Studies* 7 (Winter 1980): 65–78.

Joyner, Nancy Carol. "Toni Morrison." *Dictionary of Literary Biography Supplement*. Detroit: Gale, 1982.

LeClair, Thomas. "An Interview with Toni Morrison." In *Anything Can Happen: Interviews with Contemporary American Novelists*. Eds. Tom LeClair and Larry McCaffery. Urbana: University of Illinois Press, 1983, pp. 252–61.

McNay, Nellie. "An Interview with Toni Morrison." *Contemporary Literature* 24 (Winter 1983): 413–429.

Strouse, Jean. "Toni Morrison's Black Magic." *Newsweek*, March 30, 1981, pp. 52–55.

Willis, Susan. "Eruptions of Funk: Historicizing Toni Morrison." *Black American Literature Forum* 16 (1981): 34–42.

NANCY CAROL JOYNER

O

O'BRIEN, TIM (1946–   )

When *Going After Cacciato* (1978) won the National Book Award in 1978, Tim O'Brien and his fiction came to the attention of the American reading public and to those serious readers of postmodern fiction who might have missed the accolades of those such as John Gardner,* who had called it "the best novel on Vietnam." For the public, O'Brien's winning was a major upset; they had expected John Irving's* best-selling *The World According to Garp* to win unchallenged. O'Brien's *If I Die in a Combat Zone, Box Me Up and Ship Me Home* (1973) and *Northern Lights* (1974) soon were being reexamined by the critics, and the infantry veteran was being heralded as one of the more outstanding "Vietnam writers." Unfortunately, such a label permitted hasty assumptions about the subjects and the craft of a fiction that in many ways runs against the current of much of the postmodernist fiction while not separating itself from that tradition.

Tim O'Brien was born on October 1, 1946, in Austin, Minnesota. The son of a World War II sailor and a WAVE, he grew up in a very small, fairly conservative town that he considered "part of the prairie." From 1964 to 1968, he attended Macalester College in St. Paul, Minnesota, graduating summa cum laude and Phi Beta Kappa. Drafted into the U.S. Army in 1968, he went to Vietnam in 1969 and ended up a decorated sergeant. When he returned to the United States in 1970, he entered a doctoral program in government at Harvard University. During that first year as a graduate student, he began writing *If I Die in a Combat Zone.* During 1973–1974, O'Brien left Harvard to work for the *Washington Post* as a national affairs reporter covering such stories as U.S. Senate hearings, the oil boycott, and Washington politics. *Northern Lights* was written between newspaper stories. In 1975, 1976, and 1977, he wrote the award-winning *Going After Cacciato*, subsisting by selling chapters of the 1978 finished product to such magazines as *Redbook* and *Esquire*. Other stories and articles by O'Brien have been published by *Atlantic, Esquire, Nation, New Republic, Playboy,* and *Redbook*.

Although O'Brien resists the "Vietnam writer" label, he cannot deny the war's presence in his fiction. Begun in Vietnam, *If I Die* (1973) introduces the paradoxical fictional elements that characterize his later award-winning work. So vividly mimetic in character and place descriptions surrounding a "grunt's" tour in Vietnam, the first-person narrative was downplayed as critics focused on it as autobiography and as a document on the "wasteland of Vietnam." The 23-chaptered work also evoked complaints of being casual, anecdotal, fragmented, impressionistic, and self-conscious. The absence of a tight chronology, the multitude of allusions and philosophical monologues, and the emphasis on the discrepancies between the imagination and experience, suggest O'Brien's thematic concerns with courage, the American character, and fiction's role in personal and cultural survival.

Although one major character is an injured returning veteran from Vietnam, *Northern Lights* (1974) is not about the war. Often compared with Hemingway, this most mimetic of O'Brien's fiction tells the story of two contrasting brothers who wrestle with the issues of annihilation and ennui, courage and fear, love and isolation in a Minnesota setting familiar to O'Brien. Primarily a psychological drama of a nonveteran's emerging moral outlook in a naturalistic setting, this traditional novel is structured, paradoxically enough, around cyclical Finnish mythology.

Going After Cacciato (1978) presents three distinct narrative threads dealing with the Vietnam War: the seemingly chaotic war scenes, the philosophical Observation Post monologues, and the fantasized desertion trek to Paris. The range of narrative techniques suggests the range of responses available to America and to an individual when confronting (or trying to ignore) the dilemmas and the issues of the twentieth century as well as those involved with Vietnam. As with all of his fiction in which he uses form to dramatize the book's moral issues, *Going After Cacciato* is tightly structured, with independent chapters showing the imagination's varied ability to create order in chaos.

While eschewing experimentation for its own sake and the focus on style over the exploration of human issues, O'Brien's works exhibit qualities of the mimetic, confessional, and metafictional modes frequently found in postmodern fiction. However, their primary emphasis remains on substantive themes, universal moral choices, and the explanation of human experience.

Selected Bibliography

Primary Sources

If I Die in a Combat Zone, Box Me Up and Ship Me Home. New York: Delacorte Press/Seymour Lawrence, 1973.

Northern Lights. New York: Delacorte Press/Seymour Lawrence, 1974.
Going After Cacciato. New York: Delacorte Press/Seymour Lawrence, 1978.
The Nuclear Age. New York: Random House, 1985.

Secondary Sources

Beidler, Philip D. *American Literature and the Experience of Vietnam*. Athens, Georgia: University of Georgia Press, 1982, pp. 24–27, 99–105, 172–179.

Couser, G. Thomas. "*Going After Cacciato*: The Romance and the Real War." *Journal of Narrative Technique* 13 (Winter 1983): 1–10.

Herzog, Tobey C. "*Going After Cacciato*: The Soldier-Author-Character Seeking Control." *Critique* 24 (Winter 1983): 88–96.

McCaffery, Larry. "An Interview with Tim O'Brien." *Anything Can Happen: Interviews with Contemporary American Novelists*. Urbana: University of Illinois Press, 1983, pp. 262–78.

Raymond, Michael W. "Imagined Responses to Vietnam: Tim O'Brien's *Going After Cacciato*." *Critique* 24 (Winter 1983): 97–104.

Saltzman, Arthur Michael. "Betrayal of the Imagination: Paul Brodeur's *The Stunt Man* and Tim O'Brien's *Going After Cacciato*." *Critique* 22 (1980): 32–38.

Vannatta, Dennis. "Theme and Structure in Tim O'Brien's *Going After Cacciato*." *Modern Fiction Studies* 28 (Summer 1982): 242–46.

MICHAEL W. RAYMOND

P

PHILLIPS, JAYNE ANNE (1952–   )

Jayne Anne Phillips has said that the major influences on her work have been Sherwood Anderson, William Faulkner, Katherine Anne Porter, Eudora Welty, Flannery O'Connor, William Burroughs, and Gabriel García Márquez.* With her depiction of grotesque misfits, the banality of middle-class life, relations between family members, sex, violence, loneliness, madness, and the general sordidness and desperation of modern American life, the impact of these writers, especially O'Connor and Burroughs, on Phillips' fiction is obvious. But it is also clear that she is a highly original stylist in her own right who may influence those writers who come after her.

Phillips was born in Buckhannon, West Virginia, on July 19, 1952, and was raised there. She began writing poetry, with the strong encouragement of one of her teachers, while in high school. She told *Newsweek*, that she is grateful for having written poetry before fiction: "Poets can become good, energetic writers of prose. They've already learned to condense language" (22 October 1979, p. 118). After graduating from West Virginia University, Phillips lived briefly in California and Colorado, working as a waitress, before attending the University of Iowa where she received a master's degree in creative writing. She then taught briefly at Humboldt State University in Arcata, California.

During this time Phillips published poetry in magazines such as *Paris Review* and *New Letters* and stories in publications like *North American Review, Ploughshares*, and *Iowa Review*. *Sweethearts* (1976) and *Counting* (1978), two collections of very short stories, some of them prose poems, were published by small presses. In 1978, Phillips met Delacorte editor Seymour Lawrence at the St. Lawrence writers conference and gave him a copy of *Sweethearts*. The result was the publication of *Black Tickets*

(1979). This collection of stories made Phillips the first recipient of the American Academy and Institute of Arts and Letters Sue Kaufman Prize for First Fiction. She has also won the Fels Award in Fiction from the Coordinating Council of Literary Magazines, the St. Lawrence Award for Fiction, and a National Endowment for the Arts Fellowship.

There are three types of stories in *Black Tickets*. Sixteen are very short, usually one paragraph, many of them reprinted from *Sweethearts*. They seem to be little more than stylistic exercises, and a few reviewers complained that they would be perhaps more appropriate for a creative writing class. Of the 11 longer stories, one group deals with characters such as prostitutes and drug addicts. The best of these are "Gemcrack," narrated by a Son-of-Sam-like murderer, and "Lechery," about a 14-year-old prostitute who entices younger boys from schoolyards. Phillips' vision of this world of violence and decadence is presented without explanations, almost as reportage, without melodrama or sentimentality, but with irony and contradictions. The protagonist of "Lechery" considers herself as innocent as any middle-class girl her age. The style of these stories is occasionally somewhat flamboyant, calling too much attention to itself, but Phillips seems to feel that the desperation of contemporary American life calls for such excess.

Phillips' third type of story deals with family life in the rural South, and she employs a more subtle style to present a quieter kind of desperation. These stories examine loneliness and the need to love and be loved. In "Home," the best of the five family stories, a mother wants her daughter to feel guilty for neglecting her and cannot accept her daughter's sexuality. A former lover of the daughter visits, and when the mother overhears their lovemaking, she explodes in anger. Phillips suggests that people's prejudices and weaknesses are intensified when they are with their families.

The two strains of Phillips' fiction are seen in two stories published since *Black Tickets*. "Something That Happened," selected by Joyce Carol Oates for *The Best American Short Stories 1979*, presents a woman whose youngest daughter totally accepts the middle-class values her sisters rebel against. Phillips very economically encapsulates the mother's life through the woman's amused reflections about her life and her strangely conventional daughter. At the other extreme is "How Mickey Made It," included in *The Pushcart Prizes VII*, the bitter, profane, funny monologue of a 20-year-old punk rocker. These two stories represent growth on Phillips' part since they treat loneliness and desperation with humor and avoid the bleakness of the *Black Tickets* stories. Mickey seems to be speaking for Phillips when he says, "All you can do is turn the bad stuff into something else and not flake out on what it costs you." Phillips' most recent work is *Machine Dreams*, published by E. P. Dutton in 1984.

Selected Bibliography

Primary Sources

Sweethearts. Carrboro, N.C.: Truck Press, 1976.

Counting. New York: Vehicle Editions, 1978.

Black Tickets. New York: Delacorte Press/Seymour Lawrence, 1979.

"Something That Happened." *The Best American Short Stories 1979*. Eds. Joyce Carol Oates and Shannon Ravenel. Boston: Houghton Mifflin, 1979.

"How Mickey Made It." *The Pushcart Prizes, VII: Best of the Small Presses*. Ed. Bill Henderson. Wainscott, N.Y.: Pushcart Press, 1982.

Machine Dreams. New York: E. P. Dutton, 1984.

Secondary Sources

Adams, Michael. "Jayne Anne Phillips." *Dictionary of Literary Biography Yearbook, 1980*. Detroit: Bruccoli Clark/Gale Research, 1981, pp. 297-300.

Baker, James N. " 'Being Led by a Whisper.' " *Newsweek* 94 (October 22, 1979): 116-18.

MICHAEL J. ADAMS

PIRSIG, ROBERT (1929–   )

The immensely popular and well-reviewed *Zen and the Art of Motorcycle Maintenance* (1974) has been praised for enlarging the stock of sophisticated philosophy accessible to the general reader, for heartening and equipping countless teachers of rhetoric, for describing vividly a man's mental fragmentation and nervous breakdown, and for gripping its readers with a good mystery story. The novel's dissection of scientific rationality and its relation to the good is as rhetorically effective as its symbols of passage and Manichaean struggle are profound. Moreover, the vast majority of even the earliest critics, including George Steiner, Christopher Lehmann-Haupt, and Robert M. Adams, and others, recognized that, read as a whole, the work is even more than the sum of these parts.

Robert Maynard Pirsig was born in 1929 in Minneapolis. Blessed with an IQ of 170, Pirsig took a B.A. in chemistry and philosophy at the University of Minnesota in 1950, became a card dealer in Reno, Nevada, a student of Oriental philosophy at Benares Hindu University in India, a small-college teacher of rhetoric in Montana, and a writer of technical manuals. He finished an M.A. in Journalism at the University of Minnesota in 1953, became a motorcycle enthusiast, a graduate student in Interpretation at the University of Chicago, and ultimately a diagnosed schizophrenic.

Zen and the Art of Motorcycle Maintenance was first conceived as a short and light-toned essay in 1968 while Pirsig was writing instruction manuals for Univac in Minneapolis. When the first few pages, sent to 121 publishers, garnered 22 favorable responses, Pirsig sat down to write mornings from 2:00 to 7:00 A.M. in a tiny office over a shoe store in downtown Minneapolis.

As the manuscript grew, however, so did its philosophical density and, in the author's eyes, its pomposity, spurring Pirsig to cut section after original section concerned with Zen concepts. Frustrated with the writing project, Pirsig set out on a motorcycle trip to the West Coast that summer, with his older son, 12-year-old Chris, and (partway) with two other friends. In Los Angeles he was struck with the breakthrough idea of using the journey itself as a "matrix" for his ideas. After nearly two more years at this approach, Pirsig nearly gave up but decided on one last try at a chapter, and about halfway through suddenly hit his stride. That chapter is now the first one in the book. By this time, only James Landis, senior editor at William Morrow, remained encouraging to the project, helping to prune and reorganize hundreds of thousands of words. *Zen and the Art of Motorcycle Maintenance* slowly assumed its ultimate shape, alternating realistic descriptions with aggressive metaphysical concatenation. The final step of inventing Phaedrus (the narrator before electroshock treatments had annihilated his personality) as a separate identity eliminated the narrator's excessive self-centeredness and created crucial distance between the reader and both of Pirsig's alter egos.

Pirsig has deliberately dodged the public eye almost since his novel's publication, appearing only once since 1975 at the Modern Language Association (MLA) Convention in New York, December 29, 1981. (This was a special satisfaction for Pirsig, since certain early ideas for the novel were first presented years before in a paper to the Rocky Mountain regional MLA.) During much of this time, he has lived mostly on a small sailboat, sometimes on the coast of Finland, with his second wife, Wendy and, since 1981, with their daughter. He has been devoting himself to a second book, which will extend and challenge the ideas of his first, and will adapt another journey, this time a voyage on the Hudson river, as its structural matrix.

Although many of the events in *Zen and the Art of Motorcycle Maintenance* are shaped for the purposes of fiction, the climactic reconciliation scene with Chris is entirely factual, as Pirsig has pointed out. In addition, the father-son relationship is the key to the book's artistic structure, cementing its three spheres of action and three levels of meaning: (1) the sophisticated examination of the concept of rationality and its relation to the idea of the good; (2) the graphic account of personal disorientation and schizophrenic haunting; and (3) the frustrated efforts of a father to share a loving relationship with his son. These developments connect in threatening ways through most of the book. The narrator's monocular focus on clarifying his ideas about Quality is, ironically, the cause of Chris's bad trip. That is, metaphysics, the art of individual cerebral focusing and reflecting, necessarily menaces Pirsig's most important social relationship. At the same time, the metaphysics by which Pirsig seeks to grip his sanity actually propels his incipient schizophrenia.

The climactic cliffside reconciliation with young Chris dislodges many of the dualisms plaguing Pirsig. Chris recognizes in his once-distant father the integrity and commitment of Phaedrus' personality. Simultaneously, the force of Pirsig's metaphysics deflects from repressing Phaedrus to incorporating him in a single, whole consciousness. Furthermore, the novel's metaphysical and rhetorical structures are themselves completed by this concrete example of Quality enabling the philosopher to share and to love beyond himself.

As a work of art, *Zen and the Art of Motorcycle Maintenance* propounds its metaphysics, embodies it, and ultimately transcends it, constantly dramatizing the uneasy relations between rationality and other forms of experience. Arriving at a philosophical understanding of Quality generates further benefits as well as constant risks. If thinking outside cultural structures is a clinical form of madness, it may also reintegrate an individual consciousness. If the narrator's concentration on Quality reduces Chris, perched behind, to staring at his father's back, seeing little, saying nothing, nevertheless it is only Pirsig's study of the causes of Quality that precariously reunites him with his past and ultimately with his son.

The dissolution of subject-object duality has seldom been so forthrightly anatomized and argued for in a work of fiction. The novel's complex of movements continuously dramatizes both the perils and the raptures of deconstructing the mythos, the personal risks and satisfactions the dancer endures in becoming one with the dance, the mechanic in fixing a machine that is himself.

Selected Bibliography

Primary Sources

Zen and the Art of Motorcycle Maintenance: An Inquiry into Values. New York: William Morrow, 1974; New York: Bantam, 1974.
"Cruising Blues and Their Cure." *Esquire* 87 (May 1977): 65-68.

Secondary Sources

Allis, Una. "*Zen and the Art of Motorcycle Maintenance*." *Critical Quarterly* 20 (Autumn 1978): 33–41.
Bump, Jerome. "Creativity, Rationality, and Metaphor in Robert Pirsig's *Zen and the Art of Motorcycle Maintenance*." South Atlantic Quarterly 82 (1983): 370-80.
Rodino, Richard H. "Irony and Earnestness in Robert Pirsig's *Zen and the Art of Motorcycle Maintenance*." *Critique* 22 (August 1980): 21-31.
―――. "The Matrix of Journeys in *Zen and the Art of Motorcycle Maintenance*." *Journal of Narrative Technique* 11 (Winter 1981): 53-63.

Singer, Barnett. "Reflections on Robert Pirsig." *Durham University Journal* 73
    (June 1981): 213–19.
                                               RICHARD H. RODINO

PUIG, MANUEL (1932–)

If the Spanish-American novelistic "Boom" of the 1960s may be taken
as that area's belated but exuberant arrival at the arena of postmodernism,
then the Argentine Manuel Puig qualifies as a representative postmodern
author. Like Guillermo Cabrera Infante (Cuba), Julio Cortázar* (Argentina), José Donoso (Chile), Carlos Fuentes* (Mexico), Gabriel García
Márquez* (Colombia), and Mario Vargas Llosa* (Peru)—all in one sense
or another intellectual disciples of Jorge Luis Borges—Puig has played an
integral role in the narrative revision of Spanish America's history and
literature. With those avant-garde writers he shares an interest in questioning society's underlying myths and evolving rituals, particularly the role
allotted to the individual in such a context. Another hallmark of the fiction
of that period is a sometimes hermetic and highly ambiguous formal experimentation, including frequent changes in narrative point of view, leaps
in time and space, and the incongruous, at times humorous, montage of
heterogeneous textual fragments. Self-reflexivity and a global perspective
on local problems—the latter often the product of exile from one's homeland—are also collective concerns among these authors. Puig's unique contribution to this generation of cosmopolites (now mostly in their fifties)
perhaps lies in his personal interpretation of the importance of popular
culture in the Western experience. None of his contemporaries has evoked
with such force of consistency the voices, world view, and cultural forms
of the faceless and disenfranchised masses.

    For a little more than a decade (1968-1979) when Puig published his first
five novels, one could associate his fiction with a cinematic motif and be
at least partially correct. After his initial success with *Betrayed by Rita
Hayworth* (1968), Puig followed up with *The Buenos Aires Affair* (1973),
The Kiss of the Spider Woman (1976), and *Angelical Pubis* (1979), in all
of which film figures significantly. Only *Heartbreak Tango* (1969), evocative
of both popular music and *radionovelas*, deviates from that norm. That
Puig should have been fascinated with the movies is easily understood.
Born and raised in the isolated *pampas* town of General Villegas, Manolo's
only contact with a diverse, heterodox reality was through the filmic medium. Later, at the height of the neo-realist vogue, he studied film direction
at Rome's Centro Sperimentale di Cinematografia. Only after this experience did he realize that he did not wish to make films but rather narrate
them. To this day all his novels, ostensibly cinema inspired or not, bear a
pronounced dramatic and oral quality.

To be sure, commercial film is but one of the conventionally degraded cultural forms with which Puig works. Glamour magazines, soccer matches, mysteries, romances, and science fiction are also the stuff of his delicately poised satires and parodies. These provide his characters with archetypes for the dreams and gestures they emulate in their vulgar *petites histoires*. The result often lands on the kitsch side of bathos and melodrama. However, Puig's frequent refusal to retreat to a safe authorial distance discloses a simultaneous affection for his *cursi* creations, who are not responsible for their blindness to the nuances of their mock heroics. Reminiscent of the mass-produced artifacts that spawn them, all five of these works feature an uncannily consistent (bi-partite, 16-chapter) macrostructure.

Through most of the 1970s, when his works were set almost exclusively in Argentina, Puig resided in New York's Greenwich Village. Not until *Eternal Curse on the Readers of These Pages* (1981) does his stay in North America register as the locus of a novel. Significantly experimental in at least two senses, Puig's sixth novel deals with a political issue—the question of human rights—already raised in the guise of homosexuality in *The Kiss of the Spider Woman*. Thematically, the work is a new departure in that—rather than rely for its narrative matrix on massified artifacts—the dialogue is here generated by a popularized Lacanian psychoanalysis. The most tragic of Puig's novels in both tone and outcome, *Eternal Curse* shows the scars of being written close to the foreboding terrain of the unconscious. On a technical level the text is innovative in its mode of composition. Puig recorded conversations he had in English, translated them into Spanish, and incorporated the translations into the novel, which reads as vitally authentic but, at times, linguistically mangled.

Puig's most recent works in several ways inscribe a return to his earliest passions. In *Blood of Requited Love* (1982), one finds a soccer-playing Don Juan figure (shades of *Rita Hayworth* and *Heartbreak Tango*) who dialogues nostalgically with a woman he deceived, now apparently in a mental asylum. New in this narrative is its Brazilian setting (Puig moved to Rio de Janeiro, where he currently lives, at the end of the 1970s) and its high degree of indeterminacy. It is impossible to say with any certainty which of the two protagonists is crazy or whose version of the story, if any, is authoritative. Puig's affair with the dramatic genres reemerged with the publication of *Beneath a Blanket of Stars* (1983), a collection of theatrical pieces, as well as with screen adaptations of Silvina Ocampo's "El imposter" ("The Imposter") and José Donoso's *El lugar sin límites* (*Hell Has No Limits*). His stage version of the powerful *The Kiss of the Spider Woman*, which premiered in Mexico City in 1983, was judged to be the best play of the year by the Association of Theater Critics of Mexico. At this writing, Puig appears to be in the plenitude of his creativity, branching out in new directions (drama, psychoanalysis, indeterminacy) as he reinterprets his earlier *oeuvre*.

Selected Bibliography

Primary Sources

La traición de Rita Hayworth. Buenos Aires: Sudamericana, 1968. (*Betrayed by Rita Hayworth*. Trans. Suzanne Jill Levine. New York: E. P. Dutton, 1971.)

Boquita pintadas. Buenos Aires: Sudamericana, 1969. (*Heartbreak Tango*. Trans. Suzanne Jill Levine. New York: E. P. Dutton, 1973.)

The Buenos Aires Affair. Mexico City: Joaquin Mortiz, 1973. (*The Buenos Aires Affair*. Trans. Suzanne Jill Levine. New York: E. P. Dutton, 1976.)

El beso de la mujer araña. Barcelona: Seix Barral, 1976. (*The Kiss of the Spider Woman*. Trans. Thomas Colchie. New York: Alfred A. Knopf, 1979.)

Pubis Angelical. Barcelona: Seix Barral, 1979. (*Angelical Pubis*. New York: Random House, 1981.)

Maldición Eterna a Quien Lea Estas Páginas. Barcelona: Seix Barral, 1980. (*Eternal Curse on the Readers of These Pages*. New York: Random House, 1982.)

Sangre de Amor Correspondido. Barcelona: Seix Barral, 1981. (*Blood of Requited Love*. Trans. Jon L. Grayson, 1982. New York: Random House, 1983.)

Bajo un Manto de Estrellas. Barcelona: Seix Barral, 1983. (*Beneath a Blanket of Stars*. New York: Random House, 1984.)

Secondary Sources

Borinsky, Alicia. "Castracion y lujos: La escritura de Manuel Puig." *Revista Iberoamericana* 41, no. 90 (1975): 29-46.

Hazera, Lydia D. "Narrative Technique in Manual Puig's *Boquitas pintadas*." *Latin American Literary Review* 2, no. 3 (1973): 45-53.

Sarduy, Severo. "Notas a las notas a las notas . . . , A proposito de Manuel Puig." *Revista Iberoamericana* 37, nos. 76–77 (1971): 555-68.

Tittler, Jonathan. "*Betrayed by Rita Hayworth*: The Androgynous Text." In *Narrative Irony in the Contemporary Spanish American Novel*. Ithaca, N.Y.: Cornell University Press, 1984, pp. 78–100.

———. "Order, Chaos, and Re-order: The Novels of Manual Puig." *Kentucky Romance Quarterly* 30, no. 2 (1984): 187–201.

JONATHAN TITTLER

PYNCHON, THOMAS (1937–   )

Thomas Pynchon's work has enjoyed critical and popular success despite the formidable problems it presents to the reader. Taken together, his novels have cosmographic ambitions: they narrate a subversive version of the history and present crisis of the cultural cosmos that is the modern West, whose origins Pynchon dates to 1630, when heavy Puritan emigration to Massachusetts began. To accomplish his aims, he presses into unfamiliar service stylistic devices that originate in modern and postmodern literature: his heterogeneous heritage includes Edgar Allan Poe, William Faulkner, James Joyce, William Burroughs, Samuel Beckett, and Jorge Luis Borges. His fictions muster an army of characters and an encyclopedic range of

historical and scientific knowledge; to deploy them requires formal innovation and control of conflicting materials. *Control* becomes the central
issue of his work, even though Pynchon wants to refuse to favor order and
hierarchy, the categories of rationalized control. His attempts to deny his
work a center that controls it lead to an ironic and yet familiar self-en-
trapment: they result in a work where a decentered and diffused control
becomes the omnipresent issue. His plots enact attempts to direct sexual
desire, ballistic missiles, and interpretation (among others). His style does
succeed in making impossible the result of control that is dearest to interpreters—the production of a unified textual meaning. Instead, although
his work remains obsessively referential and minutely accurate, it ends by
enacting the anxiety of mimesis, not its self-assurance. It constantly points
to historically real events and hints at a world-embracing plot, but the unity
such a plot proffers is steadily and ingeniously undercut.

Large enterprises are part of Pynchon's heritage, which is nearly coextensive with America's Puritan past; *Gravity's Rainbow* alludes to it most
frequently. His first American ancestor, William Pynchon, sailed with John
Winthrop to Massachusetts Bay in 1630, became the colony's leading fur
trader, founded the town of Springfield, and then risked his wealth and
status by publishing an unorthodox text of Calvinist theology that was
burned in Boston. He returned to Britain, but his American descendants
were numerous and prominent. Pynchon's insistent concern with our history, with "the fork in the road America never took, the singular point
she jumped the wrong way from" (*Gravity's Rainbow*, p. 556), transforms
what might otherwise be an antiquarian interest in his family's past into a
concern with historical theme and textual form. The series of wrong turns
that brought the Christian West to the crises of the twentieth century
remains his theme, while the form of his texts is partly shaped by his desire
to gesture at the multitude of stillborn or betrayed possibilities that are
the ghosts of history. Pynchon's interest in the history of the novel also
shapes form. His gaze is fixed on the ways in which the novel became an
instrument and then a casualty of the West's epistemological arsenal. To
him, narrative is a paradoxical, ultimately untrustworthy—yet inescapable—mode of knowledge, the only available vehicle for his fictional history
of wrong turns, of those who were "passed over"—excluded from the
privileged structure of meaning which we call Western history—without
being excluded from victimage.

Although the outlines of Pynchon's personal history are clear, much
remains mysterious. He was born on May 8, 1937, in Glen Cove, Long
Island, and graduated from Oyster Bay High School as class salutatorian.
He attended Cornell University from 1953 to 1955, first studying physics
and then English, dropped out to join the Navy's Signal Corps, and returned to school in 1957. Growing up in the partitioned and oppositional
world of the Cold War, observing the 1956 conflict over Suez (to which

V. alludes), Pynchon wrote parables of adjoining yet closed worlds into which disaster erupts. A storm that destroys a town is part of the plot of his first story, "The Small Rain," which appeared in 1959, the year he graduated. Working for Boeing as a technical writer in Seattle (1960-1962), he continued to write and quickly proved successful. Two of his short stories won prizes in 1961 and 1962. *V.* won the Faulkner Prize for the best first novel of 1963, and *The Crying of Lot 49* received the Rosenthal Award of the National Institute of Arts and Letters in 1966. In 1973, *Gravity's Rainbow* received the National Book Award and was denied the Pulitzer despite the unanimous recommendation of the judges. In two decades, 16 books, a journal, and several hundred articles have been devoted to Pynchon's work. Yet he has remained inaccessible; his reluctance about publicity dates from the early 1960s. His whereabouts are a secret known to few. All this has fostered a not altogether healthy curiosity but has also had salutary results. Pynchon is coextensive with his texts, no one interpretation of which can be privileged by an appeal to interviews or self-explanatory essays. One exception is the "Preface" to a collection of his short stories, *Slow Learner* (1984), in which Pynchon sardonically works to undercut his "established" image as a scientifically knowledgeable artist celebrated by academic critics.

Themes and metaphors borrowed from science, such as entropy, provide a core for many of Pynchon's stories, which are explored less schematically in his novels. The first of these, *V.* (1963), is plotted around a deceptively simple set of characters and oppositions: Stencil/Profane, animate/inanimate, control/surrender. Stencil, whose quest is to stalk the mysterious "V", insists on imposing a constraining order on the facts he uncovers or constructs, seeking to diminish his own anxiety about meaninglessness. Everything he encounters is a malleable sign to be interpreted and fitted into his own schema. In contrast, Profane's life has more *things* in it than signs and more signs than significance; he is a reluctant interpreter. Oedipa Maas, the heroine of *The Crying of Lot 49* (1966), is also on a quest, one that obliges her to become an interpreter of the human landscape of California, in which she travels, and of European art, science, and history. Her quest is patterned on the detective story, but in this case the rewards of interpreting clues are limited. She discovers the promise of ever-elusive, deferred meanings, but no solution.

Gravity's Rainbow (1973), arguably the most important American fiction since Faulkner's *Go Down, Moses* (1942), consists of a series of intersecting quests. The figure most approximating a protagonist, Tyrone Slothrop, seeks a secret that seemingly links the sites of his erections and sexual heroics to V–2 rockets that appear subsequently to burst upon those sites. Others pursue Slothrop across the war-torn Europe of 1944–1945. They encounter, or are, the "passed over": displaced tribal remnants from Africa, dejected cadres of various competing institutions who search for the

Holy Grail, a missing rocket, and the secret of ballistic control. Although *Gravity's Rainbow* is based on scrupulous research, like its great predecessor *Ulysses* it subverts the aspiration to control the farrago of facts it amasses; only a paranoid could assemble them into a unified system. Indeed, no single interpretive synthesis can possibly account for the cornucopia of facts, language-games, and scenes of joy and suffering. As in the previous novels, so also in *Gravity's Rainbow* the reader is seduced into interminable interpretation, which offers frequent small epiphanies but no apocalyptic revelation, except perhaps that of victimage and death as our common lot. While Pynchon's work frustrates some readers, many others are captivated by the lushness of his imagination and by the compassionate vision with which he invites his readers into the labyrinths of his fiction.

Selected Bibliography

Primary Sources

V. Philadelpha: Lippincott, 1963.
The Crying of Lot 49. Philadelphia: Lippincott, 1966.
Gravity's Rainbow. New York: Viking Press, 1973.
Slow Learner. Boston: Little, Brown, 1984.

Secondary Sources

Clerc, Charles, ed. *Approaches to Gravity's Rainbow*. Columbus: Ohio State University Press, 1982.
Hite, Molly. *Ideas of Order in the Novels of Thomas Pynchon*. Columbus: Ohio State University Press, 1982.
Mendelson, Edward, ed. *Pynchon: A Collection of Critical Essays*. Englewood Cliffs, N.J.: Prentice-Hall, 1978.
Pearce, Richard, ed., *Critical Essays on Thomas Pynchon*. Boston: G. K. Hall, 1981.
Pynchon Notes. Journal, 1979–. Co-edited by K. Tololyan and J. Krafft. c/o Wesleyan University, Middletown, Conn.
Schaub, Thomas. *Pynchon: The Voice of Ambiguity*. Urbana: University of Illinois Press, 1981.
Slade, Joseph. *Thomas Pynchon*. New York: Warner, 1974.
Tanner, Tony. *Thomas Pynchon*. London: Methuen, 1982.

KHACHIG TOLOLYAN

R

REED, ISHMAEL (1938–   )

A poet as well as a novelist, Ishmael Reed is best known for his six prose narratives. His fiction borrows from poetry, with its play with images, its exploded plots, and constant homage to the power of myth and ritual. In his fiction Reed breaks from the typical pseudo-autobiographical form used by such black writers as Richard Wright, Ralph Ellison, and James Baldwin and so rejects the pattern of the slave narratives of nineteenth-century black writers. In its place Reed offers his version of the mythic past of the black man and attempts a restoration of the non-Western view of the black experience. His announced aim is to establish a black aesthetic founded on voodoo, the myth of Osiris, hoodoo, and other primitive elements of ritual belonging solely to the black character. The resulting shape of his six novels is a satire of Western religion, art, science, and rationalism.

Ishmael Reed was born in Chattanooga, Tennessee, on February 22, 1938, a propitious date, he has stated, because the number 22 is powerful in hoodoo numerology. At the age of four he moved with his mother to Buffalo, New York, where he lived until he left for New York City. He completed a degree at the University of Buffalo, and in New York he became co-founder of the *East Village Other* and *Advance*. He later became chairman and president of Yardbird Publishing Company in California and director of Reed Cannon and Johnson Communications. He has recently begun producing "spontaneous" soap operas for video consumption and has toured with his tapes to present them to live audiences. In California, he has taught at the University of California at Berkeley, and he has spent time as a visiting lecturer at the University of Washington and Yale University.

Reed's first novel, *The Free-Lance Pallbearers*, appeared in 1967. The work has an academic setting, and its aim is to demolish the typical black novel of identity crisis and search for self. Its hero, Bukko Doopeyduk, is an inversion of such figures as Ralph Ellison's Invisible Man, and the novel becomes both an hilarious allegory of the black condition and a parody of previous black novelists.

The next novel, *Yellow Back Radio Broke-Down* (1969), is what Reed called a hoodoo Western, and it takes its form from the nineteenth-century dime-novel. Its hero is the Loop Garoo Kid, who introduces what has become central for Reed in his fiction, a mythic combination of Black Osiris (the Egyptian God) and other African totems in a deadly struggle with all the West represents.

With *Mumbo Jumbo* (1972) Reed presents a fully developed aesthetic based on a revisionist reading of the myths of ancient Egypt, the voodoo practices of West Indian magic, and the elemental powers of dark people. The setting is the Harlem Renaissance of the 1920s, and the struggle is again between a character representing the hoodoo aesthetic, Papa LaBas, and American society's attempts to define and control its black members.

A fourth novel, *The Last Days of Louisiana Red* (1974), advances the career of the voodoo detective Papa LaBas as he confronts divisiveness in the black community itself, represented by Louisiana Red, a hot sauce and evil state of mind manipulating black people to fight each other. Critics pointed out that his work attacks the "posturing, rhetoric and exploitation" that infected black revolutionary organizations in the late 1960s and early 1970s. A strong anti-feminist note is also sounded in *The Last Days* in Reed's presentation of Papa LaBas' struggle with Minnie the Moocher, a black woman who represents those females who keep black men in slavery.

Reed's fifth novel, *Flight to Canada* (1976), draws back from the full-blown treatment of his hoodoo aesthetic, with its cultural diagnosticians and heroes such as Papa LaBas and the Loop Garoo Kid, to present a parodic vision of the American Civil War, the supposed historic instrument of liberation for the black in America. The plot is typically anachronistic and is inverted with such characters as Robert E. Lee and Abraham Lincoln presented as multinational businessmen who watch television and jet all over the world on deals. Raven Quickskill, a runaway slave belonging to Arthur Swille, a Virginia planter, writes a poem titled "Flight to Canada" and in so doing frees himself from his old slave identity. In this novel, art and not hoodoo sets the black self at large, and the intricately footnoted compound of Osiris, Set, voodoo, and dark power receives little credit for Raven's liberation.

Reed's most recent novel, *The Terrible Twos* (1982), continues the retreat from the earlier well-defined aesthetic to concentrate instead on an invented *Christmas Carol*, a winter's tale that pits the little black servant Peter and his master Saint Nicholas against Oscar Zumwalt, proprietor of the North Pole Development Corporation, a stealer of the nativity festival. The plot of the novel circles about the commercialization of Saint Nicholas and provides Reed an opportunity for a satiric attack on the administration of Ronald Reagan. The United States under the regime of that president conducts itself like a child in the grip of the "terrible twos," the period of development in which all identity is grasping ego and temper tantrums. "Two-year olds," states the narrator, "are what the id would look like if the id could ride a tricycle." The president in the novel is a male model who begins to have visions of past holders of his office weeping for the country in its perilous present. The long winter of 1980 begins America's Christmas blues.

The originality and power of Ishmael Reed's fiction derive from the satiric energy he achieves through the manipulation of farce, allegory, parody, and the creation of his hoodoo aesthetic. The results of his decision to concentrate on satire in his last two novels, at the expense of the Neo-Hoodoo program developed in his first four, has meant a gain in narrative movement and clarity and has led to a more accessible allegorical pillorying of his targets. So far his six novels have demonstrated his ability to shift targets and devices to meet the need he perceives, and *The Terrible Twos* marks another advance for his revisionist, deadly, and hilarious vision.

Selected Bibliography

Primary Sources

The Free-Lance Pallbearers. Garden City, N.Y.: Doubleday, 1967; London: MacGibbon & Kee, 1968.
Yellow Back Radio Broke-Down. Garden City, N.Y.: Doubleday, 1969; London: Allison & Buby, 1971.
Catechism of D NeoAmerican Hoodoo Church. London: Paul Breman, 1970.
Conjure. Amherst: University of Massachusetts Press, 1972.
Mumbo Jumbo. Garden City, N.Y.: Doubleday, 1972.
Chattanooga. New York: Random House, 1973.
The Last Days of Louisiana Red. New York: Random House, 1974.
Flight to Canada. New York: Random House, 1976.
The Terrible Twos. New York: St. Martin's Press/Marek, 1982.
Reckless Eyeballing. New York: St. Martin's Press, 1986.

Secondary Sources

Ambler, Madge. "Ishmael Reed: Whose Radio Broke Down?." *Negro Literature Forum* 6 (1972): 125, 131.
Davis, Robert Murray. "Scatting the Myths: Ishmael Reed." *Arizona Quarterly* 39 (Winter 1983): 406–420.
Duff, Gerald. "Reed's *The Free-Lance Pallbearers*." *Explicator* (May 1974), Item 69.
————. "Ishmael Reed." In *Dictionary of Literary Biography*, Volume Two. Detroit: Bruccoli Clark/Gale, 1978.
Harris, Norman. "Politics as an Innovative Aspect of Literary Folklore: A Study of Ishmael Reed." *Obsidian* 5, i–ii, (1979): 41–50.

Margareta, Peter. "An Interview with Ishmael Reed." *The Iowa Review* 13 (Spring 1982): 117–131.

Northouse, Cameron. "Ishmael Reed." In *Conversations with Writers II*. Detroit: Bruccoli Clark/Gale, 1978.

Reed, Ishmael. "The Writer as Seer: Ishmael Reed on Ishmael Reed." *Black World* 23, no. 8 (June 1974): 20–34.

Schmitz, Neil. "Neo-HooDoo: The Experimental Fiction of Ishmael Reed." *Twentieth Century Literature* 20 (April 1974): 126–40.

GERALD DUFF

ROBBINS, TOM (1936–   )

For those habituated into the expectation that a tragic vision is prerequisite to greatness in the art of the novel, Tom Robbins' fiction would probably be characterized as second rate. The wild exuberance of his style, his love of hyperbole, metaphors, and puns, and his often outrageous dealings with both the sacred and the profane are consistently playful. The theft of the corpse of Christ from the lower level catacombs at the Vatican, a disembodied brain discoursing on its own limitations, a heroine outfitted by one of nature's chance mutations with incredibly oversized thumbs, and a pyramid designed to be an exact replica of the one found on the back of a pack of Camel cigarettes would not appear the stuff out of which contemporary angst is made. And, indeed, it is not. Robbins describes himself as a philosophical writer who is "very serious about the issues" he deals with. But his is definitely a philosophy in a new key. Central to his vision of life are concepts derived from modern physics which he amplifies through analogies with Eastern mysticism to make a case against the patriarchal Judeo-Christian tradition. His novels are designed to train his readers into a perception of being in which magic and mystery appear to have a scientific foundation and in which spontaneity and playfulness are legitimized as primary modes of existence. For these reasons alone he is unique among writers of postmodern fiction.

Thomas Eugene Robbins was born in 1936 in Blowing Rock, North Carolina, where he apparently taught himself to read at age five. It was his mother, an amateur writer, whom he credits for his falling in love with language at an early age. He moved to Virginia as a preadolescent, living in a succession of small towns near Richmond. After matriculating into Washington and Lee University and discovering that its ideal of the Southern gentleman was not appealing, he set out on an extensive hitchhiking tour of America, then served in the U.S. Air Force as a meteorologist. Later, he completed a degree at Richmond Professional Institute (now Virginia Commonwealth University) and took one quarter of graduate work at the University of Washington's Far East Institute. While in Richmond he worked as a copy editor at the *Richmond Times Dispatch* and later as an art critic at the *Seattle Times*. He then moved to the East Village in New York where he researched a book on Jackson Pollock that was never written. He returned to Seattle, where he worked weekends as a copy editor at the *Seattle Post-Intelligencer*, wrote art reviews for several national publications, and participated actively in the psychedelic movement then blooming on the West Coast.

Robbins' career as novelist began to take shape when his interest in writing a story about the body of Christ occasioned research on the history of early Christianity. The result was *Another Roadside Attraction* (1971). Following modest sales and less than extravagant royalties, Robbins, by now married and the father of a child, elected to move to La Conner, a small town on Swinomish Channel about an hour and a half outside Seattle. There, in the relative isolation and privacy he still zealously seeks to protect, Robbins conceived and wrote his first truly successful novel.

Following the success in paperback of *Even Cowgirls Get the Blues* (1976), *Another Roadside Attraction* also became a commercial success in a paperback edition. Largely ignored until this point by major reviewers, Robbins' demonstrable appeal to a large reading audience made him a force to be reckoned with. The initial presumption that his audience would remain primarily college students whose adolescent concerns and unwillingness to invest in more expensive hardcover editions made them ready consumers of this fiction has slowly been displaced by the suspicion that Robbins might well be, as Thomas Pynchon* intimated in the introduction to *Cowgirls*, the harbinger of a fresh new direction in the art of the novel.

Although Robbins clearly believes that the unitary conception of being in the great religious philosophies of the East (Hinduism, Buddhism, Taoism) is more compatible with discoveries made in modern physics than the dualistic Western model, he does not presume that Eastern mysticism is the grounds for our salvation. Rather, he uses the resemblance between the Eastern emphasis on the unity and interrelatedness of all things in a cosmos that is forever moving, alive, and organic and the understanding of the character of physical reality in modern physics to make a case against several fundamental aspects of Western cosmology. Thus, self as skin-encapsulated ego, the idea of a hierarchy of being that puts the human being above all other aspects of the natural process, the view of reason as the foremost arbiter of truth, and the belief in mind-body dualism are portrayed in Robbins' fictional universe as injurious to our emotional well-being and a threat to our continued survival. What he advocates finally is a kind of psychosocial revolution that involves the reassertion of the "feminine" values of feeling, fertility, and the acceptance of the complete cycles of nature which, according to Robert Graves in *The White Goddess*, characterized the original phase of spiritual development in the West.

Robbins' *Still Life with Woodpecker* (1980) features what Robbins described as a "metaphysical outlaw" involved in a love affair with the daughter of the ousted monarchs of a small European country. Although Robbins' theme in the narrative—"When the mystery of the connection (between lovers) goes, love goes"—may be perfectly valid, and although the book spent 16 weeks on the *New York Times* Best Seller list, critical response has generally not been favorable. Robbins' next novel, *Jitterbug Perfume*, was published in November 1984.

Selected Bibliography

Primary Sources

Guy Anderson. n.p.: Gear Works Press, 1965.
Another Roadside Attraction. New York: Ballantine Books, 1971.
Even Cowgirls Get the Blues. New York: Bantam Books, 1976.
"The Purpose of the Moon." *Playboy* 26 (January 1979), pp. 78-94.
Still Life with Woodpecker. New York: Bantam Books, 1980.
"Judy Garland and the Global Death Wish, or How to Stop Worrying and Love
    Stolichnaya." *Seattle Weekly*, October 1983.
Jitterbug Perfume. New York: Bantam Books, 1984.

Secondary Sources

Gross, Beverly, "Misfits: Tom Robbins' *Even Cowgirls Get the Blues*." *North
    Dakota Quarterly* 50 (Summer 1982): 36–51.
Nadeau, Robert. "Physics and Cosmology in the Fiction of Tom Robbins." *Critique*
    20 (1978): 63–74.
———. *Readings from the New Book on Nature*. Amherst: University of Massa-
    chusetts Press, 1981, pp. 149–60.
Ross, Mitchell S. "Prince of the Paperback Literati." *New York Times Magazine*
    February 12, 1978, pp. 16–17, 66–69, 72–77 and 86.
Seigel, Mark. "The Meaning of Meaning in the Novels of Tom Robbins." *Mosaic*
    14, no. 3 (1981): 119–30.

ROBERT L. NADEAU

RUSHDIE, SALMAN (1947–   )

Salman Rushdie is two months older than the country he was born in. He is not a myth. He is a Muslim with a Cambridge M.A. and an English novelist from Bombay. He says there are ways in which he is no longer Indian and ways in which he will never be English. The language of his novels shows a discerning nose for adopted literature and a careful ear for the tongues of his native subcontinent. In allowing his roots their rhizomatic spread, he goes Conrad one better, and yet he may be less one of us. Rushdie is nearly a culture in himself, or so alienated from cultures that he can nicely mimic them.

Midnight's Children made Ahmed Salman Rushdie famous in 1981. By then, he had dropped his father's middle name from the front of his own. Anis Ahmed and Negid Rushdie told their son that he first showed a desire to be a writer in 1952. From then on he got books for his birthdays. The big book he gave the world made a cultural mirror for India out of the fictional autobiography of the first one thousand and one of her sons and daughters born during the first hour after her independence and birth as a modern nation at midnight, August 15, 1947. Ahmed Salman had been there since June 19.

In 1961 he was sent to King's College, Cambridge. His parents, meanwhile, moved to Pakistan. After receiving an M.A. with honors, he tried a return there in 1968, but knowing England better, he went back to London. There he was an actor of sorts for a year. He worked there as a free-lance advertising copywriter and wrote his first novel in 1971. It is unpublished, though still in his possession as a grim reminder of old interests and weaknesses.

He continued to produce copy and wrote another novel, *Grimus*, which was published in 1975 and earned him a listing in the *Encyclopedia of Science Fiction*. It was a fantasy of real ingenuities. Its "thought-forms" drew enough positive attention to give its young author confidence. He married its dedicatee, Clarissa, on May 22, 1976.

The purposefully lost first novel had had an Indian setting. *Grimus* had for hero an American Indian discovered by a lost European looking for India. The Indian's story is a multi-dimensional fable, rich in the quasi-sciences of the human quest. Immortalized by a pedlar's elixir, Flapping Eagle gets curious about life's meanings, just like a good character should. The problem was, he never really settled in on anything.

Grimus is another beginning that led to the big beginning for Salman Rushdie. His was called "an imagination to watch." It had made public its infatuation with an encyclopedic whimsy and philosophical self-expression. It began working out the fabric of relationship Rushdie still weaves between individuals and myths.

Myths are concepts dressed in the tribal robes of self-deceit. They are a way of telling ourselves that ideas are real. They require a willing disbelief in suspense. That is why Rushdie's narrators keep rushing ahead of themselves and then reining back their knowledge. They are anxious about their stories. Tales are only real if they have already happened, that is, if one interlocking jigsaw set of their possibilities seems to have been realized. Myths settle things down like that. How else would individuals get on with living their unsure lives?

After *Grimus*, Rushdie drafted another novel and then trashed it. Bits of it were to surface again. Meanwhile, he went on in advertising, learning the disciplines of everyday writing and economy of expression. Then, with cannibalized morsels of the scrapped draft and expanded childhood memories and a predilection for Bombay talkie film melodrama, Salman Rushdie wrote a 446-page poetic prose piece of historico-mythico-pickles for a cucumber-nosed hero to get into. It won the Booker McConnell Prize for Fiction, and he quit the other job.

The narrator of *Midnight's Children*, Saleem Sinai, absorbed a lot of selves from Rushdie. His history is a pastiche of that of populous and multi-cultural Mother India. His face is her map. His nose shows his creator new Shandy and Bergerac, but it keys into more than Western humors. Along with the names of the closest two of Saleem's midnight siblings, this nose, and later the ears of the child Aadam they three parented, will signify Ganesh. When Shiva (Destroyer-Restorer) suspected that the son his wife Parvati (Energy-Witchery) presented to him wasn't his own, he decapitated his issue right on the spot. Then he repented and grasped for a replacement. An elephant came to hand and the young deity got a trunk and flapping ears. Ganesh later sat at the feet of India's epic poet Valmiki and copied down the *Ramayana*. This god is the warp to the weft of Indian history in Rushdie's shimmering fabric of allusions, acted by Saleem's elusive and illusory selves.

Half the fun of *Midnight's Children* is following the bouncing balls of reference through the merry tunes and wailing dirges Rushdie's languages sing. Names slide from context to context. Actions echo across this text to others. Meaning interpenetrates. Form cannot be avoided, though it seems tenuous. The whole is filmy. The movies have taught people to read the techniques that bring this book to life.

In *Shame* (1983), similar techniques present a fable of Pakistan and its concept of *sharam*. More than our shame, this is "also embarrassment, discomfiture, decency, modesty, shyness, the sense of having a place in the world, and other dialects of emotion for which English has no counterparts." It stands dialectically facing both honor and shamelessness on the two axes of the mythico-cultural and the individual. These are terms which The Land of the Pure (Pakistan, as it calls itself) lives to extremes, but which are present to most all of our lives, individual and national, historical and fictional.

As universal as it is, *Shame* is built in bits. But, as in *Midnight's Children*, they take form. The narrator leans back and tells you of the efforts it takes to think and work his book of tales into your hands and eyes, but this time it is Salman talking. Bits of his real life frame the fancies. Which means he gets to us from the side of reading and from our individual memories or experience of a real world. The resulting fictional form is a questioning, an interview, between the world of *Shame* and our own.

Salman Rushdie's work is a rhetorical questioning. He writes as *mohajir*, migrant maybe in exile. In *Shame*, he writes, "I tell myself this will be a novel of leavetaking, my last words on the East from which, many years ago, I began to come loose." But his books are *hejira*, the flight that carries a truth from misunderstanding to where it may flourish. His journey is also a seeking, like the visionary quests Sufi masters make with the aid of patterns woven in their prayer rugs. A magic carpet ride.

Selected Bibliography

Primary Sources

Grimus. London: Gollancz, 1975 & Woodstock, N.Y.: Overlook, 1979.

Midnight's Children. London: Jonathan Cape & New York: Alfred A. Knopf, 1981.

Shame. London: Jonathan Cape & New York: Alfred A. Knopf, 1983.

Secondary Sources

Reviews and interviews redacted in *Contemporary Authors*, Volume III and *Contemporary Literary Criticism*, Volumes 23 and 31.

TOM MARSHALL

S

SILLIMAN, RON (1946–   )

Ron Silliman is not really a fiction writer at all; he is an influential member of the language school of poetry which thrives in San Francisco and New York City. Since 1974 he has developed a new form of plotless, creative prose. "Narrative suppresses immediate attention," Silliman has written, and his nonnarrative works intend to refocus our attention at the level of the sentence and the word, making language visible once more. For those unfamiliar with the genre Silliman is helping to invent, a sample of his writing is necessary.

Every word is either current, or strange, or metaphysical, or ornamental, or newly-coined, or lengthened, or contracted, or altered. Weathercock, scrimshaw. Between the television and the bed was an ironing board, half-finished bottles of lager atop it. When, looking out the window, you no longer see what is there, it's time to move. Narwhale, I confront you. (*Ketjak*, pp. 13-14)

In this passage, as elsewhere, Silliman emphasizes the place of language in a social, historical matrix. He presents the word as a construct, the word in transition. Working without the constraints of invented character and plot, Silliman is often able to use vocabulary from all segments of society—from technical jargon to ghetto slang. Rival codes jostle for predominance across his pages, revealing the means by which language users encode and manipulate reality.

The above quotation also demonstrates the way in which Silliman's sentences juxtapose in a fresh and humorous way, outside the expectations of logic. In its last two sentences a person (reader) turns from an overfamiliar view to be confronted by the long horn of a narwhale. Silliman never lulls his readers but provokes them to greater alertness.

Ron Silliman was raised in Berkeley, California. His father, a policeman, separated from the family when Ron was young. Silliman was raised by his mother and grandparents. He attended both San Francisco State and the University of California at Berkeley but dropped out before graduation, disillusioned by the prospects of institutional creative writing. He chose, instead, to work in grassroots political organizations such as prison reform groups and neighborhood outreach programs. These jobs allowed him access to the wide variety of language usage encountered in his writing.

Silliman began writing conventional poetry early and by the age of 23 had been published in *Poetry* and *Chicago Review*. Then his style began to change. In 1971 his first book, *Crow*, a collection of short poems, was published by Ithaca House. These poems continue William Carlos Williams' work by combining contemporary speech patterns with literary traditions. *Crow* was followed by *Nox* (1974), a collection of 60 poems in 15 pages from Burning Deck Press, and *Mohawk* (1973), a work composed of 26 words spatially arranged according to a formula involving playing cards, published by Doones. In this period Silliman made contact with a far-flung network of writers by beginning to edit *Tottel's*, a broadside literary magazine.

In 1974 Silliman began writing *Ketjak*, his first major work, published by This Press in 1978. It is a book-length prose work whose form was inspired by the repetition and elaboration of simple elements in Steve Reich's musical structures. In *Ketjak*, each paragraph contains twice as many sentences as its predecessor. Each subsequent paragraph repeats some sentences intact, while elaborating on others. Besides affording the reader the eternal pleasures of recognition and surprise, this predetermined structure seems to free Silliman to include a wide range of content without sacrificing cohesion. He focuses here on the detail of daily life in his city of San Francisco with an unmatched precision and depth, revealing a welter of common sights and sounds seldom presented within traditional literary genres.

Since *Ketjak* Silliman has published five books: *Legend* (1980), a collaboration with Bruce Andrews, Charles Bernstein,* Ray DiPalma, and Steve McCaffery; *Sitting Up, Standing, Taking Steps* (1978), a chapbook-length prose poem in which readers often fail to detect the total absence of verbs; *Bart* (1982), a chapbook written in one day while riding Bay Area Rapid Transit; *Tjanting* (1981), his longest work, published by The Figures; and, recently (1983), *ABC*, from Tuumba.

Tjanting is structured around the Fibonacci number system, so that the number of sentences in each paragraph equals the sum of those in the preceding paragraphs. The Fibonacci number system is a form of ordering found commonly in nature; in *Tjanting* it provides an asymmetrical pattern more sensed than understood by the reader. What the reader does perceive is the way these sentences are not simply repeated, as in *Ketjak*, but recast.

For instance, the sentence "A woman in a blue nightgown raises the shades," can evolve into "A woman in her shades raises a blue nightgown." The second version is more unlikely as a sentence than as a reality—and that is the kind of situation Silliman thrives on, bringing unvoiced possibility to language. As the reader grows accustomed to the constant transmutation of sentences, he or she comes to anticipate it by guessing what the next variant will be. The result is that readers are required to actively participate in the creation of Silliman's texts.

ABC is the first three sections of a long work-in-progress called *The Alphabet*. Recently, Silliman has also guest-edited a special issue of *Ironwood* magazine featuring "language poets." Combining the attention to language texture and sound native to poetry with a perceptive, detailed depiction of the contemporary scene surpassing that of most fiction, Silliman is renovating the prose poem and is bringing a new realist tradition into existence.

Selected Bibliography

Primary Sources

Crow. Ithaca, N.Y.: Ithaca House, 1971.
Mohawk. San Francisco: Doones, 1973.
Nox. Providence, R.I.: Burning Deck Press, 1974.
Sitting Up, Standing, Taking Steps. Berkeley, Calif.: Tuumba Press, 1978.
Ketjak. San Francisco: This Press, 1978.
Tjanting. Berkeley: The Figures, 1981.
Bart. San Francisco: Potes and Poets, 1982.
ABC. Berkeley, Calif.: Tuumba Press, 1983.

Secondary Sources

Davidson, Michael. "On Language Poetry." *Fiction International* 15, no. 2 (1984): 117–29.
The Difficulties 2, no. 2 (1985). Special Silliman Issue.

RAE ARMANTROUT

SORRENTINO, GILBERT (1929–   )

For a long time the works of Gilbert Sorrentino have been considered as rather elitist, nearly private products: no allowance was ever given to fashion or established convention. Indeed, his literary career has been grounded on aesthetic principles that are not palatable to many literary critics and have virtually insured that his works have been ignored by the mass audience. "I think I write everything for myself. I very rarely think of anybody reading it," confided Sorrentino, rather placidly, in a 1974 interview. His is a very personal writing, then, reserved for the chosen few whom Sorrentino considers as his peers in the "devastating, crushing" isolation of the literary avant-garde in the American 1950s and 1960s.

With Sterne, Joyce, and especially William Carlos Williams, who had transplanted the French avant-garde discoveries into a most conscious American language, Sorrentino shares that faith in the power of the word and in its multiple technical possibilities, which may be envisioned as the true leitmotiv of all his works. But even in that constant preeminence he gives to form over content, no uniformity is to be found to guide us; the linguistic patrimony is administered according to different economies: a rigorous, generative parsimony for the poetical realm; a luxurious inventiveness for his fictional language.

It might seem paradoxical that Sorrentino, although restlessly searching for new forms and techniques of representation, grounds his concept of total invention on absolute artificiality (at times even on an ingenious recycling of his own and of other writers' literature material and characters). But these sophisticated literary devices—far from constituting mere plagiarism—are rooted in the purest mannerism. A true challenge to our imaginative faculty, Sorrentino's fiction traces indigenous American landscapes through innovative means. His selected prose, elaborated and polished as an artifact, effectively succeeds in directing the reader's attention to the essence of American life.

Sorrentino was born in Brooklyn in 1929 (his father was Sicilian-born, his mother third-generation Irish), raised in Roman Catholic milieus, and grew up in the same blue-collar neighborhood that was the initial background to his lifelong friendship with Hubert Selby and that provided the fictional setting of his second and seventh novels: *Steelwork* (1970) and *Crystal Vision* (1981).

At the age of 18, Sorrentino started his migratory travels by moving across the river to the cultural centers in Manhattan to nourish his insatiable intellectual curiosity. But only in 1953, after serving in the U.S. Army and studying at Brooklyn College, did he decide to become a writer. From 1956 until 1960, he published (in collaboration with Selby) an alternative magazine, *Neon*, which was primarily a shelter for the expatriates from the faltering *Black Mountain Review* and for all the nonacademically oriented writers. For Sorrentino, *Neon* provided a connection with people like William Carlos Williams, Robert Creeley, Joel Oppenheimer, Paul Goodman, and LeRoi Jones. With Jones, Sorrentino shared also the editorship of another significant magazine of the 1960s: *Kulchur* (1960–1965). The numerous iconoclastic, critical pieces that Sorrentino contributed to *Kulchur* ("the best critical magazine of the past twenty-five years," in his words) alternated with the publication of two poetry collections—*The Darkness Surrounds Us* (1960) and *Black and White* (1964)—that were followed by his first novel, *The Sky Changes* (1966).

Although *The Sky Changes* is considered Sorrentino's most accessible work, this episodic chronicle of a marriage failure was already marked by artifictional features, such as his use of anti-conventional transitions in chronology and structure and a peculiar taste for a color-oriented system of signification. The dim, grey tinges of his first works become juicy nuances of orange in some poetry collections of his mid-career (*A Dozen Oranges*, 1976; *The Orangery*, 1978), or an all-encompassing, schizoid blue, as in his last pastoral parody on American marital life, academies, and bucolic pretension (*Blue Pastoral*, 1983).

Critics who attempt to use Sorrentino's color system as a magical pass key to his fiction are obviously misguided (behind his orange curtains he mocks us: "Nothing is the thing that rhymes with orange"), but the relevance of color as a structuring element, together with the alphabetical sequence, remains evident in *Splendide-Hotel* (1973). Here the exquisite allusiveness of some of Sorrentino's previous poetry (*The Perfect Fiction*, 1968; *Corrosive Sublimate*, 1971) is surrealistically interlaced with various technical experiments, such as the listing of pure words. Paradoxically, those enlisted words combine to render reality in a more meaningful way than a dozen sentences could do, for they trigger the readers' imagination and prove that, at one point, literature and reality become one thing, one dimension. This focus on the interaction between words and reality is also central to *Imaginative Qualities of Actual Things* (1971; the title is borrowed from Williams), and to the critically acclaimed *Mulligan Stew* (1979). Both works deal with the New York art and publishing world that he knew intimately as a writer in New York, as an editor at Grove Press (1965–1970), and as a teacher in various places, including the New School for Social Research.

No synthesis could possibly render justice to the complexity of those novels, to the arrogant and sublime quality of those authorial asides, intermissions, and zany footnotes of *Imaginative Qualities . . .* ; or even less to the shifting conglomerate of stories-within-the-story, letters, diary passages, plays, pornographic verses, baffling lists (even private ones) we are to savor in that *stew*, the original recipe for which he triumphantly borrowed from Flann O'Brien's *At-Swim-Two-Birds* (1939).

Although *Mulligan Stew* remains Sorrentino's most ambitious and audacious work to date, he has continued to publish brilliant nontraditional fiction during the 1980s including *Aberration of Starlight* (1980), *Crystal Vision* (1981), *Blue Pastoral* (1983), and *Odd Number* (1985). In 1982 he accepted a position as professor of English at Stanford University.

Selected Bibliography

Primary Sources

The Darkness Surrounds Us. Highlands, N.C.: Jonathan Williams, 1960.
Black and White. New York: Corinth, 1964.

The Sky Changes. New York: Hill & Wang, 1966.
The Perfect Fiction. New York: W. W. Norton, 1968.
Steelwork. New York: Pantheon, 1970.
Imaginative Qualities of Actual Things. New York: Pantheon, 1971.
Corrosive Sublimate. Los Angeles: Black Sparrow, 1971.
Splendide-Hotel. New York: New Directions, 1973.
A Dozen Oranges. Los Angeles: Black Sparrow, 1976.
White Sail. Los Angeles: Black Sparrow, 1976.
Sulpiciae Elegidia/Elegiacs of Sulpicia. Mount Horeb, Wis.: Perishable Press, 1977.
The Orangery. Austin: University of Texas Press, 1978.
Mulligan Stew. New York: Grove Press, 1979.
Aberration of Starlight. New York: Random House, 1980.
Crystal Vision. San Francisco: North Point Press, 1981.
Selected Poems, 1958–1980. Los Angeles: Black Sparrow, 1981.
Blue Pastoral. San Francisco: North Point Press, 1983.
Something Said. San Francisco: North Point Press, 1984.
Odd Number. San Francisco: North Point Press, 1985.

Secondary Sources

Alpert, Barry, ed. *Vort* (Fall 1975). Special Sorrentino Issue.
Baron, Dennis. "An Interview with Gilbert Sorrentino." *Partisan Review* 2 (1981): 236–46.
D'Amico, M. Vittoria. "Paradox Beyond Convention: A Note on Gilbert Sorrentino's Fiction." *Revista di Studi Anglo-Americani* 4–5 (1984–1985): 46–55.
Klinkowitz, Jerome. "Gilbert Sorrentino." *The Life of Fiction*. Urbana: University of Illinois Press, 1977, pp. 7–15.
O'Brien, John, ed. *The Review of Contemporary Fiction*, 1, no. 1 (Spring 1981). Special Gilbert Sorrentino Issue.
Thielmans, Johan. "The Voice of the Irresponsible: Irresponsible Voices? On Gilbert Sorrentino's *Mulligan Stew*." In *Representation and Performance in Postmodern Fiction*. Ed., Maurice Couturier. Montpelier, France: Delta, 1983, pp. 113–29.

MARIA VITTORIA D'AMICO

STONE, ROBERT (1937–   )

On the basis of only three novels published at regular intervals of about seven years, Robert Stone is regarded as one of the finest post-Vietnam War American novelists. He seems essentially untouched by many of the theoretical and experimental trends in recent fiction, preferring, especially with his last two works, to write novels patterned after adventure stories and thrillers. However, each of his novels contains elements of the surreal, the grotesque, the hallucinatory. The world of his books is violent, brutal, and pitiless; his main characters are troubled and angry losers who live life on the edge. Ever present are alcohol and drugs, indicating the pressures his characters feel and their need to escape. Stone is interested in the social and political—all his novels have a political background to them—but he is not a social novelist in the usual sense; his deepest interest is in individuals and finally in the spiritual condition of late twentieth-century Americans.

Stone was born in New York City on August 21, 1937 to working-class parents. Fatherless as a child, he spent three years in an orphanage when his mother was institutionalized in a mental hospital. From his relationship with his mother comes his sensitivity to the emotionally crippled. He attended a Catholic high school in New York, though he dropped out before earning a degree to join the Navy. After gaining an equivalency diploma, he briefly attended New York University and was a Stegner Fellow at Stanford University in 1962. While in California he experienced the counterculture as a member of Ken Kesey's Merry Pranksters.

Stone's first novel, partially written at Wallace Stegner's writing workshop, was *A Hall of Mirrors* (1967), which won the William Faulkner Prize for the best first novel of the year. A wild, chaotic book that frequently threatens to go out of control, *A Hall of Mirrors* uses its New Orleans setting during Mardi Gras season as a metaphor for America. The plot concerns right-wing political activity, presenting a paranoid vision of "the Big Store," in which people are manipulated and discarded by power-hungry fanatics. Focusing on a group of outsiders and dropouts, the novel suggests that those who love and care are doomed. Thus, Geraldine, a woman of wide and brutalizing experience who yet retains the desire to love and be loved, and Morgan Rainey, a devoutly religious but naive welfare worker, both die, while Rheinhardt, Geraldine's lover, survives because he avoids personal involvement and commitment. Though ending with a destructive riot worthy of comparison with the ending of *The Day of the Locust*, the novel can best be called promising but lacking in control.

The same criticism cannot be leveled at *Dog Soldiers* (1974), Stone's second novel, which was almost universally admired and won the National Book Award. Based on his observations of Vietnam as a reporter, it is much tighter in construction than *A Hall of Mirrors* and has the plot momentum of a thriller. Stone deals with the effects of the Vietnam experience on America and Americans, not by focusing on combat but by bringing Vietnam home to America in the form of smuggled heroin and violence. The novel is set primarily in California, America's dream land but here populated by burnt-out leftovers from the 1960s. The main characters are all drifters without strong moral values, seekers of sensation for its own sake. Converse, an intellectual adrift in an amoral world, initiates the smuggling scheme, involving his wife who is a pill taker and finally a heroin addict. Hicks, who actually does the smuggling, is perhaps the strongest character in the novel, a Hemingwayesque hero concerned with control and self-discipline. But through him Stone shows the Hemingway code shading toward psychopathy. All the characters live in constant fear; those who drift survive, while those who try to exert some control die. The novel presents a nightmarish vision of characters at the mercy of events and people they cannot control.

Stone's third novel, *A Flag for Sunrise* (1981), received a mixed critical reception, but it is Stone's strongest novel to date. Set in the mythical Central American country of Tecan (a combination of Honduras and Nicaragua), it deals with Americans abroad and, like *Dog Soldiers*, explores the legacy of Vietnam for Americans. With Tecan in the throes of revolution, Stone focuses on three Americans who become involved. Holliwell, like Converse, is an intellectual without values who simply drifts. Pablo, a speed freak gun runner, resembles Hicks, though he is more homicidal and less controlled than the earlier character. Sister Justin is something new to Stone's works—a nun who has lost her faith but who grasps for meaning through passionate commitment to political revolution. Holliwell is drawn to her, feeling her commitment can fill his emptiness, and they become lovers. Although his involvement with her leads to her death, she at least dies believing in something. Holliwell survives but only to live hollowly. Again, Stone's characters are manipulated by others and by the impersonal forces of history. *A Flag for Sunrise* most explicitly reveals the religious dimension of Stone's vision, for the book ultimately concerns what the world is like without God: nasty, brutal, and nightmarish.

Though working very slowly, Stone has produced two novels that are among the best of his generation. His craft has developed and his vision deepened during his career. While timely and including political, historical, and social forces as background, they are essentially psychological novels, concerning the individual hungers resulting from isolation, loneliness, and despair. Stone's novels are important, not only because they define the American condition now but also because they deal with the human condition in the absence of belief.

Selected Bibliography

Primary Sources

A Hall of Mirrors. Boston: Houghton Mifflin, 1967.
Dog Soldiers. Boston: Houghton Mifflin, 1974.
A Flag for Sunrise. New York: Alfred A. Knopf, 1981.

Secondary Sources

Beidler, Philip D. *American Literature and the Experience of Vietnam*. Athens: University of Georgia Press, 1982.
Hendin, Josephine. *Vulnerable People: A View of American Fiction Since 1945*. New York: Oxford University Press, 1978.
Karagueuzian, Maureen. "Interview with Robert Stone." *TriQuarterly* 53 (Winter 1982): 248–58.
———. "Irony in Robert Stone's *Dog Soldiers*." *Critique* 24 (1983): 65–73.
Moore, L. Hugh. "The Undersea World of Robert Stone." *Critique* 11 (1969): 43–56.

Ruas, Charles. "An Interview with Robert Stone." *Conversations with American Writers*. New York: Alfred A. Knopf, 1985, pp. 265–94.
Shelton, Frank W. "Robert Stone's *Dog Soldiers*: Vietnam Comes Home to America." *Critique* 24 (1983): 74–81.

FRANK W. SHELTON

SUKENICK, RONALD (1932–   )

Ronald Sukenick is very probably American fiction's most articulate proponent and theoretician of the anti-realist, anti-traditional novel; his own work dramatizes more clearly than any other American writer's the possibilities and liabilities implicit in that stance.

A Brooklyn native, Sukenick began writing fiction as an undergraduate at Cornell in the 1950s before beginning graduate work in English at Brandeis University, from which he received an M.A. in 1957 and a Ph.D. in 1962. The difficulties that he and other innovative fiction writers had experienced in getting their work placed with commercial publishers prompted Sukenick to join in the founding of the Fiction Collective, a writer's cooperative dedicated to the publication of serious, nontraditional fiction in the early 1970s. The continuing paucity of response to such work from established literary journals inspired Sukenick's founding of the *American Book Review* in the late 1970s, a review devoted to the sophisticated discussion of both traditional and nontraditional works of fiction. Sukenick has taught at Sarah Lawrence and Cornell, and is currently director of the Creative Writing program at the University of Colorado at Boulder.

Among the inspirators of Sukenick's theory of fiction are Laurence Sterne's *Tristram Shandy* (which balked against the conventions of fiction even before they had been codified), abstract expressionism (which, Sukenick contends, "got rid of that whole notion that art is apart from life, that it is something special which is siphoned or partitioned off from experience" [McCaffery interview, p. 294]), Joyce's *Finnegans Wake*, and the work of Samuel Beckett and Henry Miller (which undermined the notion of character in two different senses—by presenting characters who dissolve into other characters, or, alternately, by dramatizing people who deliberately seek to break down their own character structures). The major influence on Sukenick's work and thought, however, is Wallace Stevens, the subject of his dissertation and of his first published work, *Wallace Stevens: Musing the Obscure* (1967). "Adequate adjustment to the present can only be achieved," Sukenick argued there, "through ever fresh perception of it, and this is the effort of [Stevens'] poetry." It is the effort of Sukenick's fiction as well.

The aesthetic in which these disparate ideas and voices culminate is one underpinned by a few significant critical premises. The conception of the world implicit in the mimetic novel is no longer ours. Consequently, that novel must be replaced by one that reflects more accurately "the texture of our lives," it being art's fundamental struggle to "rescue the truth of our experience" from the duplicities of inadequate explanations, from outmoded forms of interpretation and sense-making. This reinvented novel insists on its existence as a physical object as well as an imaginative structure, its technological reality asserted throughout by textual self-reference and through the use of graphics, unconventional typographies, and eccentric narrative strategies. Similarly, the novel's author makes his composing process an explicit concern of his text, recognizing that that process differs little from the daily human necessity of composing one's reality, and that readers read novels in part as exemplary—if artistically heightened—models of that process. Rather than seeking to interpret this novel, the reader is led to see that its opacity discourages such analytical penetration; the process it enacts is to be experienced for its own sake, not as a representation of some other experience or as an occasion for critical excavation. And finally, because this novel is self-conscious about its own operations, it holds out greater hope than literary realism (with its suspension of disbelief and illusionist presuppositions) ever did of getting past all the constructs, including its own, to something like truth—"some truth," as Sukenick puts it, "beyond your personal vision and beyond literature itself" (McCaffery interview, p. 282).

That Sukenick's own fiction moves well beyond conventional literary realism is undeniable; whether its rejection of that mode moves it closer to the real than the method it displaces is less certain, even to the innovator. Among his experiments at introducing greater chunks of reality into fiction are "Roast Beef: A Slice of Life," which consists of a transcript of a tape recording of Ronald and Lynn Sukenick's prandial dialogue, and "Momentum," in which Sukenick recounts a moment of ecstatic happiness, attempting to seize its headlong rush by taping his response immediately afterward and transcribing that into print. ("What else is writing for . . . but . . . to capture those moments in their crudeness duplicity blind egotism," the narrator of "Momentum" wonders, but the story's contrapuntal glosses, apparently added by Sukenick in greater tranquility, effectively point up the futility of this method of appropriating life into fiction.) "The Death of the Novel," which gives Sukenick's ironically titled *The Death of the Novel and Other Stories* (1969) its name, entangles itself with the real by mixing fictional narrative, autobiography, lectures by Professor Sukenick on the state of fiction, and diverse other matters, the story operating on a "principle of simultaneous multiplicity" that closely approximates the mental atmosphere in which we live.

The same principle is at work in Sukenick's much-acclaimed first novel, *UP* (1968), which incorporates fantasies, literary parodies, autobiographical reminiscences, passages from a narrative called *The Adventures of Strop*

Banally and a review of that unpublished Sukenick work, debates between Sukenick and another character over the effectiveness of *UP*, and so on. All of these elements are presented in an unrestrained outpouring of narrative material that refuses to treat any of them as more "real" or verisimilar that any of the others. "I just make it up as I go along," Sukenick grandly confesses in the novel's final pages as he identifies a few of the characters of *UP* who are utter fabrications and then introduces Lynn Sukenick, Steve Katz,* and other "real" people who are attending his novel-completion celebration, "Though it's all true what I've written, every word of it. I insist on that" (*UP*, p. 329).

If "The Death of the Novel" and *UP* represent late 1960s-style examinations of the novel's much-touted exhaustion, Sukenick's subsequent fictions are attempts to revive or reinvent it. *Out* (1973) explores the spatial possibilities of the novel by presenting a narrative that diminishes with geometrical precision as it proceeds, its movement approximating the shape of the novel one of Sukenick's personae hopes to create: "a book like a cloud that changes as it goes." This movement corresponds to that of the novel's characters, revolutionaries traveling away from the plots, congestion, and endless interrelatedness of New York life to the openness of a California beach, their quest echoed by the novel's parallel course toward a way Out, its gathering acceleration toward the utter blankness of the book's final 11 pages. Whereas *Out* depicts the quest's goal as a blankness innocent of the preconceptions and interpretations that distort our relations with reality, *98.6* (1975) figures it as a holy land, a Palestine embraced by a new Mosaic law—"the law of mosaics, or how to deal with parts in the absence of wholes." The "children of Frankenstein" (read America) seek escape from the normality—*98.6*—of 1970s American life and find it in the "state of Israel," a not utterly actual place presided over by Tanta Golda Meir and Robert Kennedy, who has survived an Arab's attack on his life. Sukenick doesn't treat this promised land without humor (at the same time he's entering it, he's also sitting in Laguna Beach petting a cat), but the chapter nonetheless represents the realization of ideals that permeate his fiction. It is there that he learns that "Only experience can restore that lost synthesis which analysis has forced us to shatter. Experience alone can decide on truth." "In the state of Israel," Meir teaches him, "you become an illogical positivist" (*98.6*, p. 186).

Long Talking Bad Conditions Blues (1979) is what its title describes: a blues meditation in prose. Its characters are men and women confronting "new conditions"—post-1960s disillusionment, the instability of love relationships, the risk of vanishing into the world's "gaping holes" ("that nothing on the other side of something death sleep shadows phantoms ambiguities contradictions paradoxes uncertainties"), the disappearance of the Dodgers from Brooklyn—and finding no "Palestine" at the end of their journeys, the narrative's lack of punctuation reinforcing the last line's assertion that "things didn't have beginnings and endings in that sense they just start and then they stop" (p. 114). "The movement of the writing codifies the energetic life being lived" in this talking blues narrative, Jerome Klinkowitz,* Sukenick's most perceptive commentator, has argued; "more than anything else, *Long Talking Bad Conditions Blues* reads as a testimony to living in the world. The author remains so open to experience that experience is finally all we have, no more or less valuable than the record of a Charlie Parker solo or a Jackson Pollock drip painting" (*Literary Disruptions*, p. 221). Or, to use Sukenick's own metaphor from "The Endless Short Story: Dong Wang": "It's the tip of the long line we keep drawing, each one of us. It's part of the big picture we're all painting together. The big picture is that there is no big picture. That's why we keep painting it."

Selected Bibliography

Primary Sources

Wallace Stevens: Musing the Obscure. New York: New York University Press, 1967.
UP. New York: Dial Press, 1968.
The Death of the Novel and Other Stories. New York: Dial Press, 1969.
Out. Chicago: Swallow Press, 1973.
98.6. New York: Fiction Collective, 1975.
Long Talking Bad Conditions Blues. New York: Fiction Collective, 1979.

Secondary Sources

Adams, Timothy Dow. "Obscuring the Muse: The Mock-Autobiographies of Ronald Sukenick." *Critique* 20, no. 1 (1978): 27–39.
Federman, Raymond. "In." *Partisan Review* 41, no. 1 (1974): 137–42.
Karl, Frederick. *American Fictions 1940–80*. New York: Harper & Row, 1984.
Klinkowitz, Jerome. *Literary Disruptions*. 2d ed. Urbana: University of Illinois Press, 1980.
———. and Roy R. Behrens. *The Life of Fiction*. Urbana: University of Illinois Press, 1977.
Kutnik, Jerzy, *The Novel as Performance: The Fiction of Ronald Sukenick and Raymond Federman*. Carbondale: Southern Illinois University Press, 1985.
McCaffery, Larry. "An Interview with Ronald Sukenick." *Anything Can Happen: Interviews with Contemporary American Novelists*. Urbana: University of Illinois Press, 1983, pp. 279–97.
Noel, Daniel. "Tales of Fictive Power: Dreaming and Imagining in Ronald Sukenick's Postmodern Fiction." *boundary 2* 2, no. 5 (1976): 117–35.
Pearce, Richard. *The Novel in Motion*. Columbus: Ohio State University Press, 1983.

PETER J. BAILEY

T

THEROUX, ALEXANDER (1939–)

Critics aren't sure what to make of Alexander Theroux, Paul's quasi-mysterious older brother. Anthony Burgess calls him a "word-drunk Rabelais," placing him among our most revered writers of comic-satiric fiction, among Rabelais and Swift, Nabokov and Joyce; while Jack Beatty calls his prose "logorrhea": an incessant and bubbling spume of mere poison farts and gasses—the word as diarrhea. Somewhere between lies the fiction of Alexander Theroux. It is an ornate and exuberant prose style that blends wild satire, outrageous erudition, and elaborate verbal gaming. His two novels, *Three Wogs* and *Darconville's Cat*, are brilliantly spirited and fun loving—the sprawling, further adventures of *Tristram Shandy*, without all the dashes.

Alexander Louis Theroux was born in Medford, Massachusetts, in 1939, the son of a salesman. He studied at St. Francis College in Biddeford, Maine, and also did postgraduate work at the University of Virginia. He has a doctoral degree in English literature. According to one biographical source, Theroux had intense religious study, spending two years of silence in a Trappist monastery, which he later left to become a novice in a Franciscan seminary. Theroux might very well have been a monk and a novice; then again, this is the kind of outrageous "fact" he would probably delight in sneaking past unsuspecting reviewers. I prefer to let it stand, unencumbered by the petty demands of historical accuracy. (One thinks of Flann O'Brien and his relationship to Algerian basket-weavers.) Theroux has worked at various schools and universities, including Longwood College of Farmville, Virginia, and Harvard University. In addition to his novels, he has published children's books, poetry, and essays. His numerous articles have appeared in such magazines as *Esquire* and the *National Review*.

Currently, he is writer-in-residence at Phillips Academy, Andover, Massachusetts.

Alexander Theroux's first novel, *Three Wogs* (1972), is ostensibly an indictment of bigots; a wog is an English slang term for any dark-skinned non-Englishman. But social issues are all but buried beneath the wild, imaginative barrage of the author: The book is really about Theroux's unique performance with language, a writer's exploration of—and preoccupation with—style. On any given page one finds him discussing the auditory delights of the Crapper flushing system next to a philosophical argument against the doctrine of original sin; or a quick history of Wolsey, Henry VIII, Lambeth Palace, and Castlereagh (all in one page!) next to a startling pronouncement that bedwetting can be cured by "the habitual wearing of a sterilized, papally blessed rubber snood, appended to the weenie by an elastic band." Perhaps only a man with two years of utter religious silence under his alb could write a phrase like that. In *Three Wogs* one finds not merely snoods but two types of pygmies: hydrocephalic and schinocephalic. There are imported Grobians and axeheaded Harridans; Rechabites; and a poison-dart-blowing Chinaman named Yannum Fun. There are lofty discussions of Herodotus and Diocletian, along with examinations of the phrenological structures of spadoons. In short, there is the serious, the comic, the erudite, the nonsensical, the social, the philosophical, the lyrical, the historical—all of these converging and combining on the page, crossing and recrossing, vying for attention. It is the energy of this dense and magical overlay of language that makes Theroux's fiction the powerful creative gestalt that it is.

Darconville's Cat (1981) is a riotous, 704-page novel about what happens when the tumid glands of love and learning spring a leak. Darconville, a university professor, gets himself caught in an absurd, almost Lolitan love affair with one of his students. This novel in firmly set in the Nabokov-goes-to-college, anti-academic tradition; one senses the perverse, lyrical rantings of Humbert, as well as the furtive gazes of both Kinbote and John Shade, peering through the gnarled ivy and the waxwings. As in *Three Wogs*, the plot of this novel—this time unrequited love—is merely a thin outline from which the author departs in order to make elegant and outrageous language happen; in this sense, Theroux's style is self-indulgent in the very best possible way. Readers beware: his encyclopedic mind propels the narrative at a frenetic pace, manipulating and juggling a variety of tones and parallels, thematic symmetries, and rhetorical devices. He will have you scouring your Bulfinch and your dictionary. *Darconville's Cat* is grounded in Greek myth, Elizabethan drama, German romanticism, and outrageous diction (words like "dehortatory," "meditabund," and "scrobiculate"). Theroux also possesses the technical expertise needed for brilliant parody. The novel includes vulgar sermons and limericks, pornography (an "exhilarating fuel-burner," starring Rafe and Rhoda Rumpswab), sonnets, formal essays, a variety of philosophical disputations, a dialogue in blank verse, a satanic hymn for the dead, a diary, classical allusions and epigrams, a misogynist's bibliography, and a digression on ears, in the manner of Sterne's noses and Gogol's nose. These countless and elaborately skilled parodies make *Darconville's Cat* a stunning pastiche of literary modes; yet, the novel is much more than mere parody or literary imitation. Theroux uses all of these fictive devices in brilliant subordination to the novel's unifying theme: reconciling the ephemeral (passions) with the eternal (art). It is no less than the major thrust of our greatest literature: Dante and Beatrice, Cervantes and Dulcinea, Joyce and Molly Bloom, Nabokov and Lolita, all of whom, and I include Theroux and his Isabel in this group, have struggled with the contradiction inherent in passion, in time. It is no mere accident that the final line of *Darconville's Cat* reads, "Sorrow is the cause of immortal conceptions."

It is not far-fetched to mention Theroux's work in the same breath with writers like Nabokov, Dante, and James Joyce; in fact, his fiction can be seen as a kind of baroque synthesis of a variety of major writers, writers whose common thread has always been the careful and exquisite crafting of the sentence itself. This is the tradition of the prose stylist, a tradition that reflects the shimmering presence of superior creative intellects, the mastery of a craft. It is not far-fetched to consider Alexander Theroux's prose in light of this tradition; I agree with Anthony Burgess.

Selected Bibliography

Primary Sources

Three Wogs. Boston: Gambit, Inc., 1972.
Darconville's Cat. Garden City, N.Y.: Doubleday, 1981.

Secondary Sources

Beatty, Jack. "Logorrhea!" *The New Republic* 184 (April 4, 1981), pp. 38–40.
Bradham, Jo Allen. "The American Scholar: From Emerson to Alexander Theroux's *Darconville's Cat.*" *Critique* (Summer 1983): 215–27.
DeMott, Benjamin. "Awash with Lists and Catalogs." *New York Times Book Review*, May 3, 1981, pp. 9, 30–31.
Riley, Carolyn, and Barbara Harte, eds. "Alexander Theroux." *Contemporary Literary Criticism*, Vol. 2. Detroit: Gale Research Co., 1974, p. 433.

BRUCE KUTNEY

THOMAS, D. M. (1935–   )

D(onald) M(ichael) Thomas was born in Cornwall, England, on January 27, 1935. He was educated there, in Australia, and at New College, Oxford, where he got a first in English. While doing his national service he learned Russian, which was to have a profound influence on his writing. After 15 years as a senior lecturer in English at the Hereford College of Education, he went back to Oxford in 1978 to do research in problems of verse translation. At present he is a full-time writer. While at Oxford, Thomas was told by his ex-tutor John Bayley that he would be a late developer. The truth of this remark was demonstrated by Thomas' career, for in his mid-forties he made a switch from writing rather undistinguished poetry to writing genuinely innovative fiction. Although he still writes poetry and has translated Russian poetry, it is as a novelist that Thomas will continue to be known most widely. For a serious writer he has also been quite prolific, having published five novels in six years.

Despite the bewilderment critics have expressed about the meaning of Thomas' novels, he is widely recognized as one of the most inventive and resourceful novelists writing in English. His last three novels belong squarely to the spirit of postmodern experimentalism by virtue of the tension that exists in them between the compulsion to explore the individual psyche and history, and their concern with the procedures of fiction-making itself. Thomas' novels are preoccupied with vital contemporary issues: with the complex relationship between Eros and Thanatos both in the individual and in modern history, with the ambivalent relationship between totalitarianism and creativity, with the attractions and repulsions of polymorphous sexuality, with the perils of rationalism and analytic criticism, and with types and strategies of fiction writing. In his treatment of these issues he has displayed remarkable structural virtuosity and stylistic versatility.

Thomas' first novel, *The Flute Player* (1979), was the winner of the Gollanz/Picador/Guardian Fantasy Competition. It is an historically allusive (to the Holocaust and the Berlin Wall) fantasy-cum-fable set in some vaguely East European repressive state, peopled with characters who are not individuals but types. The novel poetically explores the relationship between political anarchy and artistic creativity. It provides a harrowing and yet uplifting picture of the artist *in extremis*. Repression is seen to be both a terrible threat to, and a necessary condition of, art. The central figure in the novel, Elena, the Eternal Woman, is not only a symbol of the irrepressible impulses toward art but is also, through her beauty and rich humanity and her roles as sexual therapist, a Florence Nightingale, psychoanalyst, mother-figure and repository of poems, a vital inspiration to the victimized artist. But at the same time the poetess who finds herself in the democratic, affluent West bemoans "the blankness of freedom... this urbanity and suavity, this not having anything to push against."

Thomas' next novel, *Birthstone* (1980), is original in intention but desultory in execution and unconvincing structurally. The narrator is a schizophrenic in search of domestic happiness and in futile flight from her alter egos, one of which is promiscuous and foul-mouthed and the other brutal and anarchic. The record of her adventures in Cornwall is a blend of realistic observation occasionally rooted in historical facts, much free bizarre fantasizing, and hiatuses where the alter egos violently intrude. She claims for herself a "creative power [which] seemed a compensation given to all disintegrated personalities." Hence the periods of "oceanic feeling" of both guilt and communion that the protagonist experiences. The flaws in the novel are the lack of connection between the narrator's quest and the remarkable scenes of the senior citizen Lola and the acceleration into old age of her son (both of whom have wriggled through the birthstone), and the lack of a normalizing ironic perspective to provide relief from the oppressiveness of the first-person narrative.

The White Hotel (1981), Thomas' third novel, was a close runner-up to Salman Rushdie's *Midnight's Children* for the Booker-McConnell Prize and has won international acclaim. Its film rights have recently been sold for a half million dollars. It is Thomas' most original and profound meditation on the complex relationship between Eros and Thanatos. The novel operates on the psychoanalytical, moral, and historical levels and deploys a variety of styles: epistolary, pastiche, verse, and documentary. The intricate coherence of the first four sections is due to Thomas' brilliant literary exploration of the procedures and symbolism of psychoanalysis. The process of psychoanalysis is grippingly pastiched with all the patient's avowals, retractions, hostility, and gratitude as she is led by Freud, himself limited by his own psychological make-up, toward an incomplete but satisfactory cure. Where the structure is controversial is in the articulation between the first four sections and the Babi-Yar sections. The irony of a woman who has largely freed herself from psychic repression and achieved happiness becoming a casualty of history is poignant. But despite the Freudian allusions to the death instinct in society, despite the references to Jung which imply that in the Bad-Gastein sections it is Europe's traumas that Lisa is struggling with, not just her own, and despite Lisa's capacity for precognitions, the extended fabric of images and symbols with their meanings horrifyingly accomplished or horrifyingly reversed (the corset, the bayonet) strikes the reader as being literary and superimposed. Lisa's end has little to do with her fantasies. Yet what Thomas has attempted is admirable: it is a corrective to the oversimplified socioeconomic or religious explanations of the sadistic, orgiastic deliriums of our age. The muted radiance of the final sequence posits the *possibility* of a society in which Eros reigns, but which, contrasted with the brutal historical reality of "The Sleeping Carriage," has the effect of a desperate wish fulfillment.

In *Ararat* (1983), Thomas' preoccupation with sex, genocide, and totalitarianism persists and is incorporated in an even more ingenious narrative machinery. In addition, we have a new preoccupation with the art of improvisation. The most powerful and impressive of the improvisations is the central core of the *Egyptian Nights* with its interchangeable endings that destroy any pretense to verisimilitude and that betray the lack of courage (possessed by the true creative writer, such as Pushkin) of the degenerate improviser to complete the story with the death of his own alter ego. The murderous political climate of our age is represented by the symbolic compendium of genocide, the spectral figure of Finn. In most of Thomas' novels, the narrators are peculiarly repulsive creatures obsessed with sex and power and given to obscene language. In this novel (and in the next, *Swallow*), Rozanov and Surkov are meant to be types of the fraudulent artist bred by totalitarianism. But owing to the lack of an ironic perspective, the assault on the reader's sensibilities is bought at the expense of critical placement.

Thomas' most recent book, *Swallow* (1984), is not just a sequel to *Ararat*; it swallows the previous novel. In it allusions and echoes proliferate until it becomes impossible to draw the line between fact and fiction, the mundane and the supernatural, the erotic and the pornographic, the serious and the comic, prose and poetry, the original and the pastiche, and, above all, between people's consciousnesses. The novel derives part of its inspiration from Thomas' itch to debunk critics and criticism, although in doing so he has his cake and eats it. He humorously parodies the critic's fondness for identifying levels and pouncing on plagiarism, yet there's no denying the presence of multiple levels and plagiarism, however "scandalously amended," in his novels. But the comedy of *Swallow* (already discernible in *Ararat* in Surkov's interview) is its most distinctive feature. It is present not only in the structure and styles, but also in individual episodes, such as the interview with an American President whose senility only allows him to answer the question-before-last, thereby producing absurd juxtapositions.

With this last novel, Thomas has reached an impasse. Another mirror in his hall of mirrors would surely be redundant. It will be interesting to see what direction his next novel takes from the brilliant hermeticism of *Ararat/Swallow*.

Selected Bibliography

Primary Sources

Two Voices. London: Grossman, 1968.
Logan's Stone. London: Grossman, 1971.
Love and Other Deaths. London: Grossman, 1975.
The Flute Player. New York: Viking Press, 1979.
Birthstone. New York: Viking Press, 1980.
The White Hotel. New York: Viking Press, 1981.
Ararat. New York: Viking Press, 1983.
Swallow. New York: Viking Press, 1984.

Secondary Sources

Barnsley, John H. "*The White Hotel*." *The Antioch Review* 40, no. 4 (Fall 1982): 448–60.

Kinder, Marsha. "The Spirit of *The White Hotel.*" *Humanities in Society* 4, nos. 2–3 (1981): 143–70.

ASOKE CHANDA

TODOROV, TZVETAN (1939–)

With the emergence in the late 1960s of structuralism as a movement in philosophy, science, and literary criticism, the works of Tzvetan Todorov— like those of Roland Barthes*—acquired a sudden popularity. While Barthes' theoretical shifts have often surprised his readers, Todorov has quite often been considered a didactic and orthodox structuralist. However, a closer look at his writings shows a profound evolution from the very formalistic studies of his early period to his present preoccupation with questions of ethics.

Tzvetan Todorov was born in Sofia (Bulgaria) on March 1, 1939. He studied slavic philology at the University of Sofia, where he graduated in 1961. Two years later he moved to Paris, where he still lives. In 1966 he became *docteur de troisième cycle* at the University of Paris and in 1971 *docteur d'Etat et lettres*. Since 1968 he has been a researcher at the National Center for Scientific Research, where he is now *maître de recherche*. During the 1970s he often taught and lectured in various American universities.

The fact that Todorov belongs to two different cultures puts him in the privileged position of looking at cultural alterities from outside. When he arrived in Paris in 1963, he realized just how poor the state of French literary theory was. His education in Russian formalism, German romantic theories, and Anglo-American (New) Critical texts, provided him with the background on which to base his critique of French historical and thematic criticism. His first step was to provide French-speaking scholars with the first anthology of Russian formalism (*Théories de la littérature*, 1965). In the following years, Todorov carried out his purpose of renewing French literary studies, not only through his numerous works, but also by co-directing with Gerard Genette the celebrated "Poétique" series of the Editions du Seuil, in which several studies of narratology and rhetoric were published. Furthermore, in 1970 Todorov was among the founders and editors of the international journal of literary theory, *Poétique*.

Together with Barthes and with other *nouveaux critiques*, Todorov strongly opposed traditional criticism and proposed, instead, what he called a science of literature. Science, he claimed, was not to be understood in the same terms as the natural sciences, but as analogous to structuralist linguistics: if, in linguistics, one must think of a general theory of language and not only of different languages, likewise, in literary studies, one must consider the categories of critical discourse and not only individual inter-pretations. Structuralism, then became for Todorov a synonym for the elaboration of a theory of literature, that is, a necessary theoretical basis for interpretation.

In this light, Todorov's move from semiotic studies of poetics and genres (such as the celebrated *The Fantastic: A Structural Approach to a Literary Genre*, 1970) to a general theory of the symbol (*Theories of the Symbol*, 1977; and *Symbolism and Interpretation*, 1978) and, more recently, to individual interpretations of texts, should not be viewed as a radical change of perspective, as a *kehre*, but—as he has explicitly pointed out—as a necessary evolution. In fact, after some neglected narrative and stylistic aspects of the literary analysis had received the attention they deserved, Todorov began applying the new instruments to texts.

In the last four or five years, a literary genre which Todorov calls exemplary plot has become his main object of study. In *The Conquest of America* (1982), for example, he retells the story of the conquest of America by means of quotations and reports, calling into question principles of ethics on which the problematics of alterity is based. Most recently, his interests have moved from a remote "other" (the American Indians) to the way French philosophers, writers, politicians, and scholars have treated problematics of the individual and the social, of us and the other, of primitive and civilized peoples, and of the other within us (e.g., "L'Etre et l'Autre: Montaigne," 1983).

Todorov's obsession with alterity comes from his reading of Mikhail Bakhtine's controversial notion of dialogism. (See *Mikhail Bakhtine le principe dialogique*, 1981.) Following Bakhtine, Todorov argues that both literature and criticism have a relation to human truth. Dialogic criticism, he writes in his autobiographical "Une critique dialogique?" (1984), "speaks not about the works, but to the works or rather with the works." Therefore, the critic should attempt to let *all* the voices of the text speak, questioning them and, if necessary, opposing them. This is precisely what Todorov does in his latest volume, *Critique de la critique*, a text in which, through some exemplary plots of twentieth-century literary criticism, he discusses how literature has been considered, what should be a "right" way of considering it, and what are the ideological stakes that correspond to its evolution.

If, on the one hand, Todorov has abandoned his early radical formalism rooted in a positivistic project, he has on the other, rejected an approach he calls nihilistic, such as the position of those who, following Nietzsche and Jacques Derrida,* claim that everything is interpretation. Nevertheless, he does not propose a neutral or eclectic stance. Rather, he argues, the future of dialogical criticism resides in the possible *articulations* of antinomies such as positivism and nihilism, dogmatism and scepticism, and so on. According to him, this dialogical perspective can be perceived in the radical heterogeneity of some contemporary literature, such as the fiction of Solzhenitsyn, Milan Kundera,* Günter Grass,* D. M. Thomas,* or, more explicitly, in the works of philosophers such as Jürgen Habermas and Todorov's most recent discovery, the French Luc Ferry. For many different reasons, as he puts it in his "Une critique dialogique?," our contemporary condition appears to provide a particular chance for a dialogical criticism: "one must hurry up and catch it."

Selected Bibliography

Primary Sources

Théories de la littérature, Textes des formalistes russes (Theories of Literature: Texts of the Russian Formalists). ed. Paris: Seuil, 1965.

Grammaire du "Decameron" ("A Grammar of The Decameron"). The Hague: Mouton, 1969.

Introduction à la littérature fantastique. Paris: Seuil, 1970. (*The Fantastic: A Structural Approach to a Literary Genre*. Trans. Richard Howard. Cleveland: Press of Case Western Reserve University, 1973; rpt., Ithaca, N.Y.: Cornell University Press, 1975.)

Poetique de la prose. Paris: Seuil, 1971. (*The Poetics of Prose*. Trans. Richard Howard. Ithaca, N.Y.: Cornell University Press, 1977.)

Dictionnaire encyclopedique des sciences du langage (with Osavald Ducrot). Paris: Seuil, 1972. (*Encyclopedic Dictionary of the Sciences of Language*. Trans. Catherine Porter. Baltimore: Johns Hopkins University Press, 1979.)

Poetique. Paris: Seuil, 1968 and 1973. (*Introduction to Poetics*. Trans. Richard Howard. Minneapolis: University of Minnesota Press, 1981.)

Théories du symbole. Paris: Seuil, 1977. (*Theories of the Symbol*. Trans. Catherine Porter. Ithaca, N.Y.: Cornell University Press, 1982.)

Symbolisme et interpretation. Paris: Seuil, 1978. (*Symbolism and Interpretation*. Trans. Catherine Porter. Ithaca, N.Y.: Cornell University Press, 1982.)

Les Genres du discours (Genres of Discourse). Paris: Seuil, 1978.

Mikhail Bakhtine le principe dialogique (Mikhail Bakhtine: The Dialogical Principle). Paris: Seuil, 1981.

La Conquête de l'Amérique, La Question de l'autre. Paris: Seuil, 1982. (*The Conquest of America*. Trans. Richard Howard. New York: Harper & Row, 1984.)

French Literary Theory Today, ed. Cambridge: Cambridge University Press and Paris: Editions de la Maison des Sciences de l'homme, 1982.

"L'Être et l'Autre: Montaigne." *Yale French Studies* 64 (1983): 113–44.

Critique de la critique. Paris: Seuil, 1985.

Secondary Sources

Brooks, Peter. "Introduction" to Todorov's *Introduction to Poetics*, pp. vii–xix.
Culler, Jonathan. *Structuralist Poetics*. Ithaca, N.Y.: Cornell University Press, 1975.
Hawkes, Terence. *Structuralism and Semiotics*. London: Methuen, 1977.

Scholes, Robert. *Structuralism in Literature: An Introduction*. New Haven, Conn.: Yale University Press, 1974.

STEFANO ROSSO

TOURNIER, MICHEL (1924–   )

Despite a relatively small body of fiction published to date—five novels, one collection of short stories—Michel Tournier has already achieved that enviable distinction of being both commercially successful and critically consecrated by the literary establishment. Each of his works is primarily characterized by the utilization of a mythological framework, drawn variously from antiquity, Christianity, English colonialism, or Prussia, to inform a complex metaphysical and existentialist interrogation in which the two *maîtres à penser* are undoubtedly Spinoza and Jean-Paul Sartre. Questions of transcendence, immigrant labor, solitude, intimacy, sexuality, and war are explored in texts that move with extraordinary ease and humor from the scatological to the sacred, and back again in a narrative form where a semiotics-inspired reading act is perhaps the most remarkable feature.

Tournier's early studies, both at the Sorbonne and, after the war, at Tübingen, seemed to destine him for a teaching career in philosophy: personal contacts with Gaston Bachelard and Jean-Paul Sartre were followed by academic exploration of German and Dutch metaphysics, before the shock of failure in the 1947 *agrégation* forced him to reconsider his future plans. After spending some time in translation and private radio, Tournier decided to devote some 18 months to an embryonic novel, *Friday or the Other Island*, which was published in 1967 and awarded the Grand Prix de l'Académie Française.

The novel reveals immediately many of the principal concerns that were to remain Tournier's: the transformational capacity of myth to mediate between philosophy and fiction, by providing a paradigm both recognizable and exploitable; a predilection for widespread elemental symbolism, binary oppositions, provocative and/or humorous inversions; a thematic tissue in which initiation, sexuality, solitude, and childhood are fundamental.

Three years later, Tournier's second novel, *The Erl-King* (1970), confirmed its author's rare talent amidst a generation shrivelled by arid formalism, when it became the first unanimous selection by a Goncourt jury since that prize's inception. The hero, Abel Tiffauges, is an incipient ogre. Throughout the novel he seeks, charts, and deciphers that vast multiplicity of signs that mark the stages in this ambivalent vocation: tender but devouring, serving but enslaving, carrying but carrying off. A rich mythological background is invoked, ranging from Cronos, Tiresias, Cyclops, and Hercules to Colin-Maillard, Gilles de Rais, Göring, and Hitler, but in which

Goethe's Erlkönig (*Le Roi des Aulnes*) and Saint Christopher are preeminent. This allows the writer ample scope to echo and expand the resonance of his subject. The final apotheosis, in which an all-consuming love and sense of sacrifice dominate, sees the protagonist assuming the full mantle of the mythical ogre, but also being illuminated by the beneficent light of Saint Christopher.

It was *Gemini* in 1975 which, in its regular juxtaposition of the scatological and the sacred, unleashed the fury of several critics. Tournier has quite properly argued that such a juxtaposition is part of a necessary and valid humanizing process that compels the transcendental to be rooted in reality, and thereby reflects a resolutely interrogative existentialism. The novel is certainly the most contentious to date, for it also offers a virulent attack on heterosexuality, a disdainful glance at lesbianism, but a joyful embracing of the gratuitousness of male homosexuality, alongside a supposedly principal theme which, seeking to express gradations of Otherness, becomes, not surprisingly, somewhat lost.

Perhaps not unrelated to this unsatisfactory thematic and structural balance is the continuing reduction the novel demonstrates with regard to any mythic pre-text (Genette's "hypotexte"). *Friday or the Other Island* was able to rediscover, invert, and expand the considerable body of writing on Crusoe that was Defoe's; *The Erl-King* incorporates imaginatively the multiple recorded manifestations of one central and momentous mythological type; but in *Gemini*, although the mythologizing mode of thought remains, the specific mythical substance is extremely slight, little more than the loose association of Castor and Pollux, Romulus and Remus, with twinship, meteorology, and violent dispute. From the fragility of this framework—and despite a certain coherence at the level of symbol and sign—there seems to ensue a general and unsatisfactory artistic instability overall.

The same is not true of the fourth novel, *The Four Wise Men* (1980), for, although once again Tournier reveals himself to be boldly mythopoeic, this time it is with an original substance which, however textually slight, is nevertheless solidly enshrined in every Western reader. For the laconic existing story of the three wise men, briefly told in the first 12 verses of Matthew 2 but frequently and unforgettably visualized in medieval iconography, is expanded in a work that furnishes three detailed biographies and an account of each of their quests, journeys, and discoveries. Indeed, Tournier goes further and resurrects the legend of a fourth wise man, who set off in time but arrived 33 years too late. Prince Taor, hooked on candy, sets out initially seeking *le Divin Confiseur* whose star astrologers have noted, and from whom he hopes to obtain the recipe for the celestial pistachio-flavored Turkish delight. From this derisory beginning, and after 33 years of hard labor in the salt mines of Sodome—a punishment accepted on behalf of an unknown pauper—Taor arrives at Joseph of Arimathea's house only minutes after Christ's departure from the Last Supper, but in time to enjoy the remnants of the bread and wine. He thus becomes the first partaker of Holy Eucharist and thereafter, dying, the first martyr of Christendom. Interwoven into this reanimated biblical framework in typical Tournier fashion are ideas that range from sacrifice and nonviolence to négritude and the rehabilitation of the image into Christian art.

Tournier's most recent novel, *Gilles et Jeanne* (1983), associates starkly but plausibly two powerfully evocative figures of medieval history and legend: Gilles de Rais, the source of Bluebeard, and Joan of Arc, the Maid of Orleans. The enigmatic interpenetration of two itineraries both of which led inexorably to the stake and expiation by fire—the one through heroism, glory, and selflessness, the other through satanism, sodomy, and murder—is again fiercely provocative in terms of our accepted notions of both history and morality. But what may perhaps be most interesting ultimately is an orality and a striking succinctness which, following the considerable narrative fragmentation of *The Four Wise Men*, would seem to adumbrate an evolution of potentially major proportions in which Tournier the philosopher-novelist very much becomes Tournier the novelist-philosopher. *The Four Wise Men* shows that the communication of ideas via the transformational usage of myth remains his basic mode, but the dense semiotic symbolism and reference of the early novels is in the process of being lightened in favor of a form that makes far greater demands on the creativity, rather than the cultural intelligence, of the reader. The future is indeed, it would seem, an open book.

Selected Bibliography

Primary Sources

Vendredi ou les limbes du Pacifique. Paris: Gallimard, 1967. (*Friday or the Other Island*. Trans. Norman Denny. New York: Doubleday, 1969.)
Le Roi des Aulnes. Paris: Gallimard, 1970. (*The Erl-King*. London: Collins, 1972.)
Les Meteores. Paris: Gallimard, 1975. (*Gemini*. London: Collins, 1977.)
Le Vent paraclet (The Paraclete). Paris: Gallimard, 1977.
Le Coq de bruyere. Paris: Gallimard, 1978. (*The Fetichist and Other Stories*. Trans. Barbara Wright. New York: Doubleday, 1984.)
Gaspard, Melchior et Balthazar. Paris: Gallimard, 1980. (*The Four Wise Men*. Trans. Ralph Manheim. London: Collins, 1982.)
Gilles et Jeanne. Paris: Gallimard, 1983.

Secondary Sources

Bevan, David. *Michel Tournier*. The Hague: Rodopi, in press.
Cloonan, William. *Michel Tournier*. Boston: Twayne Publishers, in press.
Delueuze, Giles, "Une théorie d'autrui," *Critique* 20, no. 241 (1982): 503-25.
Maury, Pierre. "Michel Tournier ou la perversion du myths," *Revue Générale* 113, no. 1 (1981): 15–33.

DAVID BEVAN

V

VARGAS LLOSA, MARIO (1936–   )

The Peruvian Mario Vargas Llosa stands among the three or four most lauded novelists of the "Boom" in Latin American fiction. At the age of 50, he has to his credit a formidable array of novels, which have been widely translated. Vargas Llosa's corrosive attacks on the social, political, cultural, and economic conditions of Peru reflect a deep dismay about the state of humankind. The corruption of institutions, the falsification of honor, and the fragmentation of personality are persistent themes in his work. Although he eschews the magic realism that has become the hallmark of much contemporary Latin American writing, his manipulation of popular elements such as melodrama and sensationalism, his wild sense of humor, and his attraction to the grotesque push realism to its limits and at times lend the novels a phantasmagoric quality, while the discontinuous narrations, with their abrupt shifts in perspective, time, and place, suggest the precariousness of individual personality.

Vargas Llosa was born in Arequipa, Peru, on March 28, 1936 to a family of bourgeois background. As a child, he lived in Bolivia and in different parts of his own country. In 1957, having graduated from the University of San Marcos in Lima, he accepted a grant to study literature in Madrid, where he spent a year preparing a doctoral dissertation that was never to be presented. He remained in Europe until fairly recently, living principally in Paris, London, and Barcelona. In the early years, he scraped by financially, teaching Spanish and working in the news media. Success has allowed him to live more comfortably and less frantically. He has held visiting positions at the University of London, the University of Washington in Seattle, and Cambridge University. He and his second wife and their children now live in Lima.

Vargas Llosa's first novel, *The Time of the Hero* (1963), became a critical and popular success. It won two prestigious awards in Spain, came in second for the Prix Formentor, and has been published in over ten languages. For two years as a teenager, Vargas Llosa attended the Leoncio Prado Military Academy in Lima. The novel emerged from his experiences there. Through the voices of the cadets (the "dogs" of the Spanish title), he reveals the effects of imposing a rigid code of behavior, unresponsive to human needs, on unformed human material. The boys try to beat the system by developing an equally harsh code of their own, so that their rebellion only serves to confirm this systematic inhumanity.

The next novel, *The Green House* (1966), won, among other awards, the distinguished and lucrative Premio Rómulo Gallegos for the best novel published in Spanish for the last five years. This work, which involves a broad and varied cast of characters and a wide expanse in space and time, developed from Vargas Llosa's two excursions into the Amazon region. The exploitation of the Indians by rubber barons, the Church, and society in general is a major theme of this complex narrative, but it also relates the odyssey of a Japanese fortune hunter and the epic foundation of the Green House, the brothel that brings "civilization" to Piura, the little desert city where Vargas Llosa lived for a year as a child and where he later finished secondary school.

Within three years, Vargas Llosa published an even bigger and more complex novel, *Conversation in the Cathedral* (1969). The central figure, Santiago Zavallos, a disillusioned newspaperman who has rejected his bourgeois family but never quite succeeds in embracing another ideal, suggests what might have happened to the author had he not chosen to leave Peru, but here again Vargas Llosa is as interested in the interaction of groups as in the development of the individual consciousness. Although one of two primary speakers—the "conversation" between Zavallos and a one-time family retainer takes place over a period of some four hours in a dive named The Cathedral—Zavallos shares the novel with about 70 other voices. One critic has called the book an "orchestration of consciousness around an historical period"—1948–1963, the years preceding and following the Odrista regime in Peru. Important themes are the abuse of power at every level, the ambiguity of human motivation, the dilemma of the person of conscience who cannot escape his or her background, the stratification of society and, finally, the radical solitude of every individual. The conversation is really made up of two monologues that only occasionally intersect.

Captain Pantoja and the Special Service (1973) is Vargas Llosa's first out-and-out comic novel. Pantoja, a prudish career officer with a genius for administration, is commissioned by the Army to set up a flying squad of prostitutes to service the sex-starved and therefore disruptive recruits stationed in the Amazon. This operation runs head-on into the crusade led by Brother Francis, who advocates crucifixion as a means of achieving sanctity and whose converts tend to sanctify their neighbors by force. The narration, which interpolates broadcasts by a local radio personality, military reports, letters, newspaper accounts, and dreams, provides a commentary on the bureaucratic mind, on the tendency of systems to become self-propelling, on the disparity between official and real, between the outer and the inner person and, finally, on the difficulty of sustaining any coherent notion of identity outside of the institutions that confer that identity.

The use of popular elements, of melodrama and humor that we saw in *Captain Pantoja*, is even more marked in *Aunt Julia and the Scriptwriter* (1977). Here Vargas Llosa alternates chapters describing the discovery of his vocation as a writer and his courtship of his first wife, Julia Urquidi, the widow of his uncle, with chapters that purport to be segments of soap operas written by a colleague in the radio. The problems faced by the dedicated writer in a society that sets a low value on literature and by the individual who refuses to do what his or her family expects are central issues in this novel. Too, the scriptwriter, who gets his characters and plots monumentally confused and winds up shifting them from soap to soap, is a parody of Vargas Llosa himself.

Finally, *The War of the End of the World* (1981) is an historical novel, re-creating through the perspectives of a wide number and variety of characters the 1896 Canudos War in the Northeast of Brazil. The war, between the Brazilian Army and the devotees of the Counselor, a religious leader who attracted an extraordinary following, ended in the extirpation of the faithful. Although the novel adheres to a fairly straightforward chronological order, it once again shows Vargas Llosa's fondness for organizing a lot of characters and his persistent interest in irrational psychology and fanaticism.

In addition to the big novels, Vargas Llosa has published *The Cubs* (1967), a brilliant novella about a middle-class lad who is emasculated by a Great Dane; book-length critical studies of Gabriel García Márquez* and *Madame Bovary* (which is particularly interesting), along with numerous shorter critical pieces and other essays. His is a rich and varied work, yet all the fiction reveals a world of chaos and personal disorder conveyed through highly controlled narrative structures that provide pleasure in themselves. This basic tension, between the sense of frustration and failure that is his subject and the sense of satisfaction that arises from these well-made novels is the distinctive characteristic of Vargas Llosa's narrative art.

Selected Bibliography

Primary Sources

Los jefes. Barcelona: Editorial Rocas, 1959. (*The Cubs and Other Stories*. New York: Trans. Ronald Christ and Gregory Kolovakos. Harper & Row, 1979.)

La ciudad y los perros. Barcelona: Seix Barral, 1963. (*The Time of the Hero*. Trans. Lysander Kemp. New York: Grove Press, 1966.)

La Casa Verde. Barcelona: Seix Barral, 1966. (*The Green House*. Trans. Gregory Rabassa. New York: Harper & Row, 1968.)

Los cachorros, Pichula Cuellar. Barcelona: Lumen, 1967. (*The Cubs and Other Stories*. New York: Harper & Row, 1979.)

Conversación en la Catedral. Barcelona: Seix Barral, 1969. (*Conversation in the Cathedral*. Trans. Gregory Rabassa. New York: Harper & Row, 1975.)

Historia secreta de una novela (The Secret History of a Novel). Barcelona: Tusquets, 1971.

García Márquez: historia de un deicidio (Barcelona: Seix Barral, 1971.)

Pantaleón y las visitadoras. Barcelona: Seix Barral, 1973. (*Captain Pantoja and the Special Service*. Trans. Ronald Christ and Gregory Kolovakos. Harper & Row, 1979.)

La orgía perpetua: Flaubert y "Madame Bovary" (The Perpetual Orgy: Flaubert & "Madame Bovary"). Barcelona: Seix Barral, and Madrid: Taurus, 1975.

La tía Julia y el escribidor. Barcelona: Seix Barral, 1977. (*Aunt Julia and the Scriptwriter*. Trans. Helen R. Lane. New York: Farrar, Straus & Giroux, 1982.)

La señorita de Tacna (The Young Lady from Tacna). Barcelona: Seix Barral, 1981.

La guerra del fin del mundo. Barcelona: Seix Barral, 1981. (*The War of the End of the World*. Farrar, Straus, & Giroux, 1984.)

Kathie y el hipopótamo (Kathy and the Hippopotamus). Barcelona: Seix Barral, 1983.

Contra el viento y la marea (1962-1982). (Against the Wind and the Tide [1962-1982]). Barcelona: Seix Barral, 1983.

Historia de Mayta (The Story of Mayta). Barcelona: Seix Barral, 1984.

Secondary Sources

Brotherston, Gordon. "Social Structures: Mario Vargas Llosa." In *The Emergence of The Latin American Novel*. Cambridge: Cambridge University Press, 1977, pp. 110–21.

Davis, Mary E. "William Faulkner and Mario Vargas Llosa: The Election of Failure." *Comparative Literature Studies* 16 (1979): 332–43.

Jones, Julie. "The Search for Paradise in Captain Pantoja and the Special Service." *Latin American Literary Review* 9 (Fall/Winter 1981): 41–46.

Klaren, Sara C. "Fragmentation and Alienation in La Casa Verde." *Modern Language Notes* 87 (1972): 269–86.

Rossman, Charles, and Allen Warran Friedman, eds. *Mario Vargas Llosa: A Collection of Critical Essays*. Austin: University of Texas Press, 1978.

Review 14 (1978). Focus on *Conversation in the Cathedral*.

World Literature Today 52 (1978). Special Mario Vargas Llosa Issue.

JULIE JONES

VARLEY, JOHN (1947–   )

With a series of short stories beginning in 1974, John Varley quickly made his mark as the most innovative new science fiction writer of the period, winning by age 32 the two highest honors in his field (the 1978 Nebula and Hugo awards). Although Varley's fiction is distinguished by a mastery of traditional storytelling methods, much of it also depends on experimental narrative strategies, including multiple narrators and time frames. His best writing, set in a darkly comic, technological future, presents controversial contemporary issues (such as feminism and genetic engineering) in various innovative literary forms. Indeed, among recent science fiction writers, Varley is probably the most accomplished and most accessible of the experimenters.

Varley's life has been considerably tamer than that of his bizarre fictional creations. Born in Texas in 1947, he attended Michigan State University for a few years in the mid-1960s, moved to San Francisco, then settled in Eugene, Oregon, in 1975, where he now lives with his wife, Anet Mconel, and their three sons. Varley has held few positions other than that of professional writer and maintains that he has led "a pretty dull life." One event that has directly influenced his writing is his work as a screenwriter. Commuting to Los Angeles since 1979, he has completed several scripts for MGM. Although the screenplays are literate, inventive, and well paced, none has enticed a Hollywood mogul to begin production. Varley has employed cinematic techniques in his fiction, however, and increasingly so since 1979.

Varley's early short fiction, collected in *The Persistence of Vision* (1978), combines the vernacular voice of the colloquial tradition in American literature with recent nontraditional innovations in narrative construction. In "The Phantom of Kansas," for example, Varley creates a world in which banks are the repository of individual personality and memory; at death, customers are brought back to life through genetic cloning. Varley's first-person narrator, Ms. Fox, is the victim of repeated murders and resurrections (as is the narrative text). Ms. Fox eventually discovers that the murderer is her male clone, literally (as well as figuratively) her alter ego. Victim and murderer unite sexually, and as a single unified self set out for the new frontier of outer space. Varley's variations on the structure of the mystery story produce an intricate narrative of multiple identity and romantic transcendence.

Perhaps even more technically innovative are such stories as "Overdrawn at the Memory Bank." Here Varley's hero has his memory and personality withdrawn and temporarily stored in a computer. Bungling technicians misplace the hero's body, trapping him in the computer where he sets out to "edit his world." In this holding tank for the disembodied, the narrator/narrative accordingly becomes a hallucinatory analogue of analogues. By linking solipsism with the nightmarish aspects of the individual within a computerized society, Varley fashions a technological satire with an appropriately constructed self-reflexive narrative.

Varley's two most commercially successful novels, *Titan* (1979) and *Wizard* (1980), are also his most traditional narratives, the first two books of a cyclic trilogy. These epic evocations of an alien world trace a speculative anthropology and make for splendid swashbuckling entertainment, but are not intended to be highly experimental narratives. On the other hand, Varley's overlooked first novel, *The Ophiuchi Hotline* (1977), does break new ground. Its heroine, Lilo, an "Enemy of Humanity," is sentenced to permanent death for genetic experiments she performed on herself. To escape the authorities, she clones herself several times, creating three heroines of the same name and personality to narrate the novel. Each cloning initiates a new narrative thread. These overlapping narratives are tied off neatly at the end, uniting the discontinuities of identity and place. The multiple "clone-narration" of *The Ophiuchi Hotline* is fully consonant with the novel's fragmented action and meaning. *The Ophiuchi Hotline* can be read as a quest for full individual identity in an oppressive, chaotic world.

Varley's latest novel, *Millennium* (1983), is likewise written in the experimental mode. Both a novelization of his screenplay and an expansion of his harsh, stunning short story "Air Raid" (1977), *Millennium* uses two first-person narrators, a male air disaster investigator and the female leader of a rescue team from 50,000 years in the future. Their narratives intersect at a "Time Gate" where residents of the future snatch those from the past (our present) who are about to die in air crashes. Beyond fine characterizations and a sure handling of narrative voices, *Millennium* is extraordinary in its intricate use of shifting temporal structures. Drawing on a long tradition of time-travel stories, Varley creates an experimental tour de force on the paradoxical nature of time.

In all his nontraditional fictions, however, Varley never severs the connection with the ordinary, but rich and precise, language and emotions of his characters. His fictions are not overly abstract, programmatic, or self-indulgent. Varley's experimental strategies are anchored in the psychological and emotional depths associated with the traditional literature of realism. For readers unacquainted with science fiction or postmodern literature, then, Varley provides access to the central features of both.

Selected Bibliography

Primary Sources

The Ophiuchi Hotline. New York: Dial/James Wade, 1977.
The Persistence of Vision. New York: Dial/James Wade, 1978.
Titan. New York: Berkley/G.P. Putnam's, 1979.
The Barbie Murders. New York: Berkley, 1980.
Wizard. New York: Berkley/G.P. Putnam's, 1980.
"The Phantom of Kansas" (screenplay excerpts). *The Anthology of Eugene Writers*.
    Ed. J. D. Brown. Eugene, Oreg.: Northwest Review Books, 1982, pp. 63–78.

Millennium. New York: Berkley, 1983.
Demon. New York: G.P. Putnam's, 1984.
Picknic On Nearside. New York: Berkley, 1984.

J. D. BROWN

VONNEGUT, KURT (1922–   )

Kurt Vonnegut's emergence as one of the better known postmodern novelists is in some ways ironic. This lively experimentalist began as a commercial writer—a journalist, a PR man, and a contributor of stories to glossy magazines. His popularity is now such that he is something of a public figure, yet for years he labored in obscurity, branded as a minor science fiction writer. Moreover, his popularity owes much to an experimentalism that many enjoy without being able to explain.

Vonnegut was born on November 11, 1922, in Indianapolis. He went to Shortridge High School and wrote for its daily newspaper. When he went to Cornell University, he continued the newspaper work while majoring in biochemistry. He joined the Army in 1943 and, after an emergency leave coincident with his mother's suicide, went to Europe with the Infantry. In December 1944 he was captured and taken to Dresden. He was sheltered in a meat locker below that city when it was fire bombed in February 1945, surfacing to encounter a "moonscape." Subsequent days spent laboring in the ruins uncovered horrors that intensified the trauma of his experience.

Once repatriated, Vonnegut did graduate study and worked as a journalist in Chicago. In 1947 he moved to Schenectady to work for General Electric. By 1950 his first short stories had been accepted for publication; he left his job, moved to Cape Cod, and published more stories and, by 1952, his first novel. *Player Piano* follows a traditional anti-utopian mode, though embellished with elements of science fiction and sharply ironic humor.

Although Vonnegut enjoyed success as a story writer, his novels went scarcely noticed. Meanwhile, more personal tragedies struck; first, the death of his father, and then, in the kind of grim coincidence that seems to have haunted Vonnegut, the death of his sister Alice and her husband Jim Adams within two days of each other. He adopted three of their children, doubling the size of his family. These new responsibilities coincided with the decline of the short story market, and so he turned to the paperback novel, publishing *The Sirens of Titan* in 1959. Resembling a space opera, it perpetuated his being branded as a science fiction writer. *Mother Night* (1961), a haunting novel about an American double agent in Nazi Germany, is in some ways autobiographical and follows a conventional confessional form, but its bizarre coincidences, black humor, and comic distortions are characteristic adaptations.

Cat's Cradle (1963) was the first clear indication of Vonnegut's future as an experimentalist, a postmodern writer. Its prevailing philosophy is the Bokononist religion, which announces that all of its "truths" are "shameless lies," and whose language is invented, a blend of "San Lorenza" dialect, calypsos, and Bokononist terminology. The novel begins with a metafictional joke: "Call me Jonah." In 147 fragmented, digressive, and improbable chapters, it refuses to veil its own fictionality, to rationalize, or to cohere as a metaphor lending meaning to existence. Fictions, especially religious ones, may lie in providing life with causality, purpose, or meaning; like its Bokononist religion, this fiction refuses that pretense.

God Bless You, Mr. Rosewater (1965) is a relatively conventional novel, but *Slaughterhouse-Five* (1969) culminates Vonnegut's efforts to bring together the meaning—or perhaps better, the nonmeaning—of Dresden as a personal experience and as a public event. He does not transmit Dresden into his fiction as an ordering or rationalizing or explanatory symbol. It is simply there, coupled with the ludicrous execution of a prisoner for taking a teapot from the rubble. This coupling, like the gathering of Old Testament past and sci-fi future, historical documentary and fantasy story, slapstick humor and grim pathos, insists on life's inevitable randomness. The apparently arbitrary leaps in time and place add to this resistance to causality and chronology, to the imposition of relationship and meaning on events that cry out against them.

The catharsis in completing this masterpiece left Vonnegut drained, and he cast around for new forms, including theater. *Breakfast of Champions* (1973), which incorporates numerous drawings by Vonnegut, is perhaps the most obviously experimental of all of his novels, forthrightly downgrading traditional novelistic preoccupations such as character motivation and plot development. The author appears—as author and as character—in the fiction, and notes the fictionality of the other characters. In the three novels that have followed [*Slapstick*, 1976; *Jailbird*, 1979; and *Deadeye Dick*, 1982], he refines his method. Their postmodernism continues to be marked by such techniques as metafiction, the mixing of historical documentary and fantasy, and the amusing additions of recipes and other trivia, all of which defy our expectations of genre.

Though an experimentalist, Vonnegut speaks for traditional American values. His agnosticism, pacifism, and debunking of patriotic jingoism have drawn fire but mark a bond with forbears like Mark Twain and with numerous contemporaries. His compassionate insight into the difficulties of contemporary life, his refusal to be judgmental, his warm humor, and the sharp compression of his wit contribute to his continuing broad appeal in the United States and overseas.

Selected Bibliography

Primary Sources

Player Piano. New York: Scribner's, 1952.

The Sirens of Titan. New York: Dell, 1959.
Mother Night. Greenwich, Conn.: Fawcett, 1961.
Cat's Cradle. New York: Holt, Rinehart & Winston, 1963.
God Bless You, Mr. Rosewater. New York: Holt, Rinehart & Winston, 1965.
Slaughterhouse-Five. New York: Delacorte Press, 1969.
Breakfast of Champions. New York: Delacorte Press, 1973.
Slapstick. New York: Delacorte Press, 1976.
Jailbird. New York: Delacorte Press, 1979.
Deadeye Dick. New York: Delacorte Press, 1982.
Galápagos. New York: Delacorte Press, 1985.

Secondary Sources

Klinkowitz, Jerome. *Kurt Vonnegut*. London: Methuen, 1982.
————, and Donald Lawler, eds. *Vonnegut in America*. New York: Delacorte Press, 1977.
Klinkowitz, Jerome, and Asa B. Pieratt. *Kurt Vonnegut, Jr.: A Descriptive Bibliography*. Hamden, Conn.: Archon, 1974.
————, and John Somer, eds. *The Vonnegut Statement*. New York: Delacorte Press, 1973.
Lundquist, James. *Kurt Vonnegut*. New York: Frederick Ungar, 1977.
Schatt, Stanley. *Kurt Vonnegut, Jr*. Boston: Twayne Publishers, 1977.
Reed, Peter. *Kurt Vonnegut, Jr*. New York: Thomas Y. Crowell, 1976.
————. "Kurt Vonnegut." *American Writers*, Supplement 2, Part 2. New York: Scribner's, 1981, pp. 753–84.
————. "Kurt Vonnegut." *Dictionary of Literary Biography*. Detroit: Gale Research Co., 1978, pp. 493–508.

PETER J. REED

W

WALKER, ALICE (1944–   )

As a black woman writer, Alice Walker has had to seek out and assert her own tradition outside the literary mainstream. But her distinctive voice and vision have brought her recognition and growing critical success. In her poetry and fiction Walker's experimentation is less evident than the new purposes to which she adapts preexisting forms. Her poetry is spare in line but emotionally complex in expressing sexual passion or her outrage over racist stupidity and cruelty. Her fiction explores issues of social injustice further, while being more noticeably "womanist" in intent: "womanist" seeming to Walker more inclusive than "feminist." She depicts the abuse of black women by black men, considers violence from the perspective of the victimized, and repeatedly emphasizes gradual, spiritual regeneration as necessary, even among those once oppressed, for achieving true freedom.

Alice Walker was born on February 9, 1944, in Eatonton, Georgia, the youngest of eight children in a sharecropping family. She has credited her mother in particular with having exemplified creativity against odds and having provided the enabling gifts of time to write, a suitcase, and a typewriter, these last bought with earnings from housekeeping jobs in white women's houses. In her essay "In Search of Our Mothers' Gardens," Walker explores her debt to her mother and to other black women, against a backdrop of whose lives and work she views her own.

Walker attended Spelman College in Atlanta on scholarship. From there she transferred to Sarah Lawrence, where she received her B.A. in 1965. She began to seek her spiritual roots by traveling first to Africa on a summer fellowship. She has also visited the Soviet Union and England but has always returned, as her characters do, to her home ground. During the 1960s she lived in Mississippi and worked actively for the civil rights movement. Her first volumes of poems, *Once* (1968) and *Revolutionary Petunias* (1973), reflect this political involvement. But they attest also to her commitment to beauty and love as hopeful strategies in a revolutionary time.

In her first two novels Walker's attempt to find a moral balance amid the crucial issues of this period is again evident. The focus of *The Third Life of Grange Copeland* (1970) is the violence that the struggle to survive causes within a Southern black family. Gradually, Walker's protagonist comes to reject the existence that isolation in hatred necessitates. He weighs the dilemma of justice, as Walker, evidently influenced by Camus' thought, continues to do in *Meridian* (1976). Like Camus' ideal rebel, her heroine, Meridian Hill, struggles to elude and thwart tragedy. At first her dilemma appears to be her reluctance to kill, even to advance a just revolution. Her commitment shifts nevertheless to a search for values that revolutionary murder would jeopardize. Walker complicates this search by showing the effects of Meridian's awakened responsibility for her own actions. Experiencing guilt over her personal failures, she works to atone for them.

In Walker's two volumes of short stories to date, she provides additional, striking images of black women in other roles. The emphasis of *In Love & Trouble* (1973) is on their devalued status, resulting in grotesque manifestations of thwarted sexual and creative energies. What Walker has called her "second cycle," *You Can't Keep a Good Woman Down* (1981), is more positive in tone and closer to feminism in its recurring concerns. The images of strong, self-assertive black women here are less surprising, given Walker's position for some years as an editor of *Ms.* magazine. She is also a contributory editor of *Freedomways*. Since the 1960s she has lived in New York and San Francisco and has taught or been writer-in-residence at several universities.

She has received a number of prestigious awards, including the Pulitzer Prize for her third novel, *The Color Purple* (1982). In this novel Walker departs further from traditional conventions than previously. Following Zora Neale Hurston, whose work she greatly admires, she has been interested in black folk beliefs and the possibilities of black folk English for her art. She employs the latter vividly in the voices of the characters of this novel. Thematically, it again shows her preoccupation with a spiritual evolution that alters the relationship between victimizers and victims. Yet it shows her own creative development as well, with her latest return to the sources of a tradition she cherishes. Extending that, Walker has helped to broaden and deepen an important contributory current of American literature.

Selected Bibliography

Primary Sources

Once. New York: Harcourt Brace Jovanovich, 1968.
The Third Life of Grange Copeland. New York: Harcourt Brace Jovanovich, 1970.

In Love & Trouble. New York: Harcourt Brace Jovanovich, 1973.
Revolutionary Petunias & Other Poems. New York: Harcourt Brace Jovanovich, 1973.
Meridian. New York: Harcourt Brace Jovanovich, 1976.
Good Night, Willie Lee, I'll See You in the Morning. New York: Dial Press, 1979.
You Can't Keep a Good Woman Down. New York: Harcourt Brace Jovanovich, 1981.
The Color Purple. New York: Harcourt Brace Jovanovich, 1982.
In Search of Our Mothers' Gardens: A Collection of Womanist Prose. New York: Harcourt Brace Jovanovich, 1983.
Horses Make a Landscape Look More Beautiful. New York: Harcourt Brace Jovanovich, 1984.

Secondary Sources

Christian, Barbara. "Novels for Everyday Use." *Black Women Novelists: The Development of a Tradition, 1892–1976*. Westport, Conn.: Greenwood Press, 1980, pp. 180–238.
Davis, Thadious. "Alice Walker's Celebration of Self in Southern Generations." *The Southern Quarterly* 21 (Summer 1983): 39–53.
Gaston, Karen C. "Women in the Lives of Grange Copeland." *College Language Association Journal* 24 (1981): 276–86.
Harris, Trudier. "Folklore in the Fiction of Alice Walker: A Perpetuation of Historical and Literary Tradition." *Black American Literature Forum* 11 (1977): 3–8.
McGowan, Martha J. "Atonement and Release in Alice Walker's *Meridian*." *Critique* 23 (1981): 25–35.
Steinem, Gloria. "Do You Know This Woman? She Knows You: A Profile of Alice Walker." *Ms.* 11 (1982): 36–37, 89–94.
Washington, Mary Helen. "An Essay on Alice Walker." *Sturdy Black Bridges: Visions of Black Women in Literature*. Eds. Bell, Roseann P. et al. Garden City, N.Y.: Doubleday, 1979, pp. 133–49.

                                                        MARTHA J. McGOWAN

WATTEN, BARRETT (1948–   )

As writer, theorist, editor, and publisher, Barrett Watten has exercised a critical influence on the development of new prose forms. In each of these roles, he has addressed the possibilities of prose outside the confines of normative fiction and the French-derived prose poem. Throughout, his work reflects a thoroughgoing meditation on the nature of literature and a vision that is both cohesive and intensely committed.

Barrett Watten was born in 1948 and attended the Massachusetts Institute of Technology. He later earned a science degree from the University of California at Berkeley before obtaining an M.F.A. from the University of Iowa. He currently lives in Oakland and teaches at San Francisco State University.

This, the magazine co-founded by Watten and Robert Grenier in 1971, brought together many of the poets who would later work in new prose forms. In its early issues, *This* commingled authors from different sectors of anti-academic writing to a degree not found in comparable publications. In doing so, it openly stated a dissatisfaction with the state of the art of verse.

Although *This 3* included an excerpt from Robert Creeley's *Presences*, it was the fourth issue that began to raise the question of poets' prose in a concentrated way, containing four poetic stories by Larry Eigner and prose poems from such diverse authors as Michael Palmer, Lewis Warsh, and Joanne Kyger. *This 5* featured Clark Coolidge's "Karstarts." Entitled "Prose Poetry" (*not* prose poems, and with the additional space between words indicating a tension between concepts), *This 6* made the question of new forms explicit. The number included a section of Creeley's *Mabel*, a long untitled "prosoid" by Clark Coolidge, the opening paragraphs of Ron Silliman's* *Ketjak*, four works by Watten, and contributions from Michael Palmer, Bob Perelman, Bruce Andrews, Kit Robinson, Michael Davidson, and others.

Watten's works from *This 6* are collected in *Opera—Works* (1975). Although some of these short pieces allude to dream states, a classic strategy of surrealism, the overall tone is much closer to the journals of Coleridge, Thoreau, and Ginsberg. These do less to anticipate the direction in which Watten's investigation of prose forms was to develop than some of the "poem poems" in the same book, notably "Factors Influencing the Weather" and "Place Names," in which normative connections between lines has been reduced to a minimum. Seeming almost arbitrary in their context, the individual lines acquire an autonomy that focuses the reader's attention on the immediate present.

The radical nature of this device is even more evident when executed in the form of prose in "Chamber Music," the central text of Watten's next book, *Decay* (1977). Themes occur in "Chamber Music," a series of 58 one-sentence paragraphs, but are so incidental to the reading experience that it becomes apparent that the thematic dimension, as such, is itself little more than a reiteration of signifieds. In its near-absence, the illusionist naturalism of constructed meaning is revealed. Calling into question, as this does, not only the psychological unity of a speaking subject hidden within the voice of the text, but that also of the reader, "Chamber Music" is nonetheless a work of intensity and cohesion *at another level*. The elegant construction of sentences ten to fourteen words long in such an insistently uniform format argues coherence precisely as it demonstrates totality to be an effect of construction.

If "Chamber Music" is the benchmark of Watten's mature writing, his next three books, *Plasma/Parallels/"X"* (1979), *1–10*, (1980), and *Complete Thought* (1982), extend its discoveries broadly. Of particular importance are works such as "Artifacts," in which thematic structures build and move, often with a great deal of wit, without lapsing into the simple ego-based psychology that underwrites every mode of persona-ism. The tension between sentence and paragraph is raised to perceptibility, and the paragraph itself contains many of the structural and affective attributes of both the verse line and the stanza:

Sea anemones were whispering at low tide.

Spectators have agreed to be invisible. Verisimilitude is

divided into two parts.

The valves of sensation unlock at different (various) levels.

Speakers say the words clearly. They will be replaced with a park.

One takes on chains (this haze of images) in order to better

illustrate how to throw them off (analysis).

A palm tree predicates a palm tree. The signal for "I"

resembles a rabbit or a duck.

An Articulate, winged diatribe about "everything" signs off.

"Get another linguist!" ("Artifacts," Part XI)

In addition, Watten's writing has carried the prosody and many of the social codes of prose (especially those of professional argots) back into pure verse forms, often utilizing stanzas of fixed numbers of lines, each built out of a modified syllabics. Some excellent examples of these are "Position" and "Silence" in *1–10*, and the still largely unpublished *Progress*, a work of 600 stanzas. To say that such pieces, when contrasted with something such as "Artifacts," are or are not prose (or poetry) demonstrates just how complete the collapse of old genre demarcations has been in the last decade.

Watten edited Larry Eigner's collected prose, *Country/Harbor/Quiet/ Act/Around*, which he published through This Press in 1978. Other works by This Press which extend the possibilities of prose are *Ketjak* and Carla Harryman's *Under the Bridge*. The sole editor of *This* for nine of its twelve issues, Watten presently co-edits *Poetics Journal*. A selection of his own critical writing, *Total Syntax* (1984), is available in the New Poetics series of Southern Illinois University Press. Written in 1975, "The Maintains and Later Prose," a consideration of Coolidge's early "prosoids," was perhaps the first critical account of a postgeneric poet's prose.

In 1976, Watten founded the landmark San Francisco reading series at the Grand Piano coffee house, and he currently is a member of the Board

of Directors of New Langton Arts, an alternative arts space in the same
city. Formerly 80 Langton Street, New Langton Arts often presents writers
in innovative formats and helped to pioneer Bob Perelman's concept of
"poet's talks," a mode at which Watten is a master. Several of his best
are included in *Total Syntax*.

Selected Bibliography

Primary Sources

Radio Day in Soma City. Privately printed, 1971.
Opera—Works. Bolinas: Big Sky, 1975.
Decay. San Francisco: This Press, 1977.
Plasma/Parallels/"X". Berkeley, Calif.: Tuumba 21, 1979.
1–10. San Francisco: This Press, 1980.
Complete Thought. Berkeley, Calif.: Tuumba 38, 1982.
Total Syntax. Carbondale: Southern Illinois University Press, 1984.

RON SILLIMAN

WHITE, EDMUND (1940–   )

Edmund White is a gay author of two nonfiction studies of gay life in
America—*The Joy of Gay Sex* (1977, with Charles Silverstein) and *States
of Desire* (1980)—and four widely praised, wonderfully crafted works of
fiction: *Forgetting Elena* (1973), *Nocturnes for the King of Naples* (1978),
A Boy's Own Story (1982), and *Cara Cole* (1985). Although three of White's
fictional works deal in one way or another with the nature of gay life, they
also use this focus in order to explore other, more transcendent issues: the
way in which meaning and identity are codified and exchanged via conventions; the political and personal implications of prejudice; the ways
memory and art console (and torment) us for life's loss and inevitable
decay; the effects of a twisted age on personal development. What is most
important about White's fiction, however, is not his treatment of theme
but his lush, evocative, highly lyrical prose. It is significant that many critics
have compared his fiction to prose poetry—and that Vladimir Nabokov
once referred to White as the contemporary American author he most
admired. White's use of metaphor has affinities with that of his acknowledged master, Nabokov, and it is clear that White is familiar with experimental authors, such as Alain Robbe-Grillet, John Barth,* Robert Coover,*
and Donald Barthelme.* He has also acknowledged the influence of earlier
writers, such as Marcel Proust and Ronald Firbank, as well as that of
abstract expressionist painters and of various musicians (music, he admits,
is his favorite art).

Edmund White was born in Cincinnati, Ohio, to Edmund Valentine II
(an engineer) and Oelilah (a psychologist and authority on mongolism) on

January 13, 1940. Extremely precocious, White had his first fiction published when he was nine and saw his first play presented a year later. He attended college at the University of Michigan where, in accordance with the view that studying literature was useless, even harmful for a creative writer, he majored in Chinese. There he edited the campus literary magazine and also won two Hopwood awards (student writing awards), one of which was given for his play *Blue Boy in Black* (eventually produced at the Masque Theater in New York City). After graduating in 1962, White produced numerous nonfiction works on various subjects ranging from anthropology to Japanese gardens and zeppelins for Time-Life Books. Although he was also writing fiction during his eight-year stint there, White has stated that he now regards this apprentice period as being overly long. During the 1970s and 1980s, he moved on to teach creative writing and literature at several universities (his longest stint was at Columbia) and was also a senior editor for *Saturday Review* and a contributing editor at *Horizon*. After winning a Guggenheim Award in 1982, he moved to Paris, where he recently completed a novel, *Cara Cole*.

White's first published novel, *Forgetting Elena*, immediately displays his interest in formal experimentation, his remarkable ear for prose, and his preoccupation with the sources and nature of social interaction. The novel is both a kind of existential mystery novel and a comedy of manners, vaguely suggesting an odd fusion of Kafka and Henry James. Narrated by a completely amnesiac young man—"a sleuth who strives to detect the mystery of the self," as one reviewer put it—the novel describes his efforts to construct himself on the basis of the mysterious clues (of language, of social convention, of personal nuance) that he discovers in a strange world of aesthetic elitism. In this sinister world, which is often also hilarious, as White has explained in *Library Journal*, "Every word and gesture would be governed by a subtle etiquette and would convey a symbolic meaning." One critic has referred to the "Oriental impenetrability" of the subtleties encountered by the narrator, and, indeed, in an interview in the *Mississippi Review*, White has acknowledged modeling this world on the court life of tenth-century Japan—the ultimate artistic society. *Forgetting Elena* also specifically satirized the social scene found on Fire Island during the 1960s, with its elaborate costume parties, the snobbery based on fashion, and the elegant posturing and disguises. But as Simon Karlinsky notes, this novel is not so much a study of a particular time or place as a "parable about the nature of social interaction that transcends any period and applies to the human predicament at large . . . an analysis of the drives and pressures common to all groupings, cliques and coteries" (p. 78).

White's second novel, *Nocturnes for the King of Naples*, is a densely textured "hymn to passion" which has been hailed as a "sublime piece of poetry." The novel is addressed to a famous, unnamed (possibly fictitious) older lover whom the narrator strives in vain to replace. The exact identity of the lover is problematic, as the recurring metaphors suggest that the "you" addressed might be either God or a person deified: "You are the god I wanted to celebrate or conjure." Through a carefully orchestrated sequence of reveries (musical analogies are often appropriate in describing White's fictional structures), the narrator reexperiences in language and memory what has receded into the abyss of the past. The baroque opulence of White's prose is not only beautifully rendered, but also appropriately reflects the aesthetic interplay of the Baroque period, when the divine and sensual were inextricably linked. Indeed, the chief triumph of the novel is its fusion of passion and spirituality, a fusion introduced in the book's opening image of a deserted pier used by gay men for surreptitious sex but also likened to a cathedral.

White's *States of Desire: Travels in Gay America* (1980), an examination of gay life in the 1970s, was also widely praised, despite the fact that critics often had different and even mutually exclusive expectations. *States* is not merely an exposé, an apology, or a gay Michelin guide, but could more fairly be judged as a work of New Journalism, a mixture of sociology, politics, and literature à la Alexis de Toqueville. It is filled with the sort of metaphor, insight, tentativeness, and digression (in the best sense) that we associate with our best works of fiction. What is fascinating and valuable about the book are White's deft portraits of gays in the specific circumstances of the various cities he visits. A major conclusion to be drawn is that geography matters, as does time. Here geography *is* time, in that gays living in more conservative cities are existing under the conditions that all gays did before Gay Lib. White also shows that gay America is not monolithic, that there are factions and diversity as with any other social group, and thus he provides us multiple perspectives to ponder about what it means to be gay in America.

States of Desire had an obvious effect on White's latest novel, *A Boy's Own Story*, in that while composing the former White refined his skill at developing quick character sketches and also discovered a clearer sense of how to present his own persona in his work. *A Boy's Own Story* is White's most autobiographical novel; it presents a kind of initiation formula about a young gay boy growing up in the 1950s. More episodic and amorphous than his other works, the book focuses on the trauma of growing up in a twisted age, and of being misunderstood by one's parents (loosely based on White's own parents) and by one's peers. But, again, White attains a transcendence: the book becomes a girl's own story, or an artist's—the story of everyone who grows up unable to focus and fulfill their most prized, inchoate longings. White subtly encourages the reader to identify with his narrator, whose sense of powerlessness drives him to compensatory illusions of grandeur and a hunger of power; his deformation by the spirit of the 1950s thus becomes a mirror of our own deformities as well. It is a tribute to White's scope and his craft that so many readers have identified strongly with this narrator (*A Boy's Own Story* is easily White's most popular novel to date) in spite of its sordid conclusion, where the narrator betrays a friend out of revenge.

Selected Bibliography

Primary Sources

Forgetting Elena. New York: Random House, 1973.
The Joy of Gay Sex: An Intimate Guide for Gay Men to the Pleasures of a Gay Lifestyle (with Charles Silverstein). New York: Simon & Schuster, 1979.
Nocturnes for the King of Naples. New York: St. Martin's Press, 1978.
States of Desire: Travels in Gay America. New York: E.P. Dutton, 1980.
A Boy's Own Story. New York: E.P. Dutton, 1982.
Cora Cole. New York: E.P. Dutton, 1985.

Secondary Sources

Gregory, Sinda, and Larry McCaffery. "An Interview with Edmund White." *Mississippi Review* 39 (Spring 1985): 9–27.
Karlinsky, Simon. "*Forgetting Elena.*" *Nation*, January 5, 1973, p. 78.

PAT McKERCHER

WILSON, ROBERT L. ANTON (1932–   )

With the publication of *The Illuminatus!* (with Robert Shea) (1975), Robert Anton Wilson secured a small audience ranging from the initiates of science fiction to those neurological adventurers grouped under the polite heading of Consciousness Research. During the last five years, since the initial publication of *The Schrodinger's Cat Trilogy* (1979, 1981), Wilson has gained mainstream acceptance as well as recruiting readers from what could be termed "the lunatic fringe." He began to carve his niche in this sometimes hostile realm of the Selective/Eclectic by means of a tool of his (and the Discordian Society's) own manufacture: Ontological Guerrilla Warfare, with its subtle blending of quantum mechanics theory, Western esoteric shamanism, and such metafictional devices as including anthropological reports from the Terran Archives (circa 2700 A.D.) and Galactic Archives (circa Eternity?). Wilson achieves a distancing in his texts by breaking down and questioning the reader's sense of reality—a distancing that has led him to be compared to Thomas Pynchon* and William S. Burroughs. His encyclopedic knowledge of the twentieth century, his occasional Joycean flights of prose, and a sense of humor that finds something funny in almost all of our domesticated primate behavior make Wilson a whimsical, highly effective writer who shares with Burroughs, Kurt Vonnegut,* and Pynchon a paranoiac, nightmarish, darkly humorous vision of contemporary life.

Wilson's life reads like a melodrama or a comic tragedy, but neither category fits the uncensored weirdness he's lived. Born somewhere in New York in 1932, he grew up in a working-class Irish Catholic family in Brooklyn. As a child he suffered from polio (he still has to walk with a cane at times) and was cured by a procedure known as the Sister Kenny Method. This cure, which at the time was considered by the American Medical Association as nothing more than witchcraft, seems to have been the pivotal event in his young life, for it implanted within Wilson a permanent and radical distrust of authority. This first move away from the Consensus Reality led him at the age of 14 to leave the Catholicism of his parents and to immerse himself in something almost as mystical, yet more flexible: analytical mathematics. In the mid-1950s he was also powerfully moved to further distrust societal authority when he witnessed the burning of Dr. Wilhelm Reich's books on a street in New York City. In the mid-1960s he was an editor at *Playboy*, where he once met William Burroughs (who was later to influence his prose style). With his co-editor Robert Shea, he became involved with the eldritchly comic Discordian Society, and together they eventually co-created *The Illuminatus*. Wilson left *Playboy* and civilization not long after the 1968 Chicago Democratic Convention (he was one of the protestors) to live in Mexico on savings, and he later lived in the Bay area on welfare with his wife and three children, studying Crowleyesque Shamanism and other forms of consciousness-evolving techniques.

Working with Robert Shea (circa 1970–1974?) and Discordian philosophy, Wilson wrote *The Illuminatus!* trilogy, a wacky, paranoid fantasy about the evil Bavarian Illuminati who control the world behind-the-scenes and who thus embody modern man's deepest notions that a conspiracy governs all. Both Shea and Wilson describe the trilogy as "Ontological Guerrilla Warfare." The trilogy is so structured, presenting a different yet plausible belief system about the events in the text at least once every 50 pages, that the reader is unable clearly to decide how much of Illuminatus is shameless put-on and how much is life-or-death serious. Fact and outright paranoid fantasy are mixed with such care that the fact looks like the fantasy and the fantasy looks like the fact.

Wilson later explores the function of belief systems in the *Schrodinger's Cat Trilogy*: *The Universe Next Door* (1979), *The Trick Top Hat* (1981), and *The Homing Pigeons* (1981). In these books Wilson combines the Dicordianism of *The Illuminatus!* with information theory and brings quantum mechanics, which was a minor theme in the first trilogy, into play as a system for focusing on human reality. The quantum mechanics theme is known as QUIP (for Quantum Inseparability Principle) which seems to violate commonsense implying that either (1) there are multiple universes, or (2) everything in the universe is the cause of everything else across space/time, or (3) the universe is just a function of our nervous systems or is created by the participation of the participants. Combined with Leary's concept of the individual neurological reality-tunnel(s), Wilson explodes, via methods that are often both comic and erotic, all notions of firm and fixed belief systems. In short, Wilson, in his life and work, is trying to undermine the whole continuum of that human behavior known as "belief." He thinks belief is an outmoded, Aristotelean category, and hopes that some of his readers will eventually respond to his reality-deconstructions and make their own reality-tunnels more inclusive and less robotic.

Wilson's last two novels, *Masks of the Illuminati* (1981) and *The Earth Will Shake* (1982), are more focused studies on the nature and danger of belief. *Masks of the Illuminati* deals with the initiation of a young English scholar, Sir John Babcock, into the Order of the Golden Dawn, his progressive development of a Magickal belief system, and the way his superior in the order, Aleister Crowley, manipulates his "World" into one of gothic horror and comedy. James Joyce and Albert Einstein become involved in the conspiracy when they encounter Sir John in Zurich and spend two nights trying to unravel his mystery. *The Earth Will Shake* deals with these same themes of initiation and paranoia but are set in mid-eighteenth-century Europe.

Although Wilson has affinities with shamanism, the occult, quantum mechanics theory, immortalism, and consciousness evolution, his language and characters tend toward the marvelous in the mundane. In Wilson's universe—all his books could be seen as one work, perhaps as part of that Discordian project known as Operation Mind Fuck—illumination is not just right under one's nose, it's probably right behind it, in all that grey matter. For Wilson the boredom and existential angst of postmodernist, postindustrial society is a function of Domesticated Primates (his term for "homo sap") being robotized by our DNA and our childhood and our society into conventionalized behavior. His is not a quest for any Platonic absolutes that have already divided Western civilization into hostile affinity groups but an exploration of myriad universes, each as real or irreal as the next one, that can be produced by the human nervous system.

Selected Bibliography

Primary Sources

Playboy's Book of Forbidden Words. Chicago: Playboy, 1972.
The Book of the Breast. Chicago: Playboy, 1973.
Sex and Drugs. Chicago: Playboy, 1973.
The Illuminatus! (with Robert Shea)
   Part I. *The Eye in the Pyramid*. New York: Dell Press, 1975.
   Part II. *The Golden Apple*. New York: Dell Press, 1975.
   Part III. *Leviathan*. New York: Dell Press, 1975.
Neuropolitics (with Tim Leary). Los Angeles: Starseed/Peace, 1977.
Cosmic Trigger. New York: Pocket Books, 1977.
Schrodinger's Cat: The Universe Next Door. New York: Pocket Books, 1979.
The Illuminati Papers. Berkeley, Calif.: And/Or, 1980.

Schrodinger's Cat II: The Trick Top Hat. New York: Pocket Books, 1981.
Schrodinger's Cat III: The Homing Pigeons. New York: Pocket Books, 1981.
Masks of the Illuminati. New York: Pocket Books, 1981.
The Earth Will Shake. Boston: Houghton Mifflin, 1982.
Right Where You Are Sitting Now. Berkeley, Calif.: And/Or, 1982.
Prometheus Rising. Phoenix: Falcon, 1983.

MICHAEL GLOSSAN

WITTIG, MONIQUE (1935–   )

Monique Wittig is an avant-garde French writer whose works include not only fiction, but drama and essays as well. Translated into English within a few years of their original publication, Wittig's novels quickly gained an appreciative audience, first in the lesbian-feminist community and soon after among students and teachers of literature. Challenging the traditional novel with its predetermined plot and fixed characters, Wittig evokes mythical beings in a fictional world whose discontinuity is developed through the rhythmical use of unpunctuated series—adjectives, nouns, phrases—like the evocation of mythical beings. By experimenting with forms and words, Wittig undermines the obsolete literary vision and the restrictive way of life that it projects.

A native of Alsace, Monique Wittig was born in 1935. She grew up in Rodez in the Aveyron and in Montmorency to the northwest of Paris. Her passion for words—and for other women—goes back to her grammar school days. Around thirteen she began to write mostly to win the heart of the young girl with whom she had fallen in love. Fascinated by the world of language with its seductive power and artistic possibilities, Monique Wittig took a degree in literature at the Sorbonne and studied oriental languages.

In 1964, during a six-month leave of absence from the Editions de Minuit where she worked as a proofreader, Wittig wrote *L'Opoponax.* That publishing house, whose catalogue included such writers as Sarraute, Beckett, and Butor, decided to publish Wittig's text as well; the book won the prestigious French Prix Médicis and was immediately translated into several languages. Narrated in the present tense in a style somewhere between spoken dialogue and written text, *L'Opoponax* is doubtless the first modern book on childhood; the sensory perceptions of many girls and boys having replaced the author's traditional memories of youth. Most critics have been intrigued by Wittig's repeated use of the indefinite pronoun *on*—"one," "they," or "we" in English—and they interpreted this language as a means of diffusing the point of view. But what they overlooked, as one critic has pointed out, is that Wittig's choice of the genderless, neuter *on* enabled her to recreate linguistically a world of children who grow up free from the social expectations of traditional male-female behavior.

At the beginning of 1968 Wittig started to write *Les Guérillères*. But her work was interrupted when she became politically involved in the first feminist group to unite in the wake of the May student-worker revolution in France. For nearly a year she devoted all her time to the cause of women's liberation; she resumed her writing at the end of that period and completed the book in 1969. Although *Les Guérillères* reflects the political climate of May 1968, this work clearly transcends the circumstances of a historical moment. A modern epic honoring the female warriors of the world, *Les Guérillères* brings out the long history of women's subjugation, urges women to take up arms against their oppressor, and describes the overthrow of the patriarchy through guerilla-type warfare. Appearing in translation in 1971, *Les Guérillères* was read at first as a feminist manifesto. Only when the book became the object of literary scrutiny in the mid-seventies did its complexity as well as its artful correspondence between theme, structure, and meaning become evident.

After a period of militant activism in the early stages of the French women's liberation movement, Wittig became a participant in the effort to build centers of Amazon culture; the strong females with whom she associated inspired her in the early seventies to write *Le Corps lesbien* (1973). Revealing an extraordinary inventiveness, this work defies the heterosexual attempt to reduce and naturalize lesbianism by describing it in terms of the heterosexual language. Wittig felt the need to transform sexist grammar and to discover an alternative vocabulary. Translated in 1975, *Le Corps lesbien* was praised in the French as well as in the Anglo-American presses for its power and originality, but these first critics displayed a lack of understanding with regard to the book's linguistic innovation. It was not until the 1980s, when a growing number of women scholars began to elucidate the quality of Wittig's writing, that *The Lesbian Body* assumed its rightful place in literature as an important major work, which succeeded, for the first time since Sappho, in universalizing the lesbian subject.

In 1976 Monique Wittig left her native country for political reasons and settled in the United States where she continues to be active as a creative writer, playwright, lecturer, and essayist. About this time, Monique Wittig and Sande Zeig began working together; they wrote *Brouillon pour un dictionnaire des amantes* (1976) and also translated the work under the title, *Lesbian Peoples Material for a Dictionary* (1979). Offering both a tentative lexicon and a thematic history of lesbianism, this delightful book constitutes an excellent guide to understanding Wittig's earlier novels.

With *The Constant Journey*, Wittig returned to an early love of hers— the theater. An Amazon version of the Quixote theme, this play was first performed at Goddard College, Vermont, in March 1984, then toured the Midwest and, more recently, played at the théâtre Madeleine Renaud/ Barrault in Paris. Due to the experimental nature of the staging, Wittig's play, like her novels, demands an active audience participation.

As we turn the pages of Wittig's latest novel, *Virgile, Non* (1985), we find ourselves in a strange but recognizable environment close to San Francisco. Wittig, now a character in her own book, and her guide Manastabal lead us through the circles of hell, limbo, and paradise in an allegorical journey which illustrates the female condition and which shows glimpses of Utopia here on earth. By its originality and irreverence, this fable subverts the traditional categories of literature.

It is no coincidence that a lesbian writer such as Monique Wittig, rebelling against the power relationships of the dominant sexuality, should challenge the canons of literature and the tyranny of the official language. Nor is it surprising that a long-standing literary innovator such as Nathalie Sarraute should consider Monique Wittig to be a first-rate author, a creator of new forms who is at the head of the generation that followed the *nouveau roman*.

Selected Bibliography

Primary Sources

L'Opoponax. Paris: Editions de Minuit, 1964. (*The Opoponax*. Vermont: Daughters Press, 1976).
Les Guérillères. Paris: Editions de Minuit, 1969. (*Les Guérillères*. Trans. David Le Vay. New York: Avon Books, 1973; rpt. Boston: Beacon Press, 1985).
Le Corps lesbien. Paris: Les Editions de Minuit, 1973. (*The Lesbian Body*. Trans. David Le Vay. New York: Avon Books, 1976; rpt. Boston: Beacon Press, 1986).
Brouillon pour un dictionnaire des amantes. With Sande Zeig. Paris: Grasset, 1976. (*Lesbian Peoples Material for a Dictionary*. New York: Avon Books, 1979).
Virgile, Non. Paris: Les Editions de Minuit, 1985.

Secondary Sources

Crowder, Diane Griffin. "Amazons and Mothers? Monique Wittig, Hélène Cixous and Theories of Woman's Writing." *Contemporary Literature* 24 (Summer 1983): 117–44.
Duffy, Jean. "Women and Language in Les Guérillères by Monique Wittig." *Stanford French Studies* 7 (Winter 1983): 399–412.
Ostrovsky, Erika. "A Cosmogony of O: Wittig's *Les Guérillères*," in *Twentieth Century French Fiction: Essays for Germaine Bree*. New Brunswick, N.J.: Rutgers University Press, 1975, pp. 241–251.
Rosenfeld, Marthe. "The Linguistic Aspect of Sexual Conflict: Monique Wittig's *Le corps lesbien*." *Mosaic* XVII, no. 2 (Spring 1984): 235–241.
Shaktini, Namascar. "Displacing the Phallic Subject: Wittig's Lesbian Writing." *Signs* 8, no. 1 (Autumn 1982): 29–44.

Wenzel, Hélène Vivienne. "The Text as Body Politics: An Appreciation of Monique Wittig's Writings in Context." *Feminist Studies* 7, no. 2 (Summer 1981): 264–287.

MARTHE ROSENFELD

WOLF, CHRISTA (1929–   )

"Prose makes people in the double sense. It breaks up deadly simplifications by displaying the possibilities of living in a human way. . . . Writing can only begin for those to whom reality is no longer a matter of course" (from *The Reader and the Writer*). In this way East Germany's Christa Wolf summarizes her need to write, a need that first surfaced in the early 1960s and that has catapulted Wolf into the forefront of the international literary scene. And with the publication of her last two novels, *No Place on Earth* (1979) and *Cassandra* (1983), Wolf has assumed the role of spokesperson of international feminist concerns. This is indeed an unusual state of affairs for an East German writer whose life and work have been closely tied to her socialist homeland and who, though an incessant critic of the East German system, has been an active Party member since the founding of her country in 1949. This rather contradictory situation is mirrored in her fiction, which has from the beginning focused on the difficulty of becoming oneself in a society that rewards acquiescence and conformity. Wolf's international reputation testifies eloquently to the fact, however, that her books address concerns widely felt in industrial societies, East as well as West.

Wolf was born in 1929 in Landsberg an der Warthe, a small town which today is in Poland, the daughter of a shopkeeper whose family later fled before the approaching Red Army to what is today East Germany. Although Wolf was too young to have participated in the horrors of Nazi Germany, her small-town childhood exposed her to an experiential microcosm of life in everyday fascism, a theme that forms the core of her novel *Patterns of Childhood* (formerly *A Model Childhood*; 1976). Her early education and career choices seemed headed for the track designed for the scientific-cultural elite of her society: study of German at Leipzig University, where she received her Ph.D.; editorship with a publisher and on the staff of several key literary magazines for which she wrote reviews, frequently, under the sway of Georg Lukács' Marxism, insisting on the very socialist-realist paradigms she later felt compelled to reject in her own work.

Wolf has summarized her writing as the quest for subjective authenticity, the pressing need to reconquer her subjective individuality from the insidious process of estrangement and externalization characteristic of modern

industrial society. She has endeavored to reconstitute herself—and to inspire her readers to attempt the same—as an active subject of social-
historical change.

These concerns announced themselves in Wolf's first novel, *Divided
Heaven* (1963), which she wrote shortly after the construction of the Berlin
Wall, an event, though repugnant to most in East and West alike, which
spurred a liberalization in East German social and cultural policy. *Divided
Heaven* broke down a number of taboos, among them the depiction of the
consequences of the Wall. It portrays the inner separation of two young
lovers caused by the physical division of Berlin.

The Quest for Christa T. (1968) gained Wolf the international reputation
she enjoys today. Where *Divided Heaven* challenged tenets of socialist
realism primarily in its theme, *The Quest for Christa T.*, the first East
German novel to employ stream-of-consciousness and *monologue interieur*
techniques, deviates from cultural-political norms in both style and theme,
while asking questions about the authenticity of the individual, about self-
realization, and about the clash of personal needs for self-fulfillment with
societal demands for conformity and acceptance of standardization. It questions the identity of person and personality in societies that encourage self-
subjugation and acquiescence to externally imposed norms. The novel is
a process of self-reflection and memory by a narrator who is trying to come
to grips with the unhappy life and early death of a friend whose hopes and
aspirations were crushed by an uncomprehending and inflexible society
that forced her to withdraw, first into a private sphere, later into herself,
and finally into death. The East German publication of *The Quest for
Christa T.* stirred up a political controversy that occupied Wolf for years.

In 1976 Wolf again shocked East Germany's cultural bureaucrats with
the publication of *Patterns of Childhood*, a novel that seeks to answer the
question: How have we become what we are today? The narrator, accompanied by her husband and daughter, returns to her home town in search
of her past, which lies in the Nazi period. In the multi-perspective structure
that links the present (the mid-1970s) with the past (from the late 1930s
to the present), the narrator confronts through memory her deformed past,
surrounded by millions of Nazis and fellow travelers who later became
citizens of the two Germanys. This is the first novel to draw a connection
between Nazi Germany and East Germany, a country that has insistently
portrayed itself as heir to the Communist resistance movement, as separate
from the Nazi heritage it sees alive in West Germany. And that caused a
political storm.

Her most recent two novels, *No Place on Earth* and *Cassandra*, take
Wolf's quest for personal authenticity and renewed subjectivity to the
distant past. *No Place on Earth*, the title of which invokes the Greek word
"utopia," creates a fictionalized meeting between the German romantics
Heinrich von Kleist and Karoline von Günderode, two poets who suffer

from a sense of estrangement and self-fragmentation, tormented by their inability to reconcile their existence with their time and their society. In real life, both would commit suicide within ten years of the meeting described in the novel. In portraying the bleak lives of these outsiders of the early eighteenth century, Wolf draws parallels to the position of the writer in her own society and time.

Cassandra, set in the Trojan War, tells the story of the ill-fated seer whom Apollo gave the ability to foretell the future while insuring that her prophecies would fall on deaf ears. Fulfilling Apollo's curse, her countrymen, for whom war has become an all-consuming obsession, ignore Cassandra's predictions of destruction and death. Here, Wolf again sees a distinct parallel: she comprehends herself and her fellow writers as spokespersons against nuclear madness, spokespersons who are ignored by the—largely male—military-political elite of the world. *Cassandra* underscores Wolf's feminist concerns; she sees male domination as the cause of the hyperrational thought that has led our world into the danger of self-annihilation.

Critics have asked whether Wolf's turn to history represents a withdrawal from critical portrayal of the present due to repressive measures threatening her. Although there might be some truth in this suggestion, Wolf's quest into history seems to be aimed more at examining the historical relationship of the (woman) writer and her society. This search is inspired by her desire to discover the roots of our alienation and self-destructiveness, which, she suspects, lie in the 2000-year domination of overly rational male thought, coupled with the ruthless suppression of the female thinkers who might have introduced a subjective and more humane view of the world. Wolf's work, from *The Quest for Christa T.* to *Cassandra*, has the same goal: to discover and actualize subjectivity as a potentially subversive and healing factor in social-political relationships.

Selected Bibliography

Primary Sources

Der geteilte Himmel. Eine Erzählung. Halle: Mitteldeutscher Verlag, 1963. (*Divided Heaven.* New York: Adler's Foreign Books, 1965.)
Nachdenken über Christa T. Halle: Mitteldeutscher Verlag, 1968. (*The Quest for Christa T.* New York: Farrar, Straus & Giroux, 1970.)
Lesen und Schreiben. Aufsätze und Betrachtungen. Halle: Mitteldeutscher Verlag, 1971. Expanded and revised edition published as *Fortgesetzter Versuch. Aufsätze, Gespräche, Essays.* Leipzig: Reclam, 1979. (*The Reader and the Writer.* New York: International Publishing, 1978.)
Kindheitsmuster. Berlin and Weimar: Aufbau Verlag, 1976. (*Patterns of Childhood [formerly A Model Childhood].* New York: Farrar, Straus & Giroux, 1980 and 1984.)
Kein Ort. Nirgends. Berlin and Weimar: Aufbau Verlag, 1979. (*No Place on Earth.* New York: Farrar, Straus & Giroux, 1982.)

Kassandra. Vier Vorlesungen. Eine Erzählung. Berlin and Weimar: Aufbau Verlag,
    1983. (*Cassandra. A Novel and Four Essays.* New York: Farrar, Straus &
    Giroux, 1984.)

Secondary Sources

"Documentation: Christa Wolf" (three interviews with Wolf in German). *German
    Quarterly* 57 (1984): 91–118.
Fehervary, Helen. "Christa Wolf's Prose: A Landscape of Masks." *New German
    Critique* (Fall 1982): 57–87.
Fries, Marilyn Sibley. "Christa Wolf's Use of Image and Vision in the Narrative
    Structure of Experience." *Studies in GDR Culture and Society.* Eds. Margy
    Gerber et al. Washington, D.C.: University Press of America, 1982, pp.
    59–74.
Lennox, Sara. "Christa Wolf and the Women Romantics." *Studies in GDR Culture
    and Society.* Washington, D.C.: University Press of America, 1982, pp.
    31–43.
McPherson, Karin. "Christa Wolf in Edinburgh: An Interview." *GDR Monitor* 1
    (1979): 1–12.
———. "In Search of the New Prose: Christa Wolf's Reflections on Writing and
    the Writer in the 1960s and 1970s." *New German Studies* 9 (1981): 1–13.
Paley, Grace. "A Dialogue with Christa Wolf." *Penn American Center Newsletter*
    53 (Winter 1984): 8–13.
Sauer, Klaus, ed. *Christa Wolf Materialienbuch* (materials on Wolf). Darmstadt:
    Lucterhand, 1979.
Stephan, Alexander. *Christa Wolf.* Munich: Beck, 1979.
———. "The Emancipation of Man: Christa Wolf as a Woman Writer." *GDR
    Monitor* 2 (1979/1980): 23–31.

                                                            JAMES KNOWLTON

WOLFE, GENE (1931–   )

The publication of Gene Wolfe's 4-volume magnum opus *The Book of
the New Sun* (1980–1982) revealed to a larger audience the qualities that
had been present in Wolfe's work all along: an absolute control of narrative
tone; a sardonic and subtle sense of humor; the ability to invent vivid and
complex backgrounds; extremely unusual methods of organizing a story;
and the ability to surprise and confound the reader at every turn.

Gene Wolfe was born in Brooklyn in 1931. After several moves, his
parents settled in Houston, where he grew up. He attended Texas Agricultural and Mechanical University, but dropped out and was drafted,
serving the last few months of the Korean War. After getting out of the
Army, he took a degree in mechanical engineering at the University of
Houston and remet and married Rosemary Dietz, who had once lived next
door to him. Wolfe worked as an engineer for many years, and then as a

senior editor for *Plant Engineering* magazine until his recent retirement. He and Rosemary and their four children live in Barrington, Illinois.

Wolfe's earliest stories appeared in various science fiction magazines and anthologies, most prominently Damon Knight's *Orbit*. They were characterized by extremely odd situations, too soberly set out to be surreal, that nonetheless defied conventional logic. "The Changeling" (1968) presents a series of occurrences that happen to a returning vet; each points to a science-fictional explanation, only to run into the stone wall of the next event. In the end the reader is in the heart of a maze with no way out; yet somehow there is an intuitive logic that holds the story together, if one could only add it up. "Remembrance to Come" (1970), the earliest expression of Wolfe's love for Proust, is closer to the classic one-punch story; but that punch is so out of left field that the reader is not only stunned, but disoriented. "Morning-Glory" (1970) is a variation on the Chinese fable of the man who dreamed he was a butterfly (or was it vice versa?), also incorporating in only eight pages speculations on plant intelligence and its possible application to the evolution of human society.

These stories and their fellows, however striking, were still minor achievements, and Wolfe's first novel, *Operation Ares* (1970), proved he was still groping his way. An attempt to describe the entire progress of a war within the conventional 60,000-word science fiction novel, it is universally regarded as a failure.

Wolfe found himself very suddenly with the publication of the novella *The Fifth Head of Cerberus* in 1972. The style, though noticeably "after Proust" (even echoing *Swann's Way* in its opening line), still has an individual flavor. The background, a French-colonized planet that has a sister-planet harboring a possibly mythical aboriginal race, is richly evoked. Although the nostalgic narrative is fairly linear, the plot (which involves cloning) is anything but. Wolfe does not organize the story in a classical buildup-climax-denouement structure; the meaning must be ferreted out from a complex web of allusions and buried facts, much in the way that Proust and Joyce work.

The piece was completed later that same year with two more novellas, "A Story," by John V. Marsh (one of the first story's characters), which flawlessly sustains a folktale style (in the vein of Australian aborigine myth) for over 40 pages, and *V.R.T.*, which is deliberately built up piecemeal from diary entries and other bits of raw material. The resulting book, though eccentrically structured, is entirely successful at presenting a vividly imagined future time and place and at intimating mysteries that are (somehow satisfyingly) just beyond the reader's grasp. The work stood for nearly a decade as Wolfe's most ambitious, and it clearly foreshadowed his later epic.

Another oddly connected series of stories, recently published as *The Wolfe Archipelago* (1984), began with "The Island of Doctor Death and

Other Stories" (1970), continued with "The Death of Doctor Island" (1973—winner of a Nebula Award), and was completed with "The Doctor of Death Island" (1978). Each story is completely independent of the other two, but they all deal with the same galaxy of themes: the relationship between fiction and reality, acceptable and unacceptable behavior within a society, loneliness and alienation—themes which are arranged differently in each story to cast a different light on the questions being considered.

Throughout the 1970s Wolfe continued to write excellent material at a steady rate, most notably "Against the Lafayette Escadrille" (1972), which audaciously takes up half its three pages with technical description, providing a strong contrast to the pure romantic nostalgia that ensues; "La Befana" (1973), which begins as farce, then moves inexorably in verbal counterpoint to a serious and inevitable conclusion; "Going to the Beach" (1973), a nutshell portrait of a future with robot prostitutes where only failures have to work; "Tracking Song" (1978), a kind of dry run for *Book of the New Sun*, being an odyssey through a strange landscape where human-like creatures fill all the ecological niches; "The Eyeflash Miracles" (1976), concerning a blind boy whose playmates are fictional characters and who can heal the sick and lame; and "Seven American Nights" (1979), a distinguished entry in the Third-Worlder-Visits-Decayed-America subgenre.

In 1975 Wolfe published *Peace*, which won him a Chicago Foundation for Literature Prize. A sort of ghost story, it is made up entirely of the memories of a Midwestern soft-drink magnate. Like "Fifth Head" it is organized in a mosaic fashion, and its evocation of actual times and places is every bit as vivid (and sometimes as odd) as his far future ones. *The Devil in a Forest*, a young adult medieval historical novel sparked by the carol "Good King Wenceslas," followed in 1976.

As the 1970s ended, Wolfe's reputation was in an unusual state. The cognoscenti knew him to be a major talent, but most of his best work was buried in out-of-print anthologies and magazines, and of his four books only one gave a true indication of his range and ability. The first situation was largely rectified by the generous collection *The Island of Doctor Death and Other Stories and Other Stories* (1980); the latter was changed forever by the publication of *The Shadow of the Torturer* (1980), the first volume of his tetralogy *The Book of the New Sun* (later completed by *The Claw of the Conciliator*, 1981, *The Sword of the Lictor*, 1982, and *The Citadel of the Autarch*, 1982).

Although Wolfe drew on the science fiction tradition of "the ancient future" (where the sun has dimmed and magic has returned) and on the gothic fantasies of Mervyn Peake, no one before him had imagined such a setting so rigorously; its only superior is Tolkien. The caste- and guild-ridden society is complex and believable (no mere aping of medieval feudalism); the magic-like future technology is cunningly presented bit by bit; and on practically every page the reader turns a corner to be confronted by some other truly astonishing aspect of setting or story.

Wolfe succeeds brilliantly in two self-imposed tasks: to create sympathy for the callow and callous young protagonist, a journeyman in the torturer's guild; and to keep the reader moving through a deliberately elaborate prose studded with many obsolete words that seem simultaneously brand-new and full of not-quite-grasped meaning. As before, Wolfe uses a simple narrative line (the odyssey) as the skeleton around which he weaves a convoluted web of interconnections that are so much the actual story that one could almost read the four volumes in any order and find them equally rewarding.

Wolfe's reputation is now secure: he is a master of highly textured prose and narrative recomplication, whether book length or short stories as uniquely different as crystal formations. But his most distinctive feature is his way of organizing his work so that the reader becomes a collaborator in building up the gestalt that is the story. Thus, reading him is a challenge and ultimately an unusually satisfying experience.

Selected Bibliography

Primary Sources

Operation Ares. New York: Berkley, 1970.
The Fifth Head of Cerberus. New York: Scribner's, 1972.
Peace. New York: Harper & Row, 1975.
The Devil in a Forest. New York: Follett, 1976.
The Island of Doctor Death and Other Stories and Other Stories. New York: Pocket
    Books, 1980.
The Shadow of the Torturer. New York: Timescape, 1980.
The Claw of the Conciliator. New York: Timescape, 1981.
Gene Wolfe's Book of Days. Garden City, N.Y.: Doubleday, 1981.
The Sword of the Lictor. New York: Timescape, 1982.
The Citadel of the Autarch. New York: Timescape, 1982.
The Castle of the Otter. Willimantic, Conn.: Ziesing Brothers, 1982.
The Wolfe Archipelago. Willimantic, Conn.: Ziesing Brothers, 1984.

Secondary Sources

Clareson, Thomas D. "Variations and Design: The Fiction of Gene Wolfe." In
    Voices for the Future, Vol. 3, Thomas D. Clareson, ed. Bowling Green,
    Oh.: Popular Press, 1984, pp. 1–29.
Dickinson, Mike. "Why They're All Crying Wolfe: A Few Thoughts on *The Book
    of the New Sun*." *Vector* 118 (February 1984): 13–20.

Dirda, Michael. "Gene Wolfe Talks About *The Book of the New Sun.*" *Washington Post Book World*, January 30, 1983, p. 11.

                                                                          DONALD G. KELLER

WOLFE, TOM (1931–   )

One of our most original prose stylists, Tom Wolfe has concerned himself with the liberation of thinking from what he sees as nineteenth-century patterns. Wolfe brings to his subjects a willingness not only to play with language in extraordinary ways but to sift through a mass of often contradictory information to create meaning. He brings an analytical and learned mind to bear on the changing societal landscape which most critics find either too bewildering or beneath their notice. Significantly, Wolfe presents his subjects in their full complexity and ambiguity, engaged by a human consciousness (sometimes his, other times through the eyes of a participant) in a style that seeks to capture the spontaneity of thought.

Thomas Kennerly Wolfe, Jr., entered the world in 1931 in Richmond, Virginia, where his father was an editor and professor of agronomy. At Washington and Lee University Wolfe majored in English and played baseball. A washout as a major-league pitcher, he settled for a doctorate from Yale in American Studies, a stint he compares to reading *Mr. Sammler's Planet* at a single sitting. Then, trapped "in the twisted grip of a disease of our time in which the sufferer experiences an overwhelming urge to join the 'real world,' " he worked as a furniture mover before becoming a reporter at the Springfield, Massachusetts, *Union* in 1956. In 1959 he moved to the *Washington Post*, winning awards as Latin American correspondent and as a humorist. Weary of routine assignments, he began prodigious magazine free-lancing and joined the staff of the New York *Herald Tribune*. During the newspaper strike of 1963, *Esquire* sent him to California to cover a custom car show. When Wolfe tried to force the resultant vignettes, odds and ends of scholarship, bits of memoir, short bursts of sociology, apostrophes, epithets, moan cackles and anything else that came into his head into a standard journalistic piece, he found it impossible. Under deadline pressure from managing editor Byron Dobell because a two-page illustration had already been locked into the presses, Wolfe typed his rough notes into a memorandum that began "Dear Byron." Dobell deleted the salutation and ran "There Goes (Varoom! Varoom!) That Kandy-Kolered (Thphhhhhh!) Tangerine-Flake Streamline Baby (Rahghhh!) Around the Bend (Brummmmmmmmmmmmmmm) . . . " just as it was. After this stylistic breakthrough, Wolfe found himself outside the conceptions of standard journalism, and he produced many pieces reflecting the strange, violent, paradoxical 1960s for *Esquire* and *New York* magazine, subsequently collected into *The Kandy-Kolored Tangerine-Flake*

Streamline Baby (1965) and *The Pump House Gang* (1968). *The Electric Kool-Aid Acid Test* (1969), Wolfe's extensive reportage on novelist Ken Kesey's cross-country freak odyssey with his band of Merry Pranksters, was both a critical and commercial success.

Wolfe's involvement with style in both prose and subject matter—in art, architecture, and even politics—provided the basis for most of his subsequent work. *Radical Chic and Mau-Mauing the Flak Catchers* (1970) triggered a furor; he was accused of being everything from a racist to a snob, who, according to Irving Howe, "fixates on details of manner and appearance in order to pass sentences of dismissal for inadequacies of style." But Wolfe had his defenders as well: *Newsweek* called him "some kind of great writer," and William F. Buckley declared him "an unfortunate victim of ideological ire. His wit attracts the witless among the critics." In his next book, *The Painted Word* (1975), Wolfe uncovers a literary component in the development of modern art. The following year he published *Mauve Gloves and Madmen, Clutter and Vine* which he referred to as "a higher form of writer's block." This book contained "The Truest Sport," which anticipated *The Right Stuff* (1979), his history of the early years of the space race and the impulses behind it. In *Bauhaus to Our House* (1981), he traces the development of modern architecture from its idealistic German origins to the present-day ubiquitous glass boxes.

While some critics have accused Wolfe of being too subjective, his use of proliferating points of view and vastness of detail can be seen as strategies designed to encourage readers to make their own judgments of events. Indeed, typically Wolfe uses outward details of style and status to reveal the inner workings and meanings of his subjects. As an arch-defender of New Journalism, Wolfe might suggest that his private fictions (in the sense of *fictio*, or something made) with their freely admitted biases are actually far more objective than the corporate fictions of standard journalism which conceal their prejudices behind a mask of objectivity. Conventional journalists cry foul (or rather, "subjective!") whenever this facade of objectivity is breached; however, they do not give us "all the news that's fit to print," but merely all the news that *fits* the space demands, editorial policy, and their notion of what is news.

Other critics have tried to dismiss Wolfe as a fad—a mannerist who would be co-opted or simply run dry. But because the world shows few signs of anything except becoming stranger and stranger with ever-increasing velocity, a writer with the ability to perceive, analyze, and communicate the significance of the psychic structures that underlie the cultural process won't be idle. Michael Johnson states that a writer like Wolfe "teaches us about alternate views of the popular universe, helps us tune our crap detectors, validates personal vision in an age of pre-fab and impersonal information, decodes images, and offers the world as art and thereby gives a potentially special significance to all human experience." Surely these are ends devoutly to be wished.

Selected Bibliography

Primary Sources

The Kandy-Kolored Tangerine-Flake Streamline Baby. New York: Farrar, Straus & Giroux, 1965.

The Electric Kool-Aid Acid Test. New York: Farrar, Straus & Giroux, 1968.

The Pump House Gang. New York: Farrar, Straus & Giroux, 1968.

Radical Chic and Mau-Mauing the Flak Catchers. New York: Farrar, Straus & Giroux, 1970.

The New Journalism. New York: Harper & Row, 1973.

The Painted Word. New York: Farrar, Straus & Giroux, 1975.

Mauve Gloves and Madmen, Clutter and Vine. New York: Farrar, Straus & Giroux, 1976.

The Right Stuff. New York: Farrar, Straus & Giroux, 1979.

In Our Time. New York: Farrar, Straus & Giroux, 1980.

Bauhaus to Our House. New York: Farrar, Straus & Giroux, 1981.

The Purple Decades. New York: Farrar, Straus & Giroux, 1982.

Secondary Sources

Dennis, Everette, and William Rivers. *Other Voices: The New Journalism in America*. San Francisco: Canfield Press, 1983.

Hartshorne, Thomas L. "Tom Wolfe on the 1960s." *Midwest Quarterly* 23 (Winter 1982): 144–63.

Hellman, John. *Fables of Fact: The New Journalism As New Fiction*. Urbana: University of Illinois Press, 1981.

Hollowell, John *Fact and Fiction: The New Journalism and the Nonfiction Novel*. Chapel Hill: University of North Carolina Press, 1977.

Johnson, Michael. *The New Journalism: The Underground Press, the Artists of Nonfiction, and the Change in the Established Media*. Lawrence: University of Kansas Press, 1971.

Kallan, Richard. "Style and the New Journalism: A Rhetorical Study of Tom Wolfe." *Communications Monograph* 46 (1979): 52–62.

Weber, Ronald. "Tom Wolfe's Happiness Explosion." *Journal of Popular Culture* 8 (1974): 71–79.

PAT McKERCHER

Z

ZELAZNY, ROGER (1937–   )

Roger Zelazny burst upon the science fiction scene in the mid-1960s with a flurry of short stories, novellas, and novelettes that quickly established his reputation as both a popular and highly successful commercial writer. Between 1962, when his first stories appeared, and 1969, when he quit the Social Security Administration to write full time, he won the prestigious Hugo and Nebula awards twice each and was nominated for them 19 other times. Since then, he has won the Hugo twice more and the Nebula once.

Zelazny, who was born in Euclid, Ohio, in 1937, graduated from Euclid Senior High School in 1955, received a B.A. in English from Case Western Reserve University in 1959 and an M.A. from Columbia University in Elizabethan and Jacobean Drama in 1962. From 1960 to 1963, he was in the Ohio National Guard, serving a six-month tour of active duty in 1960, mostly in Texas. In 1965, he moved to Baltimore; in 1975, he moved to Santa Fe, New Mexico.

Writing in a precise but highly poetic style and drawing heavily from mythology, literature, psychology, and the hard sciences, Zelazny explores the nature of humankind and of reality. His fiction forces readers to consider alternatives and possibilities while promoting individual psychological growth and universal renewal.

Zelazny's earliest stories, written when he was in the fifth or sixth grade, display characteristics that show up later in his work. His unpublished "Record" series, for example, is iconoclastic, experimental, humorous, and ironic. It relates the adventures of two inept but sympathetic monsters who live in the catacombs under Paris and are reluctantly sent on missions by their boss, the devil. Their fabulous luck always permits them to succeed, but in succeeding they frustrate their boss's evil intentions. The stories show a remarkable range of imagination and a capacity to create and implement a rather detailed and complicated mythology.

They also show an ability to adapt other sources to his work, a characteristic that marks his writing from the beginning. For example, in *The Dream Master* (1966), he alters the Scandinavian myth of Ragnarok to fit the moon symbolism of his tale. In *Isle of the Dead* (1969), he creates a mythology, attributes it to a race called the Pei'ans, and then uses it as background for the story. In *Damnation Alley* (1969), he uses the noh play structure to project a dream that raises the general level of the story. In *Eye of Cat* (1983), he converts the "Newsreel" and "Camera Eye" techniques of John Dos Passos' *U.S.A* triology to "Disk" sections in order to quickly and efficiently sketch in background material for the reader. Even in his pure extrapolation of science, the foundation of science fiction stories, his extraordinary creativity makes his tales unique. In "Home Is the Hangman" (1975), for example, his anthropomorphic solar system probe not only develops personality but also manages to integrate the four personalities of its creator into its own, in a metaphoric conquest of schizophrenia.

Zelazny's fiction constantly forces his readers to test reality. Whether his themes are immortality, genetic engineering, bionics, love, revenge, or renewal, underlying them is his form and chaos philosophy. Briefly, it postulates two universal, antithetical tendencies: one to create, the other to destroy. They are symbiotic. Form must be won from chaos, but even as it is being won, it is being destroyed to create raw material for new forms. This is the essence of renewal. All things change by means of this process, and in changing, they grow and evolve. The most obvious use of the form and chaos philosophy occurs in Zelazny's *Amber* novels, where chaos actually becomes a location in the drama.

Zelazny uses several means to force the reader to consider other possible realities, among them alternate worlds or universes. The *Amber* novels, for example, display a series of alternate worlds between Amber and Chaos, including our own, and end with Corwin inscribing a new universe that may have different physical laws than ours. Dilvish, the protagonist of the Dilvish the Damned stories, often shifts from one plane of existence to another. And the as-yet-unfinished *Changeling* series uses an alternate world where magic works. Zelazny explains the world as another form of reality. This, then, forces him to create laws for the use of magic. The mixing of our world with various magical worlds not only forces consideration of different possible realities but also tends to blur the traditional distinctions between fantasy and science fiction. This is seen most clearly in *Lord of Light* (1967) where a party of space colonists adopt roles from Hindu mythology and then shape a world to fit it with advanced machines and devices.

Renewal, the most persistent Zelazny theme, is a product of the form and chaos process. The physical action of his stories often results in renewal of a world, as in *This Immortal* (1966), or a universe, as in the *Amber* novels, but linked to the physical quest is a psychological quest by the hero to renew himself. It is on this quest that Zelazny builds a series of moving and compelling characters, which may eventually prove to be his greatest strength as a writer. They include Gallinger ("A Rose for Ecclesiastes," 1963), Carlton Davits ("The Doors of His Face, the Lamps of His Mouth," 1965), Sam (*Lord of Light*), Corwin (the *Amber* novels), and Billy Black-horse Singer (*Eye of Cat*).

Although Zelazny's characters are oversized in some way to meet the commercial demands of science fiction, their psychologies are entirely credible. Davits, for example, is a self-made man and the solar system's greatest fisherman, but he is very proud and must therefore fall. Traumatized by the solar system's most fearsome fish, he comes to ruin, but he rescues and renews himself by facing his fear and defeating it. This is the pattern of those Zelazny characters who evolve to psychological health under the whip of their experience. Like the existentialists, Zelazny believes that one must "make oneself" and in doing so learns what it is to be human.

If the modernist tradition in literature has reached a deadend as Norman Mailer believes, and if technology and science are altering human consciousness in a new way as philosopher William Barrett believes, and if we are searching for a new world view in our return to enchantment as editor Kathleen Agena believes, then Roger Zelazny's impact will be significant because he has already found hope for the future in his faith in the ability of people to transcend themselves.

Selected Bibliography

Primary Sources

This Immortal. New York: Ace, 1966.
Lord of Light. New York: Doubleday, 1967.
Nine Princes in Amber. New York: Doubleday, 1970.
The Guns of Avalon. New York: Doubleday, 1972.
The Sign of the Unicorn. New York: Doubleday, 1975.
The Hand of Oberon. New York: Doubleday, 1976.
The Courts of Chaos. New York: Doubleday, 1978.
Changeling. New York: Ace, 1980.
Eye of Cat. New York: Timescape, 1983.

Secondary Sources

Levack, Daniel J. H. *Amber Dreams: A Roger Zelazny Bibliography*. San Francisco: Underwood/Miller, 1983.
Sanders, Joseph. *Roger Zelazny: A Primary and Secondary Bibliography*. Boston: G. K. Hall, 1981.
Yoke, Carl B. *Roger Zelazny*. Mercer Island, Wash.: Starmont, 1979.

————. "Roger Zelazny." *Dictionary of Literary Biography: Twentieth Century American Science Fiction Writers*. Detroit: Gale Research Co., 1981, pp. 213–20.

————. "Roger Zelazny." *Twentieth Century Science Fiction Writers*. New York: St. Martin's Press, 1981, pp. 609–10.

CARL B. YOKE

Selected Bibliography of Postmodern Criticism

Aldridge, John W. *Time to Murder and Create: The Contemporary Novel in Crisis*. New York: McKay, 1966.

Allen, Mary. *The Necessary Bleakness: Women in American Fiction of the Sixties*. Urbana: University of Illinois Press, 1976.

Alter, Robert. *Partial Magic: The Novel as Self-Conscious Genre*. Berkeley: University of California Press, 1975.

Altieri, Charles. "From Symbolist Thought to Immanence: The Ground of Postmodern American Poetics." *boundary 2* 1 (1973): 605–41.

Arneheim, Rudolf. *Entropy and Art: An Essay on Disorder and Order*. Berkeley: University of California Press, 1971.

Auerbach, Eric. *Mimesis: The Representation of Reality in Western Literature*. Trans. W. R. Trask. Princeton, N.J.: Princeton University Press, 1953.

Barth, John. *The Friday Book: Essays and Other Nonfiction*. New York: G. P. Putnam, 1984.

Baumback, Jonathan. *The Landscape of Nightmare: Studies in the Contemporary American Novel*. New York: NYU Press, 1965.

Bellamy, Joe David. *The New Fiction: Interviews with Innovative American Writers*. Urbana: University of Illinois Press, 1974.

Benamou, Michel, and Charles Caramello. *Performance in Postmodern Culture*. Madison, Wis.: Coda Press, 1977.

Berger, Peter. *The Sacred Canopy: Elements of a Sociological Theory of Religion*. Garden City, N.Y.: Doubleday, 1967.

Bergonzi, Bernard. *The Situation of the Novel*. Pittsburgh: University of Pittsburgh Press, 1970.

Black, Max. *Models and Metaphors: Studies in Language and Philosophy*. Ithaca, N.Y.: Cornell University Press, 1962.

———. *The Nature of Mathematics*. London: Kegan Paul, 1933.

Blau, Herbert. *Take Up the Bodies: Theater at the Vanishing Point*. Urbana: University of Illinois Press, 1982.

Bradbury, Malcolm. *Possibilities: Essays on the State of the Novel*. New York: Oxford University Press, 1973.

Bryant, Jerry H. *The Open Decision: The Contemporary American Novel and Its Intellectual Background*. New York: Free Press, 1970.

Bulter, Christopher. *After the Writer: An Essay on the Contemporary Avant-garde.* Oxford: Clarendon Press, 1980.

Burnham, Jack. *Great Western Salt Works: Essays on the Meaning of Post- Formalist Art.* New York: George Braziller, 1974.

Burtt, E. A. *The Metaphysical Foundations of Modern Science.* Garden City, N.Y.: Doubleday, 1954.

Butor, Michel. *Inventory: Essays by Michel Butur.* Edited by Richard Howard. New York: Simon and Schuster, 1968.

Cage, John. *Writing Through "Finnegans Wake."* Tulsa, Okla.: University of Tulsa Press, 1978.

Campbell, Joseph, ed. *Myths, Dreams and Religion.* New York: E. P. Dutton, 1970.

Capra, Fritjof. *The Tao of Physics: An Exploration of the Parallels Between Modern Physics and Eastern Mysticism.* Boulder, Colo.: Shambhada, 1975.

Caramello, Charles. *Silverless Mirrors: Book, Self and Postmodern American Fiction.* Tallahassee: University of Florida Press, 1984.

Cassirer, Ernst. *Language and Myth.* Trans. Suzanne K. Langer. New York: Dover, 1946.

———. *Language.* Vol. 1 of *The Philosophy of Symbolic Forms.* Trans. Ralph Manheim. New Haven, Conn.: Yale University Press, 1964.

———. *Mythical Thought.* Vol. 2 of *The Philosophy of Symbolic Forms.* Trans. Ralph Manheim. New Haven, Conn.: Yale University Press, 1964.

———. *The Problem of Knowledge.* Trans. William H. Woglom and Charles W. Hendel. New Haven, Conn.: Yale University Press, 1950.

Christenson, Inger. *The Meaning of Metafiction.* Bergen, Norway: Universitets-forlaget, 1981.

Cohn, Dorritt. *Transparent Minds: Narrative Modes for Presenting Consciousness in Fiction.* Princeton, N. J.: Princeton University Press, 1978.

Cope, Jackson, and Geoffrey Green, eds. *Novel vs. Fiction: The Contemporary Reformation. Genre,* special issue 14 (Spring 1981).

Courturier, Maurice, ed. *Representation and Performance in Postmodern Fiction.* Montpelier, France: Delta, 1983.

Croce, Benedetto. *History: Its Theory and Practices.* Trans. Douglas Ainslie. New York: Russell & Russell, 1960.

Culler, Jonathan. *On Deconstruction: Theory and Criticism After Structuralism.* Ithaca, N.Y.: Cornell University Press, 1982.

———. *Structuralist Poetics.* London: Routledge & Kegan Paul, 1975.

Derrida, Jacques. *Of Grammatology.* Trans. Gayatri Spivak. Baltimore, Md.: Johns Hopkins University Press, 1974.

Ditsky, John M. "The Man on the Quaker Oats Box: Characteristics of Recent Experimental Fiction." *Georgia Review* 26 (Fall 1972): 297–313.

Eagleton, Terry. *Literary Theory. An Introduction.* Minneapolis: University of Minnesota Press, 1983.

———. *Marxism and Literary Criticism.* Berkeley: University of California Press, 1976.

Eisenstein, Sergei. *Film Form: Essays in Film Theory.* Ed. Jay Leyda. New York: Harcourt, Brace & World, Harvest, 1949.

Eliade, Mircea. *The Sacred and the Profane*. Trans. William R. Trask. New York: Harcourt, Brace & World, Harvest, 1959.

Federman, Raymond. *Surfiction: Fiction Now and Tomorrow*. Chicago: Swallow Press, 1975.

————, and Carl. R. Lovitt, eds. *Current Trends in American Fiction*. *Substance*, special issue 27 (1980).

Fiedler, Leslie. *Waiting for the End*. New York: Stein & Day, 1970.

Friedman, Alan. *The Turn of the Novel*. New York: Oxford University Press, 1966.

Frye, Northrup. *Anatomy of Criticism: Four Essays*. Princeton, N.J.: Princeton University Press, 1957.

Gado, Frank. *First Person: Conversations on Writers and Writing*. Schenectady, N.Y.: Union College Press, 1973.

Gardner, John. *On Moral Fiction*. New York: Basic Books, 1978.

Garvin, Harry R. *Romanticism, Modernism and Postmodernism*. Lewisburg, Pa.: Bucknell University Press, 1980.

Gass, William H. *Fiction and the Figures of Life*. New York: Alfred A. Knopf, 1970.

————. *Habitations of the Word*. New York: Simon & Schuster, 1985.

————. *On Being Blue*. Boston: David R. Godine, 1976.

————. *The World Within the Word*. New York: Alfred A. Knopf, 1978.

Gilman, Richard. *The Confusion of Realms*. New York: Random House, 1969.

————. "The Idea of the Avant-Garde." *Partisan Review* 34 (1972): 382–96.

Graff, Gerald. *Literature Against Itself: Literary Ideas in Modern Society*. Chicago: University of Chicago Press, 1979.

Grossvogel, David I. *Limits of the Novel*. Ithaca, N.Y.: Cornell University Press, 1968.

Guerard, Albert J. "Notes on the Rhetoric of Anti-Realist Fiction." *TriQuarterly* 30 (1974): 3–50.

Harris, Charles B. *Contemporary American Novelists of the Absurd*. Princeton, N.J.: Princeton University Press, 1961.

Harvey, William J. *Character and the Novel*. Ithaca, N.Y.: Cornell University Press, 1966.

Hassan, Ihab. *The Dismemberment of Orpheus: Toward a Post-Modern Literature*. New York: Oxford University Press, 1971.

————. *Paracriticisms*. Urbana: University of Illinois Press, 1975.

————. *Radical Innocence: The Contemporary American Novel*. Princeton, N.J.: Princeton University Press, 1961.

————. *The Right Promethean Fire: Imagination, Science, and Cultural Change*. Urbana: University of Illinois Press, 1980.

Heisenberg, Werner. *Physics and Philosophy*. New York: Harper & Row, 1958.

Hendin, Josephine. *Vulnerable People: A View on American Literature Since 1945*. New York: Oxford University Press, 1978.

Hellman, John. *Fables of Fact: The New Journalism as New Fiction*. Urbana: University of Illinois Press, 1981.

Hester, Marcus B. *The Meaning of Poetic Metaphor*. Paris: Mouton, 1967.

Hicks, Walter J. *The Metafictional City*. Chapel Hill: University of North Carolina Press, 1981.

Hofstadter, Douglas R. *Godel, Escher, Bach: An Eternal Golden Braid*. New York: Basic Books, 1979.

Hollowell, John. *Facts and Fictions: The New Journalism*. Chapel Hill: University of North Carolina Press, 1977.

Howe, Irving. *The Decline of the New*. New York: Harcourt, Brace, 1970.

————. *The Idea of the Modern in Literature and Arts*. New York: Horizon, 1967.

Hoy, David Couzens. *The Critical Circle: Literature and History in Contemporary Hermeneutics*. Berkeley: University of California Press, 1978.

Hutcheon, Linda. *Narcissistic Narrative: The Metafictional Paradox*. New York: Methuen, 1984.

Johsen, William R. "Toward a Redefinition of Modernism." *boundary 2* 2 (Spring 1974): 539–56.

Josipovici, R. *The Lessons of Modernism and Other Essays*. Totowa, N.J.: Rowman & Littlefield, 1977.

Kahler, Eric. *The Disintegration of Form in the Arts*. New York: George Braziller, 1968.

Kawin, Bruce F. *The Mind of the Novel: Reflexive Fiction and the Ineffable*. Princeton, N.J.: Princeton University Press, 1982.

Kellman, Steven G. *The Self-Begetting Novel*. New York: Columbia University Press, 1980.

Kellogg, Robert, and Robert Scholes. *The Nature of Narrative*. New York: Oxford University Press, 1966.

Kennard, Jean E. *Number and Nightmare: Forms of Fantasy in Contemporary Fiction*. Hamden, Conn.: Archon, 1975.

Kennedy, Alan. *Meaning and Signs in Fiction*. London: Macmillan, 1978.

Kenner, Hugh. *The Counterfeiters*. Garden City, N.Y.: Doubleday, 1968.

————. *The Stoic Comedians: Flaubert, Joyce and Beckett*. London: Will Allen, 1964.

Kermode, Frank. *The Sense of an Ending*. New York: Oxford University Press, 1968.

Klein, Marcus, ed. *The American Novel Since World War II*. Greenwich, Conn.: Fawcett, 1969.

Klinkowitz, Jerome. *The Life of Fiction*. Urbana: University of Illinois Press, 1977.

————. *Literary Disruptions: The Makings of a Post-Contemporary American Fiction*. Urbana: University of Illinois Press, 1975.

Kostelanetz, Richard. *The End of Intelligent Writing*. New York: Sheed and Ward, 1974.

Kuhn, Thomas. *The Structure of Scientific Revolutions*. Chicago: University of Chicago Press, 1962.

Laing, R. D. *The Divided Self: An Existential Study in Sanity and Madness*. Baltimore: Penguin, Pelican, 1965.

————. *The Politics of Experience*. New York: Ballantine, 1968.

Langer, Suzanne K. *Feeling and Form: A Theory of Art*. New York: Charles Scribner's Sons, 1953.

————. *Philosophy in a New Key*. Cambridge, Mass.: Harvard University Press, 1942.

LeClair, Tom, and Larry McCaffery. *Anything Can Happen: Interviews with Contemporary American Novelists*. Urbana: University of Illinois Press, 1983.

Lemon, Lee T. *Portraits of the Artist in Contemporary Fiction*. Lincoln, Neb.: University of Nebraska Press, 1985.

Lodge, David. *The Modes of Modern Writing: Metaphor, Metonymy and the Typology of Modern Literature*. London: Edward Arnold, 1977.

Lukásc, Georg. *Realism in Our Time: Literature and the Class Struggle*. Trans. John and Neale Mandar. New York: Harper and Row, 1962.

McCaffery, Larry. "The Gass-Gardner Debate: Showdown on Mainstreet." *The Literary Review* 23 (Fall 1979): 133–44.

———. *The Metafictional Muse: The Works of Coover, Gass and Barthelme*. Pittsburgh: University of Pittsburgh Press, 1983.

McConnell, Frank D. *Four Postwar American Novelists: Bellow, Mailer, Barth and Pynchon*. Chicago: University of Chicago Press, 1977.

McLuhan, Marshall. *The Gutenberg Galaxy: The Making of Typographic Man*. New York: New American Library, 1969.

Malmgren, Carl Darryl. *Fictional Space in the Modernist and Postmodernist American Novel*. Lewisburg, Pa.: Bucknell University Press, 1985.

Neff, Emergy E. *The Poetry of History: The Contributions of Literature and Literary Scholarship to the Writing of History Since Voltaire*. New York: Columbia University Press, 1947.

Nelson, Cary. *The Incarnate Word: Literature as Verbal Space*. Urbana: University of Illinois Press, 1973.

Nin, Anaïs. *The Novel of the Future*. New York: Macmillan, 1968.

Olderman, Raymond M. *Beyond the Waste Land*. New Haven, Conn.: Yale University Press, 1972.

Ortega y Gasset, José. *The Dehumanization of Art*. Garden City, N.Y.: Doubleday, 1956.

———. *The Modern Theme*. Trans. James Cleugh. New York: Harper & Row, 1961.

Pinsker, Sanford. "*Ulysses* and the Post-Modern Temper." *Midwest Quarterly* 15 (Summer 1974): 406–16.

Poggioli, Renato. *The Theory of the Avant-Garde*. Trans. Gerald Fitzgerald. New York: Harper & Row, 1971.

Poirier, Richard. *The Performing Self: Compositions and Decompositions in the Language of Contemporary Life*. New York: Oxford University Press, 1971.

———. *A World Elsewhere: The Place of Style in American Literature*. New Haven, Conn.: Yale University Press, 1972.

Popper, Karl. *The Logic of Scientific Discovery*. New York: Science Editions, 1961.

———. *Objective Knowledge: An Evolutionary Approach*. New York: Oxford University Press, 1972.

Putz, Manfred. *The Story of Identity: American Fiction of the Sixties*. Stuttgart: Metzler, 1979.

Quine, Willard V.O. *From a Logical Point of View: Nine Logico-Philosophical Essays*. New York: Harper & Row, 1961.

Richards, I. A. *The Philosophy of Rhetoric*. New York: Oxford University Press, 1936.

———. *Principles of Literary Criticism*. New York: Harcourt, Brace & World, Harvest, 1972.

Richter, David H. *Fable's End: Completeness and Closure in Rhetorical Fiction.* Chicago: University of Chicago Press, 1974.

Robbe-Grillet, Alain. *For a New Novel.* Trans. Richard Howard. New York: Grove Press, 1964.

Rochberg, George. "The Avant-Garde and the Aesthetics of Survival." *New Literary History* 3 (Autumn 1971): 71–92.

Rose, Margaret. *Parody and Metafiction.* London: Crown Helm, 1979.

Rosenberg, Harold. *The Re-Definition of Art: Action Art to Pop to Earthworks.* New York: Horizon Press, 1972.

———. *The Tradition of the New.* New York: McGraw-Hill, 1965.

Rosenblum, Robert. *Cubism and Twentieth Century Art.* New York: Abrams, 1966.

Rupp, Richard H. *Celebration in Postwar American Fiction.* Coral Gables, Fla.: University of Miami Press, 1970.

Russell, Charles. *The Avant-Garde Today.* Urbana: University of Illinois Press, 1981.

Said, Edward. *Beginnings: Intention and Method.* Baltimore: Johns Hopkins University Press, 1975.

———. "Contemporary Fiction and Criticism." *TriQuarterly* 33 (Winter 1975): 230–41.

———. "What Is Beyond Formalism?" *Modern Language Notes* 86 (1971): 933–45.

———. *The World, the Text, and the Critic.* Cambridge, Mass.: Harvard University Press, 1983.

Sarraute, Nathalie. *The Age of Suspicion: Essays on the Novel.* Trans. Maria Jolas. New York: George Braziller, 1963.

Scheffler, Israel. *Science and Subjectivity.* New York: Bobbs-Merrill, 1967.

Scholes, Robert. *Fabulation and Metafiction.* Urbana: University of Illinois Press, 1979.

Schultz, Max. *Radical Sophistication: Studies in Contemporary Jewish-American Novelists.* Athens: Ohio University Press, 1969.

Sewell, Elizabeth. *The Orphic Voice.* New Haven, Conn.: Yale University Press, 1960.

———. *The Structure of Poetry.* London: Kegan Paul, 1951.

Shattuck, Roger. *The Banquet Years.* New York: Random House, 1968.

Sontag, Susan. *Against Interpretation.* New York: Farrar, Straus & Giroux, 1966.

———. *Styles of Radical Will.* New York: Farrar, Straus & Giroux, 1969.

Spanos, William V. "The Detective and the Boundary: Some Notes on the Postmodern Literary Imagination." *boundary 2* 2 (Fall 1972): 147–68.

Spencer, Sharon. *Space, Time and Structure in the Modern Novel.* Chicago: Swallow Press, 1971.

Steiner, George. *Extraterritorial: Papers on Literature and the Language Revolution.* New York: Atheneum, 1967.

Stevick, Philip. *Alternative Pleasures.* Urbana: University of Illinois Press, 1981.

Sukenick, Ronald. *In Form: Digressions on the Act of Writing.* Carbondale: Southern Illinois University Press, 1985.

Sypher, Wylie. *Rococo to Cubism.* New York: Random House, 1960.

Tani, Stefano. *The Doomed Detective: The Contribution of the Detective Novel to Postmodern American and Italian Fiction.* Carbondale, Ill.: Southern Illinois University Press, 1984.

Tanner, Tony. *City of Words: American Fiction 1950–1970*. New York: Harper & Row, 1971.

Toulmin, Stephen. "The Construal of Reality: Criticism in Modern and Postmodern Science." *Critical Inquiry* 9 (1982): 93–111.

Turbayne, Colin M. *The Myth of Metaphor*. Columbia: University of South Carolina Press, 1970.

Vaihinger, H. *The Philosophy of "As If": A System of the Theoretical, Practical, and Religious Fictions of Mankind*. Trans. C. K. Ogden. New York: Barnes & Noble, 1966.

Valéry, Paul. *Aesthetics*. Trans. Ralph Manheim. New York: Random House, 1964.

———. *The Art of Poetry*. Trans. Denise Folliot. New York: Random House, 1964.

Wallace, Ronald. *The Last Laugh: Form and Affirmation in the Contemporary American Novel*. Columbia: University of Missouri Press, 1979.

Wasson, Richard. "From Priest to Prometheus: Culture and Criticism in the Post-Modern Period." *Journal of Modern Literature* 3 (1974): 1190–1208.

———. "Notes on a New Sensibility." *Partisan Review* 36 (1969): 460–77.

Weinberg, Helen. *The New Novel in America: The Kafkan* Mode in Contemporary Fiction. Ithaca, N.Y.: Cornell University Press, 1970.

Wheelis, Allen. *The End of the Modern Age*. New York: Basic Books, 1971.

Wilde, Alan. *Horizons of Assent: Modernism, Postmodernism, and the Ironic Imagination*. Baltimore: Johns Hopkins University Press, 1981.

Zavarzadeh, Mas'ud. *The Mythopoeic Reality: The Postwar American Nonfiction Novel*. Urbana: University of Illinois Press, 1976.

Ziolkowski, Theodore. "Towards a Post-Modern Aesthetic." *Mosaic* 2 (Summer 1969): 112–19.

Index

Pages in boldface indicate entry article.

Notes on Contributors

MICHAEL J. ADAMS has published articles about twentieth-century American and British literature and film in *Critique*, *Dictionary of Literary Biography*, *Fitzgerald/Hemingway Annual*, and *Southern Quarterly*.

RAE ARMANTROUT is the author of three books of poetry: *Extremities* (The Figures, 1978), *The Invention of Hunger* (Tuumba, 1979), and *Precedence* (Burning Deck, 1985). Her poems and essays have appeared in many magazines including *Credences*, *Ironwood*, *Partisan Review*, and *Poetics Journal*. She lives and sometimes teaches in San Diego, California.

PETER J. BAILEY teaches contemporary fiction and fiction writing at St. Lawrence University; he is the author of *Reading Stanley Elkin* (forthcoming from the University of Illinois Press) and has published essays on Robert Coover, John Gardner, Frederick Exley, and Elkin.

BARBARA BARNES received her M.A. degree from San Diego State University in English literature; her study of William Eastlake's Southwestern fiction appeared in the *Review of Contemporary Fiction*'s special issue on Eastlake.

DAVID BEVAN is Professor of French at Acadia University (Canada) and has published on various aspects of contemporary literature and film. He is editor of *Swiss-French Studies* and will have a book on Tournier appearing soon from Rodopi, The Hague.

IAN BERNARD, a native South African, is a graduate student at San Diego State University.

RICHARD A. BETTS is an Assistant Professor of English at Penn State University. His publications dealing with Edwin O'Conner, Thomas Berger, William Styron, and Gore Vidal have appeared in journals such as *Critique*, *CLA Journal*, *College Literature*, and *Ball State University Forum*.

ALFRED F. BOE teaches English and comparative literature at San Diego State University, with his main interests being comparative mythology and the Bible-as-literature.

J. D. BROWN is an editor at *Northwest Review* (University of Oregon), anthologist, reviewer, and author of books on Henry Miller, wooden boat building, and current religious practices in China (where he taught English at the Xi-an Medical College).

DOUG CAPPS received his M.A. degree from San Diego State University and has written on Mel Torme's postmodern music in *New Music Forum*.

CHARLES CARAMELLO is the author of *Silverless Mirrors: Book, Self & Postmodern American Fiction* and co-editor of *Performance in Postmodern Culture*. He is Associate Professor at the University of Maryland.

CHRIS CECIL is a graduate student at San Diego State University.

C. BARRY CHABOT chairs the Department of English at Miami University in Oxford, Ohio.

LORI CHAMBERLAIN teaches at the University of California, San Diego. She works on postmodern translation/poetics and on contemporary American and Latin American fiction.

ASOKE CHANDA received his Ph.D. in comparative literature from the University of Illinois. Currently a lecturer in English Literature at South Thames College (London), he has written articles for *Calcutta Review*, *Comparison*, and *Comparative Literature*.

RICHARD A. COHEN teaches philosophy at Penn State University, Scranton. He has translated Emmanuel Levinas' *Ethics and Infinity* and is author of several articles on contemporary Continental philosophy.

MAURICE COUTURIER is Professor of American Studies at the University of Nice. He has published a novel, *La Polka Piquée*, and books on Nabokov and Barthelme.

DAVID W. COVEY is a graduate student specializing in postmodern fiction at San Diego State University.

WILLIAM A. COVINO is Associate Professor of English at San Diego State University. His articles on Hugh Blair, Byron, DeQuincey, Kenneth Burke, and Jacques Derrida examine how these writers prefigure and illuminate postmodern developments in literature and literacy.

STEVEN CRESAP, an Assistant Professor of history at Hobart and William Smith Colleges, is a specialist in Modern European intellectual history.

G. B. CRUMP is Professor of English at Central Missouri State University. He is the author of *The Novels of Wright Morris* (University of Nebraska Press) and has published articles in *Critique*, *Contemporary Literature*, and *The D.H. Lawrence Review*.

SUSAN CURRIER is Associate Professor of English at California Polytechnic State University in San Luis Obispo. She has published essays and bibliographies on various nineteenth- and twentieth-century women writers.

MARIA VITTORIA D'AMICO is a Professor of American Literature at the University of Catania (Sicily). She has published essays on various contemporary American authors, including Thomas Pynchon and Gilbert Sorrentino.

RONALD C. DIXON heads the English Department at the Westlake School for Girls in Los Angeles. He received his doctorate in modern literature from SUNY-Binghamton.

GERALD DUFF is the author of a novel, *Indian Giver* (Indiana University Press, 1983), and a collection of poems, *Calling Collect* (University Press of Florida, 1982), as well as critical books and essays on a variety of topics. He is presently Vice-President and Dean at Rhodes College.

WELCH D. EVERMAN is the author of a novel, *Orion*, critical books on Jerzy Kosinski and Italo Calvino, and dozens of short stories, essays, and reviews.

MICHAEL GLOSSAN's fiction and essays have appeared in various magazines, including *Roadworks*.

J. KERRY GRANT, Associate Professor of English at St. Lawrence University, has written articles on Wallace Stevens, Melville, Tom McGuane, Steve Katz, and Edward Johnson.

GEOFFREY GREEN is Associate Professor of English at San Francisco State University. With Robert Scholes he is the editor of *Novel vs. Fiction:*

The Contemporary Reformation, a critical study on Eric Auerbach, and he has written numerous essays and works of fiction.

DONALD J. GREINER has edited books on Stephen Crane and contemporary American poetry, and has written books on Robert Frost, John Hawkes, and John Updike. His second book on Updike, *John Updike's Novels*, was just published by Ohio University Press. He teaches at the University of South Carolina.

DAVID S. GROSS is Associate Professor of English at the University of Oklahoma. He has published essays on E. L. Doctorow, Zola, Sartre, Flaubert, William Norris, and Blake.

JOHN Z. GUZLOWSKI's work on modern and postmodern American fiction has appeared in *Modern Fiction Studies*, *Critique*, *Journal of Evolutionary Psychology*, *Pynchon Notes*, and *Markham Review*. He is also the co-author of the annotated Kerouac bibliography. He currently teaches at Eastern Illinois University.

JOHN HELLMAN is an Associate Professor of English at Ohio State University, Lima. He is the author of *Fables of Fact: The New Journalism as New Fiction* and of numerous articles in film, American studies, and contemporary American literature.

DICK HIGGINS was among the founders of Happenings (1959) and Fluxus (1961), and founded and ran the now-legendary Something Else Press (1963–1973), developing the concept of "intermedia" (1963) along the way. He is now a composer, poet, and artist living in Tarrytown, New York.

CHARLES ISRAEL is Associate Professor of English at South Carolina State College. He is the editor of *Writer's Workshop* (Holt, Rinehart & Winston, 1982) and the author of critical essays on Barry Hannah, Gwendolyn Brooks, Lois Simpson, and George Garrett for *The Dictionary of Literary Biography*.

EDITH JAROLIM is the editor of *The Collected Poems of Paul Blackburne* (Persea Press, 1985).

JULIE JONES received her Ph.D. in English from the University of Virginia and now teaches in the Department of Foreign Languages at the University of New Orleans. Her publications include a translation of Leopoldo Alas' *Su Unico Hijo* (Louisiana State University Press) and articles on Alejo Carpentier, Mario Vargas Llosa, Jorge Tellier, Gustavo Sainz, and José Emilio Pacheco.

NANCY CAROL JOYNER is Professor of English at Western Carolina University. She is the author of numerous articles on modern fiction, especially fiction written by women, and has published *E. A. Robinson: A Reference Guide* (G. K. Hall, 1978).

DONALD G. KELLER is currently editor of *Inscape*, a journal of science fiction criticism. He has been writing for and has edited similar publications for the past 15 years. He lives in Seattle with his wife and daughter.

JEROME KLINKOWITZ is the author of numerous books, essays, and interviews dealing with contemporary American fiction, including *Literary Disruptions* and *The Life of Fiction* (both University of Illinois Press). With John Somer, he edited *Writing Under Fire: Stories of the Vietnam War* (Delta, 1978).

JAMES KNOWLTON is Assistant Professor of German at Rutgers University. He received his Ph.D. in Austria and has been an occasional visitor in East Germany, where he has done research on East German literature. He is co-editor of *Peter Handke and the Postmodern Transformation* and numerous articles on Austrian and East German literature.

JÜRGEN KOPPENSTEINER is Professor of German at the University of Northern Iowa in Cedar Falls. Born in Vienna, he was educated in Austria and has taught in the United States since 1968. Among his publications are two books, *Österreich. Ein landeskundliches Lesebuch* (Munich: Verlag für Deutsch, 1983) and *Österreich erzählt* (Vienna: Österreichischer Bundesverlag, 1984), and many articles and reviews in various journals.

MICHAEL KREKORIAN has placed fiction in *The Iowa Review*, *Kansas Quarterly*, *Fiction International*, and other magazines.

BRUCE KUTNEY has published fiction and poetry in various small presses and was nominated for a Pushcart Prize in 1984. He currently teaches English in Holt, Michigan.

JERZY KUTNIK's study, *The Novel as Performance: The Works of Ronald Sukenick and Raymond Federman*, has recently been published by Southern Illinois University Press. He teaches American Studies at the Uniwersytet Marii Curie Skłodowskiej in Lublin, Poland.

SARAH E. LAUZEN is former Fiction Editor of the *Chicago Review* (and Special Editor of two issues on Innovative/Renovative Fiction in 1983) and has written reviews and essays for such places as *New York Arts Journal*, *Antioch Review*, *American Book Review*, and *Chicago Magazine*.

THOMAS LeCLAIR's many essays and interviews have appeared in such places as *Paris Review*, *New York Times Book Review*, *The New Republic*, *Critique*, and *Fiction International*. He is co-editor of *Anything Can Happen: Interviews with Contemporary American Novelists* (University of Illinois Press) and is Professor of English at the University of Cincinnati.

MARTHA J. McGOWAN is an Associate Professor of English at the University of Lowell. She specializes in contemporary female writers and is currently working on a study of Alice Walker's short stories.

LYNN McKEAN has recently been living in a hotel near the Pantheon in Paris and has reportedly done Jacques Derrida's laundry on occasion. Her essays and reviews have appeared widely, and she was recently discussed in *The New Republic*.

PAT McKERCHER currently teaches English at San Diego State University. He has written essays on Edmund White and Tom Wolfe.

T. C. MARSHALL is a salesman and a poet, a once-and-future professor, a lapsed zenbo. He lives in and around Southern California, principally in San Diego.

CRIS MAZZA won the 1984 PEN American Center's Nelson Algren Award for an unpublished novel. Her short fiction has appeared in *Cimarron Review*, *Indiana Review*, *Fiction Magazine*, and *Kansas Quarterly*. She currently lives in San Diego, California.

STEPHEN MELVILLE teaches literary theory and related materials in the English Department at Syracuse University. He has written on criticism and theory in literature and on the visual arts. He has recently completed a book on Jacques Derrida.

ELISE MILLER is a lifelong resident of Southern California where she teaches composition, writes poetry, and hangs out with her friends.

ROBERT A. MORACE is the author of *John Gardner: An Annotated Secondary Bibliography* (1984) and has edited, with Kathryn Van-Spanckeren, a collection of essays entitled *John Gardner: Critical Perspectives* (1983). His articles on contemporary fiction have appeared in *Modern Fiction Studies*, *Studies in American Fiction*, *Studies in the Novel*,

Critique, and other journals. He teaches at Daemen College in Amherst, New York.

FRED MORAMARCO's most recent book is *Self-Portraits: Essays on Contemporary American Poetry*. His literary essays have appeared in such periodicals as *American Poetry Review*, *American Literature*, *Mosaic*, and *American Book Review*. He is Professor of American Literature at San Diego State University.

ROBERT L. NADEAU is Associate Professor of English at George Mason University. His publications include *Readings from the New Book on Nature* (University of Massachusetts Press), *Nature Talks Back: Pathways to Survival in the Nuclear Age* (Orchises Press), and numerous essays on the relationship between literature and contemporary science.

MICHAEL ORIARD is Associate Professor in the English Department at Oregon State University. His publications include *Dreaming of Heroes: American Sports Fiction, 1868–1980*, *The End of Autumn: Reflections on My Life in Football*, and essays in *Modern Fiction Studies*, *Southern Literary Journal*, *Critique*, *Studies in American Fiction*.

STEPHEN W. POTTS received his Ph.D. in English from the University of California at Berkeley. He has taught writing at San Diego State University, American literature at the Universitat Wurzburg in Germany, and science fiction at the University of California at San Diego. His publications include monographs on Joseph Heller, F. Scott Fitzgerald, and Arkady and Boris Strugatsky, as well as shorter pieces of criticism and fiction in journals and anthologies.

R. RADHAKRISHNAN is an Assistant Professor at the University of Massachusetts, Amherst, teaching critical theory. His publications have appeared in such journals as *boundary 2* and *Works and Days*.

DAVID RANDALL is a graduate student in the Department of English at SUNY/Binghamton.

MICHAEL W. RAYMOND has written essays on Tim O'Brien, Robert Pirsig, N. Scott Momaday, and Kurt Vonnegut, Jr.; he is currently Professor of English at Stetson University.

PETER J. REED received his Ph.D. from the University of Washington and has taught at the University of Minnesota since 1968. His publications include several studies of Vonnegut: *Kurt Vonnegut, Jr.* (in the *Writers for the 70's* series), the Vonnegut entry for the *Dictionary of Literary Biography*, and chapters in *Kurt Vonnegut in America.*

PENELOPE RITHNER is an author and critic currently residing in San Diego.

MARK S. ROBERTS teaches philosophy at Dowling College, Oakdale, New York. He is the editor and partial translator of Mikel Dufrenne's *In the Presence of the Sensuous: Essays in Aesthetics*, and has published articles in aesthetics, contemporary French philosophy, and social thought; he has also translated works by Jean-Francois Lyotard and Felix Guittari.

RICHARD H. RODINO is an Associate Professor of English at Holy Cross College. He has published a book, *Swift Studies 1965–1984: An Annotated Bibliography*, and about a dozen articles, mostly on Jonathan Swift, satire, and eighteenth-century literature. He has also published articles on Robert Pirsig's *Zen and the Art of Motorcycle Maintenance* and chaired the 1982 MLA Special Session on Pirsig.

MARTHE ROSENFELD, an Associate Professor of French and Women's Studies at Indiana University-Purdue University, Fort Wayne, has published articles on Monique Wittig in *Frontiers*, *Mosaic*, and *Vlasta*. She is also the author of *Edmond Jaloux: The Evolution of a Novelist.*

STEFANO ROSSO is writing his Ph.D. dissertation in the Department of Comparative Literature at SUNY/Binghamton and holds a postdoctorate research fellowship in Anglo-American Studies at the University of Genoa (Italy). He is the correspondent from New York for the journal *Alfabeta.*

SUE SANDERA RUMMEL has taught writing and literature at San Diego State University and at the University of Minnesota, Morris. Presently, she is Assistant Professor of English at Canton Agricultural and Technical College, where she teaches writing and contemporary American fiction.

RICHARD J. SCHNEIDER is Professor of English at Atlantic Christian College and has published essays on contemporary fiction in various journals, including one on William Gass in *Critique*. He is currently completing a book on Thoreau for Twayne.

MARTINA SCIOLINO is a graduate student in English at SUNY/Buffalo.

FRANK W. SHELTON is Professor of English at Limestone College in Gaffney, South Carolina. He has published numerous essays on modern fiction and drama in such journals as *Critique*, *Southern Literary Journal*, *Midwest Quarterly*, and *Southern Review*.

ALLEN SHEPHERD is Professor of English at the University of Vermont. His publications include essays, poems, and stories appearing in such places as *Kansas Quarterly*, *Southern Literary Journal*, *Mississippi Quarterly*, and *the New Yorker*.

RON SILLIMAN's current project is *The Alphabet*, a long work whose individual sections are appearing in various magazines and journals. Other books of his include *Ketjak*, *Thanting*, *The Age of Huts*, and *Bart*. He presently lives in San Francisco and roots avidly for the Giants.

GEORGE SLUSSER is Curator of the Eaton Collection at the University of California, Riverside, and writes on nineteenth-century literature and science fiction.

DEBORAH SMALL is the art editor for *Fiction International*. An artist and writer, she lives in San Diego.

CARLTON SMITH is a writer and tennis professional living in Dana Point, California.

JUDY R. SMITH is Assistant Professor of English at Kenyon College. She has published on Ellen Glasgow, John Gardner, Peter Nichols, and Nathaniel Hawthorne in such journals as *Southern Literary Journal*, *Critique*, *Literature and Medicine*, and *The Markham Review*.

DORIS SOMMER, Associate Professor of Spanish at Amherst College, has published widely in the field of Latin American literature, including articles on women's testimonials and Walt Whitman's Spanish American heirs. She is also author of *One Master for Another: Populism in Dominican Novels*.

BRIAN STABLEFORD has published widely in the field of science fiction criticism. He is a lecturer in Sociology at the University of Reading in England.

CRAIG THOMPSON is Associate Editor of *Fiction International*.

JONATHAN TITTLER is Associate Professor of Romance Studies at Cornell University, where he specializes in contemporary Latin American narratives. His publications include *Narrative Irony in the Contemporary*

Spanish-American Novel, and essays in such places as *Diacritics*, *Hispania*, and *World Literature Today*.

KHACHIG TOLOLYAN is Associate Professor of English and Associate Director of the Center for the Humanities at Wesleyan University. He has published articles on Thomas Pynchon, Jorge Luis Borges and John Barth, co-edits *Pynchon Notes*, and is writing a book on *Cosmographic Narrative: Form and Information in Fiction*.

RAYMOND L. WILLIAMS teaches Latin American literature at Washington University in St. Louis. He is the author of *Gabriel García Márquez* (Boston: Twayne World Author Series, 1984) and four other books.

MARY BITTNER WISEMAN is Associate Professor of Philosophy at Brooklyn College and the Graduate Center of the City University of New York. Her articles and reviews have appeared in *American Philosophical Quarterly*, *Ethics*, *Journal of Aesthetics and Art Criticism*, and *Philosophy and Literature*.

CARL B. YOKE is Associate Professor of English at Kent State University, and has been Associate Editor of *Extrapolation* since 1978. Among his more than 40 publications in science fiction and fantasy are monographs on Roger Zelazny and André Norton and a *Reader's Guide* to Zelazny's work.

GEORGE YUDICE, who teaches at Hunter College in New York City, has published widely in Latin American studies. He is publisher and editor of Tlon Editions, which specializes in publishing English translations of Latin American literature.

BONNIE ZIMMERMAN is Professor of Women's Studies at San Diego State University, where she teaches literature and humanities. She has published articles on George Eliot and on lesbian studies in anthologies and journals including *Criticism*, *ELH*, *Signs*, and *Feminist Studies*.

About the Editor

LARRY McCAFFERY is Professor of English and Comparative Literature at San Diego State University. His works include *Anything Can Happen: Interviews with Contemporary American Novelists, The Metafictional Muse: The Works of Coover, Gass and Barthelme*, and (with Sinda Gregory) *No Real Center: Interviews with Contemporary American Writers*. His articles on postmodern fiction have appeared in *Contemporary Literature, Critique, Fiction International, The Mississippi Review, The New York Times Book Review, The Paris Review*, and *Partisan Review*. He also co-edits the literary journals *Critique* and *Fiction International*. He is currently at work on a book examining rock music.